The Kingdom of the Hittites

❖

TREVOR BRYCE

OXFORD
UNIVERSITY PRESS

OXFORD
UNIVERSITY PRESS

Oxford University Press, Great Clarendon Street, Oxford OX2 6DP
Oxford New York
Athens Auckland Bangkok Bogotá Buenos Aires
Calcutta Cape Town Chennai Dar es Salaam
Delhi Florence Hong Kong Istanbul Karachi
Kuala Lumpur Madrid Melbourne Mexico City
Mumbai Nairobi Paris São Paulo Singapore
Taipei Tokyo Toronto Warsaw
and associated companies in
Berlin Ibadan

Oxford is a registered trade mark of Oxford University Press

Published in the United States
by Oxford University Press Inc., New York

© Trevor Bryce 1998

The moral rights of the author have been asserted

First published in paperback 1999

British Library Cataloguing in Publication Data
Data available

Library of Congress Cataloging in Publication Data
Data available

ISBN 0-19-924010-8 (Pbk.)

3 5 7 9 10 8 6 4 2

Typeset in Times
by Best-set Typesetter Ltd., Hong Kong
Printed in Great Britain on acid-free paper by
Bookcraft (Bath) Ltd., Midsomer Norton

Acknowledgements

In preparing this book I have drawn on the contributions made by many scholars to the field of Hittite scholarship. I would, however, like to express special thanks to Professor Silvin Košak who kindly agreed to read the book in its draft form and who has made many valuable comments and suggestions, particularly in relation to the passages in translation. Whatever the book's merits, it has benefited greatly from his contributions. I would also like to express my gratitude to Professor Oliver Gurney for his advice over many years on a wide range of matters relating to the Hittite world. He did much to stimulate my initial interest in this world and has always been most generous in sharing his ideas on many of the knotty problems of Hittite scholarship.

T.B.

June 1996

Note

In reference to p. 136, note 15: Details of the silver bowl, which is of unknown origin or provenance, have now been published by J. D. Hawkins, 'A Hieroglyphic Luwian Inscription on a Silver Bowl in the Museum of Anatolian Civilizations, Ankara', *Anadolu Medeniyetleri Musezi*, 1996 Yilligi, Ankara, 1997.

The Kingdom of the Hittites

❖

Abbreviations

(Abbreviations in roman type refer to publications of the original texts.)

AA	*Archäologischer Anzeiger*
ABoT	K. Balkan, *Ankara arkeoloji müzesinde bulunan Boğazköy-tableteri* (Istanbul, 1948)
AOF	*Altorientalische Forschungen*
AfO	*Archiv für Orientforschung*
ÄHK	E. Edel, *Die Ägyptisch-hethitische Korrespondenz aus Boghazköy* (Opladen, 1994)
AJA	*American Journal of Archaeology*
AM	A. Goetze, *Die Annalen des Mursilis, MVAG* 38 (1933, Leipzig; repr. Darmstadt, 1967)
AO	*Archív Orientální*
AOAT	*Alter Orient und Altes Testament*
AS	*Anatolian Studies*
AT	D. Wiseman, *The Alalakh Tablets* (London, 1953)
ATHE	B. Kienast, 'Die altassyrischen Texte des orientalischen Seminars der Universität Heidelberg und der Sammlung Erlenmeyer-Basel' (Berlin, 1960)
BASOR	*Bulletin of the American Schools of Oriental Research*
BIN	*Babylonian Inscriptions in the Collection of James B. Nies*
BiOr	*Bibliotheca Orientalis*
Bo	*Bogazköy: Istanbul and Berlin, inventory*
BoTu	E. Forrer, *Die Boghazköi-Texte in Umschrift* = *WVDOG* 41, 42 (Berlin, 1922, 1926)
CAH	*Cambridge Ancient History*
CCT	*Cuneiform Texts from Cappadocian Tablets in the British Museum*
CHD	*The Hittite Dictionary of the Oriental Institute of the University of Chicago*
CPh	*Classical Philology*
CR	*Classical Review*

CRAI	*Comptes rendus de l'Académie des Inscriptions et Belles-Lettres*
CTH	E. Laroche, *Catalogue des textes hittites* (Paris, 1971)
DS	H. G. Güterbock, 'The Deeds of Suppiluliuma as Told by his Son, Mursili II', *JCS* 10 (1956), 41–68, 75–98, 101–30
EA	*The El-Amarna letters*, most recently ed. by Moran, 1987, 1992
Fs Alp	H. Otten, E. Akurgal, H. Ertem, and A. Süel, *Hittite and Other Anatolian and Near Eastern Studies in honour of Sedat Alp* (Ankara, 1992)
Fs Bittel	R. M. Boehmer and H. Hauptmann, *Beiträge zur Altertumskunde Kleinasiens (Festschrift für Kurt Bittel)* (Mainz am Rhein, 1983)
Fs Güterbock I	K. Bittel, Ph. H. J. Houwink ten Cate, and E. Reiner, *Anatolian Studies presented to H. G. Güterbock* (Istanbul, 1974)
Fs Güterbock II	H. A. Hoffner and G. M. Beckman, *Kaniššuwar: A Tribute to Hans G. Güterbock on his Seventy-Fifth Birthday* (Chicago, 1986)
Fs Houwink ten Cate	T. Van den Hout and J. De Roos, *Studio Historiae Ardens (Ancient Near Eastern Studies Presented to Philo H. J. Houwink ten Cate on the Occasion of his 65th Birthday)* (Istanbul, 1995)
Fs Laroche	*Florilegium Anatolicum (Mélanges offerts à Emmanuel Laroche)* (Paris, 1979)
Fs Mansel	*Mélanges Mansel* (Ankara, 1974)
Fs Meriggi	O. Carruba, *Studia Mediterranea Piero Meriggi Dicata* (Pavia, 1979)
Fs Mylonas	*Festschrift for Georgios E. Mylonas, Tome A'* (Athens, 1986)
Fs Neve	*IM* 43 (1993)
Fs Otten I	E Neu and C. Rüster, *Festschrift Heinrich Otten*, (Wiesbaden, 1973)
Fs Otten II	E. Neu and C. Rüster, *Documentum Asiae Minoris Antiquae (Festschrift Heinrich Otten)* (Wiesbaden, 1988)
Fs Özgüç	K. Emre, B. Hrouda, M. J. Mellink and N. Özgüç, *Anatolia and the Near East (Tahsin Özgüce Armağan) (Studies in honour of Tahsin Özgüç)* (Ankara, 1989)

Contents

HT	L. King, *Hittite Texts in the Cuneiform Character from Tablets in the British Museum* (London, 1920)
HUCA	*Hebrew Union College Annual*
IBoT	*Istanbul Arkeoloji Müzelerinde Bulunan Boğazköy Tabletleri(nden Seçme Metinler)* (Istanbul 1944, 1947, 1954; Ankara, 1988)
IF	*Indogermanische Forschungen*
IM	*Istanbuler Mitteilungen*
JAC	*Journal of Ancient Civilizations*
JAOS	*Journal of the American Oriental Society*
JEA	*Journal of Egyptian Archaeology*
JEOL	*Jaarbericht Ex Oriente Lux*
JHS	*Journal of Hellenic Studies*
JIES	*Journal of Indo-European Studies*
JKF	*Jahrbuch für Kleinasiatisch Forschung*
JMA	*Journal of Mediterranean Archaeology*
JNES	*Journal of Near Eastern Studies*
JOAI	*Jahresheften des Österreichischen Archäologischen Institutes*
JWH	*Journal of World History*
KBo	*Keilschrifttexte aus Boghazköi*, Leipzig and Berlin
KRI	K. A. Kitchen, *Ramesside Inscriptions, Historical and Biographical I-VII*, Oxford, 1969–
kt	excavation no. of the texts from Kültepe Kanes
KTHahn	J. Lewy, *Die Kültepe-texte aus der Sammlung Frida Hahn*, (Berlin and Leipzig, 1930)
KTP	F. J. Stephens, *The Cappadocian Tablets in the University of Pennsylvania Museum*
KUB	*Keilschrifturkunden aus Boghazköi*, Berlin
LAAA	*Liverpool Annals of Archaeology and Anthropology*
LS	K. K. Riemschneider, 'Die hethitischen Landschenkungsurkunden', *MIO* 6, 1958, 321–81
MAOG	*Mitteilungen der Altorientalischen Gesellschaft*
MDAI	*Mitteilungen des deutschen archäologischen Instituts*
MDOG	*Mitteilungen der deutschen Orient-Gesellschaft*
ME	Middle Euphrates texts
MIO	*Mitteilungen des Instituts für Orientforschung*
MsK	Texts from Meşkene (Emar)

Abbreviations

MVAG	Mitteilungen der Vorderasiatisch-Ägyptischen Gesellschaft
NBC	Nies Babylonian Collection, Yale
OA	Oriens Antiquus
OJA	Oxford Journal of Archaeology
OLZ	Orientalische Literaturzeitung
Or	Orientalia
PD	E. F. Weidner, Politische Dokumente aus Kleinasien (Leipzig, 1923; repr. New York, 1970)
PRU IV	J. Nougayrol, Le Palais Royal d'Ugarit IV (Mission de Ras Shamra Tome IX) (Paris, 1956)
PRU VI	J. Nougayrol, Le Palais Royal d'Ugarit VI (Mission de Ras Shamra Tome XII) (Paris, 1970)
RA	Revue Archéologique
RAss	Revue d'Assyriologie et d'Archéologie Orientale
RHA	Revue hittite et asianique
RlA	Reallexikon der Assyriologie und vorderasiatischen Archäologie
RS	Tablets from Ras Shamra
SAK	Studien zur altägyptischen Kultur
SBo	H.G. Güterbock, Siegel aus Boğazköy I–II (Berlin, 1940, 1942)
SMEA	Studi Micenei ed Egeo-Anatolici
StBoT	Studien zu den Boğazköy-Texten
TAPS	Transactions of the American Philosophical Society
TC	Tablettes cappadociennes
TCu	Textes cunéiformes, Louvre
TTKB	Türk Tarih Kurumu Basimevi, Ankara
TTKY	Türk Tarih Kurumu Yayınları
TUAT	Texte aus der Umwelt des Alten Testament
UF	Ugarit-Forschungen
VBoT	Verstreute Boghazköi-Texte
WO	Die Welt des Orients
WVDOG	Wissenschaftliche Veröffentlichungen des deutschen Orient-Gesellschaft
WZKM	Wiener Zeitschrift für die Kunde des Morgenlandes
ZA	Zeitschrift für Assyriologie und Vorderasiatische Archäologie
ZDMG	Zeitschrift der Deutschen Morgenländischen Gesellschaft

List of Hittite Kings

Old Kingdom

Labarna	−1650	
Hattusili I	1650–1620	(grandson?)
Mursili I	1620–1590	(grandson, adopted son)
Hantili I	1590–1560	(brother-in-law)
Zidanta I ⎫		(son-in-law)
Ammuna ⎬	1560–1525	(son)
Huzziya I ⎭		(brother of Ammuna's daughter-in-law)
Telipinu	1525–1500	(brother-in-law)
Alluwamna ⎫		(son-in-law)
Tahurwaili ⎪		(interloper)
Hantili II ⎬	1500–1400	(son of Alluwamna?)
Zidanta II ⎪		(son?)
Huzziya II ⎪		(son?)
Muwatalli I ⎭		(interloper)

New Kingdom

Tudhaliya I/II ⎫		(grandson of Huzziya II?)
Arnuwanda I ⎬	1400–1360[a]	(son-in-law, adopted son)
Hattusili II? ⎭		(son?)
Tudhaliya III	1360–1344	(son?)
Suppiluliuma I	1344–1322	(son)
Arnuwanda II	1322–1321	(son)
Mursili II	1321–1295	(brother)
Muwatalli II	1295–1272	(son)
Urhi-Tesub	1272–1267	(son)
Hattusili III	1267–1237	(uncle)
Tudhaliya IV	1237–1228	(son)
Kurunta	1228–1227	(cousin)
Tudhaliya IV[b]	1227–1209	(cousin)

| Arnuwanda III | 1209–1207 | (son) |
| Suppiluliuma II | 1207– | (brother) |

Note: All dates are approximate. When it is impossible to suggest even approximate dates for the individual reigns of two or more kings in sequence, the period covered by the sequence is roughly calculated on the basis of 20 years per reign. While obviously some reigns were longer than this, and some shorter, the averaging out of these reigns probably produces a result with a reasonably small margin of error.

[a] Includes period of coregency
[b] 2nd period as king

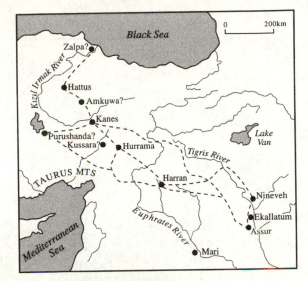

Map 1: Assyrian merchant trade routes

Map 2: Eastern Anatolia and Northern Syria today

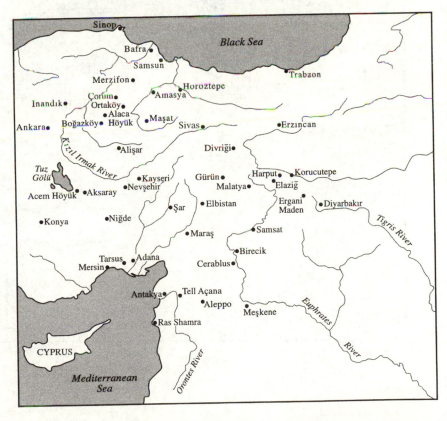

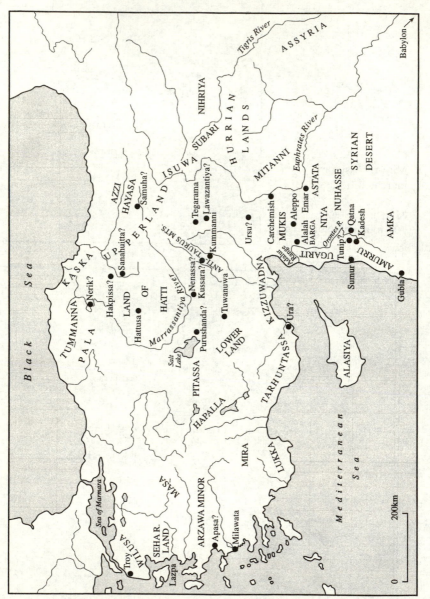

Map 3: The World of the Hittites

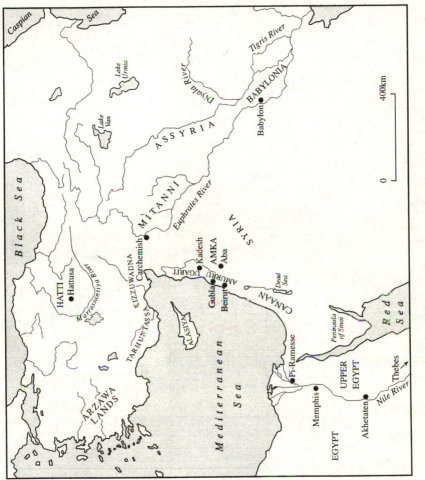

Map 4: The Near East in the Late Bronze Age

Introduction

During the last 150 years, the ancient Near East has provided a rich field of investigation for scholars from a wide range of disciplines. Archaeologists, anthropologists, historians, and philologists have all made substantial contributions to our knowledge of the ancient civilizations which rose, flourished, and fell in the land-mass extending from the Aegean coast of modern Turkey through Mesopotamia to the eastern frontiers of modern Iran. Some of these civilizations date back to the very beginnings of urban settlement in the Near East. Others of more recent origin provide evidence of highly developed political and social organizations, reflected particularly in the finds of tablet archives. These and other written sources of information have provided a basis for research into the political and social history of the Near East from the Early Bronze Age onwards. They are also of fundamental importance to the study of the scripts and languages of the region—Sumerian, Assyrian, Babylonian, Hurrian, Ugaritic, Hittite, hieroglyphic Luwian, and the Iron Age languages of the first millennium BC.

Of course none of the civilizations or languages which developed in the region can properly be studied in isolation. The Near Eastern world, then as now, was characterized by a high degree of cultural coherence as well as cultural diversity, and by a complex network of political and commercial interrelationships. It is virtually impossible to acquire expertise on a particular Near Eastern civilization unless one has an understanding of the broad political and cultural context in which it arose and ran its course.

Hittitology is a relative newcomer to the field of Near Eastern studies. Little more than a century ago, when important advances were being made in the study of the Bronze Age civilizations of Mesopotamia, the Hittites were regarded as no more than a small Canaanite tribe living somewhere in Palestine—an assumption based on a few scattered biblical references. We now know that

Hatti, the kingdom of the Hittites, was one of the great powers of
the Late Bronze Age, rivalling and eventually surpassing in the
fourteenth century its two most powerful contemporaries, the kingdoms of Mitanni and Egypt. From their capital Hattusa in central
Anatolia, the kings of the Land of Hatti controlled a vast network
of vassal states, which at the height of Hittite political and military
development in the fourteenth and thirteenth centuries extended
from the Aegean coast of Anatolia in the west to the Euphrates
river in the east.

There have been many important advances in the field of Hittite
scholarship during the last hundred years, advances which have
contributed much to our understanding of the political configuration of the Near Eastern world in the Late Bronze Age. Even in
the last decade, major discoveries have been made. Most of these
have come to light during the course of the ongoing excavations
at Hattusa, particularly in the the so-called Upper City where the
remains of no less than twenty-six temples have recently been
unearthed. Of particular value to the historian are the new discoveries of inscribed tablets, most notably the famous bronze tablet
which came to light in 1986 just inside the walls of Hattusa. Also
noteworthy amongst the new finds in Hattusa is a deposit of more
than 3,000 royal seal impressions, a collection which increases
many times over the number of such impressions previously known
to us. Recent excavations in regional centres of the kingdom have
also produced important new written sources—hieroglyphic inscriptions at several sites in southern Anatolia, cuneiform tablet
archives at Emar on the Euphrates and at (modern) Maşat,
Kusaklı, and Ortaköy in central Anatolia.

We are confronted with what is almost an embarrassment of
riches. It may be many years before the new material is fully
analysed, and the information it contains fully taken into account.
This serves to highlight the dynamic nature of the field of Hittite
studies. Long held theories or assumptions have constantly to be
revised or discarded in the light of new information. Additional
pieces are constantly being added to the incomplete jigsaw of the
world of the Hittites.

Thus now, and probably for many years to come, we can write no
more than a provisional history of this world, taking stock of what
information is available to us at the time of writing, and recognizing
that parts of such a history may already be in need of revision by

the time it appears in print. The task is made all the more difficult by the fact that on many aspects of Hittite history there is a wide divergence of scholarly views. Within the compass of the present work, it is impossible to represent these views fully or to justify in detail a particular line taken on a controversial issue. Inevitably there will be scholars who will disagree with a number of the conclusions and interpretations and reconstructions of historical events dealt with in the pages which follow. That is an occupational hazard of writing a book of this kind. The aim of the book is to present a view of Hittite history which is consistent with the evidence so far available to us, but also to indicate to the reader where there is a divergence of scholarly opinion, and where different or contrary views have been presented.

The focus will be primarily on the political and military history of the Hittite world. This provides an important context for an investigation of the many other aspects of Hittite civilization, including religion, social customs and *mores*, art, and literature. These aspects have been dealt with in a number of other works, of both a specialized and a general nature. Even so, a comprehensive, up-to-date treatment of Hittite civilization and society might well provide a valuable complement to the present work.

In writing a history of any people, ancient or modern, one should as far as possible allow the people to speak for themselves. In line with this principle, the chapters which follow contain numerous passages from the original texts. Many of the passages have already been translated elsewhere. But the general reader's access to them is limited by the several different modern languages in which the translations appear, and sometimes by the relative difficulty of obtaining these translations. As a rule, a passage included in this book has only been translated afresh if no reliable English translation of it is currently available, or if it is appropriate to render it in more idiomatic English.

But there is an important *caveat*. Hittite texts are often fragmentary, and a precise, literal translation of such texts involves a number of restorations by the translator of words, phrases, or sentences which have been lost from the original. Such restorations are conventionally indicated by square brackets in the edited texts. For ease of reading, these brackets have been removed from the passages which appear in this book, except in cases where a restoration is particularly doubtful. Readers wishing to study the texts in greater detail will need to refer to the original editions and translations of these texts, as indicated at the end of each passage or in the footnotes. In some cases the translations of other scholars have been modified, to take account of revised readings and interpretations of particular words or phrases, or to ensure consistency in the way certain terms or expressions are rendered throughout the book.

The great majority of tablets from the archives of the Hittite capital have been published, and are still being published, in two main series: Keilschrifttexte aus Boghazköi (Leipzig and Berlin), and Keilschrifturkunden aus Boghazköi (Berlin). These publications consist of copies of the original cuneiform inscriptions, and provide the basis for subsequent editions of the inscriptions in transliteration and translation. There are similar publications of tablets found at other sites; for example, the tablet archives discovered at Ras Shamra in Syria and the recently discovered Maşat archive. Most of the tablets published up to the beginning of the 1970s have been catalogued according to type and subject matter by the French scholar Emmanuel Laroche in his *Catalogue des textes hittites* (Paris, 1971). Since Laroche's *Catalogue* contains much useful supplementary information about the texts, the *CTH* number is generally included with the original publication reference for the text. For a general overview of the nature of our written sources on Hittite history, and their value and their shortcomings, the reader is referred to Appendix 2.

Hittite personal and place-names have been transliterated in a variety of different ways, depending, for example, on whether stem-forms or inflected forms are represented, and on whether Hittite *ḫ* and *š* are transliterated simply as *h* and *s*, or as *kh* and *sh*. The names produced are sometimes cumbersome and difficult to read; for example, Khattushash, Khattushilish, Shuppiluliumash, Tudkhaliyash. For ease of reading and typographical convenience, I have adopted the simplest of the commonly used transliterations; thus Hattusa, Hattusili, Suppiluliuma, Tudhaliya.

Finally, we should say something about the division of Hittite history into two or more chronological phases. (The problems of determining an absolute chronology for Hittite history are discussed in Appendix 1.) It is common practice for historians to divide the history of the ancient Near Eastern kingdoms which extended over some hundreds of years into several major phases.

Thus the history of Pharaonic Egypt and the history of Assyria are each divided into three phases, designated as the Old, Middle, and New Kingdoms. These divisions are often associated with the disappearance of one line of rulers and the emergence of another, sometimes with a considerable interval of time between the two,[1] or with a serious downturn in the fortunes of a kingdom, followed by its entry into a powerful new phase of its history—or vice versa. Sometimes there are marked differences in the political, cultural and material character of the various phases of a kingdom's history, which provides further justification for distinguishing them from each other.

Hittite history presents us with no easily distinguishable phases. In the first place throughout the 500 years of its existence, the kingdom of Hatti remained under the rule of kings who came from a single small group of closely related families. From the beginning to the end of the Late Bronze Age kingdom, there was no demonstrable change of dynasty. There were, as we shall see, a number of palace coups which unseated a king and put a pretender on the throne. However, usurpers seem (almost) invariably to have been related by blood or marriage ties to their victims.[2] And later kings traced their ancestry back to the earliest occupants of the Hittite throne.

Further, we cannot easily divide Hittite history into different phases on the basis of a major decline followed by a major upsurge in the kingdom's fortunes. The kingdom waxed and waned dramatically on a number of occasions throughout its history. It would be meaningless to attempt to represent all these as distinct phases in the history of the kingdom.

None the less, a number of Hittite scholars have followed the pattern adopted for other Near Eastern kingdoms by dividing Hittite history into three main phases—Old, Middle, and New Kingdoms. But those who do so disagree on where one ends and the other begins. This merely serves to emphasise that any attempts to split Hittite history into two or more distinctive phases is little more than an arbitrary exercise.

---

[1] As in the case of Egypt where the intervals between the main phases are designated as First Intermediate and Second Intermediate, each of which lasted several hundred years.

[2] There is some uncertainty about several of the kings who reigned between Telipinu and Tudhaliya I. We cannot be sure whether these were in fact related to their predecessors on the throne since so little is known about them.

The matter is further confused by philologists' and palaeo-graphers' use of the terms Old, Middle, and Late to designate particular phases in the development of the Hittite language and the cuneiform script in which it was written. At least in their case there is demonstrable justification for such divisions, and broad agreement amongst them. But changes in language and script cannot be assumed to have broader cultural or political significance in the absence of other significant and clearly defined factors which might support this.

While any attempt to divide Hittite history into different phases would probably be quite meaningless to the Hittites themselves, it may be advisable, if only as a matter of convenience, not to diverge too widely from a long established and generally accepted convention. With this in mind, I believe that the most acceptable solution is to divide the history of the Hittite Kingdom into no more than two main phases, an Old and a New Kingdom (to use the standard terminology), beginning the former with the reign of the first king called Labarna in the early seventeenth century and the latter with the reign of the first king called Tudhaliya in the late fifteenth or early fourteenth century.

The Hittite civilization was part of a continuum of human development which in Anatolia as elsewhere in the Near East extended back many millennia. By way of introduction to the Hittites, we shall turn our attention first to some of the antecedent civilizations in the region, especially those that emerged and flourished in central Anatolia from 3000 BC onwards, in the periods commonly referred to as the Early and Middle Bronze Ages.

CHAPTER I

The Origins of the Hittites

Anatolia in the Early Bronze Age

To the nineteenth-century scholar, Anatolia must have seemed little more than a mysterious blank on the Bronze Age Near Eastern landscape during the period when the great civilizations of ancient Mesopotamia and Egypt were in their prime. Even the excavations at Hissarlık conducted by Heinrich Schliemann between 1871 and 1890 did little to change this picture. For the material civilization which Schliemann uncovered on the alleged site of Troy was something of an enigma, a precocious development in north-west Anatolia, on the very edge of a dark subcontinent.

Since the early years of the twentieth century, that picture has changed dramatically. We now know that Anatolia was the homeland of a large complex of civilizations, the earliest of which extended back thousands of years before the beginning of the Bronze Age. Indeed we must peel back many layers of Anatolian prehistory before we see revealed, finally, the first settlements and communities of the period archaeologists have called the Bronze Age.

This period covered some 2,000 years of history and civilization in the Near East, roughly from the late fourth to the late second millennium BC. It was a period characterized by many great achievements in the development of human society and civilization within the region. Yet there was no sharp or sudden break with what had gone before: in their earliest phase, many Bronze Age sites reflect no more than a gradual and sometimes almost imperceptible cultural development out of the preceding 'Chalcolithic Age'. There was no major cultural revolution, no evident intrusion of newcomers into Anatolia, except in the Cilician Plain, and very few signs of destruction of existing communities. A number of the features of the Chalcolithic cultures persisted in the 'new age' with little or no change.[1]

For archaeologists, the hallmark of this new age was the introduction of a metal alloy called bronze, consisting of a small percentage of tin (up to 10 per cent) mixed with copper—producing a tougher, more durable metal than copper on its own. This technological advance did not lead to sudden revolutionary changes in society. Copper remained for some time the metal most commonly used by the Early Bronze Age peoples. Yet the production of the first bronze artefacts in Anatolia was a development of great significance, one which was to have a profound influence on the course of Anatolian history for the next two millennia.

There is an important reason for this. While Anatolia was richly endowed with deposits of copper, lead, nickel, and arsenic, we have yet to find evidence that there were substantial tin deposits in the region. The peoples of Anatolia had to rely largely if not exclusively on supplies of tin from foreign sources. The actual sources are still a matter of some debate. But very likely much if not all of the tin used in Anatolia came from the south-east via Mesopotamia and Syria. Increasing demand in Anatolia for raw materials like tin and other commodities which were not obtainable locally created the need for trade links with areas further afield, particularly to the south-east. This must have been an important factor in the development of stable, coherent political and administrative organizations capable of establishing and maintaining such links.

The Early Bronze Age Kingdoms

By the middle of the third millennium (the Early Bronze II phase), there were wealthy ruling houses and important centres of civilization in various parts of Anatolia. Notable amongst these were Troy and Poliochni in the north-west, Beycesultan in the south-west, and Tarsus in the Cilician Plain in the south.

But our main focus will be on central Anatolia. Here developed a number of prosperous settlements, presumably the nuclei of small kingdoms, in a region extending from just below the southern

---

[1] For an overview of the transition from the Chalcolithic to the Early Bronze Age in Anatolia, see Mellaart (1971a).

bend of the river now known as the Kızıl Irmak (Red River)[2] northwards towards the Pontic zone along the southern shore of the Black Sea. Prominent amongst these settlements was the site now known as Alaca Höyük, which lies some 200 kilometres northeast of the modern Turkish capital Ankara. The settlement which was founded here in the Late Chalcolithic period reached its peak in the Early Bronze II phase, as illustrated by its thirteen 'royal' shaft graves and their spectacular grave goods,[3] generally dated to *c.*2300–2100.[4] But it continued as a flourishing community to the end of the Late Bronze Age. Its Bronze Age name is unknown. Other important settlements were Hattus, the site of the later Hittite capital Hattusa, Alişar (probably the ancient Amkuwa),[5] Zalpa, which lay in the Pontic region, and Kanes.

The last of these, Kanes, lies in the fertile Kayseri Plain just south of the southern bend of the Kızıl Irmak river on the site with a mound now known as Kültepe. A Chalcolithic site in origin, it has a history of continuous occupation down to the Roman period. But its most flourishing phase occurred during the Early and Middle Bronze Ages.

The name of a king of Kanes called Zipani figures in a well known text which deals with a rebellion of seventeen local rulers against the Akkadian king Naram-Sin (*c.*2380–2325), whose kingdom at the height of his power extended from the Persian Gulf to central Anatolia.[6] A king of Hatti called Pamba is also included amongst the list of rebels.[7] This is admittedly a late attested tradition (*c.*1400). But it may well have a basis in historical fact. If so it provides us with valuable written evidence of the existence of organized kingdoms within the central Anatolian region during the Early Bronze Age.

In a number of respects, the Early Bronze II phase seems to represent the climax of a number of social, political, and cultural developments which had been taking place in various parts of Anatolia from the Late Chalcolithic period onwards, with little interruption and without major population changes, except

---

[2] The Halys (or Salt River) of Greco-Roman times.
[3] Brief accounts of these are given by Akurgal (1962: 15–25), Lloyd (1967: 20–9).
[4] Akurgal (1989), has suggested a later dating, to *c.*2100–2000.
[5] See the references cited in del Monte and Tischler (1978: 21). *Contra* this identification, see Ünal (1980–83: 381).
[6] For the text, see *CTH* 311, ed. Güterbock (1938: 67–76).
[7] The references to Zipani and Pamba appear in KBo III 13 (*CTH* 311.1) obv. 11'.

perhaps in the north-west and south-east (to be discussed below). But by the end of this phase, perhaps around 2300, there is evidence in some regions of major and sometimes violent changes. This is so particularly in the west and the south. In these regions there are signs of major conflagrations, and as far as we can presently determine, relatively few of the established Early Bronze II communities survived into the final phase of the Early Bronze Age.

A number of scholars associate the apparent upheavals of this period with the arrival or incursions of Indo-European newcomers into Anatolia.

The Indo-European Presence in Anatolia

Before the end of the third millennium there were three known groups of people in Anatolia who spoke Indo-European languages: in the west the Luwians, in the north the Palaians, and in central or eastern Anatolia the speakers of a language called Nesite. The names we give these groups derive from the names of their languages, as identified in the cuneiform tablets found in the archives of the Hittite capital Hattusa. These archives contain texts written in a number of languages, including several Indo-European languages identified by the terms *luwili* (in the language of Luwiya), *palaumnili* (in the language of Pala) and *nešili, našili,* or *nišili* (in the language of Nesa).[8] The locations of these groups have been determined primarily on the basis of the geographical distribution of place-names, divine names, and personal names in their respective languages.

The origins of these Indo-Europeans are disputed. Homelands in the east (eastern Anatolia, southern Caucasus, northern Mesopotamia), the north (southern Russia, north of the Black Sea), and the west (central Europe, the Balkans) have all been proposed, but no consensus has been reached.[9] Opinions also differ widely on when they came. Most scholars believe that they arrived in Anatolia some time during the third millennium. Some argue that the

[8] Or alternatively *nešumnili* (in the language of the Nesite). There is also one instance of the form *kanišumnili* (in the language of the Kanesite).
[9] For a review of the whole question, see Crossland and Birchall (1974), Diakonov (1985), Steiner (1990). Makkay (1993: 122) claims that Steiner's proposal of a western route of immigration, i.e. from the Balkan region, seems to have the support of recent archaeological discoveries. The evidence adduced remains tenuous.

Luwians were the first, entering Anatolia early in the third millennium, with the Nesites arriving towards the end of the millennium.[10] Others believe that the order should be reversed, with the Nesites (and Palaians) representing the first phase of Indo-European migration, and the Luwians arriving towards the end of the millennium.[11] Another view is that the Indo-Europeans arrived in a single mass, subsequently dispersing within Anatolia some time after their arrival.[12] Yet another view is that Anatolia had already been the home of Indo-European speakers for several thousand years, or more, before the beginning of the Bronze Age.[13]

While we still cannot reach finality on the matter of the origins of the Indo-European groups and the nature of their migration into Anatolia, there are several important questions we should at this stage address. Where do these groups belong within the context of the Early Bronze Age kingdoms? Who were the inhabitants of these kingdoms? Who were the kings who ruled over them?

The Hattians

From at least as early as the time of the Akkadian empire of Sargon, the region in which these kingdoms lay was known as the Land of Hatti. Scholars have long assumed that the predominant population of the region in the third millennium was an indigenous pre-Indo-European group called the Hattians.[14] Evidence of a 'Hattian' civilization is provided by the remnants of one of the non-Indo-European languages found in the later Hittite archives. The language is identified in several of the texts in which it appears by the term *ḫattili*—i.e. '(written) in the language of Hatti'. The few texts that survive are predominantly religious or cultic in character. They provide us with the names of a number of Hattian deities, as well as Hattian personal and place names. The material culture of the Early Bronze Age kingdoms of central Anatolia has also been pronounced to be 'definitely of native Anatolian character'.[15]

---

[10] See the references cited by Steiner (1990: 201 n. 117).
[11] The view of Steiner himself (e.g. 1981: 169, and 1990: 200–3), who bases his conclusion largely on the assumption of a west to east migration route.
[12] Thus Macqueen (1986: 27–32).
[13] See Renfrew (1987: esp. 145–75, 263–77).
[14] See e.g. Akurgal (1962: 13–15), Macqueen (1986: 32), Klinger (1996).
[15] See Akurgal (1962: 13–29; 1989: 1).

The Hattians may then have been the people who built and inhabited the Early Bronze Age kingdoms of central Anatolia. If so, where do the Indo-Europeans fit into this picture? A number of scholars believe that the royal tombs of Alaca Höyük may help provide the answer.

Attention has been drawn, particularly by the Turkish archaeologist Ekrem Akurgal, to the burial methods used at Alaca Höyük and to the 'royal standards' which the graves contained. Akurgal claims that while the style of the objects shows that they were executed by native Anatolian, or Hattian, artists, the solar discs and theriomorphic standards, of a kind also found at Horoztepe and Mahmatlar in the Pontic region, represent non-Hattian, Indo-European concepts. Similarly the method of burial has an Indo-European character; the graves remind us of later Mycenaean burials, and those of the Phrygians found at Gordion and Ankara.[16]

This has led to the conclusion that the occupants of the tombs may have been *Kurgan* immigrants from the region of Maikop in southern Russia, immigrants who spoke an Indo-European language.[17] From this Akurgal draws the further conclusion that the tombs belonged to 'Hittite princes' who installed themselves in the country of the Hattians, as rulers of a native Hattian population; hence an Indo-European invasion towards 2200 and the installation of the first Indo-European tribes in the Kızıl Irmak basin at this time.[18] But such a theory is by no means universally accepted. It has been stated, for example, that we have no firm evidence for an Indo-European invasion of Anatolia,[19] nor indeed any evidence that Hittite culture was Indo-European in origin.[20]

So the overall situation regarding the history of Indo-European settlement in Anatolia remains a confused and confusing one. Can we draw any firm conclusions at all, from the very limited data and the maze of scholarly theories available to us, about the ethnopolitical scene in central Anatolia up to the end of the Early Bronze Age (*c.*2000 BC)? In reviewing our current state of knowledge, we will have to begin with several negatives. But it is as well to state these, since in the past so many tenuously or falsely based

---

[16] Akurgal (1992: 3–4).
[17] Thus Macqueen (1986: 26, 32), Akurgal (1992: 1–2). Cf. Yakar (1981: 94).
[18] Akurgal (1992: 4).
[19] Thus Ünal (1989: 285).   [20] See Brentjes (1986: esp. 237).

assumptions about the Indo-European presence in the region have passed into conventional wisdom and from there into the realm of 'established fact'.

Briefly, the overall situation can be summarized thus:

1. None of the evidence at our disposal points *unequivocally* to a major influx of newcomers into Anatolia, whether Indo-European or otherwise, during the third millennium.

2. We are unable to determine with any certainty the predominant ethnic character of the populations who inhabited the Early Bronze Age kingdoms. It is possible, though not provable, that the dominant culture of central Anatolia in the Early Bronze Age was that of a non-Indo-European population called the Hattians. This does not exclude the possibility that there were already peoples of Indo-European origin in the same region during this period.

3. We do not know when Indo-European groups first appeared in Anatolia, whether a century, a millennium, or several millennia before their first attested appearance in written records. Archaeological evidence has not provided us with conclusive evidence as to the date of an Indo-European arrival.

4. We can however be certain of an Indo-European presence in central Anatolia by the end of the third millennium, since Indo-European personal names appear in the records of Assyrian merchants who set up trading colonies in the region early in the second millennium.

5. Whenever Indo-European immigrants arrived, whether initially as invaders or as peaceful settlers who came in small groups over a period of several centuries, they probably mixed freely with the local populations and adopted many elements of their culture.

6. Nevertheless, a number of elements that can be identified as Indo-European persisted through this and the succeeding ages. This is particularly evident in the survival of the Indo-European language called Nesite—which became the official language of the later Hittite kingdom.

7. It is possible that the burial practices and grave goods at Alaca Höyük towards the end of the third millennium reflect a predominantly Indo-European culture in at least the immediate region. If so, the persons for whom the tombs were constructed may have spoken Nesite, or an earlier form of it, and have been amongst the Indo-European ancestors of the Late Bronze Age Hittites. The

wealth of the grave goods suggest that their recipients were members of an élite ruling class. A similar conclusion may be drawn about the sites of Horoztepe and Mahmatlar in the Pontic zone. However, the theory that these sites indicate a line of foreign kings who imposed themselves on a local population has not been substantiated.

8. More generally, a large number of the Early Bronze Age settlements of central Anatolia may have included persons of Indo-European origin in their populations.

9. The close similarities between the three attested Indo-European languages in Bronze Age Anatolia indicate that those who spoke them were originally, and remained, in relatively close contact with one other. Had they arrived in Anatolia in separate migratory waves some centuries apart, the language differences are likely to have been much more marked. The differences that do exist appear to be consistent with the theory that the main dispersion of Indo-European speakers occurred within Anatolia, perhaps no more than a few centuries before the languages make their appearance in written records.

10. The likelihood is that this dispersion occurred during the course of the third millennium. It is possible that the destruction of Troy IIg towards the end of the millennium was associated with the arrival of one of the Indo-European groups in the north-west—the group identified as the Luwians.[21]

Ethnicity in the Middle Bronze Age

In the Middle Bronze Age (twentieth–eighteenth centuries), the Assyrians established a number of merchant colonies in the eastern half of Anatolia for the purpose of trading with the towns and palaces belonging to the various local kingdoms. Most of these kingdoms had already been established during the Early Bronze Age. The headquarters of the colony network was the city of Nesa or Kanes, which as we have noted lay just south of the Kızıl Irmak river.[22] In the Assyrian texts found in this city, the great majority of names are of Indo-European origin.[23] This has led scholars to conclude that Nesa was the main centre of Indo-European settlement

---

[21] Cf. Akurgal (1992: 4).

[22] On the equivalence of these two names for the one site, see Güterbock (1958), Otten (1973: 57), Bryce (1983: 29).

[23] See Garelli (1963: 133–52), Singer (1981: 126). The ratio of Indo-European to Hattian names is approximately 6:1.

in central Anatolia during the colony period; other sites were supposedly inhabited by the indigenous Hattian people. And the conflicts between a dynasty established at Nesa and the rulers of other central Anatolian kingdoms have been seen as ethnically based conflicts between Indo-Europeans and Hattians, leading to the eventual triumph of the former over the latter.[24]

However, the notion of struggles between competing ethnic groups, of conflicts fought in order to preserve or achieve the supremacy of one such group over another, is almost certainly meaningless in this period.[25] We do not know what the ethnic composition was of the other central Anatolian kingdoms, nor the ethnic identity of the rulers of these kingdoms. By the early second millennium, the population of the region may well have been a very mixed one, which included Indo-European and Hurrian as well as Hattian elements.[26]

Nevertheless Indo-European elements seem to have been particularly prominent in the city of Nesa—to the extent that the Indo-European language spoken in the region became closely identified with the name of the city. Already in this period Nesite was probably becoming established as the Anatolian language used for written records and written communications.[27] It was used by the dynasty which imposed its rule upon the city[28] and subsequently extended its sway by military conquest over much of the eastern half of Anatolia. But initially the establishment and spread of Nesite as a written language probably occurred in a commercial context, as a result of Nesa's prominence at the centre of the Assyrian trading network.[29] Moreover if Luwian was already widely spoken in other regions of Anatolia, communication with

---

[24] See e.g. the remarks by Orlin (1970: 243 n. 73), Singer (1981: 128; 1995a: 343), Steiner (1981: 153; 1990: 198).

[25] Cf. Gurney (1973a: 231).

[26] Singer (1981) attempts to delineate ethno-cultural zones by mapping the cults of the local gods belonging to different ethno-cultural circles. This procedure may have some validity, but we do not know to what extent population movements may have altered the original ethno-cultural configuration of Anatolia by the early 2nd millennium.

[27] Güterbock (1983b: 24–5) suggests that Babylonian- or Assyrian-trained scribes may have been employed for writing documents in Nesite.

[28] It is probable, but not certain, that it was the dynasty's first language. Although the names of the first two members of this dynasty, Pithana and Anitta, are commonly supposed to be Indo-European in origin, these names have so far defied conclusive linguistic analysis. See Neu (1974: 130 n. 319; 133–4) Singer (1981: 129).

[29] Cf. Steiner (1990: 198–9).

these regions would have been much easier than if the medium used was that of a closely related language.

Who Were the Hittites?

The Hittite kingdom was founded in the early or middle years of the seventeenth century. Its capital was established at Hattusa, located 150 kilometres east of Ankara. The kingdom lasted some five centuries, throughout the period known as the Late Bronze Age.

In the light of what has been said above we should discard the widely held view that the Hittites were originally a distinct ethnic group of Indo-European origin who gained political supremacy over a native Hattian population of central Anatolia. Indeed it has been argued that Indo-Europeans played only a minor role in the history of the Hittite kingdom, as subjects of kings who were Hattian in origin.[30] Certainly, a number of Hattian elements were present in Hittite civilization, although mainly in the areas of religion, art, and mythology. And Hattian personal and place-names persisted throughout the period of the Hittite kingdom. Indeed the names of some of the kings appear to have been Hattian in origin.[31] Of course the Hattian legacy is ever present in the very name by which the kingdom was known—the Land of Hatti.

But alongside this, we must set the lack of any 'perceptible trace of Hattian influence in the historical, administrative, legal and diplomatic literature of the kingdom'.[32] Even the royal titles *Labarna* (variant *Tabarna*) and *Tawananna*, long thought to be Hattian in origin, have recently been claimed to be Indo-European (see Ch. 4, n. 16). And there is the indisputable fact that the Indo-European Nesite language was the official written language of the royal court. It was used in a wide variety of documents, both religious and secular, it was the medium of communication between Hittite kings and their regional governors and other officials, and between the kings and their vassal rulers in Anatolia, particularly in the west and south west where Luwian was widely spoken. It was also the

---

[30] Thus Steiner (1990: 199).

[31] Names like Mursili, Huzziya, and Telipinu have sometimes been identified as Hattian. But this remains open to debate.

[32] Hoffner (1973: 198).

language used by the Hittite king in his correspondence with the king of Ahhiyawa.

Since Nesite was the official language of the Hittite kingdom, it is a natural assumption that this was the language spoken by its ruling class. If not, an explanation for its use has to be found.

The German scholar Gerd Steiner has offered such an explanation, along the following lines: Nesite had already been established as an important language of communication in Anatolia during the Assyrian colony period, emanating as it did from the headquarters of the colony network. Its use may have spread quite widely beyond the Nesa region, perhaps already serving as a kind of *lingua franca* in Anatolia. It would have been much more readily learnt and understood in many parts of western and south-eastern Anatolia where Luwian was spoken, than the Hattian language, or any other language spoken within the sphere of Assyrian merchant activities. Primarily for this reason Nesite (Hittite) continued to be used as the official chancellery language in Hattusa when the Hittite kingdom was established, and as the language of written communications between the royal court and the various peoples of Anatolia, particularly in the west.

One of the main problems with this theory is that the Hittite language underwent a number of changes throughout the 500 years of its use in the Hittite texts—changes which reflect not a fossilized chancellery language but a living, spoken language. Yet the theory may not be entirely without substance. Practical considerations of the kind mentioned by Steiner may well have helped ensure Hittite's survival and continuing development as the kingdom's official language, both spoken and written, irrespective of the ethnic origins of those who spoke or wrote it.

But there may have been other reasons for the continuing use of Hittite, at least within the royal court. The royal succession in Hatti remained the prerogative of a small group of families throughout the entire history of the Hittite kingdom. And those who occupied the throne frequently proclaimed their genealogical links with their earliest known predecessors. These links helped substantiate their claims to the throne. If the earliest members of the dynasty to which they belonged spoke the Indo-European Nesite language, then the retention of this language would have helped reinforce the sense of dynasty, of unbroken family continuity through a succession of generations. Nesite was to remain the language of royalty throughout the period of the Hittite kingdom. This need not indicate continuing political supremacy by a particular ethnic group. Rather it reflects the retention of an important dynastic tradition.

As a result of marriage alliances, adoptions, and coups, several ethnic elements—Hattian, Luwian, and Hurrian amongst them— were intermingled in the small number of families which provided the occupants of the Hittite throne. From the names of the kings, their consorts, and other members of their families, it is clear that membership of the élite ruling class was not based on any sense of ethnic exclusivity.[33] But once they were admitted to the ranks of royalty, all members conformed with and perpetuated its established traditions, which included the use of Nesite as the chief official language of the court.

This does not mean that the use of Nesite was confined to the members of royalty. At the very least it must have been one of the languages spoken at the highest levels of the administrative hierarchy, which included the scribes. But it may well have had much wider currency, at least in Hattusa and the upper levels of the bureaucracy in the regional centres of the kingdom.

However widespread its use, it was but one of a number of languages spoken in the kingdom. Hattian may have continued as a language in common use, and was perhaps spoken both by the kings and the members of their families as well as by their subjects. And the numbers of prisoners-of-war brought back in the wake of military campaigns must have altered significantly the ethnic composition of the homeland population and increased the range of languages spoken in the homeland. Thus the Hittites, so called, had neither a single common ethnic core, nor a single common language. They were multi-racial in character and spoke a number of different languages.

How then did the term 'Hittite' come about? It arose initially out of a few scattered biblical references to a Canaanite people after the end of the Bronze Age. The term was subsequently adopted by scholars to refer to the Late Bronze Age kingdom in Anatolia. As far as we know, the Late Bronze Age 'Hittites' never used any ethnic or political term to designate themselves, certainly not one

---

[33] It need not of course follow that a person's name always indicates his or her ethnic origin. Political and other factors may well have influenced the choice of a name in certain cases.

which reflected an Indo-European origin. They simply called them-selves 'people of the Land of Hatti'. That is, they identified them-selves by the region in which they lived, using a name which may already have been in currency for many centuries, perhaps even millennia, and perhaps long before any Indo-European presence in the region.

They were a mixed population, consisting of a number of dif-ferent ethnic elements—Indo-European (Nesites and Luwians), Hattian, Hurrian, and probably increasingly a range of other popu-lation elements from Mesopotamia and Syria. Many of them, perhaps the great majority, probably did not speak the official language of the kingdom. What gave them a recognizable common identity, in their own eyes and in the eyes of their neighbours, was not a common language, nor a common cultural or ethnic origin, but the fact that they lived within a clearly defined region which differentiated them from other subjects of the king who lived fur-ther afield in vassal states.

The region in which they lived is often referred to as the Hittite homeland. Within this region they belonged to cities, towns, or cult centres governed by laws promulgated by the king and adminis-tered by councils of elders or regional governors acting on the king's behalf. Or they lived on rural estates whose owners owed direct allegiance to the king, often in return for royal favours received or promised. Thus through a series of hierarchical inter-mediaries they too were the subjects of the king, and could be called upon to provide him with revenue in kind and to fight in his armies.

The overall picture of the Near East in the Late Bronze Age is a complex one—a picture of constantly shifting balances of power amongst the major kingdoms of the region, of expanding and con-tracting spheres of influence, of rapidly changing allegiances and alliances as Great Kings vied with one another for supremacy over their neighbours. Within this context the kingdom of the Hittites emerged, struggled for survival, triumphed, and fell. In the pages which follow, we shall be tracing the progress of this kingdom, from its beginnings in the seventeenth century, through five centuries of triumphs and disasters, until its final collapse early in the twelfth century.

But before we embark on this study, we should retrace our steps to the centuries preceding the rise of the Hittite kingdom—to the period of the Assyrian merchant colonies. This was one of the most fascinating, and one of the best documented periods of early Anatolian history. With the establishment of their colonies the Assyrians brought to Anatolia, for the first time, the art of writing. It is with this period that a study of the history of ancient Anatolia can truly begin.

CHAPTER 2

Anatolia in the Assyrian Colony Period

THE MERCHANT COLONIES

Early in the second millennium, the Assyrians established a number of merchant colonies in Anatolia. As we have noted, the appearance of these colonies marked the beginning of a major new era in Anatolian history—the era of the written record, some thousand years after the first written records were produced in Mesopotamia.[1] The Assyrian merchants kept copious accounts of their business transactions on clay tablets written in Old Assyrian cuneiform, and maintained close written contact with officials, business associates, and family connections resident in the Assyrian capital Assur. 'Contracts and judicial records of every kind recorded and validated a variety of legal transactions of which they served as written evidence, also in lawsuits. Many lists, notes, and memorandums enabled the traders to keep track of their goods and transactions, especially lists of outstanding claims which were used for collecting debts and for the periodic settling of accounts arranged by the organization of the traders, the *kārum*.'[2]

In archaeological terminology the period of the Assyrian colonies, covering the first two centuries or so of the second millennium, is commonly known as the Middle Bronze Age. During this period, the Assyrians were very active in international trading and commercial ventures. Their activities in Anatolia are but one example of these ventures. In the course of their merchant operations, the Assyrians set up a number of settlements extending from their homeland into central Anatolia.[3] Twenty-one such

[1] It may well be that there were established commercial links betwen Mesopotamia and Anatolia through the 3rd millennium; see Veenhof (1982: 154), who notes that the new texts from Ebla seem to provide evidence of early contacts with Kanes.

[2] Veenhof (1995a: 312).

[3] Balkan (1957: 31–2) cites the letter TC 18—which is the main source for the reconstruction of the routes from Assur to Kanes. See also Hecker (1981: 187), who

settlements are attested in their texts. So far we have been able to locate only three of these, two within the Kızıl Irmak basin (Hattus = Hittite Hattusa, and the settlement on the site of Alişar),[4] and one just to the south of the Kızıl Irmak river, Kültepe (ancient Kanes), in the region of modern Kayseri.

From all three sites tablets recording the Assyrian merchants' operations and transaction have been unearthed, with by far the largest number coming from Kanes.[5] More than 15,000 merchant tablets have now come to light, the great majority of which have yet to be studied in detail.[6] Two types of settlement are identified in the texts—major communities called *kāru* (singular *kārum*) and minor settlements called *wabaratum* (singular *wabartum*).[7] The latter may have functioned primarily as military posts set up by the Assyrians at strategic locations to protect the caravans of merchandise from hostile natives.[8]

The City of Kanes

The focal point of the merchant operations was the city of Nesa or Kanes, on the site now known as Kültepe.[9] There are two main sections of the site, the excavation of which was begun in 1948 under the direction of the Turkish archaeologist Tahsin Özgüç:

1. Kültepe Höyük, a 20-metre high mound, about 500 metres in diameter, rising above the Kayseri plain. This was the site of

comments that the route from Assur to Kanes was not direct, but crossed in a wide arc through northern Syria, across the Euphrates in the region between Birecik and Samsat, and then perhaps to Malatya and Maraş before making a new swing west— to Kanes.

[4] As noted in Ch. 1, this is probably the ancient Amkuwa.

[5] So far, and surprisingly, only texts from Kanes have come to light in the level II phase. Those discovered at Alişar and Hattusa belong entirely to Ib; see Larsen (1976: 52). Bittel (1983c: 55).

[6] Özgüç (1986: xxi) notes that 11,000 tablets have been discovered since 1948 and are ready to be studied in the Ankara Museum. Those found prior to the beginning of the systematic Turkish excavations at Kanes in 1948 are widely scattered in many public and private collections.

[7] On the derivation of the term *kārum*, see Orlin (1970: 25–6).

[8] Further on the possible differences between the two types of settlements, see Larsen (1976: 278). Larsen (1976: 236) notes that several of the settlements changed character in the interval between level II and Ib, so that they are attested both as *kārum* and *wabartum* settlements.

[9] See Larsen (1976: 277), with respect to the question of the Assyrians' selection of the site as the centre of their trading system.

the local Anatolian settlement, dominated by the palace of its ruler.

2. Kültepe Kārum (or Kārum Kanes), the Assyrian commercial centre on the north-east and south-east rims of the mound.[10] The *kārum* was not inhabited exclusively by Assyrian traders; it also included many Anatolians among its inhabitants, as indicated by the names of house-owners with Anatolian names, like Peruwa, Galulu, Saktanuwa, Suppiahsu.[11]

There are four major occupation levels at Kanes. The first two (IV and III) belong to the Early Bronze Age. Level III was destroyed by fire in the Early Bronze III phase. This was followed by the Middle Bronze Age, the period of the Assyrian colonies, represented archaeologically by two levels, II and Ib. On the basis of Old Assyrian chronology, the dates and duration of these two levels can be determined with reasonable accuracy. This is because a large number of the texts found at Kültepe, Alişar, and Hattusa include as a date formula the name of the eponym *limum*, an official appointed each year at Assur. Surviving lists of these officials make it possible to determine the chronological sequence of the *kārum* tablets by synchronizing the *limum* lists with the Assyrian king lists, since it was customary for an Assyrian king to be made *limum* in one of the early years of his reign.

Level II of the *kārum* at Kanes lasted some 70 to 80 years, from relatively late in the reign of Erisum I[12] until the end of the reign of Puzur-Assur, i.e. from some time in the last quarter of the twentieth century until about the middle of the nineteenth. It ended in destruction by fire. The site was left unoccupied for a period of perhaps 30 years before resettlement took place in the Ib phase—the last phase of the merchant colonies.[13] It is still not certain whether the settlement on the mound suffered destruction at the same time as the *kārum*. Quite possibly it remained intact, since a number of the tablets found in the palace at Kanes are to be ascribed to the intermediate period between levels II and

---

[10] See the reconstruction in Lloyd (1967: 46–7). On the various districts of the *kārum*, see Özgüç (1986: 14). For further details on the physical layout out of the *kārum*, see Özgüç (1964: 27–39). The *kārum* may have covered as much as 30 hectares; see Veenhof (1995b: 860).

[11] Veenhof (1989: 515).

[12] A letter from this king was discovered in level II of Kanes.

[13] See Balkan (1955: 60–1).

Ib.[14] Level Ib had a flourishing existence[15] before it too was destroyed by fire. Roughly speaking, it extended from the late nineteenth century into the first half of the eighteenth. In contrast to
level II from which several thousand tablets have been unearthed,
documentary evidence from Ib is sparse. This level has yielded no
more than about 250 tablets.

The Kingdoms of Central Anatolia in the Colony Period

From information provided in the Assyrian texts, we can conclude
that during the colony period, central Anatolia was dominated by
several kingdoms sometimes designated as *mātu* (singular *mātum*)
in the merchant texts—the kingdoms of Hatti, which probably
incorporated most of the territory lying within the Kızıl Irmak
basin, Kanes, immediately to the south, Burushattum (variant
Purushattum; Purushanda in the Hitttite texts), and Wahsusana.[16]
The latter two were probably neighbouring kingdoms south of
the Kızıl Irmak. Wahsusana was perhaps located in the vicinity
of modern Niğde.[17] Burushattum was situated on an important
trade route from Assyria passing though Washaniya, Nenassa, and
Ullamma.[18] It probably lay to the south-east of the Salt Lake, and
is today perhaps buried under the mound known as Acem Höyük
(*c.*6 kilometres west-north-west of Aksaray).[19]

In a tradition preserved in later times in a text known as the
'King of the Battle' (*šar tamḥari*),[20] the Akkadian king Sargon
(*c.*2334–2279) conducted an expedition against Nur-Dagan king of

[14] See Balkan (1955: 45, 61). Note also Larsen (1976: 366), who comments that it
is uncertain whether the gap between II and Ib was a local phenomenon, or whether
it reflects a genuine break in the Old Assyrian activities in the entire area where the
colonies existed.
[15] Özgüç (1964: 37).
[16] Cf. Singer (1981: 127). Note in the merchant texts the designations *Mat
Burušḥattum* (KTHahn 1: 3), *Mat Kaniš* (TCu 18: 42), *Mat Waḥšušana* (KTHahn
1: 3–4, KTP 10: 23).
[17] See the references cited by del Monte and Tischler (1978: 471). Larsen (1972:
101) suggested a location further west, in the plain of Konya. See also Nashef (1991:
135).
[18] See the references cited by del Monte and Tischler (1978: 324). Add Cornelius
(1958a: 382).
[19] See the references cited by Houwink ten Cate (1970: 58–9 n. 8). Add Larsen
(1976: 237), Bittel (1976a: Abb. 343 (map)).
[20] For the Hittite fragments, see *CTH* 310, and for the text, Güterbock (1934: 86–
91) and (1969); the additional fragment to which he refers in the latter publication
is Bo 68/28 (*CTH* 310.5), subsequently published as KBo XXII 6.

Purushanda. This tradition, like that associated with Sargon's grandson Naram-Sin, may well have been based on historical fact.[21] If so, it provides evidence that there was already a kingdom of Burushattum/Purushanda in the Early Bronze Age.

To the list of central Anatolian kingdoms, we can probably add Zalpa (Zalpuwa), which lay to the north of the kingdom of Hatti in or near the Pontic zone.

We cannot be sure how far the authority or influence of each of these kingdoms extended at the beginning of the colony period. However, each had as its focal point a chief city whose ruler (*rubā'um* in the merchant texts) exercised authority broadly over the communities lying within his kingdom. Some of these communities must have been quite substantial settlements with Assyrian colonies attached to them, and under the control of a local vassal, also called a *rubā'um* in the texts.[22] The local *rubā'um* probably enjoyed a large measure of autonomy in running the affairs of the community or communities lying within his immediate authority. But he was always subject to the overriding authority of the ruler of the *mātum* to which he belonged.[23]

What was the nature of the relationship between the Assyrians and the local rulers?[24] It was once believed that the colonies were established in the wake of Assyrian military conquests, reflecting Assyrian domination over the regions where they were located. But in fact the colonies were simply 'guest enclaves' based on trading pacts between Assyria and the local rulers, with the latter retaining overall control of the Assyrian merchants' activities in their region.[25]

Negotiations between the kings, or sub-kings, and the colonies in their region required the involvement of the central colony

[21] See e.g. Güterbock (1983*b*: 26–7).

[22] *rubā'um* is in fact a rather vague term. It could be used of the ruler of a *mātum*, of a local vassal ruler, or simply of the head man of a village.

[23] See also Orlin (1970: 237), and the comments by Larsen (1974: 472), on the complex political pattern of central Anatolia in this period.

[24] The political relations between the merchants and local Anatolians are discussed in detail by Garelli (1963: 321–61).

[25] Cf. Veenhof (1982: 147–8), who comments that the Assyrian presence was not based on military or imperial domination, but was in the nature of peaceful, commercial penetration on the basis of mutual interests and official agreements or treaties with local rulers; the official contacts served the establishment and maintenance of good political relations with the various Anatolian rulers by official representatives of Kanes in conjunction with envoys of Assur.

administration at Kanes. Sometimes a local ruler had to be reminded of this, as we learn from a letter written by the officials of
the kārum in Wahsusana. The letter was in response to a request
the colony had received from the *rubā'um* at Washaniya, which lay
nearby. The *rubā'um* had written to advise the merchants at
Wahsusana that he had succeeded to his father's throne and
wished to renew a treaty with them. He was informed of the correct
procedure to be followed:

We answered: 'The kārum at Kanes is our superior. We shall write so that
they may write either to you (directly) or to us. Two men from the Land[26]
will come to you and then they can make you swear the oath![27] It is up to
you now! Let your orders come here! We have given our messengers (an
allowance of) 20 minas of copper.'   (KTP 14, 9–23, adapted from trans. by
Larsen (1976: 249))

Although the reading and interpretation of this letter are not entirely certain,[28] the colony officials at Wahsusana clearly did not
have the authority to deal directly with the new king, at least in the
first instance. The matter had to be referred to Kanes, which would
send two envoys to arrange renewal of the treaty.

The Incentives for Assyrian Commercial Enterprise

What attractions did Anatolia hold for Assyrian merchant enterprises? In the first place, a stable political environment must have
been an important factor. At the beginning of the colony period,
the local rulers coexisted on relatively peaceful terms, and the
control they exercised over their own kingdoms was sufficient to
assure foreign merchants of safe and profitable trading ventures.[29]
As we know from a number of their documents, Assyrian merchants were very sensitive to such matters, and were extremely
reluctant to trade in areas where conditions were unsettled.[30] For
the Assyrian colonists, central Anatolia offered the attractions of

---

[26] For discussion of what this expression means, see Larsen (1976: 250).
[27] The term used in the texts for a commercial agreement.
[28] See Larsen (1976: 250). Cf. the earlier treatments of the text by Garelli (1963:
329–31) and Orlin (1970: 114–18).
[29] Cf. Larsen (1976: 86).
[30] Note the letters ATHE 66 (lines 9–14) and KTHahn 1 in which the Assyrian
merchants Puzur-Assur and Idi-Istar (respectively) indicate that they will not trade
in politically unstable areas where the security of themselves and their goods is at
risk. Cf. Veenhof (1989: 516).

a series of already well-established urban centres within the
framework of relatively coherent political structures conducive to
profitable commercial activities throughout the region.

However, the overall success of the enterprise rested basically on
the fact that each side had exportable goods much in demand by
the other. The main items exported to Anatolia by the Assyrians
were woollen textiles and a metal called *annukum*. Once argued
that this was the Assyrian word for lead, it now seems certain that
the metal in question was tin.[31] As we have already noted, the
Anatolian communities were largely if not solely dependent on
foreign importation of tin to make bronze. For the central and
eastern Anatolian communities, the only feasible source of supply
in this period was Assyria. The Assyrians probably obtained the
metal from the mountains of south-west Iran (ancient Elam),[32]
whence traders brought it to Assur.[33] The texts available to us
indicate the importation of some 80 tonnes of tin over a 50-year
period, which would have been used in the production of some 800
tonnes of bronze.

The textiles were manufactured in pieces about four metres
square. Some of them were produced in Assyria but the majority
were of Babylonian origin.[34] They were noted for their fine quality,
particularly in comparison with those manufactured locally in
Anatolia. Letters exchanged between the merchants stationed
in the colonies and their female relatives or business associates in
Assur[35] contain very precise instructions as to the method of manufacture and the size of textiles to be sent to Anatolia. Our most
informative source in this respect is a letter from Puzur-Assur, an
Assyrian merchant living in Anatolia, to Waqartum, a woman in
the Assyrian capital Assur:

Thus (speaks) Puzur-Assur: 'Say unto Waqartum: 1 mina of silver, its tax
added, its duties paid for, Assur-idi is bringing you under my seal. The fine

---

[31] See Garelli (1963: 269–79), Landsberger (1965).
[32] See Muhly (1973), Larsen (1976, 87–9), Yakar (1976: 122–3).
[33] See Larsen (1967: 153–5). 'The Assyrian capital was thus the centre of a transit
trade linking the tin-producing areas in Iran with Anatolia and Babylonia' (p. 155).
[34] See Larsen (1967: 178).
[35] On the role of women in the merchant enterprises, see Günbatti (1992).
Günbatti comments (p. 234) that women in Assyria were almost as active as men in
social life; not only were they the family partners, but also the business partners of
their husbands; they helped their husbands and brothers, and looked after their
interests in matters of business and judicial cases in Assyria.

textile which you sent me—keep producing similar textiles and send (them) to me with Assur-idi, and I will send you $\frac{1}{2}$ mina of silver (apiece).

Let them comb one side of the textile; they should not shear it; its weave should be close. Compared with the previous textile which you sent me, process 1 mina of wool extra (in) each (piece), but keep them thin! The other side one should comb *slightly*(?). If it is still hairy, one should shear it like a *kutanum* (i.e. a linen cloth).' (TCu 3/1, 17, 1–22, trans. Veenhof (1972: 104))

Though lacking in tin, Anatolia had rich deposits of a number of other metals, including copper, silver, and gold.[36] This was obviously what attracted the Assyrian merchants, who brought their tin and textiles to Anatolia to trade them for Anatolian metals, especially silver and gold. They supplemented their import ventures with internal commercial activities, trading wool, woollen fabrics, and copper amongst the local communities with the ultimate goal of acquiring silver and gold to be conveyed back to Assur.[37]

A loan and credit system operated widely throughout the communities of eastern Anatolia during the colony period. Rates of interest were high, ranging from 30 per cent to as much as 180 per cent.[38] There were a number of occasions when debtors were unable to repay the original loan at harvest time, particularly after a bad year, or even meet the interest repayments. Non-payment of debts was clearly a source of tension between debtors and creditors. A debtor might in fact be forced to sell a member of his family, or his whole family, including himself, to discharge a debt.[39] In some cases the local king took action to resolve problems of indebtedness by issuing a decree cancelling all debts.[40] Understandably a creditor often sought to protect at least part of his original loan in the event that such a decree was issued:

Salmuh and Iskunanika, his wife, Ispunahsu and Kiri owe 21 sacks of grain, half (of which is) wheat, half (is) barley, (and) 15 shekels of silver to Peruwa. They will give (back) the silver and the grain at harvest time. They

---

[36] See de Jesus (1978).

[37] See Özgüç (1963: 98), Veenhof (1972: 137–9; 1989: 517). There is no evidence of trade in copper between Anatolia and Assur.

[38] Balkan (1974: 30).

[39] See Balkan (1974: 30), and Veenhof (1982: 148). The latter notes that the list of Anatolians indebted and often in arrears to Assyrians far exceeds that of Assyrians in debt to Anatolians; see the lists in Garelli (1963: 379–90).

[40] The expression used is *ḫubullam masā'um*—'to wash away debt' (Balkan (1974: 32)).

themselves will haul (the grain) to (the village) Hailawakuwa. They will measure out the grain with the (measuring) pot of Peruwa. The silver and the grain are bound to their joint guarantee, (and) that of their family. Before: Kakria; before: Idi(s)-Su'in; before: Ili-(i)ddinassu.[41] If the king cancels the obligation to pay debt, you will pay me my grain.   (kt d/k 48b 5–24, trans. Balkan (1974: 35))[42]

The Organization of the Merchant Enterprises

Effective exploitation of the mutually beneficial trade links between Assyria and Anatolia obviously required organization on a large and complex scale. Anatolian society was at least one 'which could buy and absorb thousands of expensive textiles and could process considerable amounts of tin in an important bronze industry. The Anatolian palaces carried out complicated clearance operations of Assyrian imports and maintained a satisfactory balance of payments with the *Bīt Kārim*.'[43]

On the Assyrian side, the organization of the system involved the establishment and administration of the colonies, the setting up of boards to arbitrate on trading disputes, the maintenance of close contacts with the Assyrian capital Assur, the drawing up of commercial treaties with the local Anatolian rulers, and the financing of commercial enterprises.

The Assyrian state exercised some measure of control over trading operations and the conduct and administration of the colonies through the agency of the *Bīt Ālim*, literally the 'City House'.[44] But the trading enterprises themselves were financed and often operated by a wealthy Assyrian business entrepreneur or investor— *ummeānum* in the texts. He could act as an exporter-importer in his own right, or form a consortium with other entrepreneurs. He often established branch offices of his business in the colonies. The

---

[41] The witnesses to the agreement.

[42] As Balkan (1974: 32) points out, the loan contracts which refer to the possibility of the king cancelling all debts are known only in the cases of native debtors and creditors; we may assume, however, that such a cancellation of debts would also apply to debts owed by Anatolians to Assyrian merchants.

[43] Veenhof (1982: 154). *Bīt Kārim* literally means the 'Kārum House', i.e. the financial and administrative centre of the *kārum*.

[44] For a list of the responsibilities it exercised, see Orlin (1970: 58–9). But note Larsen (1974: 470), who cautions against overestimating the role of the state in these enterprises and comments on the role of Kanes at the centre of a special administrative and political structure which had its own internal coherence and which in its relations with Assur enjoyed a certain degree of autonomy (1976: 262).

branch offices were usually managed by younger male members of his family sent out to the colonies for indefinite periods of time—in some cases until the head of the business in Assur died or retired. However a number of Assyrians decided to make Anatolia their permanent home. They established or relocated their families and households there, bringing their wives or prospective wives from Assur, or marrying local Anatolian girls.[45]

As a rule, the *ummeānum* placed the actual running of his trading operations in the hands of a *tamkārum*, an agent responsible for the conduct of his affairs in Anatolia, the sale of his merchandise, the decision as to where it would be sold, and all dealings with his Anatolian customers.[46] But the most onerous responsibilities usually fell on the *kassāru*, transporters who were hired as caravan personnel to take the merchandise to Anatolia, and from Anatolia to Assyria, and to ensure that the caravans actually reached their destinations. They assumed all responsibility for payments *en route*. They spent virtually all their lives as commercial travellers, except for four winter months of each year when all trading operations ceased. In return for their services, they apparently received interest-free loans, or working capital, which would enable them to acquire merchandise of their own for sale in Anatolia or en *route* to Anatolia.[47]

Transporting and Selling the Merchandise

The caravans were made up of the so-called black donkeys of Cappadocia. They were probably bred and trained in Assyria, and were sold to the merchants for 20 shekels of silver each. An average-size caravan consisted of some 200–50 animals, with each donkey carrying about 130 minas ($= c.$ 65 kilograms) of tin or 60 minas of textiles (consisting on average of 25–6 pieces) or a mixture

[45] Veenhof (1982: 147). See further on the family-firm operation Larsen (1974: 471; 1976: 97–102). It should however be noted that while the merchant system was controlled and operated predominantly by Assyrians, others of non-Assyrian origin, including Anatolians and Syrians, also participated; see Hecker (1981: 189–93). For tablets indicating some involvement by persons from Ebla in the merchant trade, see Veenhof (1989: 516), Bilgiç (1992).

[46] The precise meaning and attributes of the term *tamkārum* seem to have varied; see Larsen (1967: 49–56; 1974: 470).

[47] See Larsen (1967: 79–80, 149–50), Veenhof (1972: 10–11, 86–7).

of the two.[48] The merchandise was placed in two packs slung on either side of the donkey, plus a top pack or saddle pack. As a rule the side packs were not to be opened during the journey, but the top pack was probably accessible and contained such items as food, animal fodder, the traveller's private possessions, and what is referred to as 'loose tin' in contrast to 'sealed tin'.[49]

Tolls and levies were demanded by every town of any significant size through which the caravan passed on the journey, in Mesopotamia, northern Syria, and Anatolia. When it passed through the territory of the various administrative centres, it was subject to a further tax, the *nishatum*, a flat rate levied by the administration of 5 per cent on textiles and 3 per cent on tin. It seems too that the palace exercised the right to buy up to 10 per cent of a consignment of textiles before it was cleared for sale on the open market. The palace also had a monopoly on rare luxury items, like meteoritic iron. In return for these privileges, the palace gave the merchants important guarantees, relating (for example) to residential rights and promises of protection when travelling in areas within the palace's jurisdiction.[50] The merchants were subject to other taxes from their own people—for example, an export tax on leaving Assur, and probably also some kind of levy on goods which was imposed by the administration of a particular colony, as payment towards general administration expenses, and for storage of goods.[51]

Once all these taxes and tolls had been cleared, the merchant then had to sell his produce. Tin was much easier to dispose of, and presumably the merchant simply discharged his cargo at one of the metallurgical centres. Textiles probably involved more effort. The merchant may have had to hawk them around, and sell them on an individual basis or in small quantities. Also, the transport costs of textiles was obviously higher since they required more than twice the number of donkeys to carry them than were needed for their equivalent weight in tin. This probably explains why the gross profit on textiles was twice that of tin.

[48] See Larsen (1967: 147–9), Veenhof (1972: 13–27).
[49] See further Larsen (1967: 169), Veenhof (1972: 23).
[50] See Larsen (1976: 245).
[51] Note by way of illustration the text TC 3/2, 165, which indicates all the taxes incurred on the journey from Kanes to Burushattum. See Garelli (1963: 308–10), Larsen (1967: 161), Veenhof (1972: 285).

How to Avoid the Taxes

Gross profits from the merchants' trading activities were high, approximately 100 per cent on tin and 200 per cent on textiles. Understandably so. The initiative and enterprise in these commercial ventures seem to have been all on the merchants' side. It was they who organized and operated the system, and they who apparently suffered all the risks. Further, their profit margins were substantially reduced by basic travelling expenses on the long, difficult, and often hazardous treks from Assyria and Anatolia, and by the succession of tolls, levies, and taxes imposed by their own officials in the colonies and by the local Anatolian authorities.[52] There was undoubtedly much incentive for finding ways of avoiding these outlays.

One way of doing so was to bypass the towns which imposed the tolls by leaving the main highway and travelling along a side road, known as the *ḫarrān sūqinnim*—literally, the 'narrow track'.[53] But this could be a hazardous undertaking, partly because such tracks were likely to be infested with brigands, and partly because they may have taken the caravans a long way from food and water. Hence the caution which the merchants showed in venturing from the beaten track, as illustrated by a letter from Buzazu to his business associate Puzur-Assur:

Let them travel on to Timilkia to reach my merchandise and, if the 'narrow track' is safe, my tin and textiles of good quality, as much as he had brought across the country, should indeed come to me with a caravan by way of the 'narrow track'. If however the 'narrow track' is not appropriate, let them bring the tin to Hurrama and let then either the native inhabitants of Hurrama bring all the tin in quantities of 1 talent each into the town, or let one make packets of 10 or 15 minas each, and let the personnel (of the caravan) bring them into the town under their loincloths. Only after they have safely delivered 1 talent are they allowed to bring another 1 talent into the town. As soon as some of the tin has safely arrived in town you should send it on to me each time with the first caravan leaving.   (BIN IV 48, 12–29, trans. Veenhof (1972: 312, 324))

As the letter indicates, the alternative method of avoiding tolls and levies was to try to convey the goods through a town secretly, without the knowledge of the local authorities. But smuggling was

[52] See Veenhof (1972: 229–302).
[53] For this translation, see Veenhof (1972: 322–3).

also a hazardous business, for discovery could mean confiscation of an entire consignment of merchandise and imprisonment for the offenders, as Puzur-Assur was warned by another of his business associates:

The son of Irra sent his smuggled goods to Pusu-ken, but his smuggled goods were caught whereupon the palace seized Pusu-ken and put him in jail. The guards are strong. The queen has sent messages to Luhusaddia, Hurrama, Salahsuwa[54] and to her (own) country concerning the smuggling, and look-outs (literally, 'eyes') have been posted. Please do not smuggle anything. (ATHE 62, 28–37, trans. Veenhof (1972, 308))

Smuggling of valuable items out of Anatolia also sometimes occurred, for example the illegal export of the rare and precious meteoritic iron (*amūtum*, *ašῑum*).

In general, the merchants had to be careful to avoid conflict with the local administrations.[55] In cases where merchants violated their agreements with them, the latter were prompt to take swift and severe action, including imprisonment and confiscation of their silver and gold.[56]

POLITICAL DEVELOPMENTS IN ANATOLIA IN THE COLONY PERIOD

One important consequence of the Assyrians' trading enterprises in Anatolia was that it almost certainly encouraged a greater sense of territorial consciousness amongst the local rulers. There were important practical considerations involved in the clear definition of territorial boundaries, both of the individual towns through which the merchants passed as well as of the kingdoms to which these towns belonged. The boundaries determined which local administration had jurisdiction over the merchants at a particular stage on their journey—and therefore the right to the various tolls and levies imposed upon them. Further, effective operation of the system must have required a high degree of co-operation amongst the various authorities through whose lands the merchants passed, on such matters as 'keeping the roads free'—i.e. ensuring that the routes travelled by the merchants were kept safe against the dangers to which commercial caravans were vulnerable. This was a

[54] The names of Anatolian towns. [55] See further Larsen (1974: 473–4).
[56] See Balkan (1974: 29).

matter on which the merchants were particularly sensitive: 'I hear that they freed the road. If they (really) freed the road, bring here my merchandise. Let me arise and go there' (CCT II, 22–5, trans. Balkan (1957: 16)).

The routes travelled by the merchants provided a regular communication network throughout central Anatolia. In this and in other ways, the merchant system must have promoted closer and more regular contacts between the kingdoms within the region where the colonies were established. Yet by bringing these kingdoms into closer contact, and by bringing into sharper focus the importance of territorial control from both a commercial as well as a political standpoint, the Assyrian colony system helped create grounds for dissension amongst and within the kingdoms. These included conflicting claims over border territory, increasing inducements for a king to seek to expand his own territory at the expense of his neighbours, and the incentives for a vassal ruler to break away from his overlord and establish himself as an independent ruler in his own right.

By the end of the first phase of the colony period (represented archaeologically by level II at Kanes), there is evidence of increasing disturbances and open conflict in the regions where the colonies were located. Thus troubles in the south forced the merchant Idi-Istar to postpone a visit to Wahsusana where he was to arrange for the dispatch of a consignment of copper held in storage there. He wrote to his colleague Assur-nada with the news: 'I have not gone to Wahsusana for there is revolt in the land of Burushattum and Wahsusana' (KTHahn 1, 2–6).

The most dramatic evidence for conflict amongst the Anatolian kingdoms is provided by the destruction of the city of Nesa/Kanes around the middle of the nineteenth century. Who or what was responsible for its destruction? We know from a text commonly called the Anitta inscription (discussed below) that the kingdom of Nesa was attacked, conquered, and looted by Uhna, the ruler of the northern kingdom of Zalpa, perhaps in collaboration with the king of Hatti. This conquest may explain the destruction of the city attested in the archaeological record. If so, we can only speculate on the reasons which had led to its attack and destruction. Nesa may have provoked it by over-exploiting its position at the centre of the Assyrian merchant system, perhaps closing off, or threatening to close off, the routes leading to the more northerly Anatolian kingdoms.

At all events, with the destruction of the hub of the colony network, the Assyrians may have ceased their trading operations in Anatolia, or at least severely curtailed them, until the return of more stable conditions several decades later, when Nesa was resettled (level Ib). But in the intervening years another kingdom had come to prominence south of the Kızıl Irmak river, probably in the mountainous area to the south-east of Nesa—the kingdom of Mama.[57]

Tensions between Mama and Kanes

Within a few years of the resettlement of Nesa/Kanes, tensions began mounting between its king Inar and the king of Mama, a man called Anum-hirbi.[58] These seem to have culminated in an invasion of Mama's territory by Inar. Subsequently peace was restored and a treaty concluded between the two kings. Yet the peace remained precarious and in the reign of Inar's son and successor Warsama, hostilities flared once more. On this occasion the instigator was the 'Man of Taisama', one of Warsama's vassal rulers, who had on his own initiative crossed into Mama and attacked and destroyed a number of its towns. Anum-hirbi wrote to the king of Kanes complaining bitterly of his vassal's conduct, and urging Warsama to keep him under control in the future:

Anum-hirbi, the king of Mama, speaks as follows: 'Tell Warsama, the king of Kanes: "You have written to me: 'The Man of Taisama is my slave; I shall keep watch over him. But will you keep watch over the Man of Sibuha, your slave?' Since the Man of Taisama is your dog, why does he quarrel with other princes? Does the Man of Sibuha, my dog, quarrel with other princes? Will a king of Taisama become a third king with us?

'"When my enemy conquered me, the Man of Taisama invaded my country, and destroyed twelve of my cities, and carried away their cattle

---

[57] On various possibilities for its location, see Balkan (1957: 33), who suggests a localization in the vicinity of modern Elbistan, or the region of Comana Cappadocia and Göksün. See also Nashef (1991: 83).

[58] Güterbock (1964*b*: 109) notes a fragment found in 1960 which mentions a certain Anum-herwa (KBo XII 3 = *CTH* 2.1)—who may be identical with Anum-hirbi. See also Helck (1983: 274–6), who transliterates and translates the fragment and supports the identification.

and sheep. He spoke as follows: 'The king is dead, so I have taken my fowler's snare.' Instead of protecting my country and giving me heart, he not only burned up my country but created evil-smelling smoke.

'"While your father Inar was laying siege for nine years to the city of Harsamna, did my people invade your land, and did they kill a single ox or sheep?"' (kt g/t 35, 1–33, based on trans. by Balkan (1957: 8))[59]

Warsama agreed to keep his vassal ruler under control, but sought a similar assurance from Anum-hirbi with regard to Anum-hirbi's wayward vassal, the Man of Sibuha. Both kings seemed anxious to restore peaceful relations and to renew the former treaty, as Anum-hirbi's letter indicates: '[you wrote] to me as follows: "Let us take an oath." Is the former oath insufficient? Let your messenger come to me and let my messenger come regularly to you.' (kt g/t 35, 49–55, trans. Balkan (1957: 8)).

In Warsama's case, the main incentive for renewing diplomatic relations was probably to ensure that the normal communication routes between the two kingdoms would be reopened: 'Today you wrote to me as follows: "Why do you not free the road for me?" I shall free the road.' (kt g/t 35, 34–7, trans. Balkan (1957: 8)). Disruption of these routes must have had serious commercial implications for Neṣa, particularly as far as the Assyrian trading operations were concerned.

Thus peace was probably restored between the two kingdoms— for the time being.

The Dynasty of Pithana

It may have been under the rule of Warsama's father Inar that Nesa/Kanes again rose to prominence, as attested by the remains of level Ib. But the Ib period seems to have been one of continuing instability. The conflicts and disputes to which Anum-hirbi refers could well have been responsible for a progressive fragmentation of the political and administrative structures of central Anatolia— the gradual breakdown of the older kingdoms into smaller units, considerably increasing the complexity of the Anatolian political scene and the potential for ongoing conflicts and disputes over borders and territorial rights. A broken text which appears to indicate a revolt of vassal communities against the king of Hattusa

---

[59] The letter is written in Old Assyrian, and is also trans. Orlin (1970: 99).

may indicate a similar process of fragmentation within the kingdom of Hatti.[60]

But then there was a dramatic turn of events, one which was to alter quite profoundly the political scene in the region both within and south of the Kızıl Irmak basin:

> The king of Kussara came down from the town in great force and took Nesa in the night by storm. He seized the king of Nesa, but inflicted no harm on the inhabitants of Nesa. Instead, he made them his mothers and fathers.   (Anitta inscript. (*CTH* 1), 5–9)

These lines come from the so-called Anitta inscription, a text preserved in fragmentary form in three copies,[61] allegedly from an original carved on a stela set up in the gate of the king's city.[62] Although once thought to have been written in Old Assyrian cuneiform, the original text was probably written in 'Hittite' (Nesite).[63] However, the earliest surviving version of it is a copy apparently made during the Hittite Old Kingdom some 150 years after the original.[64]

The inscription deals with the conquests in central Anatolia of two kings who were apparently members of a ruling dynasty based originally in a city called Kussara—Pithana and his son Anitta, the author of the text. The names of these kings are known also from several other early texts,[65] and they can almost certainly be assigned to the second phase of the colony period.[66] The city of Kussara probably lay to the south-east of the Kızıl Irmak basin in the anti-Taurus region,[67] on or near one of the main trade routes from Assyria and perhaps in the vicinity of the modern Şar (Comana Cappadociae).[68]

A number of scholars have drawn attention to Pithana's statement that on his conquest of Nesa, he did no harm to the inhabitants of the city but 'made them his mothers and fathers'. This statement is unique in cuneiform literature. Is it purely symbolical,

---

[60] See Larsen (1972), Bryce (1985*a*).
[61] The text has most recently been ed. by Neu (1974). See also the discussions of Steiner (1984; 1989*b*).   [62] Gurney (1990: 141).
[63] See Neu (1974: 3–9).
[64] See Neu (1974: 6), Hoffner (1980: 291), Güterbock (1983*b*: 24–5).
[65] See Bryce (1983: 21–2).
[66] See the references cited by Gurney (1973*a*: 232 n. 8).
[67] See Lewy, J. (1962), Singer (1981: 128), Bryce (1983: 28).
[68] For other proposals, see the references cited by del Monte and Tischler (1978: 230; 1992: 87–8).

or does it have a more literal meaning? If taken literally, it might indicate actual ethnic links between the Kussaran dynasts and the predominantly Indo-European population of Nesa, or more generally close ethnic affinities between the populations of Nesa and Kussara.[69] But this could well be reading more into the statement than is warranted. Its main intention may simply have been to convey the image of a benevolent ruler who was bent on winning the goodwill of those upon whom his rule had been imposed. He wished them to see themselves as his kinfolk, rather than as the subjects of an alien despot. The image belongs to the language of diplomacy—or propaganda. It need not reflect literal truth.

We have no firm grounds for assuming that Pithana sought to identify himself as the champion of an Indo-European ethnic group, or that the conflicts in which he and his son Anitta engaged reflect a struggle for political and military supremacy between two ethnic groups, Hattian and Indo-European. We do not know from their names alone what the ethnic origins of Pithana and Anitta were. And by the early second millennium, after several or more centuries of Indo-European settlement in Anatolia and intermingling with other groups, consciousness of ethnic differences may have largely disappeared—at least in a socio-political sense. There was no doubt a continuing awareness of basic cultural differences between various population groups or sub-groups, particularly if they continued to speak different languages, but it is most unlikely that these differences led to competition and conflict between the Anatolian kingdoms in the colony period.

After Pithana's conquest, Nesa became the new seat of the Kussaran dynasty. The discovery in 1954 of an inscribed dagger in the debris of a large building on the mound at Kültepe seemed to provide material confirmation of the establishment of Nesa as the Kussaran dynasty's royal seat. The dagger bore the inscription É GAL *A-ni-ta ru-bā-im* ((the property of) the palace of Anitta, the King).[70] Was the building where it was discovered Anitta's palace? On its own, the evidence provided by the dagger may have simply indicated that this was a regional residence of the king. But when we consider it along with other written evidence, there can be little doubt that the building on the mound was in fact the palace of Anitta.

[69] See e.g. Orlin (1970: 243 n. 73), Singer (1981: 128).
[70] See Balkan (1955: 78).

Almost certainly important strategic considerations provided the incentive for Pithana's conquest of Nesa, and the relocation of the seat of his power there. With Nesa as their base, Pithana and Anitta were well within military striking range of the Anatolian kingdoms lying both within the Kızıl Irmak basin and south of it in the region later known as the Lower Land. In view of the extensive military operations which Anitta subsequently undertook both north and south of the Kızıl Irmak, the conquest of Nesa may well have been the first step in a campaign designed to bring the whole region beneath the sway of the Kussaran dynasty.

A further incentive was the fact that the merchant colony attached to Nesa was the administrative and distribution centre of the entire Assyrian colony network in Anatolia. Of course the merchant colonies enjoyed a considerable degree of independence in their commercial operations. But as we have seen, they were none the less subject to the overall administrative and judicial control of the local administrations in whose regions they lay. That applied to the *kārum* at Kanes as well. Jurisdiction over the headquarters of the merchant network must have offered a number of significant strategic advantages to the rulers of the local kingdom. These might well be seized upon and exploited by an ambitious and enterprising king at the expense of his neighbours. In this context we need do no more than recall that one of the chief commodities imported by the Assyrians for distribution in Anatolia was tin, essential in the production of bronze weaponry.

The Empire Built by Anitta

Pithana's conquest of Nesa was the prelude to campaigns against the kingdoms which lay to the north. His campaigns were continued by his son Anitta, apparently with devastating success, from Zalpa (Zalpuwa) in or near the Pontic zone, through the kingdom of Hatti to the southern bend of the Kızıl Irmak. By the end of his first series of campaigns, Anitta had succeeded in subduing all the lands which lay within or near the Kızıl Irmak basin—from Zalpa in the far north to Ullamma in the south.

But his successes were short-lived. Subsequently he was confronted with what appears to have been a military alliance of states stretching southwards from Zalpa—an alliance in which Piyusti, the king of Hatti, and Huzziya, the king of Zalpa, played leading roles. Zalpa was conquered, and its king Huzziya was brought back in bondage to Nesa. The city of Hattusa was placed under siege, and when its population was weakened by hunger, Anitta took the city in a night assault, and destroyed it.[71] Its site was declared accursed: 'On its site I sowed weeds. May the Storm God strike down anyone who becomes king after me and resettles Hattusa' (Anitta inscript. 48–51). We shall have occasion to recall these words.

Anitta now turned his attention southwards. His immediate military objective was the subjugation of the city of Salatiwara, which lay on a road connecting the kingdoms of Wahsusana and Burushattum.[72] Two campaigns were needed to complete the conquest of Salatiwara. In the first, Anitta defeated the troops which had marched from the city to meet him, and carried them off as prisoners to Nesa. Here he took time out from his military enterprises to embark on an ambitious building programme, fortifying his city and erecting several temples where the spoils of battle were dedicated. He also marked the occasion by bringing a large and varied assortment of animals to the city—2 lions, 70 wild pigs, 9 (?) wart hogs, and 120 other beasts, including leopards, deer, and wild goats.

But once more Salatiwara rose against him. Once more Anitta took the field. Determined that he would end its resistance for all time, he captured the city and put it to the torch. Large quantities of silver and gold were removed from the city, along with infantry forces and forty teams of horse, either by the local king for safekeeping or by Anitta as the spoils of conquest.[73]

In the final stage of his recorded campaigns,[74] Anitta marched against the kingdom of Purushanda, called Burushattum in the merchant texts. During and before the colony period, it ranked as

---

[71] Its destruction is archaeologically attested by the end of level IVd on the acropolis (Büyükkale), which can be synchronized with level Ib at Kanes, partly on the basis of the archaeological context of the Assyrian tablets at Hattusa, and partly on the basis of the close similarity in ceramic ware and ritual objects from the two sites; see Bittel (1983c: 54–8).

[72] On its possible location, see the references cited by del Monte and Tischler (1978: 333–4), Nashef (1991: 101).

[73] See Neu (1974: 35) comments on line 71.

[74] Note that Wahsusana is not mentioned in the Anitta inscription. Its territory may already have been absorbed within the framework of the kingdom of Purushanda (see below), or else it had been supplanted by another southern state, perhaps Salatiwara.

one of the major kingdoms of central and eastern Anatolia. We have noted that it figures in the 'King of the Battle' tradition in which the Akkadian king Sargon undertook a campaign to the region on the urging of a delegation from the city. Subsequently it was probably one of the westernmost territories of the empire of Sargon's grandson Naram-Sin.[75] Its status in the colony period is clearly reflected in the title of its ruler—*rubā'um rabi'um* 'Great King', a title borne also by Anitta, and more imposing than that borne even by the ruler of Assur, who was simply known as *rubā'um* 'King'. The title may indicate that the ruler of Purushanda enjoyed an overlordship which extended over the neighbouring kingdoms or principalities.[76]

Anitta's southern campaigns brought him into territory which was subject to the king of Purushanda. But it seems that the latter avoided a military showdown by voluntarily submitting to the king of Nesa:

'When I [ ] went into battle, the Man of Purushanda brought gifts to me; he brought to me a throne of iron and a sceptre of iron as a gift. But when I returned to Nesa I took the Man of Purushanda with me. As soon as he enters the chamber,[77] that man will sit before me on the right.' (Anitta inscript. 73–9)

The gifts almost certainly signified a formal surrender of authority to Anitta, and an acknowledgement of him as the overlord of all territory formerly subject to Purushanda. Anitta took the Purushandan king back to Nesa with him, where he accorded him a privileged status, perhaps in part as a reward for his voluntary submission, and perhaps by way of acknowledging the high status he already enjoyed. He may then have reinstated him as a vassal ruler where he had formerly ruled as an independent monarch, or alternatively he installed him as vassal ruler elsewhere in the territories now subject to Nesa.[78] Both alternatives reflect later Hittite practice.

The establishment of the Kussaran dynasts in Nesa had dramatically altered the political landscape of the eastern half of Anatolia during the second phase of the Assyrian colony period. The

---

[75] See e.g. Orlin (1970: 228–9), and Lewy, H. (1971: 707).

[76] Cf. Otten (1951c: 38, 43). The reference to his title occurs in TTC 27, 7.

[77] An alternative reading in copy B of the text is 'As soon as he enters Zalpa'. For the possible implications of this reading, see Bryce (1983: 40).

[78] As suggested by the alternative reading in copy B referred to above (n. 77).

conquests of Pithana and Anitta had resulted in an extensive uni-
fied political structure encompassing the whole of the Kızıl Irmak
basin north to the Pontic region, and the entire region south of the
Kızıl Irmak to Purushanda. Nesa was the focal point of this structure. The old kingdoms were either totally broken up (as in the case
of Hatti) or ceased to exist as independent entities and were placed
under the immediate control of local rulers appointed by and subject to Anitta.

The Aftermath of Anitta's Conquests

The supremacy which the Kussaran dynasty established over much
of the eastern half of Anatolia proved to be very short lived. In
probably less than a generation after Anitta's conquests, the colonies had come to an end. Conflicts between the Anatolian kingdoms seem to have become much more frequent and much more
widespread in the second phase of the colonies' existence. The
impact which this had on commercial activities and diplomatic
intercourse between Assyrians and Anatolians may well be reflected in the greatly reduced number of tablets that have come to
light from this phase. We have noted the merchants' sensitivity to
unsettled conditions in the areas where they traded. Ironically,
the conquests of Pithana and Anitta which for a brief time had
imposed a fragile unity over the region within and south of the Kızıl
Irmak basin may have led ultimately to the disintegration of the
Anatolian kingdoms and the end of the Assyrian merchant enterprises which had contributed much to the region's prosperity.[79]

Yet in spite of the increasingly turbulent political landscape, the
period of the Assyrian colonies was arguably one of the most
enlightened in the history of the ancient Near East. The merchant
system as revealed by the tablets was one of considerable complexity and sophistication, and indeed foreshadowed a number of international trade and business practices of much more recent times.
Most noteworthy, perhaps, was the spirit of international co-
operation which the system reflected. With relatively few
exceptions, relations between the Assyrians and the Anatolian
communities and kingdoms with which they dealt appear to have
been remarkably harmonious. Seldom before or after this period

---

[79] Cf. Giorgadze (1991: 271). See also Yakar (1981: 108).

do we find evidence of such constructive and mutually beneficial interaction between peoples of the ancient Near Eastern world.

In the wake of the colony period, the geopolitical configuration of Anatolia was to change dramatically. From the ruins of Anitta's empire, a new power was eventually to emerge, one which was to have a much more profound and lasting impact on the Anatolian landscape—the Late Bronze Age kingdom of the Hittites.

CHAPTER 3
Territories and Early Rivals of Hatti

Reconstructing a Map of the Hittite World

The Hittite cuneiform texts and hieroglyphic inscriptions provide us with hundreds of place-names—the names of the countries, kingdoms, cities, rivers, and mountains which made up the Hittite world.[1] Unfortunately, many of these names cannot yet be assigned to particular sites or regions. Some of the sites in question may have suffered total destruction in the upheavals at the end of the Bronze Age, others may lie buried beneath layers of sediment,[2] or the foundations of towns and cities of later periods. And the majority of Bronze Age sites that have been rediscovered and excavated have yielded no written records, nor any other information which might have indicated what they were called. In attempting to identify them, we have to rely largely on information provided by texts found elsewhere.

As part of the process of using this information to reconstruct a map of the Hittite world some scholars have adopted what we might call a *homonymic* or (perhaps more accurately) a *homophonic* approach; that is, they assign Bronze Age place-names to sites or regions which had similar names in later periods. For example, it has long been argued that the country in south-western Anatolia called Lycia by the Greeks in the first millennium BC was part of the region called Lukka (or Lukka Lands) in the Late Bronze Age. A number of the cities of Lycia had names of Bronze Age origin, such as Arñna (the city which the Greeks called Xanthos), Pinara, Tlawa (Greek Tlos), Oenoanda, Kandyba. Since settlements with corresponding Bronze Age names—Arinna, Pina(ra), Dalawa, Wiyanawanda, Hinduwa—lay in or near the region of Lukka, it is tempting to regard them as earlier foundations on the sites of the later Lycian cities.

---

[1] For descriptions of the physical geography of the regions over which the Hittite kings held sway, see e.g. Lloyd (1989: 12–23), Houwink ten Cate (1995, 259–61).

[2] Cf. Macqueen (1986: 38).

But this method of identification presents a number of problems. For example, it is sometimes difficult to decide whether an assumed etymological link between two similar-sounding names is genuine, or whether the similarity is superficial and purely coincidental—what has been called 'kling-klang etymology'.[3] Even if such a link can be firmly established, we also have to take account of the fact that two or more contemporary sites or regions often had the same name; we know of two Bronze Age Pahhuwas, two Zalpas, at least two Arinnas, several Wiyanawandas, and at least two Uras.[4] In some instances, this duplication was probably due to population movements—groups of peoples shifting from one region to another and naming their new settlements after their old. Almost certainly this became an increasingly marked feature of the final decades of the Hittite kingdom and the period following its collapse. Thus even when a later city had a name with a demonstrably Bronze Age pedigree, this need not mean that it was also the site of a Bronze Age city of the same name.

In some cases homonyms, or homophones, may well contribute to the process of identifying Bronze Age sites. But they cannot be used as a primary means of establishing locations for the cities and regions of the Hittite kingdom. In undertaking this task, we must look to the texts for other types of information.

Of particular importance are texts which contain itineraries of a king's religious pilgrimages to the cult centres of his realm,[5] lists of staging posts on military campaigns, definitions of boundaries between neighbouring vassal states, or between Hittite subject territory and that of a foreign king, references to countries with a sea coast, references to topographical features like mountains or rivers. In theory, all such information helps us piece together a picture of the geopolitical configuration of the Hittite world. In practice, much of the data available to us can be interpreted in different ways and lead to different conclusions. One scholar has taken a somewhat jaundiced view of the whole process, cynically referring to it as 'the guessing game known as Hittite geography'.[6]

---

[3] Freu (1990: 53) warns us against being led astray by the 'sirènes de l'homophonie'. Cf. the comments of Košak (1981: 12), Mellaart (1986b: 217).

[4] Cf. Gurney (1992: 214).

[5] See Goetze (1957b).

[6] Mellaart, 'Troy, a Re-assessment', paper presented at the IVth International Colloquium on Aegean Prehistory, Sheffield University, April 1977.

Admittedly, scholarship on the political geography of the Hittite world is still subject to many uncertainties and many conflicting hypotheses. Even the most confidently stated proposals must remain speculative, if based purely on textual evidence, until confirmation is provided by the archaeologist's spade. But progress is steadily being made, thanks largely to new archaeological discoveries (including new text-finds) and newly established text-joins, in combination with a fresh scrutiny and revised interpretations of relevant data from other texts. As a result of the cumulative research of the past seven decades, we can provide reasonably precise locations for a number of the cities, states, and regions which constituted the geopolitical landscape of the Hittite world, and at least approximate locations for many others.

Map 3 (p. xvi) is an attempt to reconstruct the geography of the Hittite world, on the basis of information currently available to us. A number of the locations indicated on this map must be regarded as provisional, and may well require revision as new information comes to light.[7]

The Territories Comprising the Hittite Kingdom

At the height of its power in the fourteenth and thirteenth centuries, the Hittite kingdom incorporated large areas of Anatolia and northern Syria, from the Aegean seacoast in the west to the Euphrates river in the east. The kingdom consisted of four major components: (*a*) a 'core territory' in which lay the Hittite capital Hattusa; (*b*) territories peripheral to the core, under the direct control of the king or his officials; (*c*) vassal states subject to the king but under the immediate authority of local rulers; (*d*) from the reign of Suppiluliuma I onwards, two viceregal kingdoms in northern Syria.

The Core Territory of the Kingdom   The core territory of Hatti lay within the northern half of central Anatolia, in the curve of the Kızıl Irmak river. As we have noted, in Greek and Roman times the river was known as the Halys. The Hittites called it the

---

[7] A recent series of maps of the Hittite world has been published by Forlanini and Marazzi (1986), though much of the detail is highly conjectural; see the review by Gurney (1992). Del Monte and Tischler (1978; suppl. 1992) is a valuable reference work on Hittite geography; see also Cornil (1990).

Marrassantiya. We shall henceforth use its Hittite name. In the second millennium the region bounded by the river became the nucleus of the Hittite world—the homeland of the kingdom of Hatti.

The chief city of the region was Hattusa, near the modern village of Boğazköy (now called Boğazkale), the administrative and ceremonial capital of the Hittite kingdom. Still imposing in its ruins, Hattusa once encompassed at its greatest extent an area of some 165 hectares, making it one of the largest and most impressive of all ancient capitals.[8] It consisted of two main parts, a 'Lower' and an 'Upper' city. The former, situated in the northern part of the capital, dates back to the Old Kingdom. Fortified by a wall, probably in the reign of the king Hantili II (discussed in Ch. 5), it was dominated by the royal acropolis, a large outcrop of rock known today as Büyükkale (Big Castle). Here were located the palace and chief administrative buildings of the capital. To the north of the acropolis lay the city's largest and most important temple, the temple of the Storm (Weather) God.

In the thirteenth century, the city underwent an extensive building programme, with the redevelopment of the palace complex on the acropolis and a massive expansion of the city to the south. The new area, comprising what is called the Upper City, more than doubled the size of the original city. The most recent excavations at Hattusa directed by the German archaeologist Peter Neve have concentrated on this area. They have brought to light the remains of no less than twenty-six temples, in addition to the four unearthed in the Upper City in earlier excavations. These temples, which occupied a considerable part of the new area, clearly highlight the sacred and ceremonial character of the royal capital. The Upper City was enclosed by a wall which incorporated five gates, the most notable of which are the so-called Lion, King's, and Sphinx Gates.[9]

A large local population must have been required for the capital's labour force, and the wide range of support services necessary

---

[8] Although as Bittel (1983c: 33–4) points out, it was much smaller than the Babylon of Nebuchadnezzar or the Nineveh of Sargon II.

[9] In the opinion of Professor Neve, these three gates were integrated into a sacred road used for processions, which started from Temple 5, left the city at the King's Gate, and then continued to the Lion Gate where it re-entered the city. For a summary of the results of the recent excavations, and the conclusions drawn from them, see Neve (1989–90; 1993b: 16–80).

to ensure the maintenance of its administrative, religious, and ceremonial functions. Presumably residential quarters either within or
close to the city housed much of this population, including the city's
artisans and craftsmen. Future excavations may help to determine
where Hattusa's service population actually lived.

Outside the capital, the population of the homeland was distributed amongst a number of settlements, which included (*a*) regional
centres under the authority of administrators or governors, ap-
pointees of the king, who were responsible for the administration
and security of particular districts of the homeland;[10] (*b*) within
these districts, communities governed by Councils of Elders,
whose responsibilities seem to have been largely judicial and religious in nature, and who collaborated closely with the regional
administrators;[11] (*c*) holy cities (including Nerik, Arinna, Samuha,
and Zippalanda), which were amongst the most important cult
centres of the Hittite world, and the venues for a number of major
religious festivals; (*d*) frontier settlements, which grew out of garrison posts and were extremely important to the security of the
kingdom;[12] (*e*) rural estates, which were in many cases given by the
king to members of the Hittite nobility, in return for services rendered, particularly in the field of battle.[13] Much of the personnel
and livestock for these estates came from the spoils of military
conquest.

Peripheral Territories of the Homeland   The Marrassantiya river
provided the homeland with an easily recognizable natural boundary, except in the north and the north-east where there was no
clear line of demarcation between the homeland and the territories
of its neighbours. But nowhere along its frontiers was the homeland provided with an effective natural barrier against enemy incursions. The Marrassantiya is easily fordable along its entire

---

[10] Under the early kings of the Hittite Old Kingdom, the kings' sons were sent out
as governors of the territories incorporated in the kingdom through military conquest (see Ch. 4).

[11] In general on the role of the Councils of Elders in the Hittite kingdom, see
Klengel (1965*a*).

[12] With them were associated officials who bore the title BEL MADGALTI (literally
'lord of the watch-towers'). These officials had both civil and military responsibilities, on which see Beal (1992*b*: 426–36), and for the relevant texts (*CTH* 261), von
Schuler (1957: 36–65).

[13] On the system of land-grants in the Hittite kingdom, see Ch. 4, n. 85.

915-kilometre course, and presented no serious obstacle to invading forces. Within the homeland itself, there were few naturally defensible positions against a determined enemy. Indeed for significant periods of Hittite history parts of the homeland, particularly in the north and north-east, were under enemy occupation.

The homeland's vulnerability becomes clear when we consider the hostile and potentially hostile forces which were in striking distance of it. The Pontic zone to the north was inhabited by the Kaska tribes, a loose confederation of mountain kingdoms which posed a constant threat to Hittite territory,[14] invading and occupying it several times and causing widespread devastation in the homeland. To the south-east were the Hurrians, who invaded the eastern frontiers of Hatti at least as early as the reign of Hattusili I (*c*.1650–1620), and continued to threaten Hittite territories and territorial interests both in Anatolia and Syria until the conquests of Suppiluliuma I in the fourteenth century. To the south-west lay the Arzawa lands—a group of countries which in the New Kingdom became vassal states of the Hittites. But they were unreliable and frequently rebellious subjects, ready to exploit any opportunities that offered for breaking their ties with the Hittite king, establishing alliances with foreign kings, and invading the Hittite homeland from the south.

One of the important reasons for Hittite territorial expansion was to provide some measure of protection against foreign aggression, by establishing what amounted to buffer zones between the core territory of the kingdom and the countries or states which posed a direct threat to it. The buffer zones included both outlying areas within the Land of Hatti as well as countries which lay adjacent or relatively close to it. These zones played a crucial role in the defence of the homeland. They included:

1. A north-eastern zone, extending across the homeland north and north-east of Hattusa, from the lower course of the Marrassantiya in the west through the region called the Upper Land in the north-east.

---

[14] For a detailed treatment of the Kaska people and their relations and conflicts with the Hittites, see von Schuler (1965). To the sources dealt with by von Schuler, we can now add the letters from the Maşat archive, ed. Alp (1991), which are concerned largely with matters relating to Kaska, and provide detailed information on the regular dealings, exchanges, and conflicts between the Hittites and the Kaska peoples; see the comments by Klinger (1995: 83–4).

2. A south-eastern zone, extending from the easternmost territories of the homeland towards the Hurrian kingdom of Mitanni. In this region, the country of Isuwa occupied a position of considerable strategic importance in relation to both Hatti and Mitanni; during the New Kingdom it was attached first to one and then to the other of the two kingdoms.

3. A southern zone, extending south of the Marrassantiya river to the country of Kizzuwadna in the Taurus and anti-Taurus region, and westwards through the region known as the Lower Land. Kizzuwadna's political ties fluctuated between Hatti and Mitanni until its territory was annexed by the Hittites early in the New Kingdom. The Lower Land had been incorporated into the Land of Hatti early in the Old Kingdom. It provided an important buffer zone against threats to Hittite territory from the south west, notably from the Arzawa lands.

While these zones were in effect extensions of the Hittite homeland, the amount of territory over which the Hittite king could claim to exercise authority varied markedly from one reign to another. Each of the peripheral territories presented its own particular set of problems, and a range of measures were taken by various Hittite kings in their attempts to find lasting solutions to these problems. In the north one of the chief policies was to protect the core territory of the homeland by repopulation programmes in areas which had been laid waste and in some cases occupied by Kaskan peoples. In the east and south-east Hittite kings attempted to offset the threat of Hurrian encroachment on their subject territories by both military and diplomatic operations in the states which occupied important strategic locations between Hittite and Hurrian spheres of influence. In the south and south-west the Lower Land assumed the character of a military zone for both defensive and offensive purposes; it was garrisoned with Hittite troops and placed under the direct authority of a military governor.[15]

Vassal States   Beyond the homeland and its peripheral territories the Hittite kingdom at the height of its power incorporated a large

---

[15] For a more detailed discussion of Hittite frontier zones and Hittite frontier policy, see Bryce (1986–7).

number of vassal states, extending over much of Anatolia and northern Syria. The vassal system was one of the fruits of Hittite military enterprise during the New Kingdom. It reached its full development with the conquests of Suppiluliuma I and Mursili II in the fourteenth century.

Vassal states remained under the control of their own local rulers. The obligations and benefits of vassalhood were carefully spelt out and regulated by treaties.[16] In essence vassal treaties were contracts, not between two states, but between two people—the Hittite king and the vassal ruler. They were not bilateral agreements. Rather, they were imposed unilaterally by the king. Their terms and conditions were drawn up by the former and accepted on oath by the latter, whose appointment was either made or approved by the king. The individual nature of the contract was emphasized by the fact that a new treaty had to be drawn up whenever a new Hittite king or new vassal ruler came to power.

The treaty imposed certain military obligations on the vassal who was in turn promised military assistance from the king, should the need arise. A further obligation which the treaty sometimes stipulated for the vassal was an annual payment of tribute—for example, 300 shekels of gold, weighed according to the Hittite measure.[17] The pact concluded between overlord and vassal was often cemented by a marriage alliance between the vassal and a princess of the Hittite royal family. In the event of such a marriage, the treaty stipulated that the Hittite princess was to hold supreme position over the other wives, or concubines, of the vassal; and succession to the vassal throne had to pass down in the princess's line.

The vassal was obliged not only to swear allegiance to the reigning king but also to pledge support to his legitimate successors. If the Hittite throne were usurped by a pretender, the vassal was automatically freed from his treaty obligations, except that he

[16] For a detailed treatment of the vassal treaty system, see Pirenne (1950), Goetze (1957c: 96–107), Kestemont (1974), Briend *et al.* (1992). For the texts of the majority of extant treaties, see Weidner (1923; cited as *PD*), Friedrich (1926: 1930), to which add Kühne and Otten (1971), and (for the text of the treaty on the recently discovered bronze tablet) Otten (1988a). Most recently, a representative collection of the treaties has been trans. by Beckman (1996).

[17] Mursili II's treaty with Duppi-Tesub of Amurru (*CTH* 62), Friedrich (1926: 12–13 §8). Korošec (1960: 72) notes that clauses referring to the payment of tribute are found only in treaties with the Syrian vassals.

might be called upon to help restore the legitimate king to his throne. In return for his allegiance and the fulfilment of the obligations imposed by the treaty, the vassal was guaranteed sovereignty in his kingdom, and also the sovereignty of his legitimate successors.

In a few cases, local rulers bound by treaty to the Hittite king enjoyed what was called *kuirwana*, sometimes translated as 'protectorate', status. This applied to the kings of the Arzawa lands before their reduction to vassal status, and to the kings of Kizzuwadna and Mitanni (the latter after the Hittite conquest of Mitanni in the fourteenth century). In theory they were independent rulers, allies rather than subjects of Hatti, and their position was supposedly superior to that of a vassal ruler, as acknowledged ceremonially when they came to Hattusa to pay annual homage to the Hittite king. But although they enjoyed certain privileges, such as exemption from tribute, the right in some cases to annex territories which they had conquered, and the right to bilateral treaties with the Hittite king, in practice they had little more freedom of action than the vassal rulers. Above all they had no right to an independent foreign policy, and all relations with other subjects or allies of Hatti, or with foreign kingdoms, were strictly controlled by the Hittite king.[18]

One of the chief purposes of the treaties was to isolate the vassal states politically and militarily from one another. Hence the clauses which forbade the vassal ruler to enter into independent relationships with foreign powers, or to have independent political or military dealings with the rulers of other vassal states. All such dealings had to be channelled through Hattusa. Obviously the Hittite king's chief concern was to minimize, if not prevent absolutely, the possibility of anti-Hittite coalitions being formed—the greatest potential danger the Hittites faced in the west.

Hittite kings attached a great deal of importance to the matter of political fugitives. They frequently had to deal with the situation of prominent political dissidents escaping from their authority and seeking refuge in a country beyond their direct control and appealing to the local ruler for permission to settle there. In such cases the Hittite king often peremptorily demanded that they be handed

[18] Further on the conditions and privileges of *kuirwana* status, see Pirenne (1950: 378–80), Goetze (1964: 31).

back to him, and in the event of a refusal from the local ruler, was prepared to go to war to achieve this end.

How effective were the treaties in maintaining Hittite authority throughout the subject territories? The fact that Hittite kings were frequently plagued by treacherous behaviour from disloyal vassal rulers and by rebellions in vassal states which overthrew their pro-Hittite rulers may suggest that the treaties were very limited and short-lived in their effectiveness. Yet they were an extremely important instrument of Hittite influence and authority outside the homeland. They helped ensure at least temporary stability in a number of regions of the Hittite kingdom, while the king committed his resources to other regions which required more urgent and more direct attention. The stability which Suppiluliuma I had established in Syria through the network of Syrian vassal rulers and the creation of two viceregal kingdoms in the region (see below) left his son and (second) successor Mursili II largely free in the critical early years of his reign to devote his resources to the comprehensive conquest of the Arzawa lands. The vassal treaties which Mursili set up in the wake of these conquests must have contributed substantially to the high degree of stability in western Anatolia which characterized the rest of his reign.

Further, while there is much that is repetitive and formulaic in the treaties, on closer examination they often reveal careful individual tailoring and much political astuteness. Their historical preambles reflect the king's (or his advisers') close understanding of local affairs, a sensitivity to particular problems in the region where the vassal state was located, and a detailed knowledge of the region's history—coupled with a perception of how all these factors could best be turned to the Hittites' advantage. Given the large and complex range of states with which the Hittite kings often had to deal simultaneously, this was no small achievement.

The Viceregal Kingdoms   Although the majority of Hittite subject states outside the homeland were ruled by vassals of local origin, in the fourteenth century Suppiluliuma I put in place a major new development in the Syrian region. Here he established two viceregal kingdoms, one at Aleppo, the other at Carchemish on the Euphrates. Two of his sons, Telipinu and Piyassili (subsequently called Sarri-Kusuh), were appointed to the viceregal seats. Henceforth these kingdoms remained under the direct control of members of the Hittite royal family and continued to be important centres of Hittite civilization for several centuries after the collapse of the central dynasty in Anatolia. Tarhuntassa in southern Anatolia was for a brief period another (quasi-)viceregal kingdom. In the thirteenth century it was placed under the direct authority of a nephew of the Hittite king, whose appointment was recognized as equivalent in status to that of the viceroys in Aleppo and Carchemish (see Chs. 11 and 12).

Early Rivals of the Kingdom

From its early days the Hittite kingdom was confronted with challenges and threats from powerful enemies—so powerful that on more than one occasion the kingdom was brought to the verge of total extinction. We have already referred to the Kaska tribes from the Pontic zone who threatened, attacked, and sometimes occupied the northern territories of the homeland throughout the kingdom's existence. We have also referred to two other peoples who became major participants in the history of the Hittite kingdom—the Luwians in the west and south-west and the Hurrians in the southeast. For the first three centuries of the Hittite kingdom, Luwians and Hurrians presented the Hittites with some of their most formidable obstacles on their way to becoming the supreme political and military power in the Near East. Given that their own history is so closely intertwined with that of the Hittites, it may be useful at this point to summarize briefly their background and development, their political organization, the location and extent of the territories which they occupied or sought to control, and their interests and aspirations which brought them into contact and conflict with the Land of Hatti.

The Luwians   We have seen that by the early second millennium an Indo-European group called the Luwians had occupied extensive areas of western Anatolia. Indeed in the first half of the millennium, a large part of western Anatolia was called Luwiya. However, the name seems to have been used only in a broad ethnogeographical sense, with no strong political connotations. By the middle of the millennium another name had come into use for the region—Arzawa. During the Hittite New Kingdom this name embraced a number of Hittite vassal states known collectively as the

Arzawa Lands, which lay in western and south-western Anatolia. The nucleus of these lands was a kingdom called Arzawa. Scholars sometimes refer to it as Arzawa Minor, to distinguish it from other parts of the Arzawa complex. Four other western kingdoms are identified in various texts as members of this complex: Mira-Kuwaliya, Seha River Land, Hapalla, and Wilusa.[19]

On several occasions during the fifteenth and fourteenth centuries, confederacies from the whole Arzawa region seem to have been formed for specific military purposes. It is possible that the king of Arzawa Minor exercised from time to time a kind of *primus inter pares* role amongst the various chiefs and rulers of the Arzawa lands. But there is no indication that these lands ever formed a united, politically coherent kingdom under the rule of a single king. None the less Arzawa constituted a major military threat to the Hittite kingdom, and in the fourteenth century succeeded in mounting an extensive invasion of Hittite territory south of the Marrassantiya river. Indeed in these the darkest days of the Hittite kingdom before its final collapse, Arzawa was seen by Amenhotep III, pharaoh of Egypt, to be emerging as the dominant power in the whole Anatolian region.

Although Arzawa was the largest and most populous region of Luwian settlement in Anatolia, Luwian-speakers spread far beyond this region. The migrations which had led to their settlement in western Anatolia continued well into the second millennium. By the middle of the millennium, Luwian-speaking groups had occupied much of the southern coast of Anatolia, from the region later known as Lycia in the west to Cilicia and the Bronze Age country Kizzuwadna in the east.

One of the important Luwian sub-groups was the Lukka people.[20] References to Lukka and the Lukka people figure prominently in our Bronze Age texts. From these texts we can

---

[19] There is still no certainty about the precise locations and territorial limits of these countries; for various proposals see the references cited by del Monte and Tischler (1978: 44). However we may be reaching some consensus on those that apparently extended to or close to the Aegean seaboard, namely Wilusa in the north-west, with the Seha River Land and Arzawa Minor further south. See most recently Gurney (1992: 217–21). For a detailed treatment of the Arzawa Lands, see Heinhold-Krahmer (1977).

[20] It has been argued the *Lukka* should be understood as the Hittite equivalent of the Luwian name *Luwiya*; see Easton (1984: 27). But against this, see Crossland in the discussion of Easton's paper, Foxhall and Davies (1984: 58). See also Laroche (1976: 18–19).

conclude that the term Lukka, or Lukka lands,[21] referred to a region extending from the western end of Pamphylia through Lycaonia, Pisidia, and Lycia (the later Greco-Roman names).[22]

Lukka was never in any sense an organized political entity. We know of no kings of Lukka, no treaties of vassalhood between Lukka and the Hittite king, and no one person or city could act on behalf of Lukka as a whole. In other words, the term Lukka was used not in reference to a state with a clearly defined political organization, but rather to a conglomerate of independent communities, with close ethnic affinities and lying within a roughly definable geographical area. While it seems clear that there was a central Lukka region, a 'Lukka homeland', various elements of the Lukka population may have been widely scattered through southern and western Anatolia, and may in some cases have settled temporarily, or permanently, in states with formal political organizations. Singer's description of the Lukka people as 'the Habiru of Anatolia' is very apt.[23]

The Lukka people were sometime subjects of the Hittite king throughout the period of the Hittite Kingdom. But for much of this period, Hittite control over them was probably little more than nominal. This was due in part to the fact that they could not be dealt with as a single political or administrative entity, like the people of a vassal kingdom. But it must have been primarily due to the nature of the people themselves. The Hittite texts provide us with a picture of a difficult, fractious people, very prone to rebellion against Hittite authority. They seem also to have been experienced seafarers who engaged in piratical raids on coastal cities in the eastern Mediterranean.[24]

---

[21] This plurality is not so far attested before the 13th cent.

[22] See Bryce (1992*a*: 128–30).

[23] Singer (1983*a*: 208). Cf. Mellaart (1974: 497). The Habiru were nomadic or semi-nomadic groups which included social outcasts, fugitives, and marauding mercenaries. These groups inhabited and roamed through the mountains and forests of Syria, and were a particular danger to small towns, merchants and other travellers in the region.

[24] See the Amarna letter *EA* 38, from the king of Alasiya to the pharaoh Akhenaten, which refers to raids on both the coast of Alasiya and the coast of Egypt. Part of this text is translated below, Ch. 13. For a list of the texts dealing with the Lukka people, see Bryce (1979*a*; 1986*c*: 8–10). Further references to Lukka are cited by Röllig (1988). Add to these the references in the so-called Yalburt and Südburg inscriptions, discussed in Chs. 12 and 13.

Almost certainly Bronze Age Lukka people were one of the most important ethnic components of the Lycian people who emerged in south-west Anatolia, in the country called Lycia by the Greeks, early in the first millennium. The Lycians, whose language was a descendant of Bronze Age Luwian, figured prominently in Greek legendary tradition, where they were best known as the most important of Troy's allies in the Trojan War.[25]

The Hurrians   The Hurrians represent one of the most dynamic social, cultural, and political forces to emerge in the Near East from the late third millennium onwards. In a broad ethno-linguistic sense, the term 'Hurrian' applied to a diverse range of population groups whose original homeland is uncertain. One view is that they came from the Kura-Araxes region in Transcaucasia. Another view, based largely on archaeological evidence, postulates a Hurrian homeland in eastern Anatolia during the third millennium.[26] Wherever their original homeland, a common language, called Hurrian in the texts, and common onomastic features gave overall coherence to these groups—enabling us to identify the various regions where they subsequently settled or with which they came in contact. The impact which they had on these regions is reflected in the survival of various facets of Hurrian culture—notably a distinctive pantheon and body of religious tradition—long after the Hurrians themselves had ceased to be a significant political force in the Near East.

At some stage during the Mari period, in the early centuries of the second millennium, the array of small states which occupied northern Mesopotamia, where the Hurrian population was principally settled, were united into a single political entity. The process that brought this about is unknown to us,[27] but it provided the genesis of the powerful kingdom variously called Hurri, Mitanni, or Hanigalbat. The Egyptians and Canaanites referred to it by its west

[25] On the links between the Lycians and their Bronze Age ancestors, and the role of the Lycians in legendary tradition, see Bryce (1986c: 1–41).

[26] For a recent discussion of the various theories concerning the origins of the Hurrians, see Burney (1989).

[27] Astour (1978: 9) suggests that Indo-Aryans from the east (i.e. Indo-European groups who appeared in India during the 2nd millennium) may have been a catalyst in the process. Note that none of the names of the known Mitannian kings are Hurrian; all are Indo-Aryan in origin. See Wilhelm (1995a: 1246–7).

Semitic name Naharina, or Naharima.[28] The kingdom rapidly extended its influence into northern Syria and eastern Anatolia, and for the next three centuries became Hatti's chief rival for political and military supremacy in these regions. On several occasions, it seriously threatened the Hittite homeland itself.

The Hurrians made their first attested appearance in Anatolia as traders during the Assyrian Colony Period, as illustrated by Hurrian names in the colony texts.[29] These names, however, are quite rare, which suggests that they reflect the activities of a small number of enterprising merchants of Hurrian origin rather than any significant Hurrian settlement in the region where the colonies were established.[30]

Northern Syria presents a different picture. The archives of Mari and Alalah in particular indicate extensive Hurrian settlement in the region during the early centuries of the second millennium, with the establishment of Hurrian colonies or enclaves at Mari, Alalah, and Ebla. Subsequently, persons with Hurrian names appeared in Aleppo, Carchemish, and Ugarit. Hurrian immigrants in search of work and land would have been attracted by the abundant opportunities offered by the north Syrian states, which in turn had need of a stable, productive population in contrast to the fluctuating nomadic or semi-nomadic population groups in evidence there.[31] Already in the seventeenth century, when the Hittites conducted their first campaigns in the region, there was a substantial Hurrian presence in northern Syria. For example, approximately half of all the names attested in level VII of Alalah (the city destroyed by Hattusili I) were Hurrian.[32]

---

[28] On the equivalence of the various terms, see Astour (1972: 103–4). Wilhelm (1989: 24) refers to a fragmentary inscription probably from the time of the pharaoh Tuthmosis I (c. 1504–1492) which contains the name used by the natives for the first time: Maittani, later Mittani. See also von Weiher (1973). Astour (1972: 103) notes that the 14th-cent. king Tusratta who styled himself 'king of Mitanni' referred to his kingdom in his Amarna letters as Hanigalbat (*EA* 18, 9; 20, 17; 29, 49). Hanigalbat is also the name by which Hattusili I referred to the kingdom in the Akkadian version of his Annals, KBo X 1 (*CTH* 4) obv. 11 (see Ch. 4). Variant forms are Haligalbat and Habingalbat (the latter is an early form of the name).

[29] Garelli (1963: 155–8), Kammenhuber (1977: esp. 142).

[30] Cf. Bilgiç (1945–51: 19), Güterbock (1954b: 383). Hurrian names were much more common south of the Taurus, indicating that already in this period there was a significant Hurrian presence in south-eastern Anatolia.

[31] Thus Astour (1978: 8).

[32] See Wilhelm (1989: 12–13), and references cited therein.

The westward spread of Hurrian population groups was almost inevitably a forerunner to Hurrian (i.e. Mitannian) political and military expansion across the Euphrates. It was this which led ultimately to fierce competition with the kingdom of Hatti which in the same period sought to expand its influence through the same region. In the course of several centuries of conflict between Hatti and Mitanni, each side had its share of successes, each its share of disasters before one finally and irrevocably succumbed to the other.

Other Near Eastern Powers   The Hittites' territorial interests and military enterprises in Syria brought them into contact, and sometimes conflict, with two other great kingdoms who sought to establish their control over the principalities and city-states of the region—the kingdom of Egypt, and after the collapse of Mitanni as an independent power the kingdom of Assyria. A third kingdom, Babylon, was also enmeshed in the web of international relationships in the Near East during the Late Bronze Age; our records attest to frequent diplomatic communications between the rulers of the Babylonian Kassite dynasty and the other Great Kings of the Near East. But the Kassites who came to power in Babylon early in the sixteenth century after the collapse of Hammurabi's dynasty, apparently had no territorial ambitions west of the Euphrates.

There was yet another power whose rulers appear in the list of the Great Kings of the Late Bronze Age—the kingdom of Ahhiyawa. This kingdom figured prominently in the Hittites' communications and conflicts with the countries of western Anatolia. It has given rise to one of the most frequently and hotly debated controversies in Late Bronze Age scholarship. Where was Ahhiyawa located? How important a role did it play in the history of the Near East? How extensive was its influence? What brought its presence in the region to an end?

In the 1920s the Swiss scholar Emil Forrer claimed that he had discovered Homeric Greeks in the Hittite texts, as reflected in numerous occurrences of the place-name Ahhiyawa in these texts. He argued that Ahhiyawa was the Hittite way of writing the Greek name *Achaiwia*, an archaic form of Achaia.[33] And he noted that in

---

[33] See e.g. Forrer (1924*a*; 1924*b*). For a recent treatment of the philological equation, see Finkelberg (1988).

the Homeric epics, the Greeks were regularly called Achaians.[34] In historical times the name Achaia was associated with regions which in Homeric tradition were colonized by Achaians—for example, the northern Peloponnese.[35] Since Forrer made his claims, scholars have continued to debate who the Ahhiyawans were and where their kingdom was located, with Ahhiyawa being variously proposed as an Anatolian kingdom, an island kingdom off the Anatolian coast (for example, Rhodes or Cyprus), Thrace, or indeed a mainland Mycenaean Greek kingdom. Recently, however, an increasing number of scholars have come round to the view that the term Ahhiyawa must have been used in reference to the Mycenaean world, or at least to part of that world. The advocates of this view base their arguments on new readings and interpretations of the relevant Hittite texts, and on recent surveys of the material evidence for Mycenaean contacts with the Anatolian mainland.[36]

While some scholars still have serious reservations about the Ahhiyawa–Mycenaean equation, or reject it,[37] the circumstantial evidence in favour of it is becoming increasingly persuasive. There is no doubt that Ahhiyawa was a major Late Bronze Age power, whose king was accorded by the Hittites a status equal to that of the other great Bronze Age rulers—the kings of Egypt, Babylon, Assyria, Mitanni. Moreover many scholars believe that Ahhiyawa had a substantial seagoing capacity, and was in close contact during the last two centuries of the Late Bronze Age with the countries of the eastern Mediterranean as well as with western Anatolia.[38] It is in precisely this region, and in precisely this period, that we have abundant material evidence for Mycenaean activity. Further, we know from the archaeological record that the site on the western coast of Anatolia called Miletos in Greco-Roman times came

---

[34] Note, however, that Homer's name for the land of the Achaians was not Achai(wi)a but Achaiis (e.g. *Iliad* 1.254; 3.75, 258; 7.124). According to Gurney (1990: 43), the Homeric form was due to metrical considerations.

[35] See Vermeule (1960), Huxley (1960: 25).

[36] Notable among the recent supporters of the Ahhiyawa–Mycenaean equation are the scholars Güterbock, Mellink, and Vermeule. See in particular their papers published under the general title 'The Hittites and the Aegean World', *AJA* 87 (1983), 133–43. Note however that Güterbock (1986: 33) still regards the equation as 'a matter of faith', for which no strict proof is possible, either *pro* or *contra*.

[37] Thus Ünal (1989: 285).

[38] See the references cited by Steiner (1989a: 394 n. 3), although in his article Steiner himself argues at length against this view.

under strong Mycenaean influence from the late fourteenth century onwards. Most scholars agree that Miletos is to be identified with the land called Milawata (Millawanda) in the Hittite texts. From these texts it is clear that Milawata had become, by the early thirteenth century, vassal territory of the king of Ahhiyawa, in precisely the same period that we see increasing Mycenaean influence on Miletos.

If the Ahhiyawa–Mycenaean equation is *not* valid, then we must accept that there were two discrete Late Bronze Age civilizations with remarkably similar names, making their presence felt in the same region and in the same period. One of them, Ahhiyawa, is attested by documentary evidence, but has left no identifiable trace in the archaeological record; the other, the Mycenaean civilization, has left abundant archaeological evidence but no identifiable trace in the documentary record. It is difficult to write this off as mere coincidence.

Ahhiyawans made their appearance on the Anatolian mainland at least as early as the fifteenth century, when a military operation was conducted on Anatolian soil by Attarsiya, the 'Man of Ahhiya'[39] with infantry and a force of 100 chariots. From this time on our evidence indicates increasing Ahhiyawan involvement in western Anatolian affairs, either directly or through local vassals or protégés of the Ahhiyawan king. This involvement reached its peak in the first half of the thirteenth century.

At no stage, however, did Ahhiyawan enterprise in Anatolia lead to permanent occupation of substantial portions of western Anatolian territory. Rather this enterprise probably reflected (on a small scale) the practice of other major Late Bronze Age rulers, notably the kings of Hatti and Egypt, who sought to expand and consolidate their influence in the Near East by establishing a network of vassal states under the immediate control of local rulers. The Ahhiyawan presence in western Anatolia inevitably caused tensions, and sometimes conflicts, with the Hittites whose subject territories extended into the same region. In the thirteenth century in particular, Ahhiyawan strategy was to support prominent dissidents against Hittite authority in the western Anatolian states, guarantee them, if need be, refuge from Hittite authority, establish them as vassal rulers under Ahhiyawan overlordship, and use them

---

[39] The older form of the name Ahhiyawa; see Güterbock (1983*a*: 134).

as agents for the extension of Ahhiyawan influence into adjacent Anatolian states.

Yet it seems that territorial expansion was not a major object or outcome of Ahhiyawan enterprise in Anatolia. The most likely intention of this enterprise was to gain access to resources which were in demand in the Greek mainland, and which could readily be supplied by western Anatolia. These may well have been resources which have left little or no trace in the archaeological record—like slaves, horses, and metals.[40] From the Linear B tablets we know that western Anatolia was one of the regions from which labour was recruited for the Mycenaean palace work-forces.[41] And the metal-bearing and horse-breeding areas of western Anatolia may well have provided the Ahhiyawan kings with major incentives for establishing and extending their influence in the region,[42] primarily through local intermediaries.

The Ahhiyawa–Mycenaean equation, if accepted, has substantial implications for Mycenaean studies, since to date the Mycenaean world has failed to provide us with any historical sources of information beyond what can be gleaned from Homeric tradition and the Linear B tablets. Mycenaean scholars, by and large, find it difficult to accept the notion of a Mycenaean kingdom with significant political and military involvement in the Near Eastern world. Certainly the equation poses many problems for Mycenaean scholarship. If Ahhiyawa was in fact a Mycenaean kingdom, where was the seat of its power? At Mycenae itself, the kingdom of Agamemnon in Homeric tradition? Or at one of the other important centres of the Mycenaean world? How extensive was the kingdom? Did it involve a confederation of Mycenaean states, under the leadership of a single ruler—perhaps a *primus inter pares* as in Homeric tradition? Were there shifts in the centre of power during the 200 years for which Ahhiyawa is attested in the Hittite texts? We cannot rule out the possibility of other major Mycenaean centres, like Orchomenos in Boeotia or Argos in the Peloponnese, as possible nuclei of Ahhiyawan power.

We should in any case distinguish between uses of the term Ahhiyawa (*a*) as a general ethno-geographical designation (like the names *Hurri and Luwiya* in the Hittite texts) encompassing all areas of Mycenaean settlement, both in mainland Greece and

---

[40] Cf. Sperling (1991: 155).   [41] See Chadwick (1976: 80–1).
[42] See Bryce (1989*c*: 14 n. 61).

overseas; (*b*) as a designation of the nucleus of the kingdom of the Ahhiyawan rulers who corresponded with the kings of Hatti; (*c*) as a designation of this kingdom in a broader sense, including the territories attached to it as political and military dependencies.

We shall return to these matters as we survey the ever-changing picture of the world of international relationships in the Late Bronze Age.

CHAPTER 4

The Foundations of the Kingdom: The Reigns of Labarna and Hattusili I (–c.1620)

The Aftermath of the Assyrian Colony Period

An almost impenetrable veil hangs over the decades that followed the end of Anitta's reign and the disappearance of the Assyrian merchant colonies. Written records cease, and archaeological information on the aftermath of the colony period is almost non-existent. Without such information we can do no more than speculate on what brought the merchant operations to an end, and what followed in their wake.

We have witnessed, throughout the second phase of the colony period, the widespread conflicts which affected every area in Anatolia where the Assyrian merchants conducted their trading operations. Eventually the Nesa-based kingdom of Anitta collapsed, and Nesa itself probably fell victim to the conflicts, caused largely by the aggressive expansionist ambitions of its kings. Outside forces may also have been at work. The Kaska people who in later years repeatedly invaded the Hittite homeland perhaps now, for the first time, became active in the region, attacking Anatolian cities involved in trading activities with the Assyrian merchants, particularly in the north.[1] Hurrian groups from the south-east may also have disrupted the trading network, threatening and perhaps actually severing the long and hazardous routes between Assyria and Anatolia. Sensitive to unsettled conditions at the best of times, the Assyrian merchants must now have abandoned their colonies in Anatolia and withdrawn entirely from the region, never to return.

What impact did all this have on the large trading centres, the towns, the villages, and the populations with whom the merchants had conducted their business? The period following the end of the

---

[1] Cf. Mellaart (1974: 500). But there is no reliable evidence for a Kaskan presence, or at least aggressive Kaskan activity, in the northern region until the later period of the Hittite Old Kingdom; cf. Klinger (1995: 84).

Assyrian colonies is one of darkness and silence. In the view of one scholar, when a new ruling power finally emerged in central Anatolia what it inherited was 'no longer a prosperous country, but a scarred and ravaged land filled with the ruins of fire blackened palaces'.[2] The picture thus created is perhaps too imaginative, too apocalyptic. But it may reflect some elements of the scenario in which the Hittite ruling dynasty first came to power, several decades or more after the destruction of the kingdom of Anitta. What is clear is that very few of the major Anatolian cities and states of the earlier part of the second millennium retained any importance in later years; some, like the settlement on the site now called Acemhöyük, may have been abandoned and never reoccupied.

When the veil finally begins to lift, it does so on a new era in the history and civilization of Anatolia, the so-called Late Bronze Age, the era in which Anatolia was dominated by the kingdom of the Hittites.

What were the origins of this kingdom? In attempting to answer this question, we should go back to the city of Kussara, whence arose the dynasty of Pithana and Anitta. Here, very likely, the foundations of the Hittite kingdom were established—a kingdom whose early rulers launched it on a course of military and political expansion which was to make it one of the supreme powers of the Near East in the final centuries of the Bronze Age.

Its first clearly attested king was a man called Hattusili.[3] In his reign the earliest known documents of the Hittite kingdom were produced. But we know that the dynasty of which he was a member extended back at least two generations before him. For he tells us of a rebellion against his grandfather—the first known event in Hittite history.

[2] Mellaart (1974: 500).
[3] Although almost certainly Hattusili succeeded a king called Labarna (see below). It has been proposed that there was an earlier Hittite king called Tudhaliya, on the basis of the appearance of this name near the beginning of one of the royal offering lists (List C) after several names now lost. (On the offering lists, see Appendix 1). According to Forlanini (1995) this king might in fact have provided direct continuity with the colony period. But most scholars do not accept the existence of an Old Kingdom Tudhaliya, regarding his creation as a misinterpretation of his appearance in the offering lists; see e.g. Güterbock (1938: 135), Houwink ten Cate (1963: 276), Astour (1989: 85–6 n. 73). The recently discovered cruciform seal impressions have raised the possibility of another early king Huzziya; see Dinçol *et al.* (1993: 105–6).

Early Hittite Records

Our knowledge of Hattusili's reign is derived from a number of documents, three of which are of particular importance. The first, discovered in 1957, records the king's military achievements apparently over a six-year period. It is commonly referred to as the *Annals*.[4] Since Hattusili's reign probably lasted some thirty years, the *Annals* records only a small segment of his military enterprises, and we have to supplement this record as best we can with scraps of information from other sources. The extensive nature of his campaigns, conducted in many regions of both Anatolia and Syria, and the successes which they apparently achieved in such a short period, would be even more remarkable if they belonged to the early part of his reign, as most scholars assume.

But it has been argued that the text in its surviving form consists of excerpts from a much more comprehensive record covering the whole of the reign, from which the most important achievements were selected.[5] If the *Annals* do in fact present us with a series of highlights of the whole reign, then their value as a source of historical information might be thought to be considerably enhanced. But such selectivity could also lead to much distortion of the record. Even if the *Annals* were restricted to a six-year period— and that is what a literal interpretation of the text clearly conveys— the campaigns which they record probably established a pattern of military enterprises which to a greater or lesser extent recurred throughout the reign.

The text of the *Annals* is a bilingual one, with versions in both Akkadian and Hittite cuneiform. Scholarly opinion is divided on whether the original was composed in Hittite and subsequently translated into Akkadian, or vice versa.[6] The surviving copies of the text date to no earlier than the thirteenth century, some 400 years after the events to which they refer.[7] The composition is of a well-known Old Hittite type: an extended historical narrative culminating in a particular triumph of the Hittite king.[8]

---

[4] KBo x 1 + KBo x 2 (*CTH* 4), ed. Imparati and Saporetti (1965). A detailed study of the text has also been published by Melchert (1978).

[5] For recording on a small golden statue which was offered to the Sun God; see Kempinski and Košak (1982: 98).

[6] The case for the former has been argued by Melchert (1978: 2–5, 22), for the latter by Houwink ten Cate (1983).

[7] See Melchert (1978: 2), Hoffner (1980: 294), Houwink ten Cate (1983: 91).

[8] Thus Melchert (1978: 5). For a more detailed discussion of this type, see Hoffner (1980: 294–9).

The second major document of Hattusili's reign is commonly referred to as the *Testament*.[9] While the *Annals* are one of our chief sources of information on the military exploits of Hattusili, the *Testament* provides us with important details about the internal political affairs of the Hittite kingdom during his reign. It is in essence a proclamation issued by Hattusili before an assembled group of warriors and dignitaries announcing new arrangements the king has made for the succession, and his appointment of his grandson Mursili as heir to the throne. The proclamation was delivered to the assembly in the city of Kussara where the king, by now an old man, lay ill. It may in fact have been one of his final acts before his death.

Like the *Annals*, the *Testament* survives in both Hittite and Akkadian versions which are late copies of the original Old Kingdom document.[10] There has again been some dispute over the question of whether the Hittite or the Akkadian version came first. Although the Akkadian version was once thought to have been earlier,[11] the surviving Hittite text preserves a number of features of the Old Hittite language,[12] and it has been suggested that the Akkadian version was a later translation of the Hittite.[13] But it is not unlikely that both versions were composed simultaneously.[14]

A third source of information on the reign of Hattusili, as well as other early Hittite kings, is a document commonly referred to as the *Proclamation* (or *Edict*) of the king Telipinu[15] who occupied the throne some hundred years and six reigns after Hattusili's death. The lengthy historical preamble of this document recounts the early triumphs and the subsequent disasters of the Hittite monarchy up to the time of Telipinu's accession, *c.*1525. Composed originally in the last quarter of the sixteenth century, the *Proclamation* survives only in late copies—a fragmentary Akkadian version and nine exemplars of a Hittite version.

By piecing together the information contained in these and other documents dating back to the Hittite Old Kingdom, we can begin to construct a picture of the first kings who held sway over the world of the Hittites.

---

[9] KUB i 16 + KUB xl 65 (*CTH* 6), ed. Sommer and Falkenstein (1938).
[10] KBo x 1 is the Akkadian version, KBo x 2 the Hittite.
[11] Thus Sommer and Falkenstein (1938: 202–3).
[12] See Güterbock (1964*b*: 108).
[13] Otten (1951*c*: 36).
[14] Thus Güterbock (1964*b*: 108).
[15] *CTH* 19, most recently ed. Hoffmann (1984*a*).

The First Labarna

The *Proclamation of Telipinu* begins with the exploits of a king called Labarna:[16]

Formerly Labarna was the Great King. Then were his sons, his brothers, his relations by marriage, his (blood) relations and his troops united. And the land was small. But on whatever campaign he went, he held the lands of the enemy in subjection by his might. He kept devastating the lands, and he deprived the lands of power; and he made them boundaries of the sea. But when he returned from the field, each of his sons went to the various lands (to govern them). Hupisna, Tuwanuwa, Nenassa, Landa, Zallara, Parsuhanta, Lusna—these (were the) lands they governed. The large towns were assigned (to them). (*Telipinu Procl.* §§1–4, 1 2–12)

Here was a king who first came to power in what may have been one of a number of petty states and kingdoms which had survived, or emerged in the wake of, the collapse of the kingdom of Anitta. To begin with, the land ruled by Labarna was small. But a dramatic change in the political landscape was soon to take place. From the security of a kingdom firmly united under his rule, Labarna embarked on a programme of military conquests which carried his troops ever further to the south. One country after another fell before their advance, until finally Labarna established himself as overlord of the entire region stretching south of the Marrassantiya river to the Mediterranean Sea,[17] and west to the Konya Plain. Labarna brought all the conquered territories firmly under his sway, and sent his sons to govern them.

So much we learn from the historical preamble to Telipinu's *Proclamation*. Yet some scholars are sceptical. Can we really

[16] This name has long been thought to be a Hattian name or title in origin; see e.g. Sommer and Falkenstein (1938: 20–7), Kammenhuber (1959: 27), Bin-Nun (1975: 32). But recently a case has been made for an Indo-European origin (as also for the feminine term *Tawananna*, on which see below); see Puhvel (1989: 360–1), Tischler (1988: 355; 1993: 118). On the alternation between the variant forms *Labarna* and *Tabarna*, see Puhvel (1989: 351), Tischler (1988: 355) (who considers *Labarna* to be the older form).

[17] Thus I interpret the expression 'he made them (i.e. the conquered countries) the boundaries of the sea', an expression which is perhaps to be understood, as 'he made the sea their frontier' (thus Gurney (1973a: 235)); see also Heinhold-Krahmer (1977: 13–14). Or the expression may mean that the king drove the enemy back to the sea. The sea in question must be the Mediterranean. Note that Gurney (1973a: 237) assumes that the passage referring to Labarna in the *Proclamation* indicates that the countries identified—Hupisna, Tuwanuwa, etc.—already lay in Hittite hands before the time of the alleged Labarna. But later (1990: 17) he seems to follow the interpretation suggested above.

accept this Labarna, the possible founder of the Hittite royal dynasty, as an authentic historical figure? All the information we have about him comes from later sources. We have no texts from his reign, no explicit information about his relationship with his successors, or other members of the royal family, no other sources of information which might help confirm his place in Hittite history. The one document which does assign specific achievements to him—the *Proclamation*—uses almost identical wording to describe the achievements of his alleged successor Hattusili. Could it be that Labarna and Hattusili were one and the same person, that the composer of the *Proclamation* wrongly turned them into two?[18] If so, how did the error arise? Hattusili himself adopted the name Labarna as a throne-name and, the argument goes, it is possible that Telipinu, who reigned more than 100 years later, was misled into assuming that the two names indicated two different persons.[19]

This line of argument is not convincing. We know—as Telipinu obviously did—that Hattusili was not the first member of his dynasty to become king, that the tradition of a new king, or king-designate, assuming the name Labarna was already established by Hattusili's reign, and that the tradition persisted after his reign. Labarna may well have been the personal name of the founder of the first Hittite dynasty, but the name was subsequently used as a title by later members of the dynasty—in much the same way as Caesar was regularly used as a title in the nomenclature of the Roman emperors. In these circumstances, the alleged error referred to above would assume a degree of ignorance of the Labarna tradition on Telipinu's part which is inconceivable.[20]

[18] Thus Otten (1968: 104). But see Heinhold-Krahmer (1977: 12 n. 6).

[19] Cf. Gurney (1973*a*: 237–8; 1990: 17).

[20] Cf. Dinçol *et al.* (1993: 104) in the context of their discussion of the cruciform seal. The information provided by this seal clearly supports a distinction between a king called Labarna and his successor Hattusili who also assumed the name (or title) Labarna. Dinçol *et al.* assume that the first Labarna belonged to the generation immediately before Hattusili—i.e. that the Labarna of Telipinu's *Proclamation* was the uncle of Hattusili. The assumption I have made here, *contra* Dinçol *et al.*, is that the first Labarna was Hattusili's grandfather. As noted above, Dinçol *et al.* have now proposed the existence of a king Huzziya as a predecessor of the first Labarna. If they are right in assuming that the Labarna of the *Telipinu Proclamation* was the son of Hattusili's grandfather, then it may well be that the grandfather was the Huzziya in question.

The similar wording used to describe the achievements of Labarna and Hattusili in the *Proclamation* is no great cause for concern, or suspicion. It is, in effect, a formulaic way of highlighting one of the main themes of the *Proclamation*—the close link between periods of peace and stability within the kingdom and the kingdom's growth and development as a major military and political power. The link is made even more emphatic by a description in almost identical terms of the reign of Hattusili's successor Mursili. As with Labarna and Hattusili, the new king's 'sons, his brothers, his marriage relations, his (blood) relations were united. He held the enemy land in subjection by his might, and he deprived the lands of power; and he made them boundaries of the sea.'[21]

There are no good reasons for doubting the historical reality of a king Labarna, the king with whose achievements the *Proclamation* begins. From a likely power base in Kussara, ancestral home of the dynasty of Pithana and Anitta, this king made large his realm, extending his sway by military conquest over much of eastern Anatolia, as far south as the Mediterranean Sea. He was the first great warrior of the aggressive new Hittite dynasty, serving as a model and source of inspiration for those who would succeed to his throne.

But his relationship to his immediate successor in the *Proclamation* remains uncertain. It is to this man, Hattusili, that we must now turn our attention.

Rebellion in Sanahuitta

In his *Testament*, Hattusili recalls the rebellion against his grandfather:

Did not my grandfather's sons set aside his words? He appointed(??) his son Labarna in (the city of) Sanahuitta. But subsequently his servants and the great men defied his word and placed Papahdilmah (on the throne). How many years have passed and how many have escaped (their punishment)? Where are the houses of the great men? Have they not perished? (*Testament* §20, III 41–5)

[21] *Telipinu Procl.* §8, I 24–7. Güterbock (1983b: 29) comments: 'The repetitions are an impressive stylistic device (a device discussed by J. Licht, *Storytelling in the Bible*, Jerusalem, 1979) telling us that under the second and third kings things went as well—or nearly so—as under the first; equally impressive is the use of corresponding phrases for the description of bad times.'

The facts are brief and incomplete. Understandably so, for Hattusili was simply referring to an episode which occurred before his reign to point a moral, and to sound a warning. From the point of view of those to whom the warning was directed, details were unnecessary. The episode and its consequences must have been well known to the king's subjects. But from our point of view, this small snippet of information raises many questions. Where does Sanahuitta fit into the picture of the early development of the Hittite kingdom? What was the position of Hattusili's grandfather in the Hittite royal dynasty? What significance is to be attached to the fact that his son was called Labarna? What action involving his son was he attempting to take in Sanahuitta? The statement which refers to this is open to different interpretations. Why did this action provoke rebellion? Who was Papahdilmah? In attempting to answer these questions, we can do no more than provide a very tentative reconstruction of the context in which the rebellion occurred.

To begin with Sanahuitta. This name was already known, in the form Sinahuttum, in a text from the colony period.[22] The city probably lay to the north-east of Hattusa,[23] and certainly within the homeland, in the vicinity of the garrison centres Hakpissa (Hakmissa) and Istahara.[24] It thus provides further information on the extent of the Hittite kingdom before the reign of Hattusili. In addition to the territories won by Labarna in south-eastern Anatolia, the Hittites must also have controlled territories located a similar distance to the north of Kussara, at that time the centre of the Hittite kingdom. This may have been the result of a series of northern campaigns conducted by Labarna. There is no reference to such campaigns in the *Proclamation*. But if we can take at face value Telipinu's claim that the Hittite land was 'small' before Labarna's conquests, then it may be that he was also responsible for a northward as well as a southward expansion of Hittite territory.

Who was Hattusili's grandfather? The passage cited above does

---

[22] See Larsen (1972: 101).
[23] Goetze (1957b, 98) suggests a location between Mecitözü and Amasya, Cornelius (1979: 102–3) that it lay between Sivas, on the upper course of the Marrassantiya, and Malatya. Kempinski and Košak (1982: 108) place it between Alişar (Amkuwa) and Çorum.
[24] Gurney (1973a: 240).

not give his name or explicitly indicate his status. But there was no need for Hattusili to provide this information, for the grandfather was obviously a well-known figure, and had almost certainly been king. Very likely, he was the original Labarna, founder of the Hittite dynasty. If so, then the record of the rebellion provides an interesting and very significant supplement to Telipinu's account of his reign.

What role was the grandfather's son Labarna intended to fill in Sanahuitta? Unfortunately this is not clear from the passage translated above.[25] But the most likely conclusion is that the grandfather, king of Kussara, had attempted to establish his son Labarna as governor of the region in which Sanahuitta was located—an appointment which, for reasons unknown to us, proved highly unpopular. In fact it never took place. As a result of the uprising, which involved other members of the king's own family, the king's decision was rejected, and Labarna was replaced by the rebels' appointee, a man called Papahdilmah, perhaps one of the princes who had been 'made disloyal'.[26]

If all had gone according to his father's plans, the young Labarna may have succeeded to the throne in Kussara after serving as a regional ruler in the north of the kingdom.[27] His name suggests that he was his father's chosen heir. But we do not know what happened to him after the rebellion. He may not have survived it. And the rebellion must have had the effect of splitting off part of the kingdom, with a rebel regime now installed in Sanahuitta.

Hattusili Becomes King

This was the setting for Hattusili I's accession to the Hittite throne c.1650.[28] At the beginning of his *Annals*, Hattusili identified himself as: 'The Great King Tabarna,[29] Hattusili the Great King, King of the Land of Hatti, Man of Kussar(a). In the Land of Hatti he

[25] The problem lies essentially in the meaning of the verb *iškunaḫḫiš*, tentatively translated as 'appointed', which is found nowhere else in Hittite literature. For various possibilities, see Gurney (1973a: 237), Bryce (1981: 11–12).

[26] Bin-Nun (1975: 8–9, 55) suggests that he was Hattusili's father, on the basis of a textual restoration which she proposes. Cf. Sommer and Falkenstein (1938: 209), Puhvel (1989: 353).

[27] Cf. Riemschneider (1971: 99).

[28] If one adheres to the 'low chronology', the accession date should be set c.1575/70; see e.g. Astour (1989: 12).

[29] The translation is based on Melchert's restoration (1978: 7).

ruled as king, son of the brother of Tawananna' (*Annals*, I 1–3).[30] As the expression 'Man of Kussar(a)' suggests, Hattusili almost certainly began his reign at Kussara,[31] inheriting from his predecessor a kingdom which had been reduced by the rebellion in Sanahuitta, but which still controlled, apparently, extensive territory to the south of Kussara. He also inherited the account to be settled with the rebel regime in the north.

But before attending to this, Hattusili took a major new step in his kingdom's development. He established a new seat for the royal dynasty, on the site of the ruins of Hattusa! Indeed he may have adopted the name Hattusili to mark this event.[32] His resettlement of the site was in defiance of the curse imposed upon it by Anitta— a fact which some scholars see as confirming the view that Hattusili was not of the same dynasty as Pithana and Anitta. However, the site had certain natural advantages which, irrespective of Hattusili's lineage, may have outweighed any consideration of Anitta's curse. It was located in a naturally defensible position, one of the few such in central Anatolia, with its citadel on the large outcrop of rock now known as Büyükkale which was virtually impregnable from the north. Too, the region in which it lay had an abundant all-year-round supply of water, from seven springs, and at that time was thickly forested.

But from a strategic point of view, the new capital was badly situated.[33] It was much further removed than Kussara from the Hittites' southern subject territories and the routes into Syria. And it was close to the ill-defined and often shifting northern boundary of the kingdom. As we have noted, this put it within striking distance of the Kaska people and other hostile tribes in the region. Yet 'history can show many examples of the siting of a capital city at the point of danger'.[34]

Hattusili's military objectives in northern Anatolia probably also had some bearing on his selection of Hattusa as the new royal seat.

[30] Unless otherwise stated the passages from the *Annals* are translated from the Hittite version of the text (KBo x 2).

[31] This titulature was later recalled by the king Hattusili III; see Sommer and Falkenstein (1938: 105), though Melchert (1978: 7) comments that the titulature was not part of the original text, but rather a late insertion in the Hittite version.

[32] Thus Sommer and Falkenstein (1938: 20) followed by Gurney (1973*a*: 238–9), Klengel, E. and H. (1975: 59). But Kempinski and Košak (1982: 99 n. 2) comment that the name Hattusili should not be taken to imply that Hattusili rebuilt Hattusa, since it is already attested during the colony period (Bilgiç (1945–51: 5 no. 2)).

[33] Thus Gurney (1973*a*: 239), Bittel (1983*c*: 19).   [34] Gurney (1973*a*: 239).

The first target of his campaigns in this region was Sanahuitta, now within easy range of the Hittite capital. In Hattusa the king's troops were mustered. And from there the campaign against Sanahuitta was launched. But the success it achieved was a limited one: 'He marched against Sanahuitta. He did not destroy it, but its land he did destroy. I left (my) troops in two places as a garrison. I gave whatever sheepfolds were (there) to (my) garrison troops'[35] (*Annals*, I 4–8).

Hattusili plundered the lands belonging to Sanahuitta, but the city itself remained intact. There was probably a good reason for this, to which we shall return below. For the moment we must suppose that when Hattusili withdrew his troops from the territory of Sanahuitta, he had not succeeded in capturing the city or removing the rebel regime which had installed itself there during his grandfather's reign. The rebels had yet to be called to account.

In the same year as his campaign against Sanahuitta, Hattusili marched against Zalpa, very likely the kingdom which figures in the Anitta inscription, in the far north near the mouth of the Marrassantiya river:[36]

Thereupon I marched against Zalpa and destroyed it. I took possession of its gods and I gave three wagons to the Sun Goddess of Arinna. I gave one silver bull and one silver fist (rhyton) to the temple of the Storm God. The gods that were remaining I gave to the temple of Mezzulla.[37]   (*Annals*, I 9–14)

In contrast to his campaign against Sanahuitta, Hattusili apparently succeeded in capturing, looting, and destroying the city. Even so, this proved no more than a temporary setback for Zalpa, for it was to figure in a number of later conflicts with the Hittites. Indeed, as we shall see, it reappeared later in Hattusili's reign in a rebellion against his rule involving one of his sons.

Limited though they were in their long-term consequences, the campaigns against Sanahuitta and Zalpa seem to have established Hattusili's authority in central Anatolia to the point where he could now look to more distant lands to conquer. In the following year

---

[35] The fluctuation between 1st and 3rd person is a not uncommon feature of Hittite narrative texts.

[36] There was, however, more than one site called Zalpa, and some doubt has been expressed about the identification assumed here; see Cornelius (1959: 292).

[37] Mezzulla was the daughter of the Sun Goddess of Arinna.

preparations were put in place for the most ambitious campaign yet undertaken by a Hittite army as Hattusili made ready to carry his battle standards into Syria.

The Hittites Invade Syria

The earlier territorial gains which the Hittites had made south of the Marrassantiya river had already paved the way for their military enterprises in Syria. Control over the countries of south-eastern Anatolia provided them with access into Syria by several routes. One of these led through the pass later known as the Cilician Gates and no doubt came to be used regularly by the Hittites for both commercial and military purposes. This may well have been the route now taken by Hattusili's army in its march through southern Anatolia and across the Taurus mountains into Syria through the Syrian Gates (modern Beilan Pass).

Hattusili must have been well aware that a Hittite military expedition into Syria posed far greater challenges than his campaigns in Anatolia, and entailed far greater risks. For the whole of the northern part of the region was controlled by the powerful kingdom of Iamhad. From its capital Aleppo (Halap, Halab, or Halpa in the Hittite texts), Iamhad had for two centuries dominated northern Syria through a network of vassal states and appanage kingdoms which stretched from the Euphrates to the Mediterranean coast. The archives from Alalah provide the names of a wide array of states and cities which were associated with Aleppo either as subjects or as allies—Alalah, Carchemish, Ursu, Hassu, Ugarit, Emar, Ebla, Tunip. Hittite military operations against any of the north Syrian states and principalities inevitably represented a threat to the kingdom of Aleppo itself.

There can be little doubt that Hattusili already had his sights set on the eventual conquest of Aleppo. But a direct challenge lay in the future. Hattusili was not yet ready to take on the military might of the most powerful kingdom in Syria. For the present, he limited the scope of his operations to a preliminary foray into the region, in preparation for more extensive military campaigns in later years. This first probing operation was probably intended to test the strength of enemy resistance in peripheral areas of the kingdom, and where possible to eliminate some of the sources of support on which it might call in subsequent contests with the Hittites.

After entering Syria via the passes in the Amanus range, Hattusili promptly identified his first military objective. Near the northernmost bend of the Orontes river, on the road linking Aleppo with the Mediterranean coast, lay the imposing fortified city of Alalah, modern Tell Açana (Alalha in the *Annals*). It was against this city that Hattusili led his troops for their first military operation on Syrian soil. The result was an unqualified success. The troops of Alalah were routed, their city reduced to ruins.

At the time of the Hittite onslaught, Alalah was ruled by Ammitaqum, nominally the vassal of Iarimlim III who then occupied the throne of Aleppo. This information is provided by a tablet from Alalah VII mentioning Zukrasi, general of the king of Aleppo, as witness to an Alalah document in which Ammitaqum declared his will before Iarimlim.[38] Zukrasi also figures in a Hittite text referring to a Hittite attack on Hassu(wa), very likely the same event recorded in Hattusili's sixth campaign (see below). If so, then Ammitaqum and Hattusili may well have been contemporaries since Zukrasi, general of Iarimlim, appears in documents associated with both rulers. Thus we may conclude that Alalah VII, the city of Ammitaqum, was the city destroyed by Hattusili.[39] But the Hittite conquest was achieved without any apparent intervention from Iarimlim. Why did he not come to the aid of his vassal state in its hour of need?

It is possible that Alalah had taken advantage of a dynastic dispute in Aleppo to establish its independence,[40] and was thus reluctant to call upon its former overlord for support. If so, this could have been one of the factors which prompted Hattusili to attack Alalah, gambling that he could so without provoking a confrontation with Aleppo. It is still surprising that this blatant military intrusion into Syrian territory met with no response from Aleppo, unless the rapidity of the Hittite advance and conquest had caught it unawares and left it insufficient time to mount a counter-attack. At all events, before encountering any challenge from Aleppo, Hattusili withdrew from Syria. For the present, he had tested his troops' mettle on Syrian soil, and without committing them to further conflict in the region, he struck out on a north-easterly route which would eventually lead back to Hattusa.

---

[38] Cited by Otten (1964: 120), Gurney (1973*a*: 244).
[39] See also Otten (1964: 118, with n. 13), Kupper (1973: 31), Gurney (1973*a*: 241).
[40] Thus Gurney (1973*a*: 242). See also Kupper (1973: 34).

But there were other military objectives to be accomplished on the way.

An Incompetent Siege Operation

Before returning to his capital, Hattusili attacked several cities in the region lying west of the Euphrates and north of Carchemish: 'Subsequently I marched against Warsuwa. From Warsuwa I marched against Ikakali. From Ikakali I marched against Tashiniya. And I destroyed these lands. I took possession of their property and filled my house to the limit with it' (*Annals*, 1 16–21).

Warsuwa, better known by its Akkadian name Ursu,[41] figures in a later well known legendary text which records a Hittite siege of the city.[42] The siege is generally assigned to the reign of Hattusili, though we cannot be sure whether it belongs to this or to a later campaign which he conducted.[43] It does, however, throw interesting light on one of the chronic deficiencies of the Hittite military machine—its ineffectiveness in siege warfare. And as a 'literary' text it provides an interesting complement to the military record of the *Annals*. The Hittite king expresses his fury at his officers' ineptitude in conducting the siege of the city—a siege which according to the text lasted six months:

They broke the battering-ram. The king was angry and his face was grim: 'They constantly bring me bad news; may the Storm God carry you away in a flood! . . . Be not idle! Make a battering-ram in the Hurrian manner and let it be brought into place. Hew a great battering-ram from the mountains of Hassu and let it be brought into place. Begin to heap up earth. When you have finished let every one take post. Only let the enemy give battle, then his plans will be confounded.' . . . (Subsequently the king rebukes his general Santas for the inordinate delay in doing battle.) 'Why have you not given battle? You stand on chariots of water, you are almost turned into water yourself(?) . . . You had only to kneel before him and you would have killed him or at least frightened him. But as it is you have behaved like a woman.' . . . Thus they answered him: 'Eight times we will give battle. We will confound their schemes and destroy the city.' The king answered, 'Good!'

[41] For proposals on its location, see del Monte and Tischler (1978: 476).
[42] KBo I 11 (*CTH* 7) ed. Güterbock (1938: 113–38). The text has also been discussed by Klengel (1965b: 261–2), Houwink ten Cate (1984: 68–9).
[43] See Bryce (1983: 85–6).

But while they did nothing to the city, many of the king's servants were wounded so that many died. The king was angered and said: 'Watch the roads. Observe who enters the city and who leaves the city. No one is to go out from the city to the enemy.' . . . But a fugitive came out of the city and reported: 'The subject of the king of Aleppo came in five times, the subject of Zuppa is dwelling in the city itself, the men of Zaruar[44] go in and out, the subject of my Lord the Son of Tesub[45] goes to and fro.' . . . The king was furious.   (KBo I 11 obv. 2' ff., trans. Gurney (1990: 148–9))

While the text is largely anecdotal in character, and replete with dramatic embellishments, it does provide a rather more graphic picture of a Hittite military operation than the terse, bald narrative of the historical texts. And indirectly it may provide a motive for the Hittite attack on Ursu. The failure of the Hittite siege to prevent passage to and from the beleaguered city by representatives of the king of Aleppo and the king of the Hurrians was a source of acute embarrassment to the Hittite king, who had ordered all the roads leading to the city to be blocked. But the significant point is that some form of alliance apparently existed between Ursu, Aleppo, and the kingdom of the Hurrians. The last two were potential enemies of Hatti, and a pre-emptive strike against one or more of their allies might have been designed, perhaps as in the case of Alalah, to reduce their sources of military support in the event of future Hittite campaigns against them. Indeed Ursu was very likely a Hurrian subject state at the time of the early Hittite campaigns in the region.[46]

Ursu eventually fell to the Hittites. But its conquest and destruction may well have provoked the Hurrians into retaliatory action the following year—with devastating consequences for Hattusili's kingdom.

Hattusili's Arzawan Campaign

In the year following his first Syrian campaign, Hattusili turned his attention to the south-west, where he undertook a campaign against the land of Arzawa—the earliest reference we have to

[44] Astour (1989: 89 n. 104) suggests that Zaruar (Zalwar of the Alalah texts) should be located at Koyuncu Höyük, near the marshes north of the Lake of Antioch.
[45] i.e. the king of the Hurrians.
[46] See Kupper (1973: 36), Klengel (1992: 343).

Arzawa in the Hittite texts. At this time it was probably an ill-defined complex of territories spread over much of western and south-western Anatolia. How far did Hattusili venture into this region, and what did he hope to achieve? The record in the *Annals*, confined to a single sentence, tells us little: 'In the following year, I marched against Arzawa and took cattle and sheep' (*Annals*, I 22–3).

The somewhat incidental nature of this statement may indicate that the expedition was little more than a raid into Arzawan territory. Cattle and sheep were taken as plunder, but there were apparently no conquests of any significance. Quite possibly the expedition had been provoked by Arzawa. As a result of the conquests of Labarna, Hittite subject territory must have extended close to, and may even have bordered on, the territory of Arzawa. That clearly provided scope for territorial disputes and cross-border raids—then as in later times. Perhaps one or more 'border incidents' escalated to the point where the Hittite king had to intervene in person, with a punitive expedition designed to give clear warning to the people of Arzawa to keep out of Hittite territory.

In later years Hattusili may have returned to Arzawa and carried out extensive campaigns in the region, if we can attribute to his reign the conquests in Arzawa referred to in a later document.[47] And it is possible that by the end of his reign, at least part of Arzawan territory was under the control of a Hittite governor.[48]

Rebellions in the Subject States

Whatever the intended scope of Hattusili's first Arzawan campaign, it was cut short by a crisis which threatened the very survival of the Hittite kingdom: 'In my rear the enemy of the city of the Hurrians entered my land, and all my lands made war against

[47] The treaty drawn up early in the 13th cent. between the Hittite king Muwatalli II and Alaksandu, vassal ruler of Wilusa (*CTH* 76); Friedrich, 1930, 50–1 §2. But note the reservations of Heinhold-Krahmer (1977: 18–19).

[48] This is suggested by KBo III 34 (*CTH* 8A), from a 'palace chronicle', or collection of anecdotes, which may be datable to Hattusili's reign. The text makes reference to a Man from Hurma called Nunnu, who had apparently embezzled gold in Arzawa which should have been handed over to the Hittite king. Presumably Nunnu had been appointed to an important administrative post in Arzawa, perhaps that of governor. See Hardy (1941: 189–91), Gurney (1973*a*: 246), Heinhold-Krahmer (1977: 19–21). For the text, see Eisele (1970: 86–7).

me. By now only the city of Hattusa, one city, remained' (*Annals*, I 24–6).

This crisis was of a type which occurred repeatedly throughout Hittite history, exposing one of the kingdom's chronic weaknesses. Campaigns conducted to the west and south-west which drew substantially on the kingdom's military resources left the homeland dangerously exposed to attack from the north, the east, and the south-east. On this occasion the Hurrians, taking advantage of the king's absence, and perhaps in direct retaliation for the destruction of Ursu, invaded the homeland with devastating results. If we are to believe the record in the *Annals*, the whole of the homeland was lost to Hattusili, with the exception only of the royal capital.[49]

It seems that the Hurrians promptly retreated on the return of the Hittite army. But their invasion had triggered off uprisings and defections throughout all the regions incorporated into the kingdom by the conquests of both Labarna and Hattusili. The response of Hattusili was prompt and vigorous. From his base in Hattusa, he first re-established his control over the region within the Marrassantiya river boundary, and then set about the reconquest of the rebellious subject territories lying to the south.

The first city to return to the Hittite fold was Nenassa which lay just beyond the southernmost bend of the Marrassantiya.[50] On the approach of the Hittite army, it threw open its gates and surrendered without resistance. But the next city Ulma[51] was not so easily won. Twice it came in battle against the king, and twice it was defeated. Such defiance could not be tolerated a third time—and a clear message had to be sent to the other rebel cities which continued their resistance. Hattusili ordered the total destruction of the city. Its site was sown with weeds, and all future settlement was banned.[52]

Only one more city refused submission—Sallahsuwa, also known from the Assyrian merchant texts, and very likely occupying a strategically important location near one of the main east–

---

[49] Wilhelm (1989: 21) comments that though the report may be somewhat exaggerated for dramatic effect, it does give an impression of the considerable strength of the new Hurrian fighting force.

[50] See Bryce (1983: 74). The city is first attested in texts of the colony period.

[51] Variant form Ullamma, also known from the colony texts as one of the cities destroyed by Anitta.

[52] *Annals*, I 33–7.

west routes linking north Syria with Anatolia. It was promptly attacked and destroyed, bringing to an end all resistance in the south.

Hattusili's policy towards rebel and enemy states was similar to that adopted by Anitta and followed by later Hittite kings. No punitive action was taken against a rebel or enemy city if it responded to an ultimatum from the king by throwing open its gates to him. But resistance, especially persistent resistance, met with the severest reprisals. Several demonstrations of this were sufficient inducement for the other rebels in the south to surrender without further opposition, leaving Hattusili free to return to Hattusa.

There were still rebels in the north to contend with. To these Hattusili turned his attention the following year. Once more he was obliged to take the field against Sanahuitta. His campaign into the region three years earlier had left the city intact, and presumably the rebel regime was still in power there. This situation could no longer be tolerated. The city had to be conquered and destroyed.

For six months Sanahuitta held out against the king's forces. It was probably well fortified against enemy attack, which may explain why it had escaped destruction on Hattusili's earlier campaign. The conquest of a heavily fortified city almost inevitably entailed a protracted and costly siege. After sizing up the costs and the risks involved, Hattusili may have decided on his first campaign into Sanahuitta's territory to limit his operation to plundering the estates and farmlands surrounding the city.[53] But the time had now come to commit himself fully to the conquest of Sanahuitta. After six months the city fell, and no doubt with it also the regime set up there in the reign of Hattusili's grandfather. This act of rebellion was now, finally, avenged. Hattusili removed once and for all one of the chief sources of opposition to him in the region lying on the eastern periphery of the homeland. It was an event which he looked back to in later years with no small measure of satisfaction, as he issued to those assembled around his deathbed a warning of the consequences of rebellion: 'How many years have passed and how many have escaped (their punishment)? Where are the

---

[53] Wilhelm (1989: 21) comments that when a report is only of pillaging the countryside, this is usually an indication that the attack on the town had failed; cf. Klengel (1965*b*: 262–3; 1969: 158).

houses of the great men? Have they not perished?' (*Testament*, §20, III 44–5).

With the fall of Sanahuitta, resistance in other centres quickly crumbled. The city of Parmanna threw open its gates to the king, and other cities promptly followed suit. Alahha alone had the temerity to resist—and was destroyed.[54] By the end of the fifth year of the *Annals*, Hattusili's control over all his Anatolian territories lying both within and outside the Marrassantiya boundary had been fully re-established. Once more he could turn his attention to Syria: but this time he planned a more extensive campaign in the region.

The Second Syrian Campaign

In the following year I marched against Zaruna and destroyed Zaruna. And I marched against Hassuwa and the men of Hassuwa came against me in battle. They were assisted by troops from Halpa (Aleppo). They came against me in battle and I overthrew them. Within a few days I crossed the river Puruna and I overcame Hassuwa like a lion with its claws. And [ ] when I overthrew it I heaped dust upon it and took possession of all its property and filled Hattusa with it. (*Annals*, KBo x 2 II 11–19, KBo x 1 35–6.) I entered Zippasna, and I ascended Zippasna in the dead of night. I entered into battle with them and heaped dust upon them . . . Like a lion I gazed fiercely upon Hahha and destroyed Zippasna. I took possession of its gods and brought them to the temple of the Sun Goddess of Arinna. And I marched against Hahha and three times made battle within the gates. I destroyed Hahha and took possession of its property and carried it off to Hattusa. Two pairs of transport wagons were loaded with silver. (*Annals*, II 48–III 9)

The details are sketchy. The precise locations of the cities attacked by Hattusili are unknown and the identification of the Puruna river (Akkadian Puran) has led to much debate.[55] But the overall picture is reasonably clear. After crossing the Taurus mountains, Hattusili began to march east towards the Euphrates, destroying the city of Zaruna[56] *en route*. Other states in the region

[54] *Annals*, KBo x 2 II 2–10. See Melchert (1978: 15–16) on this passage.

[55] It has been variously identified with the Euphrates (Güterbock (1964a: 3–4)), the Orontes (tentatively by Wilhelm (1989: 22)), the Afrin (tentatively by Klengel (1992: 344 n. 24)) and the Pyramos/Ceyhan (e.g. Laroche (1977: 205) s.v. Purana, Astour (1989: 89 n. 102), Forlanini and Marazzi (1986)). See Gurney's review of the matter (1992: 216–17).

[56] Akkadian Zarunti; it lay not far from Alalah.

rallied against him. He was confronted by an army from the city of Hassuwa (which lay south of the Taurus and just west or east of the Euphrates)[57] supported by troops from Aleppo, and defeated their combined forces in a battle fought at Mt. Atalur (Adalur).[58] He then attacked and destroyed the cities of Hassuwa[59] and Zippasna, entering the latter's territory in the dead of night. Finally he marched against the city of Hahha on the Euphrates[60] which had made a futile attempt to come to the assistance of Zippasna. The city's defences were breached, but within its gates the Hittites met with fierce resistance. Finally the city succumbed—but only after its troops had rallied three times against its attackers.

Hattusili showed no mercy to the vanquished. Mercy was a concession granted only to those who surrendered without resistance. The conquered cities were looted, and the spoils of conquest loaded onto wagons for transport back to Hattusa. When stripped of all their precious possessions, including the statues of their gods, Hassuwa and Hahha were set ablaze, and reduced to rubble.[61] Then came the final *coup de grace*—the humiliation and degradation of the local rulers. After witnessing the looting and destruction of their cities, the kings of Hassuwa and Hahha suffered the indignity of being harnessed to one of the wagons used to convey the spoils of their cities to Hattusa: 'I the Great King Tabarna destroyed Hassuwa and Hahha and burned them down with fire and showed the smoke to the Storm God of Heaven. And I harnessed the king

---

[57] For various proposals, see the references cited by del Monte and Tischler (1978: 98).

[58] The name appears only in the Akkadian version of the text and is probably to be identified with the southern offshoot of the Amanus range, perhaps south of the mouth of the Orontes river. See Otten (1958: 82 n. 23 following Balkan (1957: 36); 1964: 116), del Monte and Tischler (1978: 54), Forlanini and Marazzi (1986), Gurney (1992: 216–17).

[59] Wilhelm (1989: 22) comments that an oracle text, KBo XVIII 151, which names both Hassu and also the Hurrians, most likely refers to this event.

[60] Perhaps on the site of modern Samsat; see Gurney (1992: 217), citing Forlanini and Marazzi (1986). For other suggested locations, see del Monte and Tischler (1978: 61–2), and add Liverani (1988), who proposes an identification with Lidar Höyük on the east bank of the Euphrates (but note Gurney's reservations).

[61] Liverani (1988: 170) notes that level 8 of Lidar Höyük, which is contemporaneous with the Old Assyrian, Old Hittite, and Mari references to Hahhum, was destroyed by a huge fire, the result of a violent attack (see also the report in *AS* 37 (1987), 204–5). Corpses were found under the collapsed walls and arrow heads sticking in the walls' plaster. He comments that the town was certainly destroyed after a war storming, and links its destruction with the wars of the Old Kingdom Hittite kings in the area.

of Hassuwa and the king of Hahha to a transport wagon' (*Annals*, III 37–42).

The magnitude of the Hittite victories during this second Syrian campaign is highlighted by an event to which Hattusili attached great significance. His conquests in the Euphrates region involved a crossing of the river itself, an achievement unprecedented in Hittite history. Indeed only the Akkadian ruler Sargon, who had crossed the river in the other direction some 700 years earlier, had accomplished such a feat before him. But Sargon had done so without the same devastating results:

No one had crossed the (river) Mala (= Euphrates, Akkadian Purattu), but I the Great King Tabarna crossed it on foot, and my army crossed it [after me](?) on foot. Sarrugina (Sargon) (also) crossed it. But although he overthrew the troops of Hahha, he did nothing to Hahha (itself) and did not burn it down, nor did he show(?) the smoke to the Storm God of Heaven.   (*Annals*, III 29–40, adapted from trans. by Güterbock (1964a: 2))

The comparison with Sargon is clearly justified, for Hattusili's conquests extended over much of the same region west of the Euphrates conquered by Sargon many generations earlier. By the end of his sixth campaign, Hattusili had subdued almost the entire eastern half of Anatolia, from the Black Sea (in the region of Zalpa) to the Mediterranean, encompassing the Lower Land and perhaps also the territory later to become the kingdom of Kizzuwadna, and had led his troops to a series of victories through northern Syria across the Euphrates to the western fringes of Mesopotamia.

What did Hattusili Achieve by his Campaigns?

In purely military terms Hattusili's campaigns were, it seems, resoundingly successful. But they raise several fundamental questions. What was their purpose? What did they actually achieve? And at what cost?

The Syrian campaigns had resulted in the destruction of a number of cities, and the accumulation of substantial spoils for the Land of Hatti. But they did not lead to the establishment of a permanent Hittite presence in the region. Attack, destroy, withdraw—that was the pattern of the campaigns. The Hittites had neither the organizational capacity nor the human resources necessary to establish and maintain lasting control over territories they had conquered in Syria. And so long as the kingdom of Aleppo remained unsubdued, the impact of the Hittites' military successes in the region could be no more than transitory.

Why then did Hattusili bother with Syria at all, particularly when he had problems enough to deal with at home? His kingdom was prone to serious political upheavals (as we shall see below) and chronically vulnerable to invasion by enemies close to its frontiers. Protracted absences of the king and his troops on distant campaigns undoubtedly increased the dangers posed by both internal and external forces to the security of the kingdom. This gives added point to our question. The kingdoms of Syria posed no direct military threat to the Hittite homeland, nor indeed to any of the Hittites' subject territories in Anatolia. Thus the Syrian campaigns can hardly be seen as defensive or pre-emptive in purpose. What then *was* their purpose?

Strategic and economic considerations may have been part of the motivation for these campaigns. As one scholar has aptly pointed out, Syria lies at the crossroads of the Near East, and its ports and land routes provided access to a wide range of products from Egypt as well as Mesopotamia.[62] The Hittites may have found that military force was the only effective means of gaining access to the international merchandise which found its way into Syrian markets, and of making secure the routes which supplied them with indispensable raw materials.

The cities attacked by Hattusili lay in important strategic locations on major routes linking Anatolia with Syria and Mesopotamia. Alalah, for example, was on or at least within striking distance of a route which led from south-eastern Anatolia through northern Syria eastwards to the Euphrates. To the north, Ursu lay in the vicinity of one of the main routes linking Assyria with Anatolia in the Assyrian colony period.[63] Given the role these routes must have played in trading enterprises from at least the time of the Assyrians' merchant operations in both Syria and Anatolia, their economic and strategic importance is obvious.

We can only speculate on the nature of most of the international merchandise to which the Hittites sought access. But one commodity in particular must have been in heavy demand. During the

---

[62] Goetze (1975a: 1).   [63] See e.g. Cornelius (1979: 101).

colony period tin, used in the manufacture of bronze, was one of the two most important commodities imported along the trade routes from Mesopotamia into Anatolia. Indeed, the Assyrian merchants may well have been the sole suppliers of the metal, which perhaps came from sources in the mountains of Elam (modern Iran)[64] to the Anatolian kingdoms. The severing of the Anatolian–Assyrian trade links at the end of the colony period must have cut off the tin supplies and brought bronze production on any significant scale in central Anatolia to an end.

The renewal of bronze production in the Late Bronze Age clearly implies renewed access to substantial sources of tin. For the Hittites, regular supplies of the metal were essential. In recent years Turkish archaeologists have claimed to have discovered several sites in Anatolia where tin could have been mined in antiquity.[65] But the evidence is disputed, particularly by the scholar James Muhly, who has long maintained, and continues to maintain, that we have yet to find evidence of workable tin deposits, at least on a significant scale, anywhere in Anatolia.[66] We must still reckon with the likelihood that most if not all of the tin used by the Hittites came from further afield.[67]

But outside Anatolia there are very few known sources of tin which could have supplied the Hittites' needs. If their supplies did not originate in the west, for example from central European sources, then they very likely came via the old trade routes from the south-east. If so, one of the objects of Hattusili's south-eastern campaigns could have been to ensure safe passage for imports—particularly tin—into his kingdom along these routes. In order to maintain control over a kingdom which had by now assumed substantial proportions, it was essential for Hattusili to have a guaranteed supply of large quantities of tin, whose most important use was in the manufacture of bronze weaponry for his army. Perhaps the destruction of cities like Ursu was intended at least in part to

---

[64] Yakar (1976: 122–3), refers to a number of fields in Iran that may have supplied Mesopotamia with tin.

[65] Notably in the Celaller region, where cassiterite and an Early Bronze Age tin mine have been discovered; see Kaptan (1995) for a summary of the results to date of the investigations of the Celaller mining complex, under the direction of K. A. Yener.

[66] See e.g. Muhly *et al.* (1991: 1992*b*).

[67] Kaptan (1995: 197) also concedes that evidence for economically feasible tin deposits in Anatolia has yet to be substantiated.

remove potential or actual threats to vital supply routes from Mesopotamia and Syria to the Hittite kingdom.

The Ideology of Kingship[68]

While economic and strategic factors may have provided an incentive for Hattusili's Syrian campaigns, there was, almost certainly, a much more powerful incentive underpinning these military adventures. Like all rulers of the great kingdoms of the Near East, the Hittite king was the supreme military commander of his people. And the ideology of kingship demanded that he demonstrate his fitness to rule by doing great military deeds, comparable with and where possible surpassing the achievements of his predecessors. 'Military expansion became an ideology in its own right, a true sport of kings.'[69] For Hattusili, Syria provided a challenge never before undertaken by a Hittite king. His Anatolian conquests gave him military status and prestige equivalent to that of his predecessor Labarna. But by his Syrian campaigns he surpassed him. And his crossing of the Euphrates, however great or little its long-term strategic value, was an act of great symbolic importance. He could now claim to be a leader whose achievements ranked him alongside the king preserved in tradition as the greatest of all known kings— the legendary Sargon. He could go further and claim to be a warlord even more ruthless than Sargon. Sargon had crossed the Euphrates and left Hahha intact. Hattusili looted it and put it to the torch! The image he presents is that of a lion pouncing upon his prey and destroying it without mercy—an image of ruthless savagery against a persistently defiant enemy. It was an image which had already been used by Anitta. And it was to become a regular symbol of Hittite royal power.[70]

Yet mercy and compassion also figured amongst the qualities of a king, as Hattusili demonstrated in his treatment of his enemy's allegedly oppressed subjects:

I the Great King Tabarna took the hands of his (the enemy's) slave girls from the handmills, and I took the hands of his (male) slaves from the sickles, and I freed them from the taxes and the corvée. I unloosed their

---

[68] For a more detailed treatment of this topic, see Gurney (1958) and Beckman (1995*b*).

[69] Gurney (1979*a*: 163).   [70] See Hoffner (1980: 297).

belts (i.e. I unharnessed them), and I gave them over to My Lady, the Sun Goddess of Arinna. (*Annals*, III 15–20)

Later kings also sought to represent themselves as conquerors who showed mercy to a submissive enemy, although it has been remarked that no other royal *Annals* casts its protagonist in the role of deliverer of oppressed subjects.[71]

Perhaps most importantly, the king held his position by divine right.[72] He was the gods' agent and representative on earth, who ruled his subjects and confounded his enemies on their behalf. And as the gods' appointed deputy on earth, he was in theory inviolable:

When the king bows to the gods, the 'anointed' (priest) recites as follows: 'May the Tabarna, the king, be dear to the gods! The land belongs to the Storm God alone. Heaven, earth, and the people belong to the Storm God alone. He has made the Labarna, the king, his administrator and given him the entire Land of Hatti.' (IBoT 1.30 (CTH 537.1), obv. 2–5, adapted from trans. by Beckman (1995: 530)) To me, the king, the Sun God and the Storm God have entrusted my country and my house (the palace), and I, the king, will protect my country and my house. (KUB XXIX 1 (*CTH* 414) I 17–19))

Hattusili's Later Campaigns

Following his triumphant crossing of the Euphrates Hattusili returned to Hattusa. For all that he may have boasted of his successes, he knew that they could have no lasting consequences while the kingdom of Aleppo remained the dominant power in Syria. He had first clashed with troops from Aleppo when they had come to the assistance of Hassuwa. But he had yet to put to the test the full might of Aleppo's military resources. The preliminary moves had been made, but the main contest had not yet begun.

We have no more than passing references to the campaigns which Hattusili conducted in the later years of his reign. As we have noted, these may have included an extensive campaign against Arzawa. But without doubt it was Syria which provided the Hittites' most important theatre of war for the remainder of Hattusili's reign. Within this theatre, the conquest of Aleppo now became the king's prime objective.

From a later document we learn that he returned to Syria and engaged the Aleppan king's forces in battle, probably on repeated

[71] Hoffner (1980: 298).   [72] See Archi (1966), Gonnet (1987).

occasions. In the process he may have succeeded in substantially weakening the kingdom—if we can so interpret the enigmatic phrase 'he caused (the days of) the kingdom (of Aleppo) to be full'.[73] Yet ultimate success was to elude him. On his death the capital of the kingdom remained intact.[74] Indeed his death was perhaps linked in some way with a final conflict with Aleppo; for subsequently his grandson and successor Mursili set out against Aleppo on a campaign 'to avenge his father's blood' (see below, Chapter 5).

The Assembly at Kussara

What was probably the final act of Hattusili's life was played out in Kussara, ancestral home of the Hittite royal dynasty. Here the king, ailing and perhaps close to death, summoned an assembly of the most powerful political and military personages in the kingdom—the warriors of the *panku* and the $^{\text{LÚ.MEŠ}}$DUGUD, high-ranking officials of the land.[75] The assembly had been convened primarily to hear Hattusili's announcement of new arrangements he had made for the royal succession.

Our chief source of information on this closing stage of the king's reign is the document we have referred to as Hattusili's *Testament*. From its last words, we learn that Kussara was the setting for the assembly convened by the king. No doubt he continued to maintain a royal residence in Kussara after the shift of the capital to Hattusa. Perhaps he sought to spend his final days there, in the city of his ancestors.

An Unruly Family

While in essence the *Testament* is an official proclamation dealing with the royal succession, it provides important information about the various members of the king's family and the events in which

[73] From the so-called Aleppo treaty, KBo 1 6 (*CTH* 75), obv. 12, thus trans. Gurney (1973*a*: 243). The treaty is discussed in Ch. 6.

[74] Astour (1989: 17) takes a different view. He translates the above words: 'he caused their kingship to be full'—i.e. 'to end'. According to his interpretation, this means that Hattusili deprived Aleppo of its status as an independent great power by forcing it to bow to his overlordship.

[75] In later times the term $^{\text{LÚ.MEŠ}}$DUGUD seems to have been used in reference to military titles of relatively low rank. In this period, it may have been a general term denoting important persons, perhaps military officers; see Beal (1992*b*: 500) and the references cited therein. The term *panku* is discussed below.

they were involved. It also gives us some interesting insights into the character of the king himself. The ruthless warlord of the *Annals* appears here as an old man, weary and disillusioned by the behaviour of members of his own family: 'Until now no member of my family has obeyed my will' (*Testament* §19, III 26).

Following the practice of his predecessor, the first Labarna, Hattusili had appointed his sons as governors of the territories incorporated by conquest into the kingdom. Yet the Hittite princes showed no greater inclination than Labarna's sons to maintain their allegiance to their father. We hear first of a rebellion in the city of Tappassanda (otherwise unknown) involving the king's son Huzziya who had been appointed governor of the city.[76] Huzziya had been persuaded by the inhabitants to rebel against his father on the grounds that Hattusili had failed to carry out a purification of the 'palaces' of the city.[77] Hattusili evidently crushed the rebellion and deposed his son. From another source we learn of a rebellion in the city of Zalpa involving Hakkarpili, another of Hattusili's sons who had likewise been appointed as a local governor.[78] The outcome of this rebellion is not known, but presumably Hattusili was again successful in crushing it and removing Hakkarpili from power.

More serious was a rebellion which broke out in Hattusa itself, one which apparently had widespread support from the Hittite nobility. Hattusili's daughter (we do not know her name) was directly implicated:

The sons of Hatti stirred up hostility in Hattusa. Then they took my daughter, and since she had (male) offspring, they opposed me: 'There is no son for your father's throne. A servant will sit upon it. A servant will become king.' Thereupon my daughter made Hattusa and the court disloyal; and the noblemen and my own courtiers opposed me. She incited the whole land to rebellion. . . . The sons of Hatti perished. (*Testament* §13, II 68–77)

When the rebellion was finally crushed, the king's daughter paid the penalty for her treachery. She was stripped of all her possessions and banished from the city.[79]

---

[76] *Testament* §12, II 63–4.
[77] *Testament* §12, II 64–7. See Sommer and Falkenstein's commentary (1938: 112–13).
[78] For the text, KBo III 38 (*CTH* 3.1), see Forrer (1922–6: no. 13).
[79] *Testament* §17, III 14–22.

Whatever the stated reasons for the rebellions in the provinces, Hattusili's sons may have had their own personal reasons for their involvement—reasons which had to do with the royal succession. Certainly this was a key issue in the rebellion in Hattusa. The right of Hattusili's dynasty to retain the kingship was clearly not in dispute. On the contrary, the point at issue was the fear that Hattusili would appoint a successor who was not his lineal descendant. In fact he had named his nephew as his successor. Almost certainly he did so only after the rebellions in which his sons were implicated.[80] The disgrace of the Hittite princes had apparently left him without a son who was worthy of kingship. In any case his choice of successor met with widespread opposition amongst his subjects, which raises two fundamental questions. Who had the right to select the successor to the throne? On what basis was the selection made?

The Selection of a New King

Scholars have long debated whether the Hittite monarchy was in origin an elective one, with the choice of successor resting ultimately with members of the noble class.[81] We have no firm evidence for an elective monarchy. But the conflicts in which contenders for the throne were repeatedly embroiled down to the reign of the king Telipinu (see Ch. 5) clearly indicate that the question of who had the right to choose the king's successor, or succeed to the throne himself, was long in dispute. It has been suggested that the insecurity of the monarchy in early times was due to a conflict of will between the nobles with their ancient rights, and the king, who was striving to establish the principle of hereditary succession. However, Professor Gurney believes it more likely that the Hittite kings were in conflict with an ancient matrilineal system of succession.[82]

A number of scholars have in fact attributed the problems over the royal succession to a fundamental clash between matrilineal and patrilineal principles of succession, the former being a vestige

[80] See Bryce (1981: 14), *contra* Bin-Nun (1975: 25).
[81] For discussion of this matter, see Güterbock (1954a: 19), Goetze (1957c: 87–8; 1964: 26), Riemschneider (1971: 80), Gurney (1973a: 253; 1990: 51), Hoffmann (1984a: 86–91), Beckman (1995: 533–5).
[82] Gurney (1990: 51).

of pre-Indo-European society, the latter a characteristic of Indo-
European newcomers.[83] But the evidence on which this theory
is based has little substance, and the case remains an extremely
speculative one. There is nothing whatever to indicate that
matrilineality was an issue in the disputes over the Hittite royal
succession.[84] Moreover while the parade of usurpers and pre-
tenders to the throne may well have attempted to use their blood-
or marriage-connections with previous kings to assert their own
claims, none of these connections conform with any underlying
principles of matrilineality. Indeed the intrigue and violence which
accompanied so many of the royal successions indicate that considerations of precedent or tradition had very little to do with who
actually succeeded in occupying the throne.

There were no formally stated regulations for determining the
right of succession prior to the reign of Telipinu. Consequently
from the very beginning of Hittite history, no king had any guarantee that his chosen successor would actually sit or remain upon
the throne so long as there were rival claimants or ambitious pre-
tenders ready to challenge his choice.

The king held his position by favour of the gods. But in spite of
his claim to divine endorsement, his authority depended largely on
the goodwill and support of a powerful landowning and military
aristocracy. He gave his nobles land-grants[85] and a share of war
booty. In return they were obliged to swear allegiance to him, and
to pledge him military assistance whenever they were called
upon to do so. But as the *Testament* illustrates, they could prove

[83] See Riemschneider (1971: 93–4), and the references therein to the proposals of
the Russian scholars Dovgjalo and Ivanov. See also Goetze (1957c: 93), Gurney
(1973b: 667–8), Bin-Nun (1975: 11–29). For a contrary view, see Hoffman (1984a:
86–91).

[84] Cf. Beckman (1986: 14–15).

[85] These are attested by a number of land-grant documents, in which estates and
landed property (including gardens, woods, meadows, and sometimes the personnel
belonging to them) were given to Hittite officials of various ranks and responsibilities either as a reward for services rendered or as a means of ensuring loyalty. It now
appears that all such documents which have survived should be assigned to the
'Middle Hittite' period (15th and 14th cents.). However there is no reason to believe
that the practice which they attest was not already in operation as early as the reign
of Hattusili. On the land-grant documents, see e.g. Riemschneider (1958), Balkan
(1973), von Schuler (1980–3), Easton (1981), Otten (1986a: 1991), Beckman (1995:
538). Beckman notes that the land given to individuals 'was not consolidated but
scattered in different localities. Thus the king sought to prevent the nobility's
establishing independent local centres of economic power which might serve to
challenge his own rule.'

dangerously unreliable and were ready to resort to rebellion if they disagreed with actions or decisions taken by the king. Military successes abroad were offset by rebellions and civil discord within the homeland, including the Hittite capital itself. Indeed the king's protracted absences on campaigns outside the homeland may well have intensified unrest and faction disputes within it.

An Abomination to the Sight!

Perhaps it was only on his deathbed that Hattusili realized the full extent of the crisis which could face the kingdom on his death. His sons had rebelled against him and had been cast off; his choice of his nephew as his successor had provoked or contributed to rebellion in his own capital. And now his nephew betrayed him. This was perhaps the cruellest blow. He had nurtured and watched over the young man, and bestowed favours upon him. No doubt this in itself had caused resentment among the more immediate members of the king's family. Then he had elevated him to the status of heir to the throne, adopting him as his son and conferring upon him the royal title Tabarna. But he had been blind to his nephew's faults—until finally came the realization that the young man was unfit to assume the role assigned to him: 'This youth was an abomination to the sight(?); he shed no tears, he was without compassion; he was cold and pitiless' (*Testament* §1, II 5–7).

Hattusili had urged his nephew to try to win over his enemies, to work towards peace and unity within a kingdom which had been torn apart by rebellion and faction strife. To no avail. The influence of his own family, particularly his mother, outweighed that of the king:

He gave no heed to the word of the king; but to the word of his mother, the serpent, he did give heed. His brothers and sisters constantly brought hostile words to him, and he listened to their words. . . . He has shown no consideration for the will of the king. How then can he be well disposed towards Hattusa? His mother is a serpent. And it will come to pass that he will always give heed to the word of his mother, his brothers, and his sisters. And he will come forth to take revenge. To the warriors, the dignitaries and the servants who are appointed as the king's people he will swear: 'Behold. Because of the king they will die.' And it will come to pass that he will destroy them. He will cause much bloodshed and have no qualms. (*Testament* §§2–4, II 9–25)

Inevitably, the nephew's accession would once more plunge the kingdom into civil chaos. Hattusili could not allow that to happen: 'My enemies abroad I have conquered with the sword(?), and I have brought peace and tranquillity to my land. It shall not happen that he will in the end plunge my land into turmoil!' (*Testament* §5, II 27–29).

Hattusili summoned his nephew to his bedside. He repudiated his adoption, and by implication his appointment as successor to the throne. The enemies of his proclaimed heir had finally triumphed. Hattusili's sister, the young Tabarna's mother, reacted with a mixture of fury and fear: 'His mother bellowed like an ox: "They have torn asunder the womb in the living body of me, a mighty ox. They have ruined him and you will kill him!"' (*Testament* §3, II 14–16.)

But there had been enough bloodshed. The nephew was banished from the city, but his personal safety and wellbeing were guaranteed. He was provided with a small estate outside the capital, stocked with cattle and sheep. And he was promised that if his good conduct could be assured, he would be allowed to return to Hattusa. All this in the spirit of reconciliation which Hattusili was to urge upon all his subjects.

A New Heir to the Throne

With his death close at hand, Hattusili could afford no delay in appointing another successor to the throne. It was for the purpose of announcing his new heir that he had hastily convened the assembly in Kussara. Mursili, Hattusili's grandson,[86] was proclaimed king's son and successor: 'Behold. Mursili is (now) my son.[87] You must acknowledge him and place him (on the throne).' (*Testament* §7, II 37–8).[88]

The assembly was not consulted on the choice of the new successor. Hattusili left no doubt that he regarded this as his own prerogative. He simply proclaimed his decision to the gathering. But he

---

[86] He is thus identified in a passage in the 'Aleppo treaty', KBo 1 6 obv. 13.

[87] i.e. Hattusili adopted him as his son in order to pave the way for his succession. There has, however, been some disagreement amongst scholars as to his actual relationship with Hattusili (son or grandson?); see the references cited by Bryce (1981: 9 n. 3).

[88] Cf. KBo III 27 (*CTH* 5) 13–14: 'See! I have given you Mursili. He will take the throne of his father and my son (is) no (longer) my son.'

took considerable pains to explain and justify what he had done. He had to convince the assembly of the wisdom and justice of his decision, and to enlist their support in ensuring that it was accepted. This support was of vital importance, especially since the new heir to the throne was still only a minor. The assembly was called upon to pledge their allegiance to Mursili. They must protect and nurture him, supervise his conduct while he was still a child,[89] and guide him towards wisdom:

When a state of war develops or a rebellion oppresses the land, you, my servants and my lords, must support my son. . . . If you do take him to the field while he is still a youth, you must bring him back safe and sound. . . . No-one must say 'The King will do in secret what he pleases, and I will justify his action whether it is right or not.' Evil conduct must never be countenanced by you. But you, who already know my will and my wisdom, guide my son towards wisdom. (*Testament* §§7–10, II 39–57)

The group charged with this responsibility included the warriors of an organization called the *panku*. This term is basically an adjective meaning 'all, entire'. In the context in which it is used here it apparently referred to some form of general assembly. We shall discuss below the question of its membership and the specific functions assigned to it by a later king. At least in Hattusili's reign, it seems to have functioned primarily as a supervisory and judicial body, with particular responsibility for dealing with offences of a religious nature. The king himself was obliged to refer such offences to this body for judgment. Thus Hattusili instructed his new heir:

You will deal mercifully with my servants and nobles. If you see that one of them commits an offence, either before a god or by uttering any (sacrilegious) word, you must consult the *panku*. Even evil speech must be referred to the *panku*. (*Testament* §22, III 59–62)

Hattusili was in effect trying to shore up the foundations of the monarchy by establishing a close partnership between the king and the representatives of the most powerful elements in the kingdom. The first and most important task of the assembly convened at Kussara was to see the kingdom through the critical period

---

[89] Cf. the instructions to kings in KBo xx 31 = KUB LVII 69 = KUB XII 21, ed. Hoffner (1992). Hoffner notes that the archaic language of this text suggests that it belongs to the Old Hittite period (p. 299).

between the death of the old king and the accession of the new.
From then on it was to act as an advisory and supervisory body to
the king, assisting him in the task of maintaining lasting unity and
stability within the kingdom.[90]

The Tawananna

One of the most powerful and influential positions in the Hittite
kingdom was that of the Tawananna, a position always held by
a female member of the royal family.[91] The first known Tawananna
was Hattusili's aunt. Subsequently the title may have been conferred upon his sister or his daughter. But in later reigns the
Tawananna seems to have gained her position by virtue of the fact
that she was the king's wife.[92] Once she became Tawananna, she
retained the title and the powers and privileges which it entailed for
the rest of her life, even if she outlived her husband.

From its origins, the position of the Tawananna may have had
religious associations. The Tawananna figured prominently in religious rituals and ceremonies as the chief priestess of the kingdom,
presiding over religious ceremonies and performing other religious
functions, sometimes in association with the king, sometimes on
her own.[93] Her religious role may have provided the basis for the
wider influence which she could exercise within the kingdom—
sometimes, it seems, for subversive purposes. But in any case, she
wielded considerable influence as mistress of the royal household,
an influence no doubt increased by the king's frequent absences on
military campaigns, religious pilgrimages, and tours of inspection.
Certain queens involved themselves in the kingdom's internal
political and judicial activities,[94] as well as in external political

---

[90] Further on the role of the *panku* in Hattusili's reign, see Marazzi (1984).

[91] The term has long been considered to be Hattian in origin, reflecting an
institution which the Hittites adopted from a pre-Indo-European Hattian culture.
This view is based largely on its appearance in archaic rituals of Hattian as well as
Palaian and Hittite origin. See the discussions (with references) in Bin-Nun (1975:
32–3), Puhvel (1989: 351–2). But a number of scholars are now inclined to the view
that Tawananna, like Labarna/Tabarna, was of Indo-European origin; see Puhvel
(1989: 360–1), Tischler (1993: 286). A Hattian origin is still maintained by Carruba
(1992: 74), and assumed by Houwink ten Cate (1995: 262).

[92] At least in those cases where the title is attested; see Carruba (1992: 74–5).

[93] Cf. Goetze (1957c: 92–4), Darga (1974: 949–50), Gonnet (1979: 29), Lebrun
(1979: 113).

[94] See Lebrun (1979: 113, with nn. 17 and 18).

affairs.[95] Yet the Tawananna's status and power were clearly anomalous in the male-oriented power structure of the Hittite kingdom, and as we shall see were never fully reconcilable with this structure.

The term 'Tawananna' first appears in the introductory passage of Hattusili's *Annals*, where the king identified himself as 'son of the brother of Tawananna'. This form of identification is unique in the Hittite texts—and raises some interesting but as yet unanswerable questions. Why did Hattusili identify himself in this way, particularly since he made no reference to the king who preceded him? Who was the woman in question? What role did she play in the royal succession? What was her relationship with other members of the Hittite royal family? There is no demonstrable justification for attempting to use this reference to her as evidence of some form of matrilineal succession, or a vestige of a former matriarchal society.[96] Nor can we assume that the identification indicates that Hattusili was his predecessor's nephew, and thus his adopted son.[97] The uniqueness of the identification may well reflect a unique set of circumstances leading to Hattusili's succession.[98] Quite possibly these circumstances were connected with the rebellion in Sanahuitta against Hattusili's grandfather and the rejection (and death?) of his son Labarna. Hattusili may have become king by default. But that is mere speculation. All we can conclude with reasonable certainty is that his relationship with the Tawananna in question—his aunt—provided, in his view at least, a legitimate basis for his own succession.[99]

[95] See Lebrun (1979: 113, with n. 19).

[96] This possibility is referred to by Gurney (1973*b*: 667). Note Haas' comments (1977: 154–5) on Bin-Nun's attempt to reconcile the nomenclatures 'son of Tawananna's brother' and 'sister's son'. Cf. Puhvel's explanation of the nomenclature (1989: 353).

[97] Thus Astour (1989: 12). See also Dinçol *et al.* (1993: 104–5), in the context of their discussion of the cruciform seal; they conclude that 'taking all the evidence together, it is safe to say that Labarna I and Tawananna represented the royal couple of the preceding generation'.

[98] For further discussion of the Tawananna's relationship with other members of the royal family, see Bryce (1981), Puhvel (1989: 353). It may well be, as Puhvel suggests, that the royal succession skipped a generation and that the definition of Hattusili's filiation indicates that his aunt was the link of legitimacy through the intermediate generation which had yielded no king, and that in the absence of an immediate regal father, Hattusili had to define himself via his grandfather and the latter's daughter.

[99] See also Beckman (1986: 21).

Apart from Hattusili's aunt, we learn of another woman who held the title of Tawananna during Hattusili's reign. Her apparent abuse of her position led the king to issue one of the most virulent royal decrees in Hittite literature:

> In future let no one speak the Tawananna's name . . .[100] Let no one speak the names of her sons or her daughters. If any of the sons of Hatti speaks them they shall cut his throat and hang him in his gate. If among my subjects anyone speaks their names he shall no longer be my subject. They shall cut his throat and hang him in his gate. (KBo III 27 (*CTH* 5) 5–12)[101]

Who was this Tawananna? What had she done to provoke such a violent reaction from the king? Was she the king's wife Kaddusi? Of her we know nothing more than her name.[102] More likely the woman in question was the king's daughter,[103] or his sister, mother of the deposed 'young Tabarna'. Both had set themselves against the king. Both had the potential for plunging the kingdom into further turmoil. But the sister was perhaps the more dangerous, for she had sons and daughters who had plotted with her and had sworn to take revenge against their enemies. Significantly, the decree was directed not only against the Tawananna but also against her sons and daughters. The king's sister may well have been appointed Tawananna when Hattusili had declared her son as his successor. Very likely it was she and her family who were seen as the greatest threat to the security of the kingdom in the future. Better to strip them of all status, rank, and official recognition, to isolate them totally from all sources of support, to make even the mention of their names a capital offence!

One other female member of the royal family figures in the *Testament*—Hastayar, who has been identified as the wife of Hattusili,[104] or possibly his mother or favourite concubine,[105] or one

---

[100] I believe this refers to a particular Tawananna, and not to the abolition of the office of Tawananna as assumed by Bin-Nun; see Bryce (1981: 15), de Martino (1991).

[101] See Carruba's discussion of this text (1992: 77–82), along with his transliteration and translation of the full text.

[102] The assumption that Kaddusi was Hattusili's wife is based on her appearance next to the king in the royal offering lists; see Beal (1983: 123).

[103] The candidate favoured by Puhvel (1989: 354).

[104] Thus Sommer and Falkenstein (1938: 188–9).   [105] Melchert (1991: 185).

of his daughters.[106] It was to her that the dying king's final appeal was made:

The Great King, the Labarna, keeps speaking to Hastayar: 'Do not forsake me!' So that the king may not say thus to her, the palace officials say: 'Look, she is interrogating the Old Women.'[107] The king responds thus to them: 'She is even now interrogating the soothsayers? . . . Do not then forsake me, do not! Interrogate *me*! *I* will give you my words as a sign. Wash me well! Protect me on your bosom from the earth.' (*Testament* §23, III 64–73, adapted from trans. by Melchert (1991: 183))[108]

In these closing words of the *Testament*, we may have 'a vivid eyewitness account of the Hittite king wrestling with his fear of death'.[109]

Some Crucial Questions

Hattusili had united under his rule a kingdom which covered much of the eastern half of Anatolia. And he had won great military triumphs in Syria. Yet the ultimate military prize, the conquest of Aleppo, had eluded him. Without Aleppo, his victories in Syria were no more than ephemeral achievements. Further, these victories had been won at great cost to his own kingdom. The kingdom's political organization was as yet unstable. To be sure, Hattusili's family had been firmly established as the ruling dynasty in Hattusa. But the king himself had no effective means of ensuring unqualified loyalty and obedience from his subjects, including the members of his own family. Without doubt his regular absences on military campaigns exacerbated the political problems he faced at home, problems which led to faction strife, rebellion, and great loss of life and property. His own children had participated in the rebellions against him, and had been banished in disgrace. So too his nephew, to whom he had shown special favour, whom he had proclaimed his heir, but who had proved unworthy of kingship. Now, with the repudiation of his nephew close to the end of his reign, the kingdom was facing a crisis of major proportions.

---

[106] Beal (1983: 123).   [107] On these, see Bin-Nun (1975: 120–5).
[108] For an interpretation and explanation of this very difficult passage, see Melchert (1991).
[109] Melchert (1991: 185).

All the king's hopes now rested on his adolescent grandson Mursili, his newly proclaimed heir to the throne. Would his nobles and warriors respond to his wishes and accept, nurture, and give their allegiance to the new boy-king? Would Mursili adhere to his grandfather's instructions, maintain unity and peace within the kingdom, and complete the old king's unfinished business in Syria? The period immediately following Hattusili's death would be critical to the very survival of the kingdom.

CHAPTER 5

The Struggles for the Royal Succession:
From Mursili I to Muwatalli I (*c*.1620–1400)

Mursili Becomes King

'Behold. Mursili is now my son. You must acknowledge him and place him on the throne.' Thus spoke Hattusili to the gathering of warriors and dignitaries summoned shortly before his death. His appeals and warnings were apparently heeded. On his death, and in accordance with his wishes, his grandson and adopted son Mursili succeeded to the throne.

Initially the royal authority may have been exercised by a regent, a prince of the royal blood called Pimpira. But we cannot be sure of this. The texts which attest the existence of Pimpira[1] are too fragmentary to indicate who precisely he was, or what role he played in the history of the Old Kingdom.[2] In any case, whatever the immediate arrangements after Hattusili's death the succession seems to have passed peacefully to the new king—in stark contrast with what happened in the reigns of his successors.

Of the small number of surviving texts which refer to Mursili,[3] the *Proclamation* of Telipinu tells us most about his reign. It speaks of harmony and unity within the Land of Hatti, at least during the first part of the reign, and the re-establishment of firm control over the regions beyond the homeland where Mursili's predecessors had been overlords. The wording is almost identical to that already used twice in describing the reigns of Labarna and Hattusili. Perhaps intentionally. Mursili may well have been obliged to assert his authority by military force in territories which had already succumbed to his predecessors. The political upheavals in the homeland towards the end of his grandfather's reign had very likely

[1] See the references cited by Laroche (1966: 144 no. 1000), Archi (1979: 39). For the appearance of the name in the offering lists (after Mursili), see Otten (1968: 104 and 122).
[2] Cf. Gurney (1973*a*: 249).
[3] *CTH* 10–13. Three of these texts may date to the reign of Mursili's successor Hantili; see Kempinski and Košak (1982: 98).

placed continuing Hittite overlordship in these territories seriously at risk. Like many of his successors, the new king had to show himself equal to the task of maintaining and consolidating the achievements of those who had occupied the throne before him. Once again the *Proclamation* stresses the close link between internal stability and external military achievement.

Of particular importance was the need to re-establish Hittite control in south-eastern Anatolia, in the region of the later kingdom of Kizzuwadna. This was a crucial preliminary to further Hittite campaigns in Syria, since through the region passed the main access routes from Anatolia into the territories belonging to the kingdom of Iamhad. The task accomplished, Mursili made ready to follow his grandfather's footsteps through Syria to the Euphrates.

To Aleppo and Beyond

The record of Mursili's Syrian enterprises is frustratingly brief— three lines in the *Proclamation*, and a couple of passing references elsewhere. But the successes he achieved firmly established his place among the great military leaders of the Hittite kingdom.

His first major objective was the conquest of Aleppo, capital of the kingdom of Iamhad. Although this once-powerful kingdom was probably much weakened by its conflicts with Hattusili's forces, it still remained unsubdued at the end of his reign. With Mursili, the final reckoning was to come: 'He (Mursili) set out against Aleppo to avenge his father's blood. Hattusili had assigned Aleppo to his son (to deal with). And to him the king of Aleppo made atonement' (KBo III 57 (*CTH* 11) 10–15).[4]

Revenge, and the obligation to complete his grandfather's unfinished business, could well have been the chief incentives for a fresh campaign against Aleppo. But there were other, broader considerations. Mursili could not hope to make any significant or lasting impact on the Syrian region while Aleppo remained unconquered. Nor could he safely bypass Aleppo and proceed to the Euphrates, where Babylon lay. The risks involved in campaigning in the Euphrates region while leaving a still dangerous enemy in his rear were too great to be contemplated.

[4] The text in transliteration appears in Forrer (1922–6: no. 20), Klengel (1965*b*: 149).

When the final test of strength came, Aleppo fell before the Hittite onslaught. Its conquest is tersely reported in the *Proclamation*: 'He went to Aleppo, and he destroyed Aleppo and brought captives and possessions of Aleppo to Hattusa' (*Telipinu Procl.* §9, i 28–9).

With the destruction of its royal capital, the kingdom of Iamhad was at an end. Henceforth its very name disappears from our records. For Mursili, the way now lay open to the Euphrates—and Babylon. Again the record is terse. But the achievement it records was momentous: 'Subsequently he marched to Babylon and he destroyed Babylon, and defeated the Hurrian troops, and brought captives and possessions of Babylon to Hattusa' (*Telipinu Procl.* §§9–10, i 29–31).

The journey from Aleppo to Babylon involved a route march some 800 kilometres in extent, east to the Euphrates and then south along the river to Babylon—an enterprise at least comparable with, if not surpassing, the greatest exploits of Hattusili.

Indeed, the conquest of Babylon marked the peak of Hittite military achievement in the history of the Old Kingdom. It also marked the end of an illustrious era in Babylonian history—for with it was associated the demise of the dynasty of Hammurabi. A Babylonian Chronicle makes reference to the Hittite offensive: 'In the time of Samsuditana, the Man of Hatti marched against Akkad' (*Babylonian Chronicle* 20, line 11, ed. Grayson (1975: 156)).[5] Samsuditana was the last member of his dynasty, and the Hittite conquest must have taken place around the time of his death, generally dated to *c.*1595 BC.[6]

The conquests of Aleppo and Babylon became firmly entrenched in Hittite military tradition, the earliest reference to them dating to the reign of Mursili's successor Hantili.[7] In a prayer of the conqueror's later namesake Mursili II, their destruction was specifically mentioned amongst the major military triumphs of the early Hittite period:

---

[5] On this text, see Grayson (1975: 45–9).

[6] Depending on which chronology is followed, the date could be raised or lowered by up to sixty years. Gurney (1974) discusses five possible dates for the raid on Babylon, favouring 1595.

[7] Kempinski and Košak (1982: 110) comment that the account by Telipinu of Mursili's expedition against these cities is a 'striking paraphrase' of a passage from the chronicle of Hantili, KBo iii 57 (*CTH* 11A) ii 10 17–18. For other fragments relating to the expeditions against Aleppo and Babylon, see *CTH* 10–12.

For of old the Land of Hatti with the help of the Sun Goddess of Arinna used to rage against the surrounding lands like a lion. And moreover whatever (cities such as) Aleppo and Babylon it used to destroy, the possessions of every country, the silver, the gold and the gods—they used to place them before the Sun Goddess of Arinna. (KUB xxiv 3 (+) (*CTH* 376A) ii 44–48; trans. Gurney (1940: 31))

Yet beyond the actual military successes and the booty which flowed from them, it is difficult to see any long-term gains from Mursili's conquests. The Babylonian expedition in particular raises some fundamental questions about its purpose and Mursili's expectations of it. He could not have hoped to convert the entire region from Aleppo to Babylon into Hittite subject territory. The vastness of this region, its remoteness from the Hittite homeland, and the very limited capacity of the Hittites to exercise permanent control over conquered territories would have made such a prospect unthinkable. In any case, the outcome of his conquest was the establishment of a Kassite dynasty in Babylon.

Conceivably, the Hittite expedition arose from an alliance between the Hittites and the Kassites, the incentive for the Hittites being the rich spoils of Babylon, and for the Kassites the prospect of creating a new ruling dynasty in the city.[8] A Hittite–Kassite alliance might also have helped offset the ever-present threat of Hurrian political and military expansion, both in Syria and Anatolia. Indeed the passage in the *Proclamation* which records the destruction of Aleppo and Babylon refers also to a Hittite conflict with the Hurrians.[9] Thus the Babylonian expedition may have been undertaken by Mursili not only for booty, but also to gain future Kassite support, if it needed to be called upon, against the Hurrian menace in the region.[10]

There may have been another, more personal, incentive for the enterprise. Hattusili had won renown as a great warrior whose exploits rivalled those of the legendary Akkadian king Sargon. To maintain this tradition, Mursili too had to perform great military deeds, at least equal to those of his illustrious grandfather. Aleppo

[8] Cf. Gurney (1973a: 250).
[9] Gurney (1973a: 251) connects this conflict with the defeat of Aleppo. However Güterbock (1954b: 385) comments that the insertion of the conflict between the destruction of Babylon and the reference to its booty seems to indicate that Hurrians attacked the Hittite king on his way home, so that he had to defend his booty.
[10] Cf. Landsberger (1954: 65).

and Babylon had been centres of the most powerful kingdoms in northern Syria and Mesopotamia since the Mari period (nineteenth and eighteenth centuries). By conquering them, Mursili demonstrated that he was not only a warrior in the mould of his grandfather, but also a worthy successor of the great kings of Syria and Mesopotamia.[11] His military exploits may have had at least as much to do with personal reputation and prestige as with any lasting political or strategic objectives.

The Hand of the Assassin

Mursili returned to Hattusa in triumph. He had re-established control over his kingdom's Anatolian territories, he had destroyed the great kingdoms of Iamhad and Babylon, and he had brought back to his capital the rich spoils of his conquests. Yet not long after his return, a few years at most, he fell victim to an assassination plot.

The assassin was his brother-in-law Hantili, husband of his sister Harapsili.[12] Hantili was aided and abetted by his son-in-law Zidanta:[13] 'And Zidanta conspired with Hantili, and they made a wicked plot. They murdered Mursili. They shed blood' (*Telipinu Procl.* §11, I 32–4). Does this provide another illustration of the dangers faced by a king who absented himself too long from the seat of his power? Perhaps so if Mursili was killed shortly after his return.[14] What his assassination does illustrate is the ultimate failure of Hattusili's attempt to ensure the security of his successor by the provisions he had made in his *Testament*. The succession was determined ultimately by whoever had the ambition, the ability, and the support to take the throne by force. Which is how Hantili became king.[15]

[11] Cf. Otten (1964: 122), Klengel, E. and H. (1975: 67).

[12] On the emendation of the text from 'wife' to 'sister', see Gurney (1973*b*: 659 n. 3), Hoffmann (1984*a*: 19 n. 2).

[13] Zidanta's relationship to Hantili is indicated by copy B of the *Proclamation* where it is stated that he was the husband of Hantili's daughter; see Riemschneider (1971: 88–9).

[14] As assumed by Gurney (1973*a*: 251) and Astour (1989: 14), though as Goetze (1957*a*: 55) points out, there is no evidence that he was murdered almost immediately after his return.

[15] There is no explicit statement in the *Proclamation* that Hantili actually became king. But his wife is referred to as queen (MUNUS.LUGAL) in the Akkadian version of the text, and the phrase referring to his approaching death—'When Hantili had

The Reign of Hantili

The few scattered references we have to Hantili's reign indicate that it was a relatively long and eventful one. For a time the new king seemed intent on maintaining Hittite influence in Syria. In the tradition of Hattusili and Mursili, he conducted military operations in the region, reaching Carchemish on the Euphrates.[16] Very likely his campaign was directed against the Hurrians. How successful this campaign was remains unknown.

On his return journey to Hattusa, he came to the city of Tegarama, probably to be identified with the modern Gürün.[17] Here, we are told, 'The gods sought (revenge for) the bloodshed of Mursili' (*Telipinu Procl.* §13, I 42). What do these words mean? They do not, apparently, refer to a disaster which befell the king himself, for he seems to have continued his journey to Hattusa without ill effects of any kind. What they probably indicate is the point in Hantili's reign where a marked decline in the kingdom's fortunes began to occur. From this time on, his reign was plagued with a series of disasters. Telipinu attributed these to divine vengeance, punishment for the criminal act which had put Hantili on the throne. *Nemesis* is a theme which surfaces repeatedly in the *Proclamation* in its account of the kings who had occupied the throne by force. It was an all-embracing vengeance, inflicted not only on the perpetrator of a crime, but on the whole land.

In the case of Hantili, the Hurrians were the first instrument of divine wrath. They apparently roamed through and plundered the Land of Hatti at will. But they were driven back across the frontiers before they captured Hattusa itself. On a later occasion Hattusa was not so fortunate.

We then come to a curious episode in a much mutilated section of the text which refers to Hantili's queen Harapsili and his two sons being taken to the city of Sugziya (perhaps to the east of Hatti in the Euphrates region).[18] According to one interpretation of the

---

grown old and was about to become a god'—recalls the standard expression which elsewhere is reserved exclusively for the death of a king.

[16] *Telipinu Procl.* §12, I 37.

[17] See the references cited by del Monte and Tischler (1978: 384).

[18] *Telipinu Procl.* §§16–17 (Akkadian version §15). For the possible location of Sugziya, see in addition to the references cited by del Monte and Tischler (1978: 363), Kempinski and Košak (1982: 101); the latter (following Bossert) place it north of Ursu which lay to the north of Carchemish.

surviving text fragments, they were taken to Sugziya by Hantili himself, and left there while presumably he continued his campaigns against the Hurrians in the region.[19] If this interpretation is correct, then he must have felt that they were safer there in his absence than at Hattusa. But a different reading of the fragments suggests that they had been deposited in this remote location by the Hurrians, who had captured them on their retreat from the homeland.[20] In any case, Harapsili fell ill in Sugziya and died there. Foul play may well have been involved, for apparently her sons shared her fate. Those held responsible were eventually arrested and brought to justice.[21]

Unlike his wife and his sons, Hantili survived the disasters of his reign and lived, apparently, to a ripe old age. He clearly intended the royal succession to continue in his own family line, and must have felt some confidence that it would—for he had a surviving son Piseni,[22] who already had offspring of his own. But his plans for the succession were dashed, and he lived long enough to see his son and his grandsons murdered by the man who had helped him seize the throne from Mursili many years before—his son-in-law Zidanta.[23]

'Now Bloodshed has Become Common'

As Hantili's accomplice in the murder of Mursili, Zidanta may long have nurtured the hope that he would one day be king. But Hantili had planned otherwise, and it was only after eliminating the legitimate heir and his sons that Zidanta was able to achieve his ambition. We have no surviving documents which can with certainty be

[19] According to the reconstruction and reordering of the relevant texts proposed by Helck (1984: 106–7).

[20] Thus Goetze (1957a: 56), following a reconstruction of the texts in question proposed by Forrer, and most recently Soysal (1990).

[21] According to the interpretation of the text fragments by Soysal (1990), the chief culprit was the queen of Sugziya, who had refused to release Harapsili and her sons from captivity (on the assumption that the text refers to two queens—a local queen as well as Harapsili); on the orders of a high-ranking Hittite functionary, she was finally arrested and executed, along with her children, in retaliation for the death of Harapsili and her children.

[22] Goetze (1957a: 56 n. 40) proposed the reading *Kasseni* in place of *Piseni*. But see Carruba (1993b).

[23] *Telipinu Procl.* §18.

attributed to Zidanta's reign.[24] It may have been very short. Once again the gods demanded blood for his crime, this time using the king's son Ammuna as the agent of their wrath. Ammuna assassinated his father and seized his throne.[25]

Under Ammuna, the decline in the fortunes of Hatti continued. A drought which caused a serious depletion of the country's crops and livestock may have contributed to this.[26] In Telipinu's view, this was yet another act of divine vengeance. The kingdom's difficulties were exploited by a range of countries which now became openly hostile—Galmiya, Adaniya, Arzawiya, Sallapa, Parduwata, Ahula. Some of these are otherwise unknown, but all of them probably lay to the south or south-west of the homeland. Adaniya was located in the region which was to become the independent state of Kizzuwadna. Its loss very likely deprived the Hittites of their access to Syria via the Taurus mountain passes.[27] Arzawiya can be identified with the country of Arzawa which lay in the south-west, and had already been in conflict with the Hittites in Hattusili's reign. Sallapa probably lay south of the lower course of the Marrassantiya river, either in the vicinity of Kayseri or further west towards the Salt Lake. Parduwata must have been situated in the same region.[28]

The *Proclamation* indicates numerous campaigns undertaken by Ammuna in his attempts to re-establish Hittite authority in the hostile countries. We may have a further reference to these campaigns in a very fragmentary text sometimes referred to as the 'Ammuna Chronicle'[29] which mentions a number of towns, including Tipiya to the north (in the heart of later Kaskan-controlled territory), Hapisna, Parduwata, and Hahha. The last of these, probably to be located on the east bank of the Euphrates, had already figured in the campaigns of Hattusili.

Ammuna seems to have applied himself vigorously to the task of holding his kingdom together, to judge from the large expanse of territory covered by his campaigns, from Arzawa in the south-west

---

[24] All the documents associated with a king Zidanta should almost certainly be attributed to the second king of this name, one of the successors of Telipinu. Further to this, see Hoffner (1980: 309).

[25] *Telipinu Procl.* §19.

[26] *Telipinu Procl.* §20.

[27] Cf. Freu (1992: 47).

[28] See Bryce (1983: 147).

[29] Fragments of three copies are preserved (*CTH* 18). Klinger (1995: 90) expresses doubts about the attribution to Ammuna.

to the Euphrates in the east. He may in fact have enjoyed some successes along the way, contrary to the impression given by Telipinu who presented his reign as a series of unmitigated disasters.[30] But ultimately he failed in his attempts to reassert his authority over the rebellious subject states.[31] By the end of his reign, the kingdom outside the homeland was close to disintegration. The loss of the subject territories in the south, the total severing of links with Syria (especially with the loss of Adaniya and Hahha) and the inroads of the Hurrians from the south-east and (perhaps already) the Kaskans from the north must not only have deprived the Hittites of most if not all of their subject territories outside the homeland, but also placed the homeland itself in serious jeopardy.

Ammuna's death, apparently from natural causes, gave rise to a fresh contest for the succession—and further bloodshed:

When Ammuna also became god Zuru, the Chief of the Bodyguards, sent secretly in those days a member of his family, his son Tahurwaili, the Man of the Golden Spear. And he killed the family of Titti along with his sons. He also sent Taruhsu, the courier, and he killed Hantili, along with his sons. Now Huzziya became king.   (*Telipinu Procl.* §§21–2, II 4–9)

Titti and Hantili were probably sons of Ammuna, and their assassins the agents of Huzziya, the man who now seized the throne. The new king was related by marriage to Ammuna's family.[32] His eldest sister Istapariya was the wife of another of Ammuna's sons, Telipinu.[33] But the marriage link with Ammuna's family was not enough to keep him on the throne as long as any of Ammuna's sons remained alive. While Telipinu lived, Huzziya's position would never be secure. Brother-in-law or not, Telipinu had to be eliminated.

[30] Cf. Hoffner (1980: 305–6).
[31] *Telipinu Procl.* §21, II 1–4.
[32] *Contra* a longstanding assumption that Huzziya was also a son of Ammuna, and the younger brother of Titti and Hantili (who had to be eliminated if Huzziya was to succeed to the throne); see Goetze (1957a: 56), Easton (1981: 26), Astour (1989: 24).
[33] In referring to his accession in the *Proclamation*, Telipinu states that he sat upon the throne of his father (§24, II 16). Since we know that he was the brother-in-law of his immediate predecessor Huzziya, then he must be referring to the previous king Ammuna. In spite of Goetze's suggestion (1957a: 56) that Ammuna was really his father-in-law, I believe, with Gurney (1973b: 663) that Telipinu's statement was literally true—that he was in fact one of the sons of Ammuna (but note Hoffner's (1975: 53) comments), apparently the only one who escaped the conspiracy which led to Huzziya's accession.

Fortunately for Telipinu, the plot against his life was discovered in time for him to take effective action against it. The usurper had probably not been on the throne for long before his intended victim staged a counter-coup, seizing the throne for himself and driving Huzziya and his five brothers into exile. That was punishment enough. Telipinu gave instructions that no further harm was to befall them. There had been enough bloodshed. He would put an end to the bloody reprisals which had become endemic among his predecessors.

That at least was his intention.

Telipinu's Attempts to Regain the Lost Subject Territories

While the new king adopted a policy of clemency towards his opponents at home, exemplary action was required against enemies abroad. The territories lost by his predecessors had to be recovered. Immediately after his accession, he applied himself to the task of doing so.

First the south-east, where he undertook an expedition against Hassuwa, Zizzilippa, and Lawazantiya.[34] These towns probably lay in the Euphrates region, north of Carchemish[35] and close to the northern frontier of the recently created country of Kizzuwadna (see below). In this and the following campaigns Telipinu had some significant successes, and a number of the lost territories were regained. Indirectly we learn of some of these from a list of Hittite storage depots in various towns and regions which had been restored to Hittite control, including Samuha, Marista, Hurma, Sugziya, Purushanda, and the river Hulaya.[36]

By the end of Telipinu's reign the Marrassantiya basin was again firmly under Hittite control, the Hittites once more commanded the region extending south of the Marrassantiya through the Lower Land and perhaps as far as the Mediterranean sea, and in the south-east, Hittite authority once more reached the Euphrates.

There was, however, one former subject territory in south-east Anatolia which remained independent of Hittite control.

---

[34] *Telipinu Procl.* §§24–5.

[35] See Bryce (1983: 80), with the references cited therein. On Zizzilippa, see Goetze (1940: 72). Lawazantiya had risen in rebellion under a man called Lahha, as indicated by a further fragmentary text relating to Telipinu's reign, KBo XII 8//9 (*CTH* 20), ed. Carruba (1974: 77–8), Hoffmann (1984*a*: 63–7).

[36] *Telipinu Procl.* §§35–44.

The Kingdom of Kizzuwadna

The name Kizzuwadna now surfaces for the first time in our records. But at least part of the territory which came to be called by this name was probably a separate political entity before then, with the name Adaniya.[37] Adaniya may previously have been incorporated into the Hittite kingdom, during Hattusili's reign or even earlier.[38] If so it had clearly broken its ties with Hatti by the reign of Ammuna, when it was listed as one of the hostile countries against which Ammuna campaigned without success. It was probably then that the independent kingdom of Kizzuwadna was established.[39]

The leader of the country's rebellion against the Hittites may have been a man called Pariyawatri. From a seal impression discovered at Tarsus we learn that he was the father of Isputahsu, contemporary of Telipinu and the first actually attested king of Kizzuwadna. The seal bears the inscription 'Isputahsu, Great King, Son of Pariyawatri'.[40] Isputahsu may have inherited his throne from his father, though as yet we have no evidence that Pariyawatri himself had ever been king.

Telipinu accepted the independent status of the newly established kingdom, and entered into negotiations with Isputahsu. In so doing, he took a major new initiative—an initiative which established one of the most important foundations of future Hittite policy. He drew up with Isputahsu a treaty of alliance.[41]

This first known Hittite treaty is too fragmentary for us to determine what precisely its intentions were. But one of its main purposes may have been to formalize agreement on territorial limits in the border region between Kizzuwadna and Hittite-controlled territory. The boundaries of Kizzuwadna seem to have fluctuated throughout the country's history, depending on how successful its kings were in asserting their claims over territories in the border region. Telipinu's expedition against Hassuwa, Lawazantiya, and

---

[37] See Beal (1986: 424, with n. 2).

[38] This is indicated particularly by a land-grant document, *LS* 28, discovered at Tarsus in the plain of Adana; see Riemschneider (1958: 344, 375) (for the text), Gurney (1973b: 661), Easton (1981: 16, 24), Beal (1986: 424–5).

[39] Cf. Gurney (1973b: 661), Beal (1986: 426), although Wilhelm (1989: 23) suggests that it may have first achieved independence during Hantili's reign.

[40] The *bulla* bearing the seal impression was first reported by Goldman (1935: 535–6). See also Goetze (1936; 1940: 73). On the possibility that the seal bears the designation 'King of Tarhuntassa', see Houwink ten Cate (1992a: 250).

[41] *CTH* 21. Fragmentary versions in both Hittite and Akkadian survive.

Zizzilippa had certainly brought him into this region. Indeed the last two of these towns are later attested as belonging to Kizzuwadna. The treaty may represent an attempt by Telipinu to secure his flank while his campaign was underway.[42] Alternatively one of its purposes may have been to confirm Hittite possession of these towns in the wake of the king's conquests. No doubt Isputahsu was required to acknowledge the Hittite claim to them, probably in return for an assurance from Telipinu that he would recognize the independent status recently won by Kizzuwadna, within the territorial limits as now defined.

But why, after his successful campaign in the border region, did Telipinu stop short of an attempted conquest of the whole of Kizzuwadna? Was he forced to come to terms with its king because he lacked the ability to reassert control over it?[43] Or were there other reasons?

The threat of more extensive Hittite military action in the region carried with it the danger of forcing Kizzuwadna into a Hurrian alliance. It has in fact been suggested that Kizzuwadna was created under Hurrian influence. The grounds for this suggestion are tenuous,[44] but in any case Hittite aggression against Kizzuwadna might well have been seen as a prelude to fresh Hittite campaigns in Syria, in regions where the Hurrian kingdom Mitanni was taking a renewed interest (see below). The last thing Telipinu could have wanted at this stage was to provoke further conflict with the Hurrians.

Even without Hurrian intervention, the conquest and subsequent control of Kizzuwadna would have dangerously stretched the kingdom's resources—at a time when priority had to be given to ensuring the security of the Hittite homeland, along with the subject territories already regained, against further threats from external forces. In the south-east, a diplomatic alliance with Kizzuwadna might achieve this objective more effectively than military force, and at far less cost.

There was another consideration. An aggressive expansionist policy, or the renewal of conflict with a major foreign power would

---

[42] Suggested by Gurney (1973*a*: 665).

[43] Thus Gurney (1979*a*: 155).

[44] It depends essentially on the claim once made by Landsberger that the name of Isputahsu's father was Indo-Aryan, implying a connection with the ruling clans associated with the expansion of Hurrian power. This claim is disputed by Gurney (1973*a*: 664–5, with 665 n. 1).

almost certainly have meant a commitment to protracted military campaigns far from the homeland—at a time when much had still to be done to restore and maintain stability within it. The reigns of Telipinu's predecessors, particularly Hattusili and Mursili, had amply demonstrated the risks a king faced by spending too long away from the seat of his power.

On this point Telipinu's policy seems clear. On the one hand he did what he could to make the territories he had recovered as secure as possible against future enemy attack. On the other hand, he applied himself to the task of ensuring that the homeland would never again fall prey to the internal political upheavals which had in the past, he believed, brought it along with the rest of the kingdom to the verge of total destruction.

The Bloodshed Continues

The task was no easy one. The bloodshed which had been a marked feature of the reigns of his predecessors seems to have continued during at least the first part of his own reign. In spite of his instructions, the deposed king Huzziya and his five brothers were secretly murdered.[45] The murderer, a man called Tanuwa, was subsequently brought to justice, along with Tahurwaili and Taruhsu, the assassins who had helped pave the way for Huzziya's accession. All three were convicted and sentenced to death by the *panku*. But Telipinu commuted the sentence to one of banishment. This act of clemency may have been a sincere attempt on his part to demonstrate a clear break with the past—supplanting the law of blood vengeance and survival of the fittest with a process of justice that was merciful and restrained, and designed to set an example for his own and future generations.

But if this was deliberate policy on his part, then in the short term it had little apparent effect—and perhaps in at least one case an unfortunate consequence. Tahurwaili, one of the assassins whose life was spared by the king, may have been the man who re-emerged on the political scene after Telipinu's death and seized the throne from the legitimate heir (see below).

Moreover, Telipinu's efforts to spare the lives of others failed to save members of his own family. From the *Proclamation*, we learn

---

[45] *Telipinu Procl.* §26, II 26. The text is fragmentary at this point, but the import of the broken passage seems clear.

of the deaths of his wife Istapariya, and later his son Ammuna.[46] The context in which their deaths are reported leaves little doubt that they too were the victims of assassination. Their assassins are unknown to us. But their deaths may have been the catalyst for the action which Telipinu now took to regularize the system of royal succession, and to protect henceforth all members of the royal family. His earnest hope was that this would end once and for all the family feuds, the dynastic disputes, and the bloodshed that had characterized the reign of every Hittite king from the time of Hattusili's grandfather.

Rules for the Succession

The *Proclamation* was originally addressed to a *tuliya*, apparently a general word for a Hittite assembly. In this case the assembly consisted of the members of the *panku*, specially convened by Telipinu to hear the arrangements he had made for the succession, and to assume responsibility for the protection and control of members of the royal family. It is clear that in making these arrangements the king was acting unilaterally. He had convened the assembly merely to hear his decisions, in much the same way as Hattusili had summoned the assembly at Kussara to inform it of his grandson's appointment as heir to the throne.

The inheritance of royal power was now firmly established on the basis of direct patrilineal succession. Only in the event that a king left no male heirs of suitable status could the son of a daughter succeed to the throne:

Let a prince, a son of the first rank, become king. If there is no prince of the first rank, let him who is a son of the second rank become king. But if there is no prince, no heir, let them take a son-in-law (i.e. a husband) for her who is a daughter of the first rank, and let him become king.   (*Telipinu Procl.* §28, II 36–9)

The establishment of the succession in one family line was not in itself a radically new development. Even if a system of elective kingship had once applied, it had effectively been discarded from at least as early as the reign of Hattusili. But it had not been replaced by any formal means of determining which male member of the king's family would succeed to the throne. The king's successor was

---

[46] *Telipinu Procl.* §27.

decided by the king himself, who might change his mind. More frequently, the throne was occupied by a usurper. Telipinu's chief intention was to remove any possibility of rival claims or random selection in the succession. In so doing he severely curtailed any free choice a future king could exercise in the appointment of his successor. The king still had some freedom, since he was not bound to appoint the eldest of the eligible candidates. Moreover, the new regulations were designed to provide some guarantee of his personal safety and that of his heir, as well as the safety of other members of the royal family. In theory at least they eliminated the possibility of any future contest or dispute amongst self-promoting candidates for the succession.

In the first instance, the succession was to pass to a son of the first rank—that is, a son of the king's chief wife who was in most cases the Tawananna. If she had no sons, then the succession would pass to a son of the second rank—presumably a son of the so-called *esertu* wife, a woman inferior in status to the chief wife though still of free birth.[47] Any male offspring of the king by women of lesser status were by implication ruled ineligible for the succession. In the event of neither the chief nor the secondary wife of the king having sons—or at least one or more sons who survived their father's death—the succession would pass to a son-in-law, husband of the daughter of the king's chief wife. This in effect formalized the eligibility of a son-in-law of the king to succeed to the throne.

Following his statement of the succession regulations, Telipinu made clear the purpose of the lengthy historical preamble to the Proclamation, and to whom it was addressed:

Henceforth whoever becomes king and plans injury for a brother or sister, you are his *panku*, and must speak frankly to him: 'Read this deed of bloodshed in the tablet. Bloodshed was once common in Hattusa, and the Gods exacted (retribution) from the royal family.'   (*Telipinu Procl.* §30, II 46–9)

The record of past events must serve as a constant reminder of the disastrous consequences of ignoring or defying these provisions.

But a mere reminder would not be sufficient to ensure adherence to the regulations. They had to be enforced. Formal disciplinary controls were instituted which would if necessary extend even to members of the royal family. Indeed the king himself may have

[47] See Goetze (1957c: 94).

been liable to the death penalty if he shed the blood of members of his own family. Admittedly we cannot be altogether sure of this, since it depends on the interpretation of a much disputed passage in the *Proclamation*.[48] But it is clear that henceforth no member of the royal family should escape legal retribution for crimes he or she committed—particularly crimes which violated or threatened to undermine the regulations for the succession.

The responsibility for enforcement was assigned to the assembly of the *panku*. We should now give further consideration to the nature and composition of this body, and the powers which it exercised.

The Panku in Telipinu's Reign

The *panku* had already exercised important judicial functions during the reign of Hattusili. But these may have fallen largely into abeyance during the reigns of his successors. There is no further reference to a *panku* prior to Telipinu's reign, and certainly no indication that such a body was able to exercise any form of control in the recurring conflicts for the succession. Under Telipinu the *panku* re-emerged as an important institution—one to which precise responsibilities were given.

Its actual composition has been the subject of much discussion.[49] The general view is that it was some form of aristocratic body. But this has been challenged on the grounds that it was 'hardly a social class, let alone a high one, but rather simply "totality of those present on a given occasion"'.[50] A passage in the *Proclamation* appears to support this:

And now from this day on in Hattusa, you, the Palace Servants, the Bodyguard, the Men of the Golden Spear, the Cup-Bearers, the Table-Men, the Cooks, the Heralds, the Stableboys, the Captains of the Thousand, bear this fact in mind. Let Tanuwa, Tahurwaili, and Taruhsu be a sign for you. If anyone does evil hereafter, ... whether low-placed or high-placed, have him brought before you as *panku*, and devour him with your teeth! (*Telipinu Procl.* §33, II 66–73.)

[48] *Telipinu Procl.* §31, II 50–2. See most recently Hoffman (1984a: 123–44, esp. 123–5), Bryce (1986a: 753–4).
[49] See Hoffman (1984a: 76–7) for a survey of these discussions. Add Marazzi (1984) who discusses the range of meanings and nuances which the term had in different contexts, particularly in Hattusili's *Testament* and Telipinu's *Proclamation*.
[50] Beckman (1982: 437).

The persons making up the *panku* for the purpose defined here apparently consisted of the personnel of the royal court, including officials highly placed in the palace administration[51] as well as less exalted members of the palace staff. But the *panku* may not have been a fixed or permanent body with regular responsibilities. More likely, it was an *ad hoc* assembly convened only in special circumstances. Its composition may have varied, depending on the situations which it was convened to deal with. In this case Telipinu had defined a specific group of officials and functionaries who were to form a *panku* in order to deal with a specific category of criminal offence.[52] The group was given little discretion in the exercise of its judicial functions. Clearly defined procedures had to be followed. For those found guilty of offences which fell within its jurisdiction, the death penalty was prescribed. But justice had to be seen to be done: 'They must not kill him in secret, in the manner of Zuruwa, Tahurwaili, and Taruhsu' (*Telipinu Procl.* §31, II 52–3).

The offender alone should suffer for his crime. No harm was to be inflicted on any other member of his family. His property was neither to be destroyed nor confiscated: 'And now, when any prince commits an offence, he must atone even with his head. But do no harm to his house or his son. It is not right to give away the persons or the property of the princes' (*Telipinu Procl.* §32, II 59–61).

The point is emphasized several times in the *Proclamation*. No member of a prince's family was to be held accountable for crimes for which the prince alone was responsible. A self-evident principle of justice, perhaps. Yet we know that on other occasions an offender's children could expect to share their father's fate, as a later king had cause to remind the son of a disgraced vassal:

Do you not know, Kupanta-Kurunta, that if in Hattusa anyone commits the offence of insurrection, and that even if the son whose father is guilty is not also guilty, his father's house and land are taken from him and either given to someone else or seized for the palace? (Mursili II: Kupanta-Kurunta Treaty (*CTH* 68), Friedrich (1926: 114–15 §7))

In the interests of the stability of the royal court, if not the whole kingdom, Telipinu stipulated that a royal offender's family and

---

[51] Cf. Beckman (1982: 442).
[52] As Beckman (1982: 440) has pointed out, the *panku* had clearly never functioned as the normal judicial organ of the Hittite state.

property had to be protected against such action. Failure to provide this protection might well have had devastating consequences for an entire branch of the royal family. It might also have encouraged the fabrication of charges against a prince by members of a rival branch, if a successful prosecution led to the confiscation and redistribution of his property and the disgrace of his children. Telipinu was determined to let nothing jeopardize his attempts to eliminate family feuds and faction strife within the royal court. Given the history of conflict amongst rival groups at the most exalted levels of Hittite society, all possible incentives for the renewal of such conflict had to be removed.

It is clear that the *Proclamation* was not concerned merely with the formalization of the rules of succession. Of equal importance were the regulations which bore directly on the power and authority of the king and the *panku*, and the safeguards which were designed to ensure the stability of the monarchy. The powers of future kings would be considerably circumscribed by the provisions of the *Proclamation*. It gave them little freedom in their choice of successor, it imposed a number of limitations on their judicial powers, and it rendered them liable to disciplinary authority by the *panku* for acts of violence committed against members of their own family. But while the king's authority was to be limited in these ways, his position and personal safety were, *in theory*, made more secure by the powers assigned to the *panku*, which was charged primarily with the responsibility of ensuring his and his family's safety, and of safeguarding the rights of succession.

Telipinu's Successors

Telipinu's reign offered prospects of a new era of order and harmony within the homeland, and a renewal of Hittite influence and authority beyond it. Yet the provisions made in the *Proclamation* had little apparent effect in the decades following his death—a period lasting perhaps for a century, sometimes arbitrarily called the Middle Kingdom. This period witnessed a succession of poorly attested rulers, some of whom found their way to the throne by the path of intrigue and usurpation—and were removed from it in the same way.

We know nothing about the end of Telipinu's reign, though he died apparently without leaving male issue. His only known son

Ammuna had predeceased him. But he was survived by a daughter Harapseki, and a man called Alluwamna, who was probably Harapseki's husband and therefore Telipinu's son-in-law.[53] In the absence of a prince of the royal blood, and in accordance with the recently formulated principles of succession, Alluwamna was the rightful heir to the throne.

Yet as events were soon to prove, the careful provisions Telipinu made for the succession gave no adequate safeguard for the security of the royal line. Alluwamna probably did succeed his father-in-law. But beyond several fragmentary texts which refer to him[54] and his appearance in the royal offering lists and land-grant documents,[55] nothing more is known of this king. Indeed he may not have been on the throne very long before it was seized from him by an interloper called Tahurwaili.[56] This name does not appear amongst those of other kings in the royal offering lists—very likely a deliberate omission from these lists.[57] But Tahurwaili's success in establishing himself as king is made clear by a tablet fragment discovered in 1963[58] and a seal impression discovered in 1969.[59] Both confirm Tahurwaili's kingly status; the latter bears the inscription: 'Seal of the Tabarna Tarhurwaili, Great King. Whoever alters his word shall die.'

Who was this Tahurwaili? What claim, if any, could he make to the throne? He *may* have been the man who has already figured in

---

[53] We conclude this from a fragmentary reference to Harapseki as DUMU.MUNUS.LUGAL (daughter of the king), KUB XXVI 77 I 2, and another to Alluwamna as DUMU.LUGAL (son of the king), KUB XI 3. See Goetze (1957a: 57), Gurney (1973b: 669). The fragments naming Alluwamna (KUB XI 3, KUB XXVI 77, KUB XXXI 74) are grouped under *CTH* 23.

[54] *CTH* 23.

[55] Most recently, those excavated at Boğazköy in 1982–4 and published by Otten (1987).

[56] There is no textual evidence to indicate the point at which Tahurwaili intruded into the royal line. However, an examination of stylistic features of the royal seals of Telipinu's successors has led Easton (1981: 29) to conclude that Alluwamna and Tahurwaili ruled successively, with the latter probably succeeding the former. Earlier Carruba (1974) and Bin-Nun (1974) had proposed the reverse order. Most recently Freu (1995: 133–4) has argued that Tahurwaili was the later king, also on the basis of stylistic considerations, though Freu makes him the successor of Alluwamna's son(?) Hantili II.

[57] Cf. Astour (1989: 27).

[58] KBo XXVIII 108 + 109 7'. See Otten (1971: 65–6), del Monte (1981: 209–13).

[59] Bo 69/200; see Boehmer and Güterbock (1987: 81, no. 252). The tablet fragment and seal impression both apparently derive from a treaty. Cf. Easton (1981: 24).

the *Proclamation* as the assassin sent to murder the family of Titti prior to the accession of Huzziya.[60] We recall that the sentence of death passed on him by the *panku* had been commuted by Telipinu to one of banishment. If this was in fact the Tahurwaili who succeeded in becoming Great King, then Telipinu's act of clemency was clearly ill-advised. For whatever Tahurwaili's immediate motives in assassinating members of the royal family, his ultimate goal may have been to secure the throne, sooner or later, for himself. While he lived he remained a threat to Telipinu's family line and the provisions made for the royal succession.[61]

It looks as if the threat became reality.[62] Tahurwaili's seizure of power, in defiance of the recent succession provisions, opened up the prospect of renewed struggles for the throne. The political stability which Telipinu had sought to leave as his principal legacy to the Hittite kingdom apparently crumbled within a generation of his death.

But beyond the homeland, Telipinu's policies seem to have had a more lasting effect, at least as far as relations with Kizzuwadna were concerned. Here Tahurwaili renewed the alliance which Telipinu had established with Isputahsu by drawing up a parity treaty with Isputahsu's successor Eheya.[63] This in fact is the only piece of information that has so far come to light about Tahurwaili's reign.

We also have very meagre information about the next three kings who appear in the offering lists—Hantili, Zidanta (Zidanza), and Huzziya. These were the namesakes of kings who reigned before Telipinu, a fact which has led some scholars to suggest that

[60] As argued by Carruba (1974) and Bin-Nun (1974: 119–20).

[61] In view of the Hittites' 'strong sense of dynasty', it is possible that Tahurwaili himself had some form of blood or marriage link with Telipinu's family; cf. Beal (1992b: 329 n. 1257). Astour (1989: 25) points out that there is no case (we should say no *demonstrable* case) in Hittite history in which kingship was held by a man who was not related to the royal house either by birth or by marriage. In Tahurwaili's case, however, any such relationship may have been quite tenuous.

[62] After removing Alluwamna from power, Tahurwaili may have sent him into exile. Evidence of this is perhaps to be found in a text which mentions the banishment of Alluwamna and his wife Harapseki, and may also refer to Tahurwaili (KUB xxvi 77 I 18). But the attribution of the text is not certain (see Bin-Nun (1974: 116–18) and Astour (1989: 27) who attribute it to Telipinu, and Easton (1981: 27)). In any case, the assumed reference to Tahurwaili involves substantial restoration of his name: [Tahurw]aili (suggested by Carruba (1974: 81) and Bin-Nun (1974: 117)).

[63] KBo xxviii 108 + 109; see Otten (1971, 66–7).

the names were mistakenly duplicated in the lists.[64] But the existence of later kings with these names is now beyond doubt.[65]

During the reign of Hantili, son(?) of Alluwamna,[66] the Kaska
people from the Pontic zone made their first recorded appearance
in Hittite history. Near the northern frontiers of the homeland they
captured the holy city of Nerik, which probably lay in the vicinity of
the Pontic region.[67] It was to be 200 years before the Hittites finally
regained control of it.[68] Also in the north, the city of Tiliura was
apparently abandoned to the northerners.[69] In response to the pressures now being exerted on the homeland from the hostile forces
outside it, Hantili claimed to have undertaken the fortification of
Hattusa,[70] along with other cities in the area. It was an admission
that the very core of the kingdom was vulnerable to enemy attack.

On the diplomatic front, Hantili may have continued the policy
of friendship with Kizzuwadna. This possibility arises from a
fragmentary Akkadian version of a treaty drawn up between a
Hittite king whose name is lost and a Kizzuwadnan king called
Paddatissu.[71] The latter probably succeeded Eheya (Tahurwaili's
treaty-partner) on the throne of Kizzuwadna.[72] In that event, his

[64] See the references cited by Gurney (1973*b*: 669 n. 7). Astour (1989: 31) believes
that all three actually existed but as non-reigning members of the royal house.
[65] As Otten (1987) has demonstrated, the new land-grant documents confirm the
reliability of the offering lists and the existence of Hantili II, Zidanta II, and Huzziya
II. See also Beal (1986: 428). For Hantili II, see Otten (1991: 345–6), Rüster (1993),
Freu (1995: 134).
[66] On the basis of the restoration of the name Han[tili], Alluwamna's son, in the
land-grant document KBo XXXII 136; see Freu (1995: 134). It does not follow, as Freu
assumes, that Hantili must have been his father's immediate successor. Tahurwaili
could well have come in between before the throne was restored to the legitimate
family line; cf. Astour (1989: 34).
[67] See Houwink ten Cate (1979*a*: esp. 160–1), and the review of possible locations
by Gurney (1992: 214–15).
[68] The loss of Nerik to the Kaskans, referred to both by Hattusili III in his so-
called *Apology* (*CTH* 81) §10b, III 46'–49', and subsequently by his son Tudhaliya,
KUB xxv 21 (*CTH* 524.1) 2–5, was once dated to the reign of Hantili I. However von
Schuler (1965: 24–7) suggested that the loss did not occur until after Telipinu's reign.
And in view of the absence of any other reference to the Kaskans up to and
including Telipinu's reign, their capture of Nerik probably occurred in the reign of
Hantili II. Cf. Klinger (1995: 84), Freu (1995: 135). The recovery of Nerik in
Hattusili III's reign is recorded in the passage from the *Apology* referred to above.
[69] Information provided by Hattusili III's treaty with the people of Tiliura, KUB
xxi 29 (+) (*CTH* 89), I 11–12.
[70] See Forrer (1922–6: no. 22).
[71] KUB xxxiv 1 + KBo xxviii 105 (*CTH* 26), ed. Meyer (1953: 112–21).
[72] See Beal (1986: 431).

treaty-partner was one of Tahurwaili's immediate successors. Hantili is a possible candidate. The document indicates what we know from later treaties was a potential source of conflict between the two kingdoms—movements of semi-nomadic communities in the border region across territorial boundaries:

If a community of the Great King, with its women, its belongings, its cattle, its sheep and goats, moves and enters into Kizzuwadna, Paddatissu shall seize and give them back to the Great King. And if a community of Paddatissu, with its women, its belongings, its cattle, its sheep and goats moves and enters into Hatti, the Great King shall seize and give them back to Paddatissu.   (KUB xxxiv i (*CTH* 26) 17–20, trans. Liverani (1990: 106–7))

Little can be gleaned from the surviving portion of the treaty about its overall nature and scope. But one of its concerns seems to have been to define clearly, or redefine, the borders between Hatti and Kizzuwadna, as in Telipinu's treaty with Isputahsu, and to control population and stock movements within the border region.

Hantili's successor Zidanta was yet another king who maintained close diplomatic relations with Kizzuwadna. We have some fragments of the treaty which he drew up with Pilliya (Pelliya), who then occupied the Kizzuwadnan throne.[73] The treaty indicates that there had been conflict between Hatti and Kizzuwadna, which involved the capture or destruction of a number of towns on each side. Very likely these towns were located in the troublesome border region between the two countries. At the best of times it must have been difficult for either side to control this region, or effectively patrol it. The earlier treaty with Paddatissu had referred to problems caused by cross-border movements of semi-nomadic groups with their livestock. Subsequently these problems may have intensified, exacerbating the tensions between the two kingdoms.

A Hitherto Unknown King   The land-grant documents discovered during the excavation of Temple 8 at Hattusa in 1984 included one which bore the impression of the royal seal of the king Zidanta,

[73] KUB xxxvi 108 (*CTH* 25). For the text of the treaty, see Otten (1951a). In spite of doubts expressed as to whether the Hittite signatory was Zidanta I or II (see Hoffner (1980: 309), Košak (1980a: 166–7)), it now appears virtually certain that the person in question was the second of that name; see Gurney (1973a: 661, 670–1), Beal (1986: 428), Freu (1995: 135); *contra*, Astour (1989: 21).

another that of a king called NIR.GÁL—in Hittite, Muwatalli.[74] The latter document is of particular interest to Hittite scholars, for it has brought to light a hitherto unknown occupant of the Hittite throne. The typology, language, and find-spot of the document and seal impression make it clear that Muwatalli was a contemporary of Zidanta, and also of Zidanta's successor Huzziya.[75]

The name Muwatalli is attested in a number of texts[76] which have previously been assigned to one or more members of the families of later kings, and most notably to the well known thirteenth-century king of that name. It is now clear that some of these texts should be assigned to the king named in the recently discovered land-grant document. Of special note is a text which refers to the murder of Huzziya by Muwatalli.[77] We can now conclude that the murdered man was the king Huzziya II, successor of Zidanta, and that his murderer Muwatalli seized the throne in his place.

In his entourage the new king included two men, Kantuzzili and Himuili, who *may* have been the sons of his victim. If so, he apparently sought a reconciliation with the rest of Huzziya's family, not only sparing the lives of his sons, and his wife Summiri, but also bestowing high office upon the sons.[78] Unfortunately for Muwatalli, this generous (if politically motivated) gesture failed ultimately to achieve the reconciliation he had hoped for. His reign ended as it had begun. With an assassination—this time his own, at the hands of Kantuzzili and Himuili.[79] Whatever their motive or

---

[74] KBo XXXII 184 and KBo XXXII 185 respectively. See Carruba (1990: 539–40).

[75] Carruba (1990: 547). Muwatalli appears to have risen to the post of GAL MEŠEDI under Huzziya; see Freu (1995: 136) with reference to KUB XXXII 187. Carruba (1990: 541) also draws attention to an Akkadian text fragment, KUB XXX 20 (*CTH* 275), which names a Mu(wa)talli two lines after a Zitanza. Note the seal of Huzziya—*SBo* I, 51, no. 85 (= Beran (1967: 32 no. 147)). *Contra* Astour (1989: 24) who assigns it to Huzziya I, it is almost certainly to be attributed to Huzziya II; see Easton (1981: 29), Freu (1995: 136).

[76] See Carruba's table I (1990: 555).

[77] KBo XVI 24 + 25 (*CTH* 251) rev. 15'. See Carruba (1990: 541–2).

[78] Himuili can perhaps be identified with the high-ranking official who held the office of GAL GEŠTIN (Chief of the Wine-(Stewards)) under Muwatalli (see most recently Freu (1995: 137), Klinger (1995: 86–7); on the term, see Beal (1992*b*: 342–57)), Kantuzzili with the holder of the office of 'Overseer of the Golden Chariot-Fighters' (for the Hittite term, see Beal (1992*b*: 410 n. 1542, and 410–11)).

[79] This follows the reconstruction of events proposed by Freu (1995: 137), on the basis of KUB XXXIV 40 (*CTH* 271) 8'–15' (ed. Otten (1987: 29–30); see also Carruba (1990: 541–2)). The text makes reference both to 'the queen, your mother' (lines 8', 12'), and to Kantuzzili and Himuili as the assassins of Muwatalli (lines 9'–10'). Freu's reconstruction may well be right, though it it is not clear from the text itself

provocation, the assassins' action led to another serious political crisis within Hatti. Once again rival factions emerged, once again the kingdom was to be plunged into internecine conflict over the royal succession.

But before turning to the events which followed the death of Muwatalli, we should review some of the developments which were occurring elsewhere in the Near East, especially those which were to have a direct impact on the future course of Hittite history.

The Wider Near Eastern Scene

In the period between Telipinu and Muwatalli, the Hittites' position *vis-à-vis* contemporary independent powers seems to have remained relatively stable. There is no indication that Telipinu's successors sustained any major losses of the territories which he had recovered—a point worthy of note since conflicts over the succession which had in the past seriously weakened the kingdom continued at least spasmodically in the decades following Telipinu's death. It is possible that these conflicts were less frequent and less intense than in the past. But we have no chronicle of events for the period, like that in the preamble to the *Proclamation*, and are therefore arguing largely from silence.

Of course the extent of Hittite influence in the Near East had diminished significantly from what it had been in the days of Hattusili and Mursili. Neither Telipinu nor his successors had the ambition, or apparently felt the need, to conduct campaigns on the scale of their two great predecessors. Without the enormous commitment of resources which such enterprises involved, it must have been easier for Telipinu's successors to maintain control over subject territories which lay closer to the homeland—in spite of any distractions caused by internal political disputes. And in regions which were strategically important to Hatti but outside its control, diplomacy rather than military force could be used to ensure that its interests were protected.

Kizzuwadna was one of these regions, probably the most important one in this period. As we have seen, the alliance which Telipinu had established with Kizzuwadna through his treaty with Isputahsu was renewed by several of his successors. One of the

that the queen in question was the wife of Huzziya or that the assassins were her sons.

ostensible purposes of the treaties was to resolve problems within the border region between the two kingdoms. But they must also have had a wider significance—to be seen within the context of the rising power of Mitanni to the south-east.

The Expanding Kingdom of Mitanni   While the kingdom of Aleppo held sway over much of northern Syria, Mitanni had apparently been content to acknowledge its sovereignty in the region and to establish diplomatic relations with it. No doubt a major incentive for a peace accord between Mitanni and Aleppo was the threat posed to the territorial interests of both kingdoms by the Hittite campaigns in Syria. Hattusili and his successor Mursili had both engaged in conflict with the Hurrians as well as Aleppo during these campaigns. But the final conquest of Aleppo, begun by Hattusili and completed by Mursili, left a power vacuum in northern Syria. Fortunately for Mitanni, the political upheavals in Hatti following Mursili's assassination prevented the Hittites from capitalizing on their military successes in Syria, providing Mitanni with an opportunity to fill the vacuum which these successes had created. Prospects for doing so were no doubt enhanced by the fact that Hurrians had already settled in substantial numbers in many parts of the region.[80]

But Mitannian enterprise in Syria was countered by Egyptian interest in the same region. This was first manifested in the campaigns of the pharaoh Tuthmosis I (accession *c*.1493), the third ruler of the eighteenth Dynasty. Shortly after his accession, Tuthmosis conducted an expedition to Syria which led to the conquest of Palestine. Subsequently he carried Egyptian arms to the Euphrates, where he erected a victory stele.[81] But his immediate successors made little or no attempt to consolidate on his military successes. In fact there was a notable shrinkage of Egyptian influence in Syria during Queen Hatshepsut's reign (*c*.1479–1457). Hatshepsut abandoned most of Tuthmosis' conquests in Syria, retaining only the southern part of Palestine.[82] This no doubt prompted the first major westward expansion of Mitannian power,

---

[80] Note that by this time the Egyptians used the term *Hurru* to refer to the Asiatic regions where they campaigned; Singer (1991*b*: 73).

[81] On Tuthmosis' Syrian campaigns, see Breasted (1906: ii §§81, 85), and on the victory stele seen by his grandson Tuthmosis III, Breasted (1906: ii §478).

[82] See Astour (1989: 20), with refs. cited therein.

in the reign of the king Parattarna (first half of the fifteenth century).

Parattarna's first main objective in Syria was to establish his sovereignty over the territories controlled by the kingdom of Aleppo. After its capture and destruction by Mursili, Aleppo itself had been rebuilt and had once more regained its independence. It had maintained this under a series of kings—Sarra-el, Abba-el, and Ilim-ilimma—and in fact expanded its territory to include a number of nearby states, notably Niya (Nii), Ama'u (Amae), and Mukis. But after the death of Ilim-ilimma, a rebellion had broken out in the kingdom. This led to the flight of Ilim-ilimma's son Idrimi to the small kingdom of Emar on the Euphrates.

His flight is recorded in the inscription on his famous statue, discovered by Sir Leonard Woolley in 1939.[83] Idrimi clearly saw himself as his father's rightful successor, and the rebellion which necessitated his flight may have been associated with dynastic disputes within his own family, perhaps not unlike those which occurred in Hatti during the reign of Hattusili. At all events, the Mitannian king Parattarna took advantage of the situation—and may indeed have helped incite the rebellion[84]—to establish his overlordship over the entire former kingdom of Aleppo.[85] Seven years in exile brought Idrimi to realize that if he was ever to claim his throne, he had to accept the reality of Mitannian sovereignty over the kingdom from which he had fled. He thus sought a reconciliation with Parattarna. Agreement was reached, a treaty was drawn up, and Idrimi was installed as one of Parattarna's vassal rulers.[86] But his kingdom was reduced to only the western parts of the former kingdom of Aleppo (Niya, Ama'u, and Mukis), with its royal seat located at Alalah.[87] The remainder of the territories comprising the old kingdom were granted virtual autonomous status by the Mitannian king.[88]

Once established on his vassal throne, Idrimi demonstrated his value as an agent of Mitannian interests by attacking and conquering seven towns lying within the south-eastern periphery of Hittite

[83] The inscription was published by Smith (1949). For a recent and substantially revised translation, see Dietrich and Loretz (1985).

[84] Cf. Klengel (1965b: 228).

[85] See Na'aman (1974: 268).

[86] Idrimi inscription, 50–8.

[87] See Na'aman (1974: 268; 1980: 41–2).

[88] See Na'aman (1974: 268, with refs. cited in n. 17).

subject territory.[89] His conquests brought him close to the borders of Kizzuwadna, and may have led to the treaty which he drew up with the Kizzuwadnan king Pilliya.[90] Since the treaty was signed under the authority of Parattarna, both Pilliya and Idrimi were tributaries of the Mitannian king at the time.[91]

Yet Pilliya had also concluded a treaty with the Hittite king Zidanta. A simultaneous alliance with Hatti and Mitanni would have been out of the question. Hence Kizzuwadna must have switched sides, presumably some time after Pilliya's accord with the Hittites.[92] The switch was probably dictated by political reality. With an aggressive Mitannian vassal campaigning near the frontiers of his kingdom, Pilliya may have had no choice other than to exchange his Hittite alliance for one with the Mitannian king and his vassal. It was a question of weighing up who posed the greater and more immediate threat to his kingdom—a hostile Mitanni or an alienated Hatti.

His dilemma was one later faced by a number of local rulers, particularly in Syria, who found themselves caught up in the contests between the major powers in the region. With which of these powers should they align themselves? Which offered the better prospects for the security of their own position and the security of their kingdom? More often than not overlordship of one or other of the major powers was forced upon them. As far as Kizzuwadna was concerned, this was neither the first nor the last time its king decided or was forced to change sides. Whether on this occasion he did so while Zidanta still occupied the Hittite throne or some time after this remains unknown.[93] At all events, Idrimi's treaty with

---

[89] Idrimi inscription, 64–77. One of the towns, Zaruna, was amongst those previously conquered by Hattusili. Smith identified it with Seleuceia, north of Antioch. For a review of the question of its location, along with the location of other place-names mentioned in context with it, see Gurney (1992, 216–17).

[90] AT 3.

[91] On this and the question of intra-empire treaties, see Beal (1986: 429 n. 26), *contra* Wilhelm (1989: 26).

[92] It should be noted that the dating of the Idrimi–Pilliya treaty has been a matter of some dispute. One school of thought assigns it and its signatories to an earlier period, making them and the Mitannian king Parattarna contemporaries of the Hittite king Ammuna; see e.g. Gurney (1973*b*: 661–2). In this case we would have to postulate an earlier king Pilliya of Kizzuwadna. However, a later dating, which removes the need for two Pilliyas and assigns Idrimi and Parattarna to the first half of the 15th cent., seems much more likely; cf. Beal (1986: 429–30), with refs.

[93] For a possible indication that it occurred after his reign, see Ch. 6 n. 53. Beal (1986: 430–1) notes that in the next generation at Alalah, Idrimi's younger son

Pilliya and his destruction of the Hittite border towns had ominous implications for Hatti. Mitanni would not long rest content with the territories it had won in Syria. Its sights must now have been set on expansion further to the west. Inevitably, this posed a major threat to Hatti and its subject territories in eastern Anatolia.

Renewed Egyptian Campaigns in Syria   Mitannian imperialist ambitions now received a major setback from the resurgence of Egyptian military enterprise under the pharaoh Tuthmosis III (*c.*1479–1425).[94] Tuthmosis' clear intention was to establish a permanent Egyptian presence in Syria, by laying the foundations of a pro-Egyptian local administration in the region.[95] In his first campaign (*c.*1458), the pharaoh defeated a coalition of Syrian forces at Megiddo, led by the king of Kadesh.[96] He then set his sights in subsequent campaigns on the conquest of Mitannian subject territories in Syria. In the process he reached and crossed the Euphrates river, thus emulating the achievement of Hattusili (and Sargon before him).

Several kingdoms acknowledged the new Egyptian overlord of Syria by seeking diplomatic relations with him and sending him gifts and tribute—notably Assyria, Babylon, and perhaps most significantly Hatti. Their overtures to Tuthmosis were perhaps designed to forestall any ambitions he may have entertained against their own territory. But more likely they reacted with no little enthusiasm to Egyptian military enterprise which effectively put a halt, at least temporarily, to the militaristic ambitions of their powerful neighbour Mitanni—ambitions which posed a much more serious threat to their own kingdoms than Egypt.

Zidanta may have been the Hittite king who sent tributary gifts to Tuthmosis on his return from his Syrian campaign in his thirty-

Niqmepa brought a dispute against Sunassura, the king of Kizzuwadna, which was to be judged by the Mitannian king Saustatar—a clear indication that Kizzuwadna was still at this stage a tributary of Mitanni.

[94] This includes a period of coregency with Hatshepsut. Tuthmosis' sole rule began *c.*1458.

[95] Thus Astour (1989: 57), who notes that his interest in the newly acquired region found expression in the metic collection of place names for his great 'Naharina List' at Karnak (citing J. Simons, *Handbook for the study of Egyptian Topographical Lists relating to Western Asia*, Leiden, 1937, List I, nos. 120–259).

[96] Tuthmosis' account of the campaign is trans. by Wilson in Pritchard (1969: 234–8).

third year.[97] Eight years later, the gesture was repeated by the same king, or his successor.[98] Quite possibly Hittite–Egyptian relations were further strengthened by a formal pact between the two kingdoms, which included an agreement to transfer inhabitants from the Hittite city of Kurustama in the north-east of Anatolia to Egyptian subject territory in Syria. This possibility arises from a document commonly known as the Kurustama treaty,[99] and referred to in two later texts.[100] While the date of the document is not certain—it could belong to a later period[101]—some form of Hittite–Egyptian pact or alliance may well have been concluded at this time.

There were obvious advantages for the Hittites in formalizing diplomatic relations with Egypt. Of course it is unlikely that Egypt ever posed a serious threat to Hittite territory in Anatolia, except on its very periphery. The pharaoh's military campaigns had already taken him far from his homeland. He would have difficulty enough in maintaining control over the territories he had already conquered without entertaining any prospects of extending his conquests even further. And there was always the threat that a resurgent Mitanni might seek to win back from him at least some of its lost subject states. On the other hand, the Hittites' main concern was to ensure the security of their existing territories in Anatolia, particularly against the threat of Mitannian aggression. In the absence of any major conflict of territorial interests between Hatti and Egypt, an alliance against the third party Mitanni could well have been to the advantage of both.

But successful as Tuthmosis' campaigns were in purely military terms, they did not lead to significant permanent Egyptian control within the regions where they were conducted. Indeed his seventeenth and final campaign was essentially an attempt to put down a rebellion by the towns Tunip and Kadesh in central Syria.[102] This

---

[97] Although without being able to determine precise or even approximate dates for Zidanta's reign we cannot be sure who the Hittite king was. It could have been Zidanta's successor Huzziya II.

[98] Breasted (1906: ii §§485 and 525).

[99] The surviving fragments are grouped in *CTH* 134.

[100] The first from the biography of Suppiluliuma I, *DS* 98, frag. 28, E iv 26–32, the second from the Plague Prayers of Mursili II, 2nd version, KUB xiv 8 (+) (*CTH* 378), obv. 13'–17'. See Sürenhagen (1985: 22–6).

[101] For discussion of the date, see Houwink ten Cate (1963: 274–5), Sürenhagen (1985: 26–38).

[102] Breasted (1906: ii §§528–40).

rebellion almost certainly had the support of Mitanni which, under the rule of its vigorous and enterprising king Saustatar I, was soon to reach the peak of its power and influence in the Near East. As the Hittite king Hattusili had discovered before Tuthmosis, and many military conquerors after him, it was much easier to win military victories than to maintain permanent control over the territories conquered, especially if these were far removed from the conqueror's home base. As subsequent events were to demonstrate, the Egyptian military successes against Mitanni were no more than a temporary setback for a kingdom whose star was still rising.

CHAPTER 6

A New Era Begins: From Tudhaliya I/II to Tudhaliya III (c.1400–1344)

The First Tudhaliya

The assassination of Muwatalli was the final episode in the history of the period we have called the Hittite Old Kingdom. The reign of his successor, a man called Tudhaliya, marked what was effectively the beginning of a new era in Hittite history. It was an era in which the Hittites embarked once more on a series of military enterprises far from their homeland in both Syria and western Anatolia— enterprises which brought them into direct conflict with other Late Bronze Age kingdoms and led ultimately to the establishment of a Hittite 'empire'. To this second period of Hittite history we have given the name 'New Kingdom'.[1]

It had an inauspicious start. Like the first recorded event of the Old Kingdom, it began with a rebellion—over the question of the succession. There were those who sought vengeance for the blood of the last king. Muwatalli had fallen victim to a palace conspiracy involving at least two highly placed court officials, Kantuzzili and Himuili. who may have been the sons of Muwatalli's predecessor Huzziya.[2] The ultimate intention of the conspirators was almost certainly to place Tudhaliya on the throne. But their actions did not have universal support. Forces loyal to the former king gathered under the leadership of Muwa, Muwatalli's Chief of the Body-guards (GAL MEŠEDI),[3] probably the highest-ranking official of Muwatalli, and perhaps his son. Backed by an army of infantry and chariotry and with Hurrian support, Muwa took the field against

---

[1] For changes in the character of the monarchy after the Old Kingdom, see Goetze (1957c: 88–92; 1964: 29–30).

[2] On the distinction between these and later princes with the same names, see Freu (1995: 138).

[3] KBo XXXII 185 rev. 12; see Beal (1992b: 333). On the importance of the office of the GAL MEŠEDI, see Beal (1992b: 327–42), esp. the summary on p. 342. Muwa also appears along with Himuili as one of the chief functionaries in the witness list on a land-grant document bearing Muwatalli's seal (KBo XXXII 185); see Otten (1991: 346).

the forces of Kantuzzili and Tudhaliya. Once again we see a kingdom divided against itself. But only briefly. Muwa and his Hurrian
allies were defeated, decisively, and Tudhaliya's occupancy of the
Hittite throne was secured:

The infantry and chariotry of Muwa and the infantry and chariotry of the
Hurrians took the field against Kantuzzili. . . . . Kantuzzili and I, the king,
defeated the army of Muwa and the Hurrians. The enemy army died *en
masse.*   (KUB XXIII 16 (*CTH* 211.6) III 4–9)[4]

We have no clear information on the position this new king held
in the kingdom before his accession. Nor do we know what part, if
any, he played in the events which led to the death of Muwatalli,
except that he was the chief beneficiary of these events. It may well
be that he was the son of Himuili, one of the assassins.[5] If so, and if
Himuili was a son of the former king Huzziya, then Tudhaliya's
accession marked the restoration of kingship to the family in whose
hands it lay before it was seized by Muwatalli. Hence Muwatalli's
reign would have been no more than a brief interlude in the history
of a royal dynasty whose tenure of power continued with little
interruption throughout the periods of both the Old and the New
Kingdoms.[6]

How Many Early New Kingdom Rulers?

Before embarking with Tudhaliya on his career as king of the
Hittites, we must briefly touch upon one of the most complex and

---

[4] The text has been ed. by Carruba (1977*a*: 162–3).
[5] The fragmentary first three lines of KUB XXIII 16 make reference to 'my (*sc.*
Tudhaliya's) father' as one of the protagonists in the conflict with Muwa. Unfortunately the father's name is lost. However, since Himuili had collaborated with
Kantuzzili in the assassination of Muwatalli, we would expect him to be a chief
participant in the conflict which followed it. And we know from KUB XXIII 16 that
there were three such participants, only two of whom, Kantuzzili and Tudhaliya, are
named. Hence the possibility that the third participant, Tudhaliya's unnamed father,
was Himuili. I am grateful to Professor Gurney for this suggestion. Freu (1995: 137)
assumes that Tudhaliya came from a different family. If so, it is difficult to see why
Kantuzzili and Himuili, after assassinating Muwatalli, should have supported the
accession of an outsider, particularly if they themselves were sons of the previous
'rightful' king. To gain their support Tudhaliya would almost certainly have had to
be a member of the legitimate royal family. By this time Kantuzzili and Himuili were
probably of relatively advanced age, and may have come to an agreement to elevate
the son of one of them to kingship. A younger man could have been seen as having
greater prospects of bringing a renewed vigour to the old dynastic line and the
demands of kingship in a very unstable period. He was also, apparently, free of the
assassin's taint, and thus more likely to win acceptance from Muwatalli's supporters.
[6] Thus Klinger (1995: 95–6 n. 81).

vexatious problems in Hittite history. What was the line of succession of the early New Kingdom rulers? Beginning with the first Tudhaliya, how many kings were there before the accession of Suppiluliuma I? This is a particular case where the absence of a reliable king-list is keenly felt by scholars. There are a wide range of uncertainties and possibilities, and much scholarly literature has been generated on the topic. But at the time of writing, the matter remains unresolved. All we can say for certain is that the first Tudhaliya preceded Suppiluliuma by three generations. But opinions differ markedly on the number of kings who occupied the throne in the intervening period. For example, should the events of the early New Kingdom which are associated with the name Tudhaliya be assigned to one or two kings so called?[7] The matter is further complicated by the possibility of several co-regencies in this period.

Further evidence will need to be produced before we are likely to get a solution to the problem which will satisfy all scholars. For the present and for the purposes of this book it seems best to assume a minimum number of kings—those whose existence is beyond doubt—and to assign all the recorded events of this period to their reigns. Thus we will assume that there was only one early New Kingdom ruler called Tudhaliya, on the understanding that the assumption may well be invalidated by new evidence. To allow for this possibility, and to preserve the conventional numbering of the later kings called Tudhaliya, we will refer to the first king so named as Tudhaliya I/II.

Tudhaliya Goes West

As soon as his occupancy of the throne was secure, Tudhaliya applied himself vigorously to the task of reasserting Hatti's status as a major international power in the Near East. The task was a formidable one. Hatti had ceased to have any effective influence in Syria since Mursili I's campaigns in the region. And by now northern Syria was firmly under the control of the Mitannian king Saustatar I. At least one of the Hittites' major routes into Syria had been cut off by Kizzuwadna's alliance with Mitanni, and the loss of Hittite subject towns in the border area.

[7] See Beal (1986: 442 n. 87) for a discussion of the various proposals to split Tudhaliya into two kings of that name.

But before looking to the recovery of lost Hittite territory in the south-east or to a new expedition into Syria, Tudhaliya had to turn his attention in the opposite direction. In western Anatolia a dangerous situation was developing which ultimately threatened Hittite subject territories bordering on the homeland in the south. No major military enterprises in Syria could be contemplated until the dangers from the west had been effectively dealt with.

During the Old Kingdom, the Hittites had limited involvement in western Anatolian affairs. Indeed, their only attested activity in the west occurred during Hattusili I's reign. Under Tudhaliya, however, Hittite armies undertook a series of extensive campaigns in the region. There were important strategic reasons for doing so. Individually, the western countries lacked the resources to make any significant inroads into Hittite territory. But they were prone to the formation of military confederacies. And when the Arzawa lands became involved, the west could eventually pose as serious a threat to Hatti as the Hurrians in the south-east and the Kaskans in the north.[8] Within this context, Tudhaliya's western campaigns were perhaps largely pre-emptive in nature, designed to break up newly forming confederacies or to pacify or intimidate states in the region before any threat to Hatti reached dangerous proportions.[9]

At the time of Tudhaliya's accession the forces in the west may already have been rallying for a major onslaught on the southern territories belonging to the Hittite kingdom.[10] Predictably, Arzawa figured prominently amongst the western forces, which had very likely come together under Arzawan leadership. But in Tudhaliya, they faced a formidable opponent. The king led his troops in a series of devastating military campaigns in the territories of his enemies. Countries belonging to the Arzawa Lands were amongst the prime targets of these campaigns—Arzawa Minor, Seha River Land, Hapalla. But alongside them were a number of other western countries and cities—Sariyanda, Uliwanda, Parsuhalda in the first campaign, and subsequently the land of the River Limiya, and the lands of Apkuisa, Pariyana, Arinna, Wallarima, Halatarsa. All succumbed to the Hittite onslaught.

---

[8] Cf. Yakar (1993: 6–7).

[9] Further on this, see Bryce (1986*b*: 3–4).

[10] News of the upheavals in the Hittite homeland could have provided the main trigger for this action.

In the aftermath of conquest, Tudhaliya attempted to eliminate, or at least minimize, the risk of further hostilities in the region by transporting back to Hattusa from the conquered lands large numbers of infantry and chariots, including 500 teams of horse. This is the earliest known example in Hittite history of a practice regularly adopted by later Hittite kings.

Much of our information about these and other Anatolian campaigns in which Tudhaliya engaged derives from the remains of the king's *Annals*.[11] They refer to four successive campaigns conducted by Tudhaliya, beginning with the conquest of the Arzawa Lands. This conquest, far from pacifying the west, merely served to provoke it to further action. Indeed, the dust of the Arzawa campaign had barely settled before Tudhaliya was confronted with a major new threat in the west. On this occasion, twenty-two countries banded together to form an anti-Hittite military alliance:

But when I turned back to Hattusa, then against me these lands declared war: [ ]ugga, Kispuwa, Unaliya, [ ], Dura, Halluwa, Huwallusiya, Karakisa, Dunda, Adadura, Parista, [ ], [ ]waa, Warsiya, Kuruppiya, [ ]luissa (or Lusa), Alatra (?), Mount Pahurina, Pasuhalta, [ ], Wilusiya, Taruisa. [These lands] with their warriors assembled themselves .... and drew up their army opposite me. (*Annals*, obv.13′– 21′, adapted from trans. by Garstang and Gurney (1959: 121–2))

Tudhaliya attacked the assembled enemy forces in a night assault:

I, Tudhaliya, brought up my forces at night, and surrounded the army of the enemy. The gods handed their army over to me, the Sun Goddess of Arinna, the Storm God of Heaven, the Protective Genius of Hatti, Zamama, Istar, Sin, Lelwani. I defeated the army of the enemy and entered their country. And from whatever country an army had come (out) to battle, the gods went before me, and the countries which I have mentioned, which declared war, the gods delivered them to me. All these countries I carried off. The conquered population, oxen, sheep, the possessions of the land, I brought away to Hattusa. Now when I had destroyed the Land of Assuwa, I came back home to Hattusa. And as booty 10,000 foot-soldiers and 600 teams of horses for chariots together with the 'lords of the bridle' I brought to Hattusa, and I settled them in Hattusa. (*Annals*, obv. 22′–36′, adapted from transl. by Garstang and Gurney, (1959: 122))

---

[11] These include the parallel texts KUB xxiii 11//12 (*CTH* 142.2), ed. Carruba (1977*a*: 158–63), also trans. Garstang and Gurney (1959: 121–3). The fragmentary text KUB xxiii 27 is also commonly assigned to these Annals, but probably belongs to a later period, perhaps the reign of Tudhaliya III; cf. Košak (1980*a*: 164).

From the reference to the destruction of the Land of Assuwa, apparently a collective term embracing all the above-mentioned countries, the enemy coalition is commonly referred to as the Assuwan Confederacy.[12] The group of states making up the Confederacy probably lay in the far west of Anatolia, covering at least part of the Aegean coast. A number of scholars believe that Assuwa is the origin of the Graeco-Roman name Asia, drawing attention to the fact that the Roman province of Asia was originally centred in this region.[13] If the first name in the list, [ ]ugga, can be restored as [L]ugga (= Lukka),[14] then the Confederacy may well have extended as far south as the region of Classical Lycia, part of the homeland of the Bronze Age Lukka people. Attention has also frequently been drawn to the last two names in the list—Wilusiya and Taruisa—with the suggestion that these are the Hittite forms of the Greek names (W)ilios (Ilion) and Troia (Troy).[15] We shall discuss this further in Chapter 14.

The Hittite victory was so decisive that the Confederacy never again reformed. And to ensure that the countries which had constituted it would pose no further threat to Hittite interests, Tudhaliya transported 10,000 infantry and 600 teams of horse along with the élite chariot contingent back to Hattusa for resettlement in the homeland.

His battle spoils from the Assuwan campaign may have included the bronze longsword which was discovered in 1991 near the Lion Gate at Hattusa.[16] The inscription on the sword, dated on stylistic grounds to around the period in which Tudhaliya reigned, indicates that the weapon was dedicated by Tudhaliya to the Storm God

---

[12] Jewell (1974: 286) notes that only four texts refer to the Land of Assuwa: KUB XXIII 11 + 12 (*CTH* 142), KUB XXIII 14 (*CTH* 211.5), and KUB XIII 9 + KUB XL 62 (*CTH* 258).

[13] Jewell (1974: 288 n. 3) cites scholars favouring the derivation, and those more cautious about it. See also Güterbock (1986: 40 n. 20), Ünal, Ertekin, and Ediz (1991: 52).

[14] Thus Garstang and Gurney (1959: 106); but see Huxley (1960: 33) who argues for the restoration Ard]ugga.

[15] Professor Hawkins has recently published details of a silver bowl of unknown origin or provenance in the Ankara Museum (1997). It bears two hieroglyphic inscriptions, one of which refers to the conquest of a place called Tarwiza by a king Tudhaliya. It is tempting to link this event with the conquest of Taruisa (and other western countries) in Tudhaliya's *Annals*. This would, however, make the inscription by far the earliest known of the hieroglyphic inscriptions apart from those appearing on seals—if the *Annals* have been correctly assigned to the first king called Tudhaliya.

[16] On the find-spot and its archaeological context, see Neve (1993: 648–52).

after a victory over Assuwa.[17] This reference to Assuwa in the inscription, and the likelihood that the sword was produced in a western Anatolian/Aegean workshop,[18] may well indicate that it was part of the booty from the Assuwan campaign.[19]

Threats from the East and the North

Tudhaliya's triumphs in the west were short-lived, and were in fact achieved at considerable cost. The concentration of Hittite forces in the west left the homeland dangerously exposed to enemies inhabiting the regions close to its northern and eastern frontiers. The Kaska tribes from the Pontic region were quick to take advantage of the situation: 'Now while I, Tudhaliya, the Great King, was fighting in the Land of Assuwa, behind my back Kaskan troops took up arms, and they came into the Land of Hatti, and devastated the country' (*Annals*, rev. 9'–12', trans. Garstang and Gurney (1959: 122)).

The crisis on this occasion was promptly dealt with by Tudhaliya on his return to Hattusa. He first drove the enemy from the homeland, then pursued them into their own territory where he defeated their combined forces, following this up in the next campaigning season with further extensive conquests in the Kaska lands. The Kaska problem was one which would continue to surface throughout the reigns of Tudhaliya and his successor Arnuwanda, as reflected in the extensive correspondence devoted to Kaskan issues in the Maşat archive.[20]

For the present, a year's respite from battle enabled Tudhaliya and his forces to regather their strength to deal with yet another major threat to Hatti—this time on the eastern frontier. Here lay the kingdom of Isuwa, between the easternmost territories of the homeland and the kingdom of Mitanni, in the region of the modern

[17] The inscription has been published by Ünal in Ünal, Ertekin, and Ediz (1991: 51).

[18] Neve (1993a: 651).

[19] See Ertekin and Ediz (1993), who refer also to another inscribed sword said to have been found in the Diyarbakır region, and probably belonging to the Assyrian colony period, discussed by Güterbock (1965).

[20] Cf. Klinger (1995: 103), who notes that the Maşat letters (which like the rest of the archive can be dated largely if not exclusively to the reigns of Tudhaliya I/II and Arnuwanda I), are concerned predominantly with the Kaska problem. The archive has been published by Alp (1991). See also Beckman (1995a: 23–6).

Turkish province of Elazığ.[21] It occupied a position of considerable strategic importance in the context of the power struggle between Hatti and Mitanni, and its allegiance fluctuated between the two of them.

Earlier in Tudhaliya's reign, it had apparently taken up arms against Hatti with the support of the Mitannian king.[22] Tudhaliya had succeeded in crushing the rebellion, and presumably re-established Hittite control over Isuwa. But a number of the rebels had escaped his authority by seeking refuge in Mitanni. He sent a demand to the Mitannian king for their extradition. The demand was refused:

> The people of Isuwa fled before My Sun and descended to the Land of Hurri. I, My Sun, sent word to the Hurrian: 'Extradite my subjects!' But the Hurrian sent word back to My Sun as follows: 'No! Those cities had previously, in the days of my grandfather, come to the Land of Hurri and had settled there. It is true they later went back to the Land of Hatti as refugees. But now, finally, the cattle have chosen their stable, they have definitely come to my country.' So the Hurrian did not extradite my subjects to me, My Sun.   (KBo 15 (*CTH* 41) 10–20, adapted from trans. by Goetze (1940: 37))

Subsequently, Hurrian troops invaded, sacked, and plundered the country of Isuwa,[23] no doubt targeting cities and areas that had remained loyal to Hatti. Tudhaliya had been powerless to prevent them, for he had committed his forces to a military campaign elsewhere, probably in the north or the west. It was only now, perhaps, after his conquests in western Anatolia and in the Kaska lands, that he could turn his attention back to Isuwa. As far as we can judge from the fragmentary passage in his *Annals* which records his campaign in Isuwa, he succeeded in restoring Hittite control over the region. But only temporarily. Isuwa was to continue to be one of the most fractious subject territories, and remained firmly pro-Mitannian in its loyalties. It was later to join the onslaught on Hittite territory which brought the kingdom close to total destruction.[24]

---

[21] See del Monte and Tischler (1978: 155).

[22] To judge from the reference in Tudhaliya's *Annals* to the king of the Hurri in association with Isuwa's military action against Hatti, KUB XXIII 11/12 rev. 27'–34'.

[23] KBo 15 20–3.

[24] Further on the relations between the Hittites and Isuwa, see Klengel (1968).

Tudhaliya's Isuwan campaigns had failed to bring any lasting security to the region. The eastern frontiers of the homeland remained dangerously vulnerable to invasion by Mitanni and its allies.

Tudhaliya's Co-regent

At least some of Tudhaliya's Anatolian campaigns were conducted jointly with the man who was to succeed him on the throne, Arnuwanda, the first of three kings of that name. Already in Tudhaliya's reign Arnuwanda was referred to as 'Great King',[25] which must mean that Tudhaliya made him his co-regent.[26] Both textual evidence and seal impressions represent Arnuwanda as the son of Tudhaliya.[27] He was also the husband of Asmunikal, who we learn from another seal impression was the daughter of Tudhaliya and his wife Nikkalmati.[28] This has raised some scholarly eyebrows, since brother–sister marriages were strictly forbidden in the Hittite world. The most logical explanation is that Tudhaliya adopted his daughter's husband as his son, prior to making him his co-regent and eventual successor to the throne.[29] Provision had clearly been made in the *Proclamation* of Telipinu for a king's son-in-law to succeed him on the throne.

Arnuwanda proved a loyal and effective comrade-in-arms to the ageing king, and no doubt played a major role in the latter's military triumphs. We learn something of this role from the remaining fragments of his own *Annals*.[30] Very likely they deal with much the same events as Tudhaliya's *Annals*, and provide rather more detailed information about the campaigns against Arzawa.[31] For example, we learn from Arnuwanda's *Annals* of action taken against

---

[25] KUB XXIII 21 (*CTH* 143) II 12, 14, 27, III 20.

[26] Cf. Houwink ten Cate (1970: 58), Carruba (1977b: 177 n. 7).

[27] For the seal impressions which associate Arnuwanda with Tudhaliya, see *SBo* I, 44, no. 76 (= Beran (1967: 33 no. 153)); see also Boehmer and Güterbock (1987: 81–2 no. 253), *Seal of Arnuwanda, the Great King, Son of Tudhaliya, the Great King*.

[28] *SBo* I, 31–2, no. 60, 44, no. 77 (= Beran (1967: 34 no. 162, 33 no. 152 respectively)).

[29] The solution proposed by Beal (1983: 117), supported by Beckman (1986: 23).

[30] Surviving in a late copy, KUB XXIII 21 (*CTH* 143); see Carruba (1977a: 166–71), Freu (1987: 135–43).

[31] See Houwink ten Cate (1970: 57–79), Easton (1984: 23), Freu (1987: 138). However Jewell (1974: 273–5) takes the view that the two sets of *Annals* deal with chronologically separate events.

the Arzawan king Kupanta-Kurunta, his defeat by the Hittites, and his escape from their clutches.[32] The Hittites were to have good reason to regret their failure to capture him! This comes to light within the context of the activities of Madduwatta—one of the most cunning and apparently one of the most unscrupulous of all Hittite vassals.

The Exploits of Madduwatta

Our chief source of information on the career of Madduwatta is a document commonly referred to as the *Indictment of Madduwatta*.[33] Originally dated to the period of Tudhaliya IV and his son Arnuwanda III towards the end of the New Kingdom, this is one of several documents which have been reassigned to the first two kings of these names (see Appendix 1). Thus the activities of Madduwatta which were once thought to reflect the weakness and ineffectiveness of the Hittite kingdom not long before its final collapse should now be seen as reflecting difficulties experienced by the first two kings of the New Kingdom.

The *Indictment* is in the form of a letter written by Tudhaliya's co-regent and successor Arnuwanda. Madduwatta, the addressee of the letter, had fled from his own country with his family and a retinue of troops and chariots, apparently because of a dispute with Attarsiya (Attarissiya), identified in the letter as 'Man of Ahhiya'. This is the earliest reference we have to Ahhiya(wa) in the Hittite texts.[34] The status of this Man of Ahhiya is unclear, but the designation suggests that he was an individual Ahhiyawan who had established a base in western Anatolia rather than an officially recognized king (LUGAL) of the Land of Ahhiyawa. He had at his disposal a small army of infantry and 100 chariots, probably of Anatolian origin.

Madduwatta's own country of origin is not made clear, although almost certainly it lay in western Anatolia.[35] Wherever its location, Madduwatta was obviously a man of some importance, to judge from the substantial retinue which accompanied him into exile

---

[32] KUB XXIII 21 II 1'–32'.

[33] KUB XIV 1 + KBo XIX 38 (*CTH* 147), ed. Goetze (1927).

[34] The shorter (older) form Ahhiya appears only here and in the oracle text KBo XVI 97 (*CTH* 571.2). See Güterbock (1983a: 134), Gurney (1990: 38).

[35] His name recalls that of the Lydian kings of the 1st millennium, Alyattes and Sadyattes; cf. Freu (1987: 123; 1990: 7).

(wives, children, troops, and chariots are mentioned), and also from the efforts Attarsiya made to seek him out and take vengeance upon him. He escaped the clutches of Attarsiya, and sought and was granted refuge with Tudhaliya.

Tudhaliya first proposed to install him as a vassal ruler in the mountain land of Hariyati, which apparently lay close to the Hittite frontier in the west or south-west. But Madduwatta declined the offer, and was set up instead in the mountain land of Zippasla. There can be little doubt that the location for the new fiefdom was chosen by Tudhaliya for a specific purpose, probably strategic in nature. The readiness with which Tudhaliya compromised on an alternative location may indicate that both were to be found in the same general area.[36] It is none the less an interesting indication of the bargaining power which Madduwatta apparently possessed. In fact we learn later in the text that Tudhaliya also handed over to his new vassal additional territory known as the Siyanti River Land, which probably became an extension to his original fiefdom.[37] The additional territory may have been a subsequent concession made to Madduwatta in an attempt to curb his territorial ambitions elsewhere.

Initially Madduwatta's installation as a Hittite vassal must have seemed a wise move. It presented Tudhaliya with the opportunity of establishing a new vassal state on the periphery of Hittite subject territory and in the vicinity of the Arzawa lands with a ready-made nucleus of a population, including troops and chariotry. The new vassal had no political or personal ties with the countries in the region. He could reasonably be expected to maintain his allegiance to his Hittite overlord who had made him his protégé and bestowed substantial favours upon him. Further, Tudhaliya probably increased the military forces under his command, to ensure adequate defence of the new vassal territory.

In return, Madduwatta's vassal status entailed a number of obligations to his overlord, particularly military obligations:

Whoever is an enemy to the father of My Sun[38] and to the Land of Hatti is also to be an enemy to you, Madduwatta. And as I, the father of My Sun,

---

[36] For a contrary view, see Houwink ten Cate (1970: 63 n. 37).

[37] Although Garstang and Gurney (1959: 92) suggested that the Siyanti River Land was another name for Zippasla, they should probably be distinguished; cf. Houwink ten Cate (1970: 64).

[38] i.e. Tudhaliya, the father or adoptive father of Arnuwanda, author of the text.

will fight resolutely against him, you must also fight him resolutely,
Madduwatta, and your troops likewise.   (*Indictment* §6, obv. 28–30)

Madduwatta was also obliged to hand over to the king anyone
guilty of seditious talk or conduct:

Whoever speaks an evil word before you, whether it be that one speaks
a word of enmity before you, or that one abuses the king and the king's
son—that person you must not conceal. Send word to My Sun and seize the
man, and send him to the father of My Sun.   (*Indictment* §7, obv. 37–9)

Similar obligations were regularly stipulated by later Hittite kings
in the treaties which they drew up with their vassal rulers.

But it soon became clear that Madduwatta had ambitions of his
own, which were not consistent with the terms of his appointment,
and which led him time and again to violate his oath of allegiance
to his overlord. He seemed intent on carving out for himself a small
kingdom of western Anatolian states, at least some of which appear
to have been nominally subject to Hatti. Arnuwanda's letter protests vigorously about the wayward vassal's conduct—his treachery, his abuse of power, his flagrant defiance of the terms of his
agreement—both in Tudhaliya's reign and subsequently in the
author's own reign.

Probably not long after his installation as a vassal ruler,
Madduwatta committed his first 'offence' by invading the territory
of Kupanta-Kurunta, king of Arzawa. He could claim that he
was justified in doing so because Kupanta-Kurunta was, after all,
a declared enemy of the Hittites. But his action was in direct
violation of his agreement with Tudhaliya, as Arnuwanda pointed
out:

You, Madduwatta, violated the oath with the father of My Sun. The father
of My Sun had given you the mountain land Zippasla to dwell in, and he
put you under divine oath as follows: 'Behold! I gave you the mountain
land Zippasla. Now you must dwell here. Further, you must occupy no
other land.' And Madduwatta took the whole land, and together with his
own troops raised forces in large numbers, and marched against Kupanta-
Kurunta to do battle.   (*Indictment* §8, obv. 42–5)

In taking this action, against the express orders of his overlord,
Madduwatta seriously miscalculated the strength of the opposition.
His expedition against Arzawa ended in disaster. His army was
destroyed, his territory was invaded and occupied by Kupanta-

Kurunta, and he was forced to flee for his life. This might well have brought his career to an ignominious end. Deservedly so! But then Tudhaliya displayed the remarkable forbearance which was to characterize all his and his son's dealings with Madduwatta. Hittite troops now came to the rescue, driving Kupanta-Kurunta back to his own land and taking substantial booty from him.[39] Tudhaliya restored Madduwatta to his vassal throne, and made him a present of the spoils of battle. Thus he emerged from the affair with his status intact, and indeed considerably better off than he had any right to expect. At least that is Arnuwanda's interpretation of the course of events. Admittedly Hittite kings were noted for, and indeed prided themselves on, their apparent leniency towards wayward vassals. But the actual rewarding of a vassal for defiance of his overlord's explicit instructions is without parallel.

There really does seem to be more to this episode than is immediately evident. We should remember that the letter to Madduwatta was written in retrospect when Arnuwanda, with the wisdom of hindsight, could see the vassal's initial attack on Arzawa as the prelude to later events, and when it had become clear that Madduwatta's intention was to carve out a kingdom of his own in western Anatolia. Thus the action that Tudhaliya might first have regarded as no more than over-zealousness on the part of a newly installed vassal took on a more ominous colour in the light of the vassal's subsequent conduct.

Further, at the time of Madduwatta's attack Arzawa posed a continuing threat to the security of Hittite-controlled territory. Kupanta-Kurunta's counter-attack provided Tudhaliya with the opportunity and the excuse for inflicting a resounding defeat on the Arzawan forces—allegedly for violating his subject territory. The very fact that he actually strengthened Madduwatta's position after the repulse of the Arzawan forces suggests a measure of tacit approval for the action which his vassal had taken, albeit without his consent. But we should note that in spite of the defeat which the Hittite army inflicted on Kupanta-Kurunta, Tudhaliya made no attempt to occupy or annex his country. Indeed it is clear from the events subsequently reported in the letter that Arzawa retained its independence.

[39] Forrer (1937: 175) suggested the possible identification of the events described here with the defeat of Kupanta-Kurunta referred to in Arnuwanda's *Annals* (see above). See also Houwink ten Cate (1970: 59), Freu (1987: 124).

Tudhaliya had a further cause for complaint. Madduwatta had been all too eager to lead his forces against the king of Arzawa. But he failed to take any action at all in support of the Hittite forces when his old enemy Attarsiya invaded Hittite territory with the prime object of capturing him and killing him:

> Subsequently Attarsiya, the Man of Ahhiya, came and sought to kill you, Madduwatta. But when the father of My Sun heard of this, he dispatched Kisnapili, troops, and chariots to do battle against Attarsiya. And you, Madduwatta, offered no resistance to Attarsiya, and fled before him. (*Indictment* §12, obv. 60–2)

Attarsiya's troops were repulsed by the Hittite commander Kisnapili, although a Hittite officer Zidanza was killed in the conflict. Once more Madduwatta was restored to his vassal throne, in spite of his failure to make any attempt to defend his own territory.

Tudhaliya must now have realized that his vassal could not be relied upon to honour his obligations in the region where he had been installed. For it seems that Kisnapili and his troops were ordered to remain there, probably with the intention of exercising some degree of vigilance and control over the region, and keeping a close eye on Madduwatta. The vassal ruler was clearly embarrassed by the Hittite presence. So he contrived to remove it.

An opportunity presented itself when two cities, Dalawa and Hinduwa, which were at least nominally subject to the Hittite king, decided to rebel.[40] Madduwatta wrote to Kisnapili suggesting that he and the Hittite commander lead a two-pronged attack on the rebellious cities; Madduwatta himself would attack Dalawa, and Kisnapili Hinduwa, thus preventing the rebels from joining forces.[41] The vassal's treachery soon became apparent. He marched his troops to Dalawa, but instead of attacking the Dalawans, he persuaded them to join forces with him, then link up with the people of Hinduwa for a combined attack on Kisnapili's army. Unaware of this, Kisnapili led his troops against Hinduwa. His

---

[40] They probably belonged to the Lukka Lands. While the Hittites exercised little direct authority in the west in this period, Tudhaliya seems to have claimed some degree of control over a number of the smaller communities in the region, perhaps in the aftermath of his western campaigns. But this may have required no more than annual payments of tribute to the king, as indicated in §24 of the *Indictment*.

[41] *Indictment* §13.

army was ambushed by Madduwatta, joined by troops from Dalawa, and the Hittite commander and his assistant Partahulla were killed.

Amazingly, Tudhaliya seems not to have retaliated, which encouraged Madduwatta to take yet another step in violation of his allegiance to his overlord. He now concluded a peace with his erstwhile enemy the Arzawan king Kupanta-Kurunta. The peace was cemented by a marriage alliance with the king's daughter.[42] Yet once more Madduwatta had breached the oath he had sworn to Tudhaliya. Yet once more Tudhaliya protested. Madduwatta replied that what he was doing was all part of a trick to win the confidence of the Arzawan king, and then to kill him. Was the Hittite king prepared to trust him, yet again? Unfortunately we do not know what his response was because of the fragmentary state of the text at this point. The end of the obverse side of the tablet and the beginning of the reverse are lost.

Yet when the text resumes, we find Tudhaliya apparently making further concessions to his vassal and drawing up a fresh contract with him. Perhaps he accepted the claim that the alliance with Arzawa was merely a means to an end—a means of gaining Kupanta-Kurunta's confidence and then disposing of him. If so, he may have tolerated this further violation by Madduwatta of his terms of vassalhood in the hope that it would result in the removal of one of the Hittites' most formidable enemies in the west without any direct involvement from Hattusa. We should be careful not to be taken in too readily by the ostensibly plaintive, self righteous tone that characterizes much of Hittite diplomatic correspondence. Many of the Hittite kings were well skilled in the art of *Realpolitik*—a quality which may be obscured by the bland, moralizing tone of their written communications.

On the other hand, the Hittites faced in Madduwatta an expert in the art of political manipulation. While the vassal ruler had clearly given the impression that his negotiations with Kupanta-Kurunta were intended to serve Hittite interests, his ulterior motive became evident when he gained control of Arzawa, probably through a combination of force and diplomacy, and added it to his own expanding kingdom. He could still reckon on avoiding military action against him by the Hittite king. Even if Tudhaliya was becoming

[42] *Indictment* §16.

increasingly alarmed at the turn events were taking near the south-western frontiers of his kingdom, Madduwatta still maintained at least the token image of a local ruler who acknowledged Hittite overlordship.

Even so, with every additional step he took, he risked pushing the Hittite king beyond the limits of tolerance. He came very close to doing so in his actions over Hapalla. The kingdom of Hapalla, one of the countries belonging to the Arzawa complex, became openly hostile to Hatti, and Madduwatta whose kingdom lay close by was called upon to pacify it on behalf of the Hittite king, now Arnuwanda. After some initial delay, Madduwatta launched an attack on Hapalla. He conquered it and added it to his own kingdom,[43] following up his success with military conquests in the Lukka lands.[44] On his return from these lands, he set his sights on the Land of Pitassa, where he succeeded in winning the elders away from their Hittite allegiance.[45]

By these actions Madduwatta was now making serious inroads into the south-western territories of the Hittite kingdom. A military showdown seemed close at hand. Arnuwanda dispatched an envoy to Madduwatta, demanding the return of the conquered lands: 'The Land of Hapalla is a land belonging to My Sun. Why have you taken it? Give it back to me now!' (*Indictment* §29, rev. 56). Madduwatta agreed to return Hapalla, but refused to relinquish his other conquests, or to hand back to the king political refugees from Hittite authority.

Finally, with much of south-western Anatolia under his control, he turned his attention to Alasiya, the island of Cyprus (or part thereof). He launched an expedition against the island, presumably using ships provided by the Lukka communities which had recently come under his control. The Lukka people had a substantial seagoing capacity, and in later times we hear of raids by Lukka ships on the coasts of both Alasiya and Egypt. The Alasiyan campaign seems to have been conducted in collaboration with Attarsiya, Madduwatta's long-standing enemy. A reconciliation must have taken place—probably after Madduwatta had achieved the status of an important and quasi-independent ruler in south-western Anatolia. Attarsiya might well have decided that such a man was now worth cultivating!

---

[43] *Indictment* §22.   [44] Ibid. §24.   [45] Ibid. §26.

With the apparent assistance of Attarsiya, Madduwatta conquered Alasiya. There was the predictable storm of protest from
Hattusa—and a disarming response from Madduwatta:

'The Land of Alasiya is a Land of My Sun and brings him tribute. Why
have you taken it?' But Madduwatta spoke thus: 'The Land of Alasiya was
afflicted by Attarsiya and the Man of Piggaya. But the father of My Sun did
not subsequently write to me, the father of My Sun never signified to me,
"The Land of Alasiya is mine. Leave it so!" If now My Sun demands
back the prisoners taken from Alasiya, I will give them back to him.'
(*Indictment* §36, rev. 85–9)

Hittite Policy towards the West

While we must make some allowance for bias and distortion, the
so-called *Indictment of Madduwatta* provides us with a number of
important insights into the the state of affairs in western Anatolia
during the reigns of Tudhaliya and Arnuwanda. In the aftermath of
his military conquests in the west, Tudhaliya made little attempt to
establish political control over the region. Most of the western
Anatolian countries retained their independence, with the apparent exception of Hapalla which lay close to the Hittite Lower Land,
and a number of communities which seem to have had the status of
token Hittite subjects. Rather than commit Hittite expeditionary
forces to continuing and ultimately inconclusive campaigns in
the west, at the expense of adequate defence of the northern and
eastern frontiers of the homeland, Tudhaliya's policy was to
strengthen and extend the frontier region which lay between the
western Anatolian countries and the homeland's south-western
frontiers. The installation of Madduwatta in the newly created
vassal state of Zippasla-Siyanti River Land was probably an important element in this policy.

We should be careful not to confuse the Hittites' reluctance to
engage more directly in western Anatolian affairs, as illustrated
repeatedly in the Madduwatta letter, with weakness and ineffectu-
ality. Their concern in the west was limited almost entirely to the
protection of the south-west frontiers, with as little involvement
and expenditure of resources as possible. On this understanding
they could well have found it politically expedient to connive at,
and in some cases tacitly approve, the activities of an enterprising
vassal ruler in the frontier zone, even conceding to him territories

which may have had a minimal attachment, but no great strategic or material importance, to Hatti.

In assessing the events recorded in the *Indictment*, we must remember that the document is written entirely from the Hittite viewpoint. One of its clear intentions was to represent its author and his father as committed to the maintenance of peace and stability, of order and right conduct, in the regions to which their influence extended. Yet in contrasting their own conduct with that of Madduwatta, the document unintentionally and to some extent misleadingly shows them up in a poor light—two apparently weak and gullible kings who were constantly deceived and outman-œuvred by a clever and unscrupulous vassal. It is this which has led one scholar to comment that under Arnuwanda Hittite power in the west did not count for anything.[46] Yet Madduwatta was probably not so treacherous as the letter makes out, nor his overlords so indulgent or so inept. There are innumerable instances in history where a ruler officially protests violations of agreements, unprovoked aggression by a second party against a third, while quietly condoning and perhaps even supporting such action if it is in his interests to do so.

Arguably, Madduwatta believed that the agreement he had made with his Hittite overlord gave him some freedom to pursue his own territorial ambitions in the west, provided he did not violate territory claimed by the Hittites.[47] In cases where this was in dispute, he seemed ready to hand back territories he had conquered if the Hittite king declared sovereignty over them, as in the case of Hapalla, and probably also Alasiya. He did however retain his hold upon territories over which the Hittites could make no justifiable claim. Thus Madduwatta may have been less treacherous and Machiavellian than his Hittite overlords would lead us to believe. His actions may in part at least reflect some ambiguities in the agreement he made with them as to what initiatives he could exercise without reference to Hattusa. Perhaps in the light of this experience later kings made sure that the rights and powers of vassal rulers were very clearly stated, and very clearly circumscribed, in the treaties they drew up with them.

The early New Kingdom rulers took a pragmatic view of Hittite involvement in western Anatolia. The region consisted of a large,

---

[46] Mellaart (1974: 503).	[47] Cf. Liverani (1990: 76–7).

heterogeneous complex of states and communities which differed markedly in their size, general character, and political organization. Even if the Hittites had sufficient human resources to establish effective control over at least the most important states in the region, without placing the homeland at risk from the enemies lying to the north and the south-east of its frontiers, they lacked the administrative capabilities necessary for organizing such a large unwieldy complex into a coherent manageable administrative structure. Given this, and the extent of Hittite involvement in the regions lying to the north, east, and south-east of the homeland, it is likely that in the early New Kingdom the Hittites intentionally confined their involvement in western Anatolian affairs to occasional military operations in the region. These were undertaken only in response to perceived military threats to Hittite territory. The most Tudhaliya could expect from his western conquests was that they would keep the region in a subdued state for long enough periods to enable him to concentrate his military resources in other regions more important to the interests of his kingdom.

Developments in Syria

The end of Tuthmosis III's Syrian campaigns and Hittite preoccupation with affairs in Anatolia provided a clear opportunity for the kingdom of Mitanni, now ruled by Saustatar I, to reassert its control over the countries of northern Syria. But before it embarked upon this task, there had to be a reckoning with Assyria. Apprehensive of the growing territorial ambitions of its powerful neighbour, Assyria had established diplomatic relations with Egypt.[48] By so doing it had become an enemy of Mitanni. With the threat of a direct offensive by Egyptian forces against Mitannian territory now virtually at an end, Saustatar felt confident enough to launch an invasion into Assyria. He struck at the Assyrian capital Assur, sacking and looting the city. Amongst the booty was a door of silver and gold, which he carried back as a trophy for his palace in Wassuganni, the capital of his kingdom.[49] With Mitannian

---

[48] See Wilhelm (1989: 26).
[49] As indicated in the treaty concluded many years later between the Hittite king Suppiluliuma I and Sattiwaza of Mitanni, this was subsequently returned to the Assyrians by the Mitannian king Suttatara (Suttarna) III, son of Artatama, during Suppiluliuma's reign; KBo I 3 (*CTH* 52) = *PD* no. 2, 38–9, obv. 8–10.

overlordship firmly established over Assyria, Saustatar then crossed the Euphrates, and swept all before him as he advanced to the Mediterranean coast. Mitannian overlordship was once more established over the north Syrian states where Saustatar's predecessor Parattarna had held sway. Alalah at that time (Alalah IV) was ruled by Niqmepa, son of Idrimi, and incorporated the former royal capital of Aleppo.

Once these territories were firmly under Mitannian control, Saustatar could turn his attention to the regions lying to the south. It may be that at this time he established an alliance with the king of Kadesh, forming a kind of Mitanni–Kadesh axis, with the latter controlling Syrian territory south of Alalah.[50] The scene was now set for a Hittite–Mitannian conflict in a Syrian theatre of war.

The Sunassura Treaty

If a Hittite challenge to Mitannian overlordship in Syria was to have any chance of success, Tudhaliya had first to reach a settlement with Kizzuwadna. As in the past control of Kizzuwadna, or at least a guarantee of benevolent neutrality from its king, was essential to the success of further Hittite campaigns in Syria[51]—to ensure unimpeded passage for a Hittite expeditionary force through Kizzuwadnan territory into Syria, and once it had arrived there freedom from the risk of being harrassed in its rear by a pro-Mitannian state in south-east Anatolia. This, very likely, provided the context of the treaty, surviving in fragmentary Akkadian and Hittite versions, which Tudhaliya drew up with the Kizzuwadnan king Sunassura.[52]

From the introduction to the Akkadian version of the treaty we learn that in the days of the Hittite king's grandfather[53]

[50] See Na'aman (1974: 270–2).
[51] Cf. Wilhelm (1988: 367–8), Freu (1992: 47).
[52] *CTH* 41. For the Akkadian version, see *PD* no. 7, 88–111, Goetze (1940: 36–9 (introduction only)). I follow Beal (1986: 432–5) in assigning all treaty fragments associated with the name Sunassura to the one treaty and making Tudhaliya, rather than Suppiluliuma I as hitherto commonly assumed, his treaty partner; cf. Wilhelm (1988: 368). For a recent contrary view, see Freu (1992: 49).
[53] i.e. Huzziya II if, as suggested above, Tudhaliya was the son of Himuili and the latter was the son of Huzziya. The statement in the first line of the Sunassura treaty that in the time of the author's grandfather Kizzuwadna was aligned with Hatti suggests that it did not switch to a Mitannian alliance until at least part way through Huzziya's reign. See also next footnote.

Kizzuwadna was on the side of Hatti;[54] but subsequently it was lost to the Hittites and reverted to an alliance with Mitanni.[55] Now it had again returned to the Hittite fold, in spite of the protests from the Mitannian king. Tudhaliya trumpeted this fact in the treaty, depicting himself as Kizzuwadna's liberator from Mitannian despotism:

Now the people of the Land of Kizzuwadna are Hittite cattle and chose their stable. From the Hurrian they separated and shifted allegiance to My Sun. The Hurrian sinned against the Land of Hatti, but against the Land of Kizzuwadna he sinned particularly. The Land of Kizzuwadna rejoices very much indeed over its liberation. Now the Land of Hatti and the Land of Kizzuwadna are free from their obligations. Now I, My Sun, have restored the Land of Kizzuwadna to its independence. (KBo 1 5 1 30–7, adapted from trans. by Goetze (1940: 39))

From this time on, Kizzuwadna was to remain firmly attached to Hatti. Indeed, at some undetermined point following the treaty, it was annexed to Hittite territory and placed under direct Hittite rule. This may in fact have happened while Tudhaliya still occupied the throne.[56] At all events with Tudhaliya's conclusion of an alliance with Sunassura, the way to Syria now lay open before him.[57]

Return to Syria

Details of the Hittites' new Syrian enterprise are sketchy. But it seems that Tudhaliya sought to follow in the footsteps of Hattusili I and Mursili I by making Aleppo his prime objective. This information comes from the historical preamble of a treaty drawn

[54] It is not clear from the relevant words of the text (KBo 1 5 obv. 5–6) whether Kizzuwadna had become part of the Land of Hatti or its ally. Goetze (1940: 37) adopts the first interpretation, Beal's translation 'Kizzuwadna was (on the side) of Hatti' (1986: 433), implies the second. Wilhelm (1988: 368) simply translates: 'Kizzuwatna das des Landes Hatti geworden (*sic*).' The alliance attested in the treaty between Huzziya's predecessor Zidanta II and the Kizzuwadnan King Pilliya may still have been in force during at least the first part of Huzziya's reign.
[55] Reflected in Pilliya's treaty with the Mitannian vassal Idrimi (see Ch. 5).
[56] Thus Beal (1986: 439–40), who tentatively suggests that a fragmentary passage from Arnuwanda's *Annals* (KUB XXIII 21, obv. 2–11) may describe the annexation; cf. Freu (1992: 47).
[57] In the list of Kizzuwadnan kings, provision has to be made for a king called Talzu, known from a land-grant document, KUB XL 2 (*CTH* 641); see Goetze (1940: 60–1). It is uncertain where he should be located in the list, although he was probably the predecessor, or a predecessor, of Sunassura. See Beal (1986: 445), Freu (1992: 51).

up more than a century later by the Hittite king Muwatalli II with Talmi-Sarruma, vassal ruler of Aleppo:[58]

Formerly, the kings of the Land of Aleppo possessed the great kingship. But Hattusili (I), the Great King, the king of the Land of Hatti made full (the days of) their kingdom.[59] After Hattusili, the king of the Land of Hatti, Mursili, the Great King, grandson of Hattusili, the Great King, destroyed the kingship of the Land of Aleppo and the Land of Aleppo. When Tudhaliya, the Great King, occupied the royal throne, the king of the Land of Aleppo made peace with him. (KBo i 6, obv. 11–16)

This last statement makes it clear that under Tudhaliya the Hittites had once more become a major force in Near Eastern affairs, and a serious threat to Mitannian overlordship in Syria. The position of the man called king of Aleppo[60] was an unenviable one. Caught in the contest between two major powers for the domination of Syria, his allegiance to one would almost certainly mean reprisals from the other. In the event, he first made peace with Hatti. But then, no doubt through pressure from the Mitannian king Saustatar, he switched his allegiance back to Mitanni (called Hanigalbat in the text). Reprisals from Hatti quickly followed:

The king of the Land of Aleppo turned and made peace with the king of Hanigalbat. Because of this he (Tudhaliya) destroyed the king of Hanigalbat and the king of Aleppo together with their lands, and he razed the city of Aleppo. (KBo i 6, obv. 16–18, adapted from transl. by Na'aman (1980: 36))

If we can accept this statement at face value, Tudhaliya's military achievement was far-reaching indeed, for it included not only the conquest of Aleppo, but extended also to the conquest of Mitanni. But almost certainly the extent of the Hittite success, particularly against Mitanni, has been exaggerated. In spite of its alleged destruction, the kingdom of Mitanni continued to exercise overlordship in northern Syria for many years to come.[61]

---

[58] KBo i 6 (*CTH* 75) = *PD* no. 6, 82–5; Goetze (1928–9). See also Klengel (1964*a*; 1965*b*: 177–8, 183–5), Beal (1986: 441). For a revised version of obv. 19–32, see Na'aman (1980). The treaty originally drawn up by Mursili II was lost, and was subsequently reissued by his son Muwatalli; see Beckman (1996: 88).

[59] As suggested in Ch. 4, this strange expression probably means that Hattusili substantially weakened (rather than brought to an end) the kingdom of Aleppo.

[60] Presumably Niqmepa, son of Idrimi, whose kingdom of Alalah included the former royal seat Aleppo.

[61] Cf. Klengel (1992: 347).

There follows a rather confused and repetitious passage which refers to the transfer on two occasions of towns and districts from the kingdom of Aleppo to the neighbouring kingdoms of Nuhasse and Astata. Presumably these towns and districts lay within the border regions which the kingdom of Aleppo shared with Nuhasse to the south, and with Astata which lay on the west bank of the Euphrates. Nuhasse and Astata had apparently first appealed to the king of Mitanni to reassign to them the territories they had requested. He had done so by way of punitive action against Aleppo for an 'offence' it had committed against him.[62] Subsequently, we are told, the people of Aleppo likewise committed an offence against a man called Hattusili, identified as king of Hatti. We shall say a little more about him below. Once again the people of Astata and Nuhasse appealed, this time to Hattusili, requesting that towns and districts belonging to Aleppo be transferred to them. Once again their request was granted.[63] If the disputed territories were the same in both cases, then presumably Aleppo had reacquired them, only to lose them again when the second appeal was made to Hattusili.

We shall not attempt to sort out here all the details of what actually happened. But we might refer briefly to the king called Hattusili, to whom Astata and Nuhasse had addressed their appeals. Scholars have long debated the identity and historicity of this king, who has been described as 'the most phantomatic of all the dubious Hittite kings', 'an extraordinarily elusive character'.[64] He apparently did not appear in the royal offering lists, nor is his existence firmly attested in any other sources. Various attempts have been made to explain the reference to him in the 'Aleppo treaty'. Most of them can be rejected.[65] We do have references to a

---

[62] The nature of this offence and subsequently the offence committed by Aleppo against the Hittite king, is not made clear in the text. No satisfactory explanation has been found by modern scholars.

[63] KBo 1 6 obv. 19–33. The interpretation followed here of the relevant passage from the text is that of Na'aman (1980). It should, however, be noted that both the reading and interpretation of this passage are problematical. A different rendering is given by Astour (1989: 39).

[64] Astour (1989: 39, 41).

[65] Note the extensive list of proposals cited by Astour (1989: 40–1). To these we can add Carruba's suggestion (1990: 552–3) that Hattusili may be identical with Kantuzzili, one of the assassins of Muwatalli I. Otten's proposal (1968, 17–18) that the document refers here in flashback to Hattusili I was refuted by Güterbock (1970: 74) but is still supported by Astour. The main grounds for rejecting Otten's proposal

Hattusili who was a member of the royal court at this time,[66] and who may have been the same man as the Hattusili who held the prestigious office of GAL GEŠTIN (Chief of the Wine Stewards) and served as a military commander in the Kaska region.[67] But as yet we lack conclusive proof that any of these references are to a king of that name. Even if there were such a king, he may have reigned only very briefly, perhaps only as a co-regent of Arnuwanda after the latter's accession as sole ruler? If so, then the events associated with him in the Aleppo treaty must have occurred some time after Tudhaliya's death.

But all this is speculative. Additional evidence will need to be produced before further light can be shed on this problem.

Arnuwanda's Sole Rule

On his death, Tudhaliya left in the hands of his co-regent Arnuwanda a vast expanse of subject territory stretching from south-western Anatolia to upper Mesopotamia. Yet the power structure which Tudhaliya had built up remained a fragile one. In the south-west Madduwatta had demonstrated the comparative ease with which an ambitious vassal could defy his Hittite over-lords, exposing time and again the tenuous nature of Hittite authority in the region. In the south-east, Tudhaliya's military successes against Mitanni and Aleppo amounted to little more than an opening move in the protracted struggle between Hatti and Mitanni for the domination of Syria. And in the north, the agreements concluded with the Kaska peoples were at best short-term

were that references to Astata and Nuhasse during the reign of Hattusili I would be anachronistic. But as Astour (1972: 103–7; 1989: 45) has pointed out, both were clearly in existence at that time. The point at issue is whether their role was significant enough already in the Old Babylonian period (contemporaneous with the reign of Hattusili I) to be compatible with the references to them in the Aleppo treaty (thus Na'aman (1980: 39)).

[66] KBo XXXII 145, KBo XXXII 224, cited and discussed by Klinger (1995: 89–90), who comments that both texts indicate the existence of a Hattusili at the royal court in this period, but provide no clear evidence that he was a king. See also Klinger's discussion of KUB XXXVI 109 (*CTH* 275), ed. Carruba (1977*b*: 190–1), which also dates to this period and mentions a Hattusili, again without any clear indication of his precise status.

[67] This appears in a 'Sammeltafel', KUB XXVI 71 (*CTH* 1) IV rev. 10', which also contains the Anitta inscription and fragments from the *Annals* of Ammuna(?). See Beal (1992*b*: 347), Klinger (1995: 90).

expedients which could not be relied upon to give lasting security to the northern parts of the kingdom.

Indeed several prayers uttered in the names of Arnuwanda and his queen Asmunikal vividly illustrate the deteriorating situation in the north where a number of Hittite cult centres were destroyed by the Kaska people:

In the Land of Nerik, in Hursama, in the Land of Kastama, in the Land of Serisa, in the Land of Himuwa, in the Land of Taggasta, in the Land of Kammama (etc.)—the temples which you, the gods, possessed in these lands the Kaskans sacked them. They smashed the images of you, the gods. They plundered silver and gold, rhyta and cups of silver and gold, and of copper, your implements of bronze and your garments; they shared out these things amongst themselves. They scattered the priests and the holy priests, the mothers-of-god, the anointed, the musicians, the singers, the cooks, the bakers, the ploughmen and the gardeners and made them their slaves . . . Thus it has come about that in those lands no one invokes the names of you, the gods, any more; no-one presents to you the sacrifices due to you daily, monthly, and annually; no one celebrates your festivals and pageants. (Extracts from *CTH* 375, adapted from trans. by Goetze in Pritchard (1969: 399)

Arnuwanda made what efforts he could to stabilize the most vulnerable parts of his realm, including in the north a series of treaties or agreements with the Kaska people,[68] and pacts with military commanders stationed in the regions of Kinnara, Kalasma, Kissiya, and Sappa who swore to maintain the security of their regions.[69] In the south, a treaty was drawn up with the city of Ura on the Cilician coast.[70] All these texts point to a climate of growing unrest and disorder in the territories around the homeland, and the need for strong and comprehensive measures to combat this.[71]

Faced with such problems, Arnuwanda seems to have made numerous attempts to assert the image of a strong ruler who would not tolerate defiance of his authority. A specific example is provided by the action he took against Mita, a Hittite vassal of the city of Pahhuwa situated near the upper Euphrates.[72] Mita had married the daughter of a declared enemy of Arnuwanda, a man called

---

[68] *CTH* 137–40.
[69] *CTH* 260, ed. von Schuler (1956: 223–33).
[70] KUB xxvi 29 + xxxi 55 (*CTH* 144). See Klengel (1965*a*: 226–8) for the text; Houwink ten Cate (1970: 68), Gurney (1973*b*: 679).
[71] Cf. Houwink ten Cate (1970: 68).
[72] On its location, see Gurney (1992: 214).

Usapa: 'And he came back to Pahhuwa and violated the oaths . . .
and even against My Sun and against the Land of Hatti he
sinned . . . and he took the daughter of the enemy Usapa for his
wife' (KUB xxiii 72 (+) (*CTH* 146) obv. 14–16, trans. Gurney
(1948: 34)).

Further acts of disloyalty followed. These could not safely be
ignored. Exemplary action was called for. Arnuwanda promptly
convened an assembly of delegates from Pahhuwa, Suhma, the
Land of H[urri], Maltiya, Pittiyarik. He outlined Mita's misdeeds to
the delegates, and then informed them that he had sent an ultimatum to the city of Pahhuwa, demanding Mita's extradition along
with his family and all his goods, and holding that city responsible
for the future good behaviour of its citizens. Should Pahhuwa fail to
abide by this ultimatum, the cities represented at the assembly
were instructed through their delegates to take immediate punitive
action, until such time as the Hittite army arrived:

And on the day when you hear a word of disloyalty among the people of
Pahhuwa, on that day you must march [to Pahhuwa(?)] and smite
Pahhuwa, chastise it thoroughly, until My Sun's army arrives. Stain your
hands immediately with the blood of the people of Pahhuwa! Whoever
does not stain his hands with the blood of the people of Pahhuwa—I, My
Sun, shall not march directly against Pahhuwa(?), but against that man I
will proceed immediately, (and) I will straightway kill him, and so I will
march on to battle against Pahhuwa.   (KUB xxiii 72 (+) rev. 27–31, trans.
Gurney (1948: 37))

The document which records Mita's misdeeds bears some similarity to the *Indictment of Madduwatta*. In the absence of any
known outcome, one wonders whether Arnuwanda's action on this
occasion proved any more successful. It may well be that Mita's
disloyalty was encouraged by Mitanni, now determined to assert
vigorously its claim to be the supreme political and military power
in the Near East.

Mitanni and Egypt come to Terms

We do not know what became of the Mitannian king Saustatar
following Tudhaliya's conquests in Syria. But an independent
Mitannian kingdom certainly continued to exist, even if part of its
territory was for a time subject to Hittite rule. With Arnuwanda

diverted by the formidable task of trying to maintain his authority in his subject territories, the time was opportune for Mitanni to emerge once more, phoenix-like, from the ashes of its defeat. A new Mitannian king Artatama had now occupied the throne, the successor and probably the son of Saustatar. Under his leadership, Mitanni sought to regain what it had ignominiously lost to the Hittites, and to stake once again its claim to overlordship over its former subject states in Syria.

But there were dangers in moving too quickly. Hatti was far from a spent force in the region, particularly while Kizzuwadna still lay under its control. Egypt might also prove problematical. Although its influence in Syria had declined substantially since the campaigns of Tuthmosis III, it retained an active interest in the region, as illustrated by a campaign in Syria during Tuthmosis IV's reign.[73] And Mitanni and Egypt were still enemies. Artatama could not risk the prospect of war on two fronts—with the Hittites in the west and the Egyptians in the south. But an alliance with Egypt was a possibility if an agreement could be negotiated with the pharaoh over a division of territories in Syria. This might satisfy the territorial ambitions of both powers, as well as providing the basis of an alliance against a future threat to either of them from Hatti.

Artatama made overtures along these lines initially to Tuthmosis' father and predecessor Amenhotep II.[74] A period of diplomatic parleying began, with much toing and froing of envoys from either side. It continued without resolution into the early years of Tuthmosis' reign. The Egyptians haggled, apparently, over the terms of a formal peace, and came up with alternative conditions to those proposed by Artatama. No doubt they were suspicious of the Mitannian king's ultimate intentions. Perhaps as a test of his good faith, they requested that as part of a final agreement he send his daughter to Egypt to become the wife of the new pharaoh. For reasons unknown to us, Artatama was reluctant to agree to the request. It was only after it had been made seven times that he finally consented:

When [   ],[75] the father of Nimmureya,[76] wrote to Artatama, my grandfather, he asked for the daughter of my grandfather, the sister of my father.

---

[73] Helck (1961: 147).   [74] See Helck (1971: 163).
[75] Presumably the prenomen of Tuthmosis IV appeared here.
[76] i.e. Amenhotep III.

He wrote five, six times, but Artatama did not give her. When he wrote to my grandfather seven times, then only under such pressure did he give her. (Letter from Tusratta to Akhenaten, *EA* 29, 16ff., trans. Moran (1992: 93))

The marriage alliance paved the way for a formal treaty. A common frontier in Syria was established, which gave Egypt control northwards to Kadesh and to Amurru and Ugarit along the coast. All territory beyond that was conceded to Mitanni. For the time being this treaty effectively ended any prospect of further Hittite intervention in Syria.

Crisis in the Homeland

This was the situation confronting the new king Tudhaliya III, son of Arnuwanda and Asmunikal,[77] and the designated *tuḫkanti* during his father's reign.[78] But as events were to prove, the Mitannian–Egyptian alliance in Syria which blocked the reassertion of Hittite authority in the region was the least of the new king's problems. Far more serious were the problems in Anatolia, which ultimately presented the kingdom with the gravest crisis it was to face before its final collapse some two centuries later.

At some undetermined time during Tudhaliya's reign, enemies swept through the peripheral subject territories of the Hittite kingdom, and invaded and sacked the homeland. Hattusa itself was captured, and burned to the ground. We learn of this crisis from the historical preamble to a decree of the thirteenth-century king Hattusili III:

In earlier days the Hatti lands were sacked by its enemies. The Kaskan enemy came and sacked the Hatti lands and he made Nenassa his frontier. From the Lower Land[79] came the Arzawan enemy, and he too sacked the Hatti lands, and he made Tuwanuwa and Uda his frontier. From afar, the Arawannan enemy came and sacked the whole of the Land of Gassiya. From afar, the Azzian enemy came and sacked all the Upper Lands and he made Samuha his frontier. The Isuwan enemy came and sacked the Land

---

[77] His Hurrian name was Tasmisarri; see Haas (1984: 7–8; 1985: 272).

[78] See Gurney (1979*b*), Alp (1980: 53–9), Beal (1983: 116). The term *tuḫkanti* is discussed below. On Tudhaliya's accession as Arnuwanda's successor, see the colophon to the *šarašši* ritual, *CTH* 700, cited by Gurney (1979*b*: 215).

[79] In place of Goetze's '*Towards* the Lower Land'; see Heinhold-Krahmer (1977: 48–50).

of Tegarama. From afar, the Armatanan enemy came, and he too sacked the Hatti lands. And he made Kizzuwadna, the city, his frontier. And Hattusa, the city, was burned down.   (KBo VI 28 (*CTH* 88), obv. 6–15, adapted from trans. by Goetze (1940: 21–2))

The impression this text gives is of a systematic and comprehensive destruction of the Hittite homeland and its neighbouring subject territories. This would seem to indicate some degree of co-ordination between the invading forces. But it is hard to imagine how such co-ordination could have been organized, given the distances separating the forces involved and their widely disparate character. More likely, a massive invasion from one direction, perhaps initially by the Kaska people, led to a hasty concentration of Hittite forces in this region, which exposed the Hatti lands to a further invasion from a different direction. The Kaskans swept through the homeland from the north as far as Nenassa on the southern bend of the Marrassantiya river, and were no doubt responsible for the destruction of Hattusa. In the south-west forces from Arzawa, which had almost certainly been building their strength even before the end of Arnuwanda's reign, were poised to invade the southern frontiers of Hittite territory, choosing the time when defence of this area was at its weakest. They swept through the Hittite Lower Land, and established their frontier at Tuwanuwa (Classical Tyana) and Uda (Hyde).

To judge from our text, Hittite territory was thoroughly devastated by the enemy invaders, and left in total ruin. But if this were literally true, there would have been virtually nothing left of the kingdom at all. We know that this could not have been so, for the king and the royal court survived, along with a sufficient fighting force to begin the task of winning back the lost territories within a few years of the kingdom's darkest days. Very likely our text has telescoped the events it records, giving the impression that a series of incursions which may have taken place over a period of years were in fact a massive simultaneous onslaught on the homeland from all directions. As the invading forces gathered, there was sufficient time for Tudhaliya to make plans for the abandonment of the capital and the re-establishment of his court in a location that provided at least temporary safe haven. Unfortunately no record of this event has survived. But it must have involved a logistical operation of major proportions, performed under conditions of great duress and danger.

Where did the king and his retinue go? The city of Samuha, an important cult centre located probably on the upper course of the Marrassantiya river,[80] was subsequently used as the Hittite base of operations in the reconquest of Anatolia. Was this where Tudhaliya set up his royal court after abandoning Hattusa? Samuha lay outside the main invasion path of the Kaska people in their advance through the homeland, although it too seems to have been captured by enemy forces from the country of Azzi. It may, however, have been the first major city to be recaptured by the Hittites, thus providing a temporary home for the royal court and a base for the regrouping of the Hittite army.[81]

But for the time being, with the Hittite kingdom close to total collapse, Arzawa seemed likely to become dominant in Anatolia. Indeed this was the perception of the pharaoh Amenhotep III, son and successor of Tuthmosis IV, who made diplomatic overtures to the Arzawan king Tarhundaradu. From two letters in the Amarna archive, we learn that Amenhotep had approached Tarhundaradu seeking a daughter of his in marriage, as a basis for an alliance between Egypt and Arzawa.[82] Clearly, he believed that the Hittites were a force now spent, remarking to Tarhundaradu: 'I have heard that everything is finished, and that the country Hattusa is paralysed' (*EA* 31, 26–7, adapted from trans. by Haas in Moran (1992: 101)[83]). The time seemed opportune for Amenhotep to establish peace with the Arzawan king, no doubt with the hope that this would further bolster Egypt's position as a major power in the Near East.

---

[80] Thus Forlanini (1979: 181), *contra* Güterbock (1961: 96), who prefers a location on the Euphrates.

[81] Cf. Haas (1985: 271), Wilhelm (1989: 32).

[82] *EA* 31, 32. These letters were written in the Nesite (i.e. 'Hittite') language, which may indicate that the international diplomatic language Akkadian was unknown to Arzawan scribes.

[83] On this statement, see also Güterbock (1976b: 145). A diametrically different rendering has been proposed by Starke (1981b), based on an earlier suggestion by Cavaignac: 'I have heard all that you said. And also the land of Hattusa is at peace.' On the latter, Moran (1992: 102–3 n. 8) comments: 'This ingenious interpretation is based on an Egyptian parallel(?), but if one takes into consideration the historical implications, it falls short of conviction.' See also Hagenbuchner (1989, 362–3). Freu, however (1992: 46–7), argues that Starke's interpretation would be compatible with the political situation in Anatolia if the correspondence between Egypt and Arzawa took place *after* Suppiluliuma had acceded to the throne and stabilized the situation *vis-à-vis* Arzawa. This argument is valid only if Suppiluliuma's accession occurred while Amenhotep III was still pharaoh.

But the approach to Tarhundaradu was premature. The Arzawan king failed, or made no attempt, to capitalize on the Arzawan military successes by asserting a claim over the former homeland territories of the Hittite kingdom. It would have been no easy task. He had established control up to the northern frontiers of the Lower Land, which brought him within striking distance of the Hittite homeland. But the homeland had already been occupied by the invaders from the Kaska region. No doubt they would have opposed any attempt by the Arzawan king to stake his own claim to the occupied territories north of the Marrassantiya.

Perhaps too the speed and the determination with which Tudhaliya set about regaining these territories took all the enemy forces by surprise.

Tudhaliya Fights Back

Fragmentary episodes of the Hittite reconquest of Anatolia are preserved for us in a document commonly known as the *Deeds of Suppiluliuma*.[84] It is a record of the military exploits of Tudhaliya's son and successor, Suppiluliuma I, composed by Suppiluliuma's own son and second successor Mursili II. The account begins before Suppiluliuma's accession with details of his father's campaigns in the northern and north-eastern regions of Anatolia.[85] Samuha provided the base for the Hittite military operations, which began with attacks against the enemies of Kaska and Azzi-Hayasa.

From Samuha, Tudhaliya embarked on the monumental task of winning back his kingdom from the enemy forces which had occupied his land, destroyed his capital, and virtually driven him into exile. That he was ultimately successful in doing so was a military achievement which must rank alongside those of his greatest

---

[84] *CTH* 40, ed. Güterbock (1956a).

[85] We might note in passing that in none of the surviving references to Suppiluliuma's father in the *Deeds* is the name of the father actually given. (A fragment originally assigned to the *Deeds* which mentions 'my grandfa[ther T]uthaliya' (p. 61, frag. 2) has now been removed; see Dinçol *et al.* (1993: 100, with refs.)). His identity was long debated. But he is now firmly identified with Tudhaliya III, on the basis of a tablet discovered in Maşat bearing the following seal impression: '[Seal of Suppilul]iuma, [the Great] King, King [of the land of Hatti, son of Tudhaliy]a, the Great King, the H[ero]' (Mşt 76/15 published by Alp (1980: Taf. 4 and Abb. 3), and described on pp. 56–7; however Hoffman (1984b: 45–8) has proposed a different solution). See also Otten (1993a: 10–13), in reference to the seal impression on the *bulla* Bo 491/1314.

predecessors—Hattusili, Mursili, and his namesake Tudhaliya. Not only did his victories re-establish Hittite control over the homeland and the subject territories lost to the Hittites; they also helped lay the foundations for the profound changes which were to occur in the political landscape of the Near East in the reign of his son and successor Suppiluliuma. Indeed we know from the *Deeds* that for many years before his accession, Suppiluliuma was his father's chief adviser, partner, and comrade-in-arms in the campaigns of reconquest. And while we should take nothing from Tudhaliya's own achievement, it was undoubtedly his partnership with his son, who was to prove the most brilliant of all Hittite military leaders, that helped ensure his ultimate success.

Fragmentary passages in the *Deeds* provide glimpses of the campaigns of reconquest. From Samuha, the Hittites launched repeated attacks on the Kaskan tribes, inflicting heavy casualties and bringing back many prisoners to their base. This was but the start of the Hittite recovery. Kaskan military strength had now been sufficiently weakened, or so Tudhaliya believed, for the Hittites to direct their operations against enemies in other regions. To the west of the homeland lay the countries of Kassiya and the Hulana River Land. These former subject territories of the Hittite kingdom had been occupied by troops from Arawanna during the general onslaught, and subsequently suffered repeated attacks by the countries of Masa and Kammala. Punitive action was swift and effective. Under the joint leadership of Tudhaliya and Suppiluliuma, the Hittite army 'liberated' the beleaguered countries, then invaded and laid waste the territory of their aggressors.[86] But Tudhaliya had little time to savour his victory, for once again there was a massing of Kaskan forces in the north, and once again the Hittites had to win back through force of arms territories they had but recently secured.

Accounts had also to be settled with another enemy in the region. To the north-east of the homeland lay the kingdom of Azzi-Hayasa, whose forces had joined in the attacks on Hittite territory, destroying the Upper Land (which as we have seen was an eastward extension of the Land of Hatti between the upper course of the Marrassantiya and the Euphrates) and advancing as far as Samuha. As the tide turned in the Hittites' favour, Suppiluliuma

---

[86] *DS* p. 65, frag. 13 E i 7 ff.

had led an expeditionary force against the enemy. They fled before him, and for a time avoided battle.[87] But finally a Hittite army under the joint leadership of Tudhaliya and Suppiluliuma invaded Azzi-Hayasa and forced a showdown with its king Karanni (or Lanni) near the city of Kummaha.[88] The passage recording the outcome of this battle is missing. But almost certainly the Hittite campaign resulted in the conquest of Azzi-Hayasa, for subsequently Suppiluliuma established it as a Hittite vassal state, drawing up a treaty with Hukkana, its current ruler.[89] In accordance with the terms of this treaty, the Hayasans were obliged to return to Suppiluliuma all Hittite subjects who had come into their territory, and also to hand back the border territory which Suppiluluma claimed belonged to the Land of Hatti.

One major enemy remained, the most dangerous of all the Hittites' opponents in Anatolia. The time had now come to deal with this enemy. Suppiluliuma sought the privilege of doing so: 'Thus (spoke) my father to my grandfather: "Oh my lord!(?) Against the Arzawan enemy send me!" So my grandfather sent my father(?) against the Arzawan enemy' (*DS* p. 68, frag. 14, 38'–40', adapted from trans. by Güterbock).

Prior to this, a successful Hittite attack had already been launched against the city of Sallapa, which lay at the junction of the main routes leading from Hatti and Syria into Arzawan territory.[90] Its destruction could well have served an important strategic purpose—to deprive the enemy forces of a base for marshalling additional troops from the Arzawa Lands against the threat of a Hittite counter-attack. Suppiluliuma's main objective now was to dislodge the enemy from the Lower Land, whose frontier lay close to the southern border of the Hittite homeland. Formerly Hittite subject territory, it was now under Arzawan occupation. So long as this occupation remained unchallenged, the homeland would never be secure.

In what may have been Suppiluliuma's first major clash with the Arzawan enemy in the Lower Land, 'The gods helped my father: the Sun Goddess of Arinna, the Storm God of Hatti, the Storm

---

[87] *DS* pp. 62–3, frag. 10.
[88] *DS* p. 66, frag. 13 D 40–4.
[89] *CTH* 42; Friedrich (1930: 103–63).
[90] *DS* p. 60, frag. 4. For the various locations proposed for Sallapa, see Gurney (1992: 220), who is inclined to favour Forlanini's proposal to put it at Classical Selma (Modern Gözören) or Selme in Lycaonia.

God of the Army, and Istar of the Battlefield, (so that) my father slew the Arzawan enemy. . . . . . and the enemy troops died in multitude' (*DS* p. 68, frag. 14, 43'–45', trans. Güterbock). The rhetoric of this passage probably disguises the strength of enemy resistance encountered by Suppiluliuma. For this was but one episode in a series of clashes between Hittite and Arzawan forces in the region.[91] The enemy was firmly entrenched there, and military operations against them may well have continued into Suppiluliuma's own reign.[92] As one group was defeated, others rose up and joined forces against the Hittite counter-offensive. We learn from the *Deeds* of clashes with the enemy around the city of Tuwanuwa, on the region's northernmost limits. The recapture of the city provided Suppiluliuma with a marshalling base for his troops and chariots. This perhaps paved the way for further attacks on the occupation forces, and their final expulsion from the entire region.

Even so, the Arzawans continued to threaten Hittite interests in the peripheral areas of the kingdom. This is illustrated by the activities of an Arzawan leader called Anzapahhaddu who refused a demand from Suppiluliuma for the return of Hittite subjects who had sought refuge with him. Suppiluliuma responded by sending an army into Arzawan territory under the command of Himuili to settle the matter by force of arms. Himuili suffered a humiliating defeat, and Suppiluliuma was obliged to take the field in person to enforce his demand.[93]

To prevent further Arzawan aggression against Hittite subject territory, Suppiluliuma (perhaps at a later stage in his own reign) installed one of his ablest military commanders Hannutti as governor of the Lower Land.

My father sent forth Hannutti, the Marshall, to the Lower Land, giving him troops and charioteers. When Hannutti had arrived in the Lower Land and the inhabitants of Lalanda saw him, they became frightened and made

---

[91] As indicated by *DS* pp. 75–7, frag. 15.

[92] We know that he continued campaigning in Anatolia throughout his reign, even during the period of his campaigns in Syria; see Bryce (1989*b*: 20).

[93] See Cancik (1976: 161–2) for a stylistic analysis of this passage from the *Deeds*. The actual status of Anzapahhaddu in the Arzawa lands is not clear. Was he one of a number of Arzawan chiefs or petty kings? Or was he perhaps the successor of Tarhundaradu (not mentioned in the surviving sections of the *Deeds*) who had been involved in negotiations with Amenhotep III? If the latter, then he may have been head of some form of Arzawan confederacy. Freu (1992: 46–7) suggests that he could have been one of the sons or vassals of Tarhundaradu.

peace. And they became again subjects of the Land of Hatti. (KUB xix 22 (*CTH* 40 vi. 52B), 4–8, adapted from trans. by Houwink ten Cate (1966: 28–9))[94]

When Hannutti had firmly reasserted Hittite authority in the region, he used it as a base for conducting military operations against neighbouring hostile lands, notably the Arzawan state of Hapalla:

However, Hannutti, the Marshall, went to the Land of Hapalla and attacked the Land of Hapalla. He burned down the Land of Hapalla, and removed it together with the population, the cattle and the sheep and brought them to Hattusa. (KUB xix 22, 8–11, adapted from trans. by Houwink ten Cate (1966: 28–9))

In spite of the Hittite successes, Arzawa still had substantial military resources at its disposal, and the support of other western states hostile to the Hittites. With these it would remain a constant threat to the security of the Hittite kingdom until such time as it could be completely subdued by force of arms. We are told that Suppiluliuma took twenty years to re-establish Hittite control in Anatolia.[95] A significant portion of this period was almost certainly devoted to campaigns in the west against the Arzawa Lands— campaigns which began in his father's reign, and continued sporadically through much of his own reign.

A Kingdom Regained

From what survives of the *Deeds*, it is difficult to determine whether any overall plan or strategy underpinned the operations which led to the Hittite reconquest of the lost territories. Were the campaigns conducted essentially on an *ad hoc* basis, as opportunities presented themselves? Or was a systematic programme of

[94] This and the lines in the passage immediately below are a duplicate of KBo xiv 42 (*CTH* 40 vi. 52A) and contain restorations from that text, proposed by Houwink ten Cate. Both passages constitute an additional fragment of the *Deeds*. Houwink ten Cate suggests that the fragment belongs towards the end of the *Deeds*, but comments that an earlier location is possible.

[95] The information comes from two documents of his grandson Hattusili III, KBo vi 28 (*CTH* 88) referred to above, and KUB xix 9 (*CTH* 83.1). The number 20 which often occurs in texts of the period, should probably not be taken too literally. It may be essentially a relative term, indicating that a particular event or series of events occupied a long period of time in comparison with other events; cf. Wilhelm and Boese (1987/9: 90–1), Bryce (1989*b*: 20), Freu (1992: 45).

reconquest mapped out for the recovery of the kingdom? Perhaps we can detect some elements of a basic strategy in the disconnected fragments. Attention seems to have focussed initially on the recovery of lost territories in the outlying regions of the kingdom, and on pursuing and attacking on their home ground the enemies who had occupied these regions. So long as enemy strength remained undiminished, a major drive by the Hittites to liberate their homeland posed serious risks. With their capital in ruins and with hostile groups still occupying the region, attempts to recover the homeland would have been highly vulnerable to a fresh wave of enemy onslaughts from all directions. The alternative was to drive the enemy out of the peripheral states formerly subject to the Hittite kingdom, carry the battle to him in his own territory, destroy his armies and devastate his lands. In this way his capacity for counter-attacks and renewed aggression would be substantially reduced, if not eliminated. And that would be the time for a concerted Hittite drive to recover the homeland, to flush out and expel the enemy groups still occupying it, as a prelude to the task of resettling and rebuilding the core territory of the Hittite world.

At what stage did the reoccupation and reconstruction of the homeland begin? Presumably it was some time after the regions lying to the north, north-east, and west had been reduced to a suitably pacific state. Suppiluliuma's subsequent campaigns against the forces occupying the Lower Land could hardly have been undertaken if much of the intervening territory between this region and the Hittite base in Samuha still lay in enemy hands. It is likely, then, that the process of reoccupation was already underway at the time Suppiluliuma began his southern campaigns. With the expulsion of the enemy from the Lower Land, the rebuilding of the Hittite kingdom could proceed with relatively little threat of outside interference—at least in the short term.

If master plan there was behind the programme of recovery of the Hittite kingdom, there is little doubt that Suppiluliuma was one of its principal architects. Indeed his father in the final years of his reign must have relied increasingly on his advice as well as on his skills in the field. The long years of almost incessant campaigning took their toll on the ageing king. Yet almost to the end of his life, and in spite of repeated bouts of illness which confined him to his bed in Samuha, Tudhaliya led his forces in person against his enemies.

It is unfortunate that we do not know more about this king. Indeed, Tudhaliya's great-grandson, Hattusili III, in recalling the devastation of the Hittite kingdom in the dark days of Tudhaliya III's reign attributes the campaigns of reconquest which restored the kingdom's supremacy in Anatolia solely to his son Suppiluliuma.[96] But however much the Hittites' success in winning back the kingdom was due to the son, its survival, after it could so easily have disappeared entirely from the pages of history, must have been due in very large measure to the father—perhaps one of the most courageous and most determined, if one of the least known, kings of the Hittites.

[96] In the documents cited in the previous note.

CHAPTER 7

The Supremacy of Hatti: The Reign of Suppiluliuma I (c.1344–1322)

Suppiluliuma Seizes the Throne

In spite of his close partnership with his father, and in spite of the role he had played in the restoration of the kingdom, Suppiluliuma was not intended for the mantle of kingship after his father's death. The heir to the throne was another, presumably older, son called Tudhaliya the Younger. Initially, Suppiluliuma pledged his support for the new king, and the chief dignitaries of the land followed suit. Suppiluliuma's son Mursili refers to the oath of allegiance sworn to him:

As Tudhaliya the Younger was the master of the Land of Hatti, the princes of Hattusa, the lords, the military chiefs, the nobles, the entire infantry, the cavalry swore allegiance to him, and my father also swore allegiance to him. (Mursili II's 1st Plague Prayer, KUB xiv 14 (+) (*CTH* 378.1), obv. 13–15)[1]

But secretly Suppiluliuma may well have felt aggrieved, after all he had done for the kingdom, at being relegated to a position of subordination to his brother. He had ambitions of his own which were incompatible with this. And he had his supporters! A quarrel broke out between the two brothers, perhaps deliberately engineered by Suppiluliuma, and blood was shed:

When my father revolted against Tudhaliya, on the departure from Hattusa the princes, the lords, the military chiefs and the nobles were all ranged alongside my father, and the conspirators seized Tudhaliya, and they killed Tudhaliya. (1st Plague Prayer, obv. 16–19)

By this act of fratricide, Suppiluliuma seized the Hittite throne. As we shall see, it was an act which many years later was to have disastrous consequences for the whole kingdom. That at least was the advice conveyed by the gods to his son Mursili.

---

[1] For the full text and translation of this prayer, see Lebrun (1980: 193–203).

Opening Moves in the Conflict with Mitanni

On occupying the throne, Suppiluliuma applied himself vigorously to two major tasks still to be undertaken before the reconquest of the lost Hittite territories could be regarded as complete.[2] To the east of the Lower Land lay the kingdom of Kizzuwadna, which had been sacked and occupied by the enemy of the Land of Armatana. Further to the north Tegarama, somewhere between Kummanni and the Upper Land and on the main route between Hattusa and Carchemish,[3] had fallen to the enemy of the Land of Isuwa. Fragmentary passages in the *Deeds* may refer to the Hittite attacks on Armatana and Isuwa in reprisal for their invasion and occupation of Hittite subject territory.[4] Unfortunately the mutilated state of the text deprives us of details of these attacks or their outcomes. But both countries were subject-allies of Mitanni.

An invasion of Isuwa meant an expedition across the Euphrates river and close to the heartland of the Mitannian kingdom. During the period of their reconquests of their Anatolian territories, the Hittites had avoided hostilities with Mitanni. Now, by marching against Isuwa, Suppiluliuma could hardly fail to bring the two kingdoms into direct conflict. Far from shrinking from such a conflict, Suppiluliuma may have welcomed it. Almost certainly he had long nursed the ambition of confronting and destroying once and for all the Hittites' chief rival for the domination of the Near East. Now that Hittite supremacy had been all but re-established throughout Anatolia, the time for a military showdown with Mitanni was at hand.

The political situation in Mitanni may also have prompted Suppiluliuma to make his move at this time. Artatama I had been succeeded on the Mitannian throne by his son Suttarna II, perhaps the king responsible for re-establishing Mitannian control over the Land of Isuwa.[5] He may also have incited the Isuwan attack on Hittite territory during Tudhaliya III's reign. But on Suttarna's

---

[2] We have no record of Suppiluliuma's accession since the passage in the *Deeds* where this was reported is missing. The report of the accession must be assigned, at the earliest, to the short gap of *c*.11 lines (thus Güterbock) at the beginning of col. IV of the second tablet, since extant references to Suppiluliuma's father continue to the end of col. III of this tablet; see further, Bryce (1989*b*: 20).

[3] Probably to be equated with modern Gürün on a tributary of the Euphrates; see Garstang and Gurney (1959: 47), Gurney (1979*a*: 156).

[4] *DS* pp. 82–4, frags. 23–5.

[5] Cf. Cornelius (1979: 163), and Wilhelm (1989: 30).

death, dynastic rivalries broke out in the kingdom. The king's son and successor Artasumara was assassinated by a military officer Utkhi, and replaced on the throne by his younger brother Tusratta.[6]

Tusratta's elevation to the kingship did not go unchallenged. There was another claimant to the throne, a second Artatama whose name suggests that he too was a member of the Mitannian royal family (there was a lawsuit pending between them before the gods). Since, apparently, Artatama commanded the loyalty of a significant element of the Mitannian population, and was actually styled as 'king', he posed a serious threat to the young Tusratta and to the stability of his kingdom.[7] The Hittites themselves had learnt from bitter experience the vulnerability to outside forces of a kingdom split by internal dissension. What better time than now for the Hittite king to capitalize on the political situation within Mitanni? What better time to lead his forces against a Mitannian ally lying on the very borders of the heartland of the Mitannian kingdom?

Yet initially Suppiluliuma may have underestimated the opposition. In a letter written to the pharaoh Amenhotep III Tusratta claimed to have won a victory over the enemy of Hatti, and stated that he was sending part of the spoils of victory to the pharaoh:

When the enemy came to my country, Tesub My Lord delivered him into my power, and I conquered him. There was no one who returned to his country. I am sending to you with the present letter one chariot, two horses, one male and one female servant, as part of the booty of the Land of Hatti. (*EA* 17, 30–8)

The victory claimed by Tusratta may have occurred during a Hittite expedition across the Euphrates in an abortive attempt by Suppiluliuma to regain control of Isuwa.[8] If so, it would have given Suppiluliuma clear warning that he was dealing with a still powerful and dangerous enemy. But humiliating though his defeat must have been, it was no more than a temporary setback—and Tusratta may

---

[6] *EA* 17 indicates the circumstances of his accession.

[7] Wilhelm (1989: 31) notes that opinions differ on whether Artatama actually ruled over a region in the north-east of the Mitannian kingdom (Goetze (1957a, 67–8)), or was no more than a king by name, a grace and favour status accorded by the Hittites (Kühne (1973: 19 n. 82)).

[8] Cf. Houwink ten Cate (1963: 271), and Gurney (1979a: 157).

well have exaggerated the extent of his victory. In any case Suppiluliuma had learnt a salutary lesson: there should be no further venture into his enemy's territory until he had carefully prepared the way in advance—diplomatically as well as militarily. This he undertook to do. As one scholar aptly comments: 'all sources available on Suppiluliuma's tactics concur in offering us a clear picture of a very capable military commander who carefully planned his attacks beforehand with intricate diplomatic moves and dealings.'[9]

As part of his preparation for a major onslaught on Tusratta's kingdom and its subject territories and allies, Suppiluliuma sought to isolate his opponent from all major sources of support by a series of diplomatic alliances. Thus he negotiated a treaty with Artatama. Although the treaty itself has not survived,[10] it was almost certainly drawn up as a pact between equals, in which Suppiluliuma recognized Artatama as 'Great King' and the rightful claimant to the Mitannian throne. The treaty presumably required benevolent neutrality from Artatama in the Hittites' forthcoming conflict with Tusratta, in return for an undertaking by Suppiluliuma to support Artatama's accession to the Mitannian throne when Tusratta had been defeated and driven from it.

Suppiluliuma was also intent on developing friendly relations with Egypt, whose throne was now occupied by the pharaoh Akhenaten.[11] Although Egypt's influence in Syria seems to have diminished significantly in Akhenaten's reign, none the less it still retained at least token control over a number of kingdoms of southern Syria and all of Palestine. And an Egyptian–Mitannian alliance still remained in force.[12] Moreover, from various letters in the Amarna correspondence it is clear that Akhenaten kept

---

[9] Houwink ten Cate (1963: 271).

[10] Reference to it is made in the treaty later concluded between Suppiluliuma and Tusratta's son Sattiwaza; *PD* no. 1 (*CTH* 51) 2–3, obv. 1–3. The treaty is discussed below.

[11] According to the most recent revision of Hittite-Egyptian synchronisms; see Wilhelm and Boese (1987/9: 94), and Bryce (1990: 100–1). It is possible that his accession occurred during the period of Akhenaten's co-regency with Amenhotep III. This would certainly be so if Tusratta's defeat of the Hittite forces recorded in the letter *EA* 17 occurred after Suppiluliuma's accession, since the letter was addressed to Amenhotep.

[12] It had been cemented by a marriage alliance when Tusratta, in the same manner as his father Suttarna and grandfather Artatama, sent his daughter Taduhepa as a bride for the pharaoh (*EA* 19, 17 ff., *EA* 22 iv 43–9).

himself closely informed of political and military developments in the region. Suppiluliuma therefore took some pains to minimize any risk of Egyptian involvement in his conflict with Mitanni by cultivating diplomatic relations with the pharaoh, no doubt assuring him that he had no designs on his subject territory in southern Syria and Palestine. A letter which he wrote probably to Akhenaten's immediate successor Smenkhkhare stresses the pact of friendship which had been established between the two kings:

Neither my messengers whom I had sent to your father, nor the request which your father had made in these terms: 'Let us establish between ourselves nothing but the friendliest of relations'—I have not refused these, o King. All that your father said to me, o King, I did absolutely everything. And my own request, o King, that I made to your father, he never refused it; he gave me absolutely everything.   (*EA* 41, 7–13)

His relations with Akhenaten may not have been as close or as cordial as he suggests. But his policy towards Egypt was consistent with an overall strategy of establishing diplomatic links with foreign powers on whose support Tusratta might call in the forthcoming conflict with Hatti.

This was probably Suppiluliuma's chief motive for the marriage alliance which he contracted with the Kassite ruling family in Babylon.

Suppiluliuma's Family

Seals and inscriptions associate three queens with Suppiluliuma during his reign—Daduhepa, Henti, and Tawananna in that order.[13] The first of these, Daduhepa, was Suppiluliuma's mother, wife of his father Tudhaliya.[14] She must therefore have outlived her husband and retained her status as queen after his death, in the standard Tawananna tradition.

On her death, her place as reigning queen was taken by Suppiluliuma's first (known) wife Henti. Henti's status is indicated

---

[13] See *SBo* I, 4–9, nos. 5–11. To these we can now add the seal impressions discovered in the Nişantepe seal archive which associate Suppiluliuma with Henti and Tawananna. The archive has produced three more seal impressions in which Henti is paired with Suppiluliuma, and more than fifty in which Suppiluliuma and Tawananna (= Malnigal; on this name see below) appear together; see Otten (1994; 1995: 13–16) for a description of the Suppiluliuma–Henti seals. The three queens are also listed (after Walanni, Nikkalmati, and Asmunikal) in the *nuntarriyašḫa* festival text, KUB xxv 14 (+) (*CTH* 626.IV) I 28′ ff., 46′ ff., III 10′ ff. For transliteration and translation of part of this text, see Bin-Nun (1975: 199–200).

[14] See Gurney (1979*b*: 218–21).

in a decree appointing Suppiluliuma's son Telipinu priest in Kizzuwadna.[15] But her enjoyment of this status was short-lived, for within a few years of her husband's accession she disappeared from the scene, and Suppiluliuma took a new wife and queen, the daughter of the king of Babylon. The new queen apparently assumed the name Tawananna as a personal name after her marriage, alongside her original name Malnigal.[16]

Tawananna is associated with her husband on a number of seal impressions. These include several which belong within the context of Suppiluliuma's alliance with the Ugaritic king Niqmaddu II,[17] an alliance which can be dated to Suppiluliuma's 'First' or 'One-year' Syrian war (discussed below).[18] At this time Burnaburias II was ruler of Babylon, and therefore Tawananna's father. It may well be that the marriage alliance with the Kassite ruling family was strategically motivated—to ensure at least benevolent neutrality if not active support from Babylon while Suppiluliuma was campaigning against Mitanni.[19]

What of the queen Henti? Her fate remains a mystery. But just possibly it is referred to in a fragmentary text from the reign of Suppiluliuma's son Mursili II, which makes mention in consecutive lines of the king's father, his mother, and a banishment to the land of Ahhiyawa.[20] Since much of the right hand side of the tablet on which the text appears is missing, we cannot draw any firm conclusions about its overall content. But if a commonly accepted interpretation of the text is correct, it provides an explanation for what happened to Henti—she had been banished by her husband.[21] The prospects of an important strategic marriage alliance with the ruling dynasty of Babylon may have provided incentive enough for him to remove her from the scene. As Suppiluliuma had demonstrated by his seizure of the throne from his brother, he was quite

[15] KUB XIX 25 + 26 (*CTH* 44), discussed below.

[16] On the latter name, see *SBo* I, 46–7, no. 84, Laroche (1956: 100), Beran (1967: 33, 74), Bin-Nun (1975: 17–72).

[17] *SBo* I, 6–7, nos. 9–11. See RS 17.227, 17.373, 17.340 (Schaeffer (1956: 2–6)). The legend in Akkadian cuneiform reads: 'Seal of Suppiluliuma, the Great King, King of the land of Hatti, beloved of the Storm God; seal of Tawananna, the Great Queen, Daughter of the King of Babylon.'

[18] See *PRU* IV, 32–4, with Dossier IIA 1–3.

[19] Cf. Goetze (1975a: 13). We have suggested that a Hittite–Kassite alliance may have served a similar purpose in Mursili I's reign; see Ch. 5.

[20] KBo XIV 2, ed. Sommer (1932: 298–306).

[21] Cf. Freu, 1990 (23). Steiner (1964: 375 n. 78), Jewell (1974: 326), Košak (1980c: 41) have expressed doubts about this interpretation.

prepared to deal ruthlessly with members of his family who stood
in the way of the achievement of his objectives.

Whatever the reasons for Henti's sudden disappearance
from our records, she had left Suppiluliuma with one of the most
important mainstays of his reign—for she was almost certainly
the mother of all his sons. We know of five sons—Arnuwanda,
Telipinu, Piyassili (later Sarri-Kusuh), Zannanza, and Mursili.
With the possible exception of Mursili, these sons had all reached
manhood during their father's reign, and had all provided him with
consistently loyal and able support.

Arnuwanda, probably the eldest, was the crown prince. From
early in his father's reign he had been the designated heir to
the throne. His status is first indicated in the decree which formalized the appointment of his brother Telipinu, second son of
Suppiluliuma, as priest in Kizzuwadna. The decree was issued in
the name of Suppiluliuma, the queen Henti, Arnuwanda as crown
prince, and Suppiluliuma's brother Zida, the Chief of the Bodyguards.[22] By this time Kizzuwadna had lost its independent status
and was now under direct Hittite rule. Telipinu is also referred to
in several other documents as 'the priest' or 'the great priest'.[23]
But his role in the kingdom was not confined to religious duties. He
had important political and military responsibilities as well. The
terms of his appointment in Kizzuwadna were similiar in several
respects to those imposed by treaty upon vassal rulers of the kingdom. Like them he was obliged to have the same friends and the
same enemies as the Hittite king, and to denounce those guilty of
acting or speaking against him. Given that Telipinu's appointment
was made only a short time before Suppiluliuma led his forces
into Syria, it was almost certainly connected with the king's
political and military preparations for his first major campaign
against Mitanni.

The Great Syrian War

Within a few years, perhaps no more than four or five, of his seizure
of the Hittite throne, Suppiluliuma's preparations were complete.
He now embarked on what was to prove the most momentous

---

[22] KUB xix 25 + 26 (*CTH* 44), ed. Goetze (1940: 12–16). Zida's relationship
with Suppiluliuma is indicated in the Annals of Mursili II, *AM* 152–3.
[23] References cited in Bryce (1992*b*: 9 n. 15).

undertaking of his career. The magnitude of his task can hardly be overestimated. Not only was he preparing to take on the military might of the Mitannian king on his own territory, but in order to establish his supremacy in Syria he had also to confront a formidable coalition of enemy forces mustered from the kingdoms of the region. So long as these kingdoms could call on the support of their Mitannian overlord, a Hittite campaign against them could well end in failure. A direct, all-out attack on the heartland of the Mitannian kingdom had to be the first priority.

Unfortunately the section of the *Deeds* which records this undertaking is entirely lost to us, with the possible exception of one small fragment.[24] But a reasonably detailed account is preserved in two other documents.[25] The Hittite campaign was apparently triggered by two events in particular: Tusratta's attack on the Syrian country of Nuhasse, whose king Sarrupsi had established an alliance with Suppiluliuma,[26] and a further anti-Hittite uprising in the Land of Isuwa.[27]

After dispatching an expeditionary force to Nuhasse to support Sarrupsi (see below), Suppiluliuma led the main Hittite army across the Euphrates, conquered the Land of Isuwa to the border of the kingdom of Alse,[28] and then struck south into Mitannian territory, occupying and plundering its capital Wassuganni. Unprepared for the speed and ferocity of the Hittite advance, Tusratta could offer no effective resistance. He had no option but to flee the capital, with whatever troops he could muster, before it fell to the Hittites.[29]

Suppiluliuma then turned westwards, recrossing the Euphrates. In a series of lightning conquests, he reduced all the local kingdoms subject to Mitanni from the Euphrates to the Mediterranean coast—Aleppo, Mukis, Niya, Arahtu, Qatna, and Nuhasse—as far south as Aba (Apina, Upi, the later Damascus) which lay in the border region of Egyptian territory.[30] Only the Mitannian

---

[24] *DS* pp. 84–5, frag. 29; see Wilhelm and Boese (1987/9: 89).
[25] The account appears in the historical preambles to the treaties which Suppiluliuma drew up with Sattiwaza, *PD* no. 1 (*CTH* 51) and Tette, king of Nuhasse, *PD* no. 3 (*CTH* 53).
[26] *PD* no. 3, 58–9, 1 obv. 1–13.
[27] *PD* no. 3. 58–9, 1 obv. 14 ff.
[28] Which he passed through apparently with the consent of its king Antaratli, *PD* no. 1, 8–9, obv. 26, *PD* no. 3, 58–9, 1 19–20.
[29] *PD* no. 1, 6–9, obv. 17–29; cf. *DS* pp. 84–5, frag. 26.
[30] *PD* no. 1, 10–15, obv. 30–41.

stronghold Carchemish on the Euphrates remained unsubdued. The rulers of the conquered states were deposed and transported along with their families to Hattusa.

Amongst the states which fell victim to the Hittite onslaught was one which Suppiluliuma had intended to leave unmolested— Kadesh on the Orontes river. Formerly an ally of Mitanni, the Land of Kadesh had been forced to accept Egyptian sovereignty during the campaigns of Tuthmosis III; a coalition of Syrian forces led by the kings of Kadesh and Megiddo had been decisively defeated by Tuthmosis on his first campaign,[31] and in a subsequent campaign Kadesh itself had fallen to the Egyptians.[32] This might have proved a source of ongoing tension and conflict between Egypt and Mitanni. But by the terms of the accord reached between the two kingdoms during Tuthmosis IV's reign, Kadesh was officially recognized as subject to Egyptian overlordship while still, it seems, providing a possible focus of Mitannian influence and support in the region.

Nevertheless, true to his policy of avoiding conflict with Egypt, Suppiluliuma had intended to bypass Kadesh. But he was provoked into action by its king Suttarna (Sutatarra) who led his troops against him. Suppiluliuma was quick to retaliate. The Kadesh force was defeated, and its king and leading citizens, along with the king's son Aitakkama, were led off in captivity.[33] Although this must have put some strain on Hittite–Egyptian relations, there was no apparent immediate reaction from Egypt. Suppiluliuma subsequently allowed Aitakkama to return to Kadesh, where he occupied his father's throne, and probably formalized his status as a Hittite vassal by drawing up a treaty with him (though no record of this has survived). Aitakkama used his Hittite backing both to establish regional alliances with other rulers, notably Aziru, king of Amurru, and to extend his own territory.[34] So long as it suited his purposes, he remained loyal to his Hittite allegiance.[35] But the loss of Kadesh rankled in the Egyptian mind, and some years later, in the reign of the pharaoh Tutankhamun, the Egyptians tried to recapture it (see below).

---

[31] For the relevant texts, see Pritchard (1969: 234–7).
[32] Breasted (1906: ii. 465, 585).
[33] *PD* no. 1, 14–15, obv. 40–3.
[34] *EA* 140, 25–32.
[35] He finally broke his ties with Hatti in the ninth year of the reign of Suppiluliuma's son Mursili II, when he participated in a rebellion of Syrian princes against Hittite rule (see Ch. 8).

It was with no little satisfaction that Suppiluliuma recounted all that he achieved within the space of a single campaign:

Because of the hostility of Tusratta, the king, I plundered these lands all in a single year, and conveyed them to the Land of Hatti. I incorporated them into my territory from Mount Niblani and from the opposite bank of the Euphrates. (Suppiluliuma:Sattiwaza Treaty, *PD* no. 1 (*CTH* 51), 14–15, obv. 45–7)

The Kingdom of Ugarit

Suppiluliuma's successes were not achieved purely by force of arms. Even in the midst of his Syrian campaign, he sought to strengthen his position by diplomatic alliances. Thus, perhaps while he was in the Land of Aleppo, he made overtures to Niqmaddu II, the king of Ugarit, to join him in an alliance against the kings of Mukis and Nuhasse.[36]

An alliance with Ugarit had much to offer. Ugarit was endowed with many natural advantages. With its thickly wooded mountains, it was a valuable timber-producing region, and its rich, fertile steppes and plains were excellent for grazing purposes and for the production of a wide range of goods, including grain, wine, oil, and flax. It was also the centre of thriving manufacturing industries, where the arts of bronzesmiths and goldsmiths flourished and a wide range of linen and woollen goods were produced for export. Its 50-kilometre-long coastline contained four or more seaports, making it an important link between the Mediterranean world and the lands stretching to the Euphrates and beyond. And through its territory passed some of the major land-routes of Syria, north through Mukis to Anatolia and east through Aleppo to Mesopotamia. With its rich natural resources, its commercial prosperity, and above all its important strategic location, it inevitably attracted the keen interest of the major Near Eastern powers. The substantial tribute payable by Ugarit, as recorded in its treaties with Hatti, indicates that it became the richest of the Hittite vassal states in north Syria. Its possession very likely provided the Hittite kingdom with an important source of revenue.[37]

We know little of the history of Ugarit before the beginning of the Amarna archive. From the letters in this archive, we see the pressures brought to bear on the Ugaritic king to ally himself with

---

[36] *PRU* iv, 32–52, Dossier II A.   [37] See Korošec (1960: 72–3).

one or other of the major powers. In one of these Niqmaddu's father and predecessor Ammistamru declared his allegiance to the pharaoh Akhenaten,[38] in spite of apparent attempts made by Suppiluliuma to win him over to the Hittite side. Ammistamru must have died shortly after this, and Suppiluliuma renewed his attempts to establish an alliance with Ugarit by his overtures to the new king Niqmaddu. No doubt he had in mind the long-term advantages of such an alliance. But for the moment his chief concern was to hem in the enemy of Mukis and Nuhasse between his own forces, perhaps now based in Aleppo, and the forces of Ugarit which bordered on the enemy states to the west.

In pursuit of an alliance with Ugarit, Suppiluliuma wrote to Niqmaddu in the most courtly and persuasive terms. His letter is an excellent example of the diplomatic skills which the Hittite brought to bear in persuading a potential ally to join his side:

Although the Land of Nuhasse and the Land of Mukis are my enemies, you, Niqmaddu, do not fear them, have confidence in yourself! Just as formerly your ancestors were friends and not enemies of the the Land of Hatti, now you, Niqmaddu, be the enemy of my enemy and the friend of my friend ... Be faithful, o Niqmaddu, to the alliance of friendship with the Land of Hatti, and you will see then how the Great King deals with the kings of Nuhasse and the king of Mukis who abandoned the alliance of friendship with the Land of Hatti and became the enemies of the Great King their master. If then all these kings launch an attack on your country, do not be afraid, Niqmaddu, but immediately send one of your messengers to me. But if you, Niqmaddu, attack first with your armies the troops of Nuhasse or Mukis, let no one take them from your hands. And if it happens that for want of troops from Nuhasse, troops from Mukis come to your land as fugitives, let no one take them from your hands. If it happens that certain towns within your borders become hostile to you and you engage in combat with them and defeat them, in the future let no one take them from your hands.   (RS 17.132 = *PRU* IV, 35–7, Dossier II A 1)

The offer was tempting. Niqmaddu was presented with the double incentive of guaranteed protection by the Hittite king in the event of an attack upon his territory, and the prospect of retaining any territory he conquered in the course of conflict with the enemy kingdoms. But the letter also contained a subtle threat of the consequences of refusing an alliance with the Hittite king.

[38] *EA* 45.

Niqmaddu was faced with a dilemma. By refusing the overtures of the other Syrian kingdoms to join their alliance,[39] he was also putting himself at risk. He must have carefully weighed up the consequences of both options, before finally deciding to go with Suppiluliuma.[40]

As expected, his decision met with prompt reprisals from the coalition of local kingdoms whose overtures he had rejected. His kingdom was invaded and plundered.[41] But when he appealed to his Hittite overlord, the latter honoured the terms of the alliance, sent an expeditionary force to drive the enemy from his kingdom, and restored to him the booty which they had taken.[42] Further benefits from the alliance were to be bestowed upon Niqmaddu, with little apparent effort on his part. After his conquest of Mukis and Niya, Suppiluliuma transferred substantial portions of their territory to the kingdom of Ugarit—which may have led to an almost fourfold increase in its own territory.[43]

The Nuhasse Lands

The Nuhasse lands occupied a region stretching west of the Euphrates to the Orontes river, between Hamath and Aleppo, and bordering on the kingdoms of Mukis and Kadesh.[44] The name Nuhasse figures in the Mari and Alalah VII archives, but seems not to have designated a coherent political entity prior to the period of Suppiluliuma's campaigns in Syria.[45] At the time of the Syrian war, Nuhasse was at least nominally subject to Mitannian over-lordship.[46] The texts refer to the 'kings of Nuhasse', suggesting that

[39] RS 17.227, 7–11 (*PRU* IV, 40–1).
[40] For reference to the pact he made with Suppiluliuma, see RS 17.227, 16–53 (*PRU* IV, 41–3), and the following texts in *PRU* IV, 44–52.
[41] RS 17.340, 2–8 (*PRU* IV, 49).
[42] RS 17.340, 9–21 (*PRU* IV, 49–50).
[43] Drower (1975: 138). See *PRU* IV, 63–70, Dossier IV A. Astour (1969: 404) calculates that the amount of territory given by Suppiluliuma to Niqmaddu covered 4,000–4,500 square kilometres.
[44] See Klengel (1969: 18).
[45] As Klengel (1969: 33) points out, at the time of the Mari archives the north part of Nuhasse belonged to the territory of Iamhad, the south part to the territory of Qatna. Cf. Na'aman (1980: 38). On the history of Nuhasse before the Hittite conquest, see Klengel (1969: 33–7).
[46] For Nuhasse's hostility to the Hittites at the time of their invasion of Syria, see KBo x 12 (*CTH* 49.II), the Hittite version of the treaty between Suppiluliuma and Aziru, king of Amurru, ed. Freydank (1959/60), 15'; cf. Klengel (1969: 38).

the Nuhasse region was made up of several kingdoms, each with its own ruler of whom one may have been a kind of *primus inter pares*.[47]

We have noted that prior to the Syrian war, and no doubt as part of his preparation for this war, Suppiluliuma had managed to establish an alliance with a king of Nuhasse called Sarrupsi. This was clearly contrary to any claims of allegiance the Mitannian king may have had on him, and Tusratta was quick to seek revenge. But it seems that Suppiluliuma was as quick to respond when he received an appeal for assistance from Sarrupsi:

When the king of the Land of Mitanni plotted to kill Sarrupsi, thereupon the king of the Land of Mitanni along with his élite troops and his chariots invaded the Land of Nuhasse. And when he had attacked it, thereupon Sarrupsi sent his messenger to the king of the Land of Hatti: 'I am the servant of the king of the Land of Hatti. Rescue me now!' And I, My Sun, sent warriors and horse to his support, and he drove out the king of the Land of Mitanni along with his troops and his chariots from the Land of Nuhasse.   (Suppiluliuma: Tette Treaty, *PD* no. 3 (*CTH* 53), 58–9, I 2–11)

However, the Hittite response failed to save Sarrupsi. While the Mitannian troops may have been driven from the land, Sarrupsi was murdered by members of his own family,[48] very likely because he had thrown his lot in with Hatti.[49] When Suppiluliuma recrossed the Euphrates after his sack of Wassuganni, Nuhasse was once more in the enemy camp, and Sarrupsi had been replaced by a new king Addu-Nirari. Presumably he was another member of Sarrupsi's family, one who was willing to declare his allegiance to Mitanni.

But his kingship was short-lived. Following his reconquest of Nuhasse, Suppiluliuma transported to Hattusa all members of the royal family. No doubt he held them accountable for Sarrupsi's death and the change of allegiance back to Mitanni. He now appointed a man called Takibsarri, apparently a loyal supporter of Sarrupsi, to the kingship of Ukulzat, a city in Nuhasse.[50]

---

[47] Cf. Astour (1969: 387).

[48] *PD* no. 1, 12–13, I obv. 38.

[49] I see no good justification for Klengel's assumption (1969: 40) that Sarrupsi realigned himself with Mitanni. It seems more likely that he did not survive, or survive long, the Mitannian attack on Nuhasse.

[50] *PD* no. 1, 12–13, obv. 39–40. It was not, however, the capital; see Klengel (1969: 48 n. 15).

The Kingdom of Amurru

At the time of Suppiluliuma's Syrian campaigns, Amurru was one of the most prominent of the local kingdoms. It also proved one of the most troublesome, both to its neighbours and to the major powers who sought to establish their dominance over the region.

The name *Amurru* first appears in texts of the third and early second millennium as a geographical term, referring to a broad expanse of territory covering much of the region of modern Syria and extending westwards from Mesopotamia towards the Mediterranean coast. However from the time of the Mari and Alalah archives, the term came to be used of a more restricted region of central and southern Syria.[51] Subsequently, with the expansion of Egyptian military power in Syria under Tuthmosis III, it was incorporated into Egyptian subject territory, as a clearly defined geo-political unit extending between the Orontes river and the central Levantine coast.[52]

Semi-nomadism seems to have been a traditional feature of the population groups associated with Amurru. Prominent amongst these groups were the Habiru[53] who roamed the mountains and forests of the region. With their numbers swelled by criminals, fugitives, refugees, marauding mercenaries, and social outcasts, they posed a constant threat not only to merchants and other travellers, but also to the more settled communities of the region. Left to their own resources, they were highly disruptive of social and political order and stability. But a leader who had the skills and the enterprise to organize and unite them would have a very formidable force at his disposal.

From the Amarna correspondence we know that in the fourteenth century such a leader did emerge, a man of unknown but possibly royal origin called ʿAbdi-Asirta.[54] Banding groups of Habiru from the highland regions into a powerful fighting force under his command, ʿAbdi-Asirta embarked on a series of

[51] Thus Singer (1991*a*: 137; 1991*b*: 69), who notes that the broad sense of the term never disappeared entirely.

[52] See Singer (1991*a*: 138; 1991*b*: 69).

[53] ʿ*apiru* or SA.GAZ in the texts. On the SA.GAZ movement in Syria, see Waterhouse (1965: 192–9), with references. For a more recent general survey of the Habiru, see Loretz (1984).

[54] Singer (1991*a*: 141) suggests that he was probably from one of the royal families of the coastal cities of Amurru.

conquests which brought the whole of Amurru under his sway. This caused no little consternation amongst Amurru's neighbours.

To the south of Amurru lay the kingdom of Gubla (Byblos), whose king Rib-Addi viewed the Amurrite's progress with increasing alarm. Urgent letters were dispatched to the pharaoh Akhenaten, reporting the conquest of one Amurrite city after another by ʿAbdi-Asirta and the Habiru, and the slaughter of their leaders:

Let the king pay attention to the words of his servant: 'The Habiru killed Aduna, the king of Irqata, but there was no one who said anything to ʿAbdi-Asirta, and so they go on taking territory for themselves. Miya, the ruler of Arasni, seized Ardata, and just now the men of Ammiya have killed their lord. I am afraid!' (*EA* 75, 24–30, trans. Moran (1992: 145))[55]

After taking Sigata for himself, ʿAbdi-Asirta said to the men of Ammiya: 'Kill your leader, and then you will be like us and at peace.' They were won over, following his message, and they are like the Habiru. (*EA* 74, 23–30, trans. Moran (1992: 143))

To the north the city of Sumur, one of Egypt's three major strongholds in the region, also fell to ʿAbdi-Asirta.[56] The other two were Ullaza (Ullassa) and Tunip. All three had succumbed to Egypt during Tuthmosis III's Syrian campaigns.[57] ʿAbdi-Asirta was perhaps encouraged by the withdrawal of the Egyptian commissioner Pahannate to occupy Sumur.[58] The cities lay in Egyptian subject territory, for Amurru was the northernmost of Egypt's possessions in Syria. Surely the pharaoh would not tolerate these blatant acts of aggression against his own territory. But Rib-Addi's protests and appeals fell on deaf ears. He was politically outmanoeuvred by his Amurrite rival. The latter also wrote to the pharaoh, representing himself as the protector of Egyptian interests in Amurru, and seeking to have himself recognised as deputy to the Egyptian governor of the region:

Look, there is Pahannate, my commissioner. May the king, the Sun, ask him if I do not guard Sumur and Ullassa. When my commissioner is on a mission of the king, the Sun, then I am the one who guards the harvest of the grain of Sumur and of all the lands for the king, my Sun, my Lord. May

[55] On Irqata and Ardata, see Klengel (1969: 252). Further on *EA* 75, see Bryce (1989b: 22–3).
[56] *EA* 84, 11 ff., *EA* 91, 6.
[57] See Singer (1991b: 69).   [58] *EA* 62; cf. *EA* 67.

the king, my Lord, know me and entrust me to the charge of Pahannate, my commissioner. (*EA* 60, 19–32, trans. Moran (1992: 132))

ʿAbdi-Asirta had correctly calculated that Akhenaten had no wish to embroil Egyptian troops in further conflicts in Syria if they could be avoided, and would be only too willing to accept his protestations of loyalty. The support ʿAbdi-Asirta sought from Egypt was no doubt also assured by the threat of Hittite intervention in Amurru. If the pharaoh refused to accommodate him, ʿAbdi-Asirta might well throw his lot in with the Hittites. In the face of such considerations, Rib-Addi's record of unwavering loyalty to his Egyptian overlord carried little weight when he appealed for action against ʿAbdi-Asirta.

His worst fears were soon to be realized. Emboldened by his military and political successes, and confident that there was little risk of Egyptian intervention, ʿAbdi-Asirta now turned his attention to the Land of Gubla. In desperation, and no doubt with a sense of utter frustration, Rib-Addi wrote once more to the pharaoh:

So now ʿAbdi-Asirta has written to the troops: 'Assemble in the temple of Ninurta, and then let us fall upon Gubla. Look, there is no one that will save it from us. Then let us drive out the mayors from the country that the entire country be joined to the Habiru . . . Should even so the king come out, the entire country will be against him, and what will he do to us?' Accordingly, they have made an alliance among themselves and, accordingly, I am very, very afraid, since in fact there is no one who will save me from them. Like a bird in a trap so I am in Gubla. Why have you neglected your country? I have written like this to the palace, but you do not heed my words. (*EA* 74, 30–50, trans. Moran (1992: 143))

Again, apparently, there was no response from the pharaoh. Appeals by Rib-Addi to his southern neighbours, Beirut, Sidon, and Tyre, also went unanswered. One by one the cities of the highlands and the coast fell to ʿAbdi-Asirta and the Habiru. Soon only two towns and the royal capital remained to the king.[59] But just when the fall of the capital seemed imminent, it was spared— by the death of ʿAbdi-Asirta.[60]

Mystery still surrounds the circumstances of his death. Was he assassinated by dissidents amongst his own countrymen,[61] or

---

[59] *EA* 74, 19–22; 78, 7–16; 79, 7–12.
[60] Referred to in *EA* 101, 27–31; see Moran (1969: 94).
[61] Thus Moran (1969).

officers of the pharaoh acting on their own initiative?[62] Did he die
of natural causes after a serious illness?[63] Or was he in fact seized
and taken to Egypt by the Egyptian task force which reoccupied
Sumur?[64] The likelihood is that 'Abdi-Asirta did in fact overstep
the limits of Egyptian patience, and that Akhenaten did finally
respond to Rib-Addi's appeals, and ordered the reassertion of
Egyptian control over the territories occupied by 'Abdi-Asirta—
and the permanent removal of 'Abdi-Asirta from the scene.[65]

But whatever the manner of his removal, 'Abdi-Asirta's death
provided no more than a very temporary respite from the problems
which Amurru caused both to Egypt and to its own neighbours,
especially Gubla. Shortly after his death, he was succeeded by his
son Aziru—who proved no less of a threat to his neighbours than
his father had been, and even more politically astute than his father
in the international political arena.

Aziru is one of the best documented and undoubtedly one of the
most colourful personalities of Late Bronze Age Syria. Fifteen of
his letters to the pharaoh have survived, and there are numerous
references to him in other letters in the Amarna archive and a
range of other documents. But abundant though this material is, it
leaves us with many unresolved problems, particularly relating to
the chronology of important events in Aziru's career.[66]

Aziru must have come to power around the time Suppiluliuma
was preparing for his first major thrust into Syria. Given Amurru's
proximity to the expanding sphere of Hittite influence, the situation might well be exploited by an astute local ruler seeking to play
one of the major powers off against the other.

The respite Rib-Addi gained from the death of 'Abdi-Asirta
proved extremely short-lived. If anything the luckless king of

[62] Murnane (1985: 14).

[63] Klengel (1969: 257–8), following *EA* 95, 41 ff.

[64] On the basis of *EA* 95, 41–2, Altman (1977) argues that 'Abdi-Asirta was in fact
arrested and removed to Egypt, where he ended his life.

[65] See also Singer (1991*a*: 146). Note his arguments, 146–7, against the view that
the reason for 'Abdi-Asirta's removal was his alleged co-operation with Mitanni
and/or Hatti.

[66] For more detailed treatments of this wily ruler and the role he played in the
international power games, the reader is referred to such publications as Klengel
(1964*b*; 1969: 264–93), Helck (1971: 174–9), Krauss (1978: 59–62), Singer (1991*a*:
148–58). Note the revised chronology of Aziru's career presented by Izre'el and
Singer (1990: 128–69), and Singer (1991*a*). Although I have followed a more traditional line here, the new proposals warrant serious consideration and may well be
right.

Gubla found in his successor an even more formidable and ruthless opponent. Cities like Irqata, Ambi, Sigata, and Ardata, previously captured by ʿAbdi-Asirta, had scarcely been 'liberated' before they were again occupied, by the forces of the new Amurrite leader and his brothers.[67] For a while Sumur, reinforced by Egyptian troops, held out against Aziru. Once again Rib-Addi sent a stream of letters to the pharaoh,[68] stressing how desperate the situation was and begging for reinforcements. If the pharaoh failed to act, then Sumur would certainly fall. Yet again there appears to have been no response from the pharaoh. In the struggle to defend the city the Egyptian commissioner was killed, and in the face of the Amurrite siege, there was large-scale evacuation of the city's inhabitants.[69]

Yet Aziru also made representations to the pharaoh. Far from being an enemy of Egypt, he was the pharaoh's loyal subject, he claimed. His wish was but to serve the pharaoh, and to protect his territories against his enemies. And his attempts to do so were being frustrated by the Egyptian officials in Sumur who refused him entrance to the city:

My Lord, from the very first, I have wanted (to enter) the service of the king, my Lord, but the magnates of Sumur do not permit me. Now of dereliction of duty or the slightest thing against the king I am innocent. The king, my Lord, knows (who the real) rebels (are). And whatever the request of the king, my Lord, I will grant it. (*EA* 157. 9–19, trans. Moran (1992: 243))

Aziru went on to refer to Hittite aggression against him, and asked for Egyptian troops and chariots in support of his efforts to defend Egyptian territory against the Hittites. But in spite of all his protestations of loyalty, his complaints against the local Egyptian officials and his request for assistance against the Hittites conveyed a very explicit warning: should the pharaoh prove unco-operative, he might have no alternative but to join the Hittite king and hand over to him the territories he had conquered.[70]

Without doubt Akhenaten was faced with a dilemma of major proportions. Suppiluliuma had apparently sought to assure him of his wish to maintain friendly relations with Egypt and his intention

---

[67] *EA* 98; 104; 140. [68] e.g. *EA* 107. [69] *EA* 106. 23 ff.

[70] Goetze (1975a: 12) suggests that some understanding may already have existed between Suppiluliuma and Aziru, citing a passage from Mursili II's treaty with Aziru's grandson Duppi-Tesub, *CTH* 62; Friedrich (1926: no. 1, 4–5, obv. 2–3).

to respect Egyptian subject territory in Syria. And Akhenaten can hardly have wanted to provoke a conflict with him. But the scales were very delicately balanced. To respond to Rib-Addi's requests for action against Aziru would almost certainly have driven the latter into the Hittite camp. Yet to refuse support to Rib-Addi meant virtually surrendering to Aziru whatever territory he managed to acquire for himself by force of arms. To go even further and strengthen Aziru's hand by sending him reinforcements would exacerbate the crisis in his subject territories; further, use of these forces against the Hittite king might well be construed as an open declaration of war.

There appeared to be no immediate way of solving this dilemma. But it did have an immediate victim—Rib-Addi. The vacillation of the pharaoh, understandable though it was, left the king of Gubla in a hopeless position. Stubbornly refusing the urgings of his own family that he come to terms with Aziru, Rib-Addi went to Beirut where he stayed four months or more and concluded an alliance with its king(?) Ammunira. But on returning to his capital, he found that a coup had taken place. He had been unseated from his throne by his younger brother Ilirabih. He now sought refuge with Ammunira, while seeking support from Egypt for restoration to this throne.[71] In spite of promises from Egypt, the requested support never materialized, and Rib-Addi had to resort to the ignominious alternative of appealing to his mortal enemy Aziru for assistance in getting back his throne. This was a desperate gamble, and it failed to pay off. Once he had Rib-Addi in his power, Aziru promptly handed him over to the rulers of Sidon,[72] and it was almost certainly at their hands that he met his death.

Belatedly, Akhenaten responded angrily to the news of Aziru's action.[73] He had earlier summoned Aziru to Egypt, but the latter in letters both to the pharaoh[74] and to his officials[75] had put off the visit with the excuse that the Hittite king was in Nuhasse and an invasion of Amurru was feared. It soon became clear that this was largely a pretext on Aziru's part—to gain time for strengthening his own position in the region, while avoiding outright defiance of his overlord's command. He may well have pondered on how he could best turn the highly unstable political scene in Syria to his own

[71] A succession of letters from Rib-Addi to the pharaoh relate these events: *EA* 136–8; 141; 142.
[72] *EA* 162.   [73] *EA* 162, 7–21.   [74] *EA* 165.   [75] *EA* 164; 166–7.

advantage, and whether his interests would best be served by switching his allegiance to the Hittite king.

Akhenaten clearly suspected this. He became increasingly concerned at reports he received from his other vassals in the region—Aziru's seizure of cities in Qatna, his capture of Sumur in association with Zimrida of Sidon,[76] and his alliance with Aitakkama, king of Kadesh.[77] This alliance in particular must have alarmed the pharaoh, for Aitakkama had been placed on the throne of Kadesh as a Hittite vassal.

With a scarcely veiled accusation of outright treachery, Akhenaten now issued a peremptory demand that Aziru or his son now appear before him:

Now the king has heard as follows: 'You are at peace with the ruler of Qidsa (Kadesh). The two of you take food and strong drink together.' And it is true. Why do you act so? Why are you at peace with a ruler with whom the king is fighting? . . . But if you perform your service for the king, your Lord, what is there that the king will not do for you? If for any reason whatsoever you prefer to do evil, and if you plot evil, treacherous things, then you, together with your entire family, shall die by the axe of the king . . . And when you wrote, saying, 'May the king, my Lord, give me leave this year, and then I will go next year to the king, my Lord. If this is impossible, I will send my son in my place'—the king, your Lord, let you off this year, in accordance with what you said. Come yourself, or send your son, and you will see the king at whose sight all lands live. (*EA* 162, 22 ff., trans. Moran (1992: 249))

We cannot be sure what precisely Akhenaten's intentions were, or what he hoped to achieve by summoning Aziru to Egypt. His first concern may have been to remove at least temporarily from Egyptian territory in Syria the man who had been so active in destabilizing it. But he may also have entertained hopes that Aziru could still be used as an effective instrument of Egyptian authority in the region, provided satisfactory terms could be negotiated with him.

In spite of the pharaoh's threats, it is difficult to see why Aziru would have been prepared to comply with his summons had there been no positive incentives for him to do so. Given the volatility of the Syrian scene, especially with the Hittites' intrusion into the region, and the tenuousness of Egyptian authority over its subject

[76] *EA* 149, 37–40, 67–70.   [77] *EA* 151, 69–73.

territories, an attempt by Akhenaten to enforce his demand would simply have driven Aziru into the Hittite camp. As an astute political strategist, Aziru must have carefully weighed up the consequences of either complying with or defying the pharaoh's ultimatum. His conclusion was that at this stage he had more to gain by complying. And so he did, while no doubt in his own mind keeping open the question of where his future allegiance would lie.[78]

Yet Aziru may not have reckoned on the length of time that the pharaoh would keep him in Egypt—it was at least a year. Indeed there were rumours that Aziru would never leave Egypt, that his son Duppi-Tesub had sold him to the pharaoh for gold. This information is revealed to us in a letter written to Akhenaten probably by Duppi-Tesub, urging the pharaoh to allow his father to return home immediately;[79] his continued absence was placing the kingdom of Amurru at serious risk from hostile neighbours. This was reinforced in a letter to Aziru from his brothers(?) Ba'aluya and Batti'ilu,[80] with the alarming news that Hittite troops under the command of Lupakku had captured cities in the territory of Amka (Amki).[81] There was an even more alarming report, yet to be confirmed, that a further force of 90,000(??) Hittite infantry under the command of Zitana had arrived in the country of Nuhasse.[82] The news was grave, and seemed to point to an imminent and massive Hittite-led offensive against Amurru, from both north (Nuhasse) and south (Amka).

These circumstances may have persuaded the pharaoh to allow Aziru to return home immediately, to rally his forces for the defence of his kingdom. It was not only the Amurrite kingdom that was at stake. By invading Amka the Hittites had violated Egyptian subject territory, and might well mount a more comprehensive challenge to Egyptian territorial possessions in Syria, if their depredations proceeded without check.

We do not know what agreements were reached between Akhenaten and Aziru while the latter was in Egypt. But Aziru's return to Syria allegedly to protect Egyptian interests there must

---

[78] For his compliance, see *EA* 168.   [79] *EA* 169.   [80] *EA* 170.

[81] The Biqāʿ valley between Lebanon and Antilebanon; Gurney (1990: 49). For a discussion of the sources of information on the Hittite attack, see Sürenhagen (1985: 40–51).

[82] On the number, see Murnane (1990: 19 n. 101).

reflect clear assurances by the Amurrite king that he would remain firm in his loyalty to the pharaoh. Akhenaten's options were very limited. By detaining Aziru in Egypt, he faced the almost certain loss of Amurru and other Egyptian territories in Syria to the Hittites. By releasing Aziru, he could do little more than hope that Aziru would honour any undertakings he had given to defend Egyptian interests in Syria. The risks were great—but there really was no viable alternative.

For a short time after his return, Aziru apparently demonstrated his loyalty to his Egyptian overlord by continuing a dispute with Niqmaddu II, king of Ugarit and now a Hittite vassal, begun during his absence by his brother(?) Ba'aluya. But a settlement was reached between the two rulers.[83] This was followed, probably with little delay, by a treaty with Suppiluliuma.[84] There may well have been further protests, threats, and demands from the pharaoh that Aziru return to Egypt.[85] But confident in the protection of the Hittite king, and with the consolidation of his position through regional alliances (for example, with Niqmaddu and Aitakkama) Aziru could safely ignore his former overlord. He remained faithful to his new Hittite overlord until his death.

Suppiluliuma Consolidates his Syrian Conquests

The Hittite conquests in the one-year Syrian campaign, and the events which followed in the aftermath of this campaign resulted in the establishment of a network of Hittite vassal states extending through almost the entire region of Syria north of Aba (Apina). Niqmaddu II had pledged his allegiance to Suppiluliuma at Alalah, and had been installed as vassal ruler on the throne of the kingdom of Ugarit. Tette had been installed as vassal ruler of Nuhasse. Kadesh was removed from the Egyptian orbit and became a Hittite vassal state when Suppiluliuma put Aitakkama on its throne. Aziru had eventually thrown his lot in with Suppiluliuma and brought the kingdom of Amurru into the Hittite fold. And both Aitakkama and Aziru used their status as Hittite vassals to extend their own territories at the expense of neighbouring states who remained faithful to their Egyptian allegiance. Protests and appeals by these states to

[83] *PRU* IV, 281–6, Dossier II C (for the suggested order of events, see p. 283).
[84] *PD* no. 4 (*CTH* 49), 70–5. See Singer (1991*a*: 154).
[85] See Singer (1991*a*: 153–4).

the pharaoh apparently went unanswered, as in the case of Abi-
Milki of Tyre, Akizzi of Qatna, and most notably as we have have
seen, Rib-Addi of Gubla. Thus Qatna, whose ruler Akizzi held firm
to his Egyptian allegiance, fell victim to Aitakkama,[86] who had both
Hittite support and the support of Aziru.

But Suppiluliuma could not yet claim total victory. Tusratta still
eluded him. And there was still one Mitannian stronghold to be
conquered—Carchemish on the Euphrates. While the Mitannian
king and a major centre of Mitannian power remained beyond
his grasp, Suppiluliuma's conquests were incomplete. In what is
commonly referred to as the Second Syrian War, or Hurrian War,
Suppiluliuma launched a series of military operations, over a
period of some six years,[87] which resulted in the final subjugation
of Mitanni and the consolidation of Hittite control over Syrian
territory north of Aba.

Akhenaten had died some ten years before this war, and with the
abandonment of his capital Amarna within three to four years of
his death, the Amarna archive came to an end. Thus we lose one
of our chief sources of information on developments in Syria.
Unfortunately the section of the *Deeds* covering the period after
Akhenaten's death is too fragmentary for any significant information to be gained from it. We do know, however, that by the year
immediately preceding the Second Syrian War Suppiluliuma was
back in Anatolia, engaged in further operations in the Kaska region.[88] Military operations in Syria were left in the hands of dep-
uties, notably his son Telipinu.

We have seen that Telipinu was originally appointed by
Suppiluliuma as 'priest' in Kizzuwadna—though with powers and
responsibilities which went considerably beyond a priestly role.
Subsequently his father appointed him as king (LUGAL) of the Land
of Aleppo.[89] In contrast to the other kingdoms in Syria the throne
of Aleppo was not reoccupied by a local ruler after the Hittite
conquest. Suppiluliuma had decided to establish direct rule over it

    [86] *EA* 55.   [87] See KUB XIX 9 (*CTH* 83.1).
    [88] *DS* p. 92, frag. 28 A ii 1–14.
    [89] Reference to the appointment is made in two documents, already cited, from
the reign of Hattusili III—KUB XIX 9 I 17 ff. and KBo VI 28 obv. 19 ff. We cannot be
sure when this appointment was conferred upon him, but it may well have occurred
shortly after Suppiluliuma's conquest of Aleppo in the First Syrian War; see Bryce
(1992*b*: 12–14) and cf. Cornelius (1979: 156).

by appointing his son as his viceroy there—an appointment which presumably meant that Telipinu relinquished his post in Kizzuwadna.[90]

The Hittite king's departure from Syria prompted one final attempt by the forces of Tusratta to reassert Mitannian power west of the Euphrates. Hostilities flared up in the Euphrates region around the territory of the Mitannian stronghold Carchemish. But the Hittite prince Telipinu, if he had already been installed as viceroy in Aleppo, was well placed to meet any fresh challenge from across the Euphrates—which may indeed have been one of the main reasons for his appointment. He now moved swiftly to deal with the situation. Leading an expedition against the enemy forces, he subdued the countries of Arziya and Carchemish—though not the city of Carchemish—and established a winter camp in the town of Murmuriga.[91]

But at this point he was summoned from the region for a meeting with his father, leaving behind a Hittite garrison of 600 troops[92] and chariotry under the command of Lupakki. The situation in Syria remained unstable. The city of Carchemish had yet to be taken, and Mitannian forces invaded the Euphrates region and laid siege to the Hittite garrison at Murmuriga.

The meeting between Suppiluliuma and his son took place in Uda in the Lower Land, where Suppiluliuma was involved in the celebration of religious festivals. The chief purpose of the meeting was probably to provide the king with first-hand information on the current military situation in Syria, particularly in the region of Carchemish, to assess whether his own return was warranted.[93] With the absence of both the king and his son from Syria, Hittite control in the region came under increasing pressure. The Hittite garrison at Murmuriga was in danger of falling to the Mitannian besieging force. At the same time the Egyptian pharaoh, now Tutankhamun, sensing a weakening of the Hittites' grasp on the subject territories they had taken from Egypt, and seeking to

---

[90] It is unlikely that he held both posts simultaneously, as Goetze (1940: 12 n. 51) suggests.

[91] *DS* p. 92, frag. 28 A ii 1–14.

[92] Or 700? See *DS* p. 92 n. 27.

[93] *Contra* Goetze (1975a: 17), who says that the purpose of Telipinu's return was to attend to urgent religious duties. The reference to Suppiluliuma's religious activities in Uda seems quite incidental.

regain some of Egypt's prestige and influence in the region, launched an attack on Kadesh.[94]

The danger of a renewed and strengthened alliance between the weakened though still unconquered Mitannian king and a pharaoh who sought to restore Egypt's lost power in Syria might well have assumed major proportions. Decisive action, taken by the king in person, was essential. As soon as the winter had passed, Suppiluliuma began his march into Syria. He paused at Tegarama, where after reviewing his troops and chariotry he sent ahead of him an army under the command of his son, the crown prince Arnuwanda, and his brother Zida, the Chief of the Bodyguards. Their military successes paved the way for Suppiluliuma's own arrival in the region, to undertake the last remaining task that would complete the total destruction of the Mitannian empire—the conquest of the city of Carchemish.

As he was preparing to lay siege to the city, he also sought to settle a score with Egypt. In spite of his apparent attempts to maintain peaceful relations with the pharaoh, the Egyptians had attacked Kadesh, which the Hittites claimed as their own territory.[95] This allegedly unprovoked act of aggression had infuriated Suppiluliuma. Now that Egypt's Mitannian ally was close to total collapse, retaliatory action could be taken. A detachment of troops was dispatched under the command of Lupakki and Tarhunta-zalma for a quid pro quo attack against the Egyptian subject state Amka. As Suppiluliuma was later to say to the Egyptian envoy Hani:

I myself was [   ] friendly, but you, you suddenly did me evil. You came(?) and attacked the man of Kadesh whom I had taken away(?) from the king of the Land of Hurri. When I heard this, I became angry, and I sent forth my own troops and chariots and the lords. So they came and attacked your territory, the Land of Amka.   (*DS* p. 97, frag. 28, E3 iv 1–8, adapted from trans. by Güterbock)[96]

But was this sufficient to satisfy the Hittite king's wrath? The Egyptians might well have feared that once the destruction of

[94] *DS* p. 93, frag. 28 A ii 21–3.
[95] Although as we have noted it had formerly belonged to Egypt before it was conquered by Suppiluliuma.
[96] The Hittite attack referred to here was the second of two such attacks on Amka, both perhaps by the same commander. For discussion of the relationship between the attacks, see Houwink ten Cate (1963: 275), Bryce (1990: 103 n. 28).

Mitanni was complete, the full force of Hittite military might would be turned their way. To make matters worse, the Egyptian monarchy was suddenly plunged into crisis. It was this which gave rise to one of the most extraordinary, and one of the most puzzling, episodes in the history of the ancient Near East.

'Such a Thing has Never Happened to me in my Whole Life!'[97]

As Suppiluliuma prepared for his final onslaught on Carchemish, he received word that a messenger had arrived from Egypt, with an urgent letter from the Egyptian queen. With some surprise, he listened as the letter was read to him. It began with a simple statement. 'My husband is dead.' Then followed an extraordinary request. Surprise turned quickly to amazement as the Hittite king realized the full implications of what the queen was asking of him. 'Such a thing has never happened to me in my whole life!', he exclaimed. He hastily convened a council of his nobles, seeking their reaction and advice. Could the queen be trusted? Was she attempting to deceive them? A decision was made to send the royal chamberlain Hattusa-ziti to Egypt. The king's instructions to him were clear: 'Go and bring me back the truth!'

The request as recorded in the *Deeds* was baldly stated: 'I have no son. But they say that you have many sons. If you would give me one of your sons, he would become my husband. I will never take a servant of mine and make him my husband!' (*DS* p. 94, frag. 28, A iii 11–15).

The pharaoh whose sudden death had led to this request is called Niphururiya (Nibhururiya) in the *Deeds*. This is a precise rendering in cuneiform of Tutankhamun's prenomen Nebkheperure. Although a number of scholars have attempted to equate the pharaoh in question with Akhenaten,[98] the case for Tutankhamun seems virtually irrefutable.[99]

---

[97] For a stylistic analysis of the account of the following episode, see Cancik (1976: 163–7). The translated extracts from the account are adapted from Güterbock's translation.

[98] e.g. Krauss (1978: esp. 9–19). Further arguments in favour of Akhenaten have recently been reiterated by Helck (1994: 16–22) in support of his previously stated position. Smenkhkhare has also been suggested; see Wilhelm and Boese (1987/9: 101–2).

[99] See Edel (1948: 149), Kitchen's review of Krauss (1985: 44), and most recently Bryce (1990), supported by van den Hout (1994: 85).

The widow of the pharaoh is called Dahamunzu in the *Deeds*. The name simply means 'the wife of the king'.[100] But we know from Egyptian records that this was the queen Ankhesenpaaten (after the restoration of the Theban gods, she was called Ankhesenamun).[101] She was the third eldest of Akhenaten's and Nefertiti's six daughters. At the time of her husband's death she was probably 21 or 22 years old, three years or so older than Tutankhamun. This was the woman whose request to Suppiluliuma had aroused such surprise and suspicion. Hostilities had recently flared between the two kingdoms. They were now virtually on a war footing. Yet within a matter of a few weeks the Egyptian queen had asked for a marriage alliance! Leaving aside the context in which this request was made, it was certainly not uncommon for such alliances to be arranged between Near Eastern rulers. The difference here was that Tutankhamun's widow was not merely offering a marriage alliance. She was offering, to a foreign prince, her kingdom's throne! Little wonder that Suppiluliuma decided to send his chamberlain Hattusa-ziti to Egypt to determine the sincerity of the queen's request before he acceded to it.[102]

In the meantime, Suppiluliuma turned his attention back to the siege of Carchemish:

He had besieged it for seven days, and on the eighth day he fought a battle against it for one day and took(?) it in a terrific battle. When he had conquered the city—since my father feared the gods—on the upper citadel he let no one into the presence(?) of (the deity) [Kubaba (?)] and of (the deity) LAMMA, and he did not rush close to any one of the temples . . . But from the lower town he removed the inhabitants, silver, gold, and bronze utensils and carried them to Hattusa.   (*DS* p. 95, frag. 28, A iii 28–41)

When the city finally fell, Suppiluliuma installed his son Piyassili, who now adopted the Hurrian throne-name Sarri-Kusuh, as viceroy in the Land of Carchemish.[103]

[100] See Federn (1960).

[101] This identification depends of course on the understanding that Niphururiya = Tutankhamun. If the pharaoh in question is Akhenaten, then 'Dahamunzu' must be one of his wives; Helck (1994: 20) suggests Kiye (as in his earlier publications).

[102] Cf. the comments by Liverani (1990: 278–9) on this episode.

[103] *DS* pp. 95–6, frag. 28, E3 17–20. The appointment is also referred to in KUB xix 9 1 17ff. and KBo vi 28 obv. 19ff. Both documents refer to the appointment of Telipinu as king (i.e. viceroy) of Aleppo in the same context.

It was about this time that Tusratta finally met his end. He had avoided capture by the Hittites, and his whereabouts remained unknown. But reports were received that he had fallen victim to a group of assassins, which included his own son Sattiwaza.[104] Suppiluliuma could now begin his homeward trek to Hattusa, confident that all his main objectives in his conflict with Mitanni had been accomplished.

By appointing his sons as viceroys in Syria—Telipinu in Aleppo and Sarri-Kusuh in Carchemish—he had taken the unprecedented step of imposing direct Hittite rule over subject territories beyond the homeland. He had good reason for doing so. The destruction of the Mitannian empire had been achieved. But Egypt remained a constant threat to Hittite interests in Syria and might well try to win back its lost territories. Assyria, now released from Mitannian bondage, was also beginning to loom menacingly on the horizon. When we add to this the fluctuating loyalties and the inherently volatile relationships between the local Syrian kingdoms, it must have been very clear to Suppiluliuma that his hold on the region would remain tenuous without a permanent strong Hittite presence to enforce it. It was only after completing his arrangements for viceregal rule in Carchemish as well as in Aleppo, that he felt he could leave Syria, with reasonable hopes for a lasting *pax Hethitica* in the region.

Once back in Hattusa, he awaited the return of his envoy Hattusa-ziti from Egypt.

An Aborted Marriage Alliance

The following spring, as soon as the winter snows had begun to thaw, Hattusa-ziti returned to the Hittite court. He was accompanied by one of the queen's special envoys, a man called Hani. The meeting with Suppiluliuma took place in the pillared audience chamber of the Hittite palace. Here Hattusa-ziti presented his king with a furious letter from the Egyptian queen:

Why did you say 'they deceive me' in that way? Had I a son, would I have written about my own and my country's shame to a foreign land? You did not believe me, and you even spoke thus to me! He who was my husband is dead. I have no son! Never shall I take a servant of mine and make him

---

[104] *PD* no. 1, 14–15, obv. 48.

my husband! I have written to no other country. Only to you I have written. They say you have many sons; so give me one son of yours. To me he will be husband. In Egypt he will be king!   (*DS* pp. 96–7, frag. 28, A iii 50–A iv 12)[105]

As Suppiluliuma listened to the letter being read to him, his own anger mounted. What right had the Egyptians to complain? Had he not good reason to suspect their intentions? Had they not recently made a treacherous, unprovoked attack on Kadesh, and suffered the consequences when Amka was attacked in retaliation? Fear and further treachery were the motives underlying the Egyptian queen's approach. That at least was Suppiluliuma's conclusion: 'When they (the Hittite expeditionary force) attacked Amka, which is your country, you probably were afraid; and (therefore) you keep asking me for a son of mine (as if it were my) duty. He will in some way become a hostage. You will not make him king!' (*DS* p. 97, frag. 28, E3 iv 8–12).

The signs for a successful outcome to the queen's mission were decidedly unfavourable. But then it was the turn of the Egyptian envoy Hani to speak. Hani's name occurs a number of times within the context of Egyptian diplomatic missions. He was well known as an experienced and highly accomplished representative of the Egyptian court. His approach to Suppiluliuma was conciliatory—and ingratiating:

Oh my Lord! This is our country's shame! If we had a son of the king at all, would we have come to a foreign country and kept asking for a lord for ourselves? Niphururiya who was our lord is dead. He has no son. Our Lord's wife is solitary. We are seeking a son of our Lord (i.e. Suppiluliuma) for the kingship in Egypt. And for the woman, our Lady, we seek him as her husband! Furthermore, we went to no other country, only here did we come! Now, oh our Lord, give us a son of yours!   (*DS* pp. 97–8, frag. 28, E3 iv 13–25)

The king was finally won over: 'Since my father was kind-hearted, he complied with the word of the woman, and concerned himself with the matter of (supplying her with) a son' (*DS* p. 97, frag. 28, A iv 13–15).

Suppiluliuma had already made arrangements for three of his five sons. His eldest son Arnuwanda was crown prince. His next

---

[105] The actual letter which the queen sent to Suppiluliuma, KBo xxviii 51, survives in fragmentary form and has been ed. by Edel, *ÄHK* I no. 1, 14–15. The text is written in Akkadian.

two sons, Telipinu and Sarri-Kusuh, had been appointed viceroys in Syria. His youngest son Mursili was still only a child, or young adolescent. That left only the fourth son—a young man called Zannanza. It was Zannanza who now set off for Egypt to marry the Egyptian queen.

If the reason Mursili gives for the decision his father finally made is true—a concession made to the young widowed queen out of the kindness of his heart—then it was an extraordinary act of gallantry on Suppiluliuma's part. We can be justifiably sceptical. Throughout his career Suppiluliuma had proved himself a shrewd political operator as well as an able military commander. Skilful diplomacy could often achieve important political objectives—at far less cost than force of arms. Undoubtedly Suppiluliuma found great attraction in the prospect of one of his sons becoming king of Egypt. In this way he could extend Hittite power and influence a far greater distance than he could hitherto have dreamed of—without one drop of Hittite blood being spilt. And at one diplomatic stroke he could put an end to any future threat Egypt might pose to Hittite territory in Syria. But his son's safety was his paramount concern. It was only after being convinced that Zannanza would come to no harm that he dispatched him to Egypt.

Zannanza began the journey. Back in Hattusa, Suppiluliuma waited anxiously for news of his son's safe arrival in Egypt. Several weeks passed. Then a messenger arrived at the Hittite court. Zannanza was dead. He had been killed on the journey to Egypt.

Who was responsible? His father had no doubts about this. When the news of Zannanza's death was broken to him, Suppiluliuma's grief and fury knew no bounds. He held the Egyptians directly responsible for the crime: 'When my father heard of the murder of Zannanza, he began to lament for Zannanza, and to the gods he spoke thus: "Oh Gods! I did no evil, yet the people of Egypt did this to me! They also attacked the frontier of my country!"' (*DS* p. 108, frag. 31, 7'–11').

Vengeance was inevitable. For the Egyptians, the crisis caused by Tutankhamun's death, the last king of the eighteenth dynasty, was serious enough in itself. They were now faced as well with the threat of all-out war with Hatti. It was imperative for a new king to be installed on the throne without further delay.

The man who now became pharaoh is depicted on one of the
walls of Tutankhamun's tomb, performing the final ceremonies
before the tomb was sealed. His name was Ay. Suspicion inevitably
falls on him as the person most likely to have ordered the murder
of the Hittite prince. Though not of royal blood himself, it is possible that he was related by marriage to the royal family. He had
been one of Akhenaten's closest and most trusted advisers, and
continued to exercise a strong influence in the Egyptian court
throughout the reign of Tutankhamun. On Tutankhamun's death,
he might well have seen himself as the rightful successor to the
Egyptian throne. It is scarcely surprising that Suppiluliuma—and
posterity—should blame Ay for the Hittite prince's death. But he
was probably innocent of the crime.

From the fragmentary remains of a letter written by
Suppiluliuma to the new pharaoh, it is clear that Ay denied all
responsibility for Zannanza's death.[106] Anticipating the possibility
of Hittite military retaliation for the prince's death, Ay warned
Suppiluliuma of the strength of the Egyptian forces. He none the
less hoped that Suppiluliuma would accept his declaration of innocence, and earnestly sought to establish friendly relations with him.
To no avail. Suppiluliuma rejected the pharaoh's attempt at reconciliation, and demanded vengeance. On his orders, a Hittite army
under the command of his son Arnuwanda crossed the Egyptian
frontiers in southern Syria and launched a vigorous attack on the
cities in the region.[107] Many thousands of prisoners-of-war were
taken, and transported back to the Hittite homeland.

The sequel to this has an ironic twist. The prisoners brought with
them a plague, which for the next twenty years ravaged the kingdom and decimated its population (see Chapter 8).

The murder of the Hittite prince still remains a mystery. It
presents us with one of the intriguing 'what ifs' of history. What if

---

[106] KUB xix 20 (*CTH* 154), ed. Hagenbuchner (1989), no. 208, 304–9. For a
suggested reconstruction of the letter's contents, see Murnane (1990: 25–7). Van
den Hout (1994) has established a join with the small fragment KBo xii 23 (*CTH*
832), and has produced a fresh edition of the combined texts. On the basis of
the join, van den Hout argues that KUB xix 20 (+) is a draft letter written in
response to a tablet brought by the Egyptian envoy Hani with official word of
Zannanza's death, and a disclaimer by the new pharaoh of any involvement in his
death.

[107] *DS* p. 111, frag. 36. Van den Hout (1994: 85) suggests that Suppiluliuma may
have appointed his son to lead the campaign instead of going himself because of his
ongoing involvement in further campaigns in Kaskan and Hurrian territory.

Zannanza had in fact reached Egypt and ascended the Egyptian throne? Would this have been the beginning of a powerful Egyptian–Hittite alliance which might have changed the course of history? What the murder did lead to, on the contrary, was an intensification of the enmity between Hatti and Egypt which culminated some fifty years later in a showdown at Kadesh.

Problems on the Eastern Flank

For the remaining years of his reign, Suppiluliuma had pressing problems to deal with on the eastern flank of his empire. The conquest of the Mitannian kingdom had left a political vacuum east of the Euphrates, which the newly liberated Assyrian kingdom, then under the rule of Assur-uballit, was hastening to fill. The kingdom of Mitanni was despoiled by troops from both Assyria and the kingdom of Alse. Its treasures were carried off to Assyria, its charioteers to Alse where they suffered death by impalement. The northern part of the former Mitannian kingdom was now divided between Assyria and Alse.[108]

The throne of what was still left of the old kingdom was occupied by Tusratta's son Sattiwaza. This was a cause for further inter-dynastic disputes. Suppiluliuma had almost certainly promised to support Artatama as the rightful king of Mitanni when he drew up his treaty with him before the First Syrian War. If so, he apparently reneged on his promise after Tusratta's downfall. The succession had passed to Tusratta's son. This provoked a bitter reaction from Artatama's son Suttarna III. If Tusratta was a usurper, then his son had no right to the throne. A struggle ensued, which ended with Sattiwaza being forced to abandon the throne and flee for his life, first to Babylonia and then to Hatti where he sought Suppiluliuma's assistance in reinstating him.

Contrary to any previous agreement he had made with Artatama, Suppiluliuma may have subsequently promised to back Sattiwaza in the succession stakes. The murder of his father Tusratta, along with an undertaking that Sattiwaza would rule what was left of his father's kingdom as an ally of the Hittite king, was probably the price the Mitannian prince was called upon to pay for this backing.

---

[108] See *PD* no. 2, 36–9, obv. 1 ff.

But Sattiwaza had been overthrown, and the new regime which replaced him must have been decidedly hostile to the regime in Hattusa. For Suppiluliuma the situation was intolerable, particularly with the Assyrian threat to the region looming ever larger. Indeed the new Mitannian king Suttarna had probably aligned himself with Assyria, ingratiating himself with its king by sending him rich gifts including booty which the former Mitannian king Saustatar I had seized from Assur.[109] If the remainder of the Mitannian kingdom were to be established firmly within the Assyrian orbit, the Hittites' subject territories west of the Euphrates, and particularly the viceregal kingdom of Carchemish, would be at grave risk.

Suppiluliuma decided to act. After consolidating an alliance with Sattiwaza by marrying one of his daughters to him, he sent the Mitannian prince to Carchemish to prepare for a joint campaign across the Euphrates with the viceroy Sarri-Kusuh—with the object of re-establishing Sattiwaza on the Mitannian throne:

Having supported by my hand Sattiwaza, son of Tusratta the king, I will let him sit upon his father's throne. And in order that the Land of Mitanni—which is a great country—be not destroyed, I, the Great King, King of Hatti, will let the Mitanni country live. (Suppiluliuma:Sattiwaza Treaty, *PD* no. 1 (*CTH* 51), 18–19, obv. 56–8, trans. Liverani (1990: 74))

Irrite and Harran fell before the army of the Hittite and Mitannian princes, who finally led their troops in triumph into the Mitannian capital, with much rejoicing from the local populace.[110] Enemy resistance seems to have been minimal. Apart from some minor skirmishing with the invaders, the Assyrian king Assur-uballit decided to avoid becoming embroiled in a major conflict with the Hittites—for the time being.

The Boundaries are Redrawn

Following the military success won by Sarri-Kusuh and Sattiwaza, Suppiluliuma drew up a treaty with Sattiwaza, now restored to the Mitannian throne, which bound him in a close alliance with his military partner, the viceroy of Carchemish.[111] But the kingdom

---

[109] *PD* no. 2, 36–9, obv. 4–7.

[110] See *PD* no. 2, 44–7, obv. 37 ff., *DS* pp. 110–11, frag. 35.

[111] The treaty survives in two forms—one prepared by Suppiluliuma (*CTH* 51), the other by Sattiwaza (*CTH* 52). The Akkadian versions of the treaty appear in *PD* nos. 1 and 2 respectively. Fragmentary Hittite versions also survive.

ruled by Sattiwaza was but a pale shadow of the kingdom over which his father had held sway. It was now much reduced in size, and was little more than a puppet state of the Hittite king. By contrast, the list of countries detailed in the new boundary provisions in the treaty indicates a significant expansion of the kingdom of Carchemish both east and west of the Euphrates:

I, the Great King, the King of Hatti, I conquered the Mitanni lands. In the time of the king's son Sattiwaza, I conquered them, in the time of Tusratta I conquered them. I established the Euphrates river in my rear and Mount Niblani as my boundaries. All the cities of the Land of Astata on this bank: Murmuriga, Sipri, Mazuwati, Surun, these cities in the district of [   ] I allotted to my son Piyassili. All the cities of the Land of Astata on the other bank, which are located in the Land of Mitanni: Igal[   ], Ahuna and Tirqa, these cities of the Land of Astata, since the king's son Piyassili together with the king's son Sattiwaza crossed the Euphrates and entered Irrite, all these cities on the other bank that Piyassili took, let him keep them; they belong to Piyassili.   (Suppiluliuma:Sattiwaza Treaty, *PD* no. 1, 22–5, rev. 14–21, trans. Liverani (1990: 82))

The territory to the east served as a frontier defence zone against Assyrian encroachment across the Euphrates. West of the Euphrates, the kingdom extended to the borders of Mukis. Almost certainly this meant that it absorbed part of the territory formerly belonging to the Nuhasse lands.[112] Southwards along the Euphrates, the kingdom incorporated territory formerly belonging to the kingdom of Astata.[113] To Sarri-Kusuh fell the daunting task of governing this large and inherently unstable conglomeration of subject territories.

Within the region of Astata, a new city was built under Hittite direction and inaugurated by Suppiluliuma's son Mursili II.[114] This was the city of Emar, uncovered by the French in excavations during the period 1972 to 1976 at the site of Tell Meskene Khadime on the right bank of the middle Euphrates, in what is now

---

[112] Cf. Na'aman (1980: 39–40). For the kingdom's westward extension, see *PD* no. 1, 22–5, rev. 16–21, and also the fragmentary remains of Suppiluliuma's treaty with Sarri-Kusuh, KUB xix 27 (*CTH* 50), 4' ff., trans. Forrer (1926b: 48–9). Cf. Klengel (1965b: 51, 73) who discusses the boundaries of the latter's kingdom. For the suggestion that the land of Mukis was actually incorporated in the kingdom of Carchemish, see Klengel (1965b: 78); cf. *PRU* iv, 63 n. 1.

[113] *PD* no. 1, 22–5, rev. 18–21. On the location of Astata, see del Monte and Tischler (1978: 49).

[114] See Arnaud (1987b: 9).

commonly referred to as the 'Big Bend' of the Euphrates.[115] The
name Emar was already well known from earlier references in the
Mari archives and other contemporary documents.[116] In the early
second millennium it was evidently a prosperous centre involved
in the economic and commercial activities of Mesopotamia and
northern Syria. However, the 'Hittite city' was a new foundation
which has revealed no trace of earlier settlement. Presumably the
site of old Emar lay somewhere close by, where it still awaits
discovery.[117] The new kingdom of Emar extended along the
Euphrates to the borders of Carchemish on the north and Aleppo
on the west.[118]

Texts from the new city make clear that Emar was subject to
Hittite control from the fourteenth to the early twelfth centuries,
under the immediate jurisdiction of the viceroy at Carchemish.[119]
But although the Hittites were actively involved in the daily affairs
of the kingdom, administrative responsibilities were divided between the Hittite viceroy and a local king. The latter was supported
by a local body of elders. This body, based apparently on a clan
system, seems to have exercised an important consultative role,
which in effect considerably circumscribed the powers of the local
king. Hence at Emar political negotiations between Hittite viceroy
and the local authorities were probably more complex than in
the case of other vassal states where the Hittite king or viceroy
dealt directly and in most cases exclusively with the local vassal
ruler.[120]

---

[115] For the excavations and layout of the site and the discoveries made there, see
the papers assembled in Beyer (1982). Earlier publications on the excavations are
listed by Beyer, pp. 141–2. See also Margueron (1995).
[116] e.g. it was referred to in the Idrimi inscription (see Ch. 5) which indicates that
it was the city whence Idrimi's mother came, and to which he fled as a place of refuge
(Idrimi Inscription, 3–8).
[117] Margueron (1982a: 11–13).
[118] See Arnaud (1987: 11).
[119] As revealed by the Akkadian texts from the site, ed. Arnaud (1986, 1987a).
For further references to publications of the texts, see Arnaud (1987b), van der
Toorn (1994: 39–40 n. 4), Yamada (1995: 297–8). Note also the seals found there of
Ini-Tesub, viceroy of Carchemish during the reign of Tudhaliya IV (Msk 73.58 and
Msk 73.1025); see Laroche (1982: 55 no. 3 and 56 no. 4, respectively). Already
before the French excavations Astour (1969: 407) concluded from the Ugaritic
document RS 17.143 (*PRU* IV 217–18) that Emar was part of the kingdom of
Carchemish in this period.
[120] See Arnaud (1987b: 10–11). Further on the administration of Emar, see
Beckman (1995a: 26–32).

While the Hittites seem to have taken no part in the economic activities of Emar, they did involve themselves directly in the administration of justice, even down to a very mundane and routine level.[121] Thus the Hittite king received an appeal from a local priest involved in a dispute with the garrison commander over property and taxes, and made a judgment in favour of the priest:

Thus (speaks) My Sun: Say to Alziyamuwa: 'Look, this Zu-Baʿal, a priest, man of Astata, has prostrated himself before me (in these terms): "The house of my parent, AN-damali, and the vineyard, Alziyamuwa takes from me and gives it to Paluwa. As for the tax, formerly I did not pay it at all. But now it has been imposed upon me." So now, let no one take it from him, and let no one take from him either his estate or his vineyard. As for the tax which he has never paid, why have you now imposed it upon him? What he did before, let him do now.' (MsK 73. 1097 = Laroche (1982: no. 1) based on Laroche's trans. (1982: 54))

The Roles of the Viceroys

There may well have been marked differences between the roles and functions of the viceroys Sarri-Kusuh and Telipinu whom Suppiluliuma appointed in Syria. By virtue of his appointment in Carchemish, and the powers and responsibilities which this appointment entailed, Sarri-Kusuh seems to have played the more influential and more active role in Syrian affairs, and was perhaps generally regarded as the chief representative of Hittite interests in the region. The territories assigned to him on his appointment must have meant that his kingdom reached the very boundaries of the kingdom of Aleppo, which apparently had not been extended on Telipinu's appointment beyond the limits of the former vassal state.[122]

Telipinu on the other hand is conspicuously absent from the record of political and military activities in Syria after his brother's appointment in Carchemish. While he clearly did have a military role in Syria prior to the Second Syrian War, this role was apparently taken over by, or reassigned to, Sarri-Kusuh at the end of the first year of the war. From this time onwards Telipinu took no

---

[121] Cf. Arnaud (1987b: 13).

[122] Some of the territories taken from the kingdom by the Mitannian king may have been restored to it by Suppiluliuma at the time of Telipinu's appointment; see Na'aman (1980: 38, 40).

further part, as far as we can determine, in the political or military affairs of the region as a whole. He may, however, have exercised important religious and judicial responsibilities throughout the Syrian region, by deputizing for his father in the fulfilment of religious responsibilities in his capacity as 'Great Priest', and by performing viceregal judicial responsibilities, which included the arbitration of disputes between local vassal rulers.

Thus in the broad context of Hittite authority in Syria, Telipinu's role as Great Priest in the chief religious centre of the region, and as arbiter of disputes between neighbouring vassal states, complemented Sarri-Kusuh's predominantly military role in the region. In the religious, judicial, and military functions assigned to them, the viceroys in Carchemish and Aleppo exercised in Syria the three most important functions of the Hittite king himself within the Hittite realm as a whole.[123]

Suppiluliuma's Legacy

Some six years after his capture of Carchemish, Suppiluliuma died, probably a victim of the plague brought by Egyptian prisoners-of-war to Hatti. He is generally regarded as the greatest of all Hittite kings, and his reputation is in many respects well merited. He had brought the kingdom of Hatti from the brink of annihilation to become the most powerful kingdom of the Near Eastern world. He had achieved the destruction of the Mitannian empire, which had long been the greatest threat to Hittite expansion in Syria, and a major threat to the security of Hittite territories within Anatolia, including the homeland itself.

Yet his achievements need some qualification. In the last years of his reign, Assyria was rapidly replacing Mitanni as a major threat to Hittite territory west of the Euphrates—a threat which was to pose an ever-increasing problem to the king's successors. Tensions between Hatti and Egypt remained high, and with the emergence of a strong new Egyptian dynasty, it was only a matter of time before

---

[123] I can see no justification for Klengel's suggestion (1965*b*: 73) that Aleppo was actually under Sarri-Kusuh's control, or that Telipinu was in any sense his brother's subordinate. According to the documents from Hattusili III's reign, the title LUGAL was conferred upon both Telipinu and Sarri-Kusuh without distinctiion. I see no reason for doubting this statement (*contra* Klengel (1965*b*: 73, 196–7)), or for assuming that there was in fact some differentiation in the *formal status* conferred upon the brothers.

serious conflict would erupt over subject territory in Syria. In the west, the Arzawa lands had only temporarily been pacified. And the widespread uprisings throughout Anatolia which followed shortly after the king's death demonstrated how tenuous Suppiluliuma's control had been over the territories which he held in subjection. The problems faced by the Hittite kingdom were exacerbated by the plague which had carried off the king and continued to ravage the homeland for many years. Further, the king left his immediate successors with a major problem to deal with in the royal household itself: his wife, the Babylonian princess Tawananna.

CHAPTER 8

A Young King Proves his Worth: The Reign of Mursili II (c.1321–1295)

The Brief Reign of Arnuwanda II

In spite of the mounting external pressures faced by the kingdom of Hatti at the time of Suppiluliuma's death, the prospects for maintaining control over the territories won or regained during his reign appeared reasonably promising. The responsibility for governing the kingdom lay primarily in the hands of the king's three eldest sons, to each of whom Suppiluliuma had allocated specific roles and spheres of authority. All were experienced in administering the affairs of the kingdom, and all had proved capable and successful military commanders. In this respect at least Suppiluliuma had made good provision for the security of his kingdom after his death.

In Hattusa the succession passed to the crown prince Arnuwanda. Although we know little about his career,[1] it is clear that he came to the throne as an experienced military commander, widely respected by his kingdom's subjects and enemies alike. In Syria the permanent presence of the viceroys Sarri-Kusuh and Telipinu was an important deterrent against Assyrian and Egyptian encroachment on Hittite subject territory in the region, and served also to keep the Syrian vassal states under control.

In the regions closer to the homeland, the situation was more volatile. To the west and south-west, the Arzawa lands remained hostile, and a constant threat to Hittite subject territories adjacent to them. However, the appointment of the veteran commander Hannutti as governor of the Lower Land[2] had ensured that for the

[1] We have no information about him beyond his expedition to Syria which paved the way for his father's siege of Carchemish, and a subsequent expedition into Egyptian territory, *DS* p. 111, frag. 36. On a seal impression from the Nişantepe archive he is associated with his stepmother Tawananna; see Otten (1995: 17–19).

[2] The appointment of such governors was rare, and confined to a few key territories close to the homeland—notably Pala-Tummanna, and the Upper and Lower Lands; see Goetze (1964: 32).

time being there was no fresh outbreak of aggression from this region. Of more immediate concern were the threats confronting the Hittites from the Kaska zone and neighbouring territories. Already before the end of Suppiluliuma's reign, Kaskan aggression against Hittite territory which had continued sporadically throughout the reign was gathering fresh momentum,[3] due to the king's preoccupation with affairs in Syria:

Furthermore since my father was in Hurrian territory, as long as he fought with the Hurrian countries and stayed there, many enemies were levied from behind, from Kaska, and they oppressed the Land of Hatti and part they destroyed and part they even occupied and held in possession. (*Comprehensive Annals*, *AM* 152–3, trans. Houwink ten Cate (1967: 49–50))

Serious though the situation was, it was not yet out of control. But then an unexpected turn of events precipitated a crisis which once more imperilled the very existence of the Hittite kingdom. Not long after his accession Arnuwanda fell ill, probably another victim of the plague which had carried off his father. News that the new king was ailing, probably terminally ill, spread rapidly, encouraging widespread enemy attacks on Hittite territory. Hannutti, the governor of the Lower Land, was ordered to leave his post, and proceed north without delay. He promptly obeyed, and headed for Ishupitta in the Kaska zone—but died shortly after his arrival. His death must have been a tragic blow to Arnuwanda's hopes of restoring control in the northern regions. The crisis intensified. With the loss of one of its most able commanders, Hatti was now faced with rapidly escalating enemy action and rebellion.[4]

This was the situation confronting Suppiluliuma's youngest son Mursili, when on the death of his brother Arnuwanda, perhaps no more than eighteen months after his accession, the mantle of kingship was suddenly thrust upon him.[5]

---

[3] See Houwink ten Cate (1967: 59–61).

[4] *AM* 18–19.

[5] The succession would normally have passed to a son of Arnuwanda. We do know of one such son, Tulpi.LUGAL.ma, who appears in a fragmentary sacrificial list, KBo XIII 42 (*CTH* 661.9), referred to by Bin-Nun (1975: 279–80). But there is no other mention of this son, and he may have predeceased his father, or have been a young child at the time of his father's death.

The 'Child' upon the Throne

The reaction of Hatti's enemies to the news of Mursili's accession was one of undisguised contempt:

When my brother Arnuwanda became a god, the enemy lands who had not yet made war, these enemy lands also made war. And the neighbouring enemy lands spoke as follows: 'His father, who was king of the Land of Hatti and a Hero-King, held sway over the enemy lands. And he became a god. But his son who sat upon his father's throne and was previously a great warrior fell ill, and he also became a god. Yet he who has recently sat upon his father's throne is a child. He will not preserve the Land of Hatti and the territory of the Hatti lands.' (*Ten-Year Annals, AM* 16–21)

You are a child; you know nothing and instil no fear in me. Your land is now in ruins, and your infantry and chariotry are few. Against your infantry, I have many infantry; against your chariotry I have many chariotry. Your father had many infantry and chariotry. But you, who are a child, how can you match him? (*Comprehensive Annals, AM* 18–21)

A young and inexperienced king, perhaps. But almost certainly not a child when he mounted the throne. He must already have reached an age when he was capable of ruling in his own right.[6] Had this not been the case, then other arrangements, if only temporary, would undoubtedly have been made to ensure the stability of the monarchy. There were, after all, two surviving elder brothers of Mursili, the viceroys of Carchemish and Aleppo, who would surely have seen to it that the kingdom did not collapse for want of a credible successor to the throne.

The young king was probably in his early twenties at the time of his accession. But exaggerated statements about his youth and inexperience were worth recording, for in retrospect they would make the achievements of the early years of his reign seem all the greater. Undoubtedly his first years on the throne were very critical ones. He clearly needed the advice and support of his older brothers, particularly Sarri-Kusuh, with whom he seems to have collaborated closely up to the time of the latter's death nine years later.[7]

---

[6] See Bryce (1989*b*: 28–9).

[7] Bin-Nun (1975: 283–5, 288–9) has suggested that Mursili was forced to make concessions to Sarri-Kusuh regarding the succession in Hattusa in order to dissuade him from laying claim to the Hittite throne himself. Her suggestion is based largely on her interpretation of KBo I 28 (*CTH* 57), the co-called miniature treaty which Mursili drew up with Sarri-Kusuh, probably shortly after his accession. But both her reading and interpretation of this text have been refuted by Gurney (1983: 100–1).

But the credit for restoring Hittite authority throughout Anatolia was due very largely to the young king himself. In response to the crisis confronting him on his accession, he acted with exemplary promptness and vigour, in a series of intensive campaigns of pacification and reconquest.

The Critical Early Years of Mursili's Reign

The *Annals* of Mursili provide us with a record of the military campaigns conducted throughout the king's reign. They appear in two series: (1) a summary account of Mursili's personal military achievements during the first ten years of his reign; (2) a detailed account of Hittite campaigns including the first ten years of the reign, but extending over a period of some twenty-seven years and including a record of the exploits of the king's military commanders.[8] We shall refer to each series respectively as the *Ten-Year Annals* and the *Comprehensive Annals*.

Punitive campaigns against the Kaska people occupied the first two years of Mursili's reign. When the young king felt confident that he had effectively, if only temporarily, relieved the pressures on the homeland's northern frontiers, he turned his attention to the west. Here Hittite interests were being seriously threatened by the aggressive activities of Uhhaziti, king of Arzawa Minor, the nucleus of the Arzawa complex. Uhhaziti was attempting to win, or to force, Hittite subject states in the region away from their allegiance, apparently in collaboration with the king of Ahhiyawa. The latter probably controlled a group of islands in the eastern Aegean, close to the Anatolian mainland, which could serve as a place of refuge for fugitives from Hittite authority, as well as a base for the extension of Ahhiyawan influence on the mainland.[9] Uhhaziti had also formed an alliance with other Arzawan kings in the region—an alliance which if left unchallenged might ultimately pose as serious a threat to Hatti as the Arzawan drive towards the homeland prior to Suppiluliuma's accession.

At the beginning of Mursili's third year Milawata (Millawanda), a Hittite subject state on the Aegean coast, allied itself with Ahhiyawa. The alliance, very likely engineered or facilitated

[8] Both series are catalogued as *CTH* 61 and ed. Goetze (1933) (cited as *AM*). The *Ten-Year Annals* has also been ed. by Grélois (1988).

[9] See Easton, 1985, 192, Bryce, 1989*a*, 299–300, Freu, 1990, 10 ff.

by Uhhaziti, provided the trigger for direct Hittite action in the west:

> But when it was spring, because Uhhaziti joined the side of the king of the Land of Ahhiyawa, and the Land of Millawanda had gone over to the king of the Land of Ahhiyawa . . . I sent forth Gulla and Malaziti and troops and chariots; and they destroyed the Land of Millawanda. (*Comprehensive Annals*, AM 36–7)[10]

Successful though the Hittite expeditionary force appears to have been on this particular mission, it failed to deter Uhhaziti from further provoking Mursili by providing asylum for refugees from Hittite authority. A demand from Mursili that he return them was refused. This in itself was tantamount to a declaration of war on Hatti. The time had come for a decisive showdown:

> I sent a messenger to Uhhaziti, and I wrote thus: 'When I asked for the return of my subjects who went over to you, you did not give them back to me. You treated me like a child, you despised me. Now, let us do battle, and the Storm God, My Lord, will make judgement on our dispute!' (*Ten-Year Annals*, AM 46–7)

Under Mursili's personal command, a Hittite army set out from the homeland for a major campaign in the west, aimed primarily at settling the Arzawan problem once and for all. At Sallapa, Mursili was joined by his brother Sarri-Kusuh with a contingent from Syria.[11] The combined Hittite forces now advanced into Arzawan territory.

They had divine support on their side—or so Mursili claimed:

> When I marched forth and when I reached Mount Lawasa, My Lord, the mighty Storm God, revealed to me his divine power. He unleashed a thunderbolt and my army saw the thunderbolt and the Land of Arzawa saw it. The thunderbolt proceeded and struck the Land of Arzawa and struck Apasa, the city of Uhhaziti, and brought Uhhaziti to his knees, and he fell ill. Since Uhhaziti fell ill, he did not therefore come against me in battle. He sent forth his son Piyama-Kurunta along with infantry and chariotry against me. Piyama-Kurunta confronted me in battle at the river Astarpa in Walma,[12] and I, My Sun, did battle with him. And My Lady, the

---

[10] This follows the reading of Goetze, which is supported by Güterbock (1983*a*: 135).

[11] AM 48–9.

[12] This river subsequently formed part of the boundary of the Arzawan state Mira-Kuwaliya.

Sun-Goddess of Arinna, and My Lord, the mighty Storm God and
Mezzulla and all the gods supported me. I defeated Piyama-Kurunta, son
of Uhhaziti, together with his infantry and chariotry, and I struck him
down. I pursued him again and went across into the Land of Arzawa, and
went into Apasa, the city of Uhhaziti. Uhhaziti offered me no resistance,
but fled before me and went across the sea to the islands,[13] and there he
remained. However the whole Land of Arzawa fled. (*Ten-Year Annals,
AM* 46–53)

There remained two Arzawan strongholds to be captured before
the conquest of Uhhaziti's kingdom was complete—Mount
Arinnanda and the city of Puranda, where some of the refugees
who had sought asylum from Hittite authority had gathered.
Others had fled with Uhhaziti 'to the islands', probably the group
of islands in the Aegean which were then under Ahhiyawan sovereignty. Arinnanda was blockaded by Mursili's troops, and its occupants starved into surrender:

I, My Sun, went to Mount Arinnanda. This mountain is very steep and
extends out into the sea. It is also very high, difficult of access, and rocky,
and it is impossible for horses to advance up it. The transportees[14] held it
en masse and the infantry were above *en masse*. Since it was impossible for
horses to advance up the mountain, I, My Sun, went before the army
on foot and went up Mount Arinnanda on foot. I beleaguered the
transportees with hunger and thirst. And under pressure of hunger and
thirst, they came down and fell at my feet: 'Our Lord, do not destroy us.
Our Lord, take us into subjection, and lead us up to Hattusa.'
(*Comprehensive Annals, AM* 54–7)

The other stronghold Puranda remained unconquered at the end
of the campaigning season. After withdrawing to the Astarpa river
where he set up a winter camp, Mursili returned to Arzawa the
following year, laid siege to Puranda and captured it.[15] His conquest of Uhhaziti's kingdom was now quickly completed. Uhhaziti had died in exile, and only one of his sons, Tapalazunawali,
had returned to his father's kingdom to attempt to defend it.
But with the fall of Puranda, Arzawan resistance was at an
end. Tapalazanuwali alone managed to escape. His fate remains

[13] For this interpretation of *guršawananza* (to the islands), formerly translated by
Goetze as 'zu Schiffe(???)', see Starke (1981a).
[14] i.e. those who were destined for transportation back to the homeland, as part of
the spoils of conquest.
[15] *AM* 62–5.

uncertain, though he may have sought refuge with the Ahhiyawan king, who handed him over to Mursili.[16]

Mursili had another score to settle. Before returning to Hattusa, he set out on a punitive expedition against one of the other states in the Arzawa complex, the Seha River Land,[17] whose king Manapa-Tarhunda had formed an alliance with Uhhaziti. Manapa-Tarhunda panicked when he received news of the Hittite king's approach, fresh from the victory over Uhhaziti's kingdom and bent on further vengeance. He had no alternative but to throw himself on the king's mercy: 'Manapa-Tarhunda sent a messenger to me and wrote to me as follows: "My Lord, do not kill me! Take me into subjection, my Lord. The people who have fled to me, I will hand over to my Lord."' (*Comprehensive Annals*, AM 68–9)

Mursili remained unmoved. Manapa-Tarhunda had forfeited all right to merciful treatment. The son of the previous king Muwawalwi,[18] he had once been forced to flee his country because of a dispute with two of his brothers who had sought to kill him, and had found refuge in the country of Karkisa. Mursili had intervened on the refugee's behalf, demanding of the people of Karkisa that they protect him. Subsequently when one of the brothers, Ura-Tarhunda, had violated his oath, Manapa-Tarhunda was restored to his country with Hittite support and placed on the throne. But he had proved disloyal, as Mursili reminded him:

Once when your brothers expelled you from your land, I recommended you to the people of Karkisa and also rewarded the people of Karkisa on your behalf. In spite of that you did not come to my side, and you joined sides with my enemy Uhhaziti. Am I now to take you into subjection? (*Comprehensive Annals*, AM 68–71)

Intent on revenge, Mursili was about to attack the kingdom of his treacherous vassal when something happened which caused him to have a change of heart:

I would certainly have marched against him and destroyed him utterly, but he sent forth his mother to meet me. She came and fell at my knees and

[16] This depends on the restoration of a fragmentary section of the *Annals*, AM 66–7 §25. Cf. Goetze (1975*b*: 122).

[17] Generally located in one of the river valleys of western Anatolia. The river itself is commonly identified with the Maeander but could be the Caicos (the Classical names of these rivers); see Gurney (1992: 221).

[18] See Laroche (1966) no. 839.1, Heinhold-Krahmer (1977: 75 n. 50, 381–2).

spoke to me as follows: 'My Lord, do not destroy us. Take us, my Lord, into subjection.' And since a woman came to meet me and fell at my knees, I gave way to the woman and thereupon I did not march to the Seha River Land. And I took Manapa-Tarhunda and the Seha River Land into subjection. (*Comprehensive Annals, AM* 70–3)

The episode seems to represent a remarkable last-minute change of heart by Mursili.[19] A signal example of Hittite chivalry and gallantry? That may well have been the impression Mursili wanted to create—a display of mercy in response to the old woman's appeal, an act of magnanimity towards her renegade son. This was very much in the nature of Hittite royal diplomacy—to make a show of merciful and generous conduct in situations where it was little deserved.[20] But the outward gesture may have had a strong underlying practical motive. Hittite kings were often ready to accept last-minute surrenders by recalcitrant vassal rulers and other protégés, to avoid unnecessary commitment of troops to a military campaign or a protracted siege. Mursili and his troops had already spent two years away from the homeland campaigning in Arzawa. Rather than committing himself to further campaigning in the region, the king decided to exploit the diplomatic advantages offered by the occasion. His willingness to accept a last-minute surrender, when his army was apparently on the verge of conquest, could be presented as a noble and magnanimous gesture. Hittite kings regularly took the view that a subject state was more likely to remain submissive under a contrite vassal than if it had been crushed into submission and needed a continuing Hittite presence to ensure it remained that way.[21]

Manapa-Tarhunda was accepted into Hittite vassalage and a treaty was drawn up with him. So too the other Arzawan states, Hapalla and Mira, were quick to acknowledge Hittite overlordship. Targasnalli was reinstated as vassal ruler of Hapalla,[22] and a man called Mashuiluwa was appointed ruler of Mira. We shall have more to say about him below. Thus within four years of his

---

[19] It is also recorded in Mursili's treaty with Manapa-Tarhunda, *CTH* 69; Friedrich (1930: 6–9 §4).
[20] Cf. the reason given in the *Deeds* for Suppiluliuma's eventual compliance with the Egyptian queen's request, *DS* p. 97, frag. 28, A iv 13–15.
[21] Compare, or rather contrast, the view expressed by Liverani (1990: 148), that Mursili's final acceptance of the surrender was 'only for ethical/social reasons, not for (and actually against) political reasons'.
[22] *CTH* 67.

accession, Mursili accomplished a feat which had eluded his father Suppiluliuma after many years of campaigning in Anatolia—the final conquest and subjugation of all the lands making up the Arzawa complex.

What became of the kingdom of Uhhaziti, the nucleus of the Arzawan complex? Nothing more is heard of this kingdom. It had long posed a serious threat to Hittite interests in Anatolia, it had allied itself with foreign powers hostile to Hatti, and it had almost certainly led the forces which had brought the Hittite kingdom close to extinction in the reign of Mursili's grandfather. There is a strong possibility that Mursili resolved to remove any further threat it might pose to Hittite interests in the region by destroying it totally, evacuating its population and dividing its territory amongst the other vassal states in the region.[23] He states that after he conquered the kingdom, he transported from it no less than 65,000 (or 66,000) of its inhabitants to the homeland.[24] If this figure is correct, then the kingdom must have been almost entirely depopulated.[25] Indeed in the texts following Mursili's Arzawan conquests, there is no further clearly identifiable reference to the kingdom once ruled by Uhhaziti.[26] Mursili sought to maintain control over other states in the region which he had conquered or which had submitted to his overlordship through a network of vassal treaties.[27]

Campaigns in the North

With Hittite authority firmly established in the west and south-west, Mursili was again obliged to turn his attention to the regions

---

[23] See Heinhold-Krahmer (1977: 136–47).   [24] *AM* 76–7.

[25] Košak (1981: 15) comments that the total numbers of transportees could have been no less than 50,000 and might have been as high as 100,000. As he further remarks, the impact of such a number of displaced persons is difficult to imagine. Were they all transported back to the Hittite homeland, or were some settled in other regions?

[26] See Jewell (1974: 319), Mellaart (1986b: 218–19). There are, however, references to a Land of Arzawa in texts from the reign of Mursili's son Hattusili; notably KUB xxxi 69 (*CTH* 590), a vow of the queen Puduhepa, in which divine assistance is sought for the king in a campaign against the Land of Arzawa (obv. 7'), and KBo VIII 23 (*CTH* 209.7) = Hagenbuchner (1989: 80–1 no. 48), a fragment of a letter written probably to Puduhepa, which also mentions the Land of Arzawa. In both cases, however, it is arguable that the name Arzawa is being used in its broader sense. Without more specific information, I am inclined to agree with Heinhold-Krahmer (1977: 243) that these texts provide no evidence that the kingdom of Uhhaziti continued to exist after Mursili's campaigns in the region.

[27] On the nature and purpose of the vassal treaties, see Ch. 3.

to the north and north-east of the homeland. Once more, the northern frontiers of the homeland, and the subject territories beyond, were imperilled by fresh outbreaks of aggression from Kaska. The prolonged absence of the king in the Arzawa lands was no doubt the incentive for these. Mursili responded promptly. In the year after his return from Arzawa, the fifth year of his reign, he attacked the Kaskan forces from the mountain land of Asharpaya, who had cut the route to Pala, and laid waste their territory. In the same year he invaded and conquered the Land of Arawanna.[28]

The following year savage reprisals were carried out against the Kaskans from the Land of Ziharriya who, the king claimed, had attacked Hattusa. If such an attack did in fact take place, it under-lines the chronic vulnerability of the Hittite capital to enemy action from the north, even at a time when the security of the homeland had apparently been firmly re-established. But Mursili may have exaggerated the danger to Hattusa in order to justify the ruthless retaliatory measures which he took. The Kaska land was attacked and conquered, its population slaughtered, and its city put to the torch.

The security of Hittite territories bordering the homeland to the north-east, particularly the region called the Upper Land, re-mained a constant problem. Prior to Mursili's campaigns against Kaska, a Kaskan tribal chief called Pihhuniya from the Land of Tipiya had captured the Upper Land and incorporated it into Kaskan territory.[29] Pihhuniya's conflict with the Hittites is recorded at some length in the *Annals*. Mursili tells us that he was unlike other Kaskan leaders: 'Pihhuniya did not rule in the Kaskan man-ner. But suddenly, where in the Kaskan town the rule of a single man was not (customary), Pihhuniya ruled in the manner of a king' (*Ten-Year Annals*, AM 88–9). This made him a formidable and very dangerous opponent. The Kaskans caused problems enough as disunited groups. But if amongst them there arose a leader with aspirations to kingly status, and with the ability to weld the frag-mented groups into a single united fighting force, they could well prove invincible. It was essential that Pihhuniya be dealt a decisive blow before this happened.

Mursili was determined to force the issue. He demanded that Pihhuniya hand back the Hittite subjects who had come under his

[28] AM 78–81.   [29] AM 88–9.

control. The demand was dismissed with contempt: 'I will give nothing back to you. Even if you come to fight me, I will not fight in any way on my land. I will meet you in your land and will join battle in your land' (*Ten-Year Annals*, *AM* 90–1). Whether this was mere bravado or a genuine belief in his ability to match military strength with the Hittite king, Pihhuniya eventually paid the penalty for his defiance. He was defeated in battle, his land was ravaged, and he was forced into a humiliating surrender and taken back to Hattusa in captivity.

The restoration of Hittite authority in the Upper Land was short-lived. Two years later, in Mursili's ninth year, it was again invaded, this time by troops from Hayasa. But for the present, the main theatre of action shifted to the south-east. Here there were escalating problems which required urgent attention.

Rebellion in Syria

Early in Mursili's seventh year, trouble once more flared in Syria. Unfortunately there are large gaps in the *Annals* for the early part of this year. We learn of a rebellion in the Nuhasse lands, but have only fragmentary information about the events which led up to it. It may, however, be possible to fill some of the gaps from another document, which deals with a communication between Mursili and a local ruler Abiradda, king of Barga, over a town called Yaruwatta in the border region between the Nuhasse lands and the kingdom of Barga.[30] From this we can attempt to reconstruct some of the events which led up to the Nuhasse rebellion:

Mursili received word that Tette, whom Suppiluliuma had installed as king in the Nuhasse lands, had rebelled, along with a lesser king in the region called EN-urta. Apparently Kadesh was also involved in the rebellion.[31] The uprisings in Syria presented Mursili with a serious dilemma. It was essential that they be dealt with promptly, but the king was still preoccupied with affairs in Anatolia. In the interests of the security of the homeland, he could

---

[30] KBo III 3 (*CTH* 63). See Klengel (1963), Bryce (1988*a*). Barga is probably to be located south of Aleppo and east of the Orontes river; see del Monte and Tischler (1978: 304), under Parka.

[31] If we can assign to this period the rebellion of Kadesh and Nuhasse recorded in Mursili's treaty with the Amurrite king Duppi-Tesub (*CTH* 62), Friedrich (1926: 6–7 §3) rather than to Mursili's 9th year when Mursili's *Annals* records rebellions by both Nuhasse and Kadesh (*AM* 110–15). See Bryce (1988*a*: 26).

not afford to cut short his campaigns in the north and divert his forces to Syria to deal with the rebellion there.

But the rebellion could perhaps be dealt with in another way. Mursili's intelligence sources revealed that support for Tette's action within his own family was far from secure. This could be exploited. In addition, the rebellion had brought EN-urta into conflict with Abiradda, who ruled the neighbouring land of Barga as a loyal Hittite vassal. Abiradda had lost Yaruwatta, one of his cities in the border region, to Tette's grandfather Sarrupsi, probably through the intervention of the Mitannian king Suttarna II, and now made overtures to Mursili for its return. Negotiations were conducted secretly with Tette's brother Summittara (perhaps by the viceroy Sarri-Kusuh on Mursili's behalf) with the object of deposing Tette, and either killing him or holding him prisoner until he could be handed over to the Hittites. The incentive for Summittara was that he could then assume the vassal throne for himself, and be acknowledged by Mursili as the legitimate ruler, provided he declared allegiance to him.[32] He would also be allowed to keep the border town of Yaruwatta.

Summittara was persuaded, and the coup took place. Tette was deposed, and taken into custody by his brother. That left only EN-urta to be dealt with. With the scale of the crisis now considerably reduced, Mursili took time out from his northern campaigns for a brief expedition into Syria, probably the first Syrian campaign in which he was directly involved. EN-urta was defeated, and his kingdom handed over to Abiradda, who was no doubt still smarting over his failure to get back Yaruwatta. The acquisition of EN-urta's kingdom would have been more than adequate compensation. Mursili also used the opportunity to draw up a pact between Abiradda and the new regime in Nuhasse, to ensure that there would be no further hostilities between the two kingdoms. While in Syria, he may also have re-established Hittite control over Kadesh.[33]

Surprisingly, Mursili did not take custody of the rebel Nuhasse king Tette during his Syrian operations. His failure to do so was soon to have unfortunate consequences. Probably within a short time of the Hittite king's departure from Syria, Tette staged a

---

[32] See Bryce (1988*a*: 23–4).
[33] As recorded in Mursili's treaty with Duppi-Tesub (*CTH* 62), Friedrich (1926: 18 §13).

counter-coup and regained his throne.[34] Unfortunately for the Hittites, the counter-coup was staged before Mursili had troops available to prevent it. And when rebellion broke out afresh under Tette's leadership, the crisis was intensified by the arrival of an expeditionary force from Egypt to support the rebels.

The responsibility for crushing the rebellion fell upon the viceroy Sarri-Kusuh. Mursili was too heavily involved in his northern campaigns to make a second expedition into Syria, and could do no more than send an expeditionary force under the commander Kantuzzili to support his brother. Even with this support, and particularly in view of the reinforcements which the rebel king had received from Egypt, Sarri-Kusuh had serious concerns about the adequacy of his resources to deal with the rebellion. It was probably in this context that he sought to establish against Tette a military alliance with Niqmaddu II, the king of Ugarit:

The king of Nuhasse being at war with me, I instructed Niqmaddu thus: 'If, Niqmaddu, you go to war against Tette, and before I arrive in Nuhasse you take the initiative and attack the country of Tette—whatever Niqmaddu takes from Nuhasse by his own force of arms, or whoever come as fugitives into his country, he will have nothing to return to Tette should Tette reclaim his subjects in the days that follow. But if Niqmaddu does not go to war with Tette and does not perform the things I have said, the proposition contained in this tablet will be rescinded.'   (RS 17.334 (*PRU* IV, 54–5) 1–19.)[35]

It is possible that Niqmaddu, who appears to have remained consistently loyal to his alliance with the Hittites after the treaty drawn up with him by Suppiluliuma at the time of the First Syrian War, died before the agreement could be implemented, or was replaced by his son Arhalba who pursued an independent policy and engaged in diplomatic contacts with the pharaoh Horemheb.[36] Irrespective of this, the combined Hittite forces succeeded in driving the Egyptians from the region. Mursili himself had indicated his readiness to advance to meet the Egyptian force. But on reaching Ziluna he received word that the Egyptians had been defeated, and

---

[34] We have no surviving evidence of a coup, but such an event could well have been covered in the missing first column of KUB XIV 17 from the *Annals*, dealing with events in Mursili's 7th year; see Bryce (1988*a*: 28).

[35] See further Kitchen (1962: 37), Klengel (1965*b*: 75–6; 1969: 51), Spalinger (1979: 66).

[36] See Kitchen (1962: 37).

had returned to their homeland.[37] Once again Mursili diverted his attention northwards, to the Upper Land and the Kaska zone.

In spite of the success of the combined Hittite operation against the troops from Egypt, there is no indication that Sarri-Kusuh and Kantuzzili succeeded at this time in crushing the rebellion in Nuhasse. Even if they did, within two years the rebellion had broken out afresh.

War on Three Fronts

To the north-east of the homeland, Mursili was confronted in his seventh year with further problems in the kingdom of Azzi-Hayasa, previously reduced to vassal status by his grandfather Tudhaliya III. It was currently under the rule of Anniya, who had advanced on and attacked the Land of Dankuwa, and transported its population back to his kingdom.[38] Mursili marched to the borders of the king-dom and wrote to Anniya demanding the return of his subjects. When Anniya refused, Mursili immediately attacked the border fortress of Ura.[39] His campaigns against Azzi-Hayasa may well have continued through the eighth year of his reign, for which the record is all but lost. It is clear, however, that before he could complete the reconquest and pacification of the country other events intervened, some of grave moment.

By the beginning of Mursili's ninth year, Anniya was still unsubdued, and continued to defy the Hittite king's demands for the return of his subjects. And trouble erupted in the Land of Pala, when the city of Wasumana broke away from it. Nuwanza was sent to assist Pala's governor Hudupiyanza (Hutupiyanza) with its recapture.[40]

Mursili himself took time off from campaigning, in order to go to Kummanni in Kizzuwadna and attend as a matter of urgency to the festival of the goddess Hepat, a task neglected by his father:

When I went to the Land of Kummanni—my father had promised the festival of adoration to the (goddess) Hepat of Kummanni, but he had not yet performed it for her. Thus it became urgent for me. Therefore I went to Kizzuwadna and spoke as follows: 'I have come to make restitution for my father's default(?). Be gracious to me, to my wife, my son, my house,

[37] *AM* 86–7. [38] *AM* 94–5. [39] *AM* 96–9. [40] *AM* 106–7.

my country and to the [   ], Hepat of Kummanni, My Lady.'   (KUB xiv 4
(*CTH* 70) iii 23ff., trans. Goetze (1940: 10))[41]

He also used the opportunity to arrange a meeting with his
brother Sarri-Kusuh, who had been summoned from Carchemish.
Generally regarded as one of the most pious of all the Hittite kings,
Mursili had apparently postponed pressing military matters in or-
der to celebrate the festival of Hepat. But the meeting with Sarri-
Kusuh was probably at least as important a reason for the journey
to Kummanni,[42] which was located approximately halfway between
Hatti and the viceregal kingdom at Carchemish.

Although we have no information on the purpose of the meeting,
there were urgent matters to be discussed by the two brothers,
particularly with regard to developments in Syria. The Nuhasse
problem had still to be resolved, Assyria was becoming an increasing threat, and Egypt under Horemheb might seek to renew its
territorial ambitions in the region. Further, it is likely that Mursili's
other surviving brother Telipinu had recently died, leaving vacant
the viceregal seat in Aleppo. A successor was available in the
person of Telipinu's son Talmi-Sarruma. But no doubt Mursili
wished to discuss his appointment with Sarri-Kusuh, and call upon
him to provide support to the fledgling viceroy in the early days of
his reign. Given the volatile situation in the nearby Nuhasse lands,
it was imperative to demonstrate that the death of the old viceroy
in no way weakened continuity of Hittite control in the region.
There was also a serious family matter on which Mursili may
well have wanted his brother's advice (see below, § *The King's
Stepmother*).

But then came a tragic and presumably quite unexpected blow
for the king. While at Kummanni Sarri-Kusuh suddenly became ill
and died.[43] Mursili had yet another crisis on his hands. The death of
both Syrian viceroys, within probably no more than a few months
of each other, placed Hittite control in Syria in serious jeopardy.
Once again the Nuhasse lands rose in revolt. But the troubles were
not confined to Nuhasse. In Kadesh, Aitakkama who had been
installed as vassal ruler by Suppiluliuma also seized the opportunity to break ties with Hatti. Even more serious, the news of Sarri-

---

[41] Cf. *AM* 108–9.
[42] It recalls the meeting held between Suppiluliuma and his son Telipinu at Uda
in the Lower Land, where Suppiluliuma was celebrating religious festivals.
[43] *AM* 108–9. There is no evidence of foul play, as Bin-Nun (1975: 289) suggests.

Kusuh's death prompted the Assyrians to invade and occupy the kingdom of Carchemish.[44] At the same time to the north-east of the homeland, the king of Azzi-Hayasa launched a counter-offensive, invading once more the Upper Land, destroying the Land of Istitina and placing the city of Kannuwara under siege.[45]

Faced with conducting campaigns in three regions simultaneously, Mursili again displayed the decisive action which had characterized the first years of his reign. He dispatched his general Kurunta to deal with the rebellion of the Syrian vassals. He sent another of his generals, the experienced and able Nuwanza, to expel the Azzi-Hayasan enemy from the Upper Land. And the king himself set out for Astata on the Euphrates to make preparations for driving the Assyrians from Carchemish.

Nuwanza had already figured in campaigns in Mursili's second year when he was sent with an army to Kadesh to provide reinforcements for Sarri-Kusuh against the threat of an invasion from Assyria.[46] The campaign in the Upper Land could safely be left in his hands. But he delayed for some time before taking any action, insisting that the augurs and soothsayers had to be consulted first. No doubt irritated by the news of the delay, and the reason for it, Mursili took the omens himself, and sent word to Nuwanza assuring him that he could proceed.[47] When he finally did so, he inflicted a resounding defeat on the occupation forces and restored the Upper Land to Hittite control. As far as we can determine, the Upper Land remained firmly in Hittite hands for the rest of Mursili's reign, under the immediate authority of a local governor appointed by the king.

But the campaigning season had come to an end before the Hittites could follow up their success by invading and reconquering Azzi-Hayasa itself. This was a task which Mursili effectively completed in his tenth year,[48] although its formal submission did not take place until the following year. The failure to complete the reconquest in the ninth year may have been due partly to Nuwanza's delay in taking action against the occupation forces in the Upper Land. But it may also have been due to a serious family crisis which needed the king's urgent attention (see below, § *The King's Stepmother*).

---

[44] *AM* 116–19.   [45] *AM* 110–11.   [46] *AM* 26–9.   [47] *AM* 116–19.
[48] *AM* 130–3.

The campaigns in Syria were more decisive. Kurunta crushed the rebellion in Nuhasse and ravaged its territory,[49] and re-established Hittite control over Kadesh. This was facilitated by the assassination of Aitakkama by his son Niqmaddu:[50]

Aitakkama was king of Kadesh and Niqmaddu was his eldest son. As he saw that they were besieged and short of grain, Niqmaddu killed his father Aitakkama. Thereafter Niqmaddu and the Land of Kadesh turned to my side again and submitted to me. (*Comprehensive Annals, AM* 112–13, trans. Liverani (1990: 136–7))

Kurunta subsequently brought the assassin to Mursili at Carchemish. Mursili found himself in a dilemma. By eliminating the traitorous vassal Aitakkama, Niqmaddu had done him a favour. Yet in so doing he was guilty of the act of parricide, a crime which the conscience-plagued Hittite king found abhorrent. He could hardly reward the prince for this crime, and at first angrily rejected him: 'Under these circumstances, I did not accept Niqmaddu into vassalage. Since they had violated the oath, I said to them: "Let the gods of the oath carry out the curse: let son kill father, let brother kill brother, let everyone extinguish his own flesh!"' (reference as above). Nevertheless political considerations finally prevailed over moral scruples, and Niqmaddu was eventually formally installed on his father's throne.

Mursili himself succeeded in regaining from the Assyrians control of the kingdom of Carchemish. Before leaving Syria, he installed Sarri-Kusuh's son Sahurunuwa on the throne of Carchemish, and then proceeded to the investiture of Telipinu's son Talmi-Sarruma as king of Aleppo.[51] He further consolidated Hittite control in Syria by replacing Arhalba on the throne of Ugarit, after a reign of probably no more than two years,[52] by his younger brother Niqmepa and drawing up a treaty with him.[53] By the terms of this treaty the territory of Ugarit, which had been considerably expanded under the terms of Suppiluliuma's treaty with Niqmaddu, was now reduced to perhaps only one-third of its

---

[49] *AM* 110–13.

[50] Formerly read NIG.BA-Tesub (thus *AM* 112). For the revised reading, see Albright (1944: 31–2).

[51] *AM* 124–5. For the treaty which Mursili drew up with Talmi-Sarruma, KBo 1 6 (*CTH* 75), see *PD* 80–9, no. 6.

[52] See Klengel (1969: 359–60).

[53] See *PRU* IV, 84–101, Dossier IV D. The treaty has subsequently been ed. by del Monte (1986).

previous size,[54] with a substantial portion of it, including the king-dom of Siyannu, now being assigned to the territory of the viceroy of Carchemish.[55] But the boundary fixed by Suppiluliuma between Ugarit and Mukis was confirmed.[56]

Mursili's personal *Annals* cease with the end of the tenth year of his reign. The king could be well satisfied with what he had achieved in these years. He had been confronted, and had dealt successfully with, two major crises in these years. The first was at the very beginning of his reign, following the sudden death of Arnuwanda, when there was widespread rebellion amongst the subject states and a major threat of attack on the homeland by the enemy lands. The second was in his ninth year, when both his remaining brothers Telipinu and Sarri-Kusuh died, which led to a fresh outbreak of rebellion in Kadesh and the Nuhasse lands, sup-ported by an expeditionary force from Egypt, and prompted the Assyrian invasion and occupation of the kingdom of Carchemish. In both cases Mursili, supported by able commanders, responded promptly and decisively. Campaigns to the north and north-east successfully countered the mounting aggression from the Kaska lands, already evident in the last years of Suppiluliuma's reign, and eventually reduced once more to vassal status the hostile and aggressive kingdom of Azzi-Hayasa. Campaigns in the west and south-west resulted in the conquest and reduction to vassal status of the Arzawa lands. And campaigns in Syria firmly re-established control over the rebellious vassals in the region, and for the time being held in check the rapidly rising power of Assyria.

Plague

Mursili's achievement is the more remarkable when we consider other major problems which he faced during his first ten years on the throne. One of these was a virulent plague which broke out in the last years of Suppiluliuma's reign, and swept the Hittite land, decimating its population and continuing well into Mursili's reign. A graphic account of the plague and its effects appears in a series of prayers by Mursili,[57] in which the king remonstrates with the

---

[54] See RS 17.382 + 380, 22–3 (*PRU* iv, 81), Korošec (1960: 68).
[55] See *PRU* iv, 71–83, Dossier IV B–IV C. On Siyannu, see Astour (1979).
[56] See *PRU* iv, 63–70, Dossier IV A.
[57] Notably *CTH* 376, Prayer of Mursili to the Sun Goddess of Arinna, and *CTH* 378, the so-called Plague Prayers which appear in four versions. The prayers have

gods for punishing his land so severely, warns them that the kingdom is becoming a prey to the enemy forces which surround it, and
desperately seeks reasons for the divine wrath.

What is this, o gods, that you have done? A plague you have let into the
land. The Land of Hatti, all of it, is dying; so no one prepares sacrificial
loaves and libations for you. The ploughmen who used to work the fields
of the god are dead . . . Man has lost his wits, and there is nothing that we
do aright. O gods, whatever sin you behold, either let a prophet rise and
declare it, or let the sibyls or the priests learn about it by incubation, or let
man see it in a dream! O gods, take pity again on the Land of Hatti! On the
one hand it is afflicted with a plague, on the other hand it is afflicted with
hostility. The protectorates beyond the frontier, (namely) the Land of
Mitanni and the Land of Arzawa, each one has rebelled . . . Moreover
those countries which belong to the Land of Hatti, (namely) the Land of
Kaska, also the Land of Arawanna, the Land of Kalasma, the Land of
Lukka, the Land of Pitassa—these lands have also renounced the Sun
Goddess of Arinna . . . Now all the surrounding countries have begun to
attack the Land of Hatti. Let it again become a matter of concern to the
Sun Goddess of Arinna! O God, bring not your name into disrepute!
(Mursili's Prayer to the Sun Goddess, KUB xxiv 3 (+) (*CTH* 376) ii 3'–53',
adapted from trans. by Goetze in Pritchard (1969: 396))

    Determination of the cause of divine wrath was essential before
suitable propitiation could be made. In this case, through a lengthy
process of oracular consultation, Mursili identified offences committed by his father as the source of the gods' wrath—neglect of a
sacrifice for the river Mala (Euphrates),[58] and on two occasions the
violation of an oath. The first violation occurred when Suppiluliuma broke his oath of allegiance to his brother Tudhaliya the
Younger by seizing his throne and killing him.[59] On the second
occasion, Suppiluliuma had allegedly violated a treaty with Egypt,
the so-called Kurustama treaty (referred to in Ch. 5), by twice
attacking the Land of Amka, on the frontier of Egyptian subject
territory in Syria.[60] Suppiluliuma might well have disputed at least

been ed. by Lebrun (1980: 155–79, 192–239). For an English translation of a number
of passages, see Goetze in Pritchard (1969: 394–6). The plague had been brought to
Hatti by Egyptian prisoners taken by Suppiluliuma in his attack on Egyptian territory in Syria in reprisal for the murder of his son Zannanza; see the 2nd Plague
Prayer, obv. 25'–31'.

[58] 2nd Plague Prayer, obv. 9'–12'.
[59] 1st Plague Prayer, obv. 10–12.
[60] 2nd Plague Prayer, obv. 13'–20', 33'–46'.

the second of these alleged offences, on the grounds that he was simply retaliating against unprovoked aggression from Egypt. But the responsibility now lay with his son for bringing the plague to an end. When all other measures had failed, Mursili was not disposed to debate the legalities of his father's actions in seeking to appease his divine overlords. He himself had no part in these actions. But he fully accepted that sons should bear the responsibility for offences committed by their fathers.

At all events, he had no doubt that the plague was the instrument of divine wrath, and once the causes of this wrath had been ascertained the appropriate propitiation rites were performed. Whether the plague now came speedily to an end—or by that time had almost run its course—remains unknown. It was, however, but one of the unfortunate legacies Mursili inherited from his father.

The King's Stepmother

We have referred above to Suppiluliuma's marriage, around the time of the First Syrian War, to the Babylonian princess who assumed the name Tawananna as a personal name. As the years went by, this second wife of Suppiluliuma, stepmother of his sons, seems to have played an increasingly prominent role in the political affairs of the kingdom. We have noted her name appearing alongside that of her husband on seals impressed on documents involving diplomatic negotiations with Niqmaddu II, king of Ugarit. She seems also to have become a powerful figure in the royal household, probably increasingly so in Suppiluliuma's later years. Her domineering behaviour, her extravagance, and her introduction of undesirable foreign customs into the kingdom went apparently unchecked by her husband. Her conduct was a cause of deep concern to her stepsons. But no action was taken, or else complaints to the king fell on deaf ears.

Even after Suppiluliuma's death, she continued to dominate the royal household, and to engage in conduct which outraged the new king Arnuwanda. But still no action was taken against her. She was, after all, the reigning queen, with all the powers and privileges that her office carried with it, an office which in the traditional Tawananna mould would continue throughout her lifetime whether or not she outlived her husband.

Mursili refers to the remarkable forbearance which he and his brother displayed towards her:

But when my father became a god, Arnuwanda, my brother, and I did no harm to Tawananna, nor in any way humiliated her. As she governed the house of the king and the Land of Hatti in the lifetime of my father, likewise in the lifetime of my brother she governed them. And when my brother became a god, I did no evil to Tawananna, nor in any way humiliated her. As she governed the house of the king and the Land of Hatti in the lifetime of my father and of my brother, likewise then she governed them. And the customs which in the lifetime of her husband [were dear to her heart(?)] and the things which in the lifetime of her husband were in no way permitted to her, [these she clung to??]   (KBo xiv 4 (*CTH* 70) I 5–13.)[61]

She allegedly stripped the palace of its treasures to lavish on her favourites, or on those whose support she sought. And her postion as *šiwanzanni*-priestess[62] with its powers of allocating sacrifices, votive offerings, perhaps even temple lands, allowed her considerable control over assets of the state cult:[63]

Do you gods not see how she has turned the entire house of my father into the 'stone house' (mausoleum) of the Tutelary God (the god LAMMA) and the 'stone house' of the God? Some things she brought in from the Land of Sanhara (i.e. Babylon). Others in Hatti [   ] to the populace she handed over(?). She left nothing . . . My father's house she destroyed.   (KUB xiv 4 II 3–12, adapted from trans. by Hoffner (1983: 191))[64]

Initially Mursili refrained from taking action against his stepmother. Indeed the association of his name with hers on a number of seal impressions.[65] indicates that for a time he fully acknowledged her formal status as the reigning queen. But tensions within

[61] For the most part this translation follows the restorations proposed by Laroche (1956: 102).
[62] *šiwanzanni* = 'mother of god'; see Bin-Nun (1975: 190–1).
[63] Thus Hoffner (1983: 191). For a discussion of the charges brought against Tawananna, see Bin-Nun (1975: 186–9).
[64] For the complete text, see Forrer (1926: ii.1, 1–3). Bin-Nun (1975: 187–8) remarks that the oracle text KUB xxii 70 (*CTH* 566) 'gives a true picture of the tyranny which this old lady exercised on the king and his family by her continuous threats of divine anger, and by her demands to punish the daughters of the royal house. Her priestly office enabled her to rule the people with the terror of divine oracles'.
[65] Neve's table (1992a: 313), indicates sixteen seal impressions bearing the names Mursili and Malnigal (Tawananna's original name). See now Otten (1995: 19–21).

the royal household ran high. There was, apparently, little Mursili could do. His lengthy absences from the capital on military campaigns must have substantially reduced his ability to act as a restraining influence on Tawananna's conduct. This was to have tragic personal consequences for him.

He was married to the princess Gassulawiya.[66] Her name is associated with his on a conventional seal impression[67] and on the recently discovered impressions of the cruciform seal naming Mursili and Gassulawiya as the seal owners and listing a number of the king's ancestors.[68] Mursili was devoted to his wife, and became deeply alarmed when she was struck down by a mysterious illness. At first the illness was attributed to the goddess Lelwani (an underworld deity), as punishment for the princess's alleged neglect of her cult. In an ancient prayer adapted for the present occasion an appeal was made to the goddess, protesting Gassulawiya's innocence and begging that she be restored to health.[69]

But the prayers were to no avail, and Gassulawiya died in her husband's ninth year.[70] In his grief, Mursili now turned upon his stepmother, convinced that she was guilty of his wife's death, and

[66] The name also appears as Gassuliyawiya; see Laroche (1966: 89 no. 539). The shorter form will henceforth be used in this book.

[67] *SBo* I no. 37 = Beran (1967: no. 220).

[68] For a detailed treatment of the seal, see Dinçol *et al.* (1993), who point out that it now places beyond doubt the husband–wife relationship of Mursili and Gassulawiya (*contra* Tischler (1981: 67–8), who argued that the latter was the king's daughter).

[69] KBo IV 6 (*CTH* 380), ed. Lebrun (1980: 248–55), Tischler (1981: 11–45). For the attribution of the text to the reign of Mursili II, see also Kammenhuber (1976: 29–30). In another prayer, KUB xxxvi 81, ed. Tischler (1981: 46–54), Mursili again made an appeal for his wife's recovery, this time to the Sun Goddess. De Roos (1985–6: 77–9) doubts that the subject of KBo IV 6 is Mursili's wife, suggesting an attribution to a later Gassulawiya, daughter of Hattusili III and Puduhepa; see also his comments (1985: 133). Winkels (1985: 185) has claimed that the text does not belong stylistically to the context of the other prayers of Hattusili's reign. More recently, Singer (1991c: 329) has supported the attribution to the later Gassulawiya on the basis of the ductus of the text which he says must be dated to the 13th cent. In his view, KUB xxxvi 81 is the only one of the two prayers that can be attributed to Mursili's reign. However, account needs to be taken of the fragmentary text 335/e which is one of three additional small fragments to be added to KBo IV 6. See Otten (1984: 298–300) for the significance of this fragment in relation to the identification of Gassulawiya in KBo IV 6 (particularly in view of the reference to sa]L *ta-wa-an-na[-* in line 3'), and also Neu (1995: 121 n. 21). On balance, I still prefer to attribute this text to the reign of Mursili II.

[70] We know this from KUB xiv 4, one of two texts in which Mursili refers to her death and holds his stepmother responsible. The other text is dealt with below. She died in the year Mursili went to Kizzuwadna to celebrate the festival of Hepat at

that she had brought it about by black magic. Ironically the step-mother seems to have been the person who had uttered the prayer for Gassulawiya's health.[71] While this may seem surprising in view of the way Tawananna was depicted by her stepson, she may simply have been performing a duty expected of her as reigning queen. Indeed if she really were guilty of contriving the princess' death, she would would hardly have drawn suspicion upon herself by withholding her priestly services.[72]

Mursili had no doubt that his stepmother had caused his wife's death. His sense of devastating loss, and his bitterness against the woman who had allegedly been responsible, are clearly revealed in his prayers:

My punishment is the death of my wife. Has this become any better? Because she killed her, throughout the days of life my soul goes down to the dark netherworld on her account. For me it has been unbearable(??). She has bereaved(?) me. Do you gods not recognize whose is the punishment? (KBo iv 8 (*CTH* 71) ii 24–6, iii 1–4, adapted from trans. Hoffner (1983: 188))

Oracular consultation confirmed the queen's guilt, and indicated to the king what action it was appropriate for him to take. The gods determined that she had committed a capital offence. The oracle sanctioned her removal from office and execution by her stepson.[73] But in spite of his stepmother's long catalogue of offences, in spite of the alleged murder of his wife, Mursili shrank from inflicting the extreme penalty upon her. It may well be that one of the purposes of his meeting with his brother Sarri-Kusuh in Kummanni was to discuss what action should be taken against the queen.[74] Under the circumstances, it was milder than she might have feared. She was put on trial, deposed from office, and banished from the palace. But her life was spared:

Kummanni. Mursili's *Annals* indicate that he did this in the 9th year of his reign (*AM* 108–9).

[71] On the assumption that the duplicate fragment 335/e which identifies *Tawana[nna]* as the author (line 3′) represents the same prayer as KBo iv 6; see Dinçol *et al.* (1993: 98).

[72] Cf. Dinçol *et al.* (1993: 98).

[73] KBo iv 8 ii 1–8.

[74] Kitchen (1962: 5 n. 1) notes that his visit to Kizzuwadna is also recorded in KUB xiv 4, and that it was subsequent to this visit that Mursili decided on the queen's punishment.

I did not execute her, but I deposed her from the office of *šiwanzanni*-priestess. And because it was determined by oracle that she should be removed from office, I removed her from office, and I gave her a place of residence. Nothing is lacking to her desire. She has food and drink. Everything stands at her disposal. Nothing is lacking to her. She is alive. She beholds the sun of heaven with her eyes. And she eats bread as one of life.[75] Mine is only this one punishment: I punished her with this one thing, that I sent her down from the palace: I deposed her from the gods in the office of *šiwanzanni*-priestess. Mine is only this one punishment.   (KBo IV 8 II 9–20, adapted from trans. by Hoffner (1983: 188))

Of the queen's guilt there can be little doubt. She had motive enough for contriving Gassulawiya's death. Already Gassulawiya's name was linked with that of her husband on royal seals where she bore the title 'Great Queen'.[76] It seems extraordinary that such seals should have been produced while Tawananna still lived and held the office of reigning queen. Such an act might well lead her to suspect that her days in this office were numbered, that she would soon be completely supplanted by her stepson's wife.[77] She would not let this happen. But by murdering Gassulawiya she precipitated her downfall, provoking the king into taking action which, he believed, was long overdue.

The decision not to execute her must have been made only after long and careful consideration. While she lived, she was a constant threat to the security of the royal household, particularly if she had the support of those upon whom she had lavished favours. Yet Mursili could not bring himself to kill a member of his own family, even if the oracles had advised and authorized it. He had seen the consequences of his father's act in murdering his uncle. This act had been identified as one of the reasons for the plague inflicted by divine wrath upon the kingdom. He may well have been loath to bring divine retribution upon his land yet again by a further royal execution, whatever the justification for it. Indeed Mursili's son Hattusili later even questioned the legality of deposing the queen, and pointed out that he was in no way involved:

---

[75] Or 'eats the bread of life'.

[76] *SBo* I, no. 37 and the cruciform seal, in both of which Dinçol *et al.* (1993: 97) now read Gassulawiya's title as MAGNA REGINA (according to the convention used in transliterating hieroglyphic texts).

[77] Alternatively Dinçol *et al.* (1993: 98) suggest that Tawananna had already been dismissed from her office, perhaps on the ground of her extravagances as mentioned by Mursili, and replaced by the already ailing Gassulawiya.

But when in the palace the trial of Tawananna, your servant, took place, when my father humiliated Tawananna the queen . . . you (were the only one) who knew perfectly if the humiliation of the queen was in accordance with your will or if it was not . . . As for me, I was in no way implicated in this affair.[78]   (Prayer of Hattusili III and Puduhepa to the Sun Goddess of Arinna, KUB xiv 7 + KUB xxi 19 (*CTH* 383) i 20–9)[79]

Mursili's Second Wife

Some time after Gassulawiya's death Mursili married again, on this occasion a woman perhaps of Hurrian origin called Tanuhepa. The surviving texts from Mursili's reign are completely silent about her. This is the more remarkable since from his *Annals* and his *Prayers* we have more information about this king's family and personal circumstances than we have about any other Hittite king—apart from his youngest son Hattusili. We know of Tanuhepa's association with Mursili only from a few seal impressions.[80] This might suggest that Mursili married her only a short time before the end of his reign. However, the above prayer to the Sun Goddess refers to Tanuhepa's sons,[81] which presumably she had by Mursili. She must have been married to him for several years at least before his death in order to have produced these sons.

Seal impressions also link her with Mursili's first two successors on the throne, his son Muwatalli and grandson Urhi-Tesub.[82] Unless there was another queen called Tanuhepa,[83] she appears to have held the office of reigning queen for some thirty years, spanning the reigns of three kings.[84] But her career like that of her husband's stepmother, became embroiled in scandal. We shall return to this below.

A New Rebellion in the West

In the twelfth year of his reign, Mursili received word of a fresh outbreak of rebellion in Arzawa. The ringleader on this occasion

---

[78]   Because at the time he was still only a child.

[79]   The text of the prayer has been ed. by Lebrun (1980: 309–28), Sürenhagen (1981: 88–108).

[80]   *SBo* I, nos. 24–9 = Beran (1967: nos. 221–5, 228 abc), Gonnet (1979: no. 192f).

[81]   KUB xiv 7 obv. i 18' + KUB xxi 19 obv. ii 4.

[82]   *SBo* I, nos. 42–4. To these can now be added the seal impressions linking Tanuhepa with Muwatalli and Urhi-Tesub in the Nişantepe archive; see Neve's table (1992a: 313).

[83]   See the discussion in Laroche (1956: 105).

[84]   Cf. Houwink ten Cate (1974a: 124).

was named É.GAL.PAP.[85] His status and origin are unknown to us, although he may have been a person of some eminence from the Land of Masa.[86]

Trading on the Hittite king's preoccupation with affairs in the north-eastern and south-eastern regions of his kingdom, É.GAL.PAP saw an opportunity for setting himself up as the leader of a new anti-Hittite movement in the west. The rebellion was reported to Mursili by Mashuiluwa, the vassal ruler of the Arzawan kingdom Mira-Kuwaliya, who had to this point remained true to his Hittite allegiance. But subsequently Mashuiluwa quarrelled with his over-lord, broke his Hittite allegiance, incited the land of Pitassa to rebellion against the king, and joined forces with É.GAL.PAP.[87] Mursili learned from an outsider of the rebellious activities of these two men.[88]

The Hittite response was a measured one. With the situation in Syria still potentially volatile, and with the Kaska tribes in the north still far from subdued, Mursili had no wish to become embroiled in a further series of campaigns in the west. The mounting crisis there might yet be resolved without the need for military conflict, if pressure were brought to bear on Mashuiluwa to return to his Hittite allegiance. Mursili took personal command of a Hittite expedition to the region, with the hope that as his forces approached Mashuiluwa's kingdom, the rebel vassal could be intimidated into submission. But the ploy failed: 'When I reached Sallapa, I wrote to Mashuiluwa: "Come here to me!" But because Mashuiluwa was aware of his offence, he refused me, My Sun, and he fled before me and went over to the Land of Masa' (Mursili: Kupanta-Kurunta Treaty §5).

There had been other occasions when Masa had provided refuge for rebellious Hittite vassals. It could no longer be allowed to do so with impunity. Mursili pursued his wayward vassal into the territory of Masa where he carried out a campaign of reprisal. This was followed by an ultimatum delivered to the people of Masa:

---

[85] Mursili II: Kupanta-Kurunta Treaty (*CTH* 68); Friedrich (1926: 128–9 §18). The Hittite reading of the name is unknown.

[86] See del Monte (1974: 364 n. 38, 367–8), supported by Houwink ten Cate (1979*b*: 28).

[87] These events are recorded in the Kupanta-Kurunta treaty §§4 and 18. See also *AM* 142–3.

[88] KBo xix 76 (+) i 1'–8' = KUB xix 34 (+) i 1'–13'; see Houwink ten Cate (1979*b*: 284).

Mashuiluwa was my liegeman; and he quarrelled with me and stirred up my subjects against me, and would have begun conflict with me. Now he has fled before me, and see, he has come to you. Now seize him and hand him over to me! If you do not seize him and hand him over to me, I will come and destroy you along with your land.   (Mursili: Kupanta-Kurunta Treaty §6)

The people of Masa bowed to the ultimatum. They were aware that dignitaries from the land of Mira had already disassociated themselves from Mashuiluwa's actions, appearing in person before Mursili, protesting their innocence, reaffirming their loyalty, and requesting that Mashuiluwa be replaced on the vassal throne by his adopted son.[89] Mashuiluwa had now become a dangerous liability. The nobles of Masa withdrew their protection from him, and demanded that he give himself up to his Hittite overlord. When he refused, they seized him and handed him over to Mursili, who removed him to Hattusa.[90] Here he was assigned a place of residence, and held as a virtual hostage to ensure the loyalty of the man now appointed vassal ruler in his place.

The man in question was Kupanta-Kurunta, Mashuiluwa's nephew and son of his brother. Suppiluliuma had given his daughter Muwatti in marriage to Mashuiluwa. But the union had proved childless, and Mashuiluwa had on his accession asked permission of Mursili to adopt his nephew as son and heir to the vassal throne. The request was granted: 'And I gave you, Kupanta-Kurunta, to Mashuiluwa, in place of a son. Then I placed the Land of Mira and the Land of Kuwaliya under oath to Mashuiluwa, to Muwatti, and also to you, Kupanta-Kurunta' (Mursili: Kupanta-Kurunta Treaty §4).

But Mashuiluwa's rebellion had raised a serious question about the succession. In Hittite custom, if not in law, a son could be held responsible, and pay the penalty for, the sins of his father:

Do you not know, Kupanta-Kurunta, that if in Hattusa anyone commits the offence of insurrection, and that even if the son whose father is guilty is not also guilty, nevertheless the house of his father is taken from him, and either given to someone else or seized for the palace? And because

---

[89] *AM* 144–5.
[90] Kupanta-Kurunta treaty, §6; *AM* 144–7 = KUB xiv 24, 17′–24′, to which add KUB xix 39 iii; for the joining of the latter to KUB xix 24, on the basis that KBo ix 77 1′–8′ duplicates KUB xiv 24 19′–24′ and KBo ix 77 8′–14′ duplicates KUB xix 39 iii 1′–6′, see Houwink ten Cate (1979*b*: 267).

your father Mashuiluwa was guilty, and you, Kupanta-Kurunta, were Mashuiluwa's son, even if you had not been guilty too, I, My Sun, could have cast you out at that very time, if it had ever occurred to My Sun to do you harm. Even now I could have taken your father's house and land from you. I could have given them to someone else and made another ruler for the land. (Mursili: Kupanta-Kurunta Treaty §7)[91]

But Mursili was conscious of the support that Kupanta-Kurunta enjoyed amongst the nobles of Mira, who in disassociating themselves from Mashuiluwa's treachery had asked that Kupanta-Kurunta be appointed king in his place. By implication, this seemed to clear Kupanta-Kurunta of any involvement in his adoptive father's rebellious activities. Mursili himself was convinced of the young man's innocence.[92] In any case, there appeared to be no viable alternative to his appointment. Thus Kupanta-Kurunta became the next king of Mira. Mursili's decision to appoint him was no doubt dictated by sound political considerations. But in the treaty which he drew up with his new vassal he represented it as an act of royal grace and favour:

Because Mashuiluwa, your father, offended against My Sun, and you, Kupanta-Kurunta, were the son of Mashuiluwa, although you were in no way guilty, I, My Sun, could none the less have rejected you if My Sun were disposed to do evil, and could have taken from you the house of your father and the land, and given it to another, and could have made another ruler in the land. But now because My Sun is not disposed to do evil, I have not rejected you and taken from you the house of your father and the land, and have not made another ruler in the land; and I have given back to you the house of your father and the land, and have made you ruler in the land. (Mursili: Kupanta-Kurunta Treaty §§21–2)

He also united Kupanta-Kurunta under one oath with two other rulers in Arzawa—Manapa-Tarhunda, king of the Seha River Land, and Targasnalli, king of Hapalla.[93]

We hear of no further rebellion or unrest amongst the vassal states in western Anatolia for the remainder of Mursili's reign, which occupied another fifteen years or so. This may well be indicative of the success which the king achieved in imposing firm control over the region. It must certainly rank as the most significant of

---

[91] The translation of the lines beginning 'And because your father' is adapted from that given in *CHD* 3/2, 142.
[92] See e.g. §§11 and 21 of the treaty.
[93] Kupanta-Kurunta treaty §27.

Mursili's contributions to the development and consolidation of the kingdom he had inherited from his father. This is the more remarkable when we reflect that it was achieved within the first twelve years of Mursili's reign, at a time when the king had also to deal with a number of crises in Syria, which seriously threatened the loss of many if not all of the territories secured by the intensive campaigns and diplomatic manœuvrings of his father.

To the North Once More

But problems to the north of the Hittite homeland remained unresolved. Much of the second half of Mursili's reign was devoted to further campaigns in this region, directed mainly against the Kaska enemy. These campaigns generally resulted in short-term military successes. Indeed in his nineteenth year Mursili claims to have gone further afield than any other Hittite king, in his conquest of the Lands of Takkuwahina and Tahantattipa,[94] and in his twenty-second year to have been the first king since Telipinu to reach the land of Hatenzuwa, which he conquered.[95]

Further, he could claim with some satisfaction a decisive result from a campaign which he undertook in his twenty-first year to the Land of Tummanna. Here his chief opponent was Pitaggatalli, who had first come to light towards the end of Suppiluliuma's reign when he mobilized his forces against Suppiluliuma during the latter's campaigns in the region.[96] In spite of the positive way in which Mursili's reports them in the *Deeds*, Suppiluliuma's campaigns in Tummanna clearly had no lasting impact. It was not until the showdown with Mursili, some twenty years later, that Pitaggatalli was finally and decisively defeated. His base Sapidduwa was captured, along with his military forces. Pitaggatalli alone, apparently, eluded the Hittite king by taking to the hills.

But successes in some areas were matched by setbacks in others. Thus in his twenty-second year, Mursili was confronted with a rebellion in the land of Kalasma, which refused to provide him with troops. This seems to have caused him particular distress, for the land had a history of continuous loyalty to the Hittite crown from the time of his grandfather Tudhaliya, and had maintained its loyalty up to this point in Mursili's reign. Mursili was unable to deal

---

[94] *AM* 150–1.   [95] *AM* 164–5.   [96] See *DS* p. 109, frag. 34.

with the rebellion in person as he had wished, since he was
overladen with booty from the Tummanna campaign, and sent his
general Nuwanza to resolve it by force of arms.[97] In spite of
Nuwanza's initial success the rebellion continued to smoulder, and
several years later broke out afresh when the Kalasman Aparru
attacked the (presumably neighbouring) Hittite subject state of
Sappa.[98] Although Aparru was defeated and had to flee for his life,
it took a further campaign by Hutupiyanza (whom we have previously met as the governor of Pala) the following year before
Kalasma was fully restored to Hittite control.

In spite of his catalogue of successful campaigns and conquests to
the north of the homeland, it is doubtful whether Mursili's overall
achievements in this region were any more substantial or lasting
than those of his father. He certainly failed to achieve the degree of
authority which he had imposed on the western Anatolian territories. But such an achievement was well nigh impossible. Continuing Kaskan aggression while constituting a major threat to Hittite
security in its own right, must also have had a continuing destabilizing effect on the Hittites' northern subject states. There was little
that the Hittites could do about this on a long-term basis. Reduction
of the Kaska tribes, in any comprehensive way, to the status of
Hittite subjects was not a prospect which could be seriously entertained. In the absence of any clear coherent political structure
amongst the Kaska people, of a kind which characterized, for example, the Arzawa Lands, the Hittites had no firm foundation on
which to attempt to build a vassal state system in the Kaska region
in the wake of conquest. To ensure the security of their northernmost territories, there seemed no feasible alternative to constant campaigning in the Kaska region, accepting that such
campaigns would at best result in only very limited periods of peace.

A greater measure of security could perhaps be achieved by
repopulating with Hittite subjects some of the peripheral territories
which had been largely abandoned since the Kaskan invasions in
the reign of Hantili II. Such repopulation might at least create a
buffer zone against enemy encroachment on the homeland. Mursili
made some preliminary efforts along these lines, for example by
partially resettling the city of Tiliura on the border of Kaskan
territory. Tiliura had been abandoned since Hantili II's reign. But

[97] *AM* 160–3.   [98] *AM* 188–9.

it was not until the reign of Mursili's son Muwatalli II that full resettlement was achieved (see Ch. 10).

Mursili was also the first king to attempt to regain possession of the holy city of Nerik which had been seized by the Kaskans during the Old Kingdom.[99] A journey which he made to Nerik to celebrate the festival of the Storm God and to liberate the countryside from the Kaska enemy was no doubt hailed as an event of great symbolical importance. For the first time in almost 300 years a Hittite king had now reclaimed, and worshipped in, one of the holiest of Hittite cities. Yet the event had little more than token significance. Mursili failed to resettle the city with his own subjects, and it was not until the reign of his grandson Urhi-Tesub that the Hittites could claim that Nerik had been fully restored to them.

Transportation

In the aftermath of conquest, Mursili regularly followed a practice which had been instituted at least as early as the reign of the first Tudhaliya—the transportation of large numbers of persons from the conquered territories for resettlement in the Hittite homeland or other regions of the kingdom.[100] It was a practice also adopted by the rulers of the Assyrian New Kingdom. Rough parallels can be found in a number of later civilizations as well. But nowhere else did it operate as extensively as in the Hittite world. Under Mursili in particular transportation followed almost invariably in the wake of a successful military operation. Given the number of campaigns in which he engaged throughout his reign of almost thirty years, and the number of transportees involved, running to hundreds in the smaller communities and many thousands in the larger states, the logistical problems associated with the transportation system and the resettlement of the transportees in the homeland must have been enormous.

Transportation served important practical purposes. On the one hand, it helped reinforce the effectiveness of a treaty drawn up with the ruler of a conquered, or reconquered, territory; it served to diminish the threat of future anti-Hittite activities in the region by removing a large part of the population and placing the remainder

---

[99] Haas (1970: 8–10) discusses texts from the reigns of Hattusili III and Tudhaliya IV which deal with campaigns in the Nerik region by Mursili II and also Muwatalli II. See also Houwink ten Cate (1973: 78).
[100] The Sumerian logogram NAM.RA^MEŠ or NAM.RA^HI.A (Akkadian *šallatu*) is used in Hittite texts to refer to the transportees.

under a loyal vassal. Almost certainly a significant component of the transportees were the able-bodied men of a conquered state. On the other hand, resettlement in Hatti helped restock both the military and the agricultural personnel of the homeland—an important consideration, given the substantial drain on Hittite manpower caused by year after year of military campaigns, and the apparently serious depletion of the Hittite population by the ravages of the plague.

We might well wonder how the Hittites coped with this constant influx of new settlers into their homeland—large, disparate, hostile groups of conquered peoples forced to leave their countries against their will. Yet we have no evidence that the transportees caused any major social or political problems when resettled in Hatti, apart from one instance recorded in the *Annals* of Tudhaliya I.[101] The new arrivals were apparently assimilated into the Hittite system quickly enough to avoid such problems. The fact that they were rarely mentioned outside military contexts might in itself be an indication of their rapid and peaceful integration into the population of their conquerors.[102]

How did this integration occur? After they had been selected for transportation, the transportees were usually divided into two categories—those the king claimed for his own service, and those allocated to his military officers. Transportees in the second category were frequently accompanied by livestock from the conquered state. In this case at least they probably covered a broad cross-section of the local population—men, women, and children; and for the most part they were probably settled on the estates owned by the aristocracy to whom they were assigned as war booty.[103]

The transportees assigned to the service of the king became in effect his own property, and could be disposed of as he saw fit. Very likely a large number of the men of military age became part of the king's own militia, whose duties included the garrisoning of frontier

---

[101] In this case, the 10,000 infantry and 600 chariotry taken as booty from the land of Assuwa rose in rebellion under the leadership of a man called Kukkulli (KUB XXIII 11//12 rev. 1–6).

[102] There is e.g. just one passing reference to them in the Laws. Clause 40 of the Laws makes provision for the king to allocate transportees for the purpose of working the land.

[103] Goetze (1964: 28) comments that they were not allowed to move freely from town to town, but were shifted around by the authorities presumably as the needs of state required.

posts. Other transportees were assigned to temple duty in various cult centres within Hatti.[104] Others served as a labour force, for example on a farm that had been abandoned by its tenant, or on various state works projects. Transportees may also have been used to populate or repopulate sparsely inhabited or abandoned settlements situated in peripheral areas of the homeland[105]—particularly in the reigns of Mursili's successors (see Ch. 10). They could also be used as a medium of exchange for the recovery of Hittite subjects held by enemy countries as hostages or prisoners-of-war.[106]

The actual removal of the transportees to the homeland, along with wives, children, and livestock, must often have proved a long, difficult, and laborious operation, especially when their home country was hundreds of kilometres from their place of resettlement. And transportees sometimes escaped from their conquerors during the journey and sought refuge in neighbouring regions. Hittite kings took strong measures to discourage the practice. Explicit extradition clauses were written into the treaties demanding that local rulers promptly hand back any fugitives from Hittite authority who had sought refuge with them. Failure to do so was likely to meet with military retaliation, as happened when Uhhaziti refused to hand over to Mursili the Hittite transportees who had escaped to his land and sought his protection.[107] A rebellious vassal or hostile independent ruler who suddenly found his population swelled by large numbers of able-bodied, disaffected Hittite subjects could become an even greater threat to the stability of Hittite-controlled territory in the region.

The King's Speech Affliction[108]

In the course of a journey to Til-Kunnu,[109] Mursili suffered the first symptoms of an affliction, allegedly induced by the shock of a

---

[104] For the provision of transportees for service to the deity, see KUB xv 21 (*CTH* 590) 4–6, cited by Alp (1950: 117).

[105] Bryce (1986*b*: 8) suggests that Madduwatta's NAM.RA$^{HI.A}$ (referred to in the *Indictment of Madduwatta* §9) were originally transportees to the Hittite homeland subsequently reassigned to Madduwatta by the Hittite king.

[106] See e.g. *AM* 106–7.

[107] See *AM* 40–1.

[108] The text which records this affliction (*CTH* 486) has been ed. by Goetze and Pedersen (1934).

[109] On this name, see Goetze and Pedersen (1934: 14).

thunderstorm, which affected his speech. Initially he was alarmed, but gradually came to terms with the affliction. Or so he thought. It continued to prey on his subconscious mind, and eventually to figure in his dreams. What had he done to warrant it? Which god had inflicted it upon him? During one of his dreams, the illness suddenly increased in severity:

Thus speaks My Sun Mursili, the Great King: 'I travelled to Til-Kunnu . . . A storm burst forth and the Storm God thundered terrifyingly. I was afraid. Speech withered in my mouth, and my speech came forth somewhat haltingly. I neglected this plight entirely. But as the years followed one another, the cause of my plight began to appear in my dreams. And in my sleep, the god's hand fell upon me, and my mouth went sideways. I consulted the oracles, and the Storm God of Manuzziya was ascertained (as responsible for my plight). (*CTH* 486, obv. 1–10)

As far as we can determine from the expression 'my mouth went sideways', the king appears to have suffered a minor stroke, which caused partial speech paralysis. We do not know when this affliction occurred. It is possible that it was induced by cumulative stress associated with a number of factors—not only the stress of years of constant warfare, sometimes on several fronts simultaneously, but also the king's despair and frustration over the plague which had decimated the Hittite population, and perhaps above all the emotional strain caused by the crises in his own family. All these may well have taken a heavy toll upon his health, leading to a medical condition which characteristically he attributed to divine origin.[110]

In order to appease the god identified as the cause of the affliction, the king sought oracular advice, and was instructed on the appropriate ritual to be performed. The ritual involved sending a 'substitute ox' along with various paraphernalia (including the garments he had worn on the day the symptoms of the disease first appeared) to the temple of the Storm God in Kummanni. Here the ox and the accompanying paraphernalia were to be burned as an offering to the Storm God.

We do not know whether the ritual was followed by any improvement in the king's condition. But whatever the actual cause of

---

[110] Cf. the explanation of Oppenheim (1956: 230–1). For a recent translation of the text, see Kümmel (1987: 289–92).

the affliction, the treatment prescribed, which was consonant with the king's belief in the divine origin of such afflictions and the efficacy of appropriate divine appeasement, may have brought about at least a partial cure. No other surviving text makes any reference to the affliction. The whole episode is a curious one, and the affliction appears not to have affected, at least in any recognizable way, the king's ability to provide sound military and political leadership in the years following the first onset of the disease. But it adds another interesting personal dimension to the record of Mursili's reign.

By the end of this reign, Mursili had effectively answered his critics who had so contemptuously dismissed him on his accession as a mere child, with none of the qualities of his illustrious father. But his years on the throne took their personal toll, both physically and emotionally. In the field of battle he could be no less ruthless than his father had been. But there are many texts which reveal him as a man blessed—or afflicted—with a strong sense of conscience. The 'sins of his father' weighed heavily upon him, and he sought to do all he could to gain absolution for them as he saw the plague, which he had no doubt was due to divine wrath, take increasingly greater toll of his subjects. And he must long have wrestled with the problem of what to do with his stepmother before finally taking action. In spite of her offences she was the legitimate reigning queen. No doubt he continued to agonize over the decision he made to strip her of all power. His military records reveal him as a determined and sometimes ruthless warlord, in the traditional royal warrior mould. But his prayers and appeals to the gods show him as a humane and sensitive man who sought always to act in accordance with the dictates of his conscience and what he perceived to be the divine will.

Through the traumas of his personal life, and the intimate glimpses which he provides into his feelings and emotions, we can understand and relate more readily to this king than we can to any of his predecessors or successors who held sway over the world of the Hittites.

CHAPTER 9

The Showdown with Egypt: The Reign of Muwatalli II (c.1295–1272)

The Re-Emergence of Egypt

On his death, Mursili left to his son and successor Muwatalli a relatively stable kingdom. In the west, the vassal network which Mursili had established appears to have remained submissive to Hittite overlordship during the last half of his reign. In the north, repeated campaigns in the Kaska region had provided temporary respite from the constant threat of Kaskan incursions, and the rebellious vassals had been firmly restored to their Hittite allegiance. In the south-east, control over the vassal kingdoms established by Suppiluliuma had been maintained, in spite of the increasing menace of Assyria. And after the crises in Mursili's ninth year, precipitated by the deaths of the viceroys Telipinu and Sarri-Kusuh, the viceregal kingdoms of Carchemish and Aleppo remained securely under Hittite control.

But further to the south a major new threat was building, in the land of the Nile. In the aftermath of the Amarna period and the end of the eighteenth Dynasty, there had been no serious challenge from Egypt to Hittite overlordship in Syria. Although still holding some territories in southern Syria, particularly military establishments in Palestine (for example, Beth-Shan), Egypt could claim no more than token influence in the region as a whole. But the tensions between Hatti and Egypt had persisted. They were now to take a turn for the worse. After some four years on the throne, Tutankhamun's successor Ay died, and was replaced by Horemheb[1] whose reign paved the way for the beginning of the nineteenth Dynasty. A powerful new era was dawning in Egyptian history.

Under Horemheb, Egyptian military activity had begun afresh in Syria when an expeditionary force was sent to the region to support

[1] He may have occupied the throne for some 30 years (c.1323–1291 max.). But the length of his reign is uncertain. See Aldred (1975: 72).

the rebellion against Hittite rule in the Nuhasse lands during
Mursili's ninth year. On this occasion, the invading force was
repulsed. But the very fact of Egyptian intrusion into territory
claimed by the Hittites made it clear that Egypt had by no means
relinquished its political and military interests in Syria. It was only
a matter of time before it would once more pursue these interests
with determination and vigour.

Contrary to popular opinion, Horemheb himself seems to have
made little impact on the international scene.[2] Rather, he devoted
himself to a programme of reunification and reconstruction within
his own kingdom, in the process rooting out the administrative
corruption and abuse of bureaucratic power which had apparently
become rife in Akhenaten's reign.[3] In so doing, he prepared the
ground for the early rulers of the nineteenth Dynasty, when Egypt
emerged as the Hittites' most serious contender for political and
military supremacy in Syria.

Repopulation Programmes in the North

Probably from the very beginning of his reign Muwatalli realized
that he would soon be forced into a major contest with Egypt,
particularly over the Syrian kingdoms which had formerly been
subject to the pharaoh. Successful defence against a determined
challenge from Egypt would necessitate a substantial concentration
of Hittite military resources in Syria. The Syrian viceroys could not
on their own be expected to muster sufficient resources to deal
effectively with such a challenge.

Yet Muwatalli knew all too well from the experience of his
predecessors the dangers of diverting to Syria Hittite troops who
would otherwise be used for the defence of the homeland, particularly against threats from the north. The series of campaigns which
his father had conducted throughout his reign and particularly
towards its end may have provided some temporary easing of the
pressures on the homeland's northern and eastern frontiers. But in
their long-term effects, they were likely to prove no more conclusive than the campaigns Suppiluliuma, or indeed any of his predecessors, had conducted in the region.

[2] On possible though dubious evidence for a major Egyptian offensive against the
Hittites in Horemheb's reign, see Murnane (1990: 30).
[3] See the Edict of Horemheb, Breasted (1906: iii, 22–33 §§45–67).

The clear lesson to be learned from this experience was that no matter how frequently and how intensively the Hittites campaigned against the Kaska lands, they would never succeed in permanently subjugating these lands or in establishing any form of lasting control over them. The only alternative was to strengthen the outlying areas of the homeland which were most prone to enemy attack and occupation and provided a route to the very heart of the Hittite kingdom. As we have noted, the siting of the Hittite capital close to enemy territory to the north and north-east made it chronically vulnerable to attack from these regions.

The major incursions into Hittite territory prior to Suppiluliuma's reign had resulted in the loss of almost the entire region extending across the Marrassantiya basin north and north-east of Hattusa, from the lower course of the Marrassantiya in the west towards the Euphrates in the south-east (although much of this region may have been in enemy hands even earlier). Foreign invasion or encroachment had led to large numbers of the Hittite subject populations dispersing or resettling in areas still under the protection of the Hittite king. However, Suppiluliuma's campaigns against the Kaskans had succeeded in reducing the enemy presence in this region and forcing their evacuation of some of the settlements which they had occupied. In the wake of their retreat, Suppiluliuma instituted a policy of repopulating the settlements with their original inhabitants after fortifying these settlements against future enemy attack.[4]

Like his father, Mursili followed up his military successes with some attempts to repopulate settlements abandoned or partly abandoned as a result of the Kaskan incursions.[5] But the military conquests and the sporadic repopulation programmes carried out by Suppiluliuma and Mursili failed to provide a lasting solution to the Kaska problem, and Muwatalli was again faced with Kaskan invasions in the territories to the north and north-east of Hattusa. Before he could commit to Syria the forces necessary to counter the resurgence of Egyptian military power in the region, he had first to put in place more effective arrangements for the protection of the homeland, and above all, the royal capital.

---

[4] See *DS* p. 65, frag. 13, D iv 12–16.
[5] As indicated in the preamble of a decree which Hattusili III drew up for the town of Tiliura (*CTH* 89), ed. von Schuler (1965: 145–51), excerpts trans. by Garstang and Gurney (1959: 119–20).

What he did was to formulate and implement a plan of astonish-
ing boldness—one totally without precedent in the history of the
Hittite kingdom. We shall return to this below. But for the moment, we must once more turn our attention westwards.

Introducing Piyamaradu

After almost two decades of relative peace, a dangerous situation
was again beginning to develop in the west. This was due largely to
a man who was to prove one of the most provocative, and one of
the most elusive, of the Hittites' enemies—a renegade Hittite of
high birth called Piyamaradu.[6] Piyamaradu had apparently fallen
out of favour with the king, presumably for nurturing ambitions
beyond the reasonable expectations of a Hittite subject, albeit a
high ranking one, and had fled to the west. Here he began building
his own power base amongst the Hittites' western subject territories—probably with the support of, perhaps in alliance with, the
king of Ahhiyawa. He confirmed his links with Ahhiyawa by marrying his daughter to Atpa, the Ahhiyawan vassal ruler of the land
of Milawata (Millawanda).

We have noted that Milawata had previously belonged to Hatti,
and that in the third year of Mursili II's reign Hittite control
had been re-established over it when it had attempted to form
an alliance with Ahhiyawa. But subsequently, perhaps during
Muwatalli's reign, Milawata had become subject to Ahhiyawa. It is
possible that Muwatalli had agreed to relinquish the vassal kingdom, which had by now assumed a predominantly Mycenaean
character, in the hope that this would satisfy Ahhiyawan territorial
ambitions on the Anatolian mainland, and in return, perhaps, for a
guarantee from the Ahhiyawan king of co-operation in maintaining
general stability within the region. This was particularly important
now that the Hittites needed to focus their attention increasingly
on developments in Syria.

The ceding of Milawata to Ahhiyawa may have occurred within
the context of a more general agreement reflected in a fragmentary
text which lists a number of Anatolian states and their boundaries.[7]
The surviving portion of the text refers to Tarhuntassa, Mira, and
Ahhiyawa. Since the text indicates boundaries, it probably defined

---

[6] For a detailed treatment of Piyamaradu's career, see Heinhold-Krahmer (1983).
[7] KUB xxxi 29 (*CTH* 214.16), ed. Sommer (1932: 328).

the limits of Ahhiyawan-controlled territory in Anatolia. This suggests some form of pact or understanding, if not a formal treaty, between the Hittite king and his Ahhiyawan counterpart.[8] At all events, relations between Ahhiyawa and Hatti seem for a time to have been peaceful, even amicable.[9]

We know frustratingly little about the career of Piyamaradu, one of the most notorious 'villains' of Hittite history, since the majority of texts which refer to him are fragmentary and open to different interpretations. But from what we can piece together, it appears that he sought to create a kingdom of his own out of the Hittites' vassal states in the west. In the early years of Muwatalli's reign he gained control of the Land of Wilusa, which lay in the north-west of Anatolia, in the region later known as the Troad (see Ch. 14). Whether he was willingly accepted by the people of Wilusa or occupied their country by force remains unknown; the fact that Muwatalli subsequently referred to Wilusa as one of the most consistently loyal of the Hittites' western vassal states suggests the latter. In either case, before the Hittites could take any effective action against him, he had firmly entrenched himself in Wilusan territory.[10] Indeed the only opposition he encountered was from the veteran Manapa-Tarhunda, vassal ruler since the beginning of Mursili's reign of the nearby Seha River Land.

We recall that Manapa-Tarhunda had disgraced himself not long after his appointment by breaking his allegiance with Mursili II and forming an alliance with the king of Ahhiyawa. But Mursili had forced his surrender, accepted his assurances of future loyalty, and reconfirmed his appointment. From that time on Manapa-Tarhunda apparently remained faithful to his Hittite allegiance.[11] In keeping with this allegiance, and perhaps out of concern for the

---

[8] The reference to Tarhuntassa suggests (but does not prove) that the text belongs to Muwatalli's reign since the kingdom of Tarhuntassa was apparently newly created by Muwatalli (see below). For the possibility of an earlier treaty with Ahhiyawa in Mursili II's reign, see Košak (1980c: 41).

[9] Cf. Jewell (1974: 326), Bryce (1989c: 8 n. 36).

[10] The account of Piyamaradu's activities at this time and the response to these activities is provided by the so-called Manapa-Tarhunda letter, KUB xix 5 (*CTH* 191), augmented by the join-piece KBo xix 79, on which see Houwink ten Cate (1983–4: 33–64).

[11] He participated in a campaign late in Mursili's reign which appears to have begun in Mira-Kuwaliya (*AM* 186–7); see Heinhold-Krahmer (1977: 221), Houwink ten Cate (1983–4: 59). Although the text is broken, it is likely that he acted in support of the Hittite king (*contra* Jewell (1974: 331)).

threat Piyamaradu might pose to his own kingdom, he seems to have made an attempt to drive Piyamaradu out of Wilusa. But without success. Piyamaradu inflicted a humiliating defeat on him, and followed this up by attacking what was apparently one of his dependent territories, the island of Lazpa (Lesbos).

Muwatalli must have received news of these events with considerable alarm. With his commitment to increasing the security of the northern frontiers of his kingdom, and his concerns about the growing threat posed by Egypt to his Syrian territories, he could ill afford to commit resources to a military campaign in the far west. Yet failure to respond to the provocative actions of Piyamaradu could well lead to an escalation of anti-Hittite activities in the region. Given the clear interest of Ahhiyawa in extending its own influence in western Anatolia, an exemplary show of force was imperative. This task Muwatalli assigned to a Hittite expeditionary force under the command of Gassu, with the prime objective of dislodging Piyamaradu from Wilusa, and presumably bringing him back as a prisoner to Hattusa.[12]

Reinforced by a contingent from Mira-Kuwaliya under the command of Kupanta-Kurunta, who had been ruler of the vassal state since the twelfth year of Mursili's reign, Gassu advanced to the Seha River Land on his way to Wilusa. No doubt he counted on additional support from Manapa-Tarhunda. But the latter, who had already experienced a drubbing from Piyamaradu, suddenly fell ill—or so he pleaded in a letter to Muwatalli apologizing for his inability to join the Hittite expeditionary force: 'I, however, became ill. I am seriously ill, illness holds me prostrated!' (KUB XIX 5 (*CTH* 191) + KBo XIX 79 5–6, trans. Houwink ten Cate (1983–4, 40)).

The outcome of the Hittite expedition against Piyamaradu is not recorded in our surviving texts. But from the subsequent renewal of Hittite control over Wilusa, it is clear that the Hittites succeeded—temporarily—in curbing the rebel's activities in the region. Unfortunately for them, Piyamaradu himself eluded their grasp, probably withdrawing to the protection of the king of Ahhiyawa as he did on later occasions—and was thus able

---

[12] This may be the campaign referred to in §6 of the Alaksandu treaty (discussed below). See Heinhold-Krahmer (1977: 152, 160–3, 175–6), Bryce (1979b: 63), Singer (1983a: 206).

to continue his anti-Hittite activities once the Hittite army had departed.

Some time following the Hittite campaign in the west, Muwatalli drew up a treaty with Alaksandu,[13] the duly acknowledged occupant of the Wilusan throne.[14] Muwatalli stressed in the treaty the outstanding loyalty displayed by Wilusa in the past, particularly by its king Kukunni,[15] and the obligations of its current ruler both to act as watchdog of Hittite interests in the west and to provide reinforcements in the event that a Hittite army again campaigned in the region:

If you hear any wicked words about rebellion, (involving) either a man from the Seha River Land or a man of Arzawa and you know about the rumour in time . . . write about it immediately to My Sun. . . . If I, My Sun, am called to the field from that land, either from Karkisa or Masa or Lukka or Warsiyalla, then you must march out on my side with infantry and chariotry. Or if I send any commander from this country to make war, then you too must take the field regularly by his side. (Muwatalli: Alaksandu Treaty §§11, 14, adapted from trans. by Garstang and Gurney (1959: 102))

At the time the treaty was concluded, Muwatalli knew that he would soon be calling on all his available military resources to defend his territories in Syria. The various arrangements and provisions contained in the treaty probably reflect his efforts to ensure the stability of his western territories at this time with as little direct Hittite involvement as possible. Wilusa could play an important role in this regard. In addition, the king expected his vassal to provide troops for his campaigns in Syria. Egypt might not be the only enemy he had to contend with in the region:

Also the following campaigns from Hattusa are obligatory on you: the kings who are of equal rank with My Sun, the king of Egypt, the king of

---

[13] *CTH* 76, ed. Friedrich (1930: 42–102). For translated excerpts, see Garstang and Gurney (1959: 102–3). The chronological order of the Manapa-Tarhunda letter, the Alaksandu treaty, and the so-called Tawagalawa letter (discussed in Ch. 11) has been debated by a number of scholars. In this book I have followed the sequence adopted by Houwink ten Cate (1983–4: 62–4).

[14] Presumably he had been installed, or re-installed, as Hittite vassal ruler after Piyamaradu's expulsion from the kingdom.

[15] Alaksandu treaty, §§3–4. Kukunni was probably the immediate predecessor and perhaps the adoptive father of Alaksandu, according to the restoration proposed by Friedrich (1930: 54–5) to §5 of the text (followed by Garstang and Gurney (1959: 102)). Cf. Freu (1990: 18).

Sanhara,[16] the king of Hanigalbat, or the king of Assyria; if thence anyone marches against me, or if from within anyone stirs up rebellion against My Sun, and I write for infantry and chariotry from you, let infantry and chariotry at once come to my help.   (Muwatalli: Alaksandu Treaty §14, trans. Garstang and Gurney (1959: 102))

Manapa-Tarhunda still occupied the throne of the Seha River Land at the time the treaty with Alaksandu was drawn up.[17] But he was becoming an increasing liability to his overlord, particularly at a time when it was essential to ensure strong and stable leadership amongst the vassal rulers in the west as the Hittites prepared for their campaigns in Syria. This probably prompted Muwatalli's decision to depose the old vassal and banish him from his kingdom,[18] appointing his son Masturi in his place.[19] Presumably the latter had given promise of being a more reliable and effective agent of Hittite influence in the west than his aged and ailing father.

When he felt confident that this influence had been firmly re-established, Muwatalli began final preparations for his confrontation with Egypt.

The Rise of Egypt's Nineteenth Dynasty

During Horemheb's reign, a youth called Pramesse from an undistinguished noble family in the north-eastern part of the Egyptian Delta rose to prominence through a succession of increasingly important military posts, and was eventually appointed as the pharaoh's vizier. His advancement was almost certainly due to Horemheb's direct patronage. Himself childless, the pharaoh had recognized the promise shown by the young Pramesse and had

---

[16] i.e. Babylon. See Laroche (1956: 103 n. 3).

[17] He is almost certainly referred to in §17 of the treaty as one of the kings of the Arzawa Lands; see Heinhold-Krahmer (1977: 146–7), Houwink ten Cate (1983–4: 62, 66).

[18] Houwink ten Cate (1994: 241) comments that his banishment can easily be explained as having been caused by his military and diplomatic setbacks known from the Manapa-Tarhunda letter, IV 8'–11'.

[19] The appointment is referred to in a later treaty, between Tudhaliya IV and Sausgamuwa, king of Amurru, KUB XXIII 1 (*CTH* 105) II 15–19. See the discussions of Stefanini (1964: 25–8), Houwink ten Cate (1974a: 127–8), Heinhold-Krahmer (1977: 228–31). Manapa-Tarhunda was apparently later restored to his country, but probably not to his throne, by Muwatalli's son and successor Urhi-Tesub (see Ch. 10).

probably spent some years grooming him as his successor. On his death c.1295, Pramesse ascended the throne of Egypt as Ramesses I. His accession marked the beginning of Egypt's Nineteenth Dynasty, one of the most famous dynasties in the history of pharaonic Egypt.

Its founder had little time to fulfil the expectations held of him, for his reign lasted little more than a year. But before he died, he had made his son Seti I co-regent. This second pharaoh of the new dynasty was responsible for launching Egypt on an aggressive new programme of military expansion. From the very beginning of his reign, Seti applied himself to the task of regaining the status his kingdom had once enjoyed as a major international political and military power. (In so doing, he sought to emulate the achievements of his most illustrious predecessors, looking to Tuthmosis III in particular as his source of inspiration.) Restoration of Egyptian prestige and authority in Syria was essential to the achievement of this task.

A graphic though now fragmentary record of how he set about it is provided by the battle scenes from his reign, carved in two groups east and west of the central doorway of the Hypostyle Hall at Karnak.[20] To begin with, he dealt with rebellious groups in the regions in Syria still subject, if only nominally, to Egyptian authority. A successful campaign in his first regnal year against the Shosu bedouins in Canaan [21] was followed by a campaign in Palestine which led to the defeat and submission of a coalition of local rulers.[22] Once Egyptian authority had been firmly reasserted in these regions, Seti prepared for a more ambitious undertaking—the reconquest of the kingdoms of Kadesh and Amurru.

As we have seen, these kingdoms had in the past fluctuated in their allegiance between Egypt and Hatti. Although they had been Hittite vassals since the latter part of Suppiluliuma's reign, Egypt had never accepted the legitimacy of Hittite control over them. But there had been little it could do to reassert its own claims—until now. A pharaoh had emerged who had the determination, the ability, and the resources to win them back.

---

[20] See Murnane (1990: 39–40).
[21] Bottom register, eastern group. On the Shosu campaign, see Murnane (1990: 40–2).
[22] Second register, eastern group; see Murnane (1990: 42–5).

As Seti's war monument at Karnak records, both Kadesh and Amurru fell to the pharaoh.[23] His success had wider implications. The attack on Hittite subject territory amounted to a declaration of war against Hatti itself and clearly posed a serious challenge to continued Hittite supremacy in the whole of Syria. Muwatalli could not afford to let this challenge go unanswered. Direct conflict between the two kingdoms now seemed inevitable.

But a year or more elapsed before the conflict took place, probably because of Muwatalli's preoccupation with affairs in Anatolia. If so, Seti had chosen his time well, re-establishing his hold over the southern Syrian kingdoms and depriving the Hittite king of two of his vassal states before he could muster sufficient troops in Syria for a counter-offensive. It was fortunate for Seti that the Hittites did not retaliate promptly, for he had to postpone further military operations in Syria for a year or so in order to undertake a campaign closer to home against the Libyans.[24]

With the successful completion of this campaign, he returned to Syria—prepared for a direct test of strength with the Hittites in defence of the vassal states he had taken from them. Even if they had been willing to concede him these states, his territorial ambitions in Syria would not have been satisfied. In the tradition of Tuthmosis III, he undoubtedly sought to extend his conquests further afield. He had to be stopped now.

The confrontation between the armies of Hatti and Egypt probably took place in the region of Kadesh, a region which a few years later was to figure as the arena for the most famous of all clashes between Hittite and Egyptian forces. An account of the present confrontation, and its alleged outcome, appears on Seti's war monument at Karnak:

... mighty Bull, [ready]-horned, [mighty]-hearted, smiting the Asiatics, beating down the Hittites, slaying their chiefs, overthrown in their blood, charging among them like a tongue of fire, making them as that which is not ... Chiefs of the countries that knew not Egypt, whom his Majesty brought as living captives ... The victor returns, when he has devastated the countries. He has smitten the land of Hatti, causing the cowardly rebels to cease.   (Extracts from Seti's war monument, trans. Breasted (1906: iii, 72–3 §§144, 148))[25]

---

[23] See Murnane (1990: 52–8).   [24] See Breasted (1906: iii, 58–70 §§120–39).
[25] The conflict with the Hittites is recorded on the bottom-most of the three registers on the western wing of the war monument. The Kadesh and Amurru

As far as we can distinguish the facts amongst the bombast, it appears that the battle honours went decisively to Seti, who took a substantial number of Hittite prisoners back to Egypt.[26] Kadesh and Amurru probably remained under his control for the rest of his reign. This effectively made him overlord of the whole of southern Syria.

For the moment, Muwatalli had little choice but to accept the territorial gains made by Seti, and to acknowledge that political and military supremacy in Syria had now to be shared with Egypt. It is possible that this was ratified in a treaty between the two kings.[27] If a treaty was in fact concluded at this time, it no doubt specified a demarcation of territory between the kingdoms and an obligation on the part of each king to respect the boundaries as defined; the territories within the region from Kadesh southwards and the coastal strip as far as the northern limits of the kingdom of Amurru were probably acknowledged as being under Egyptian sovereignty, with the territories north of Kadesh confirmed as Hittite.

Whatever agreement, if any, was reached between the two kings, Muwatalli had no qualms in breaking it once he had assembled sufficient military resources in Syria to do so. But for the few remaining years of Seti's reign, an uneasy peace seems to have prevailed between Hatti and Egypt. This gave Muwatalli the respite he needed to implement some radical changes within his kingdom.

The Shift of the Royal Seat to Tarhuntassa

Probably during the middle years of his reign, Muwatalli transferred the seat of Hittite power from Hattusa to a city called Tarhuntassa located in the region later known as Cilicia.[28] A record

campaign appears in the topmost register. There has been some debate about the chronological sequence to be followed in reading these registers; see Murnane, (1990: 51–2).

[26] Those depicted in the pictorial record were clearly Hittites. See Murnane (1990: 58).

[27] If one can so conclude from a reference in the treaty between Ramesses II and Hattusili III (see Ch. 11) to a treaty which existed in the time of Muwatalli (*KRI* ii 228: 1–3). Further on this, see Murnane (1990: 37–8).

[28] On the location of Tarhuntassa see e.g. Bryce (1992a: 122–3). It seems to have been a new entity created by Muwatalli and incorporating the country known as the Hulaya River Land; see Otten (1988a: 46), Hoffner (1989b: 47), Beckman (1989/90:

of this momentous change has been left us by Muwatalli's brother, the man who later ascended the throne as Hattusili III:

When, however, my brother Muwatalli at the command of his (patron) deity went down to the Lower Land, leaving the city of Hattusa, he took the gods and the *Manes*[29] of Hatti . . . and he brought them down to the city of Tarhuntassa and made it his place of residence.   (*Apology of Hattusili (CTH* 81),[30] §6, I 75–II 1–2 §8, II 52–3)[31]

That this was no mere temporary relocation, for military or other reasons, is indicated by the wholesale removal of the state deities to the new site. Muwatalli intended the move to be a permanent one. Now, probably, he assumed the title 'Great King of Tarhuntassa'.[32]

   The transfer of the capital may well have met with strong opposition from many of the king's subjects. For all the weaknesses of its location, Hattusa had been the heartland, if not the original ancestral home, of Hittite power from the early days of the Old Kingdom. Muwatalli's predecessors had fought vigorously to protect it, and to regain it when it had fallen into enemy hands. It was the spiritual as well as the material symbol of the might of the Hittite kingdom, the location of the great Temple of the Storm God, and the temples of many other deities. It was indisputably the greatest city of the Hittite world, and had become virtually synonymous with Hittite power—not only to the Hittites themselves, but to their vassal kings, many of whom came annually to the city to pay homage to their Hittite overlord.

   Yet this royal city was now being abandoned by its king for a new location several hundred kilometres to the south, and at that time apparently insignificant and largely unknown. Indeed we have no certain references to Tarhuntassa before the royal seat was established there.[33] The practical reasons for the transfer must have been

---

290 n. 3). Gurney (1993: 26–8) argued that Tarhuntassa and Hulaya River Land were two different names of the same country, but elsewhere (1992: 221) that the names referred to different countries. Most recently Hawkins (1995c: 50) has argued that the Hulaya River Land was in fact the frontier zone of the Land of Tarhuntassa—i.e. it was a part of Tarhuntassa, not synonymous with it.

[29] The spirits of ancestors.

[30] The text, ed. Otten (1981), is referred to and discussed at greater length in Ch. 10.

[31] On the question of whether the transfer took place in two stages, see Houwink ten Cate (1983–4: 69 n. 100).

[32] See Houwink ten Cate (1994: 234).

[33] But see Houwink ten Cate (1992a: 250), who suggests that a geographical notion Tarhuntassa may have existed much earlier. He refers to the possibility that

very strong indeed to outweigh arguments for maintaining the royal seat at Hattusa. Even so there were those who remained unconvinced. Many years later Hattusili III still questioned the wisdom of his brother's action. In a prayer to the Sun Goddess he stressed that he had no part in it:

Whether [the transfer of the gods] was in accordance with your wishes or whether it was not in accordance with your wishes, you, My Lady, are the one who knew that in your divine soul. But I was not involved in the order to transfer the gods. For me it was a matter of coercion, (while) he was my master. But the transfer of the gods was not in accordance with my wishes and I was afraid for that order. And the silver and gold of all the gods, to which god he gave the silver and gold of each of them, in that decision, too, I was not in any way involved.   (KUB XIV 7 (*CTH* 383) 13′–15′, adapted from trans. by Houwink ten Cate (1974*a*: 125–6))

Political and military developments in Syria may well have been an important factor in the action taken by Muwatalli. And once taken, he held firm to it. Tarhuntassa provided him with a much more geographically convenient base than the old Hittite capital for launching his campaign into Syria. Further, the massive diversion of the kingdom's military resources to Syria for the confrontation with Egypt would leave the old capital dangerously exposed to the enemies in the northern regions—the Kaska enemy above all. It would make better sense, so Muwatalli may have reasoned, to re-establish the permanent administrative and spiritual centre of the kingdom in a new location far removed from the menace of the northern enemies.

What became of Hattusa? Although it was to suffer a substantial decline in status, the king certainly had no intention of abandoning it entirely. On his departure from the city he placed it under the immediate authority of a man called Mittannamuwa.[34] The latter had been a distinguished functionary in Mursili's reign, rising to the rank of 'Great Scribe' (GAL DUB.SAR), a post now conferred upon his son Purandamuwa. But while Mittannamuwa became the administrator of Hattusa itself, the city was probably included in the region which Muwatalli assigned to the control of his brother Hattusili,[35] and thus lay within Hattusili's overall jurisdiction.

the seal impression bearing the name of the 16th-cent. Kizzuwadnan king Isputahsu may contain the designation 'King of Tarhuntassa'.

[34] KBo IV 12 (*CTH* 87) rev. 17.
[35] As suggested by two royal prayers from Hattusili's own reign (*CTH* 383 and 384). Cf. Houwink ten Cate (1994: 233–4).

From very early in Muwatalli's reign, Hattusili had exercised considerable power within the Hittite kingdom. Shortly after his accession, Muwatalli had conferred upon his brother the highly prestigious position of GAL *MĚSEDI*, Chief of the Royal Bodyguards. He also assigned to him a number of important military commands, and appointed him governor of the Upper Land. The appointment meant displacing the current governor Arma-Tarhunda, who protested vigorously at his removal from office (see Ch. 10). But it was to prove critically important to the maintenance of Hittite authority in the north while Muwatalli prepared for his conflict with Egypt.

There was a need for other measures to ensure that the region would remain secure. Many of the old Hittite settlements located within it now had only a sparse population, or were inhabited by Kaska settlers, or were abandoned ghost towns. Muwatalli assigned the whole region to Hattusili, with the particular brief of repopulating .abandoned or sparsely populated settlements, and establishing a Hittite population in areas where there was already a substantial Kaskan presence. Hattusili became in effect the ruler of a buffer kingdom which included the countries of Ishupitta, Marista, Hissashapa, Katapa, Hanhana, Darahna, Hattena, Durmitta, Pala, Tummanna, Gassiya, Sappa, and the Hulana River Land.[36] In broad terms the region incorporating these countries must have extended across the northern half of the Marrassantiya basin probably from the region of present-day Merzifon in the north-west to Sivas or beyond in the south-east.

Muwatalli also conferred upon his brother the status of king (LUGAL) in the Land of Hakpissa (Hakmissa).[37] The location of the city of Hakpissa was strategically important, for it lay on the route from Hattusa to the holy city of Nerik and thence into Kaskan territory. It also served as an important administrative centre, in effect a royal capital from which Hattusili ruled the northern region as a whole.[38] We shall consider below some of the measures taken by Hattusili to repopulate the 'empty countries' (KUR.KUR[MEŠ]

---

[36] *Apol.* §8, II 56–60.

[37] Generally located at Amasya; see del Monte and Tischler (1978: 66). However Kempinski and Košak, 1982, 109, suggest that the city lay in the area of modern Çorum in the Upper Land. On the m/p variation, see Cornil and Lebrun (1972: 21).

[38] See further on Hakpissa/Hakmissa Haas (1970: 7, 11, 13–15; 1972–5: 49–50).

dannatta) in the north and to reassert Hittite control throughout this region.

What is clear is that Muwatalli's decision to shift his capital to Tarhuntassa had the effect of virtually partitioning the Hittite kingdom, with the northern part of the kingdom, including much of the homeland, now directly ruled by Hattusili. This was to have some major political repercussions, not to become fully evident until after Muwatalli's death. For the present, it enabled Muwatalli to concentrate his efforts on his forthcoming confrontation with Egypt. Following the death of his old adversary Seti I, an ambitious and enterprising new pharaoh had now ascended the throne—Seti's son Ramesses II.

Preparations for the Conflict

From his early years Ramesses had been prepared by his father for the succession, and probably in his mid-teens was officially designated as prince-regent. On Seti's death in 1279,[39] Ramesses ascended the throne as Ramesses II. The first three years of his reign were taken up largely with internal affairs. But by the summer of his fourth year, he was ready to follow up his father's successes in Syria with a fresh assertion of Egyptian authority in the region.

The Syrian campaign which he conducted in 1275 paved the way for a more extensive campaign the following year. Much of the territory through which he passed in his first campaign was already firmly under Egyptian control, including Canaan and the cities of Tyre and Byblos. It is possible that the kingdom of Amurru which Seti had wrested from Hittite control had by this time been regained by the Hittites, and Ramesses may have been obliged to reconquer it. But more likely it had remained with Egypt since its conquest by Seti.[40] If so, Ramesses' expedition in his fourth year

---

[39] Bolger (1991: 426), in his review of Åström (1987/9), notes that four papers from the 1987 Gothenburg colloquium (by Hornung, Helck, Kitchen, and Bietak) address the existing chronologies for the Middle and New Kingdoms. With the exception of Kitchen they unequivocally support the low New Kingdom chronology which sets the start of Ramesses II's reign at 1274. Most important in the view of Hornung and Bietak is the fact that the new chronology has been determined without the use of Sothic dating. I have none the less adopted an accession date of 1279, following Kitchen (and others).

[40] Cf. Murnane (1990: 55–6), Klengel (1995: 164).

was probably little more than a probing exercise, which provided the opportunity for confirming the loyalty of Egyptian vassals in the region, ensuring their support in the forthcoming confrontation with Hatti, and gaining direct knowledge of the terrain where the contest would take place.

By the summer of Ramesses' fifth year, preparations in Egypt were complete for a return to Syria and a decisive test of strength between the two great military powers of the day. Ramesses' prime object was to destroy Hittite power in Syria, and to restore Egypt fully to the pre-eminent position it had enjoyed in the days of Tuthmosis III.

At the time of this campaign, the dividing line between Hittite- and Egyptian-controlled territory in Syria was a vaguely defined frontier in the region of Kadesh, which lay on the left bank of the Orontes river. We have noted this kingdom's fluctuating loyalties through several centuries as it changed sides from one major power to another. It had recently fallen to Seti, along with Amurru. However, it must have reverted to Hittite control, perhaps in the first year of Ramesses' reign, for it was clearly on the Hittite side at the time of Ramesses' second Syrian campaign.[41]

The Battle of Kadesh (1274)

The contest which finally took place between the armies of Hatti and Egypt in the vicinity of the city of Kadesh is recorded on the walls of five Egyptian temples—the Ramesseum (Ramesses' temple near the Valley of the Kings), and the temples at Karnak, Luxor, Abydos, and Abu Simbel. The record generally appears in two versions on the temple walls—the lengthy 'Poem' or 'Literary Record', and a shorter version, the so-called 'Report' or 'Bulletin', which is closely associated with one of the reliefs which depict episodes from the campaign. Both versions deal not only with the battle itself, but also with events leading up to it, including the progress of the Egyptian forces from the time of their departure from Egypt. Unfortunately we do not have a Hittite account of the battle, and obviously have to allow for bias, distortion, and exaggeration in what we learn from the Egyptian account. None the less this account provides us with one of the most detailed records of all

---

[41] Cf. Murnane (1990: 58).

ancient battles, and enables us to reconstruct a reasonably complete picture of what actually happened in the days leading up to the battle as well as on the day of the battle itself.[42]

On the Hittite side Muwatalli, determined to crush once and for all Egyptian military aggression against his Syrian territories, had amassed a vast army in Syria. It was made up of a substantial body of regular Hittite troops, contingents from a wide range of vassal states, and large numbers of mercenaries. The Egyptian record provides a valuable source of information on the composition of this armed force:[43]

And now the wretched Fallen one of Kadesh had come and had collected together all the foreign countries so far as the end of the sea; the entire Land of Hatti had come, that of Nahrin (i.e. Mitanni) likewise, that of Arzawa, Dardany,[44] that of Keshkesh (i.e. Kaska), those of Masa, those of Pitassa, that of Arawanna, that of Karkisa, Lukka, Kizzuwadna, Carchemish, Ugarit, Kedy, the entire land of Nuhasse, Musanet, Kadesh . . . They covered mountains and valleys and they were like the locust by reason of their multitude. He left no silver in the land, he stripped it of all its possessions, and gave them to all the foreign countries in order to bring them with him to fight. (Kadesh Inscription P40–53, adapted from trans. by Gardiner (1975: 8))[45]

The total number given by Ramesses for the enemy forces is 47,500, including some 3,500 chariotry and 37,000 infantry.[46] While Ramesses *may* have exaggerated the figures, it is quite conceivable that the Hittites did in fact gather such a force from the sources available to them.[47]

Ramesses had mustered his forces at the city of Pi-Ramesse in the eastern Delta. His army was made up of four divisions, recruited from four Egyptian cities—from Thebes the army of the god Amun, from Heliopolis the army of Re, from Memphis the army of Ptah, and probably from Tanis in the Delta the army of Sutekh. In late May, 1274, this large military assemblage left Egypt

---

[42] See Liverani (1990: 178–9), for a quite different interpretation, from the one which follows, of the Kadesh engagement.

[43] See the discussion of the list of Hittite allies in Goetze (1975c: 253).

[44] The assumed identification of the 'Dardany' (Drdny) with the 'Trojan' Dardanoi is doubted by Mellaart (1986a: 82), but supported by Gurney (1990: 47).

[45] P (= Poem) designates the Literary Record. On the likelihood that the troops from Masa, Karkisa, and Lukka participated in the battle as mercenaries, see Bryce (1979b: 63). Cf. Singer (1983a: 206).

[46] See Beal (1992b: 291–6).   [47] Ibid. 296.

and began its march into Syria, proceeding northwards up the coast of Palestine towards the territories of the king of Hatti.

Ramesses led the way with his imperial entourage and the Amun division, advancing post-haste towards the city of Kadesh. His progress was swift, unhindered by any resistance worth noting along the way, and within a month he was within striking distance of his objective. But normal military precautions had been thrown to the winds, and the pharaoh's whole progress was characterized by poor planning and lack of reconnaissance. The risks he ran were substantial. He was now in enemy territory, and if attacked, he could call only on the resources of the Amun division, for the other three divisions were spread out over a considerable distance in the rear. Before proceeding any further, he had need to consolidate his forces by awaiting the arrival of the three lagging divisions, and carrying out at least some basic reconnaissance to determine the whereabouts of the enemy. Such must have been the advice given to him by his military advisers. If so, it was ignored.

Indeed just as he was preparing to cross the Orontes along with the Amun division by a ford near Shabtuna, his confidence received a considerable boost when two Shosu bedouins came to him, claiming that they and their fellow tribesmen wished to leave the service of the Hittite king and join the Egyptian forces. Under interrogation, they stated that their tribal chiefs were still with the Hittite army, which was far to the north, in the Land of Aleppo:

'Our brothers who are headmen of tribes with the Fallen One of Hatti have sent us to His Majesty to say that we will be servants of Pharaoh and will separate ourselves from the Ruler of Hatti.' Then said His Majesty to them: 'Where are they, your brothers who sent you to report this to His Majesty?' And they said to His Majesty: 'They are where the wretched Ruler of Hatti is, for the Fallen One of Hatti is in the Land of Aleppo to the north of Tunip, and he feared Pharaoh (too much) to come southward when he heard that Pharaoh had come northward.' (Kadesh Inscription B8–18, adapted from trans. by Gardiner (1975: 28))[48]

The story was a fabrication. The bedouins had been sent by Muwatalli to spy out Ramesses' position. Incredibly, Ramesses accepted what they told him without any further investigation.

[48] B (= Bulletin) designates the inscriptions associated with the Pictorial Record.

Failing to make even a token reconnaissance he crossed the ford with the Amun division, and took up a position north-west of Kadesh. The Amun division was thus isolated from the Re division, which was still occupied with crossing the ford. The Ptah and Sutekh divisions were still many kilometres to the south.

As his troops were setting up camp in preparation for laying siege to Kadesh the following day, and while awaiting the erection of his royal pavilion, Ramesses received a severe shock. Two Hittite scouts sent by Muwatalli to ascertain the exact position of the Egyptian army were captured and under a beating revealed the true location of the Hittite army:

Then said His Majesty: 'What are you?' They replied, 'We belong to the Ruler of Hatti! He sent us to see where Your Majesty was.' Said His Majesty to them, 'Where is he, the Ruler of Hatti? See, I heard it said that he was in the Land of Aleppo, north of Tunip.' They replied, 'Behold, the Ruler of Hatti has (already) come, together with the many foreign lands that he brought as allies . . . See, they are poised, armed, and ready to fight behind Old-Kadesh!'   (Kadesh Inscription B35–51, trans. Kitchen (1982: 54–6))

The entire Hittite army was in a concealed position just across the Orontes, ready to attack!

After summoning and venting his fury upon his officers for this disastrous breakdown in the Egyptian intelligence service (for which he himself was largely to blame), Ramesses quickly dispatched two of his personal officials to hurry on the divisions of Ptah and Re, the latter still many kilometres distant; the division of Sutekh was too far away to be of any use at all. But then the Hittite army passed to the south of Kadesh, crossed the river, and charged into the midst of the Re division. Caught completely unawares, it broke apart before the onslaught. Its troops fled in panic and confusion to the camp still being set up by Ramesses and the Amun division, with the Hittite chariotry in hot pursuit.

A total rout of the Egyptian forces, and the capture or death of the pharaoh, seemed inevitable. But Ramesses, making up for his earlier recklessness and gullibility, stood his ground with an exemplary show of courage and leadership—at least according to his own version of the events. As the Hittite chariotry surrounded his forces in an ever-tightening circle, the pharaoh launched a desperate counter-attack:

Then His Majesty started forth at a gallop, and entered into the host of the fallen ones of Hatti, being alone by himself and none other with him. . . . And he found 2,500 chariots hemming him in on his outer side, consisting of all the fallen ones of Hatti with the many foreign countries which were with them . . . I called to you, My Father Amun, when I was in the midst of multitudes I knew not. All foreign countries were combined against me, I being alone by myself, none other with me, my numerous infantry having abandoned me, not one looking at me of my chariotry. I kept on shouting to them, but none of them hearkened to me as I called . . . I found Amun come when I called him; he gave me his hand and I rejoiced . . . All that I did came to pass. I was like Mont. I shot on my right and captured with my left . . . I found the 2,500 chariots, in whose midst I was, sprawling before my horse. Not one of them found his hand to fight . . . I caused them to plunge into the water even as crocodiles plunge, fallen upon their faces one upon the other. I killed among them according as I willed . . . (Kadesh Inscription, extracts from P80–140, adapted from trans. by Gardiner (1975: 9–10))

The outcome, according to the Egyptian record, was a decisive victory for Ramesses:

Then my army came to praise me, . . . my high officers having come to magnify my strong arm, and my chariotry likewise boasting of my name and saying, '. . . You are great of victory in the presence of your army, in the face of the entire land . . . You have broken the back of Hatti forever!' (Kadesh Inscription, extracts from P235–50, adapted from trans. by Gardiner (1975: 12))

Muwatalli, allegedly, acknowledged the Egyptian victory, paying homage to the pharaoh, and begging mercy for his subjects:

Thereupon the wretched Ruler of Hatti sent and did homage to my name like that of Re, saying 'You are Sutekh, Baal in person. The dread of you is a brand in the Land of Hatti . . . As for the Land of Egypt and the Land of Hatti, they are yours, your servants, they are under your feet . . . Be not hard in your dealings, victorious king. Peace is better than fighting. Give us breath!' (Kadesh Inscription, extracts from P295–321, adapted from trans. by Gardiner (1975: 13–14))

What truth is there in all this? To begin with, Ramesses must have had considerably more military support than he claimed to have lived to tell the tale. While we should not detract too much from the personal leadership he gave at the moment of crisis, the Hittite attack might well have resulted in a complete rout of the

Egyptian forces but for what appears to have been a very timely arrival of reinforcements from Amurru. While these reinforcements are not mentioned in the literary record, the relief sculptures of the battle illustrate a large orderly array of troops approaching the Egyptian camp. For his own purposes Ramesses would have played down their role. But their arrival may well have distracted the Hittite attacking force sufficiently to prevent the complete destruction of the first two divisions, providing time for the arrival of the third and fourth.

Ramesses may also have been helped by another factor. As we have noted, the Hittite army was made up of a motley collection of vassal troops and mercenaries in addition to the regular Hittite troops. After the success of the initial shock assault on the Egyptians, it is quite possible that discipline in the Hittite ranks broke down when the Egyptian camp was reached, with its enticing prospects for looting and plunder.

Even if we make allowance for exaggerations in the Egyptian account, there can be little doubt that the Hittites suffered substantial losses. Detailed lists of Hittite officers slain in the battle appear on the walls of the Ramesseum, and some of the names also appear in the temples of Ramesses at Abydos and Abu Simbel. There is no reason to doubt the accuracy of these details.

But to which side were the overall battle honours due? Both sides claimed victory. The Egyptian records clearly depict the battle as an overwhelming triumph for the pharaoh. On the other hand our Hittite records, while they contain no surviving account of the battle itself, represent it as a victory for Muwatalli. The likelihood is that after a desperate rally from Ramesses and the forces immediately at his disposal, the Egyptian army was saved at the eleventh hour from a devastating defeat, and the battle itself ended in a stalemate; both sides sustained heavy losses and neither emerged as the decisive victor.

In the longer term, however, Muwatalli was the ultimate victor. After fending off the Hittite onslaught, Ramesses promptly withdrew his forces far to the south. Not only had he failed to regain for Egypt Hittite subject territories north to Kadesh, but his retreating forces were pursued by Muwatalli into Egyptian-held territory, as far south as the Land of Aba. Aba fell to the Hittites, and before returning to Hatti, Muwatalli placed it under the control of his brother Hattusili, as the latter tells us:

Because my brother Muwatalli campaigned against the king of Egypt and
the king of Amurru, when he defeated the kings of Egypt and Amurru, he
went back to Aba. When Muwatalli, my brother defeated Aba, he . . . went
back to Hatti, but he left me in Aba.   (KUB XXI 17 (*CTH* 86) I 14–21, with
duplicate KUB XXXI 27 2–7,[49] trans. Beal (1992*b*: 307))

For Muwatalli, the most important sequel to the battle of Kadesh
was his recapture of the kingdom of Amurru. Control of this kingdom was of critical importance to the security of Hittite rule in
Syria, particularly in view of its strategic location on the south-
western flank of Hittite subject territory. So long as Amurru was in
enemy hands, the Hittite vassal kingdoms in northern Syria were at
risk. The loss of Amurru to Seti I had been a severe blow to Hatti,
and from that time Muwatalli was determined to regain it. Indeed
it was this determination which provided on the Hittite side the
immediate motive for the confrontation with Ramesses. Amurru
was itself held partly responsible for succumbing to Egypt, its 'defection' being represented as an act of treachery:

When Muwatalli, the brother of the father of My Sun, became king, the
people of Amurru broke faith with him, and had this to say to him: 'From
free individuals we have become vassals. But now we are your vassals no
longer!' And they entered into the following of the king of Egypt. Thereupon Muwatalli, the brother of the father of My Sun, and the king of Egypt
did battle with each other over the people of Amurru. Muwatalli defeated
the king of Egypt and forced the Land of Amurru to the ground with his
weapons and subjected it to himself.   (Tudhaliya IV: Sausgamuwa Treaty
(*CTH* 105),[50] I 28–38)

In particular, Muwatalli's wrath was directed against the
Amurrite king Bentesina (*c*.1290/80–1235) who was blamed for his
kingdom's defection. Once the kingdom was restored to Hittite
control, Bentesina would be deposed and taken prisoner: 'On
whatever campaign My Sun marches, if then you Gods support me
and I conquer the Land of Amurru—whether I conquer it with
weapons, or whether it makes peace with me—and I seize the king
of Amurru, . . . I will bestow gifts upon the Gods' (KBo IX 96 (*CTH*
590) 7–9, 14).[51]

The accusation of treachery which was levelled against
Bentesina was probably unjustified. The vassal had little choice but

---

[49] Ed. Edel (1950: 212).   [50] Ed. Kühne and Otten (1971).
[51] Extract from a votive text, trans. and discussed by Klengel (1969: 213).

to submit to Egyptian overlordship, with Seti's forces on the very borders of his kingdom and no prospect of immediate military support from Muwatalli. Amurru was recaptured, and Bentesina was taken prisoner and transported to Hatti. He was replaced on the vassal throne by a man called Sapili, about whom nothing else is known.[52] But Bentesina's career was far from over. He had found favour with Muwatalli's brother Hattusili, who apparently accepted his protest that he had been compelled to submit to Egyptian overlordship, and now requested that Bentesina be placed in his charge. Muwatalli agreed. Bentesina was resettled in Hattusili's own northern capital Hakpissa.[53] But only temporarily. He would one day reoccupy his throne in Amurru (see Ch. 10).

In spite of Ramesses' claims to victory in the battle of Kadesh, the substantial loss of territory as well as loss of face which he suffered in the aftermath of the battle must have been a serious blow to Egypt's status and authority in Syria, in the eyes of its subjects as well as its enemies. And in the two years immediately following Kadesh, local rulers in Canaan and Palestine openly defied Egyptian authority. Ramesses responded by conquering the centres of resistance in a rapid and decisive series of military operations.

These operations were a prelude to more extensive campaigns in the north in his eighth and ninth years, once again deep into Hittite subject territory. Advancing down the Orontes valley, Ramesses captured the cities of Tunip and Dapur. When firmly entrenched in this region, Egypt once more posed a serious threat not only to the kingdoms of Amurru and Kadesh, but to all the subject territories Muwatalli had but recently acquired, from Amurru south to Aba. For the remainder of Muwatalli's reign, and indeed for the next sixteen years, tensions remained high between Hatti and Egypt. The prospect of another major confrontation was ever-present.

Yet it was a confrontation that neither power could afford. The conflict at Kadesh had seriously drained the resources of both kingdoms. From this they would never fully recover. And Assyria continued to lurk menacingly on the sidelines.

---

[52] Details of the above are provided by Hattusili's treaty with Bentesina, *PD* no. 9 (*CTH* 92), 126–7, obv. 11–13, and Tudhaliya IV's treaty with Sausgamuwa, 1 39.
[53] Bentesina Treaty, 1 13–15.

Muwatalli's Reign in Review

Muwatalli had proved himself a worthy successor to his father Mursili. Undoubtedly he is best remembered as the opponent of Ramesses on the field of Kadesh, and in terms of its outcome, the overall success of the Hittite–Egyptian confrontation was undoubtedly his. Had there been a less able or less determined occupant of the throne in Hattusa, Ramesses may well have succeeded in emulating the exploits of his great predecessor Tuthmosis III, and gaining control of much of the region over which Tuthmosis had held sway.

Yet before meeting the challenge posed by Egypt's resurgence, Muwatalli had first to reassert Hittite authority firmly and comprehensively amongst the territories and kingdoms of Anatolia. This had meant further campaigns in the west, particularly to counter the threats posed to Hittite subject territories in the region by disaffected subjects like Piyamaradu, probably with Ahhiyawan backing. It had also meant seeking more lasting solutions to the kingdom's vulnerability to enemies closer to the homeland. Repeated military campaigns against the Hittites' northernmost enemies, notably the Kaska people, had provided no more than temporary relief from attacks by these enemies. With the need now for a major concentration of Hittite resources in Syria, it was imperative for Muwatalli to ensure, first of all, the security of his Anatolian territories. The virtual partitioning of the kingdom, with the royal seat transferred to Tarhuntassa and the king's brother Hattusili appointed as ruler of the northern regions of the kingdom, was a radical attempt by Muwatalli to bring about this security.

For a time he appears to have succeeded, at least long enough for him to achieve his objectives in Syria, while ensuring that Hittite territory in Anatolia was reasonably secure from enemy attack. But the arrangements he had made in Anatolia barely survived his death.

The Trial of Tanuhepa

In the final years of his reign, Muwatalli was confronted with a serious crisis in the royal court. It involved his stepmother Tanuhepa, second wife of his father and predecessor Mursili. In the time-honoured tradition, Tanuhepa continued to exercise the functions of Hittite queen after her husband's death, and was linked with Muwatalli by the appearance of her name with his on royal seals. But her relationship with her stepson seems to have been fraught with tension. Matters reached a head when he placed her on trial, apparently for acts of profanation in the service of the deity. In this respect, her career seems to have borne an ominous resemblance to that of her predecessor, the notorious Babylonian Tawananna, wife of Suppiluliuma.

We learn of the trial from the prayers of Muwatalli's son Hattusili—who sought to distance himself from any responsibility for the action taken against both queens. In referring to the trial of Tanuhepa, he stated:

I wish that my father and the queen would not be adversaries in a lawsuit! And may no evil whatsoever jeopardize me! Why should I pass judgment on those lawsuits? That is a lawsuit pertaining to the god! And if my father, as compared to the queen, would not (appear to) be in the right in the lawsuit, would I then be obliged to make him the losing party in the lawsuit with respect to Tanuhepa, the queen? For my life's (or my soul)'s sake I repeatedly made the following remark: 'May no evil, whatsoever, jeopardize me!' (KUB xxxi 66 + IBoT iii 122 (*CTH* 297.7) A iii, trans. Houwink ten Cate (1974a: 132))[54]

Tanuhepa was found guilty of the charges laid against her. She was stripped of office and presumably banished from the court and the city.[55] Her sons and retinue were also victims of her downfall.[56] In looking back to the trial, Hattusili raised serious questions about the justification for what his father did, and whether his actions had divine sanction. One suspects that these actions were inspired, in part at least, by political motives.

Indeed, there is a strong possibility that the chief cause of the dispute between Tanuhepa and Muwatalli was the question of the succession. Was Tanuhepa seeking to advance the claims of one of her own sons to the kingship over that of Muwatalli's son Urhi-

---

[54] Cf. KUB xiv 7 i 17'–21' + KUB xxi 19 ii obv. 1–22 (from the prayer of Hattusili and Puduhepa to the Sun Goddess). Archi (1971: 212) notes that in KUB xvi 32 (*CTH* 582) (a prayer by Hattusili's son Tudhaliya IV), another reference is made to the case of Tanuhepa, which therefore could not have been considered resolved even in Tudhaliya's reign. See also KUB xvi 16 (*CTH* 570) obv. 1 and 23, cited by Archi, which refers to an investigation relating to both Tanuhepa and Urhi-Tesub.

[55] Cf. Houwink ten Cate (1994: 243).   [56] KUB xiv 7 obv. 1 16'–21'.

Tesub?[57] As we shall see, the latter was not the son of a first wife, merely of a concubine or secondary wife. And his eventual appointment as king was to cause major upheavals in the kingdom. The Niṣantepe seal archive has presented us with an intriguing enigma. Amongst the *bullae* found in the archive are two which bear the seal impression of Tanuhepa along with that of an 'unknown king'. Was this yet another king with whom Tanuhepa was associated? And if so, could it have been one of her own sons, set up with her support in defiance of Muwatalli's own plans for the succession? No doubt these questions will provide scholars with a fruitful field for speculation.

At all events, unlike her husband's stepmother, Tanuhepa was eventually restored to royal favour. The evidence provided by seals indicates that in the reign of Muwatalli's successor Urhi-Tesub, she once more held the status of the reigning Hittite queen,[58] quite possibly with the support of Hattusili. The career of this remarkable woman thus extended through the reigns of three Hittite kings—Mursili, Muwatalli, and Urhi-Tesub. Presumably she married Mursili at a young age, but not too young, it seems, to have presented him with offspring before his death. It is frustrating that we know so little about her, or her part in the palace intrigues which may well have bedevilled the reign of her stepson and were to continue through the reigns of at least his first two successors.

We do not know whether the trial and downfall of Tanuhepa took place before or after Muwatalli's Kadesh campaign. But the former seems more likely. All military campaigns in which the king personally participated involved the risk that the king would be captured or killed in action. And the risk increased substantially for a king taking on the full might of the Egyptian army. Muwatalli must have been anxious to ensure that his plans for his son's succession would proceed without challenge in the event of his own death. This no doubt was one aspect of the careful and detailed

---

[57] Houwink ten Cate (1994: 240) suggests that this is hinted at in the broken lines KUB XXI 19 II 3–6 of Hattusili's and Puduhepa's prayer.

[58] See Beran (1967) nos. 226–7 (Urhi-Tesub + Tanuhepa), no. 228 (Mursili (III) + Tanuhepa), nos. 180–2 (Mursili III). (Urhi-Tesub assumed the throne-name Mursili on his accession.) In addition to these, numerous seal impressions from the Niṣantepe archive bear the joint names of Tanuhepa and Urhi-Tesub or Mursili (III); see Neve (1992a: 313). These seal impressions show that for at least part of the time he occupied the throne Urhi-Tesub reigned with Tanuhepa.

preparations he made within his kingdom before setting forth to confront Ramesses.

In any case, the history of the Hittite monarchy made all too clear a king's vulnerability to court conspiracies while he himself was on campaign. Tensions between Muwatalli and his stepmother may have been increasing for some years. If she did in fact have ambitions for placing one of her own sons on the throne, she posed a serious threat both to her stepson and to his sons. This was a matter which Muwatalli very likely sought to resolve before he set out for Syria. Matters were brought to a head when he put the queen on trial and subsequently banished her from the capital, thus preempting any attempt on her part to conspire against him or stage a coup in his absence.

It is possibly in this context as well that he decided to hand over to his brother Hattusili the safekeeping and upbringing of his second son Kurunta.[59] This may have occurred several years before the Kadesh campaign. Presumably Kurunta was sent to Hakpissa where Hattusili had been installed as king. At least while he was under Hattusili's protection he should be safe from the queen and her supporters. If the worst came to the worst and Muwatalli's designated successor Urhi-Tesub fell victim to Tanuhepa's machinations, there would still be a surviving son of Muwatalli to claim the throne.

The 'worst case' scenario was avoided on this occasion. But in avoiding it, Muwatalli had laid the foundations for ongoing disputes within his own family which in the long term may have contributed to the kingdom's final collapse.

---

[59] Bo 86/299 (Bronze Tablet), §2, I 12–13.

CHAPTER 10

The Ill-Fated Reign of the Second-Rank Son: The Reign of Urhi-Tesub (c.1272–1267)

A Sickly Child

While I was still a child . . . My Lady Istar sent my brother Muwatalli to my father Mursili in a dream (with the message): 'For Hattusili the years (are) short. He will die soon. Therefore give him into my service, and let him be my priest. (If you do so) he will continue to live.' (*Apology of Hattusili*, §3, I 13–17)

There were grave fears for the health of the prince Hattusili, the youngest of Mursili's four children.[1] The chances were that he would not survive childhood. Certainly, none who saw the condition of this sickly child could have foreseen the long and illustrious career that lay ahead of him. But his father had faith in the goddess's advice. Obedient to her command, he gave the child into her service. 'Under the protection of My Lady Istar I saw prosperity. She took me by the hand, and led me on the right course' (*Apol.* §3, I 20–1). Under Istar's care, Hattusili did indeed survive and prosper. In the reign of his brother Muwatalli he was to become, next to the king, the most powerful figure in the Land of Hatti, even though illness seems to have dogged him for much of his life.[2]

Much of our information about Hattusili's early career comes from a document commonly known as the *Apology*,[3] a self-

---

[1] Mursili had three sons (the other two were Muwatalli and Halpasulupi), and a daughter DINGIR^MEŠ-IR-i (= Massan(a)uzzi); see Laroche (1966: 155 no. 775). For the phonetic reading of the daughter's name and her identification with Matanazi who figures in Hittite correspondence with Ramesses II (see Ch. 11), see Imparati (1992: 307 n. 8), and the references cited therein. Imparati (1992: 307) suggested that Hattusili's claim to be the youngest child (*Apol.* §1, I 12) might be no more than a literary *topos* frequent in documents of this kind, although she has subsequently commented (1995: 144 n. 8) that we must keep in mind that this was a case of recent fact, easily verifiable by Hattusili's audience.

[2] As is clear from the numerous votive prayers of his wife Puduhepa, discussed below. See also Ünal (1974: I, 45–6).

[3] Ed. Sturtevant and Bechtel (1935: 64–99), and more recently by Otten (1981). A shorter version of this account, with some variation in details, appears in KBo VI 29

laudatory and self-justificatory account of Hattusili's progress through a succession of administrative and military appointments to his seizure of the Hittite throne. We shall refer frequently to this document—but always with the proviso that it presents a very one-sided view of Hattusili's actions and achievements, and those of his enemies. This is more marked than in most personal records of the Hittite kings, due no doubt to the fact that a number of Hattusili's actions, particularly against the rightful occupant of the Hittite throne, were both illegal and unpopular with many of his subjects. Hattusili's concern to justify what he had done has inevitably led to a biased treatment of the events in which he was involved. Above all he sought to portray his successes as due not to superior brute force but rather to 'the prevalence of reason and justice over military and political power'.[4] In using the *Apology* as a source of information on Hattusili's career, as well as that of the man whom he displaced from the throne, we must take into account the strongly propagandist flavour of the document.

The Ruler of the Northern Kingdom

Perhaps shortly after his accession, Muwatalli assigned to his brother Hattusili the responsibility for governing the northern regions of the kingdom, beginning with his appointment while GAL MEŠEDI as governor of the Upper Land.[5] The appointment did not meet with universal approval. Indeed, it caused deep resentment in certain quarters, for it meant displacing the current governor Arma-Tarhunda, son of Zida.[6] Arma-Tarhunda reacted bitterly at his removal from office:

My Sun and Arma-Tarhunda came into conflict and were estranged for this reason, that the Upper Land was given to Arma-Tarhunda to govern. But when Muwatalli, my brother, gave me the Upper Land to govern,

---

(+) (*CTH* 85.1), ed. Goetze (1925: 47ff). As to the primary purpose of the document, a different view is proposed and argued at some length by Imparati (1995). She sees the document as intended to create a favourable climate for the king's decision to name his son Tudhaliya as his successor in place of an older son who had been designated for this position. For perhaps the best analysis of the document, see Cancik (1976: 41–5).

[4] Liverani (1990: 155).
[5] *Apol.* §4, I 25–6.
[6] And possibly a relative of Hattusili, to judge from *Apol* §10a, III 25. Cf. Hoffner (1975: 55).

Arma-Tarhunda began to betray my brother and kept harassing me further. (KUB xxi 17 (*CTH* 86.1) i 3–9, adapted from trans. by Archi (1971: 198))[7]

He was not alone in protesting the king's action. Others rallied to his support. Charges were laid against the new appointee in an attempt to discredit him. Although we do not know the nature of the charges, the hostility which Hattusili's appointment generated suggests that they were serious, and perhaps not without foundation. None the less, Hattusili successfully defended himself against his enemies, claiming the support and guidance of his patron goddess Istar. But the final reckoning was yet to come.

For the time being, however, Hattusili had survived the opposition to his appointment, and was given a number of military assignments in the northern regions. To judge from his own account, he accomplished these with unqualified success: 'To whatever land of the enemy I turned my eyes, none of the enemy could turn my eyes back. I conquered the lands of the enemy, one after the other. The favour of My Lady Istar was always with me. I drove out of the lands of Hatti whatever enemy had occupied it' (*Apol.* §5, i 67–72).

But the severest test of his abilities came when Muwatalli left Hattusa for his new royal capital at Tarhuntassa. The king's departure prompted widespread rebellion and attacks on Hittite territory:

In his rear all the lands of Kaska, the Land of Pishuru, the Land of Daistipassa rose up. They destroyed the Land of Ishupitta, the Land of Marista, and the fortified cities. Then the enemy crossed the Marrassantiya river and began to attack the Land of Kanes and the city of [ ]. Ha[ ], Kurustama and Gazziura immediately declared enmity and attacked the ruined cities of Hatti . . .   (*Apol.*§ 6, ii 2–10.)

The text continues in this vein. Hattusili was left to deal with the situation—apparently with little help from his brother who provided him (Hattusili claimed) with a pitifully small force for the defence of the beleaguered territories: 'The enemy had 800 teams of horse and a countless number of infantry. But my brother Muwatalli sent me (against the enemy), giving me only 120 teams of horse and not even one infantryman' (*Apol.* §7, ii 34–7).

[7] Cf. *Apol.* §4, i 32–4.

Although this statement has been seen as directly critical of Muwatalli,[8] this was probably not Hattusili's intention. Rather, he was simply seeking to highlight the magnitude of his task and subsequently his achievement, probably exaggerating in the process the disparity between his own and the enemy's forces. This is of course a standard *topos* characteristic of many military memoirs, both ancient and modern. But in Hattusili's case, it was not purely or even primarily a case of self-aggrandisement. Hattusili attributed his success to divine intervention. Above all else, it was divine support and favour that validated his actions (according to his own arguments), leading up to and including his seizure of the throne. Right and justice were on his side. It was this rather than the size of his forces or indeed his own military prowess that ensured his success.

With Istar marching before him, he firmly restored Hittite control over the regions which lay within his charge, and thus paved the way for the establishment under his authority of what was in effect a viceregal kingdom in the north, extending from Pala and Tummanna to the Upper Land. As we have noted, Muwatalli conferred upon his brother the title of king, establishing the seat of his authority in the important northern centre of Hakpissa. This served as a clear signal to the populations of the region, and the enemies who threatened it, that there would be no slackening of Hittite control in the north, despite the shift of the royal capital to the south. The northern region would be ruled virtually as a kingdom in its own right, by the king's own brother and most able supporter.

One of Hattusili's most pressing tasks was the repopulation of ruined, abandoned, or sparsely populated towns and countries within his kingdom.[9] This meant coming to terms with the Kaska population who lived in or near the areas where he sought to implement his repopulation programme. His policy towards the Kaska people in these areas is illustrated by the terms of a treaty which he drew up with the town of Tiliura, located on the Hittite–Kaskan border. Originally abandoned in the reign of Hantili II, Tiliura was eventually rebuilt by Mursili. But he only partly resettled it, using transportees from conquered territories for the

---

[8] Thus Liverani (1990: 122): 'In the case of Hattusili . . . the boast for victories won in conditions of numerical inferiority is linked to a polemic towards Muwatalli.'

[9] See Bryce (1986–7: 88–90).

purpose. Hattusili claimed the credit for full-scale resettlement, transferring to the town the remnants of its original population. He was critical of his father for failing to do this:

The city of Tiliura was deserted from the time of Hantili. My father Mursili built it up again, but did not resettle it properly, rather he resettled it with his labour force (i.e. his transportees) whom he had conquered with the sword. But I, My Sun, have transferred such of the former population of Tiliura as remained and have brought them back and resettled them in Tiliura.   (KUB XXI 29 (+) (*CTH* 89) I 11–19, trans. Garstang and Gurney (1959: 119))

Most importantly, Hattusili wanted to ensure that the town was resettled by its former population, as distinct from the transportees whom Mursili had earlier settled in the town and also, more particularly, from the Kaska people who were explicitly banned from settling in or even entering the town. The treaty seems to be a reflection of a more general Hittite policy of allowing, or at least accepting, some degree of peaceful intercourse between Hittite subjects and Kaskans in the Hittite–Kaska border area, while strictly excluding Kaskans from inhabiting newly settled or resettled Hittite frontier towns. But this policy apparently applied only to Kaska groups who were formally recognized as Hittite 'allies', as distinct from other Kaska groups who belonged to the 'enemy' category. The 'allied' group were bound by a number of regulations which gave them controlled access into Hittite territory and sometimes grazing rights in this territory, but generally barred them from settling in or otherwise occupying Hittite urban settlements.[10]

The resettlement programme in the northern region was temporarily brought to a halt as final preparations were made for the Hittite showdown with Egypt. Unwilling to confront the pharaoh without the support of his most experienced and able military commander, Muwatalli now summoned his brother to join forces with him in Syria, as commander of the infantry and chariotry recruited from the northern kingdom.[11]

---

[10] This information is provided by two treaties in particular, namely *CTH* 137 (von Schuler (1965: 130–4)) and *CTH* 138 (op. cit. 117–30). These treaties date to the early period of the New Kingdom (see Neu and Klinger (1990: 141)), and are probably indicative of Hittite policy towards 'allied' Kaska groups from this period onwards.

[11] *Apol.* §9, II 60–74.

Hattusili's Marriage to Puduhepa

In the aftermath of the battle of Kadesh, Hattusili was left in command of the land of Aba following the defeat of the Egyptian forces there. We do not know how long he held this post. But his prolonged absence from his kingdom must have caused him increasing anxiety. The kingdom was still far from secure. Enemies from within as well as external enemies would certainly seek every opportunity to exploit his absence.

When finally Muwatalli gave him permission to relinquish his Syrian commmand, he at once began his homeward journey. But he had an important obligation to fulfil on the way. *En route* to his northern destination, he visited the Kizzuwadnan city of Lawazantiya, now assuming increasing importance as a religious centre. The purpose of his visit was to carry out rituals in honour of Istar, the goddess who had watched over and protected him from his early years. Her continuing support would be essential to him in grappling with the problems he would face on his return to his kingdom.

The visit had another important outcome. In Lawazantiya he met and married Puduhepa, the daughter of Pentipsarri, priest of the goddess Istar, and herself a priestess in the goddess' service.[12] According to Hattusili, it was not a marriage of his own choosing. Rather, it was one which quite literally had been made in heaven. He married Puduhepa at the command of Istar, whose wishes were revealed to him in a dream.[13] The goddess had chosen well. On a personal level, a close and lasting bond was to develop between the royal couple; the goddess gave them 'the love of husband and wife'.[14]

Puduhepa's role was not restricted to that of a loyal and devoted wife. She was destined to come into high prominence in the affairs of the kingdom, particularly after her husband's accession to the throne. Apart from being a major source of support and comfort to

---

[12] Darga (1974: 950) comments that the goddess whom the Hittites represented with the sign of Istar was very different from the Mesopotamian Istar, goddess of love; the texts indicate that the Istar of Lawazantiya was not a goddess of love but a warrior goddess.

[13] According to KBo vi 29 (+) (*CTH* 85.1) i 18–21, a passage from the shorter version of the *Apology*. Whatever the propaganda value of this claim, there may well have been political and strategic incentives for the marriage; cf. Klengel (1991; 225).

[14] *Apol.* §9, iii 3.

her husband, she became an astute diplomatist in the international arena. We shall return to her below.

The nuptials completed, Hattusili could not afford further delay in Lawazantiya, for there was news of alarming developments in the north. As he must have feared, the Kaskans had been quick to seize upon his absence in Syria to renew their attacks on the northern frontier of Hatti. Worse still, Hakpissa, the seat of the viceregal kingdom, had risen in revolt.[15] On his return, Hattusili dealt promptly with the situation. He drove the Kaskans back across the frontiers and restored his control over Hakpissa, where he resumed the viceregal throne and installed his bride as queen. It was an eventful beginning to her life as Hattusili's consort.

Further Dealings with Arma-Tarhunda

The uprisings had left Hattusili with a clear message. In spite of all his efforts to establish lasting security and stability in the north, Hittite authority in this region remained fragile. And the revolt in Hakpissa made it plain that even in the seat of his power there were significant elements of the population who were hostile to him. Much still had to be done to ensure the security of the region as a whole, and to reconcile the population to his rule.

The uprising in Hakpissa may have been triggered at least in part by Arma-Tarhunda, the man who had been deposed from governorship of the Upper Land to make way for Hattusili. Still deeply resentful of being cast aside, he too took advantage of Hattusili's absence in Syria to plot against him, even resorting to witchcraft.[16] He further attempted to discredit Hattusili by bringing another indictment against him. Hattusili responded with a counter-indictment. Arma-Tarhunda lost the case, and Muwatalli handed him over to Hattusili (presumably as the aggrieved party) for punishment. Now was his chance to rid himself of his arch enemy once and for all. But Hattusili was disposed to be merciful:

I did not respond against him with malice. Rather, because Arma-Tarhunda was a a blood-relation, and was moreover an old man, I took pity on him and let him go free. And I let (his son) Sippaziti go free and took no (further) action against them. I sent Arma-Tarhunda's wife and

---

[15] *Apol.* §9, III 10.
[16] *Apol.* §10a, III 17–18.

his (other) son to Alasiya, and I took half of Arma-Tarhunda's estate and gave it back to him.[17]   (*Apol.* §10a, III 24–30)

He might have hoped that this gesture would help pave the way for an eventual reconciliation with Arma-Tarhunda's family. If so, it apparently failed. As we shall see, Arma-Tarhunda's son Sippaziti remained implacably hostile to him.

A Second-Rank Son Occupies the Throne

Up to the time of Muwatalli's death, perhaps shortly after these events, Hattusili's status and influence, and the powers accorded him, must have set him far above all others amongst the king's subjects. Not without good reason. He had played an important role in Syria, he had confounded the attempts of his personal enemies to discredit him, and most importantly he had brought some measure of peace and stability to the northern regions of the kingdom. Thus when the king died without leaving a male heir of the first rank, he might have been sorely tempted to claim the throne for himself.

Muwatalli did in fact have a son whom he had designated as his successor. But the son, Urhi-Tesub, was the child of a concubine (DUMU EŠERTI).[18] He still had a right to the throne, in terms of the succession principles laid down by Telipinu. But he was not the son of a first wife, and at least one vassal ruler, Masturi, Manapa-Tarhunda's successor in the Seha River Land, was later to refuse him his support. 'Should I protect a second-rank son?' he protested.[19] But Muwatalli clearly intended that his son should succeed him. And for the time being, Hattusili honoured his brother's intention, while giving the distinct impression that the bestowal of kingship lay entirely within his own authority: 'Out of esteem for

---

[17] The other half was dedicated to the service of Istar; *Apol.* §12b, IV 66–73.

[18] *Apol.* §10b, III 41. On the term [LÚ]*pahhurzi* used in reference to such a son, see *CHD* Vol. P, fasc. 1, 17. The usual translation of this term is 'bastard' although in a society where concubinage was regularly practised the Hittite term does not have the strong stigma of illegitimacy which the English word implies. None the less it was clearly used as an expression of contempt for a person whose status was inferior to that of a 'son of the first rank'.

[19] As recorded by Hattusili's son Tudhaliya IV in his treaty with the Amurrite king Sausgamuwa, KUB XXIII 1 (+) (*CTH* 105) II 29. This statement probably belongs within the context of the conflict between Hattusili and Urhi-Tesub which led to the latter's overthrow (see below).

my brother, I did no evil against him. And since he had left no son of the first rank, I took Urhi-Tesub, the son of a concubine (by him), and placed him on the throne of Hatti. I put all Hattusa into his hands, and he was Great King in the lands of Hatti' (*Apol.* §10b, III 38'–44').[20]

On ascending the throne, Urhi-Tesub adopted the name Mursili (III).[21] This, the name of his grandfather, was perhaps in itself an implicit statement of his right to sit upon the throne of his predecessors, and might help enhance his status in the eyes of his subjects. Throughout his reign he used it alongside his original name.[22] But as far as we know, Hattusili never called his nephew Mursili.[23] For all his outward declarations of loyalty, he must have found it very difficult to accept subjection to this son of a concubine, and may have particularly resented his adoption of so illustrious a name.

If these were in fact his feelings about his nephew, he kept them well hidden for a time, and remained faithful to his brother's wishes. In the early days of Urhi-Tesub's reign, uncle and nephew probably worked closely together. In view of Hattusili's experience and standing in the kingdom, and his declared support for the new king, it would have made good sense for Urhi-Tesub to cultivate him and use him as his constant mentor. Indeed, behind a number of the actions taken by Urhi-Tesub, we can probably see the influence of Hattusili at work.

[20] Also relating to this: KUB xxi 19 (*CTH* 383) II 23–31 (prayer of Hattusili and Puduhepa to the Sun Goddess of Arinna) and KUB xxi 27 (*CTH* 384) I 33–48, esp. 38–40 (prayer of Puduhepa).

[21] As we know from seal impressions bearing the name Mursili and clearly attributable to Urhi-Tesub. The first of these were found at Boğazköy in 1953. See Güterbock (1956c), and cf. Otten (1955: 19–23). The number has now been substantially increased by the recent discovery of the Nişantepe seal archive. Some 600 of the *bullae* found in this archive have been attributed to Urhi-Tesub/Mursili (III), second only in number amongst Hittite kings to the 700 *bullae* of Tudhaliya IV; see Neve (1992a: esp. 313 and 315).

[22] Güterbock (1956a: 121) comments that evidence that Urhi-Tesub used both names when king is provided by the seals *SBo* I no. 13 on the one hand and nos. 43 and 44 on the other. This is further confirmed by the evidence provided by the Nişantepe seal archive.

[23] Although all references which Hattusili makes to Urhi-Tesub date to the period after the latter's overthrow. Perhaps it was only then that Hattusili refused to use his nephew's adopted name. Cf. Goetze (1975c: 256). Note too that Hattusili's son Tudhaliya in his treaty with Sausgamuwa also refers to Urhi-Tesub only by this name and not by his throne-name Mursili.

Hattusa Becomes the Royal Capital Again

'He took up the gods from Tarhuntassa and brought them back to Hattusa' (KUB xxi 15 (*CTH* 85 1B) 1 11–12, trans. Houwink ten Cate (1974*a*: 125)).[24] This brief statement records the most important initiative taken by Urhi-Tesub during his brief reign—his reinstatement of Hattusa as the Hittite royal capital. Its loss of status can have lasted no more than twenty years or so, during which time it had been entrusted to the governorship of Mursili's former chief scribe Mittannamuwa. The position of chief scribe had been assigned to Mittannamuwa's son Purandamuwa.[25] Although the move back to Hattusa was almost certainly contrary to Muwatalli's intentions, it seems to have met with little or no opposition from the king's subjects. Indeed, Urhi-Tesub may have come under pressure from a number of quarters to reinstate Hattusa as the capital—and did so partly in order to fortify his position on the throne. Hattusili seems not to have disputed his nephew's action, and may in fact have encouraged it. The fact that he later denied having any part in his brother's decision to relocate the capital in Tarhuntassa (see below) suggests that he was not unhappy to see this decision reversed.

Thus Tarhuntassa lost its short-lived status as the Hittite royal capital. It would, however, continue to function as one of the most important regional centres of the kingdom, under a ruler whose status placed him on a par with the viceroys in Syria.

There were other cases where Urhi-Tesub overturned decisions made by his father. Some of these appear in a curious text which has caused much debate amongst scholars. The text in question[26] records actions taken by Urhi-Tesub[27] which clearly ran counter to

---

[24] On the sources relating to Urhi-Tesub's shift of the capital back to Hattusa, see Houwink ten Cate (1994: 234 n. 5) and the references cited therein.

[25] As recorded in KBo iv 12 (*CTH* 87), Hattusili III's decree in favour of the members of Mittannamuwa's family.

[26] KUB xxi 33 (*CTH* 387).

[27] The king is called Mursili in the text, and is almost certainly Mursili III, i.e. Urhi-Tesub; see Meriggi (1962 70–6), Archi (1971: 201), Houwink ten Cate (1974*a*: 128) (*contra* Stefanini (1964), Heinhold-Krahmer (1977: 228–9), who assign the text to the reign of Mursili II). The text has recently been reconsidered by Houwink ten Cate (1994: 240–2), who emphasizes the close link between it and the oracle-enquiry text KUB xxxi 66 (+) (*CTH* 297.7). Also in a recent consideration of KUB xxi 33, Mora (1992) proposed that the Mursili of this text while probably identical with Mursili III, was a different person from Urhi-Tesub. This hypothesis is now ruled

his father's wishes. The recall of Manapa-Tarhunda, the former king of the Seha River Land sent into banishment by Muwatalli, was one of these actions. The vassal throne was now occupied by his son Masturi. Contrary to Muwatalli's wishes, Urhi-Tesub allowed Manapa-Tarhunda to return from exile,[28] although Masturi apparently retained the vassal throne. His ailing father presumably lived out his final days in peaceful obscurity.

The link between Masturi and the Hittite throne was strengthened by the vassal's marriage with Muwatalli's sister Massanauzzi. We cannot be entirely sure when this took place. While credit for the marriage was later given to Muwatalli,[29] we are told in KUB xxi 33 that it was Urhi-Tesub arranged it: 'My Lord did not give(?) Massanauzzi to Manapa-Tarhunda as daughter-in-law(?)[30] [ ] but Mursili (i.e. Urhi-Tesub) gave her to him' (KUB xxi 33, iv? 12–13).

Other actions of Urhi-Tesub that nullified his father's decisions included the restoration of Bentesina to the throne of Amurru. This former vassal king had been deposed by Muwatalli for his alleged disloyalty in joining forces with Egypt, and replaced by a man called Sapili. He had subsequently been assigned to the custody of Hattusili, at Hattusili's own request, in the city of Hakpissa. Here he resided for some years as Hattusili's protégé, in conditions of considerable comfort.[31] Some scholars believe that his reinstatement did not take place until Hattusili himself became king.[32] Indeed Hattusili later claimed the credit for putting the deposed king back on his throne, without any mention of Urhi-Tesub.[33] But it is more likely that he regained his throne during Urhi-Tesub's

out by evidence from the Nişantepe seal archive which confirms that Urhi-Tesub and Mursili (III) were one and the same; see Otten (1993a: 25).

[28] KUB xxi 33, iv? 8–11, trans. Heinhold-Krahmer (1977: 299).

[29] Tudhaliya IV: Sausgamuwa treaty, ii 16–18.

[30] For the term of relationship in question, see Heinhold-Krahmer (1977: 229–30).

[31] Singer (1991a: 168) speculates on the reasons for Hattusili's warm treatment of Bentesina, and asks whether at this stage he already foresaw his own usurpation of the Hittite throne and the reinstatement of Bentesina in Amurru. Or was he simply motivated by personal friendship?

[32] Thus e.g. Singer (1991a: 168, with n. 50), who notes that in KUB xxi 33 the name of the king who reinstated Bentesina is missing (but see n. 34), and that in the Sausgamuwa treaty Tudhaliya reports that his father was responsible.

[33] Hattusili: Bentesina treaty (*CTH* 92), obv. i 16–17. Hattusili's son Tudhaliya also attributed Bentesina's restoration to his father in the Sausgamuwa treaty, i 40–5.

reign,[34] although almost certainly because of Hattusili's influence. In Bentesina Hattusili clearly had a loyal supporter—and once he was back in the strategically important kingdom of Amurru, a valuable ally.

If the text we have been considering does in fact belong to Urhi-Tesub's reign, then it seems to be a remarkably frank admission of the new king's defiance of a number of his father's wishes. According to one view, it is probably to be assigned to a high official of Urhi-Tesub who composed it at Urhi-Tesub's request—a 'penitential' text made up at a time when the king felt obliged to excuse himself for his conduct.[35] Alternatively, the text might have been composed after Urhi-Tesub's reign, at the instigation of Hattusili III, in order to highlight some of the 'offences' committed by Urhi-Tesub by way of justifying his removal from the throne.[36]

There is a further question. Did Urhi-Tesub carry out the actions recorded in our document while his father was still on the throne, or after his death? Some scholars have argued for the former.[37] But it is difficult to believe that during his own reign Muwatalli would have assigned to his son such extensive authority, including the power to restore disgraced vassals to their kingdoms both in the west as well as the east of the Hittite kingdom—particularly when their restoration had been expressly forbidden. Even if his son had been granted such power, his father would surely have overruled any decisions he made which were counter to his own decisions.

Another no doubt highly controversial action taken by Urhi-Tesub was the reinstatement of the queen Tanuhepa after her

[34] See Houwink ten Cate (1994: 247 n. 42), who adduces evidence which virtually confirms the restoration of Mursili (III)'s name in the relevant passage. On Hattusili's suppression of information (for political reasons) relating to Bentesina prior to his (Hattusili's) accession, see Houwink ten Cate (1994: 247).

[35] Thus Houwink ten Cate (1974a: 128), taking up Stefanini's categorisation of the text, as well as Meriggi's proposal regarding authorship of the text. See also Houwink ten Cate (1994: 240–3), for further development of, and some revision to, the views he expressed in his (1974) article.

[36] Cf. Meriggi (1962: 73, 76), Bin-Nun (1975: 281 n. 228).

[37] e.g. Houwink ten Cate (1974a: 128). A particular reason advanced by Houwink ten Cate is that Muwatalli's sister Massanauzzi would not have been a suitable candidate for marriage by the time of Urhi-Tesub's reign because of her mature age. Yet if we accept that she was about 50 shortly after the signing of the Hittite–Egyptian peace treaty (on the basis of Hattusili's claim to this effect in his letter to Ramesses), then she would probably have been in her mid-thirties during Urhi-Tesub's reign—perhaps an unusually late but by no means an impossible age for marriage.

removal from office by Muwatalli. Further, the king recalled from exile Sippaziti, son of his uncle's bitter enemy Arma-Tarhunda.[38] This action almost certainly did not have Hattusili's support, and was probably taken at a time when tensions were mounting between uncle and nephew towards the end of the latter's reign. Very likely there was an ulterior motive behind it (see below).

But prior to this Hattusili seems to have exercised considerable influence with his nephew in matters relating to the restoration of a particular person's or family's former status. A further illustration of this is provided by action taken on behalf of Mittannamuwa's family. The former chief scribe Mittannamuwa was now old and sick. On appointing him as administrator of Hattusa, Muwatalli had conferred his scribal office on his son Purandamuwa. Subsequently, for reasons unknown to us, the office had been taken from his family. However, Hattusili had interceded with his nephew on behalf of the family, with whom he had close and longstanding personal bonds. On this occasion Hattusili prevailed and another of Mittannamuwa's sons, Walwaziti (UR.MAH-ziti), was appointed 'Great Scribe'.[39]

There is little doubt that the record of Urhi-Tesub's reign was subject to a good deal of revisionism by his immediate successors. On the one hand he was criticized for acting against his father's wishes. On the other hand, any 'positive' actions taken by him, or at least under his authority, were credited to his successor, like the restoration of Bentesina to the throne of Amurru. In a number of actions and decisions taken by Urhi-Tesub, we can see Hattusili's influence at work. But other actions, like the recall of Sippaziti, must have been taken by the king entirely on his own initiative, and for his own personal reasons—which were later to become apparent.

Trouble Across the Euphrates

Probably during Urhi-Tesub's reign, news reached Hattusa of alarming developments east of the Euphrates. Here Sattuara I, king of Hanigalbat (what remained of the former kingdom of

[38] *Apol.* §10c, IV 3–6.
[39] Information on the fortunes of Mittannamuwa's family is provided by KBo IV 12 (*CTH* 87) 15–30; see Goetze (1925: 42–3).

Mitanni),[40] had launched an attack on Assyria, then ruled by the king Adad-Nirari (*c.*1295-1264).[41] The reasons for his attack are unknown. But it may not have been unprovoked. In the past, the Hittites had managed to curb Assyrian aggressive enterprises in the Euphrates region. But they were unable to deter the Assyrians from pursuing their territorial ambitions in this region whenever appropriate opportunities arose. Inevitably, the remnants of the Mitannian kingdom would be engulfed in any major Assyrian advance westwards.

Sattuara's attack on Assyria may have been intended as a preemptive strike against such a threat. It was carried out entirely on his own initiative. The Hittites were apparently not consulted beforehand or asked for support. Under other circumstances, this might have been expected. Although nominally independent of Hatti, with its ruler accorded a status equal to that of the Hittite king,[42] Hanigalbat had provided Muwatalli with troops at the battle of Kadesh and at least in theory enjoyed Hittite protection. But if his kingdom was now under serious threat from Assyria, Sattuara could have had little confidence that a new and inexperienced Hittite king, preoccupied with the affairs of his own kingdom, would provide him with effective support. It was this realization, perhaps, which led him to take matters into his own hands. Predictably, his quixotic enterprise ended in failure:

When Sattuara, king of the Land of Hanigalbat, rebelled against me, and committed hostilities: by the command of Assur, My Lord and Ally, ... I seized him and brought him to my city Assur. I made him take an oath and then allowed him to return to his land. Annually, as long as he lived, I regularly received his tribute within my city, Assur. (Assyrian royal inscription, adapted from trans. by Grayson (1972: 60–1 §392))

Sattuara was reinstated in his kingdom, but lost his independence. His kingdom now became a vassal territory of Assyria.

The Hittites apparently made no attempt to intervene in the conflict. But Adad-Nirari's conquest of Hanigalbat must have

[40] Singer (1985: 102) notes that 'the geographical extent of Hanigalbat, on the northern rim of the Mesopotamian plain, is provided by Adad-Nirari's and Salmaneser's descriptions of the conquered territory—from the Tur 'Abdin westwards, across the upper reaches of the Habur and the Balih to the Euphrates'.
[41] The dates in the short chronology proposed by Wilhelm and Boese (1979).
[42] Muwatalli in his treaty with Alaksandu of Wilusa (*CTH* 76) lists its king amongst those of equal status with himself; see Friedrich (1930: 68–9 §14, III 11).

exacerbated tensions between Hatti and Assyria. Diplomatic relations between the two kingdoms continued, but relations were
strained, as we hear subsequently, though in a somewhat muted
way, in a letter from Hattusili to Adad-Nirari: 'The ambassadors
whom you regularly sent here in the days of Urhi-Tesub usually
had sad experiences' (KBo 1 14 (*CTH* 173), rev. 15–16, trans.
Goetze (1940, 31)).

This may have emboldened Sattuara's son and successor
Wasasatta to attempt to break away from Assyrian overlordship.
He clearly looked to support from Hatti in doing so.[43] The hoped
for support did not eventuate, and the rebellion was crushed:

After Sattuara's death, his son Wasasatta revolted, rebelled against me,
and committed hostilities. He went to the Land of Hatti for aid. The
Hittites took his bribes, but did not render him assistance. With the strong
weapons of the god Assur, My Lord, . . . I captured by conquest the city
Taidi, his great royal city, the cities Amasaku, Kahat, Suru, Nabula, Hurra,
Sudubu, and Wassuganni. I took and brought to my city, Assur, the possessions of those cities, the accumulated wealth of Wasasatta's fathers, and
the treasure of his palace. I conquered, burnt, and destroyed the city Taidi
and sowed *kudimmus* over it. The great gods gave me to rule from the city
Taidi to the city Irridu, the city Eluhat and Mount Kasiyari in its entirety,
the fortress of the city Sudu, the fortress of the city Harranu, to the bank
of the Euphrates. As for the remainder of Wasasatta's people, I imposed
corvée upon them. But as for him, I took out from the city Irridu his 'wife
of the palace', his sons, his daughters, and his people. Bound I brought
them and his possessions to my city, Assur. I conquered, burnt, and destroyed the city Irridu and the cities within the district of the city Irridu.
(Assyrian royal inscription, adapted from trans. by Grayson (1972: 60–1
§393))

Exasperated by this further outbreak of hostilities against his kingdom, Adad-Nirari probably withdrew Hanigalbat's vassal status
and annexed it to Assyrian territory, establishing a royal residence
in the city of Taidi.[44]

Such a development must have been viewed with considerable
alarm in the Hittite capital, as well as in the viceregal kingdom of
Carchemish. It was bad enough that Hanigalbat, which had provided an important buffer against Assyrian encroachment on
Hittite subject territory, had been reduced to Assyrian vassal

---

[43] See Weidner (1930–1).
[44] See Rowton (1959: 1). According to Rowton, this conquest dates to no more
than six years prior to Adad-Nirari's death.

status. But far worse was the news that Hanigalbat had now been fully absorbed into Adad-Nirari's kingdom. Assyrian territory now extended to the very borders of the Land of Carchemish. Indeed a letter written by Hattusili shortly after his accession to Adad-Nirari virtually acknowledged full Assyrian sovereignty over the former kingdom of Hanigalbat.[45]

We cannot be entirely certain when Wasasatta's abortive rebellion took place. But it may well have occurred before the end of Urhi-Tesub's reign. If so, it must have been a serious blow to the young king's credibility. What confidence could there be in his ability to defend his kingdom's Syrian territories against invasion from across the Euphrates if he was unable to provide support for Hatti's former ally in this region? Yet Adad-Nirari apparently had no immediate plans to follow up his success with a campaign into Hittite territory. In fact, he seems to have wanted to preserve what was at best a very uneasy peace with Hatti.

He wrote to the Hittite king, claiming for himself the title of 'Great King', and requesting acknowledgement as his 'Brother'. To this request he received an angry response. After grudgingly acknowledging his victory over Wasasatta, and accepting that he had become a 'Great King', the Hittite letter continues:

With respect to brotherhood ... about which you speak—what does brotherhood mean? ... With what justification do you write about brotherhood ... ? Are not friends those who write to each other about brotherhood? And for what reason should I write to you about brotherhood? Were perhaps you and I born of the same mother? As my father and my grandfather did not write to the king of Assur about brotherhood, even so must you not write about brotherhood and Great-kingship to me! (KUB XXIII 102 (*CTH* 171) (= Hagenbuchner (1989: 260–4, no. 192) 15–18, trans. Goetze (1975c: 258))[46]

Very likely the author of the letter was Urhi-Tesub.[47] The young king was forced to acknowledge the Assyrian as the permanent

[45] KBo I 14, discussed below.
[46] Some scholars have identified the addressee of this letter as Salmaneser, Adad-Nirari's successor. For a brief discussion of this alternative possibility, see Harrak (1987: 75–7). The traditional view, that the addressee was Adad-Nirari, is the one favoured by Harrak, and is adopted here.
[47] Although it is usually attributed either to his father or more commonly his uncle (after the latter's accession), or even to his uncle's son Tudhaliya IV. For the attribution to Urhi-Tesub, see Hagenbuchner (1989: 263), supported by Beckman (1996: 138).

overlord of Mitannian territory. But he refused to accept that Adad-Nirari had by his actions attained a status which warranted addressing the Hittite king as 'Brother'. This form of address was not merely a matter of courtesy. It implied a relationship of full diplomatic equality between two rulers of equal status, often linked by family ties, and at least on the surface committed to friendship and cooperation. And this Urhi-Tesub, whose regime was already insecure and had now been humiliated by the Assyrian king's military successes, was not willing to concede.[48] Hence his angry, somewhat petulant response.

In the interests of *Realpolitik* he might well have considered the benefits of establishing closer diplomatic links on terms of full equality with Adad-Nirari, particularly in view of the threat still posed by Egypt to Hittite territories in Syria. If through an accommodation with Assyria greater stability could be achieved in the Euphrates region, the Hittites would be in a stronger position to deal with any renewal of Egyptian aggression from the south, in the knowledge that their eastern flank was secure. There could have been distinct advantages in responding positively to the Assyrian king's overtures, even if Urhi-Tesub suspected his ultimate intentions.

It was perhaps Urhi-Tesub's failure to do so that helped bring matters to a head in his own kingdom.

The Overthrow of Urhi-Tesub

What may have begun as a reasonably harmonious relationship between Urhi-Tesub and his uncle eventually turned sour. Unfortunately, we have only Hattusili's version of the reasons for this, a version which predictably assigns all blame to Urhi-Tesub. According to Hattusili, his nephew's jealousy was the chief cause of the increasing hostility between them: 'When Urhi-Tesub saw the goddess's goodwill towards me, he envied me and sought to do me

---

[48] Although Muwatalli had earlier listed the king of Assyria amongst those whom he acknowledged as equal in rank to himself (Alaksandu treaty, Friedrich (1930: 68 §14, III 12)). With regard to the above letter, Liverani (1990: 200) comments: 'The Hittite king has to reluctantly accept the Assyrian king as a "great king"; this is a formal definition, based on factual evidence that cannot be denied. But he refuses the terminology of brotherhood, which is a voluntary option and a social metaphor, implying a personal agreement, and which is otherwise too easy to dismantle and make ridiculous.'

harm. He took away from me all my subjects. Further, he took away from me all the depopulated lands which I had resettled and made me weak' (*Apol.* §10c, III 54–9).

In actual fact, Urhi-Tesub probably had good reason for distrusting his uncle, to the point where he was forced to strip him of much of his power. There was no denying the substantial contributions Hattusili had made to the kingdom, particularly in strengthening the northern regions against enemy attack, and recapturing and resettling areas which had long been under enemy control and occupation. Further, in the early days of Urhi-Tesub's reign one of Hattusili's crowning achievements had been the reoccupation and rebuilding of the holy city of Nerik,[49] which had been captured and sacked by the Kaskans during the reign of Hantili II some 200 years earlier,[50] and left in ruins since that time:

My Lady, Sun Goddess of Arinna, you know how former kings neglected Nerik. To those kings of the past you gave weapons, My Lady, Sun Goddess of Arinna, and they subdued the surrounding enemy lands. But no one made the attempt to capture the city of Nerik. However your servant Hattusili, even when he was not a king but only a prince—it was he who captured the city of Nerik. (from Puduhepa's prayer to the Sun Goddess of Arinna, KUB XXI 27 (*CTH* 384) obv. 16–25)

Convinced that divine right was on his side, conscious of the personal support which he commanded in the kingdom, and conscious too of all that he had achieved for the kingdom, Hattusili might now have set his sights on greater rewards. In so doing he would undoubtedly pose a serious threat to the man to whom his first allegiance was due. He had been content to support the young king, so long as he maintained a strong influence over him and the latter relied heavily on his advice and support. But as Urhi-Tesub began acting independently of his uncle and against his advice—his response to Adad-Nirari may have been a case in point—tensions between the two must have grown. If his own position were to remain secure, Urhi-Tesub could no longer allow his uncle to exercise the substantial powers which had been assigned to him.

[49] *Apol.* §10b, III 46'–48'. Hattusili himself clearly regarded it as one of the highlights of his career. Cf. von Schuler (1965: 57), Archi (1971: 194). *CTH* 90 contains further fragments relating to the restoration of Nerik; see also Cornil and Lebrun (1972).

[50] Its destruction is also referred to in KUB XXV 21 (*CTH* 524.1) III 2–5, which states that it remained uninhabited for 500 years. This is obviously a 'round number', and an inflated one at that.

He began by stripping him of the territories where he exercised direct authority, though still leaving him in control of Hakpissa, the seat of his power, and Nerik, where he was priest of the Storm God. There may have been other reasons as well for taking from his uncle the regions where he had once held sway. His appointment as king in the northern regions had been closely associated with Muwatalli's transfer of the Hittite capital to Tarhuntassa and his forthcoming confrontation with Egypt. But with the return of the Hittite capital to Hattusa, and with the chief objectives of Hattusili's appointment in the north now having been accomplished, there was arguably less justification for a continuation of the arrangements which Muwatalli had made.

Initially Hattusili accepted his reduced status and remained submissive to his nephew's authority—because, he claimed, of his own sense of right conduct and out of respect for and loyalty to his brother's memory. But as long as he controlled Hakpissa and Nerik, he still remained a threat to the king.[51] Eventually Urhi-Tesub tried to deprive him of these as well. This was the final straw:

For seven years I submitted. But at a divine command and with human urging, Urhi-Tesub sought to destroy me. He took Hakpissa and Nerik from me. Now I submitted to him no longer. I made war upon him. But I committed no crime in doing so, by rising up against him with chariots or in the palace. In civilized manner I communicated thus with him: 'You have begun hostilities with me. Now you are Great King, but I am king of only one fortress. That is all you have left me. Come! Istar of Samuha and the Storm God of Nerik shall decide the case for us!' Since I wrote to Urhi-Tesub in this manner, if anyone now says: 'Why after previously making him king do you now write to him about war?' (my reply would be): 'If he had not begun fighting with me, would Istar and the Storm God have now subjected him to a small king?' Because he began fighting with me, the gods have subjected him to me by their judgement. (*Apol.* §10c, III 63–79)

The die was now cast. Hattusili sought to present the conflict not as a rebellion, but 'as a legal contest based on correctness of conduct and on legitimacy of roles'.[52] The issue would be decided not by superior force of arms, but by divine judgement: 'You are a Great King, while I am a small king. Let us go in judgement before

---

[51] See KUB XXI 19 (+), rev. III 26′–35′ (from the prayer of Hattusili and Puduhepa to the Sun Goddess of Arinna).

[52] Liverani (1990: 155–6).

the Storm God My Lord and Sausga of Samuha My Lady. If you prevail in the trial, they will raise you; but if I prevail in the trial they will raise me' (KBo VI 29 (*CTH* 85.1) II 1–8, trans. Liverani (1990: 156)).

Whether or not he was confident that he had the forces to over-throw his uncle, Urhi-Tesub could delay no longer. Hastily gathering his troops in Hattusa, he took the initiative by marching into the Upper Land to confront him. By so doing he would at least avoid bloody conflict between his own and his uncle's forces within Hattusa itself. But there were major risks. He could not be sure of what support he would get from his own subjects, how many of them would rally round Hattusili. Further, he was forcing a show-down on what had become his uncle's home territory. Admittedly Hattusili had met with opposition in the region. But there must have been many who identified closely with the man who had brought them peace and stability, who had for many years been their king. It was surely with such a man rather than the undistin-guished and largely unproven occupant of the throne of Hattusa that loyalties in the region would lie.

Conscious of this Urhi-Tesub appointed Arma-Tarhunda's son Sippaziti, whom he had recalled from exile, to gather troops for him in the Upper Land. The price of Sippaziti's support may well have been a promise of reinstatement of his family in the region, and the appointment of Sippaziti to his father's old position as governor of the Upper Land. Presumably Arma-Tarhunda's family still had its supporters there, including those who had protested Arma-Tarhunda's removal from office. If so, this might be turned to Urhi-Tesub's advantage.[53]

But it was a desperate ploy. Sippaziti failed to gather the support in the Upper Land that was essential to Urhi-Tesub's success. Hattusili, on the other hand, was able to amass a considerable force in the region, which included elements of the Kaska peoples who

---

[53] The western vassal states may also have taken sides in the conflict. Masturi, king of the Seha River Land, had refused to recognize the legitimacy of Urhi-Tesub's succession and had supported Hattusili (Tudhaliya IV: Sausgamuwa Treaty (*CTH* 105) II 24–9, discussed in Ch. 12), whereas the kings of other Arzawan lands apparently remained loyal to Urhi-Tesub. Included amongst the latter was the king of Mira, as indicated by his correspondence with the pharaoh Ramesses II (*CTH* 166, discussed in Ch. 11), and another unnamed Arzawan king (KUB xxxi 69 obv. 7 = KUB xv 6 II 12 (*CTH* 590)). However, the conflict was probably brought to an end before the western vassals became actively involved in it.

had been permitted to settle within Hittite territory. But perhaps most importantly a significant number of the Hittite nobility seem to have rallied to Hattusili's side. At least some of these were disaffected subjects who had apparently been exiled by Urhi-Tesub.[54] Some may have acted out of contempt for the king's 'illegitimacy'.[55] But the majority may simply have been eager to ensure that they were on the winning side—and judged that the odds, with or without divine intervention, clearly favoured Hattusili.

The conflict ended in a decisive defeat for Urhi-Tesub. He had managed to reach Samuha, where he established his base. But Hattusili placed the city under siege, shutting Urhi-Tesub up in it 'like a pig in a sty',[56] and eventually forcing his surrender. Urhi-Tesub had left Hattusa as the king of the Hittite realm. He now suffered the ignominy of returning to the city as his uncle's prisoner, probably only a few years after he assumed the royal power.[57] He was formally deposed, and his uncle seized the throne.

Hattusili Becomes King

In a formula unique amongst the rulers of the New Kingdom, Hattusili proclaimed his genealogy:

'Thus (speaks) the Tabarna Hattusili, the Great King, King of Hatti, the Hero, beloved of the Sun Goddess of Arinna, the Storm God of Nerik, and Istar of Samuha; Son of Mursili, the Great King, King of Hatti, the Hero; Grandson of Suppiluliuma, the Great King, King of Hatti, the Hero; Great-Grandson (= Descendant?) of Hattusili, the Great King; (one) of the seed of Kussar (who was) singled out by the gods.'   (KBo vi 28 (*CTH* 88), adapted from trans. by Güterbock (1973: 101))

By tracing his ancestry back to his earliest namesake, and claiming that the gods were on his side, Hattusili sought to leave no doubt

---

[54] *Apol.* §12, IV 19–20.   [55] As Goetze (1975c: 257) suggests.

[56] *Apol.* §11, IV 25–6.

[57] The length of his reign is uncertain. Hattusili states that he 'submitted to him for seven years' (*Apol.* §10c, III 62). This may indicate the period of overt tension between uncle and nephew, which was perhaps preceded by several years of relative harmony following Urhi-Tesub's accession. However, it has been claimed that Urhi-Tesub's reign may have been much shorter, its length being exaggerated by Hattusili to emphasize how long he had put up with the injustice done to him by his nephew. This view may need some re-evaluation in the light of the substantial number of *bullae* attributed to Urhi-Tesub in the Nişantepe seal archive.

that he was indeed the legitimate successor to his brother's throne.[58]

But his coup did not have the wholehearted support of his subjects. In a proclamation to the people of Hattusa he acknowledged the division in the population between his own supporters and those who supported Urhi-Tesub.[59] Indeed there may well have been conflict in Hattusa itself, leading to the looting and destruction of what was perhaps the royal treasury.[60] Hattusili's first task was to reunite the population, and reconcile them to the coup. He tried to project the image of the aggrieved party, who had been steadfastly loyal to Muwatalli, and initially to his successor Urhi-Tesub; it was the latter's ingratitude in stripping him of all his power that had forced him to take the action which led to his seizure of the throne. Now was the time for reconciliation. There would be no recriminations against those who had taken sides with Urhi-Tesub in the conflict. But henceforth the succession would remain within Hattusili's family line. Henceforth Urhi-Tesub's sons, and thus the direct descendants of Muwatalli, were explicitly excluded from the right to occupy the throne:

In future you must support the sons of My Sun. If something should happen to a son of mine, you, people, must support in kingship those sons that I, My Sun, have with the queen. Do not take anyone of other descent. No one should look for a son of Urhi-Tesub. (KUB xxi 37 10–14, adapted from trans. by van den Hout (1995: 1114))

The Exile

What was to be done with Urhi-Tesub? Indefinite imprisonment in Hattusa was clearly not an option. Banishment from the capital was the traditional punishment imposed on members of the royal family who had fallen from grace or been removed from power. And traditionally the king who imposed this punishment had sought to ensure that the person banished would continue to live in reasonable comfort. But if the dethroned king were exiled to a location

---

[58] Cf. Archi (1971: 196). This assumes that in the expression 'Great-Grandson of Hattusili' the term of relationship is used in the vague sense of 'descendant' (cf. Gurney (1979b: 223 n. 35)), in reference to Hattusili's earliest namesake Hattusili I.

[59] KUB xxi 37 (*CTH* 85), ed. Archi (1971: 203–8).

[60] This is indicated in a letter subsequently written by Puduhepa to the pharaoh Ramesses, discussed in Ch. 11.

close to the capital, the possibility of an attempted counter-coup could not be ruled out. Removal to a location far from the seat of power, but still under Hittite control, was the better option. Hattusili chose the Nuhasse lands in Syria as the place of exile.[61]

It was to be seen as an 'honourable exile',[62] and entailed the exercise of some responsibility—for Urhi-Tesub was appointed governor of a number of fortified cities in the region. Perhaps Hattusili hoped that by keeping his nephew occupied with some administrative functions, he might divert his thoughts from attempting to regain his throne. The new king might also have relied on his former protégé Bentesina, now restored to the vassal throne of the nearby kingdom of Amurru, to keep a close eye on Urhi-Tesub's conduct and alert him to any suspicious activities in which Urhi-Tesub might engage.

But whatever considerations led to Urhi-Tesub's banishment to this region, the decision proved a major blunder whose consequences were to haunt Hattusili for the rest of his reign. He had seriously underestimated Urhi-Tesub's determination to regain his throne. Within a short time of his arrival in Nuhasse, Urhi-Tesub apparently began surreptitious dealings with the Babylonians.[63] The specific purpose of these is unknown, but almost certainly Urhi-Tesub intended them as a first step in building up foreign support within the Euphrates region and strengthening his position to the point where he could restake his claim to the Hittite throne. His communication with the Assyrian king Salmaneser I, who came to power not long after Hattusili's accession, may also have had the same ulterior purpose.[64]

The coup in Hattusa must have created some perplexity in the foreign courts.[65] Who was the rightful occupant of the throne in Hattusa? With whom—Hattusili or Urhi-Tesub—should foreign

---

[61] *Apol.* §11, IV 32–3.

[62] Thus Gurney (1990: 28).

[63] *Apol.* §11, IV 34–5. The *Apology* states that he would have proceeded to the Land of Karaduniya (i.e. Babylon) if Hattusili had not aborted this plan. Urhi-Tesub may already have paved the way for a visit to Babylon with at least preliminary negotiations with Babylonian officials, if not with the Babylonian king Kadasman-Turgu himself.

[64] This may have been the subject of the letter he wrote to Salmaneser, which the latter's son and successor Tukulti-Ninurta subsequently returned to Tudhaliya IV, as indicated in Tudhaliya's letter to Tukulti-Ninurta, KUB XXVI 70 (*CTH* 209.21); see Otten (1959: 67–8), Hagenbuchner (1989: 266–7 no. 194).

[65] Thus Archi (1971: 208).

rulers negotiate in establishing or maintaining diplomatic relations with Hatti? So long as Urhi-Tesub remained at large, the doubts about who the legitimate king of Hatti was would persist. Prompt action was needed.

On receiving word of his nephew's dealings with the Baby-lonians, and seeking to prevent any move he might have made to escape altogether from his authority, Hattusili ordered his removal to a new place of exile, either somewhere on the coast, or offshore in the Land of Alasiya (Cyprus).[66] Urhi-Tesub remained defiant. He was determined to escape from his uncle's clutches, and to find the means of winning back his throne.

As soon as the opportunity presented itself, he eluded his Hittite custodians, fled his place of exile, and eventually resurfaced at the court of the man who had been his father's bitterest enemy— Ramesses, pharaoh of Egypt![67] Hattusili promptly wrote to Ramesses, demanding his nephew's extradition. Ramesses curtly refused, as indicated in a letter which Hattusili wrote to the Babylonian king Kadasman-Enlil II:

My enemy who fled to another country went to the king of Egypt. When I wrote to him 'Bring my enemy', he did not bring my enemy. Then I and the king of Egypt became enemies of one another, and to your father I wrote: 'The king of Egypt went to help my enemy.' So your father kept the messenger of the king of Egypt at bay. (KBo I 10 + KUB III 72 (*CTH* 172) obv. 67–9, trans. Wouters (1989: 230)).[68]

Ramesses' failure to hand over Urhi-Tesub must have been a serious blow to Hattusili's credibility as the legitimate sovereign of the Hittite world, at least in the eyes of those kings with whom Hattusili sought to establish diplomatic relationships. Now more than ever it was imperative for Hattusili to remove all doubt in foreign courts that the reins of power in Hatti were firmly in his own hands.

[66] The new place of exile was A.AB.BA *ta-pu-ša*. This phrase means either 'across the sea' or 'along the sea'—i.e. on the coast. If the latter, Houwink ten Cate (1974*a*: 139) suggests the Arzawan country Mira as a possibility.
[67] Houwink ten Cate (1994: 246) suggests that his flight to Egypt may be alluded to in a letter from Hattusili to Bentesina, KUB III 56 (*CTH* 208.4) = Hagenbuchner (1989: 379–82 no. 267).
[68] The king's enemy who fled to Egypt is unnamed in this passage, but his identification with Urhi-Tesub is virtually certain; cf. Helck (1963: 96), Houwink ten Cate (1974*a*: 139), Wouters (1989: 230).

CHAPTER 11

Hatti and the World of International Diplomacy: The Reign of Hattusili III (c.1267–1237)

Hattusili as International Diplomat

Vigorous military campaigner though he was before he occupied the throne, the predominant image of Hattusili in his own reign is that of diplomat and conciliator. This may in part be a reflection of his advancing years. He was in his fifties at the time of his accession, and was perhaps already suffering increasingly from bouts of ill health. He had no apparent ambitions to expand Hittite territory beyond the frontiers established by his great predecessors, and indeed undertook personal military campaigns both in Anatolia and further afield with considerable reluctance. The emphasis now was on ensuring the security of his kingdom's subject territories by establishing formal diplomatic alliances with foreign kings whose territories bordered his own. This was all the more important in view of the stigma of illegality associated with his occupancy of the Hittite throne, and the persistent efforts of the deposed king Urhi-Tesub to regain the throne—if necessary with foreign support. Above all, Hattusili needed to persuade his royal counterparts—particularly the kings of Assyria, Babylon, and Egypt—that he and not Urhi-Tesub was the rightful king of Hatti, that it was with him that all diplomatic negotiations should now be conducted.

Shortly after his accession, he had established an alliance with the Babylonian king Kadasman-Turgu, drawing up a treaty with him and persuading him to sever his links with Egypt. But within a year or so of the treaty, Kadasman-Turgu died, and was succeeded by his son Kadasman-Enlil II,[1] who quickly restored diplomatic

---

[1] According to the standard reconstruction of Babylonian chronology, Kadasman-Turgu reigned from 1281 to 1264 and Kadasman-Enlil from 1263 to 1255; see Brinkman (1976: 31). These dates may require some revision as further information comes to light; see Brinkman (1983).

relations with Egypt. Hattusili was angered and frustrated by the news. Yet ill-considered protests and threats might only serve to strengthen the Babylonian king's links with Egypt, and seriously jeopardize any hope of persuading him to renew his father's alliance with Hatti. Hattusili was also aware that the young king's policies were strongly influenced by his powerful vizier Itti-Marduk-balatu, leader of an anti-Hittite, pro-Assyrian faction in the Babylonian court. In view of the potential threats posed by both Egypt and Assyria to Hittite subject territories in Syria, Hattusili must have set great store on cultivating good relations with Kadasman-Enlil.

Thus he wrote to him in very measured terms, reminding him of his father's accord with the new regime in Hattusa, and mildly reprimanding him for his failure to renew and maintain this accord:

When your father and I established diplomatic relations[2] and when we became like loving brothers, we did not become brothers for one day only; did we not establish permanent brotherly relations based on equal understanding? We then made the following agreement: We are only human beings; the survivor shall protect the interests of the sons of the one of us who has gone to his fate. While the gods have kept me alive and preserved my rule, your father passed away and I mourned him as befits our brotherly relationship. When I had done what is proper(?) after the death of your father, I dried my tears and dispatched a messenger to the Land of Babylon, and sent the following message to the high officials of Babylon: 'If you do not keep the son of my brother as ruler, I shall become your enemy, I will go and invade Babylon; but (if you do, then) send me word if an enemy rises against you or if any difficulty threatens you, and I will come to your aid!' My brother was a youngster in those days and so I assume that no-one ever read these tablets to him; now these old scribes are not alive any more, and none of the tablets are even kept in the archives so that they could be read to you now. (Extract from KBo i 10 + KUB iii 72 (*CTH* 172), trans. Oppenheim (1967: 139–40))

Unfortunately the outcome of Hattusili's long and carefully worded letter to the young Kadasman-Enlil remains unknown.

It was probably in the same period that Hattusili formalized his relationship with the Amurrite king Bentesina by drawing up a treaty with him—a treaty which, apparently, Bentesina himself

[2] Houwink ten Cate (1974*a*: 145) dates the treaty between Kadasman-Turgu and Hattusili to the period after Urhi-Tesub's earlier dealings with Babylon and his removal from Nuhasse.

requested in order to confirm the legitimacy of his regime and to secure the succession for his lineal descendants.[3] Hattusili no doubt responded to the request with alacrity. Every formal agreement he concluded with either vassal or foreign ruler served to strengthen his position on the Hittite throne and broaden the base of support he could call upon if that position became imperilled. The vassal was reminded that he had Hattusili to thank for his restoration to the throne of Amurru (even if the formal decision to reinstate him had been made by Urhi-Tesub). And his relationship with Hattusili was strengthened by a double marriage alliance between the two royal families:

My son Nerikkaili will take the daughter of Bentesina of the Land of Amurru in marriage.[4] And I have given the king's daughter Gassuliyawiya[5] to the Land of Amurru into the royal house to Bentesina for marriage.[6] In the Land of Amurru she will have the status of queen. The son and grandson(s) of my daughter will forever hold kingship in the Land of Amurru. (Hattusili: Bentesina Treaty, *PD* no. 9 (*CTH* 92), 128–9, obv. 18–21)

Hattusili had a plentiful supply of sons and daughters available for political marriages with vassal rulers or foreign kings. In addition to the double marriage with the royal house of Amurru, we learn of a double marriage with the royal house of Babylon, the provision of two of Hattusili's daughters for the pharaoh Ramesses, the provision of a daughter(?) Kilushepa for the vassal king of Isuwa,[7] and during Tudhaliya's reign, another daughter of Hattusili

---

[3] Hattusili's treaty with Bentesina, *PD* no. 9 (*CTH* 92), 128–9, obv. 24–6. According to Houwink ten Cate (1994: 244) there may be indirect references to the treaty in letters sent by Bentesina to Hattusili (KBo VIII 16 (*CTH* 193) = Hagenbuchner (1989: no. 260, 370–2)) and Puduhepa (KBo XXVIII 54 = Hagenbuchner (1989: no. 263, 375–7)).

[4] For the interpretation of this statement as referring to future rather than (as originally read) past time, see Hagenbuchner (1992: 112 n. 6), Houwink ten Cate (1992a, 259–60 n. 41 (referring to a reading proposed by del Monte); 1994: 248). This would mean that the treaty was concluded before Nerikkaili's marriage took place.

[5] She thus had the same name as her grandmother, the ill-fated first wife of Mursili. On the uncertainty regarding the allocation of the texts containing the name Gassul(iy)awiya between grandmother and granddaughter, see most recently de Roos (1985–6: 77–9), Singer (1991c: 328–9), and in this book Ch. 8, n. 69 (with reference to the prayer KBo IV 6).

[6] The marriage is also referred to in a letter of Puduhepa, KUB XXI 38 (*CTH* 176).

[7] See KUB XV 1 (*CTH* 584.1) III 54–5, KUB XV 3 (*CTH* 584.2) IV 10–12, both trans. and discussed by Güterbock (1973b: 139–40), and KUB LVI 14 IV 1. For

was married to the Amurrite king Sausgamuwa. Political marriages were a long-established means of consolidating alliances between royal families.[8] Those contracted by Hattusili also helped provide him with the recognition which he so keenly sought from foreign rulers as the true king of Hatti.

Yet in spite of all his diplomatic efforts, both on the international scene and amongst his vassal rulers, Hattusili could never feel secure on the throne he had won by force while his deposed predecessor remained at large and under the protection of the most powerful of his royal counterparts, Ramesses, pharaoh of Egypt. This undoubtedly exacerbated tensions between Hatti and Egypt, and was to have a major impact on Hittite–Egyptian relations for some years to come.[9]

Before considering this further, we should retrace our steps a little in order to pick up several other strands, both domestic and foreign, which became woven into the fabric of events impacting on the reign of Hattusili.

Another Potential Claimant to the Throne

On Sunday 20 July 1986, during the course of the German excavations of Hattusa, a bronze tablet was discovered in a state of perfect preservation, with over 350 lines of Hittite cuneiform text. It came to light under a paved area of the city just inside the city's south wall, near the Sphinx Gate.[10] The significance of this chance discovery can scarcely be overestimated. It is the only bronze tablet known to us from the Hittite world, it throws important new light on the political geography of Anatolia during the Late Bronze Age, and it provides important and hitherto unknown information about political developments in the Hittite kingdom in the final century of its existence.

recent discussions of the identification of Kilushepa, see de Roos (1985–6: 76), who argues that she was either a daughter or sister of Puduhepa, and Singer (1991c: 327–8).

[8] On political marriages in the ancient Near East, see Röllig (1972–5; 1974).

[9] There is some debate as to whether Urhi-Tesub's flight to Egypt took place before or after the treaty which Hattusili finally concluded with Ramesses, discussed below. Houwink ten Cate (1974a: 140, 145, etc.; 1994: 243) assigns the flight to the period after the treaty, *contra* Edel (1958), Helck (1963: 96; 1971: 214); cf. Rowton (1959: 6 n. 31; 1966: 244–9).

[10] The text, Bo 86/299, has been published by Otten (1988a). See also Otten (1989a).

The text of the tablet is that of a treaty drawn up between Hattusili's son and successor Tudhaliya IV and a man called Kurunta. Before the discovery of the tablet Kurunta was already known to us as a nephew of Hattusili,[11] a 'powerful king' during Hattusili's reign,[12] and the man appointed by Hattusili as ruler of the Land of Tarhuntassa.[13] The bronze tablet confirms that Kurunta was a Hittite prince, a second son of the king Muwatalli,[14] and thus a brother of Urhi-Tesub. It also provides much valuable additional information about the role Kurunta played in the Hittite kingdom after the throne was seized from his brother.

At the time of Muwatalli's death, Urhi-Tesub clearly had priority over Kurunta in the royal succession. The latter was presumably of the same status as his brother (i.e. son of a concubine) but younger than him. While preparing Urhi-Tesub for the succession, Muwatalli had entrusted Kurunta to the care of his uncle Hattusili: 'Already had Muwatalli, the king, entrusted Kurunta to my father Hattusili to raise; and thus had my father raised him.' (Bronze tablet §2, I 12–13).

Though not destined to become king, he was no doubt marked out for high office and a distinguished career within the kingdom. Muwatalli saw in his brother Hattusili an appropriate guardian and tutor for the young prince in preparing him for his future role. We have suggested (in Ch. 9) that Muwatalli's decision to send Kurunta to his brother in Hakpissa may have been influenced by intra-family disputes in the royal court, and his wish to ensure that at least one of his sons would be protected from the possible consequences of these disputes.

Hattusili discharged his tutelage responsibilities conscientiously. He brought up his nephew as one of his own sons, and a particularly

---

[11] *Apol.* §12b, IV 62.

[12] He is thus referred to in the so-called Tawagalawa letter, KUB xiv 3 (*CTH* 181) I 73–4, discussed below; for the reading there of the name ᴰLAMMA-a (ᴰKAL-a) as Kurunta, see Houwink ten Cate (1965: 130), Laroche (1966: 101 no. 652), Gordon (1967: 71 n. 6).

[13] *Apol.* §12b, IV 63–4. Two other texts refer to this appointment; namely (*a*) KUB III 67 (*CTH* 163) obv. 12 ff. (letter from Ramesses II to Hattusili, discussed in Ch. 12), (*b*) *CTH* 96 obv. 3′–12′: 'Hattusili, the Great King, was my lord, and I was indeed in his heart. [   ] And I was a prince . . . Then Hattusili, the Great King, my lord, and Puduhepa, the Queen, took me back into their concerns, set me in the place of his brother (i.e. Muwatalli), made me lord of the Land of Tarhuntassa, and installed me in kingship in the Land of Tarhuntassa. And he made treaty tablets for me' (trans. Beckman (1989/90: 291)).

[14] See Otten (1988*a*: 3–4, c and D), Güterbock (1990: 162).

close friendship developed between Kurunta and his cousin Tudhaliya. If we can take at face value what the bronze tablet tells us, this greatly strengthened the bond between Kurunta and the family of Hattusili. In the upheavals which accompanied Hattusili's seizure of the throne, Kurunta apparently remained loyal to his uncle. For this he was rewarded with the prestigious appointment of king of the Land of Tarhuntassa: 'But when my father removed Urhi-Tesub from the kingship, thereupon my father took Kurunta and made him king in the Land of Tarhuntassa.' (Bronze tablet §3, I 14–15).

Apparently Kurunta's appointment followed very soon after Hattusili's seizure of the throne. The timing was probably deliberate. Given that the coup had led to civil war in the homeland and serious division within Hattusa itself, Urhi-Tesub must have had a significant following amongst his subjects, at least in the royal capital. He had lost his throne and been banished—but there was still Muwatalli's other son. The supporters of Urhi-Tesub might well have redirected their support to this second son if he had remained in Hattusa. At the very least his continuing presence in Hattusa would have been a constant embarrassment to the new king. It was understandable, perhaps imperative, that Hattusili should remove both sons from the capital at the earliest possible opportunity. Hence as soon as Hattusili had seized the throne, Kurunta was dispatched to Tarhuntassa.[15]

Although no longer the Hittite capital, Tarhuntassa continued to play an important role in Hittite affairs. No doubt this was largely because of its strategic location, extending as it did to the southern coast of Anatolia, and bordering on the country of Kizzuwadna. As we shall see, this region assumed increasing significance in the last decades of the kingdom. Thus the appointment of Kurunta to the former royal seat of his father was not only a reward for his loyalty. By placing Tarhuntassa under the direct rule of a prince of the royal line Hattusili made clear that it would henceforth function as one of the highest ranking and most important dependent territories of the kingdom. In recognition of his status, concessions and favours were heaped upon the prince, both by Hattusili and his successor Tudhaliya.

We should mention here the controversy surrounding a king of

---

[15] Cf. van den Hout (1995*a*: 86).

Tarhuntassa called Ulmi-Tesub and a surviving treaty which he concluded with a Hittite king (whose name is broken off in the text)—the so-called Ulmi-Tesub treaty.[16] Who was Ulmi-Tesub, and who was his treaty partner?

A number of scholars have argued, or assumed, that Ulmi-Tesub was a third son of Muwatalli, and thus the brother as well as the successor of Kurunta, and that the treaty in question was drawn up with him by Tudhaliya.[17] But a contrary argument is that Kurunta and Ulmi-Tesub were one and the same person: Kurunta was the Luwian name adopted by the prince Ulmi-Tesub when he was appointed by Hattusili as ruler of Tarhuntassa, which lay in a Luwian area; the Ulmi-Tesub treaty was drawn up not by Tudhaliya, but by his father Hattusili, as the fourth in a series of treaties with Ulmi-Tesub/Kurunta.[18] On the assumption that Ulmi-Tesub was Kurunta, the treaty further illustrates the concessions and favours which were conferred upon the young prince.

Hattusili granted one of these concessions during a visit to Tarhuntassa, where he found that the *šaḫḫan* duties (a form of payment or levy or tax in kind, often of a religious nature)[19] were imposing a heavy burden on the land. Thus he abolished the garrison duties for the kingdom, so that the garrison troops could be redeployed to meet the commitments of the *šaḫḫan*

When I, My Sun, came to Tarhuntassa, I saw that the *šaḫḫan* of the god (as imposed by) the treaty was onerous and could not be fulfilled. Formerly Muwatalli made Tarhuntassa his place of residence and celebrated the gods of Tarhuntassa, and all the Hittites honoured them.[20] But now the king and queen have made Kurunta king in Tarhuntassa. He could not fulfil the *šaḫḫan* of the god from (the resources) of his own land. So the

---

[16] KBo IV 10 + KUB XL 69 + 1548/u (*CTH* 106), ed. van den Hout (1995a). Extracts from this treaty are trans. by Garstang and Gurney (1959: 66–9).

[17] Thus Otten (1988a: 6), Hoffner (1989b: 47), van den Hout (1989b), Houwink ten Cate (1994: 233). Van den Hout has reiterated this view, with further arguments, in his edition of the Ulmi-Tesub treaty (1995a: 11–19).

[18] See Gurney (1993: 14–21). The equation was earlier suggested by Güterbock (1961: 86 n. 3). Further support for it and for assigning the treaty to Hattusili III is provided by Klengel (1991: 231–2), Sürenhagen (1992), Beal(1993: 31–2 n. 10). Van den Hout apparently did not have the opportunity of taking account of Gurney's discussion of this matter before his edition of the Ulmi-Tesub treaty went to press. The points raised by Gurney need to be addressed and effectively countered before finality can be reached on the identification of Ulmi-Tesub and the date of the treaty.

[19] See Giorgadze (1991: 280), Gurney (1990: 84; 1993: 15–16).

[20] i.e., the *šaḫḫan* was met out of the resources of the whole kingdom.

king and queen have made for you this (revised) treaty: My Sun has waived the previous requirement for chariotry and troops from the Hulaya River Land. In future, only 200 men will be required for a Hittite campaign. No further troops will be sought from him. (Hattusili: Ulmi-Tesub Treaty, KUB iv 10 (*CTH* 106), obv. §7, 40′–4′)[21]

This act of generosity may have been one of the measures designed to maintain Kurunta's goodwill towards his overlord and keep him loyal. It was important to ensure that his duties and obligations in Tarhuntassa gave him no grounds for complaint or defiance, which might encourage him, with the support of his father's former subjects in the region, to break his allegiance and perhaps attempt to exchange his throne in Tarhuntassa for the one in Hattusa. As a son of Muwatalli, Kurunta had a right to the Hittite throne. But unless he forced his claim, he could never hope to become Great King. Hattusili had made it quite clear that after his death the succession was to remain within his own family line.

But who within his family would succeed him?

Hattusili's Heir

Tudhaliya was not his father's first choice as successor to the throne. From the bronze tablet we learn that an older brother of Tudhaliya had originally been designated as the *tuḫkanti*, the crown prince.[22] But Hattusili subsequently took the title from the older brother and appointed Tudhaliya in his place.[23] Unfortunately the brother is not named in our text. Who was he, and why was he replaced?

The most likely candidate is the prince Nerikkaili, whom Hattusili married to the daughter of the Amurrite king Bentesina.[24] Already in Hattusili's reign Nerikkaili had been appointed *tuḫkanti*. He is referred to by this title at the head of a list of witnesses in the Ulmi-Tesub treaty,[25] and he may also have been

---

[21] This corresponds to the first five of the eight lines of ABoT 57 (*CTH* 97), which as Laroche (1947–8: 48) has noted, is a particular protocol for inserting in a general treaty.

[22] Bronze tablet, §14, ii 43. The precise meaning of the term *tuḫkanti* has been much debated. For its interpretation as 'crown prince', see Gurney (1983). Alternatively, it has been interpreted as 'heir presumptive'; see Houwink ten Cate (1992a: 262–3).

[23] Bronze tablet §14, ii 43–4.   [24] Cf. Klengel (1991: 230–1).

[25] §16, rev. 28.

the *tuḫkanti* sent to the west by Hattusili to negotiate with Piyamaradu.[26] But if he were in fact the older brother who was removed from office,[27] the reason for his removal remains unknown. It is unlikely that he suffered demotion because he had fallen into disgrace, for he apparently continued to play a prominent role in the kingdom. He was the first person called upon, as DUMU.LUGAL ('king's son'), to witness his brother's treaty with Kurunta.[28] And later in Tudhaliya's reign he appears once more with the title of *tuḫkanti*.[29] It may well be that at the time Tudhaliya drew up his treaty with Kurunta, probably one of the first official acts of his reign, he had not yet appointed a crown prince;[30] subsequently he reappointed Nerikkaili to the office, but perhaps as an interim measure and on the understanding that it would eventually be assumed by one of his own sons.

If Nerikkaili was in fact the older brother replaced by Tudhaliya in the office of *tuḫkanti*,[31] we are still left with the question of why Hattusili took this action. Did the queen Puduhepa have a hand in it? If Nerikkaili was Hattusili's son by a former marriage,

---

[26] In the context of the events recorded in the Tawagalawa letter, discussed below.

[27] It has been argued that he was the son of a former wife of Hattusili, prior to the latter's marriage to Puduhepa; see Klengel (1989: 186–7 n. 8), Hagenbuchner (1992: 118). This argument depends at least in part on the assumption that he was already married to Bentesina's daughter at the time of Bentesina's treaty with Hattusili, probably early in Hattusili's reign; if he were of marriageable age at this time, he must have been born before Puduhepa appeared on the scene. The argument is weakened, though not necessarily invalidated, if Nerikkaili's marriage was merely envisaged when the treaty was drawn up rather than an event which had already taken place. See also Houwink ten Cate (1994: 246–7).

[28] Bronze tablet §27, IV 30.

[29] At the head of a list of persons called upon to witness a document which made a land-grant to Sahurunuwa, king of Carchemish, KUB XXVI 43//50 (*CTH* 225) obv. 28, where he is referred to as both DUMU.LUGAL and *tuḫkanti*. However Hagenbuchner (1992: 121) doubts the identification of this Nerikkaili with the son of Hattusili.

[30] Perhaps because at that time he had no direct heirs. Cf. Imparati (1992: 318; 1995: 152).

[31] We might note here the alternative suggestion that Kurunta was the 'brother' who was removed from office; see Houwink ten Cate (1992a: 239–40, 265–8), van den Hout (1995a: 94). This would imply that Hattusili had actually adopted Kurunta as his son, and appointed him as *tuḫkanti*, which would in effect mean that Kurunta held the positions of *tuḫkanti* and king of Tarhuntassa simultaneously. *Contra* van den Hout, 1995a, 89, this seems unlikely. In fact on the basis of earlier precedents with the viceroys of Carchemish and Aleppo, appointment to a viceregal position, to which Kurunta's position was tantamount, virtually excluded the incumbent from any expectation of occupying the Hittite throne.

she may have persuaded her husband to set him aside in order to advance the claims of her own son Tudhaliya.[32] But this is mere speculation. There may have been other reasons for the new appointment.

Quite possibly the personal relationship between Tudhaliya and Kurunta was an important factor in Hattusili's decision. Kurunta had sworn to give unqualified loyalty and support to Tudhaliya, whatever position the latter was assigned in the kingdom:

But at that time when my father appointed my older brother as *tuḫkanti*, I was still not at that time marked out for kingship. But Kurunta (already) showed his loyalty to me and gave me in person the following oath: 'If your father does not appoint you to kingship, in whatever position your father places you, I will be loyal only to you and (be) your (loyal) servant.'   (Bronze tablet §13, II 35–41)

Hattusili was very conscious of the close bond between his son and Kurunta.[33] This might in the long term provide the strongest guarantee of the security of the succession in his family line. If in spite of his own eligibility for kingship Kurunta remained true to his oath, he would be bound to support Tudhaliya's accession to the throne. But his loyalty to any other member of Hattusili's family, even Nerikkaili who had long had a prior claim upon the throne, could have been open to question. Perhaps this influenced Hattusili's decision to appoint Tudhaliya as the new *tuḫkanti*. The last thing he wanted was yet another conflict over the succession. To avoid this, he set great store by the long-standing friendship between Kurunta and Tudhaliya, on their mutual assurances of loyalty to and support for each other, and on the substantial compensation Kurunta received in the form of the throne of Tarhuntassa.

It was essential that both Hattusili and his son and successor Tudhaliya ensure Kurunta's loyalty—by rewarding him with the prestigious kingdom of Tarhuntassa and granting him a range of privileges and honours. For a time Kurunta seemed satisfied. But was he simply biding his time?

[32] Suggested by Otten (1989*a*: 11), Klengel (1991: 228), Hagenbuchner (1992: 122), Imparati (1995: 154). The suggestion that Tudhaliya was also a son from an earlier union (thus van den Hout (1995*a*: 86)) is negated by a seal impression from Ugarit, which reads: 'Seal of Tudhaliya, Great King, King of Hatti, the Hero, Son of Hattusili, Great King, the Hero; and of Puduhepa, Great Queen of Hatti; Grandson of Mursili, Great King, the Hero' (RS 17.159; Laroche (1956: 111)). Cf. Klengel (1991: 225).
[33] See e.g. bronze tablet, §14, II 45–8.

The Lead-Up to the Treaty with Ramesses

From the beginning of his reign, Hattusili seemed intent on improving relations with Assyria and Egypt, Hatti's two main adversaries in the south-east. Shortly after his accession, he had written to the Assyrian king Adad-Nirari in conciliatory terms. Relations between Hatti and Assyria had become severely strained during Urhi-Tesub's reign, particularly with the Assyrian conquest of Hanigalbat and the extension of Assyrian territory to the borders of Carchemish. But Adad-Nirari had stopped short of an invasion of Hittite territory and had attempted, apparently, to strengthen diplomatic ties with Hatti. With little success. The missions which he had sent to Hatti had merely served to increase the tensions between the two kingdoms, and he had been soundly rebuked by Urhi-Tesub when he wrote to him as one 'Brother' to another.

Hattusili sought to dissociate himself from the previous regime. He had more than one motive for doing so. In the first place he had no wish to become embroiled in further conflict in the south-east. But just as importantly, he was anxious to gain recognition abroad for the legitimacy of his own regime. This becomes very evident from the text of his letter to Adad-Nirari, who had failed to provide the usual tokens of acknowledgement when Hattusili became king:

Did not my father send you fine gifts? When I assumed kingship, you did not send me an ambassador. It is the custom that kings assume the kingship, and (other) kings and their nobles send him fine gifts, a royal mantle, and pure oil for unction. But up (until) now, you have not done this.   (KBo I 14 (*CTH* 173) rev. 4–10, trans. Archi (1971: 208))[34]

The main purpose of the letter was to provide a basis for a more positive relationship between the two kingdoms. Indeed there was already an opportunity for demonstrating mutual goodwill. On the Hittite–Assyrian frontier the people of the town of Turira, once part of the kingdom of Hanigalbat, had recently taken to raiding the neighbouring territory of Carchemish. This had the potential for escalating into conflict between Hittite and Assyrian forces, which Hattusili clearly wanted to avoid. If Adad-Nirari claimed sovereignty over the territory (he wrote), then he should take

---

[34] Further on this letter, see Goetze (1940: 27–33), Rowton (1959: 2–4), Harrak (1987: 68–75), Hagenbuchner (1989: 267, no. 195), Liverani (1990: 104–5).

action to stop the raids. If not, then Hattusili would himself take action against the offenders:

> The men of Turira keep raiding my territory. From over there they raid the Land of Carchemish, from over here they raid the Land of . . . The king of Hanigalbat used to write 'Turira is mine, or Turira is yours, and a matter affecting Turira is no (more) a concern of the king of Hanigalbat.' But must you not recognise that the (men of) Turira are raiding the country and taking booty into Turira? My subjects who ran away have likewise the habit of going up to Turira. Now, if Turira is yours, smash it! But as to my subjects who stay in the city, do not touch their belongings. If Turira is not yours, write to me so that I may smash it. But as to your soldiers who stay in the city, their belongings will not be touched. Why do the people of Turira sniff at the gift of me, the lion?   (KBo 1 14 6–19, trans. Liverani (1990: 104–5))

It is clear from this appeal that Hattusili had accepted Assyrian sovereignty over the territories belonging to the former kingdom of Hanigalbat as a *fait accompli*. But in Hanigalbat itself, the spirit of resistance continued to smoulder. On Adad-Nirari's death after a reign of some thirty-three years[35] Sattuara II, the nephew and successor of Wasasatta, rebelled against Assyria and sought to realign his kingdom with Hatti, counting on both Hittite support and the assistance of some local Aramaic tribes. It was a courageous venture, though doomed to failure. Sattuara was setting himself against the formidable new Assyrian king Salmaneser I (c.1263–1234).[36] There was little likelihood that Hattusili would come to the assistance of the rebel. He had already written off Hanigalbat. And he was too preoccupied with other matters, including the Egyptian question, to contemplate a change of heart. Further, he had written to Salmaneser, probably shortly after the latter's accession, in very amicable terms, acknowledging him as a Great King, and probably coming to terms with him over territorial claims in the Euphrates region.[37] In such a context, Sattuara's rebellion against the Assyrian king may have been a distinct embarrassment to Hattusili, and so he probably chose to ignore any appeals

---

[35] See Rowton (1959: 1).

[36] On the basis of Wilhelm and Boese's lower chronology (1979).

[37] KBo XVIII 24 = Hagenbuchner (1989: 242–5, no. 188). The authorship of this letter has been attributed to either Hattusili or Tudhaliya; the latter is assumed by Harrak (1987: 187). But in my opinion Hattusili is the more likely candidate; cf. Hagenbuchner (1989: 243).

Sattuara may have made to him, or at best provided him with only token assistance.

Salmaneser claimed a crushing and decisive victory over the rebel kingdom, capturing and sacking numerous cities and settlements throughout the kingdom and taking many thousands of prisoners. Although the reliability of his account is open to question on matters of detail,[38] there is little doubt that he was responsible for dealing the final death blow to the kingdom of Hanigalbat:[39]

When, by command of the great gods and with the exalted strength of Assur, My Lord, I marched to the Land of Hanigalbat, I opened up the most difficult of paths and passes. Sattuara, king of the Land of Hanigalbat, with the aid of the armies of the Hittites[40] and Ahlamu, captured the passes and watering-places in my path. When my army was thirsty and fatigued, their army made a fierce attack in strength. But I struck back and brought about their defeat. I slaughtered countless numbers of their extensive army. As for Sattuara, I chased him westward at arrow-point. I butchered their hordes, but 14,400 of them which remained alive I blinded and carried off. I conquered nine of his fortified cult centres (as well as) the city from which he ruled and I turned 180 of his cities into ruin hills. I slaughtered like sheep the armies of the Hittites and Ahlamu, his allies. (Assyrian royal inscription, trans. Grayson (1972: 82 §530))

The Treaty with Egypt

In the mean time, Hattusili was intent on bringing about a final peaceful settlement with Egypt. The ever-present threat of Assyria has been seen as one of Hattusili's chief incentives for concluding a peace with Ramesses; an alliance between Hatti and Egypt would help safeguard the interests of both in Syria against the increasingly ambitious and belligerent upstart power across the Euphrates.[41] But the 'Assyrian factor' has probably been over-emphasized. Rather, Hattusili was motivated much more by

---

[38] See Wilhelm (1989: 40).

[39] See Astour (1994: 228), who refers to tablets of Salmaneser's reign which show that a regular Assyrian administration was now installed in the cities of the conquered kingdom, that part of their population was being transported eastward, and that land estates and enslaved local persons were distributed to Assyrian aristocrats.

[40] This almost certainly exaggerates the extent of Hittite involvement in the conflict, which was probably only minimal.

[41] Thus argued by Rowton (1959).

personal considerations in initiating the steps which led to the conclusion of a treaty with Ramesses. The treaty would in effect provide him with formal recognition from the pharaoh of the legitimacy of his rule.[42] Such recognition would serve to strengthen his credibility amongst other foreign rulers, as well as his own subjects.

We know from his correspondence with foreign rulers how sensitive he was on this matter. Perhaps with good reason. The diplomatic overtures he had made to the Assyrian king, probably Adad-Nirari, had met with a gratuitously offensive response: 'You are (no more than) a substitute for the Great King!' Ramesses took some pleasure in reminding Hattusili of this.[43] He clearly saw how important the treaty was to Hattusili in helping to gain for him the international recognition which he so earnestly sought. Indeed Hattusili had written to Ramesses some time before the treaty complaining about the pharaoh's failure to treat him with the respect that his status deserved. He reminded him that he and not Urhi-Tesub was now king of Hatti. All this is evident from Ramesses' rejoinder:

I have just heard these harsh words that my brother wrote to me (saying): 'Why did you write to me all these words as though I were a servant?' It is simply not true that I wrote to you as I would to one of my servants. Have you not attained the kingship? Do I not know this? Is it not firmly instilled in my heart? Fulfil your role as king! Moreover, I have heard about this business of Urhi-Tesub of which you have written. You have written to me about him saying: 'I have become king in his place!' (KUB III 22 (*CTH* 155) + KBo XXVIII 3 (= *ÄHK* I no. 20) obv. 5–9)

Attempts to persuade Ramesses to extradite Urhi-Tesub to Hatti had so far failed. But a treaty with the pharaoh would at least have the effect of gaining from him an agreement that he would not support any attempts Urhi-Tesub might still make to regain the throne of Hatti. Indeed it might induce Ramesses, finally, to

---

[42] Cf. Spalinger (1981: 357).

[43] The Assyrian king's statement is recorded by Ramesses in one of his letters to Hattusili, KBo VIII 14 (*CTH* 216) (= *ÄHK* I no. 5), 24–5, obv. 10'. It may have been a rejoinder to Hattusili's complaint that Adad-Nirari had failed to send him the usual tokens of acknowledgment on his accession. If so, this must have occurred shortly after Hattusili's seizure of the Hittite throne. Although that was now some years in the past, Ramesses could not resist the temptation of reminding his treaty-partner of what the Assyrian king had said to him. However, Edel, *ÄHK* II, 41, suggests that the statement in question was made much later, in the context of Ramesses' attempts to persuade Hattusili to visit Egypt (see below). If so, the Assyrian king who made it was Salmaneser.

surrender Urhi-Tesub to Hattusili's authority. The treaty would also endorse the right of succession in Hattusili's own line. This was an important consideration, particularly in view of the existence of a second son of Muwatalli and the possibility that attempts might be made to restore the throne to Muwatalli's lineal descendants. By the terms of the treaty, Ramesses was bound to oppose any such attempts.[44]

What did Ramesses hope to gain from the treaty? Here again we can only speculate. While in the years immediately following the conflict at Kadesh he had continued to maintain an active military presence in the Syrian region, his campaigns had tapered off considerably in more recent years. And any ambitions he originally had entertained for emulating the achievements of Tuthmosis III were now, he had to acknowledge, completely unrealizable. He had not even been able to recover former Egyptian territories lost to the Hittites in the aftermath of the battle at Kadesh. Nor did he achieve any territorial gains from the treaty, which made no reference to territorial matters and thus by implication confirmed the status quo.[45]

It is possible that the growing power of Assyria was a factor in Ramesses' decision—though as yet Assyria posed no direct threat to Egyptian territory in Syria. But Ramesses was now two decades into his reign, and may have felt the need for some significant achievement in the international arena to bolster his image amongst his subjects. In the absence of any significant military triumphs abroad in recent years, perhaps the next best thing was a major diplomatic achievement—an alliance with the long-term enemy of Egypt. Ramesses could represent the treaty as a settlement sought by the Hittite king, abjectly suing for peace with Egypt—in itself an acknowledgement that under the pharaoh's rule Egypt was still regarded as a major power in the international scene. It provided good propaganda value for the pharaoh.

The treaty was concluded in the twenty-first year of Ramesses' reign (November/December 1259) in the city of Pi-Ramesse:

Year 21, 1st month of Winter, Day 21, under the Majesty of . . . Ramesses II. This day, behold, His Majesty was at the city of Pi-Ramesse, doing the pleasure (of the gods . . .). There came the (three royal envoys of

---

[44] See the Hittite version of the treaty, Pritchard (1969: 203), under *Succession to the Throne*.
[45] Cf. Goetze (1975c: 259).

Egypt . . .) together with the first and second royal envoys of Hatti, Tili-Tesub and Ramose, and the envoy of Carchemish, Yapusili, bearing the silver tablet which the Great King of Hatti, Hattusili, sent to Pharaoh, to request peace from the Majesty of Ramesses. (Introduction to the Egyptian version, trans. Kitchen (1982: 75))[46]

Two independent versions were composed, one in Hattusa, the other in Pi-Ramesse. Each version presented the terms of the treaty from the respective treaty-partner's viewpoint. The Hittite version was originally written in Akkadian, from a first Hittite draft, inscribed on a silver tablet, and then sent to Egypt, where it was translated into Egyptian. Copies of this version were inscribed on the walls of the temple of Amun at Karnak and the Ramesseum. Correspondingly, the Egyptian version of the treaty was first composed in Egyptian, and then translated into Akkadian on a silver tablet before being sent to the court of Hattusili.[47] (Thus the version of the treaty written in Egyptian represents the original Hittite version, and the version in Akkadian the original Egyptian version.) We have here a classic illustration of the importance of Akkadian in the Late Bronze Age world as the international language of diplomacy.

While the two versions of the treaty were independently prepared, it is clear from the fact that there are no significant discrepancies between them that the critical issues had been thoroughly discussed and negotiated in advance of their preparation. Thus both versions essentially formalized agreements that had already been reached, after extensive diplomatic communication. Important provisions in the treaty included mutual assurances that neither treaty-partner would invade the territory of the other, that each would come to the aid of the other, if called upon, in the event of aggression by a third power or rebellion in his own country, that each would return fugitives from the other's country seeking asylum with him, on the understanding that an amnesty for persons so extradited would be provided in their own country.

Although the treaty marked a major step forward in Hittite–

---

[46] A full translation of both the Egyptian and the Hittite versions of the text appears in Pritchard (1969: 199–201, Egyptian version trans. Wilson; and 201–3, Hittite version trans. Goetze).

[47] The production and dispatch of these tablets were referred to in several letters from Ramesses to Hattusili around the time the treaty was concluded; see KUB III 52 (*CTH* 165.7) (= *ÄHK* I no. 3), 20–1, KBo XXVIII 1 (= *ÄHK* I no. 4), 22–3. In passing, it is interesting to note that a copy of the Akkadian version is mounted at the entrance to the Security Council of the United Nations in New York.

Egyptian relations, it did not result in a total relaxation of the tensions between the treaty-partners. The memories of past hostilities lingered on. We know, for example, that Hattusili wrote to Ramesses protesting about the pharaoh's depiction of the battle of Kadesh—in a way that was deeply humiliating to his new ally. In his reply Ramesses made no apology at all for what he had said about Kadesh. After all, he was speaking no more than the truth! And he repeated his version of his 'victory' at Kadesh, and the events leading up to it, to emphasize the point.[48] But he then went on to assure his Hittite Brother of his total personal commitment to the treaty, and of his adherence to its terms:

See, the Great Gods of our lands, they are witnesses to the word of the oath, which we have made. Further: I have not set aside the oath. I have obeyed the oath. And I will adhere closely to it, the peace and the brotherhood . . .   (KBo I 15 (+) (*CTH* 156) (= *ÄHK* I no. 24) rev. 6–8)[49]

Most important from Hattusili's point of view was the fact that the treaty provided him with explicit Egyptian acknowledgement of the legitimacy of his regime. Hattusili wanted this to be made quite clear. The pharaoh obliged:

Certainly you are the Great King of the lands of Hatti. The Sun God has granted to you and the Storm God has granted to you, to sit in the Land of Hatti, in the place of the father of your father.   (NBC 3934 (*CTH* 155) (= *ÄHK* I no. 22), obv. 13′–15′, adapted from trans. by Archi (1971: 209)))[50]

By implication, Ramesses was thus endorsing the legitimacy of Hattusili's action in deposing his nephew Urhi-Tesub from the kingship, as he made clear in his response to the king of Mira, who questioned him on this matter. Although the passage containing this response is incomplete, there can be no doubt that the pharaoh was now declaring his full support for Hattusili over the Urhi-Tesub affair:[51]

Take note of the good alliance which the Great King, the king of the Land of Egypt, made with the Great King, the king of the Land of Hatti, my brother, in good brotherhood, in good peace. The Sun God and the Storm

---

[48]   KBo I 15 (+) (*CTH* 156) (= *ÄHK* I no. 24), 58–61, obv. 15′–33′.
[49]   This translation is based on the German translation and restorations proposed by Edel in *ÄHK*. For a detailed discussion of the letter, see Edel (1950). See also Fecht (1984: 41–5).
[50]   Text also ed. Goetze (1947*b*).   [51]   Cf. Archi (1971: 209).

God have granted this for ever. Note further: (regarding) the matter of Urhi-Tesub about which you have written to me, the Great King, the king of the Land of Hatti, handled it as I would have wished. (KBo I 24 + KUB III 84 (*CTH* 166.1) (= *ÄHK* I no. 2), obv. 9–13)

Equally important, the treaty provided Hattusili with a guarantee of military support from the pharaoh, should there be an uprising against him by members of his own nobility. This in itself seems to be a further reflection of what Hattusili saw as the continuing insecurity of the Hittite monarchy, particularly over the question of the succession. So long as both sons of Muwatalli lived, his determination to place his own son upon the throne might be open to serious challenge, by his own subjects. It is this possibility which must have been foremost in Hattusili's mind when he included the following provision in his treaty with Ramesses—a provision which has no corresponding obligation demanded by Ramesses:

The son of Hattusili . . . shall be made king of Hatti in the place of his father Hattusili, after the many years of Hattusili, king of Hatti. If noblemen of the Land of Hatti do a sin against him, then Ramesses, the king of the Land of Egypt, will send infantry and chariotry in order to take revenge on these. (Akkadian version, 40–3, trans. Spalinger (1981, 338–9))

Relations between Hatti and Egypt Following the Treaty

Notwithstanding Ramesses' stated position with regard to Urhi-Tesub, and Hattusili's persistent requests for his nephew to be handed over to him, Urhi-Tesub defied all attempts by his uncle to get him back. This might well have imperilled the peace accord right from the outset. The tensions caused by Urhi-Tesub's flight to Egypt, whether before or after the treaty, are evident from Hattusili's letter to Kadasman-Enlil, referred to above.[52] Urhi-Tesub apparently continued to enjoy the pharaoh's protection, or at least never again fell within his usurper's grasp.[53]

The reasons for Ramesses' stubbornness on this matter are hard

---

[52] See in particular KBo I 10 obv. 67 ff., and Edel's discussion (1958: 131). See also Singer (1988a: 330).

[53] Singer (1988a: 330) comments that it appears he was still in Egypt when the subsequent marriage between Ramesses and Hattusili's daughter was negotiated, citing KUB XXI 38 obv. 12, and referring to Helck (1963: 88). But see below.

to fathom, since in other respects his commitment to an alliance and peaceful relations with Hatti seems to have been quite sincere. One wonders if his retention of Urhi-Tesub was a means of ensuring that his treaty-partner would himself abide strictly by the terms of the treaty, particularly with regard to Egyptian interests in Syria. In the knowledge that his nephew had by no means abandoned his hopes of regaining his throne, and might well make a serious attempt to do so if he had Egyptian backing, Hattusili would have been careful to avoid taking any action likely to jeopardize his peace accord with the pharaoh.

On the other hand, it is possible that Ramesses did not deliver up Urhi-Tesub because he was no longer under his protection, that Urhi-Tesub, fearing the possible consequences to himself of the Hittite–Egyptian treaty, had taken the first opportunity to flee from Egypt, and that his present whereabouts were unknown. This at least is what Ramesses told his treaty-partner, suggesting that he should look elsewhere for him. Hattusili had angrily rejected the suggestion. As far as he was concerned, Urhi-Tesub was still in Egypt. Yet again Ramesses wrote declaring that he had no idea where he was. The bird had flown the coop:

As for what you have written to me regarding the matter of Urhi-Tesub: 'It is not the case that he went to the Land of Kadesh or the Land of Aleppo, or the Land of Kizzuwadna!'—thus you have written. Look, I don't understand these words you have written about this matter of Urhi-Tesub, as follows: 'Bring him into the Land of Egypt!' I do not know where he is lodged. [He has flown like a bird.]   (KBo I 15 (+) (*CTH* 156) (= *ÄHK* I no. 24), rev. 22–5)[54]

Ramesses' claim that Urhi-Tesub's whereabouts were unknown to him had failed to convince Hattusili. But the latter may finally have resigned himself to the fact that for all his efforts Urhi-Tesub would for ever remain beyond his control.

A Royal Wedding   In other respects, the conclusion of the treaty marked the beginning of a significant improvement in Hittite–Egyptian relations.[55] Ramesses and Hattusili exchanged a series of

---

[54] For a discussion of the composite text from which this passage comes, see Edel, *ÄHK* II, 95–121. See also Wouters (1989).

[55] Reflected in the regular diplomatic exchanges between the two kingdoms following the treaty. Singer (1995: 92) notes that Megiddo (Makkitta) in the Jezreel valley was an important station on the diplomatic route between the two royal courts.

cordial letters regarding the treaty,[56] and relations between the royal families were consolidated thirteen years later by the marriage between Ramesses and a daughter of Hattusili (thirty-third year of Ramesses' reign, autumn of 1246). The marriage was preceded by extensive correspondence between the two royal houses relating to terms of the marriage settlement, the dowry to be provided, arrangements for the Hittite princess's journey to Egypt, and guarantees that royal messengers from Hatti and members of the Hittite royal family would henceforth be permitted to visit the princess after her marriage. The correspondence was not without some acrimony. There were, for example, complaints from Ramesses about delays on the Hittite side in finalizing arrangements for the marriage. Much of the responsibility for these arrangements fell to the queen Puduhepa. It was to her that Ramesses wrote complaining of Hittite prevarication—but his complaint received a brusque response from Puduhepa, who took the opportunity to bring up again with him Urhi-Tesub's alleged continuing sojourn in his kingdom. Who was Ramesses to complain about his 'Brother's' failure to accede to his wishes?

Now you my Brother wrote to me as follows: 'My Sister has written to me: "I will send you a daughter." But you hold back before me and are ill disposed (towards me). Why have you failed to give her to me?' You should not distrust me. You should have faith in me. I would have sent you the daughter by now. Do I not know the 'House of Hatti-land' as well as you, my Brother, know it? [ ] The House is destroyed by fire.[57] What remained Urhi-Tesub gave to the Great God. As Urhi-Tesub is there, ask him whether it is so or not![58] What daughter in heaven or earth should I then give to my Brother? . . . Should I then marry him to a daughter of Babylon, or Zulabi, or Assyria? (KUB xxi 38 (*CTH* 176) (= *ÄHK* i no. 105) obv. 7′–13′)[59]

Puduhepa spent much of her letter explaining to Ramesses that the delay in sending him his bride was due to the time taken to

[56] See *ÄHK* i, nos. 2–6.
[57] The passage 'Do I not know . . . destroyed by fire' (obv. 10–12) is trans. Houwink ten Cate (1994: 237).
[58] The reference to Urhi-Tesub is generally assumed to indicate that he was still in Egypt at the time (e.g. Singer (1988*a*: 330)). But could it not simply be a sneer by the Hittite queen, in response to Ramesses' no doubt oft-repeated claim that Urhi-Tesub had left Egypt and his present whereabouts were unknown? Such a sneer need not indicate the actual truth of the matter.
[59] For the full text of this draft letter to Ramesses, see Helck (1963). See also Hagenbuchner (1989: no. 222, 325–7), and Houwink ten Cate (1994: 237–8).

collect a suitable dowry. A fire in Hattusa which destroyed the 'House of Hatti-land' had been at least partly responsible for this. What this 'House' was remains uncertain. It may have been a royal treasury of some kind, from which suitable items for a royal dowry might normally have been collected.[60]

Finally Ramesses received word from Puduhepa that all arrangements had been finalized in Hatti. The princess was on her way. The pharaoh was delighted, and wrote in fulsome terms to Puduhepa:

I have seen the tablet that my Sister sent me, and I have noted all the matters on which the Great Queen of Hatti, my Sister, has so very, very graciously written to me . . . The Great King, the King of Hatti, my Brother, has written to me saying: 'Let people come, to pour fine oil on my daughter's head, and may she be brought into the house of the Great King, the King of Egypt!' . . . Excellent, excellent is this decision about which my Brother has written to me . . . (our) two great countries will become as one land for ever! (KUB III 63 (*CTH* 159.2) (= *ÄHK* I no. 51) obv. 12–20, trans. Kitchen (1982: 85))

Inscriptions from Egypt provide details of the pomp and ceremony of the wedding.[61] The princess's Hittite name is unknown, but her Egyptian name was Mahornefrure or Manefrure, which means 'She who beholds Horus who is the beauty of Re'.[62] From Puduhepa's correspondence with Ramesses, it seems very likely that the Hittite queen requested that her daughter be recognized as Ramesses' principal wife.[63] This request may initially have been agreed to, although subsequently the Hittite princess was apparently sent to live in the pharaoh's harem near Fayum.[64]

At all events, the peace accord between Hatti and Egypt was now consolidated, and remained firm throughout the remaining years of the Hittite kingdom.

[60] 'House of Hatti-Land' is the translation offered by Houwink ten Cate (1994: 238) for the term É KUR ^URU*Hatti*, contrary to earlier assumptions that it was a reference to the royal palace. As Houwink ten Cate points out, there is no archaeologically attested evidence for a major fire in Hattusa during Hattusili's reign. He sees the term as one perhaps used in reference to 'an economic or administrative institution, presumably situated in the capital, but not necessarily forming part of the palace on the citadel'.

[61] Copies are found in the temple of Karnak on the ninth Pylon, in Elephantine, and at the entrance to Ramesses' temple at Abu Simbel. See Edel (1976: 27–30), Kitchen (1982: 85–7). The inscriptions are collected in *KRI* II, 233–81. For a translation, see Kitchen (1995: 768).

[62] On the reading of this name see Gardiner (1965: 294, 484 no. 56).

[63] See Singer (1991c: 333). [64] See Kitchen (1982: 88–9, 110).

Further Communications between the Royal Courts The royal correspondence provides further evidence of regular personal communications between the two royal houses, particularly between Puduhepa and members of the Egyptian royal family. There is also a well-known instance in which Hattusili wrote to Ramesses requesting the services of an Egyptian doctor to assist his sister Massanauzzi (wife of Masturi, king of the Seha River Land), to have children. In Egyptian texts, the sister's name appears as Matanazi.[65] The assignment was a difficult one since, Hattusili claimed, Matanazi was 50 at the time. Ramesses' undiplomatic response to the request could hardly have endeared him to his Hittite Brother:

Thus to my Brother: (Concerning) what my Brother has written to me regarding his sister Matanazi: 'May my Brother send to me a man to prepare medicines so that she may bear children.' So has my Brother written. And so (I say) to my Brother: 'Look, Matanazi, the sister of my Brother, the king your Brother knows her. A 50-year-old!! Never! She's a 60-year-old! Look, a woman of 50 is old, to say nothing of a 60-year-old! One can't produce medicines to enable *her* to bear children! Well, the Sun God and the Storm God may give a command, and the order which they give will then be carried out continually for the sister of my Brother. And I, the king your Brother, will send an expert incantation-priest and an expert doctor to assist her to produce children.   (KBo xxviii 30 (= *ÄHK* i no. 75), obv. 8–rev. 8)[66]

The arrogant, patronizing tone of this letter surfaces elsewhere in Ramesses' communications with the Hittite court. On a personal level, Ramesses sometimes adopted a lofty, condescending attitude towards his northern ally. None the less he was curious to meet the Great King, brother of his opponent at Kadesh and usurper of the

[65] Thus her name appears in the response from Ramesses. As we have seen, her name was written Massan(a)uzzi/Massana-IR-i in Hittite. Edel, *ÄHK* ii, 271, suggests that as Hattusili's sister was married in Arzawa, *matana-* could be a dialect form in the regional Arzawa language for *maššana-*.

[66] The letter was originally ed. Edel (1976: 67–75; see also 1976: 31 ff., 53 ff.). Beckman (1983a: 254) comments: 'It is the Hittite attitude which is of interest here. If there were persons at the Hittite court expert in the use of medicines for the treatment of gynaecological problems, they would certainly have informed Hattusili that his hopes in regard to the possible fertility of his sister were misplaced.' Hoffner (1977: 78) cites Güterbock who showed in his article 'Hittite Medicine' in *Bulletin of the History of Medicine* 36 (1962), that the Hittites did not approach a medical practice deserving of the name 'medicine' and were even more primitive than their contemporaries in Egypt and Mesopotamia.

Hittite throne. Indeed he issued Hattusili with an invitation to visit him, shortly after the conclusion of the treaty.

Hattusili was surprised by the invitation, and enquired what the purpose of such a visit would be. Concealing any annoyance he might have felt at this less than enthusiastic response, Ramesses renewed the invitation and offered to meet the Hittite king in Canaan,[67] whence he would escort him personally to his residence in the eastern Delta:

The Sun God (of Egypt) and the Storm God (of Hatti) and my gods and the gods of my Brother will cause my Brother see his Brother—and may my Brother carry out this good suggestion to come and see me. And then we may see each other face to face at the place where the king (Ramesses) sits enthroned. So, I shall go (ahead) into Canaan, to meet my Brother and see him face (to face), and to receive him into the midst of my land! (KBo xxviii 1 (= *ÄHK* i no. 4) obv. 19′–24′, trans. Kitchen (1982: 90))[68]

Ramesses probably represented the proposed visit primarily as a goodwill mission which would consolidate further the good relations between the two kingdoms. But no doubt his curiosity to meet his Hittite counterpart and his desire to impress him with the splendours of Egypt were also important motives. Moreover a visit from Hattusili offered considerable scope for enhancing Ramesses' image amongst his own subjects. It could be depicted as a major act of homage paid to the pharaoh in his own court by the ruler of the Land of Hatti.

As far as we are aware, Hattusili never took up the pharaoh's invitation. Initially he postponed acceptance of it, perhaps making the excuse of a personal indisposition. We know that he suffered from inflammation of the feet,[69] and may have used this as a reason for not responding more enthusiastically. But he probably had no great wish to go to Egypt, and may well have been suspicious of Ramesses' motives in issuing the invitation. In any case problems within his own kingdom, particularly in the west (see below), meant that he could ill afford a lengthy absence from his homeland—on a diplomatic mission of very dubious benefit to himself.

---

[67] Where the pharaoh probably had a royal residence; see Edel (1960: 18).

[68] See also Edel (1960: 17–18). A further reference to the proposed visit occurs in KBo viii 14 (*CTH* 216) (= *ÄHK* i no. 5), obv. 3′–5′.

[69] The text referring to his affliction is translated below. Apparently news of the king's indisposition was sent to Egypt, quite possibly in the context of a reply to the pharaoh; see Edel (1960: 20).

Nevertheless the close links between the two royal houses continued, and were further strengthened some years later when another Hittite princess was sent to Egypt to marry the pharaoh. Details are provided on a stele discovered by Petrie in 1896 in the Great Temple at Coptos:[70]

The great chief of Hatti caused to be brought the exceeding rich booty of Hatti, the exceeding rich booty of Keshkesh (i.e. Kaska), the exceeding rich booty of Arzawa, and the exceeding rich booty of Qode—they could not be known in writing—to Ramesses, (and) likewise, many droves of horses, many herds of cattle, many flocks of goats and many herds of small cattle before his other daughter whom he caused to be brought for Ramesses, given life, to Egypt, for what was the second time. (Coptos Stele, 7–11, trans. Kitchen and Gaballa (1969–70: 17))

It is possible that this second marriage took place after the death of Hattusili. In any case, we can have little doubt that the chief negotiator on the Hittite side was the queen Puduhepa.

Puduhepa

The marriage correspondence between Puduhepa and the Egyptian royal court (we have fifteen letters written to Puduhepa by Ramesses or members of his family) well illustrates the respect which the Hittite queen was accorded by foreign rulers. She was held in high esteem by Ramesses in particular, whose four surviving letters to her are couched in terms virtually identical to those used in his correspondence with the Hittite king himself.

This was but one instance of the extensive and largely unparalleled role which Puduhepa played in international affairs, as exemplified by her frequent communications with both foreign and vassal rulers.[71] It was a role which she continued to fulfil following her husband's death, in the reign of their son Tudhaliya.[72] There is

---

[70] It was found in a fragmentary state, but another fragment was discovered a few years later, making it almost complete. For the publication of the full inscription, see Kitchen and Gaballa (1969–70: 14–17).

[71] An example of the latter is the Amurrite king Bentesina's letter to her, KUB III 56 (*CTH* 208.4) (= Hagenbuchner (1989: 379–82, no. 267)), which may refer to Urhi-Tesub's flight to Egypt (see Houwink ten Cate (1994: 244)).

[72] See Singer (1985a: 116; 1987: 415).

little doubt that her international profile had the blessing, and indeed the active encouragement, of her husband. She was included with him in the loyalty oath in the Ulmi-Tesub treaty,[73] and important documents of state, including the treaty with Ramesses, bore the names of both king and queen as co-signatories.[74] Puduhepa also issued seals in her own right.[75]

Amongst her many activities, she played a role as royal matchmaker, claiming the credit for arranging the double marriage between the Hittite and Amurrite royal families, and taking responsibility for deciding on a wife for Urhi-Tesub's brother Kurunta. She also arranged marriage alliances with the family of the king of Babylon. It was probably a Babylonian princess who became the wife of her son Tudhaliya (see Ch. 12).

After her husband's death, Puduhepa became increasingly active in the judicial sphere, sometimes intervening in legal disputes,[76] and making pronouncements on cases brought to her attention in the vassal states. We learn of a case probably early in Tudhaliya's reign in which she found against a defendant for wilfully damaging a ship and ordered that he pay compensation to the plaintiff, a shipowner in Ugarit:

Thus (speaks) My Sun: Say to Ammistamru: 'When this man from Ugarit came with Sukku for judgement before My Sun, Sukku said: "His boat broke itself against the quay." But the man of Ugarit said: "(No!) Sukku deliberately broke up my boat." My Sun has made the following judgement: "Let the chief man of the boatsmen of Ugarit swear: Sukku

---

[73] KBo IV 10 rev. 5, 8, 9.

[74] *SBo* I, nos. 49–51 = Beran (1967: 42–43 nos. 231–33; 42 nos. 229–30), Boehmer and Güterbock (1987: 82 no. 257). See also Gonnet (1979: 20, 71–3 nos. 182–7, 83 no. 220), and the discussions by Darga (1974: 946–9) and Otten (1975: 24–5). The silver tablet of the Egyptian version of the treaty with Ramesses was impressed with 'The Seal of the Re of the town of Arinna, the Lord of the Land; the Seal of Puduhepa, the Princess of the Land of Hatti, the Daughter of the Land of Kizzuwadna, the [*Priestess*] of [*the town of*] Arinna, the Lady of the Land, the Servant of the Goddess' (trans. Wilson in Pritchard (1969: 201)). The seals of Hattusili and Puduhepa appeared on the obverse and reverse sides of the tablet respectively.

[75] Neve (1992a: 313), identifies fourteen seal impressions from the Nişantepe archive with the name of Puduhepa alone.

[76] Already very early in her marriage to Hattusili Puduhepa appears to have been active in judicial matters, to judge from her appearance with her husband in the preamble to KUB XXI 17 (*CTH* 86.1) I 1–2, which contains the so-called 'case against Arma-Tarhunda'. Cf. Imparati (1995: 146 n. 21).

must reimburse (the aggrieved party) for his boat and the goods therein."'   (RS 17.133 (*CTH* 95) = *PRU* IV 118–19)

The document is in the form of a letter written to Ammistamru II, king of Ugarit, informing him of the Hittite queen's decision. It was signed with her personal seal. The use of the royal title 'My Sun' indicates that she was acting on behalf of the Hittite king, and clearly with full authority to make such decisions on his behalf. It may be that such authority had originally been delegated to her by Hattusili, and then continued after his death during at least the early part of her son Tudhaliya's reign.[77]

Puduhepa had been a priestess before her marriage to Hattusili, and for the rest of her life she seems to have devoted much time and attention to the religious affairs of the kingdom. Her role as chief priestess of the Hittite realm is visually illustrated by the well-known relief sculpture on the rock face at Firaktin, approximately 100 kilometres south of Kayseri. Here she is engaged in a religious ceremony conducted jointly with her husband. He is making a libation to a god, she to the goddess Hepat.[78] Her participation in the ceremony as her husband's equal is one further example of the close working partnership between king and queen which characterized the reign of Hattusili.

In her capacity as chief priestess, Puduhepa seems to have ordered a comprehensive collection and organization of religious texts, and to have made extensive revisions to religious ceremonies and rituals. She may also have organized a major rationalization of the vast array of deities who had accumulated in the Hittite pantheon, establishing a number of syncretisms between Hittite and Hurrian deities in particular. The most important of these syncretisms is reflected in the opening lines of her prayer to the Sun Goddess of Arinna:

To the Sun Goddess of Arinna, My Lady, the Mistress of the Hatti lands, the Queen of heaven and earth. Sun Goddess of Arinna, you are Queen of all countries! In the Land of Hatti you bear the name of the Sun Goddess of Arinna; but in the land which you made the cedar land you bear the

---

[77] For the queen's involvement in other matters which were judicial in nature, see Darga (1974: 944–5).

[78] See Bittel (1976*a*: 187–8) and Abb. 198 (176–7). For the hieroglyphic script on the monument, see Güterbock (1978).

name Hepat.   (KUB xxi 27 (*CTH* 384) i 1–6, trans. Goetze in Pritchard (1969: 393))

Amongst all the prayers uttered by Puduhepa, the most poignant were those in which she sought divine protection for the life and health of her husband.[79] Ill health seems to have dogged Hattusili in his later years as well as in his youth. Puduhepa begged that his health be restored, that he be granted long life:

Hattusili, that servant of yours who is ill . . . If Hattusili is accursed, and if Hattusili, my husband, has become hateful in the eyes of you, the gods; or if anyone of the gods above or below has taken offence at him; or if anyone has made an offering to the gods to bring evil upon Hattusili—accept not these evil words, O Goddess, My Lady! Let evil not touch Hattusili, your servant! O gods, prefer not our adversaries, our enviers, (and our) [   ] to us! If you, Goddess, My Lady, will grant him life and relay to the gods, your peers, the good (word), and if you will tread underfoot the evil words and shut them out—O Lelwani, My Lady, may the life of Hattusili, your servant, and of Puduhepa, your handmaid, come forth from your mouth in the presence of the gods! To Hattusili, your servant, and to Puduhepa, your handmaid, give long years, months, and days!   (KUB xxi 27 (+) (*CTH* 384) iii 14'–35', adapted from trans. by Goetze in Pritchard (1969: 393–4))

Along with her prayers, the queen made numerous heartfelt appeals to Lelwani, goddess of the Underworld, with offers of votive gifts if her appeals were answered and the king were restored to health and granted long life.[80] Her requests were often quite specific. One of them sought that the king be cured of an inflammation of his feet:

A dream of the queen: Somebody said again and again to me in a dream: 'Make a vow to the goddess Ningal as follows: "If that (disease) Fire-of-the-Feet of His Majesty will pass quickly, I shall make for Ningal ten (?) *talla* (oil flasks) of gold set with lapis lazuli!"'   (KUB xv 3 (*CTH* 584.2) i 17 ff. trans. Güterbock in Oppenheim (1956: 255))

Other votive prayers refer to an eye-illness from which the king suffered.[81] He was already subject to this affliction at the time of his

---

[79] For Hittite vows and dream texts, see *CTH* 583–90. Add the texts published by Klengel in KUB lvi (1986).

[80] *CTH* 585. For the texts, see Otten and Soucek (1965).

[81] e.g. KUB lvi 13 obv. 11. Klengel in his summary of this prayer (KUB lvi, Inhaltsübersicht) compares KBo viii 61, KUB xxii 61, KUB xlviii 119, KUB xlviii 121.

treaty with Ramesses. Among the gifts which the pharaoh sent him to mark the signing of the treaty were some medicines to help alleviate it.[82] In all Puduhepa's votive prayers, we see expressions of 'the love and loyalty of this queen, who always lived under the threat of losing her beloved husband.'[83]

The death of Hattusili brought to an end one of the closest and one of the most enduring and constructive royal partnerships of the ancient world. For this much credit must be due to Puduhepa. In contrast to certain earlier Hittite queens who had played a prominent role in the kingdom, it is worth noting that history has left us with a very positive impression of Puduhepa. Our records give little indication that she used her substantial powers for purely personal ends, or that she ever provided her husband with less than total dedicated support. This must have been of inestimable value to the king in helping him to deal with the crises over the royal succession, and in establishing the credibility of his regime in the eyes of foreign rulers.

In forming such a picture of Puduhepa, we are of course dependent on the chance survival of documents—which in this case present a very favourable picture of the former priestess of Lawazantiya. Whether or not there was a more sinister dimension to her role as the Hittite queen, as in the case of Suppiluliuma's wife Tawananna, is a matter on which we can only speculate. There is no doubt that she was an extremely powerful figure in the royal court, who was almost certainly influential in many of the decisions which her husband made. Indeed as illness and old age took their toll upon the king in his final years, Puduhepa may well have increasingly become 'the power behind the throne'. In such a role, she could not have failed to make enemies.

She continued to play an active role in Hittite affairs for many years after her husband's death, and may have still been alive as late as the reign of the Ugaritic king Niqmaddu III at the end of the thirteenth century.[84] If so, she must have lived at least to the age of

---

[82] KUB III 51 (*CTH* 170) (= *ÄHK* I no. 2, 16–19), rev.(?) 2'–3', 10'. The letter was sent to Hattusili before the silver tablet on which the treaty was inscribed had been produced; see Edel, *ÄHK* II, 27.

[83] Darga (1974: 953–4).

[84] This conclusion is based on a letter from the Ugarit archives, RS 17.434, assumed to have been written by Puduhepa to Niqmaddu III (thus Nougayrol, *PRU* IV 199; cf. van den Hout (1995b: 1112)). But see Klengel (1969: 397), and the reservations expressed by Otten (1975: 31). If this conclusion is correct,

90, even if she was only 15 when she married Hattusili not long after the battle of Kadesh.

Campaigns in Anatolia

Hattusili's peace accord with Ramesses made a welcome and significant contribution, at least in the short term, to political stability within Syria. In effect it confirmed existing territorial boundaries between Hatti and Egypt, and the authority of each over the respective local kingdoms within these boundaries. In the past much of the volatility of the region had been due to vassals who had sought to increase their own territory and status at the expense of their neighbours by exploiting the rivalry between the two major powers for overall supremacy. The treaty virtually ruled out opportunities for the local vassals to attempt to play off one power against the other. Further, the new alliance between Hatti and Egypt might also help keep the Assyrians out of Syria.

There were other reasons why a permanent settlement of affairs in Syria needed to be finalized as quickly as possible. As Hattusili negotiated his way through the complexities of his treaty with Ramesses, he became aware of further serious unrest in his Anatolian territories. In the north the Kaskans continued to menace the Hittite frontiers, and regular campaigns were needed to keep them at bay.[85] But it was in the west and the south that the most serious problems were emerging. We learn from the small surviving fragments of the king's *Annals*[86] of a major uprising in the Lukka lands, which extended through the region of the later Lycaonia,[87] Pisidia, and Lycia. Rebel groups from these lands had apparently carried out extensive conquests in neighbouring Hittite subject territories in southern Anatolia.[88]

then Puduhepa was still alive, and politically active, down to the end of the 13th cent.

[85] Hattusili's son Tudhaliya seems to have played an important role in these, while holding the office of GAL MEŠEDI, and possibly from a very early age. See Ch. 12.

[86] KUB xxi 6 + 6a (*CTH* 82).

[87] Laroche (1976: 17) comments that the name Lycaonia is a Hellenized derivative of Luwian *Lukawani-*, 'inhabitant of Lukka'.

[88] Note Gurney (1992: 218) with reference to the fact that the countries listed in *CTH* 82 are either part of or at least adjacent to the Lukka Lands. Forlanini (1988: 157–9) draws a parallel between the Tawagalawa letter (see below) and *CTH* 82, and identifies Piyamaradu's attack against Lukka, referred to in the Tawagalawa letter, with the invasion referred to in *CTH* 82; cf. Freu (1990: 49).

Further evidence of problems involving the Lukka people is provided by a letter commonly referred to as the Tawagalawa letter, written by Hattusili to a king of Ahhiyawa.[89] The letter refers primarily to the activities of the Hittite renegade Piyamaradu, whom we met in Chapter 9.[90] Piyamaradu had already been harrassing the Hittites' western vassal states in Muwatalli's reign, and was still active in the region, apparently with the support, or at least the connivance, of the king of Ahhiyawa.

The uprising in the Lukka lands was ripe for exploitation. As the Hittites prepared for retaliatory action, a large group of the rebels sought asylum with Tawagalawa, the brother of the Ahhiyawan king,[91] who had apparently come to western Anatolia to receive the fugitives. Piyamaradu had brought them to Tawagalawa, probably to arrange their relocation in Ahhiyawan territory. But loyalties amongst the Lukka people seem to have been divided. For another group of them who had adhered to their Hittite allegiance were forcibly removed from their homeland by Piyamaradu, and now appealed to Hattusili to rescue them.[92]

In response, Hattusili set out for the west in order to reassert Hittite authority over the region occupied by Piyamaradu, and to effect the liberation of his subjects. It was a campaign which he undertook with great reluctance, and even while he was on the march, he attempted to reach a settlement with Piyamaradu. For a time Piyamaradu appeared willing to negotiate. But the negotiations broke down:

Now when I came to Sallapa, he sent a man to meet me (saying) 'Take me into vassalage and send me the *tuḫkanti*[93] and he will conduct me to My Sun!' And I sent him the *tartenu*[94] (saying) 'Go, set him beside you on the

[89] KUB xiv 3 (*CTH* 181), ed. Sommer (1932: 2–194), and trans. in part by Garstang and Gurney (1959: 111–14). Although the author is not identified in the surviving portion of the text, its attribution to Hattusili is virtually certain; see Güterbock (1983a: 135), Heinhold-Krahmer (1983: 95–7), Houwink ten Cate (1983–4: 34), and other references cited by Singer (1983a: 209 n. 18). *Contra* this attribution, see Freu (1990: 22). Further on the text, see Heinhold-Krahmer (1986).

[90] 'Tawagalawa letter' is thus something of a misnomer; see Singer (1983a: 210–13).

[91] On the filiation, see Güterbock (1983a: 136).

[92] Tawag. letter, i 4–5.

[93] As suggested above, the person in question may have been Hattusili's son Nerikkaili.

[94] On the apparent interchangeability of the terms *tuḫkanti* and *tartenu*, see Gurney (1983: 97–8).

chariot and bring him here!' But he—he snubbed the *tartenu* and said 'no'. But is not the *tartenu* the proper representative(?) of the king? He had my hand. But he answered(?) him 'no' and humiliated him before the lands; and moreover he said this: 'Give me a kingdom here on the spot! If not I will not come.' (Tawag. letter, 1 6–15, trans. Garstang and Gurney (1959: 111))

This truculent demand from his former subject could not be tolerated. Hattusili continued his march westwards, determined to give an exemplary demonstration of Hittite force to his subjects and to his enemies, and to put an end once and for all to the activities of Piyamaradu. Word reached him that Iyalanda near the Aegean coast[95] had been occupied by the forces of Piyamaradu. Hopeful that even now Piyamaradu could be intimidated into submission, he sent him an ultimatum. To no avail:

When I reached Waliwanda I wrote to him: 'If you desire my overlordship, see now, when I come to Iyalanda, let me not find any of your men in Iyalanda; and you shall not let anyone go back there, and you shall not trespass in my domain. . . .' But when I came to Iyalanda, the enemy attacked me in three places. (Tawag. letter, 1 16–23, trans. Garstang and Gurney (1959: 111))

Hattusili conquered the land. But not promptly enough to lay hands on Piyamaradu, who fled to the Land of Millawanda (Milawata), still at that time subject to Ahhiyawa. Hattusili had no wish to provoke a conflict with the Ahhiyawan king, and later assured him that he had no designs on Millawandan territory. Nevertheless, more determined than ever to bring Piyamaradu to justice, he entered Millawanda, and demanded that its local ruler Atpa (Piyamaradu's son-in-law) hand the renegade over to him. Again Piyamaradu eluded him, making a hasty departure from Millawanda by ship and presumably seeking refuge in Ahhiyawan territory—off the Anatolian mainland but close enough to it for him to make continual raids on Hittite subject territory once the Hittite forces had left the area.

This much we know from Hattusili's letter, which is in part a letter of complaint to the Ahhiyawan king about his apparent support of Piyamaradu's activities. But the letter was written in a largely conciliatory tone, for Hattusili's main intention was to seek

---

[95] = Classical Alinda? See Garstang and Gurney (1959: 78), Bryce (1974*b*: 398, 402), Freu (1990, 31).

the addressee's co-operation in putting an end to Piyamaradu's activities:

According to this rumour, during the time when he leaves behind his wife, children and household in my Brother's land, your land is affording him protection. But he is continually raiding my land; whenever I have pre-vented him in that, he comes back into your territory. Are you now, my Brother, favourably disposed to this conduct? (If not), now, my Brother, write at least this to him: 'Rise up, go forth into the Land of Hatti. Your lord has settled his account with you! Otherwise come into the Land of Ahhiyawa, and in whatever place I settle you, [you must remain there]. Rise up with your prisoners, your wives and children, and settle down in another place! So long as you are at enmity with the king of Hatti, exercise your hostility from (some) other country! From my country you shall not conduct hostilities!' (Tawag. letter, III 55–IV 5, adapted from trans. by Garstang and Gurney (1959: 113))

With disarming frankness, Hattusili admitted that his expedition to the west had been unsuccessful. He had failed to secure the return of his subjects, and had failed either to capture Piyamaradu, or to put a stop to his constant raids on Hittite territory. But he had no wish to commit his forces to further campaigns in the west, if this could be avoided. These resources were needed elsewhere. His letter should be seen in this light. It has been described as abject, soft-spoken, apologetic, and is certainly written in very restrained and carefully measured terms. But the underlying sense of frustra-tion and humiliation is evident—above all, humiliation at having to appeal for Ahhiyawan assistance where he himself had failed, in the knowledge that Piyamaradu had been operating with Ahhiyawan support. Hattusili could rely on little more than hope that the Ahhiyawan king would not seek to exploit the Hittites' fragile authority in the west by further expanding his own influence in the region.

We do not know the outcome of Hattusili's appeal. The likeli-hood is that it was ignored. And although we hear no more of Piyamaradu, there is no reason to believe that his activities in western Anatolia were in any way curtailed. The need for a firm resolution of the deteriorating situation in the west was but one of the problems which Hattusili left to his son Tudhaliya. Above all, it must have been clear to Hattusili and his successor that so long as the Ahhiyawan king maintained a firm foothold on Anatolian soil, there could never be any lasting security for Hittite subject territories in the region.

Hattusili's Legacy

Hattusili ran the risk of being a king who reigned too long. He was already in his fifties when he seized the throne from Urhi-Tesub, and had then occupied it for at least the next twenty-five years. He was at least in his seventies when he died.[96] In his final years, his ability to perform effectively the responsibilities of kingship must have been seriously limited. There were many problems, some becoming increasingly serious, which required the direct attention of a fit and able monarch. The physical demands of travel, whether on goodwill missions, religious pilgrimages, or military campaigns, must have become increasingly difficult for him to cope with in his later years, particularly if he suffered from chronic ill health. But divisions between the various branches of his own family and the potential these had for erupting into open conflict were amongst his most immediate concerns.

The longer he lived, and the more enfeebled he became, the greater the likelihood that intra-family disputes would throw into disarray his plans for the succession. Challenges could come from several different quarters. There was his brother's son Kurunta. So far he had been loyal. But could he be trusted to remain so if the political situation in Hattusa became increasingly unstable as the king's death approached? There was Urhi-Tesub, apparently still alive[97] and still at large. By now he must also have been a man of advanced years. But the possibility could not be ruled out that he would make a further bid for reclaiming his throne after Hattusili's death. In any case, he had sons[98] who might also seek to restore the

[96] Wilhelm and Boese (1979: 36 n. 65) assume that he lived until at least the 42nd year of Ramesses' reign—i.e. until 1237, which would make him at least 75 on his death, given that he was the youngest child of Mursili's wife Gassulawiya, who died in 1212. However van den Hout (1984: 90), believes that this assumption is not compelling, and comments that the *terminus post quem* for his death remains the 34th year of Ramesses' reign (1245), for he was still alive at least as late as the marriage of his first daughter to Ramesses. Even if he died very shortly after this, he would still almost certainly have lived to his seventies.

[97] This is to be inferred from the oracle text KUB xvi 32 (+) (*CTH* 582) which makes reference to Urhi-Tesub and implies that he was still alive in the final years of Hattusili's reign; see van den Hout (1991: 295–6), Houwink ten Cate (1994: 250). Further on this, see Ch. 12.

[98] Referred to in KUB xvi 32 (+) obv. ii 14'–15', ii 28'–30' (in the latter passage in connection with possible territorial compensation for Urhi-Tesub's sons), and

sovereign line to the descendants of Muwatalli. And what of the sons of Tanuhepa, or their sons? Did they have kingly aspirations? What of Hattusili's older son Nerikkaili? He had, apparently, submitted with good grace to his father's will when he had been removed from the position of *tuḫkanti*. But might not his ambitions have been rekindled as his father's end drew near? Apart from him, Hattusili had other sons by a previous marriage, who in a letter to Ramesses Puduhepa claimed she raised and made into military officers:

When I entered the palace, the princesses that I found inside gave birth under my care, and I raised them (i.e. their children). Those that I found already born, them I raised as well, and I made them army commanders. (KUB xxi 38 (*CTH* 176), obv. 59–62, adapted from trans. by van den Hout (1995*b*: 1110))[99]

The considerable number of potential claimants for the royal succession probably weighed heavily on the mind of Puduhepa. Her pleas to the gods for the health and longevity of her husband may not have been entirely altruistic. On her husband's death, her own position could have become precarious if the succession did not proceed in accordance with his (and probably her) plans. The influence she wielded in the royal court and the kingdom at large had almost certainly made her many enemies within the extended royal family. If any of these succeeded in seizing power, her days as reigning queen might well have been numbered. There were after all precedents for ridding the court of a troublesome, domineering queen.

rev. iii 32–3 (where reference is made to his sons 'choosing his side'). See also van den Hout (1991: 295–6).

[99] Note also the passage from the Mittannamuwa decree, KBo iv 12 (*CTH* 87) rev. 8–9 (Goetze (1925: 44–5)), where Hattusili appears to distinguish two groups of his lineal descendants, those deriving apparently from an earlier union, and those from his union with Puduhepa: 'our sons, our grandson, the son of My Sun, the grandsons of My Sun, the descendants of Puduhepa, the great queen.'

CHAPTER 12

New Enterprises, New Threats: The Reign of Tudhaliya IV (*c*.1237–1209)

The Preparation of Tudhaliya for Kingship

In his early years, the prince Tudhaliya could have had little thought that he would one day become king. His cousin Urhi-Tesub, son of Muwatalli, had succeeded to the throne, with the endorsement and support of his uncle Hattusili, Tudhaliya's father. In the normal course of events the succession would continue in Muwatalli's family line. Even after Hattusili had deposed Urhi-Tesub and seized the throne for himself, Tudhaliya's prospects of following his father upon the throne must still have seemed remote. For his older brother Nerikkaili had been appointed to the office of *tuḫkanti* which carried with it the expectation, if not the certainty, that he would one day be king.

But subsequently Hattusili had deprived Nerikkaili of his post, and appointed Tudhaliya 'for kingship' (LUGAL-*iz-na-ni*).[1] Political considerations, particularly recognition of the close bonds between Tudhaliya and his cousin Kurunta, may have played an important role in prompting the action which Hattusili took. But whatever the role of such considerations, the removal of Nerikkaili from office and the elevation of Tudhaliya was probably not a decision suddenly made. Rather Hattusili had decided upon Tudhaliya as his heir some time before his formal announcement, and was waiting for an appropriate time to make this announcement. It may have been no coincidence that Tudhaliya's early career followed a similar path to that of his father. Hattusili probably planned it that way.

---

[1] Bronze tablet §14, II 44. *Contra* van den Hout (1991: 275–6), who uses this passage in support of his argument for a period of coregency between Hattusili and Tudhaliya, LUGAL-*iznani tittanu-* must be an elliptical expression for appointment to (a position which will be followed by) kingship, i.e. the *tuḫkanti*-ship, the same as LUGAL-*iznani tapariya-* in §13, II 36, and must be translated 'appoint *for* kingship'. I am grateful to Professor Gurney for this comment.

Thus he had assigned his son to the service of his own special patron goddess Istar (of Samuha),[2] just as in his own childhood he had been assigned by his father Mursili to the goddess' service. And he had appointed him priest of the Storm God of Nerik,[3] again a significant appointment in view of his own special associations with the holy city; its restoration had been one of the great achievements of his early career, and here he too had been priest of the god. He also bestowed upon him governorship of the city of Hakpissa, formerly the seat of his own power,[4] and appointed him to the post of GAL *MEŠEDI* (Chief of the Bodyguards).[5] Hattusili too had been GAL *MEŠEDI* early in his career.

It was while holding this post that Tudhaliya campaigned extensively in the Kaska region, thus gaining the battle experience that would help equip him for his eventual role as commander-in-chief of the Hittite forces. Indeed Hattusili credited his son with a military victory in the region, the conquest of Hatenzuwa, which he himself had not been able to achieve.[6] How much credit for this victory was due to Tudhaliya personally is open to question. He may have been no more than 12 years old at the time of the campaign.[7]

The career path which Hattusili had mapped out for Tudhaliya may well indicate that he had been grooming his son for the succession for some years. Indeed, his so-called *Apology* may have been intended as much to justify his choice of successor, and to pave the way for his succession, as to defend his own course of action in

---

[2] *Apol.* §12b, IV 76–8.

[3] KUB xxv 21 (*CTH* 524.1) III 13–16 (ed. Goetze (1951: 24–5), von Schuler (1965: 186–7)), KUB xxxvi 90 (*CTH* 386.1) obv. 15–17 (ed. Haas (1970: 175–9)).

[4] KUB xxxvi 90 obv. 15–17; see Haas (1970: 7, 11, 13–15, 175).

[5] See *Apol.* §12a, IV 41–2, and KUB xix 8//9 (*CTH* 83.1); on the identification of the GAL *MEŠEDI* Tudhaliya in the latter text as Hattusili's son, see Riemschneider (1962: 118–19).

[6] KUB xix 8//9 III 25–31. He may well have had a political motive for highlighting this achievement. His own apparent failure to capture Hatenzuwa may have been due to the fact that he was occupied with military operations elsewhere when it declared its hostility, or to illness. But his primary aim could well have been to promote the image of his son Tudhaliya as a military leader of proven ability; cf. Riemschneider (1962: 120), van den Hout (1991: 298). The text belongs to the reign of Hattusili III (see Riemschneider (1962: 115–21)) and is one of the fragments surviving from a historical review of the reigns of Suppiluliuma I, Arnuwanda II, Mursili II, Muwatalli II, Urhi-Tesub, and Hattusili III (*CTH* 83).

[7] If line 27 of the text has been correctly interpreted; see Riemschneider's discussion (1962: 118–19).

seizing the throne.[8] Almost certainly the *Apology* was composed in the later years of his reign, after the conclusion of his treaty with Ramesses[9] and in the period when the question of the succession was assuming increasing importance.

Perhaps Hattusili went further than merely proclaiming Tudhaliya his successor and actually shared the throne with him. In view of his age and state of health in the later years of his reign, and particularly in view of the potential for conflict among a number of possible claimants upon the throne after his death, this might have been an extremely wise move. Indeed several scholars have concluded that Tudhaliya was for a time his father's co-regent. The case for a co-regency has rested largely on a seal impression from Ugarit which features the name Tudhaliya in the inner ring and, allegedly, Hattusili in the outer.[10] This would clearly indicate joint kingship. However it has now been demonstrated that the name Tudhaliya should be read in both the inner and the outer rings.[11] This leaves only one dubious piece of evidence for a co-regency between Tudhaliya and his father—an oracle text which *may* indicate that Tudhaliya bore the title 'My Sun' in the lifetime of his father.[12]

A Wife for the Heir to the Throne

In order to help secure the succession in Hattusili's family line, the future king needed a wife. Strangely, we can find no explicit

---

[8] Cf. Imparati (1995: 153–4).

[9] This is probably indirectly alluded to in the *Apology* §12b, IV 58–9. See Otten (1981: 27 n. on lines 58f.), supported by Imparati (1995: 154 n. 59).

[10] The impression appears on the tablet RSL 2 from Ras Shamra (*PRU* VI, 129, no. 179). See Mora (1987) and cf. van den Hout (1991: 278).

[11] See Otten (1993*b*: 107–10) who suggests that the name in the outer ring refers to Tudhaliya's earlier namesake at the beginning of the New Kingdom (pp. 109–10).

[12] KUB XVI 32 (*CTH* 582) II 14′–22′: 'As it was not established (with oracles) for My Sun to make offering according to the *mantalli* ritual in favour of the sons of Arma-Tarhunda, as I did not harm to them; (but) the man who did do harm to them, as he (is) still living, as his soul (is) not placated, then (it is) through his (fault) (that) it was not established to offer the *mantalli* ritual' (adapted from trans. by Archi (1971: 212)). For the attribution of this text to Tudhaliya, see Ünal (1974: I. 107, 172), and for the conclusion that it dates to the period before Hattusili's death, see van den Hout (1991: 294–7); cf. Houwink ten Cate (1994: 249). In view of Hattusili's earlier conflicts with Arma-Tarhunda and the punishment he inflicted on his family, the assumption is that Hattusili was the man still living who 'did harm to them'; therefore 'My Sun' must be Tudhaliya. But if, as is quite possible, the man in question was someone else, then the king referred to here may well be Hattusili and not Tudhaliya.

reference to a wife of Tudhaliya, either in texts or in seal impressions. Yet it would be remarkable if a suitable marriage had not been arranged for him at the earliest feasible opportunity, in view of the precarious nature of the succession and all the other steps apparently taken to prepare him for kingship. In fact Tudhaliya probably had married some years before he succeeded to the throne. His wife may be referred to in the draft of one of the letters written by Puduhepa to Ramesses regarding his forthcoming marriage to her daughter.[13] In the course of this long letter the Hittite queen refers to two other Hittite marriages with foreigners: 'The daughter of Babylon and the daughter of Amurru whom I, the Queen, took— were they not indeed a source of praise for me before the people of Hatti?[14] This I did, taking as daughter-in-law a foreigner, the daughter of a Great King' (KUB xxi 38 (*CTH* 176) obv. 47–9).

The 'daughter of Amurru' was married to Tudhaliya's older brother Nerikkaili. The 'daughter of Babylon' probably became the wife of Tudhaliya.[15] Puduhepa seems to have taken the initiative in arranging these marriages.[16] Such unions were of course a regular feature of Bronze Age international relationships. Indeed the Hittite and Babylonian royal houses were now linked by two marriages, since Hattusili had provided one of his daughters as a wife for the king of Babylon.[17] A similar double marriage had already taken place between the Hittite and Amurrite royal families in Hattusili III's reign.

Ramesses reacted with some contempt to the news of the marriage links with Babylon, on the grounds that the occupant of the throne of Babylon no longer deserved recognition as a 'Great King'. To this Puduhepa made a curt response: 'If you say "the king of Babylon is not a Great King", then you do not know the status

[13] KUB xxi 38 (*CTH* 176), ed. Helck (1963: 87–93).
[14] This statement is treated as a rhetorical question, following Helck (1963: 91), and Beckman (1983*b*: 109), *contra* Singer (1991*c*: 331), whose translation 'they were not indeed a source of praise for me' would give precisely the opposite sense. In the light of the overall context of this passage, a rhetorical question seems more convincing.
[15] See Beckman (1983*b*: 109), Singer (1991*c*: 330–2).
[16] That Puduhepa played an active role in arranging royal marriages is clear from the bronze tablet §19, ii 84–6, where it appears that the Hittite queen assumed the responsibility of finding a wife for Kurunta. However Tudhaliya seems to have given his cousin the option of choosing his own wife, regardless of any choice made by Puduhepa (bronze tablet §19, ii 88–9). This may well have caused some tension between Puduhepa and her son early in his reign.
[17] KUB xxi 38 obv. 55.

of Babylon' (KUB xxi 38 obv. 55–6, trans. Singer (1991c: 331)).
Since her letter was written some time before 1246, i.e. before
the marriage of the first Hittite princess to Ramesses, then the
Babylonian king who had aroused Ramesses' contempt was
Kudur-Enlil, who occupied the Babylonian throne from *c.*1254–
1246 following the reign of Kadasman-Enlil II.[18] If the Babylonian
princess became Tudhaliya's wife, then this must have been the
period in which his marriage took place—some years before he
acceded to his father's throne.

In spite of Ramesses' dismissive statement about the Babylonian
king, the Hittite court still recognized him as the ruler of a Great
Kingdom, and continued to do so down to the time when the
kingdom finally succumbed to the forces of the Assyrian king
Tukulti-Ninurta.[19] Moreover there were two important incentives
for a Hittite–Babylonian marriage alliance. In the first place the
alliance further strengthened the ties between Hatti and Babylon,
which Hattusili no doubt saw as very important in the face of
the threats posed to both powers by a sword-brandishing Assyria.
In the second place, it must also have helped promote the personal status of Tudhaliya above that of his brother Nerikkaili.
Nerikkaili's wife was merely the daughter of a vassal king. In this
respect the influence of Puduhepa may well have been at work,
particularly since she claimed to have taken the initiative in arranging the marriage.

She may later have had cause to regret this initiative. A lengthy
oracle text which enquires into the reasons for the illness of a
Hittite king indicates factions within the royal court involving the
women of the court who had divided themselves into two groups—
supporters and opponents of the Great Queen.[20] The text is almost
certainly to be assigned to the reign of Tudhaliya.[21] The queen in
question must be Puduhepa, who in the manner of the Tawananna
continued to exercise her official powers after Hattusili's death,

---

[18] See Brinkman (1980–3). The king could not have been Kadasman-Enlil who
was apparently only a minor when he came to the throne and reigned only for a
short time (1263–1255 on the most common reckoning); see Brinkman (1976: 31;
1976–80: 285).

[19] As indicated in Tudhaliya's treaty with Sausgamuwa of Amurru, where the
king of Babylon is listed amongst the kings of equal rank with the king of Hatti (see
below).

[20] KUB xxii 70 (*CTH* 566), ed. Ünal (1978).

[21] See Ünal (1978: 22, 52), Singer (1991c: 330).

both in foreign and domestic spheres. She was still a formidable figure in the royal court, seeking to maintain her role as the chief power-broker within court circles. It was this no doubt that led to the hostility and intrigues against her—by those who had fallen foul of her.

The leader of the anti-Puduhepa faction was apparently the DUMU.SAL GAL, the Great Princess, very likely Tudhaliya's wife.[22] An attempt seems to have been made by Puduhepa to discredit her by bringing charges against her supporters Ammattalla and Pattiya; the latter, who had apparently enjoyed a very privileged position in the royal court, may have been the king's mother-in-law.[23] Caught between the two factions, with his powerful, still very active mother on the one side, and his wife and her supporters on the other, Tudhaliya no doubt felt that he had been placed in a well-nigh impossible situation! The immediate outcome of this royal wrangle is unknown. It has been suggested that Puduhepa was expelled from the palace.[24] But in the long term, she appears to have triumphed over her enemies and even strengthened her position. Indeed she continued to be a powerful force in both the foreign and domestic affairs of the kingdom for much if not all of her son's reign.

Other Problems Confronting the New King

Tudhaliya inherited from his father a formidable list of problems and potential crises. To begin with, many vassal rulers appear to have held back from pledging their allegiance to the new regime. They adopted a 'wait and see' attitude.[25] In the west, Hittite control over the vassal states was becoming ever more shaky, particularly with the consolidation of Ahhiyawan influence in the region. The ability of men like Piyamaradu to raid Hittite territory and escape with impunity, even when a Hittite army had been dispatched to the region under the personal command of the Hittite king, merely served to underline the Hittites' inability to guarantee the security of their western territories. It was a problem which Tudhaliya needed to address, as a matter of urgency. To the south-east,

---

[22] Thus Singer (1991c: 332).   [23] Suggested by Ünal (1978: 52).
[24] Thus Singer (1991c: 332).
[25] If §15, ii 53–4 of the bronze tablet can be so interpreted. Tudhaliya gives the impression that Kurunta's immediate and unqualified support was in sharp contrast with that of other regional kings.

peaceful relations with Egypt had provided a strong measure of stability within the Syrian region. Even so, Tudhaliya did not entirely dismiss the possibility of further conflict with the pharaoh.[26] But Assyria was cause for the greatest concern. The tensions in the south-eastern frontier region caused by an increasingly ambitious and aggressive Assyrian kingdom, were soon to take a dangerous new turn.

Closer to home, the people of Lalanda in the Lower Land, 'notorious troublemakers',[27] broke out in rebellion. Tuhaliya wrote to his mother Puduhepa about the situation, and also expressed deep concern that the rebellion might spread throughout the Lower Land.[28] This was an ominous symptom of the perceived weakening of Hittite authority in regions where there had been relative peace and stability for many years.

In Hattusa itself, Tudhaliya had fears for his own safety. He was very conscious of the threats posed by the wide array of family members who might stake their own claims to his throne, as indicated in his instructions to his dignitaries and high officials:

My Sun has many brothers and there are many sons of his father. The Land of Hatti is full of the royal line: in Hatti the descendants of Suppiluliuma, the descendants of Mursili, the descendants of Muwatalli, the descendants of Hattusili are numerous. With regard to kingship, you must acknowledge no other person (but me, Tudhaliya), and protect only the grandson and great grandson and descendants of Tudhaliya. And if at any time(?) evil is done to My Sun—(for) My Sun has many brothers—and someone approaches another person and speaks thus: 'Whomever we select for ourselves need not even be a son of our lord!'—these words must not be (permitted). With regard to kingship, you must protect only My Sun and the descendants of My Sun. You must approach no other person.   (KUB xxvi 1 (*CTH* 255.2) 1 9–29)[29]

These are the words of a king who recognized that his throne was at constant risk, particularly from possible rival claimants within his own family.[30]

---

[26] This is evident from the treaty which he concluded with his vassal Sausgamuwa, in which he still saw Egypt as one of the potential threats to Hittite territory in Syria (KUB xxiii 1 (*CTH* 105) rev. iv 4–7).

[27] Thus Houwink ten Cate (1966: 30).

[28] KUB xix 23 (*CTH* 192).

[29] For an edition of the full text of this document, see von Schuler (1957: 8–21). Cf. KUB xxvi 12 (*CTH* 255.1) ii 2–11; von Schuler (1957: 24).

[30] In this context Imparati (1992: 319) also draws attention to the fragment KUB xxvi 18 (*CTH* 275) ii 9'–10', 16', which mentions Nerikkaili, Huzziya (the latter

In another text, a treaty or protocol in which the king calls upon the unconditional loyalty and support of an (unnamed) ally, the risks he faced of being opposed or abandoned by his subjects are even more dramatically highlighted:

Likewise, if the king is preoccupied because not a single palace official is left, and nobody is left to yoke the horses (to the king's chariot), and he has not even one house where to enter: in such a situation you must show even more support for your king. . . . Likewise if the situation becomes so serious for the king that the chariot-driver jumps down from the chariot, that the chamber-valet flees from the chamber, that not even a dog is left, and I do not even find an arrow to shoot against the enemy, your support for your king must be all the greater. (KBo IV 14 (*CTH* 123) III 42–9, adapted from trans. by Liverani (1990: 191))[31]

Some years later, in the treaty which he drew up with Sausgamuwa, son and successor of Bentesina on the throne of Amurru, Tudhaliya still showed an obsessive although probably realistic concern about his personal security and the security of his throne:

Because however, I made you, Sausgamuwa, my brother-in-law, so protect My Sun in his kingship. Thereafter protect also the sons and grandsons and descendants of My Sun in the kingship. Those however who are legitimate brothers of My Sun and those who are sons of *ešertu* wives of the father of My Sun, all those who are of royal descent including those who are second-rank sons—desire none of them for kingship. Do not act like Masturi! (Tudhaliya: Sausgamuwa Treaty, II 8–15)

This last command reflects a deep and probably long-held concern by Tudhaliya:

This Masturi, who was king of the Seha River Land—Muwatalli took him, made him his brother-in-law by giving him his sister in marriage, and installed him as king in the Seha River Land. But when Muwatalli became a god, his son Urhi-Tesub became king. But my father (i.e. Hattusili) took the kingship away from Urhi-Tesub. Masturi, however, joined the plot, and he whom Muwatalli had made his brother-in-law, did not protect the latter's son Urhi-Tesub but rather sided with my father (saying) 'Should

probably also a brother of Tudhaliya), and Kurunta, and indicates Tudhaliya's concern to protect the succession against the possible pretensions of his brothers or members of the family of Muwatalli.

[31] For the attribution of this text to Tudhaliya (*contra* Liverani, who assigns it to Tudhaliya's successor Arnuwanda III), see Singer (1985a: 109–19), supported by Hawkins (1990: 313).

I protect a bastard?' Would you ever act like Masturi? (Tudhaliya: Sausgamuwa Treaty, II 16–30, trans. Güterbock (1983b: 29–30))

Comment has been made about this surprising display of frankness from Tudhaliya.[32] Indeed his criticism of Masturi may seem somewhat hypocritical. After all, Hattusili took considerable pains to justify his seizure of power from Urhi-Tesub and the establishment of the succession in his own family line. Masturi had apparently provided him with welcome support for his action, by refusing support for the 'bastard' Urhi-Tesub. Now, apparently, he was being reproached for this.

But the legitimacy of Urhi-Tesub's claim to the throne was not an issue in the conflict between him and his uncle. Hattusili had never raised any doubt about his nephew's eligibility to succeed his father, and had openly endorsed and supported his accession. The justification for his removal from the throne was the alleged injustice of his actions, particularly towards his uncle, and more generally his alleged unfitness to retain royal power. Thus the reason stated by Masturi for his opposition to Urhi-Tesub was quite spurious. What was most alarming was that a vassal ruler should have seen fit to decide for himself whether or not he would support a particular successor to the Hittite throne. This was in breach of the standard treaty regulations whereby a vassal ruler was bound to give allegiance to his overlord's duly appointed heir. Urhi-Tesub clearly fulfilled that criterion.[33]

Tudhaliya sought to make it absolutely clear to Sausgamuwa that he was bound by the terms of the treaty to maintain allegiance to the king and his descendants, and to them only. Within the context of his concern about so many potential claimants upon the throne from within his own family, his admonition to Sausgamuwa had particular significance.[34]

Favours Bestowed on Family Members

Tudhaliya did take a number of positive steps in an effort to ensure unity within his extended family and to gain support from its

[32] Thus Güterbock (1983b: 30).

[33] In spite of Tudhaliya's criticism of Masturi's conduct, the latter seems to have held a high place in the king's regard, to judge from his position immediately next to the viceroy of Carchemish in the list of witnesses in the bronze tablet (§27, IV 31–2).

[34] Cf. Imparati's treatment of this passage (1992: 308–9).

disaffected members. The reinstatement of his brother Nerikkaili as *tuḫkanti* may have been one of these steps. There are indications that he saw his brother as a threat to his position,[35] and perhaps tried to counter this by continuing to involve Nerikkaili at a high level in the affairs of the kingdom. Favours were also bestowed on other branches of the royal family. Thus a decree which Tudhaliya issued probably early in his reign in association with his mother Puduhepa was designed to ensure that the descendants of Sahurunuwa, son of Sarri-Kusuh and his successor as viceroy at Carchemish, received fair and adequate land apportionments from the viceroy's substantial estate.[36] And even before his accession, Tudhaliya apparently sought to make his peace with the descendants of Muwatalli, sons of Urhi-Tesub. In an oracle enquiry text dating to this period Tudhaliya considered the question of territorial compensation for Urhi-Tesub's sons.[37]

Such actions were no doubt intended as goodwill gestures designed to win extended family support for the new king, or at least acceptance of his kingship. But Tudhaliya probably relied most on Kurunta as his greatest source of support. This second son of Muwatalli had been one the few members of his family who had already declared his unconditional loyalty to him. But just to make sure of his loyalty, Tudhaliya must have lost no time in concluding his treaty with him after his accession, and bestowing further concessions and favours upon him. These went sigificantly beyond the concessions already made in earlier treaties concluded by his father. Additional territories not included in earlier agreements were given to Kurunta.[38] He was granted freedom of choice in the matter of his successor in Tarhuntassa.[39] The taxes and corvées imposed upon his kingdom were further reduced.[40] Most importantly, Tudhaliya formally acknowledged his status as a king equivalent to the Syrian viceroys and second only to the Great King in Hattusa.[41]

---

[35] Cf. Imparati (1995: 152 n. 53).

[36] KUB xxvi 43 (+) (*CTH* 225), ed. Imparati (1974). Cf. Darga (1974: 944–5), Klengel (1991: 233).

[37] KUB xvi 32 (*CTH* 582), ed. Ünal (1974: ii. 104–11, obv. ii 29'). Cf. Houwink ten Cate, 1994, 249.

[38] Bronze tablet §§4, 6, 9, 16.

[39] Bronze tablet §19.

[40] Bronze tablet §§12, 22, 24. See further on this Houwink ten Cate (1992a: 241–2).

[41] Bronze tablet §18.

It was thus with great concern that Tudhaliya received news that his cousin had suddenly been stricken with illness, which was sufficiently serious and prolonged to warrant an urgent request for Egyptian medical expertise. He received the following advice from the pharaoh:

See, I have now dispatched the scribe and doctor Pareamahu. He has been sent to prepare medicines for Kurunta, the king of the Land of Tarhuntassa, and he will allocate all, all medicines as you have written. As soon as he comes to you, place Kurunta, the king of the Land of Tarhuntassa, in his charge so that he may prepare medicines for him. And dispatch these two doctors, who are there with Kurunta and let them go to Egypt. As soon as the scribe and doctor Pareamahu reaches him, on that day these two doctors must adjust their activity. See, I have understood what you have said. By this time the scribe and doctor Pareamahu is on his way, and he is to share all, all (types of) medicines as you have written. (KUB iii 67 (*CTH* 163.3) obv. 12' rev. 1–12)[42]

Kurunta obviously recovered, thanks to Egyptian medical science. Tudhaliya may subsequently have had cause to regret the skills of the Egyptian doctors! But in the mean time, after taking what steps he could to consolidate his hold upon the throne, the king had pressing matters to attend to in other parts of his kingdom.

Vale *Masturi*

In the west, Tudhaliya faced a rapidly deteriorating situation. His father's campaign recorded in the Tawagalawa letter had almost certainly proved an embarrassing failure. Indeed it probably strengthened the hands of those who had already seriously undermined Hittite influence in the region and were now ready to exploit any opportunity for destabilizing it further. The Lukka people again figured prominently. From a hieroglyphic inscription found in 1971 at Yalburt to the north-west of Konya, we learn of military operations conducted by Tudhaliya against the Lukka Lands and

---

[42] This is one of two parallel letters referring to Kurunta's illness; the other is KUB iii 66 (*CTH* 164.2). See Edel (1976: 46–50, 82–91), van den Hout (1984: 90; 1995*a*: 91–4 with n. 113). On the dating of this correspondence to the period between the 42nd and 56th year of Ramesses' reign (i.e. 1237–1223), see Edel (1976: 20, 29–30).

Wiyanawanda.[43] Lukka also figures in another text of Tudhaliya's reign as enemy territory along with the country of Azzi and the Kaska lands.[44]

There can be little doubt that one of the key factors in the problems faced by the Hittites in the west was Ahhiyawa. Hattusili had appealed to the Ahhiyawan king for his cooperation in maintaining peace and stability in western Anatolia. Whatever his response, it is most unlikely that it led to any reduction in Ahhiyawan enterprise in the region. On the contrary, in Tudhaliya's reign Ahhiyawa continued to support insurrectionist activity in the Hittites' western states. This emerges from a text which refers to offences committed against the regime in Hattusa by the Seha River Land:

Thus speaks Tabarna Tudhaliya(?), the Great King: 'The Seha River Land transgressed again for a second time(?). They said(?): "In the past(?) the great(?)-grandfather of My Sun did not conquer us by force of arms; and when the grandfather of My Sun conquered the countries of Arzawa, he did not conquer us by force of arms. He would have conquered us, but we erased(??) for him the transgression." Thereafter Tarhunaradu waged war and relied on the king of Ahhiyawa. And he took refuge on Eagle Peak (i.e. Mt. Harana). But I, the Great King, set out [and   ] and raided Eagle Peak. I brought home 500 (teams of) horse and . . . troops to the Land of Hatti(?), along with Tarhunaradu together with his wives, his children, his possessions(? etc.) I transported [to   ] and led him to Arinna, the city of the Sun Goddess. Ever since the days of(?) Labarna[45] no Great King went to the country. I made [personal name], a descendant of Muwawalwi, king in the Seha River Land and enjoined him to deliver *xxx* teams of horse and *xxx* troops.   (KUB XXII 13 (*CTH* 211.4), adapted from trans. by Güterbock (1992: 242))[46]

---

[43] The inscription, formerly known as the Ilgin inscription, was published by Özgüç (1988: pls. 85–95), in the form of photographs of the 18 blocks discovered; see also Özgüç (1988: xxv–xxvii) for a description of the site ('a rectangular stone basin . . . lined with walls on all four sides. The walls on three sides have Hittite Hieroglyphic inscriptions on large limestone blocks') and excavations, and 172–4 for plans of the site. Wiyanawanda lay in the border zone of the kingdom of Mira-Kuwaliya; see Bryce (1974a: 105–6). Further on the inscription, see Masson (1979), Hawkins (1992; 1995c: 66–85).
[44] KUB XXVI 12 (+) (*CTH* 255.1) II 15'.
[45] The first Labarna? Cf. Güterbock (1992: 242).
[46] In the past this text has been variously assigned to the reigns of Muwatalli, Hattusili, or Tudhaliya. It can now be confidently assigned to the last of these, since

The text begins by referring to Manapa-Tarhunda's transgressions against Tudhaliya's grandfather Mursili II in the first years of his reign. As we have seen, Mursili was on the point of taking punitive action when Manapa-Tarhunda made an abject plea for mercy, which Mursili finally accepted. Subsequently, he had provoked the wrath of Mursili's successor Muwatalli, who had replaced him on the vassal throne with his son Masturi. Henceforth the Seha River Land appears not to have caused any serious concern to its Hittite overlords until the reign of Tudhaliya.

But some time after Tudhaliya's treaty with Kurunta there was a fresh outbreak of rebellion in the Seha River Land. It was led by a man called Tarhunaradu who may have unseated Masturi, or seized power in the vassal kingdom after his death. Masturi was still alive at the time of Tudhaliya's accession, since he was one of the signatories of the treaty with Kurunta. But by then he was an old man. He had been appointed to the vassal throne of the Seha River Land some forty years earlier by Muwatalli, and was probably already a man of mature years at the time of his appointment.[47] He was the husband of Hattusili's sister Massanauzzi. We recall that the couple had been unable to produce an heir for the vassal throne. Understandably this had caused much concern in Hattusa, for the Seha River Land was one of the most important, and hitherto one of the most stable kingdoms in the west. Its stability might be seriously endangered if there were no suitable successor to Masturi.

The Hittites' worst fears were realized. Masturi's reign ended with a rebellion, and the vassal throne was seized by the upstart Tarhunaradu. Otherwise unknown to us, Tarhunaradu may have had no direct family connections with the previous rulers. What he did have, however, was the backing and perhaps the direct assistance of the king of Ahhiyawa.[48] With this he led the vassal kingdom

the events to which it refers took place after the reign of Masturi in the Seha River Land, and we know from the bronze tablet that Masturi was still on the vassal throne when Tudhaliya drew up his treaty with Kurunta (bronze tablet §27, IV 32). Cf. Güterbock (1992: 235).

[47] To judge from the fact that his father had occupied the vassal throne for thirty years or more when he was finally removed from it. His advanced age at this time suggests that his son was no youngster when he took his place.

[48] On the basis of Güterbock's revised interpretation of the words referring to Ahhiyawa in the passage translated above, dealing with the 'offences' of the Seha River Land. See also Güterbock (1983a: 138), Bryce (1989a: 303).

in rebellion against Hatti. Tudhaliya lost no time in responding. If he was to maintain any authority at all in the west, retention of the Seha River Land was vital. The rebellion was crushed, and Tarhunaradu and his family were captured and transported to Hatti, to the city of the Sun Goddess of Arinna, along with many prisoners and 500 teams of horse. Tudhaliya was also quick to restore the vassal throne to the family of the previous rulers, by placing upon it a 'descendant of Muwawalwi' who was the father of Manapa-Tarhunda.[49]

His success in dealing with the rebellion in the Seha River Land no doubt gave a significant boost to Hittite authority in the west. But the political situation in the western vassal states would remain volatile while Ahhiyawa maintained an active presence and interest in the region. It was clear that in spite of Hattusili's appeals, the Ahhiyawan king was still giving support, and probably active encouragement, to rebels and dissidents who set themselves in opposition to the regime in Hattusa. And Milawata continued to serve as the base from which this support was being provided. This was a problem which now had to be resolved once and for all. Tudhaliya set himself the task of doing it.

The 'Milawata Letter'

One of our important sources of information on political developments in western Anatolia during Tudhaliya's reign is a document commonly called the Milawata letter. Originally only the left-hand side of the tablet on which it was inscribed had come to light[50]— enough to tell us that in its complete form it contained important historical information, but too little to be of use for the purpose of detailed historical analysis. Then in 1981 Dr Harry Hoffner of the Oriental Institute, University of Chicago, discovered that a fragment in the Hittite tablet collection in Berlin fitted precisely along one of the broken edges of the document.[51]

Once the join was made, it was possible to start correlating the incomplete scraps of information, and to provide a context for the

---

[49] The new ruler (whose name is lost in the break) is called 'offspring of Mu[   ]'. Güterbock (1992: 242) notes that Sommer restored this name as Mu[-wa-UR.MAH], the name of the father of Manapa-Tarhunda (*AM* 68–9), which can now be read as Muwa-walwi.

[50] KUB XIX 55 (*CTH* 182), trans. Garstang and Gurney (1959: 114–15).

[51] KUB XLVIII 90. See Hoffner (1982).

personal and place names referred to in the letter. As a result of these correlations, the combined fragments have given us valuable information about the history of western Anatolia towards the end of the Late Bronze Age. We now have the name of a hitherto unknown king of the region, and information about a new administrative arrangement in western Anatolia in the last decades of the Hittite kingdom—an arrangement for which we have no precedent in Hittite history.[52]

Neither the author of the letter nor the addressee is identified in the surviving portions of the text. While there is little doubt that the author was Tudhaliya,[53] we have no clear idea who the recipient of his letter was. He may have been the son of Atpa, the Ahhiyawan puppet ruler in Milawata during Hattusili's reign and the son-in-law of Piyamaradu.[54] But there are other possibilities.[55]

Of particular interest is the information which the text-join provides about a king of Wilusa called Walmu, and the events in which he was caught up. (We recall that Wilusa was one of the Hittites' western vassal states.) The following extract from the letter demonstrates how the text-join has advanced our knowledge of these events. The roman type indicates the text contained in the first identified fragment of the letter, the italicized type the additional material provided by the fragment discovered in Berlin:

But Kuwalanaziti[56] *kept* the documents which [*I/they(?) made*] for Walmu. Now behold *he is bringing them* to you, my son.[57] *Examine them! Now, my son*, as long as you protect the welfare of My Sun, *I, My Sun, will trust your good will.* Now, my son, send Walmu to me, and I will install him as king *again in Wilusa.* And just as previously *he was the king of Wilusa, now let him be so again!* (KUB XIX 55 + KUB XLVIII 90, rev. 38′–42′, based on trans. by Hoffner (1982: 131))

---

[52] For discussion of the combined fragments and the historical information which they provide, see Singer (1983*a*: 214–16), Bryce (1985*b*).

[53] See Güterbock (1983*a*: 137), Bryce (1985*b*: 17).

[54] See Bryce (1985*b*: 21–2).

[55] See e.g. Singer (1983*a*: 216).

[56] On this reading of the name, in place of *Kuwatnaziti* as read by Hoffner, and the possible identification with the Hittite envoy Kulaziti who figures in Egyptian correspondence with Hatti, see van den Hout (1995*a*: 91, with n. 112).

[57] For an alternative reading of this line (rev. 39′), including a proposed reference to Kurunta, see van den Hout (1984: 91) and (1995*a*: 91).

Even with the text-join, we are still unable to reconstruct fully the events to which the letter refers, and the following must be regarded as no more than a tentative attempt to do so.

It seems that with Hittite support, the addressee of the letter had established himself as the ruler of Milawata, whose throne had previously been occupied by his father. The latter had been openly hostile to the Hittites and had used Milawata as a base for conducting attacks on Hittite territory, and for depositing hostages from the cities he raided. Utima and Atriya are specifically mentioned in the letter. His refusal to return the hostages provoked a retaliatory Hittite attack on Milawata, in conjunction with the Milawatan ruler's son who had decided to throw in his lot with the Hittites in opposition to his father. The kingdom was conquered and the former ruler's son was installed as its new ruler.[58]

During this period, there had been further trouble in the north, in the kingdom of Wilusa. Its king Walmu had been deposed, and had fled his country. He was now in the custody of the new ruler of Milawata. From the fact that Tudhaliya wanted him restored to his throne, it seems clear that he had remained loyal to his Hittite allegiance, and may have been deposed for this reason. Now with a Hittite ally on the throne in Milawata, Tudhaliya was in a better position to reassert Hittite authority in the west. One of his first objectives was to put Walmu back on his throne. He asked the new ruler of Milawata to deliver Walmu to him as the first step towards his restoration, and had sent an envoy Kuwalanaziti with documents confirming the legitimacy of Walmu's claim to the throne.

Tudhaliya addressed the Milawatan ruler as 'my son'. This almost certainly means that he was joined to the Hittite royal family by a marriage alliance, and was perhaps adopted as the king's son. But his status was clearly more exalted than that of a standard vassal ruler or subject ally, and he appears to have exercised a role as a kind of regional overlord in the west. The Wilusan king Walmu was apparently answerable to him as well as to Tudhaliya, who

---

[58] This is deduced from Güterbock's reading of lines 47–9 of the text: 'When we, My Sun, and you, my son, established/fixed the border of Milawata for ourselves ... I did not give you [such and such a place] within the borders of Milawata' (1986: 38 n. 17). The clear implication is that the attack on Milawata had been successful, and that in the wake of conquest, the new ruler was installed, and the boundaries of Milawata were redefined with certain conditions imposed by the Hittite king. A slightly different reading proposed by Gurney (1992: 220–1 n. 58) would not materially alter the sense of this passage.

states in his letter: 'As Walmu was previously our *kulawanis* vassal, so let him (again) be a *kulawanis* vassal!'[59] This suggests a new power-sharing arrangement in the west, with a local ruler being granted direct authority over at least one other vassal kingdom in the region.

Such an arrangement would have marked a distinct divergence from previous Hittite policy which gave no local ruler precedence over any other, and insisted that each deal directly with and be answerable exclusively to the Hittite king.[60] But times had changed. Hattusili's western campaign had demonstrated how difficult it now was to reassert and maintain, even for a short time, Hittite authority in the region. Tudhaliya had no wish for a repetition of his father's humiliating experiences in the west. By conceding more extensive authority to a local ruler he might succeed in achieving greater and longer lasting stability in the region, keeping it within the Hittite sphere of influence but with minimal Hittite involvement. There were, besides, pressing matters to attend to in other parts of his kingdom, particularly in the south-east. These required a substantial commitment of his military resources, and he could ill afford to deplete these by redeploying part of them for further campaigns in the west.

Even so, Tudhaliya took care not only to stress to the Milawatan ruler the need to protect his own territory but also to warn him against attempting to extend the boundaries of his kingdom. There is more than one hint in the letter that Tudhaliya did not fully trust its addressee.[61] He clearly had no intention of abandoning Hittite interests in the west, and would doubtless have been prepared to take the field again in this region if he believed that these interests were in serious jeopardy.

The End of Ahhiyawan Involvement in the Near East?

What impact did the new developments in western Anatolia have on Ahhiyawan enterprise in the region? With the establishment

---

[59] Rev. 43'. The meaning of the term *kulawanis* is not clear; see Hoffner (1982: 135 n. 14), and the references cited therein.

[60] It may be that the previous ruler of Milawata had already exercised a regional overlordship role, on behalf of Ahhiyawan interests, which extended his activities well beyond the borders of Milawata. Perhaps Tudhaliya adopted the same practice when Milawata reverted once more to a pro-Hittite regime.

[61] See Bryce (1985b: 21).

of a pro-Hittite regime in Milawata, Ahhiyawan political and commercial activities must have been seriously curtailed, if not altogether terminated. The reversion of Milawata to Hittite over-lordship would have deprived the Ahhiyawan king of his most important base on the Anatolian mainland—the base which the Hittites had conceded to Ahhiyawa several generations earlier, and from which Ahhiyawan kings had extended their influence either directly or through local agents into Hittite vassal territory. They had succeeded in doing so without provoking a major conflict with Hatti. Relations between Hatti and Ahhiyawa had remained cool, but relatively peaceful. That was now at an end. The Ahhiyawan king had lost his control over Milawata, and Tudhaliya now sought to end any further involvement by Ahhiyawa in the political and commercial activities of the Near East.

In the surviving draft of the treaty which Tudhaliya drew up with Sausgamuwa, ruler of the Syrian state of Amurru,[62] Tudhaliya placed a ban on traffic between Ahhiyawa and Assyria (with whom Hatti was then at war; see below) via the harbours of Amurru.[63] In this draft, the name of the king of Ahhiyawa was included in, and then erased from, the list of kings whom Tudhaliya considered to be of equal rank with himself:

And the kings who (are) of equal rank with me, the king of Egypt, the king of Karadunia (= Kassite Babylonia), the king of Assyria, the king of Ahhiyawa, if the king of Egypt is a friend of My Sun, let him also be a friend to you, if he is an enemy of My Sun, let him be your enemy also . . . (Tudhaliya: Sausgamuwa Treaty, IV 1–7)

Why was the Ahhiyawan king removed from the list? The eras-ure of his name might well indicate that he 'was not, and could not be thought to be, a mighty sovereign of the same rank as that of the other kings mentioned'.[64] But if this were so, why was his name put there in the first place? Was it simply a scribal error? Or had there been a sudden reversal in the fortunes of Ahhiyawa, of sufficient moment to warrant the removal of its king's name from the treaty while it was actually being drawn up? Some years earlier

---

[62] KUB XXIII 1 (+) (*CTH* 105), ed. Kühne and Otten (1971).
[63] KUB XXIII 1 IV 23. But note Steiner (1989*a*), who argues that the generally accepted restoration *Aḫ-ḫ]i-ia-u-ua-aš-ši* [GIS]MÁ (Ahhiyawan ships) in this line is incorrect. He proposes [*laḫ]ḫi-ia-ua-aš-ši* [GIS]MÁ (warships), a restoration which Singer (1991*a*: 171 n. 56) considers most unlikely.
[64] Hooker (1976: 130).

Hattusili III had explicitly acknowledged the Ahhiyawan king as his equal.[65] But at that time the latter was still overlord of a part of western Anatolia.

It is possible that the erasure was associated with the loss of Ahhiyawan control over Milawata. With it once more under Hittite, or pro-Hittite, control, and in the absence of any other known Ahhiyawan base for political and military activity in Anatolia, the Ahhiyawan king could no longer claim to exercise any significant influence on the Anatolian mainland.[66] In his treaty with Sausgamuwa, Tudhaliya was concerned only with the Great Kings who controlled territories within the regions of the Near East. These were the kings whom he regarded as his equals, and with whom he had to deal, either as allies or as enemies. Once excluded from these regions, the Ahhiyawan king was no longer considered a Great King, irrespective of what power he may have continued to exercise elsewhere.

Reasonably confident that the Ahhiyawan problem had now been finally resolved, and with the situation in western Anatolia now under control, at least for the time being, Tudhaliya could turn his attention to the south-east. Here the situation was cause for much greater concern. In his treaty with Sausgamuwa Tudhaliya envisaged the possibility of hostilities with three other major powers in the region—Egypt, Babylonia, and Assyria.[67] Of these Assyria posed the most serious and most immediate threat. The support of Amurru might well be needed for the defence of Hittite subject territories in Syria against an attack from across the Euphrates. Assyria had long had ambitions to expand its territory westwards to the Mediterranean coast.

A Problematical Marriage Alliance

Hattusili had already laid the foundations for an ongoing close alliance between the royal houses of Hatti and Amurru. He had been instrumental in restoring Bentesina to the vassal throne, and had then consolidated Bentesina's links to him by arranging a double marriage between his and his vassal's family (see Chs. 10

[65] See Güterbock (1983a: 136), in reference to the Tawagalawa letter, KUB XIV 3 II 13–14.
[66] Cf. Klengel (1995: 170).
[67] Sausgamuwa treaty, IV 4–13.

and 11). Bentesina had remained true to his Hittite allegiance until his death,[68] probably early in Tudhaliya's reign. The succession now passed to his son Sausgamuwa,[69] whose appointment was confirmed by Tudhaliya.[70] The links between the two royal houses were further strengthened by the marriage of Tudhaliya's sister to the new Amurrite king.[71]

As we have noted, diplomatic marriages were a long-established means of consolidating political alliances between kingdoms. But a marriage which turned sour could have serious political repercussions. Such proved to the case with a marriage link contracted between the royal families of Ugarit and Amurru.

In order to build further on the peaceful relations between Ugarit and Amurru which had lasted more than a century, a daughter of Bentesina (unnamed in the texts) and his Hittite queen Gassulawiya[72] was married to the young king Ammistamru II, who had succeeded his father Niqmepa on the throne of Ugarit. Unfortunately the royal couple did not live happily ever after. The princess apparently committed a serious offence against her husband, perhaps adultery.[73] A divorce followed:[74]

Before My Sun Tudhaliya, Great King, King of Hatti: Ammistamru, king of Ugarit had taken as his wife the daughter of Bentesina, king of Amurru. With regard to Ammistamru, she has only sought to do him harm. (Therefore) Ammistamru, king of Ugarit, has repudiated the daughter of Bentesina for all time. (RS 17.159 (*PRU* IV, 126) 1–10)

The Amurrite princess returned in disgrace to her homeland. In accordance with the standard divorce provisions, all possessions she had acquired since her marriage would remain in Ugarit.[75] But she took her original dowry home with her:

---

[68] Sausgamuwa treaty, I 45–8.

[69] Perhaps the son of Hittite princess Gassulawiya; see Klengel (1969: 313).

[70] Sausgamuwa treaty, II 3.

[71] Sausgamuwa treaty, II 1–3; bronze tablet §27, IV 32.

[72] On the identification of Gassulawiya as her mother, see most recently Singer (1991c: 334).

[73] The actual nature of the offence is not known; see Kühne (1973a: 183–4).

[74] Recorded in the texts RS 17.159, 17.396, 17.348 (*PRU* IV, 125–8, Dossier V c). See also Yaron (1963), Singer (1991a: 174–5). Brooke (1979: 83) supports Pardee (1977) in the view that the Ugaritic letter RS 34.124 is also concerned with this divorce.

[75] The items she had acquired from her marriage included objects of gold, silver, copper, servants, and garments (RS 17.396, 5–9).

The daughter of Bentesina is to take back all that she has brought to the house of Ammistamru, and is to leave the house of Ammistamru. If Ammistamru holds back anything, the sons of Amurru should testify to this on oath, and Ammistamru is to reimburse them. (RS 17.159, 12–21)

But this was not the end of the matter. Brooding further over his wife's offence, Ammistamru refused to accept that justice had been done. He demanded that the princess be extradited to Ugarit, for punishment,[76] and was prepared to use force to back up his demand.[77]

Initially it seems that Sausgamuwa resisted any attempts to have his sister extradited, knowing that she faced certain execution. The affair looked like escalating into a crisis of major proportions. Hittite intervention became imperative. The last thing Tudhaliya could have wanted was a major conflict between two of his loyal vassals. There were obvious dangers in taking the side of one vassal against the other in the dispute. Yet clearly Ammistamru was the aggrieved party—and he may well have been acting under pressure from his own advisers, particularly if his position on the throne was not yet fully secure. He had been involved in an earlier dispute, perhaps over the succession, with his brothers Hismi-Sarruma and ARAD-Sarruma. At the instigation of the queen mother Ahat-milku, who had apparently acted for a short time as regent following her husband Niqmepa's death, the brothers had been exiled from Ugarit.[78] This action had Tudhaliya's support. But now, the Amurrite princess's conduct had been a serious humiliation to the king, and could well have undermined his standing in the eyes of his subjects, and his enemies, if he failed to insist on exemplary vengeance.

Protracted negotiations followed, involving both Tudhaliya and Ini-Tesub, the current viceroy at Carchemish with overall responsibility for Syrian affairs.[79] Considerable pressure was brought to bear on Sausgamuwa by his Hittite overlords:

[76] RS 16.270 (*PRU* IV 134–6), RS 17.372 A + 360 A (*PRU* IV 139–41), RS 17.228 (*PRU* IV 141–3). Singer (1991c: 174) notes that contrary to earlier views it is now proved beyond doubt that there was only one Amurrite princess married to Ammistamru.

[77] RS 18.06 + 17.365 (*PRU* IV 137–8), 1′–6′.

[78] RS 17.352 4–28 (*PRU* IV 121–2).

[79] See the texts in *PRU* IV, 129–48, Dossier V D.

If Sausgamuwa, son of Bentesina, king of Amurru, does violence to
Ammistamru, son of Niqmepa, king of Ugarit, or does violence to the
boats or the soldiers who go to retrieve the daughter of the Great Lady,
Heaven and the Earth will know it . . . (a list of deities follows) May these
gods do him violence, may they make him disappear from the house of his
father and from the country of his father, and from the throne of his
fathers! (RS 18.06 + 17.365 (*PRU* IV 137–8) 1′–15′)

Sausgamuwa was left with no option but to send his sister back to
Ugarit, and to certain death. But to soften the blow for the grieving
brother, an agreement was drawn up which specified compensation
to be paid to him by the aggrieved king of Ugarit:

Ammistamru, son of Niqmepa, king of Ugarit, has given 1,400 (shekels of)
gold to Sausgamuwa, son of Bentesina, king of Amurru. If Sausgamuwa,
son of Bentesina, king of Amurru, happens to say to Ammistamru, son of
Niqmepa, king of Ugarit: 'This is not enough. Give (me) more gold!'
the present tablet will take it from him. (RS 17.228 (*PRU* IV 142–3), 30–
41)

One final footnote to this episode relates to Utri-Sarruma, the
son of the divorced couple. Tudhaliya gave him the option of
remaining behind in Ugarit where he would inherit the throne from
his father, or returning to Amurru with his mother.[80] He apparently
chose the latter option, for Ammistamru was succeeded on the
throne by Ibiranu, his son by another wife.

The Assyrian Menace Resurfaces

The name of Ini-Tesub, who was involved in the divorce proceedings above, occurs several times in the context of Syrian affairs. Son
of Sahurunuwa and grandson of Sarri-Kusuh,[81] he was the cousin of
Tudhaliya, and the third viceroy of Carchemish. The role which he
played in Syria, particularly in arbitrating on judicial disputes between the local kingdoms, was vital to the maintenance of regional
stability, and enabled Tudhaliya to devote his attention to maintaining, as best he could, peace and stability elsewhere in his

[80] RS 17.159 (*PRU* IV 126–7) 31–9; cf. RS 17.348 (*PRU* IV 128).
[81] See RS 17.128 (*PRU* IV 179) with the seal impression whose cuneiform legend
reads: 'Seal of Ini-Tesub, King of Carchemish, Servant of Kubaba, Son of
Sahurunuwa, Grandson of Sarri-Kusuh, Great-grandson of Suppiluliuma, Great
King, King of Hatti, Hero—Sarruma' (Cf. Laroche (1956: 121)). Other seals of Ini-
Tesub include RS 17.146, 17.59, 17.158. See also Schaeffer (1956: 20–9).

kingdom. We learn, for example, of a dispute over compensation demanded by the king of Tarhuntassa for the murder of one of his subjects while trading in Ugarit. The case was brought to Ini-Tesub who resolved it with an award of 180 shekels of silver to the aggrieved party.[82] He was also directly responsible for the administration of the city of Emar, where his authority is attested by seal impressions. His communications with Hattusa provided valuable information on local affairs, particularly on relations between the vassal kingdoms.

Ini-Tesub must also have kept his king well informed of developments in the Euphrates region. This was of critical importance to the security of Hittite territory in Syria in view of the increasing menace posed by Assyria. Ever since the Assyrian conquest of Hanigalbat, now irretrievably lost to the Hittites, tensions between Hatti and Assyria had remained high. While Salmaneser occupied the Assyrian throne, there was little prospect of any improvement in the relations between the two kingdoms. Indeed with Assyrian power now firmly established up to the east bank of the Euphrates it seemed but a matter of time before the Hittites would be faced with a major Assyrian onslaught west of the river.

But then came news of Salmaneser's death, and his replacement on the Assyrian throne by his young son Tukulti-Ninurta (c.1233).[83] Tudhaliya was no doubt relieved and delighted by the news. Perhaps conflict with Assyria might yet be avoided. Tudhaliya wrote to the new king in very conciliatory terms, congratulating him on his accession, praising the exploits of his father Salmaneser, urging him to protect the frontiers established by his father (and thus acknowledging that Hanigalbat was now part of Assyrian territory), offering assistance in the event of rebellion by any of his subjects, and making explicit offers of friendship.[84]

Initially the new Assyrian king made a pretence of responding positively to these overtures, acknowledging the former enmity between Tudhaliya and his father, but expressing his own friendship with the Hittite king.[85] His letter was written specifically in

[82] RS 17.158 (*PRU* IV 169–71).
[83] On the basis of the lower chronology proposed by Wilhelm and Boese (1979), who date Tukulti-Ninurta's reign to the years 1233–1197.
[84] KUB XXIII 92//XXIII 103//XL 77 (*CTH* 178), ed. Hagenbuchner (1989: 249–60 no. 191). See also Otten (1959–60).
[85] KUB III 73 (*CTH* 216) 10' ff. = Weidner (1959: 40 no. 36), Hagenbuchner (1989: 275–8 no. 202).

response to a complaint from Tudhaliya about repeated Assyrian raids on Hittite border territory. Tukulti-Ninurta firmly denied that the complaint had any substance.

But Tudhaliya remained unconvinced. With good reason. Even while Tukulti-Ninurta went through the motions of establishing and maintaining amicable relations with his Hittite counterpart, he was preparing for a major offensive against the Hurrian states constituting the land of Subari, between the Tur ʿAbdin and the upper Tigris. The states in question were Paphi (Assyrian Papanhi), Katmuhi, Buse, Mumme, Alzi, (A)madani, Nihani, Alaya, Tepurzi, and Purukuzzi.[86] Tudhaliya reacted with alarm when he received word of the planned offensive. With the subjugation of the Subari lands, Tukulti-Ninurta would thereby have gained control over the most important routes leading across the Euphrates into Anatolia, as well as the strategic copper mines at Ergani Maden.[87] Amidst his continuing protestations of friendship for the Assyrian king, Tudhaliya warned the Assyrian chancellor Bâbu-ahu-iddina of the dangers faced by an Assyrian army in the impenetrable mountains of the land of Paphi/Papanhi.[88] Tukulti-Ninurta could have had no doubt about the real motive behind the warning, and contemptuously disregarded it. Delaying only to quell some local rebellions, he led his forces northwards against the Subari lands.

With attempts at diplomatic settlement now clearly at an end, Tudhaliya made overt preparations for the inevitable confrontation with Assyria. He reinstated Ugarit's obligation to provide him with military aid when called upon to do so,[89] after previously cancelling this obligation in exchange for a payment of 50 minas of gold.[90] It was perhaps in this context that he drew up his treaty with

---

[86] Grayson (1972: 106 §701, 108 §715, 118 §773).

[87] Cf. Munn-Rankin (1975: 285), Singer (1985a: 104–5). Machinist (1982: 266) comments: 'While the sources describe Assyrian–Hittite contact mostly in military-political terms, there was clearly also an economic side. This becomes especially clear in the documents bearing on the period of Tukulti-Ninurta, whose interest in the Upper Euphrates and Tigris must have included the rich mineral deposits of the region, particularly the copper mines of Ergani Maden. And the economic motive becomes explicit in the sanctions established by Tudhaliya against Tukulti-Ninurta, attempting to cut off the latter's access to Syrian and Mediterranean trade (see KUB XXIII I IV 14–26).'

[88] KUB XXIII 92//XXIII 103//KUB XL 77, rev. 20 f.

[89] RS 17.289 (*PRU* IV 192).

[90] RS 17.59 (*PRU* IV 150–1).

the Amurrite king Sausgamuwa.[91] The instructions to Sausgamuwa regarding Assyria were very clear. The Assyrian king was now the Hittite king's declared enemy:

> As the king of Assyria is the enemy of My Sun, so must he also be your enemy. No merchant of yours is to go to the Land of Assyria, and you must allow no merchant of Assyria to enter your land or pass through your land. If, however, an Assyrian merchant comes to your land, seize him and send him to My Sun. Let this be your obligation under divine oath! And because I, My Sun, am at war with the king of Assyria, when I call up troops and chariotry you must do likewise.   (Tudhaliya: Sausgamuwa Treaty, IV 12–20)

The attempt to impose commercial sanctions on Assyria may have been no more effective then than similar sanctions have been in more recent times. Ultimately the sanctions may simply have served to strengthen the Assyrians' resolve to gain the unrestricted access which they had long sought to the ports of the Mediterranean—by force if necessary. Military confrontation was the only possible effective means of putting an end to Assyrian aggression. A prayer of Tudhaliya appealing for divine assistance against the Assyrian king, with the promise of three stelae as a thank-offering if success was granted,[92] probably portended the forthcoming clash between the two powers.[93]

Where and when did this clash take place?

Following his conquest of the Land of Subari, Tukulti-Ninurta might next have turned westwards, across the Euphrates. But his first objective was the Nairi lands. These lay beyond the northern frontier he had now established and were likely to pose a continuing threat to the security of this frontier. Nairi can almost certainly be equated with Nihriya known from Mesopotamian, Hittite, and Urartean sources. It probably lay in the region north or north-east of modern Diyarbakır.[94] A campaign against it presented formidable problems, both because of the region's mountainous terrain, and the likely fierce resistance the Assyrians would encounter from the local tribes and the forty kings who ruled over them.

This may have been the point at which Tudhaliya entered the fray. A letter written by Tukulti-Ninurta to the king of Ugarit

[91] Singer (1991c: 172) comments that the treaty would best fit either at the beginning of Tukulti-Ninurta's reign, or the very end of Salmaneser's.
[92] KBo XXXIII I 5′–8′, trans. Otten (1962: 76), ed. de Roos (1989).
[93] Thus Singer (1985a: 109).   [94] See Singer (1985a: 105–6).

provides evidence of the conflict.[95] The letter reports that Hittite troops had occupied Nihriya. Tukulti-Ninurta presented Tudhaliya with an ultimatum, demanding the withdrawal of his troops:

> I sent this message to the king of Hatti: 'Nihriya is at war with me; why are your troops in Nihriya? Legally you are at peace with me, not at war. Why then have your troops fortified Nihriya? I am going to lay siege to Nihriya; send a message ordering your troops' withdrawal from Nihriya.' (RS 34.165, rev. 6–13)

In spite of this peremptory demand, Tukulti-Ninurta still sought to maintain peace with Hatti, clearly not wishing to become embroiled in a conflict with the Hittite king at the same time as he was at war with the kings of Nairi. Tudhaliya refused to withdraw his troops, but Tukulti-Ninurta persisted with his attempts at peace:

> When I heard these words (i.e. Tudhaliya's refusal to withdraw his troops from Nihriya), I had a treaty tablet written, and had it conveyed to him (with these words): 'According to your custom, touch(?) this tablet before the Sun.' He refused to touch(?) the tablet before the Sun. Then I withdrew my troops from Nihriya, and installed them . . . ? at Surra . . . (RS 34.165, rev. 16–22, based on French trans. by Lackenbacher (1982: 148))

Tudhaliya ordered his troops to advance against the Assyrian forces. There could be no better time, he must have reasoned, to try to humble the Assyrian king than when the latter was facing the formidable obstacles which the conquest of Nairi presented. But it was a major gamble. While he might have expected some support from the beleaguered Nairi kings, his troops were campaigning far from their base, close to the territories controlled by their powerful opponent and almost certainly without the support of auxiliary forces from the Syrian vassal states.

The Hittite and Assyrian armies clashed somewhere between Nihriya and the Assyrian base at Surra.[96] Tukulti-Ninurta hastily prepared for battle when a fugitive brought him news that the Hittites were advancing. He gave an account of the battle and its outcome to the king of Ugarit:

---

[95] RS 34.165, ed. Lackenbacher (1982). For the attribution of this letter to Tukulti-Ninurta, see Singer (1985*a*: esp. 107–8).

[96] Thus Singer (1985*a*: 108). According to Singer, Surra is probably located at Savur on the northern slopes of Tur Abdin. The battle may also be recorded in a Hittite text, KBo IV 14 (*CTH* 123), which refers to a Hittite–Assyrian engagement at Nihriya, but has generally been ascribed to one of the last two Hittite kings—Arnuwanda III or Suppiluliuma II, e.g. by Liverani (1990: 191).

When I heard the words of the fugitive, I called my camp herald (and said to him): 'Put on your cuirasses and mount your chariots. The king of Hatti arrives in battle order.' I harnessed [   ] my chariot and made a charge, [shouting(?) 'the king(?) of Ha]tti comes ready to do battle!' . . . Certainly I won a great victory.   (RS 34.165, rev. 29–37, based on French trans. by Lackenbacher (1982: 148))

Tukulti-Ninurta followed up this victory by completing his conquest of the Nairi lands, and imposing his sovereignty over the forty local kings who had resisted him.[97] Flushed with success and with his Hittite opponent at least temporarily humbled, he might well have set his sights on the conquest of Hittite territory west of the Euphrates. Indeed his letter to the king of Ugarit could have been intended to win this important Syrian vassal away from his Hittite allegiance in preparation for a campaign in the region. Two later inscriptions from his reign do in fact seem to indicate a major offensive against the Hittites' Syrian possessions. They refer to the capture of 28,800 (eight *šar*) Hittites from across the Euphrates.[98] But the figures may be greatly exaggerated, and the whole episode indicative of no more than a minor border clash.[99]

Nevertheless, Tudhaliya had been severely humiliated by the Assyrian. In the aftermath of his defeat at Nihriya, he sent an angry letter to one of his vassal rulers, almost certainly the king of Isuwa,[100] upbraiding him for his loss of nerve and failure to come to the support of his Hittite overlord:

As (the situation) turned difficult for me, you kept yourself somewhere away from me. Beside me you were not! Have I not fled from Nihriya alone? When it thus occurred that the enemy took away from me the Hurrian lands, was I not left on my own in Alatarma?[101]   (KBo IV 14 II 7 ff., trans. Singer (1985a: 110))

Yet in view of the grave situation in which Tudhaliya found himself following his defeat, punitive action against his disloyal vassal would have been impractical, or at least politically unwise. He could do no more than demand his vassal's loyalty and support when it was called upon in the future.[102]

---

[97] Grayson (1972: 108 §715).   [98] Grayson (1972: 118 §773).
[99] See Munn-Rankin (1975: 291), Singer (1985a: 104).
[100] KBo IV 14 (*CTH* 123). Singer's attribution of this letter to Tudhaliya has been referred to above.
[101] A town lying to the east of the Euphrates; see Singer (1985a: 110 n. 61).
[102] Cf. Singer (1995: 110).

Much to Tudhaliya's relief, this proved unnecessary. Tukulti-Ninurta pursued his conflict with the Hittites no further, but instead turned his attention to the conquest of Babylon. The result was the defeat and capture of the Babylonian king Kastilia (IV) and the total subjugation of his kingdom:

With the support of the gods Assur, Enlil and Samas, the Great Gods, My Lords, and with the aid of the Goddess Istar, Mistress of Heaven and Underworld, (who) marches at the fore of my army, I approached Kastilia, king of Babylon, to do battle. I brought about the defeat of his army and felled his warriors. In the midst of that battle I captured Kastilia, king of the Kassites, and trod with my feet upon his lordly neck as though it were a footstool. Bound I brought him as a captive into the presence of Assur, My Lord. Thus I became lord of Sumer and Akkad in its entirety and fixed the boundary of my land as the Lower Sea in the east. (Assyrian royal inscription, trans. Grayson (1972: 108 §715))

This marked the pinnacle of Tukulti-Ninurta's military achievements, and it was accomplished by the end of the first decade of his reign (*c.*1223). It also marked the end of his military adventures into foreign lands. For the remainder of his reign he seems to have devoted his attention to the internal affairs of his kingdom, including building programmes and the founding of a new capital Kar-Tukulti-Ninurta.[103]

In hindsight it is difficult to see what lasting benefits he hoped would come from his conquest of Babylon. Babylonia offered none of the material rewards in terms of raw materials and the expansion of commercial opportunities which had been one of the prime objectives of Assyrian imperialist enterprises. Indeed the main beneficiaries of the Babylonian conquest were the Hittites, for the vast resources required to maintain control over the territories conquered by Tukulti-Ninurta effectively ended any future threat he might have posed to Hittite territory. Moreover he was faced with mounting opposition within his own kingdom, perhaps partly or even largely inspired by the ruinous cost of maintaining control over Babylonia for little apparent benefit, at the expense of adequate protection of Assyrian territories elsewhere in his empire. His depleted defence forces in other regions suffered several military defeats, and for all his efforts he eventually lost control of Babylonia. Such was the legacy he left to his successor

---

[103] Grayson (1972: 121–2 §785).

Assur-nadin-apli when he eventually fell victim to an assassination plot (*c.* 1197).

A Royal Coup in Hattusa?

In spite of the favours and concessions conferred upon Kurunta, the burning question still remained. How long would he continue to be satisfied with rewards which left him short of the main prize? Why settle for an appanage kingdom, no matter how much Tudhaliya jacked up the prestige of his appointment, if he believed that the Hittite throne was rightfully his, and he had the means to force his claim to it? Did he in fact attempt to do so?

The answer to this question may be provided by the recent discoveries of seal impressions in Hattusa bearing the inscription *Kurunta, Great King, Labarna, My Sun.*[104] There appears to be only one possible interpretation of these words: that the Kurunta so identified became king in Hattusa.[105] To achieve this, he would almost certainly have had to take the Hittite throne by force, wresting it from his cousin Tudhaliya.[106]

His coup would have occurred some years after Tudhaliya's accession, perhaps in the context or aftermath of the king's unsuccessful campaign against Assyria. Kurunta may have considered this an appropriate time to make his move and seize the capital.[107] During the course of Tudhaliya's reign, parts of Hattusa suffered destruction, particularly the walls and temple quarter.[108] This could have been caused by armed conflict in the city, between the forces of Kurunta and those loyal to Tudhaliya. But if coup there was, the usurper's triumph was short-lived. If Tudhaliya lost his throne for a time, he succeeded in regaining it, and shortly after commenced an ambitious restoration and rebuilding project in the upper city.[109]

---

[104] See Neve (1987: 401–8, Abb. 20*a.b*; 1993*b*; Abb. 40–2).

[105] Cf. Otten (1988*a*: 4), Neve (1989–90: 8), Beckman (1989/90: 293), Freu (1990: 58–9). Hoffner (1989*b*: 50) tentatively raises the question of whether this could have been a later Kurunta, perhaps successor of the last known king Suppiluliuma II. That possibility cannot be entirely ruled out, although in the absence of any clear evidence for a second Kurunta, it seems unlikely.

[106] Cf. Hawkins (1990: 313), Neve (1993*b*: 19).

[107] Cf. Neve (citing Otten) (1987: 403).

[108] Neve (1987: 403–5, with table, 404; 1989–90: 9–10).

[109] See Neve (1984: 377; 403 and table, 404).

The tablets have yet to provide evidence for a coup by Kurunta. Perhaps that reflects the increasing paucity of our records in the final decades of the kingdom. On the other hand it is possible that after Kurunta's fall, every attempt was made to expunge from the records all trace of his career, culminating in his seizure of the Hittite throne. The unique find-spot of the bronze tablet, beneath the pavement near the Yerkapı Gate, would be consistent with this. Professor Neve has advanced the theory that after Tudhaliya regained control of Hattusa, he took the tablet and gave it a desacralizing burial under the pavement, where it remained hidden until it was unearthed in 1986.[110]

But the coup must remain no more than theory until such time as we have more direct evidence of it. And of Kurunta's ultimate fate, we know nothing. If he had rebelled against his overlord he may, like his brother Urhi-Tesub, have spent his remaining days in exile. It is hardly likely that he would have been reinstated as ruler of Tarhuntassa. Indeed a large question mark hangs over the subsequent relationship between Hatti and Tarhuntassa. If Muwatalli did in fact have a third son Ulmi-Tesub, then almost certainly Tudhaliya now appointed him to the kingship of Tarhuntassa in place of Kurunta, and drew up with him the treaty we have called the 'Ulmi-Tesub treaty' (see Ch. 11). But if Ulmi-Tesub was simply another name for Kurunta, then as yet we have no clear information on what became of the kingdom of Tarhuntassa after Kurunta. Very likely Tudhaliya lost control of it. There may well be indirect evidence, some of it new evidence, that Tarhuntassa now broke from its Hittite allegiance and became openly hostile to the kingdom of Hatti.

We shall take this up in the next chapter.

The Conquest of Alasiya

The military threats facing the Hittites in almost all parts of their kingdom made it imperative for Tudhaliya to ensure that his forces were kept at full strength and in a constant state of alert, ready to be deployed at short notice to defend Hittite territory against enemy attack, wherever it occurred along the kingdom's frontiers.

---

[110] Cited by Hoffner (1989*b*: 47–8). Cf. Beckman (1989/90: 293 n. 20). Beckman points out that the tablet was found beneath reconstruction work done under the aegis of Tudhaliya.

With some surprise, then, we find Tudhaliya committing his forces to a campaign on the island of Alasiya.

Information about the campaign appears on a tablet from the reign of his son Suppiluliuma II.[111] The tablet contains a cuneiform copy of two Luwian hieroglyphic inscriptions. The first, originally appearing on a statue of Tudhaliya, commemorates Tudhaliya's conquest of Alasiya and the imposition of tribute on the land:[112]

I seized the king of Alasiya with his wives, his children, [and his   ]. All the goods, including silver and gold, and all the captured people I removed and brought home to Hattusa. I enslaved the country of Alasiya, and made it tributary on the spot.   (KUB XII 38 I, 3–8, adapted from trans. by Güterbock (1967a: 77))

A list of the tribute imposed, including gold and copper, then follows.

What was the object of this campaign? What did Tudhaliya hope to gain from it—especially when it must have meant a significant redeployment of forces needed for the defence of his mainland empire? Hittite kings had certainly claimed Alasiya as a Hittite possession in the past.[113] But this control can have been no more than nominal, and obviously relied on the support of seagoing vassal states like Ugarit. Important practical considerations probably provided the chief incentive for Tudhaliya's campaign.

A number of scholars have claimed that the Hittite world suffered a severe and prolonged famine in the last decades of the Hittite kingdom.[114] Whether or not food shortages were as severe or prolonged as has been suggested, it does seem clear that the Hittites became increasingly dependent on shipments of grain from abroad, probably from the reign of Hattusili III onwards.[115] The chief sources of such grain appear to have been Egypt and Canaan,[116] whence it was transported to Ugarit and from there to the Hittite port of Ura in western Cilicia (the later Classical name for the region).[117]

---

[111] KBo XII 38 (*CTH* 121), ed. Güterbock (1967a), and also trans. Kümmel (1985).
[112] The second describes a further campaign against Alasiya by Suppiluliuma II and will be discussed in Ch. 13.
[113] e.g. Arnuwanda I, as indicated in his letter to Madduwatta; see Ch. 6.
[114] See e.g. Klengel (1974), and for further discussion, Ch. 13.
[115] In a letter to Ramesses, KUB XXI 38 I 17–18, Puduhepa makes reference to the lack of grain in her lands; see Singer (1983b: 5).
[116] Singer (1983b: 4–5).
[117] See Klengel (1979b: 77–8), Singer (1983a: 217). Overland transportation was then provided by caravans of donkeys; see Heltzer (1977).

During Hattusili III's reign a trip was made to Egypt by a prince of the Land of Hatti called Hesmi/Hismi-Sarruma[118] to organize a shipment of grain back to his homeland.[119] In the past, scholars have suggested that the prince in question was Tudhaliya, and that Hesmi-Sarruma was his birth-name.[120] But since we now know, from the bronze tablet, that there was another prince called Hesmi-Sarruma,[121] this was probably the king's representative who visited Egypt.[122] In the wake of Hattusili's treaty with Ramesses grain was probably imported from Egypt into Anatolia via the Levantine ports on a regular basis, rather than on an occasional basis in response to a particular food shortage.

Hatti may have come to rely heavily on grain importation during the last century of the kingdom. But whether this was due to a prolonged drought or series of droughts in the homeland, or to other factors such as substantial redeployment of Hittite manpower from agricultural to military activity, remains unknown. We shall return to this in the next chapter. In any case, shortfalls in local grain production would have posed no serious problems as long as the Hittites could count on regular grain shipments from Egypt and Syria. But problems could arise if the grain routes began to be threatened by hostile forces.

This may well have a bearing on Tudhaliya's campaign in Alasiya. Because of its abundant resources of timber and copper, as well as its strategic location in the north-east corner of the eastern Mediterranean, Alasiya had come into increasing prominence in the last century of the Bronze Age.[123] It provided an extremely

---

[118] Identified as a Hittite prince in a letter from Ramesses II to Hattusili, KUB III 34 (*CTH* 165.1) rev. 15.

[119] Cf. Klengel (1974: 167), Singer (1983*b*: 5).

[120] e.g. Kitchen (1982: 89), and (more tentatively) Güterbock (1956*a*: 121), Laroche (1956: 118–19; 1966: 69 no. 371).

[121] Listed in §27, IV 34, as one of the witnesses to the treaty.

[122] Imparati (1992: 311–12) remarks that we cannot be certain whether such a prince was in fact a member of the Hittite royal family; his place about midway in the list of witnesses in the bronze tablet and several names after the vassal rulers Masturi and Sausgamuwa, would suggest that his provenance was elsewhere, even if Ramesses called him a prince of the Land of Hatti. Van den Hout (1989*a*: 138 ff) also argues that Hesmi-Sarruma was not Tudhaliya but his son or more probably his younger brother; further on this, see Mora (1992: 141). Klengel (1991: 229) still considers that the identification with Tudhaliya is possible, though not compelling. For the most recent and most comprehensive treatment of the whole question, including the possible identification of the names Hesmi-Sarruma and BU-LUGAL-(ma), see van den Hout (1995*a*: 127–32).

[123] As attested by its material remains in this period. See Knapp (1983: 43), Muhly (1992: 19).

attractive prospect for exploitation by outsiders, either through alliance or conquest. Under the control of a native or foreign regime hostile to Hittite interests, it had considerable potential for disrupting transhipments of grain from Egypt and Syria to a port on the southern Anatolian coast. We do not know what the regime in Alasiya had done to provoke the Hittite attack. But clearly Tudhaliya could not tolerate a hostile Alasiya which could itself threaten his kingdom's grain supplies, or provide naval bases for other enemy forces to do so.

These other forces might have included elements of the so-called Sea Peoples, soon to figure prominently in Egyptian records. But it is also possible that Tarhuntassa, which extended along the Anatolian coast directly north of Alasiya, had now broken its ties with Hatti and had become involved in anti-Hittite activity in the region.

Tudhaliya apparently succeeded in defeating the Alasiyan king and establishing a pro-Hittite regime in his place. But his victory had little long-term effect in reasserting Hittite authority in this part of the eastern Mediterranean. Within the space of a few years enemy forces were again active in the region, and Tudhaliya's son Suppiluliuma was forced to undertake a naval campaign off the coast of Alasiya, almost certainly to protect the supply routes which were becoming increasingly vital to the provisioning of the Hittite world.

The Achievements of Tudhaliya

The majority of our records for Tudhaliya's reign convey the impression of a kingdom coming under mounting pressures from both within and beyond its boundaries, and of a king preoccupied with his attempts, both military and diplomatic, to keep his kingdom intact and to hold at bay the hostile forces which threatened to engulf it. Undoubtedly the problems Tudhaliya faced were complex and far-reaching in their possible consequences. On the one hand he was faced with the possible disintegration of his western vassal states, on the other with the ever-present threat of the loss of his Syrian possessions to the warlords of Assyria. And the military action he took against Alasiya may well foreshadow the mounting crisis in the eastern Mediterranean associated with the last years of the Hittite kingdom.

Closer to home, we find evidence of increasing unrest in Hittite subject territories, with a rebellion in the Lower Land probably early in Tudhaliya's reign, and later the possible loss of the kingdom of Tarhuntassa. We also have glimpses of tensions within the Hittite royal family itself, stemming from Hattusili's usurpation of the Hittite throne and the potential to which this gave rise for ongoing rival claims upon the throne by various branches of the royal family.

Yet severe though these pressures undoubtedly were, the reign of Tudhaliya was characterized by a number of substantial achievements both at home and abroad. In the west the king seems to have accomplished considerably more than his father or even his uncle Muwatalli. He had crushed a rebellion in the Seha River Land, he had regained overlordship of the land of Milawata, in the process probably removing any future threat of Ahhiyawan interference in the region, and very likely he restored the deposed king of Wilusa to his vassal throne. The Yalburt inscription provides further evidence of successful campaigns which he undertook in the west. In the east the Syrian vassal states remained under Hittite control. And although Tudhaliya's forces may have suffered a major military defeat at the hands of the Assyrian king Tukulti-Ninurta, no serious attempt seems to have been made by Tukulti-Ninurta to expand his kingdom westwards across the Euphrates. Indeed, although Tudhaliya took little direct part in Syrian affairs, it is clear from documents like the Sausgamuwa treaty that he was fully committed to maintaining firm Hittite control within the region. And to the south of the Anatolian mainland, he appears to have won a significant victory against enemy forces on Alasiya which for the time being at least he restored to Hittite sovereignty.

Within Hattusa itself, Tudhaliya may have been temporarily removed from his throne by his cousin Kurunta. But if so, he soon regained it. Whether or not the coup did lasting harm to the monarchy must remain at present an open question. The destruction by fire of parts of the capital at this time may indicate that coup and counter-coup left substantial damage in its wake. Yet these setbacks were more than matched by substantial restoration and new building projects during Tudhaliya's reign. Indeed this king has left some enduring tangible monuments to his reign—more enduring than those left by the kings who reigned in what might be regarded as peak periods of Hittite power.

The rock sanctuary at Yazılıkaya, one kilometre to the north-east of the capital, and probably associated with the Hittite New Year festival, provides evidence of a florescence in Hittite material culture. The sanctuary had been in use for some considerable time, extending back before the Hittite period, but underwent its most significant development during the reigns of Hattusili and Tudhaliya. To Tudhaliya was due the sculptural decorations and hieroglyphic inscriptions which appear on the walls of the two natural rock chambers. Tudhaliya himself is represented three times in the reliefs, once in close association with his patron deity Sarruma. While the artistic concepts embodied in the reliefs may owe something to Egyptian influence, the depiction of the procession of Hurrian deities in the main chamber represents the culmination of a programme of religious reform initially undertaken by Hattusili and his Hurrian queen Puduhepa and completed by Tudhaliya. The sanctuary in its fully developed form, clearly representing the Hurrian pantheon as the national Hittite pantheon, is the most sophisticated surviving artistic achievement of the Hittite world.

From recent excavations carried out in Hattusa, we know that Tudhaliya engaged in a major building programme in his capital.[124] Of particular importance was the development of the upper city, which included an extensive temple-building programme and extended over an area which more than doubled the size of the original city. In this period the Hittite capital assumed its most impressive proportions, and could justly be regarded as one of the greatest cities of the ancient Near East.

When we review the reign of Tudhaliya, it is very difficult to detect in this reign clear signs of a kingdom in irreversible decline.

---

[124] See Bittel (1983a: 501–5), Neve (1984: 349–70, esp. 369–70), van den Hout (1995c).

CHAPTER 13

The Fall of the Kingdom and its Aftermath

On the death of Tudhaliya, the succession passed to his son Arnuwanda (III). But the latter's death after perhaps only a year or so on the throne has left him as no more than a passing footnote in the history of the Hittite monarchy. Apart from seal impressions bearing his name,[1] and a reference to him in a coronation oath to his successor, we have no further information about him in our texts. He had left no issue, and after his death the succession passed to another of Tudhaliya's sons, Suppiluliuma, whose name was usually written *Suppiluliama*.[2] Two texts contain oaths of allegiance by high-ranking subjects on his coronation.[3] One of these indicates that the new king was faced with serious unrest in Hatti which had erupted during his brother's short reign:

The inhabitants of Hatti rebelled against him (i.e. Arnuwanda). But I was not at fault. If he had had descendants, I would not have passed over them; I would, rather, have acknowledged these descendants. (Because) he had no descendants, I enquired about (whether there was) a pregnant wife; but there was no pregnant wife. As now Arnuwanda has left no descendants, could I have offended by passing over his descendants and making another lord? (KUB xxvi 33 (*CTH* 125) ii 3 ff.)[4]

---

[1] To *SBo* I, 64 = Beran (1967: 34 no. 161) we can now add the (maximum of) 45 seal impressions found in the 'seal archive' at Nişantepe (Neve's table (1992a: 313)). This is a significantly greater number than those so far attributable to some of Arnuwanda's more illustrious predecessors. Of course we have to be careful not to place too much emphasis on absolute numbers of seal impressions when we do not know the circumstances which led to their production.

[2] For the discovery of this king, see Laroche (1953). His name also appears on a number of seal impressions. To Boehmer and Güterbock (1987: 83 no. 261) add the seal impressions on clay bullae discovered during the excavations at Hattusa in 1987 and 1990. Five were found in temple 2 (Neve (1988: 374–6, Abb. 23a–c)) and six in the Nişantepe archive (Neve (1991: 332; 1992a: 313, 315)). The attribution of the seals to the second rather than the first Suppiluliuma seems virtually certain; see Neve (1992b).

[3] *CTH* 124 and 125.

[4] See also Otten (1963: 3–4).

The unrest may have been provoked by intrigues within the royal court arising from still unresolved questions over which branch of the royal family had legitimate claims to the throne.[5] Indeed an oath taken by one of the scribes may imply this:

I will acknowledge only the descendants of my lord Suppiluliama. I will not appear on the side of another man, (whether) a descendant of Suppiluliuma the Older (i.e. Suppiluliuma I), a descendant of Mursili, a descendant of Muwatalli or of Tudhaliya.   (KUB xxvi 32 (+) (*CTH* 124) iii 10′–14′)[6]

Whatever its causes, unrest and disunity within the homeland could have seriously limited the new king's ability to deal effectively with the external forces which were threatening his kingdom. His first task was to restore the kingdom's internal political stability. The majority of surviving documents from his reign indicate his commitment to this task.[7] He also devoted his efforts to the mortuary shrine of his father and to other religious establishments. One scholar sees this as typical of a civilization in decline: 'Rather than reflecting self-confidence and security, it is a mute plea to the gods and spirits to grant salvation where the sceptre and the sword have failed.'[8]

The subject territories required urgent attention. Here too the king was faced with outright defiance and disobedience from his vassals, as illustrated by a letter of reprimand from his son Pihawalwi to Ibiranu, king of Ugarit, who had failed to provide the usual tokens of loyalty after his accession:

Thus (speaks) Pihawalwi, son of the king: to Ibiranu, my son, say: '. . . Since you have assumed royal power at Ugarit, why have you not come before My Sun? And why have you not regularly sent messengers? This has made My Sun very angry. Therefore send messengers to My Sun with all haste, and see that gifts are brought for the king.'   (RS 17.247 = *PRU* IV 191)[9]

We know of no direct involvement by Suppiluliuma in Syrian affairs. These may have been left largely in the hands of others,

---

[5] Cf. Otten (1976: 31).

[6] The full text appears in Laroche (1953). See also Otten (1963: 3).

[7] See Singer (1985*a*: 120). The documents in question, protocols and instructions, are listed in *CTH* 121–6, 256. See Otten (1976) for a comprehensive survey of these documents.

[8] Singer (1985*a*, 121).

[9] On the use of the expression 'my son' in addressing Ibiranu, see Nougayrol, *PRU* IV 191 n. 1.

notably the current viceroy of Carchemish, Talmi-Tesub, son of Ini-Tesub. Fragments survive of a treaty between Suppiluliuma and Talmi-Tesub,[10] but insufficient of it remains to determine what precise responsibilities were assigned to the viceroy. Quite possibly he exercised an almost independent role in Syria.[11]

We do know that he was responsible for supervising a divorce settlement apparently between a daughter of the Hittite king and Ammurapi, king of Ugarit.[12] Unfortunately, the circumstances which led to the dissolution of the marriage are not recorded. But the divorce of a Hittite princess by a local vassal ruler or a member of his family was, as far as we know, without precedent in the Hittite world. It may provide yet more evidence of the increasingly tenuous nature of the relationship between vassal and overlord in the last years of the Hittite kingdom, and the diminished respect in the vassal states for the authority of the Hittite king.

Final Campaigns in the West

On at least some occasions the flouting of royal authority or acts of outright defiance or rebellion in the subject states did meet with retaliation, as indicated by an inscription on a building discovered in Hattusa in 1988. Commonly referred to as the Südburg structure, the building includes a stone chamber, 4 metres long, embellished with reliefs of a deity and a king called Suppiluliuma,[13] and inscribed with a text in the hieroglyphic script.[14] Although some scholars have suggested that the building was the king's tomb, it is more likely to have been what the Hittite texts refer to as a ^{d}KASKAL.KUR—an entrance to the Underworld (in this case a symbolical one).[15]

The inscription records Suppiluliuma's conquest and annexation of the lands of Wiyanawanda, Tamina, Masa, Lukka, and Ikuna,

---

[10] KBo XII 41 (*CTH* 122.1); see Otten (1963: 7).

[11] Cf. Klengel (1992: 352).

[12] RS 17.226, 17.355 (*PRU* IV 208–10, Dossier VIII A). See Astour (1980).

[13] His status is confirmed by the royal cartouche bearing his name. For arguments in favour of attributing the text to Suppiluliuma II rather than to the first king of that name, see Otten (1989b: 336).

[14] See Neve. (1989: 316–32; 1989–90: 12–14; 1990: 279–86), Otten, (1989b), Hawkins (1990).

[15] See Gordon (1967), Hawkins (1990: 314).

which all lay within or near Lukka territory in south-western Anatolia.[16] These campaigns indicate continuing unrest amongst the western vassal states in spite of Tudhaliya's efforts to bring about greater stability and more lasting peace in the region. What conclusions can we draw from his son's conquests? We might take the view that in spite of the problems Suppiluliuma faced elsewhere in his kingdom, he was still determined to maintain control over his western territories.[17] Alternatively, the western campaigns may have been simply rearguard actions designed to protect or buffer Hittite territories to the south of the homeland from concerted onslaughts against them from the west. The risk of such onslaughts may have increased significantly if the Hittites were now confronted with a hostile regime in the kingdom of Tarhuntassa on the southern coast. Indeed the inscription goes on to report the conquest and annexation of Tarhuntassa.

Food Shortages in Hatti?

Tarhuntassa was probably lost to the Hittites in Tudhaliya's reign, in the aftermath of Kurunta's presumed seizure of and removal from the Hittite throne. Whatever Kurunta's fate, Suppiluliuma's later conquest of the appanage kingdom over which he had ruled is a clear indication that it had broken its ties with Hattusa and become openly hostile to its former overlord.[18]

There were several pressing reasons why a hostile Tarhuntassa could not be tolerated. One of the most important of these was the location of the port of Ura within or at least very close to its borders.[19] We recall that Ura was the Anatolian port to which grain shipments were brought from Egypt and Canaan via Ugarit for transhipment to Hatti. Particularly at times of food shortages in the Hittite kingdom, it was vital that the grain route be kept open. Ura's location was thus of considerable strategic significance. So

---

[16] Ikuna probably = Hittite Ikkuwaniya and should very likely be identified with Ikonion-Konya; see Hawkins (1990: 312; 1995c: 51).

[17] Cf. Yakar (1993: 6–7).

[18] But note the contexts suggested by Hoffner (1989b: 50–1), for the operations described in the Südburg inscription.

[19] Several scholars have identified Ura with modern Silifke (Classical Seleucia); see Davesne *et al.* (1987: 373–6), in support of a proposal made originally by Albright. More recently it has been equated with modern Gilindere (Classical Kelenderis); thus Beal (1992a: 68–9).

long as it remained under the control of an independent and particularly an enemy regime, Hittite communications with Syria and
Egypt would be seriously imperilled.[20]

We have already referred to the Hittites' apparent increasing
dependence on grain supplies from abroad (Ch. 12). This dependence may well have intensified in the final years of the Hittite
kingdom. Several texts dating to Tudhaliya's reign seem to indicate
the critical importance to the Hittite world of imported grain. Thus
the pharaoh Merneptah in his Karnak inscription recording his
victory over Meryre and the Libyans referred to a shipment of
grain which he had sent to 'keep alive the land of Hatti'.[21] A
particular note of urgency was sounded in a letter sent from
the Hittite court to the Ugaritic king, either Niqmaddu III or
Ammurapi (his name is not preserved in the text), demanding a
ship and crew for the transport of 2,000 *kor* of grain (*c.*450 tonnes)
from Mukis to Ura:

And so (the city) Ura [acted(?)] in such a way ... and for My Sun the food
they have saved. My Sun has shown them 2,000 *kor* of grain coming from
Mukis. You must furnish them with a large ship and a crew, and they must
transport this grain to their country. They will carry it in one or two
shipments. You must not detain their ship! (RS 20.212, 17′–26′, adapted
from trans. by Heltzer (1977: 209))[22]

The letter stresses the need for the Ugaritic king to act without
delay.[23] It ends by stating that it is a matter of life or death![24]

Suppiluliuma's Sea Battles

Very likely it was in the context of increasing threats to supply
routes in the eastern Mediterranean that Suppiluliuma undertook

[20] Cf. Hoffner (1989*b*: 49).
[21] Breasted (1906: iii §580)
[22] For the full text, see Nougayrol *et al.* (1968 (*Ugaritica* V): 105–7, no. 33). Cf. RS
202.141 B (op. cit., 107–8, no. 34), RS 26.158 (op. cit., 323–4, no. 171). See also
Astour (1965: 254–5).
[23] Cf. the Hittite text Bo 2810, ed. and discussed by Klengel (1974: 170–4). It
refers to the urgent need of a large shipment of grain to relieve a famine 'in the
lands'. Unfortunately the identity of both the author of the letter and the addressee
is uncertain.
[24] But Hoffner (1989*b*: 49), comments that the Ugaritic text does not mention a
famine or catastrophe, and considers that the shipment may not have been a special
case in response to an emergency but part of a standing arrangement between the
two states. Cf. Klengel (1974: 168).

the only recorded sea battles in which Hittites engaged—battles fought off the coast of Alasiya. Information about these battles is provided by the second of two texts inscribed in cuneiform on a clay tablet during Suppiluliuma's reign. We have referred above to the first of these texts which describes a campaign undertaken by Tudhaliya IV against Alasiya, and the establishment, or re-establishment, of Hittite control over the kingdom. The second text, which like the first is probably copied from an original hiero-glyphic inscription,[25] records three naval engagements and a subse-quent land engagement—against the 'enemies from Alasiya':

My father [   ]I mobilized and I, Suppiluliuma, the Great King, immedi-ately [crossed/reached(?)] the sea. The ships of Alasiya met me in the sea three times for battle, and I smote them; and I seized the ships and set fire to them in the sea. But when I arrived on dry land(?), the enemies from Alasiya came in multitude against me for battle.   (KBo XII 38 (*CTH* 121) III 1′–13′, trans. Güterbock (1967a: 78))

It is clear from this account that Tudhaliya's earlier campaign against Alasiya had succeeded in establishing no more than tem-porary Hittite control over the island, and that his son had to undertake the task all over again. But it is not clear whether the enemy forces encountered by Suppiluliuma were (*a*) the same as those who had fought against Tudhaliya, (*b*) native Alasiyans, (*c*) foreigners who had occupied Alasiya or used its ports as their bases, or (*d*) belonged within the context of the so-called Sea Peoples.[26]

Whoever the enemy, the Hittite forces on this occasion appar-ently fought a successful campaign against them. Of course, the Hittites had no naval resources of their own. Their success could only have been achieved by having at their disposal a war fleet from an allied state, probably Ugarit. Under its last kings Ugarit seems to have played a valuable role in helping to prop up the belea-guered Hittite kingdom.

When disaster finally struck, it was but one of many disasters which devastated large parts of the Near Eastern world in the early years of the twelfth century. For this the so-called Sea Peoples are generally held responsible.

---

[25] See Güterbock (1967a: 81), Hoffner (1989b: 48).
[26] Cf. Astour (1965: 256 n. 23), Otten (1983), Singer (1983a: 217; 1985a: 122), Muhly (1984: 44).

The Sea Peoples

The final collapse of the Hittite kingdom has traditionally been associated with massive movements of peoples who swept through Anatolia, Syria, and Palestine, and across the eastern Mediterranean to the coast of Egypt early in the twelfth century. On the walls of his funerary temple at Medinet Habu, the pharaoh Ramesses III presented a graphic description of the havoc and devastation which they caused before reaching Egypt:

The foreign countries made a conspiracy in their islands.[27] All at once the lands were removed and scattered in the fray. No land could stand before their arms, from Hatti, Qode, Carchemish, Arzawa and Alasiya on, being cut off at one time. A camp was set up in one place in Amurru. They desolated its people, and its land was like that which has never come into being. They were coming forward toward Egypt, while the flame was prepared before them. Their confederation was the Peleset, Tjeker, Shekelesh, Denyen, and Weshesh, lands united. They laid their hands upon the land as far as the circuit of the earth, their hearts confident and trusting: 'Our plans will succeed!' (Medinet Habu inscription of Ramesses III's 8th year, lines 16–17, trans. Wilson in Pritchard (1969: 262))

A letter from Ammurapi, the last king of Ugarit, provides further evidence of the crisis engulfing the Near Eastern world. The letter is a dramatic response to an appeal for assistance from the king of Alasiya, and highlights the desperate situation confronting Ugarit:

My father, behold, the enemy's ships came (here); my cities(?) were burned, and they did evil things in my country. Does not my father know that all my troops and chariots(?) are in the Land of Hatti, and all my ships are in the Land of Lukka? . . . Thus, the country is abandoned to itself. May my father know it: the seven ships of the enemy that came here inflicted much damage upon us. (RS 18.147 = Nougayrol *et al.* (1968 (Ugaritica V): 87–9 no. 24), trans. Astour (1965: 255))

Ammurapi appealed also to the viceroy of Carchemish. But all the latter could do was to offer him encouragement, and some words of advice:

---

[27] 'Islands' is the usual translation of Egyptian *rww*. But Drews (1993: 52) comments that the Egyptian language has no word or concept equivalent to our 'islands', and that the two Egyptian words that sometimes mean 'islands' are frequently used for continental coasts; a less prejudicial translation would therefore be: 'As for the countries, they made a conspiracy in their sealands.'

As for what you have written to me: 'Ships of the enemy have been seen at sea!' Well, you must remain firm. Indeed for your part, where are your troops, your chariots stationed? Are they not stationed near you? No? Behind the enemy, who press upon you? Surround your towns with ramparts. Have your troops and chariots enter there, and await the enemy with great resolution!   (RSL 1 = Nougayrol *et al.* (1968: 85–6 no. 23))[28]

There can be little doubt that the end of the Late Bronze Age in the Near East was marked by cataclysmic upheavals and the collapse and disappearance of many of the old centres of power. But was this caused by marauding groups of northerners collectively identified as the Sea Peoples? Who *were* these Sea Peoples? Whence did they come? Early theories represented them as barbarian invaders from some homeland to the north of Anatolia who swept through the Near East, massacring, pillaging, destroying everything in their path—the Huns and Goths of the Late Bronze Age world—until they were eventually stopped on the coast of Egypt.

But theories of dramatic invasions by bloodthirsty northern barbarians against long-established, sophisticated civilizations are no longer fashionable in Bronze Age scholarship.[29] We need to re-examine very carefully the meagre information available to us before drawing any firm conclusions as to who the Sea Peoples were and what role they played in the final decades of the Bronze Age.

Seaborne attacks were by no means a new phenomenon. Already in the fourteenth century the pharaoh Akhenaten complained to a king of Alasiya about piratical raids conducted on his coastal cities by people from the Lukka lands. He accused the Alasiyan people of aiding and abetting their enterprises. But the Alasiyan king disclaimed responsibility, declaring that his country too was suffering from raids by the Lukka people: 'Why does my brother speak in these terms to me? "Does not my brother know what is going on?" As far as I am concerned, I know nothing of the sort! Indeed each year the Lukka people seize towns in my own land!' (EA 38 7–12).

[28] Note also Astour (1965: 255–6), who refers to a letter to the king of Ugarit from Eshuwara, Grand Supervisor of Alasiya, RS 20.18 (Nougayrol *et al.* (1968: 83–5 no. 22)), which states that some of the king's subjects, who stopped at Alasiya with their ships, surrendered a flotilla to the enemy.
[29] Cf. Drews (1993: 53–4)

We also learn of a raid on the Egyptian coast during Ramesses II's reign by Sherden pirates, who were already raiding the Egyptian coast in the time of Amenhotep III and figure later in the list of Sea Peoples. From the inscription which records the raid it is clear that they had long been a threat in the region: 'the unruly Sherden whom no one had ever known how to combat, they came boldly sailing in their warships from the midst of the sea, none being able to withstand them' (Inscription on a stele from Tanis, trans. Kitchen (1982: 40–1)).

On this occasion, Ramesses succeeded in repelling the invaders. But the pressures continued to mount, and the Egyptian Delta was subjected to further and more concerted attacks in the reign of his son and successor Merneptah (c.1213–1204). In a long inscription carved on the eastern wall of the temple of Karnak, Merneptah recorded his conflict with large groups of invaders. They included bands of Libyans who had previously made attacks on the Delta, no doubt attracted by the rich, fertile soil of the region, and were now joined by other peoples from across the sea, under the Libyan chief Meryre:

The wretched fallen chief of Libya, Meryre, son of Ded, has fallen upon the country of Tehenu with his bowmen . . . Sherden, Shekelesh, Ekwesh, Lukka, Teresh,[30] taking the best of every warrior and every man of war of his country. He has brought his wife and children . . . leaders of the camp, and he has reached the western boundary in the fields of Perire. (Inscription of Merneptah, trans. Breasted (1906: iii. §579)

Of the groups that joined the Libyans for this onslaught on Egypt we have already referred to the Sherden, who were active in the region at least as early as Amenhotep III's reign, and may have eventually occupied the island of Sardinia in the western Mediterranean at the end of the Bronze Age. The Shekelesh were another group, possibly of Anatolian origin, and probably like the Sherden they eventually moved westwards, settling in Sicily. The Lukka people are well known from the Hittite texts, and from their raids on Alasiya and Egypt during Akhenaten's reign. The Teresh group may be identifiable with the Tyrsenoi, referred to later in Greek texts, and were perhaps the ancestors of the Etruscan people of southern Italy. The Ekwesh (Akaiwasha) are commonly identified with the Ahhiyawans of the Hittite texts.

---

[30] Vocalizations of *Šrdn, Škrš, Ikwš, Lk, Trš* respectively.

Merneptah's Karnak inscription indicates that the pharaoh succeeded in driving the invaders from Egypt. But their invasion was
little more than a prelude to the main movements of these groups
in the reign of Merneptah's eventual successor Ramesses III
(*c*.1185–1154), founder of the Egyptian Twentieth Dynasty after
the preceding Nineteenth Dynasty had died out in a succession of
short reigns bedevilled by dynastic intrigues.

According to the records of his reign, Ramesses was confronted
with several major onslaughts in the north of his kingdom, by both
land and sea. In the fifth year of his reign, he was at war with the
Libyan invaders,[31] in his eighth year, with peoples from across the
sea,[32] in his eleventh year, with Libyans once more.[33] We have two
sources of information for these conflicts: inscriptions from the
walls of Ramesses' temple at Medinet Habu, and a document now
known as the Great Harris Papyrus. Compiled by Ramesses III's
son and successor Ramesses IV, it is the longest known papyrus
from Egypt, with some 1,500 lines of text, and covers the entire
period of Ramesses III's reign.[34]

The list of the peoples from across the sea included Peleset,
Tjekker, Shekelesh, Weshesh, and Denyen.[35] Only one of these
groups, the Shekelesh, had figured amongst the invaders during
Merneptah's reign. The most notable group, the Peleset, can be
confidently identified with the Philistines who eventually settled
in Palestine.[36] The Denyen (Danuna) were associated with
Cilicia.[37]

Ramesses' Medinet Habu inscription vividly illustrates in both
word and picture the strenuous preparations the pharaoh made to
meet the enemy, and the decisive defeat which he claimed to have
inflicted upon them:

I equipped my frontier in Zahi (Djahi) prepared before them. The chiefs,
the captains of infantry, the nobles, I caused to equip the harbour-mouths,
like a strong wall, with warships, galleys, and barges [   ] They were

---

[31] Medinet Habu I 27–8 = *KRI* v 20–7.
[32] Medinet Habu I 46 = *KRI* v 37–43.
[33] Medinet Habu II 80–3 = *KRI* v 58–66.
[34] For the text, see Breasted (1906: iv. 110–206).
[35] These are common vocalizations of the following names: *Plst/Prst* (Peleset,
Pulesati, Philistines), *Tjkr* (Tjekker, Tjikar, Zeker, Teucrians?), *Shklsh* (Shekelesh),
Wshsh (Weshesh), *Dnyn* (Danuna, Denyen, People of Adana, Hittite *adanawanai*,
Egyptian *daniuna*, Greek *Danaoi*?).
[36] See Barnett (1975*a*: 371–8).
[37] Cf. Barnett (1953: 87), Laroche (1958), Gurney (1990: 108).

manned completely from bow to stern with valiant warriors, soldiers of all the choicest of Egypt, being like lions roaring on the mountain tops. The charioteers were warriors [   ], and all good officers, ready of hand. Their horses were quivering in their every limb, ready to crush the countries under their feet . . . Those who reached my boundary, their seed is not; their heart and their soul are finished forever and ever. As for those who had assembled before them on the sea, the full flame was their front, before the harbour mouths, and a wall of metal upon the shore surrounded them. They were dragged, overturned, and laid low upon the beach; slain and made heaps from stern to bow of their galleys, while all their things were cast upon the water. (Extracts from Medinet Habu inscription, trans. Breasted (1906: iv. §§65–6))

It should be stressed that the invasions were not merely military operations, but involved the movements of large populations, by land and by sea, seeking new lands to settle.[38] Their land forces were moving south along the Levantine coast and through Palestine[39] when they were confronted and stopped by Ramesses' forces at the Egyptian frontier in Djahi (in the region of later Phoenicia). However, their fleet reached the coast of Egypt, where it was destroyed by the Egyptian fleet.

We must now examine the identity and provenance of these invaders and the part they played in the collapse of the Late Bronze Age civilizations. The term 'Sea Peoples' was coined in the late nineteenth century to refer to the invaders from across the sea described in Egyptian sources, and has been widely used by historians and archaeologists ever since. Yet it is a misleading term, for there can be little doubt that a number of the groups of peoples covered by it had neither an island nor a coastal origin, and indeed their movements and activities were not confined to the sea or to coastal regions, but encompassed almost the entire Near Eastern world.

Their possible origins have also caused much debate and speculation. We can, however, assign an Anatolian origin to at least the Lukka element amongst the groups that attacked Egypt in Merneptah's reign, and very likely to the Denyen (Danuna) group who figure in the records of Ramesses III's reign. Indeed it is quite possible that all groups listed in the Egyptian records originated in Anatolia, particularly western Anatolia. The Teresh may, as we

[38] Note e.g. that the Peleset and Tjekker warriors who fought in the land battle are accompanied in the reliefs by women and children loaded in ox-carts.
[39] See Albright (1975: 507–16).

have noted, be identical with the Tyrsenoi whose original home-land according to the Greek historian Herodotos was in Lydia.[40] The Ekwesh, if the name can be equated with Hittite Ahhiyawa/ Greek Akhaia, may represent the remnants of Achaian/ Mycenaean settlement at various points along the western Anatolian coast after Ahhiyawa lost the significant presence and influence it had enjoyed in the region for two centuries. The Peleset may also have originated from western Anatolia.[41] A further sug-gestion is that the name Tjekker is associated with Teucer, one of the heroes of the Trojan War, and ancestor in Greek literary tradi-tion of the Troad people known as the Teucri. But we are now getting into the realms of pure speculation.

Nevertheless the western Anatolian region may well have pro-vided the genesis for the movements of the 'Sea Peoples'. For this seems to have been the region where the political structures estab-lished by the major Bronze Age powers first began to crumble and disintegrate. We have seen the problems which the Hittites had in controlling the region, very marked in the reign of Hattusili III, and the probable loss of Ahhiyawan political and military influence in the same region during the reign of Hattusili's son Tudhaliya. However much foreign control may have been resented by the subject states upon whom it was imposed, the overlordship of the Hittite and Ahhiyawan kings in western Anatolia probably helped ensure some protection for the regions where vassal states were established, at least for limited periods of time.

On the other hand, the overlords also helped create the con-ditions for ever-increasing population instability. They did so through their practice of removing and relocating in their home territory large groups of transportees from rebellious vassal states, a practice which led to prisoners or disaffected subjects trying to escape their authority by seeking refuge in other nearby kingdoms. The tensions and rivalry between Hatti and Ahhiyawa in western Anatolia merely served to exacerbate these unsettled conditions. With the decline and disappearance of both Hittite and Ahhiyawan influence in the region, the movements of population groups, large and small, gained increasing momentum. Local rulers could no longer call on the support of an overlord, or guarantee protection to their own subjects. In an environment of increasing insecurity

---

[40] Herodotos i. 94.   [41] See in particular Singer (1988c).

and anarchy, groups began abandoning their old homelands in search of new lands to settle.

These groups were not in themselves the cause of the cataclysmic events which brought about the collapse of the Bronze Age kingdoms. Rather they were associated with the gradual disintegration of these kingdoms, and were at least in part the victims of it. In the widespread unsettled conditions of the period, they took on a marauding aspect in their search for new lands. By so doing they may well have accelerated the final collapse of the main centres of power.

Yet the actual nature, extent, and duration of their activities leave much room for doubt. The view that they were participants in a carefully planned military operation[42] is not sustainable. Rather, they were a largely disorganized array of groups, who banded together from time to time in their wanderings and sometimes joined forces for raids and, on occasions, more extensive military operations. They may have had much of the character of the roving, marauding bands that are frequently depicted by science fiction writers in a post nuclear war environment.

The perception of them as a united organized enemy depends very largely on their depiction in Egyptian records, most notably the account of Ramesses III. Yet questions have been raised about the historical validity of these records. The graphic account of Ramesses' conflict with and triumph over his enemies has been seen as a 'narrative condensation of a continuous long-lasting process, consisting in small skirmishes and rebuffs of repeated attempts at assault and penetration, into a single great military event, to serve a precise propagandistic purpose'.[43] Another scholar expresses a similar view: 'It is most probable that a series of small episodes were joined together in order to artfully build up a "battle" that as such never took place, but was required by tradition and by functionality in the propagandistic celebration—even by way of symmetry to the real and decisive battle won against the Libyans.'[44] Such 'deconstructionism' markedly reduces the dramatic impact of the Egyptian narrative, and considerably scales down the extent of the Egyptian military achievement. But it may well provide us with something closer to the truth.

---

[42] Thus Mellaart (1984: 77).   [43] Cifola (1988: 303).
[44] Liverani (1990: 121).

There is also a disappointing lack of unequivocal archaeological evidence for the movements of the displaced peoples. The combination of both written records and archaeological evidence reveals a clear break in occupation of many sites along the Syro-Palestine littoral, and of some inland sites c.1200.[45] However, it is virtually impossible to identify the authors of the destruction of the cities of the Levant—Egyptian, Israelite, or Sea Peoples—even if the last of these remains a prime suspect for sites along the coast.[46] As far as the Levant is concerned, the debate over assigning responsibility for the destructions at the end of the thirteenth century to the Sea Peoples, to invading Hebrews or rebellious dispossessed Canaanites on their way to becoming Hebrews, really highlights the lack of any evidence from which we can draw meaningful conclusions.[47]

The Collapse of the Hittite Kingdom

Many theories have been proposed to account for the collapse of the Hittite kingdom and other contemporary powers in Greece and the Near East at the end of the Late Bronze Age.[48] Amongst these theories several have attributed the demise of the Late Bronze Age kingdoms largely to natural forces, such as earthquake and drought.

A strong advocate of the earthquake theory was C. F. A. Schaeffer who proposed that many of the cities of both Anatolia and Syria, including Hattusa and Alalah, fell victims to earthquake c.1200.[49] The destructions of Knossos (in Crete) and Troy VI were similarly explained by Sir Arthur Evans and Professor Carl Blegen respectively. Such theories are no longer given much credence. In the great majority of cases, there is little or no demonstrable archaeological evidence of earthquake activity, at least on such a scale as to have caused the total destruction and abandonment of a site.[50] Even in the few cases where earthquake may have played some part (such as at Troy; see Ch. 14), the evidence is equivocal and inconclusive.

---

[45] Millard (1984: 8).   [46] Ibid.
[47] Thus Muhly (1992: 14).
[48] For a recent survey of these, see Drews (1993: chs. 3–8).
[49] In Nougayrol *et al.* (1968: 753–68).
[50] See Drews (1993: 47).

The theory of a prolonged drought in the Greek and Near Eastern worlds has had wider currency amongst scholars.[51] Rhys Carpenter, the most influential advocate of this theory,[52] argued that *c.*1200 the eastern Mediterranean world suffered a drought of such length and severity that many of the peoples of this world were forced to abandon their homes. Spurred on by hunger, they attacked and destroyed the major Bronze Age centres, in order to gain access to their storehouses of grain and other food supplies. We have referred to a number of texts which indicate food shortages, if not actual famine, in the Hittite world during the reigns of the last Hittite kings. But such shortages may have been due largely to human factors, such as the disruption of grain supply routes, rather than to a disastrous change in weather patterns. We simply do not have evidence of a drought of such length and intensity and extent that it brought about, or contributed substantially to, the collapse of the Bronze Age centres of power.

This does not of course rule out the possibility of periodic droughts in Greece and the Near East, which in the last decades of the Late Bronze Age exacerbated the mounting pressures and problems faced by the rulers of the Near Eastern and Mycenaean worlds.[53] If the kingdom of Hatti in particular was becoming increasingly dependent on importation of grain supplies, even temporary shortfalls in local grain production caused by drought would have given an increased urgency to ensuring that regular shipments from abroad were not disrupted. And if other factors intervened which seriously affected the Hittites' ability to maintain political stability throughout their kingdom, then food shortages caused by drought or the disruption of supply routes might well have led to a crisis of major proportions.

A further theory that the introduction of ironworking technology which placed weapons of iron in the hands of Anatolian rebels and enabled them to overthrow the Bronze Age kingdoms[54] has been justifiably dismissed.[55]

---

[51] Discussed by Drews (1993: 77–84).   [52] See e.g. Carpenter (1968: 9).

[53] Drews (1993: 79) refers to physical evidence from Gordion, in the form of a series of narrow tree rings in a juniper log unearthed at this site, pointing to an Anatolian drought *c.*1200.

[54] As once argued by Childe (1954: 182–3).

[55] Drews (1993: 73–6). Cf. Sandars (1985: 174–7). On the use of iron in the Hittite world, see Muhly *et al.* (1985). The Hittite texts which refer to iron have been collected by Košak (1986).

A 'systems collapse' has also been adduced as a prime reason for the decline and collapse of the major centres of power in the Late Bronze Age world, in Anatolia and Syria, and Mycenaean Greece.[56] In the case of the Mycenaean world, it has been argued that complex commercial operations absolutely demanded conditions of reasonable security,[57] that the prosperity of the Levant and the Aegean was commercial and depended on the existence of markets for surplus products, that the Mycenaean kingdoms were over-specialized, over-dependent on central bureaucracies, that dependence on the palace and the over-specialized economy became an acute danger point,[58] and that increasingly unstable conditions in the region led to economic breakdown and ultimate general collapse. Increasing disruption of commercial networks and trading operations may well have been a prominent feature of the last decades of the Late Bronze Age kingdoms in both Greece and the Near East. But they are in themselves symptomatic of a period of general decline and disintegration rather than one of the root causes. We must look elsewhere for these causes.

Another theory is that the 'Catastrophe' at the end of the Bronze Age was the result of a radical innovation in warfare, which suddenly gave the 'barbarians' the military advantage over the long-established and civilized kingdoms of the eastern Mediterranean.[59] The argument goes that the 'barbarians'—in Libya, Palestine, Israel, Lycia, northern Greece, Italy, Sicily, Sardinia etc.—with their swarming infantries and equipped with javelins, long swords, and a few essential pieces of defensive armour were able to overwhelm the chariot-based forces on which the great kingdoms relied, assaulting, plundering, and razing the richest palaces and cities. But even if we were to admit the possibility of such a scenario, or a modified version of it, we are still left with one fundamental question. What finally had so weakened these centres, which had long stood firm against the forces which now allegedly overwhelmed them, that they succumbed? The theory of changes in style of warfare, or weapons used, does not in itself address this question, even if it could be proved to be true.

Should we look for signs of decline and disintegration within the kingdoms themselves as a major factor in their final collapse? We

---

[56] See e.g. Sandars (1985: 47–9, 77–9, 197), Zaccagnini (1990), and the comments by Drews (1993: 85–90).
[57] Sandars (1985: 49).   [58] Ibid. 79.   [59] Drews (1993: 97).

have seen that at a much earlier period in its history the Hittite kingdom had suffered serious internal political upheavals which encouraged aggression by outside forces and led to a substantial reduction of Hittite territory. In the aftermath of the assassination of Mursili I, struggles for the succession had allegedly brought the kingdom to the verge of extinction. Yet the situation had been saved when control was seized by a strong leader, Telipinu, who committed himself to uniting the kingdom beneath his sway. As Hattusili I and subsequently Telipinu had both pointed out, so long as the kingdom remained united, it could resist all foreign aggression. But if it became weak and divided against itself, it would easily fall prey to its enemies.

Until recently, the Hittite New Kingdom was generally considered to have enjoyed much greater internal stability than the Old. Hattusili III's coup against his nephew Urhi-Tesub was seen as the only significant exception to an otherwise peaceful series of royal successions down to the end of the Hittite empire. Recent discoveries, most notably the bronze tablet and the seal impressions of Kurunta, have made it necessary for us to reconsider this view, and to look afresh at other texts dating to the last years of the kingdom. Even before the discovery of the bronze tablet one scholar had commented: 'Without diminishing the role of the outside enemies in the fall of the Hittite Empire, I feel that more weight should be given to the symptoms of inner decline and disintegration.'[60]

Texts from both Tudhaliya IV's and Suppiluliuma II's reign indicate that the monarchy was under constant threat from elements within the higher echelons of Hittite society, particularly members of the extended royal family. In spite of the efforts made by these last Hittite kings to shore up their authority, the threats continued, apparently, to have a destabilizing effect upon the monarchical structure and may well have seriously undermined the king's authority in the eyes of many of his subjects. This is reflected in the rebellion in Hatti and perhaps also in the insubordination of vassal rulers, both reported in Suppiluliuma's reign. If the king had difficulties in securing his own position in Hattusa, what confidence could his vassals have that he could protect them and their kingdoms if they came under threat, from outsiders or disaffected elements amongst their subjects? What incentives were there for

---

[60] Singer (1985*a*: 120).

them to maintain a strong allegiance to their current overlord in Hattusa? As yet we cannot prove that there was a direct connection between a perceived weakening in the central power structure and an apparent crumbling of Hittite authority in the subject territories. It does however remain a distinct possibility, particularly if we give credence to the warnings sounded many generations earlier by Hattusili I and Telipinu.

But in attempting to find reasons for the collapse of the Hittite kingdom, we should be careful not to give undue prominence to any specific set of factors, whether internal or external. Further, its collapse did not occur in isolation. The fact that a number of centres of the Mycenaean world were destroyed in roughly the same period as the fall of Hatti and other Near Eastern kingdoms gives some credence to the view of a series of widespread upheavals and disasters, at least within the Greek and Near Eastern worlds, which led to, or helped precipitate, the downfall of the major centres in both regions. Hence the theories of a long-lasting and ruinous drought, or of simultaneous or contemporaneously related onslaughts by 'Sea Peoples' upon both the Greek and Near Eastern worlds, or of a widespread 'systems collapse'. While we should be mindful that there were significant differences in the patterns of decline and collapse of the Mycenaean and Near Eastern centres of power,[61] it is difficult to believe that there is not some relationship between the course of events in both regions in the last decades of the thirteenth and the early twelfth century. But given the apparent paucity of contact between the Mycenean and Hittite worlds, particularly from the middle of the thirteenth century onwards, we must at present avoid the temptation of devising too precise a set of common factors to explain the pattern of events in both regions in this period.

Historical records of the Hittite kingdom end abruptly in Suppiluliuma II's reign with the account of the naval battles off the coast of Cyprus and the record of military events in the Südburg inscription.[62] The final, violent destruction of Hattusa must have followed soon after, perhaps while the Egyptian throne was

[61] In the Greek Argolid, for example, archaeological evidence indicates a 'destruction horizon' which occurred in several phases over a century or more rather than a single devastating apocalyptic event.

[62] Hoffner (1989b: 48), comments that if Suppiluliuma had a successor, it is likely that his reign was so short and chaotic that there was no opportunity to accumulate a tablet archive.

occupied by the pharaoh Ramesses III who included Hatti in the list of countries that fell before the onslaught of the 'northerners in their islands/sealands'.[63] Archaeological evidence for the destruction indicates that the capital was consumed in a great conflagration.[64] This probably occurred in the very early years of the twelfth century. Satellites of the Hittite kingdom must have fallen around the same time, possibly even earlier in the case of Ugarit.[65] Archaeological evidence further indicates that in addition to central and western Anatolia, the eastern (mainly Hurrian) and southern (mainly Luwian) Hittite districts were also being invaded from almost all directions.[66]

Were the Kaska people responsible for the final sack of Hattusa, as they had been for its destruction in the past?[67] However one explains the weakened state which led to its destruction—internal political instability—severely depleted defence capabilities—communication networks and supply lines in disarray—critical shortages of food and other resources—the royal capital perhaps fell victim, finally and irretrievably, to an enemy who had plagued the Hittites from almost the beginning of their history, an enemy over whom they had often triumphed, but from whose menace they had never been completely secure. Was this the enemy who now delivered the *coup de grace* to the very heart of a kingdom already on the verge of total disintegration?

Other Major Powers in the Aftermath

Egypt escaped relatively unscathed from the upheavals at the end of the Bronze Age. In fact Ramesses III claimed to have followed up his victory over the Sea Peoples with further campaigns in Syria. At least this is what he depicted in scenes on the walls of his temple at Medinet Habu, though the scenes are considered to be

---

[63] See, however, Güterbock (1989: 55), who raises the question of what was actually meant by 'Hatti' in Ramesses' account.

[64] See Bittel (1976b; 1983b: 26–7).

[65] See Singer (1987: 416, 418), who notes that the fall of Ugarit is usually dated shortly before Ramesses III's alleged land battle with the Sea Peoples in Amurru (p. 416, with references cited in nn. 22–4), but could conceivably have been 15–20 years earlier (p. 418).

[66] Yakar (1993: 22).

[67] Cf. Hoffner (1973: 206), Mellaart (1984: 79), Bittel and Otten, cited by Güterbock (1989: 55).

anachronistic copies taken from a building of Ramesses II.[68] In any case, apart from an apparent fresh incursion from Libya in year 11, Egypt seems to have remained secure from any major external military threats in the last twenty years of Ramesses' reign, and his inscriptions record a number of peaceful enterprises, including an expedition to the Land of Punt.[69] But within his kingdom, the pharaoh was faced with serious troubles during his final years, apparently due to administrative incompetence and disloyalty on the part of his officials.

The Twentieth Dynasty to which he belonged continued for almost a century after his death. But under his successors, the kingdom of the pharaohs was but a pale shadow of what it had been during the ascendant years of the two previous dynasties. While it outlasted its northern counterpart, the kingdom of Hatti, it was never again to regain the initiatives which had led to its becoming one of the dominant powers in the Near East. Finally, in the seventh century, Egypt was conquered by Assyria (see below). The future course of Near Eastern history was to be determined by other powers which were now beginning to emerge and would come to full strength during the course of the first millennium.

In Assyria, we have seen that Tukulti-Ninurta's reign had limped to an inglorious finale, ending with his assassination. Although Assyria seems not to have been directly affected by the chaos and devastation occurring in other parts of the Near Eastern world in the years following his death, it none the less experienced a period of continuing political and military decline under his immediate successors.

At the beginning of the first millennium it was no more than a remnant of the great kingdom it once had been in the days of Adad-Nirari and Salmaneser. Its territory was reduced to a narrow strip of land extending some 150 kilometres along the Tigris river; to the south its prospects for expansion were limited by the kingdom of Babylonia, and to the north and east it was in constant danger from warlike tribes—particularly the Arameans—who encroached upon its frontiers and threatened its cities.

But then, early in the first millennium, Assyria entered upon a new era of aggressive militarism and territorial expansion. This was initiated by the king Adad-Nirari II (*c.*911–891). After driving the

[68] See Faulkner (1975: 243).
[69] Information provided by the Harris Papyrus; Breasted (1906: iv. §407).

Arameans out of the Tigris valley, the new Assyrian warlord conducted campaigns into Babylonia where he defeated the king Samas-Mudammiq, seized a large slice of his territory, and incorporated it afresh into the Assyrian kingdom. These campaigns laid the foundations for further expeditions by his successors beyond the kingdom's frontiers. By the reign of the king Sargon (*c*.721–705), Assyrian authority extended through the entire Fertile Crescent, westwards into Anatolia, southwards to the Persian Gulf, and eastwards into Elam (part of modern Iran). In the reign of Sargon's grandson Esarhaddon (*c*.680–669), Assyrian military enterprise extended as far afield as Egypt. The once-great kingdom of the pharaohs was conquered after a short campaign and added to the long list of subject states of the Assyrian empire.

Ultimately, then, Assyria proved to be the only major survivor of the great Late Bronze Age powers. But its survival proved short-lived. For in the late seventh century it too was to fall, the final blow being delivered by a coalition formed between the Chaldaean rulers of Babylonia and the newly emerging kingdom of the Medes.

What Happened to the Hittites?

With the final destruction of the Hittite capital early in the twelfth century, the kingdom over which it had held sway was at an end. Within but a few generations, all trace of it seems to have been lost to human memory. But how complete was the actual destruction of the Hittite centres outside the capital? Or of the vassal kingdoms subject to Hatti? What was the fate of those who populated the Hittite world? Who inherited what survived the devastation which brought about its final collapse?

While centres like Hattusa and Ugarit succumbed to total destruction, the evidence for devastation elsewhere in the regions they once dominated is far less marked. The sites destroyed by fire seem to have been limited to the regions east of the Marrassantiya river, with Karaoghlan (south of Ankara) the only site west of it; there is no visible evidence of such a catastrophe further west.[70]

---

[70] See Bittel's map (1983*b*: 32, Abb. 2), indicating the pattern of destruction. This is quite contrary to the assertion by Goetze (1975*c*: 266) that 'wherever excavations have been carried out they indicate that the Hittite country was ravaged, its cities burnt down'. Cf. Mellaart (1984: 78–9).

Indications from archaeological excavations are that only a small number of sites of the Hittite world were actually destroyed; the majority were simply abandoned, as Bittel has demonstrated, for example, in the case of the Late Bronze Age level at Gordion. In summary, 'the conclusion to be drawn from the very small number of sites that can be proved to have been burnt *c.*1176 BC and the very large number that just seem to have been deserted in the Hittite homeland is that though politically the attack by its neighbours was disastrous for Hatti, the loss of life must not be exaggerated'.[71]

The overall, though still far from complete, picture we have of the centuries immediately following the collapse of the Hittite kingdom is not one of widespread destruction and massacre, but of large-scale movements of peoples—abandoning their homelands, grouping and regrouping with other peoples on the move, then finally dispersing, sometimes to lands far from their places of origin. Some groups, like the Sherden, Shekelesh, and Teresh, and a group of Pelasgians may have gone west, to Italy, the Adriatic region, and the islands of the western Mediterranean. Others, most notably the Peleset, or Philistines, settled on the coast of Canaan, where sites like Ashdod, Eqron, and Ashqelon are revealing important aspects of the Philistines' material culture.[72]

Other groups seem to have remained in or returned to their original homelands. Notable amongst these were the Luwian-speaking inhabitants of the Lukka Lands in south-west Anatolia. These became prominent in the countries which in the first millennium BC the Greeks called Lycaonia and Lycia. The countries in question were almost certainly part of the original Lukka homeland. In Lycia the native population was joined by immigrants from other regions, probably including Crete.[73] But the original inhabitants retained a number of features of the civilization and culture of their Bronze Age Luwian ancestors, most evident in the names of their deities[74] and in their Luwian-derived language.[75] Further, there is a notable persistence of Hittite and Luwian place-names in this region in the first millennium; thus Arñna (the Lycian name for

[71] Mellaart (1984: 78–9).
[72] In general on the settlement of the Sea Peoples in Canaan and Palestine, see Singer (1988c: 240).
[73] See Bryce (1986c, 29–35).
[74] Ibid. 175–8.
[75] See e.g. ibid. 64–6, and the refs. cited therein.

Xanthos) derives from Late Bronze Age Awarna-Arinna, Pinara from Pina-Pinale, Tlawa (the Lycian name for Tlos) from Dalawa, Oenoanda from Wiyanawanda.[76] The survival of such a contingent of names from the Bronze Age seems to reflect a stable population group which remained relatively unaffected by the upheavals which were associated with the demise of the major Bronze Age kingdoms,[77] although this still requires confirmation by archaeological evidence.

In any case, Luwian elements amongst the Late Bronze Age peoples of Anatolia continued with some vigour beyond the end of the Bronze Age through the succeeding 'Dark Age', and figured prominently in the Iron Age civilizations of the first millennium.[78] The kingdom of Tarhuntassa which extended through the region later known as Cilicia and Pamphylia and had a predominantly Luwian-speaking element in its population, may well have continued to exist as an independent kingdom in the centuries which followed the collapse of the Hittite kingdom. Even as late as the Roman imperial period, Luwian names figured prominently in the inscriptions of Cilicia Aspera as well as Lycia.[79] It is also significant that the majority of hieroglyphic inscriptions, attributable to the rulers of the early Iron Age kingdoms in south-east Anatolia and northern Syria, date to the first two centuries or so of this period.

The communities along the Aegean coast of Anatolia were no doubt affected by the unsettled conditions in the centuries which followed the end of the Bronze Age. And there may well have been a southward shift of some of the peoples in this region.[80] But major centres like Millawanda/Milawata (Classical Miletos) survived, as did other settlements along the coast. They continued to be occupied by local inhabitants, while absorbing large numbers of Greek-speaking immigrants from across the Aegean.[81] Indeed it was the influx of Aiolian and Ionian settlers from the Greek world around the end of the second millennium, and their admixture with the native Anatolian inhabitants, which helped give the region to become known as Ionia its rich and distinctive character in the first millennium.

[76] Cf. Mellink (1995: 189–90).   [77] Ibid. 193.
[78] Ibid. 188, with regard to Tarsus and Adana.
[79] See Houwink ten Cate (1965).
[80] See Košak (1980c: 43).   [81] See Yakar (1993: 7–8).

In spite of its inclusion in Ramesses III's list of countries devastated by the Sea Peoples, the kingdom of Carchemish on the Euphrates, one of the two viceregal seats in Syria from the time of Suppiluliuma I, seems to have survived the upheavals at the end of the Bronze Age relatively unscathed.[82] Indeed at Carchemish a branch of the Hittite royal dynasty continued for at least several more generations after the collapse of the central dynasty at Hattusa. From royal seal impressions discovered in 1985 at Lidar Höyük on the east bank of the Euphrates,[83] we know that Talmi-Tesub, the great-great-great-grandson of Suppiluliuma I and the viceroy at Carchemish during the reign of Suppiluliuma II, was succeeded by his son Ku(n)zi-Tesub.[84] The fact that he styled himself 'Great King' suggests that the central dynasty at Hattusa was now defunct and that he saw himself as the one true heir of the line of the great Suppiluliuma. Further inscriptional information from Arslantepe established the names of two brothers, kings of Melid (Classical Melitene, modern Malatya), who were the grandsons of Kuzi-Tesub,[85] thus enabling us to extend further the genealogy of the Bronze Age Hittite kings.

The central line of this dynasty did not, apparently, survive the catastrophe which brought about the end of Hattusa. This left Kuzi-Tesub from the collateral line as the dynasty's sole heir. Yet the Anatolian kingdom had disintegrated, and Kuzi-Tesub's domain extended through no more than part of the eastern territories of this kingdom, along the west bank of the Euphrates from Malatya through Carchemish to Emar.[86]

This may well have provided a new homeland for a number of groups from the old homeland, particularly perhaps the more elite elements of Hittite society, including members of the royal court. Although Carchemish no doubt retained a predominantly Hurrian character, the establishment of a Hittite viceregal seat there with its accompanying social and administrative infrastructure must have created an environment not unlike that of the palace society at

---

[82] Although immediately to the south Emar seems to have fallen victim to 'troops of foreigners' at this time; see Arnaud (1987: 20 n. 3), in reference to the text ME 73, which mentions their siege of Emar.

[83] See Sürenhagen (1986).

[84] See Sürenhagen (1986), Hawkins (1988), Hoffner (1989b: 49).

[85] Hawkins (1988: 101).

[86] Hawkins (1995a: 1300–1).

Hattusa.[87] It had obvious attractions for those who had the means to relocate themselves there. Yet this kingdom was not long to survive in the form in which Kuzi-Tesub inherited it. Perhaps even in his lifetime it too began to follow the pattern of fragmentation into smaller units that occurred elsewhere in the Near Eastern world. There would be no return to the political coherence which in the Bronze Age had been established to a greater or lesser degree by a succession of Mitannian, Egyptian, and Hittite overlords.

From this process several new kingdoms emerged in Syria, including the kingdom of Melid where Kuzi-Tesub's grandsons ruled. To the south was the kingdom of Kummukh, the Commagene of Graeco-Roman times, and further south again the kingdom of Hamath in central Syria. The fragmentation may have been caused in part by an influx of new settlers, most notably the Arameans who settled in large numbers across the Fertile Crescent from *c.*1100 onwards, and the Phoenicians who settled along the Mediterranean coast. These new groups significantly altered the political and cultural climate and configuration of the region. Even so, a Hittite veneer persisted. Tangible illustrations of this are provided by Hittite-type monuments and sculptures, and above all by the 'Hittite' hieroglyphic inscriptions of the region.[88] Assyrians, Urartians, and Hebrews continued to refer to Syria and the Taurus region as 'the Land of Hatti', and the Bible makes reference to the local Syrian rulers as 'Kings of the Hittites'.[89] Indeed in Assyrian records a number of the kings of the region continued to have names strongly reminiscent of those of the Late Bronze Age Hittite kings—names like Mutallu (cf. Muwatalli) and Lubarna (cf. Labarna). And although the cuneiform script disappeared entirely from both Anatolia and Syria the hieroglyphic inscriptions of the region helped perpetuate Hittite traditions.[90] Because of the persistence of this Hittite veneer, the kingdoms which emerged in Syria out of the obscurity of the Dark Age are sometimes known as the Neo-Hittite, or Syro-Hittite kingdoms.[91]

[87] Cf. Liverani (1978: 153–5).
[88] The language of the inscriptions was Luwian, as in the Bronze Age.
[89] 2 Kings 7: 6, 2 Chron. 1: 17, discussed further below.
[90] Cf. Hawkins (1974: 68), Gurney (1992: 32).
[91] Liverani (1992: 143 n. 36) comments: 'It is to be underscored that the extent of the Neo-Hittite states is coincident with those areas (Carchemish, Tarhuntassa, Isuwa) that had already an autonomous status at the close of the empire.'

The Hittites' Successors in Anatolia

Who were the heirs of the Hittite homeland and adjacent regions? In southern Anatolia, we see a pattern of development similar to that in Syria, with the persistence of elements of Hittite civilization, for example in eastern Cilicia at the site now known as Karatepe (ancient Azatiwataya). An important bilingual inscription, in Phoenician and Luwian hieroglyphs, was discovered here in 1946. Also important are a group of inscriptions discovered on the mountain-top sanctuary Karadağ and in the city of Kizildağ[92] in the region of the Konya Plain. These, composed by a 'Great King' Hartapu, who also designated his father Mursili as a Great King, are closely linked stylistically with the 'Yalburt inscription' of Tudhaliya IV.[93] In 1971, a further hieroglyphic inscription came to light in the same region on the western slope of a hill called Burunkaya to the north-east of modern Aksaray. Here again the name Hartapu, the Great King, appeared along with the name of his father, the Great King Mursili.[94]

In the past, this group of inscriptions was generally considered to date to a much later period than the last years of the Bronze Age Hittite kingdom. This is because a figure in relief, which is next to one of the inscriptions (Kizildağ 1) and presumed to be a representation of Hartapu, has been dated to the eighth century. But the inscriptions can now almost certainly be assigned to the period immediately following the fall of Hattusa.[95]

Who then were Hartapu and his father Mursili? It is very tempting to see them as genealogically linked to the royal house of Hattusa. Indeed, more than twenty years ago it was suggested that the Mursili in question was Mursili III, i.e. Urhi-Tesub; if so, then Hartapu was Urhi-Tesub's son.[96] The stylistic linking of the Hartapu inscriptions with inscriptions of the last known Hittite kings has led to further consideration of this suggestion.[97] In any case, we can now see in Hartapu and his father the inheritors of a southern Anatolian kingdom which survived the collapse of

[92] Two from the former, five from the latter, published by Alp (1974).
[93] See Hawkins (1988: 106–7; 1992).
[94] Alp (1974: 20).
[95] They are assumed to be 'post-Empire' on the grounds that no Anatolian ruler would refer to himself as 'Great King' while the throne of Hattusa was still occupied; see Hawkins (1992: 270).
[96] Mellaart (1974: 514–16).
[97] See Hawkins (1992: 270; 1995c: 64).

Hattusa. Perhaps the seat of their power was Tarhuntassa, whose history becomes very obscure after the treaty which Tudhaliya IV drew up with its appanage king Kurunta. Indeed it is possible that the two post-Empire kings were descendants of Kurunta.[98]

That still leaves the sculpture to be explained. The suggestion has been made that it was added to the inscription some four centuries later, in the eighth century, by a southern Anatolian king called Wasusarma, son of Tuwati, whose royal seat was probably at Kululu near Kayseri. 'Possible military success in the Konya plain could have placed the city Kizildağ and the mountain top sanctuary Karadağ in the hands of Wasusarma. Could we suppose that he felt moved to add to the inscriptions of the Great King (an ancestor real or pretended) an anachronistic likeness accompanied by a repeat of his royal cartouche?'[99]

Hieroglyphic inscriptions indicate the existence of a country called Tabal (biblical Tubal) in the region of what in Hittite times was called the Lower Land, and which included the cities of the Classical Tyanitis—Tuwanuwa, Tunna, and Hupisna. Tabal seems originally to have consisted of a series of small independent states, or petty kingdoms, whose rulers sent gifts to the Assyrian king Salmaneser III (c.858–823). During the course of the eighth century, Tabal became united into a single confederacy ruled by the dynasty of Burutas.

From the inscriptions of Tabal, we learn of the prominence of the goddess Kubaba in Tabalic cult. Kubaba was a later version of the Hurrian goddess Hepat, who had figured prominently in the Hittite pantheon at least from the time of Hattusili III. The worship of Kubaba and the monumental hieroglyphic inscriptions give good reason to suppose that the ethnic and cultural affinities of the people of Tabal were predominantly Luwian, perhaps with some admixture of Hurrian. Here too there seems to have been a significant continuity of traditions from the Late Bronze Age Hittite world through the succeeding Dark Age down into the first millennium.

The Tabalic texts make mention of a people called the Kasku, whose territories apparently bordered on those of the country of Tabal. These were almost certainly the descendants of the Late

---

[98] Suggested by Hawkins (1992: 270; 1995c: 64).   [99] Hawkins (1992: 272).

Bronze Age Kaska people. We have suggested that Kaskans may have been directly responsible for the final destruction of Hattusa. With the disappearance of the Hittite kingdom, they may well have swept through the former Hittite homeland from their own homeland in the Pontic region and occupied large expanses of former Hittite territory, to the southern bend of the Marrassantiya river, and east to the Euphrates. Indeed the Assyrian king Tiglath-Pileser I (*c*.1112–1072) was confronted by Kaska forces as far east as the upper Euphrates.[100] Almost certainly they were one of the great survivors, and one of the principal beneficiaries, of the upheavals at the end of the Late Bronze Age.

We also learn from Assyrian records of another people, the Muski, with whom Tiglath-Pileser was involved in conflicts in a region yet to be precisely identified to the south-east of the old Hittite homeland:[101]

In my accession year: 20,000 Muski with their five kings, who had held for 50 years the lands Alzu and Purulumzu—bearers of tribute and tithe to the god Assur My Lord—(the Muski) whom no king had ever repelled, being confident of their strength, they came down and captured the land of Kadmuhu. With the support of the god Assur, My Lord, I put my chariotry and army in readiness and not bothering about the rear guard, I traversed the rough terrain of Mount Kashiyari. I fought with their 20,000 men-at-arms and five kings in the Land of Kadmuhu. I brought about their defeat. Like a storm demon I piled up the corpses of the warriors on the battlefield and made their blood flow into the hollows and plains of the mountains. I cut off their heads and stacked them like grain piles around their cities. I brought out their booty, property, and possessions without number. I took the remaining 6,000 of their troops who had fled from my weapons and submitted to me and regarded them as people of my land. (Assyrian royal inscription, trans. Grayson (1976: 6–7 §12))

The origins and ethnic affinities of the Muski, who may have formed an alliance with the Kasku, are far from certain. They may, however, have entered Anatolia in the west from Thrace and Macedonia in the course of the twelfth century, subsequently advancing through Anatolia, then southwards and finally encountering the Assyrians. They are often closely associated with another

[100] See Grayson (1976: 9 §18), where reference is made to '4,000 Kasku (and) Urumu, unyielding troops of the Hittites'.
[101] On the location of the region occupied by the Muski, either in the upper catchment area of the Euphrates or further to the south-east in the upper Tigris region, see Bartl (1995: 205–6).

group of foreign invaders from the west, the people referred to in Greek sources as the Phrygians. According to Homer's *Iliad*, the Phrygians were already well established in their new homeland at the time of the Trojan War,[102] although most scholars follow the Greek geographer Strabo[103] and date their arrival slightly later. At all events, they appear to have become firmly established in central Anatolia, particularly within the region of the old Hittite homeland, before the end of the second millennium. Originally they may have been quite separate in origin from the Muski, but subsequently amalgamated with them towards the end of the eighth century. Very likely this amalgamation was brought about by the Muski king Mita, who is referred to in the *Annals* of the Assyrian king Sargon (who claims to have inflicted a defeat on him),[104] and can be identified with the well-known Midas of Greek tradition.

In Mita's reign, Phrygia attained a high level of material prosperity, and by the end of the eighth century was a major political power in Anatolia. Mita established the city of Gordion, about 96 kilometers from modern Ankara, as his capital. From here he ruled a kingdom which extended southwards to the Cilician plain, and westwards as far as the Aegean sea. More than any of the other tribal groups in evidence in Anatolia in the centuries which followed the end of the Bronze Age, the united Muski-Phrygian peoples were the true heirs to the role of the sovereign people of Anatolia, a role which the Hittites in spite of their chequered fortunes had filled with distinction for half a millennium.

The Hittites in Biblical Tradition

The Bible contains a number of references to Hittites and Hittite kings. What connections, if any, do these 'Biblical Hittites' have with the kingdom which dominated Anatolia and parts of Syria in the Late Bronze Age, and its successors in the centuries which followed?

A number of references place the Hittites in a Canaanite context, clearly as a local Canaanite tribe, descendants of the

---

[102] *Iliad* 3. 184 ff.
[103] *Geography*, 14. 5. 29.
[104] Luckenbill (1927: 8 §18). Further refs. to the Muski occur in texts from the reigns of the Assyrian kings Tukulti-Ninurta II and Assurnasipal; see Luckenbill (1926: §§413, 442).

eponymous patriarch Heth,[105] and encountered by Abraham around Hebron. The names of these 'Hittites' are for the most part of Semitic type; for example, Ephron, Judith, Zohar.[106] These were presumably the Hittites who were subject to Solomon,[107] and who were elsewhere in conflict with the Israelites.[108] They were a small group living in the hills during the era of the Patriarchs and the later descendants of that group,[109] and clearly to be distinguished from the Hittites of historical records.

Yet there are other biblical references to the Hittites and their land which are not compatible with the notion of a small Canaanite hill tribe.[110] Most notable among these is 2 Kings 7: 6: 'The Lord had made the army of the Syrians hear the sound of chariots, and of horses, the sound of a great army, so that they said to one another, "Behold, the king of Israel has hired against us the kings of the Hittites and the kings of Egypt to come upon us." '

This conveys the impression that the Hittite kings were at least commensurate in importance and power with the Egyptian pharaohs. A similar impression is conveyed by 2 Chron. 1: 17: 'They imported a chariot from Egypt for six hundred shekels of silver, and a horse for a hundred and fifty; likewise through them these were exported to all the kings of the Hittites and the kings of Syria.'[111] In these cases there can be little doubt that the references are to the neo-Hittite kingdoms of Syria.

Is there any connection between the two sets of references, any relationship between the local Canaanite tribe and the neo-Hittite kingdoms? The name similarity could be due simply to chance conflation.[112] Certainly there is no evidence that at any stage in their history the Hittites either settled in or extended their influence into Palestine or other states in southern Syria. On the other hand, one scholar has commented that Hittite cultural influence reaching the Israelites indirectly via the Canaanite kingdoms, after

---

[105] Gen. 10: 15.

[106] See Hoffner (1973: 214).

[107] 1 Kings 11: 1–2, 1 Kings 9: 20–1, 2 Chron. 8: 7–8.

[108] For example, Deut. 20: 16–17, Judges 3: 5–6. See further references in McMahon (1989: 71 ff.).

[109] Hoffner (1973: 213–14).

[110] Cf. McMahon (1989: 73–4).

[111] Note also Joshua 1: 4, where the area around the Euphrates is described as Hittite territory and is clearly to be distinguished from the territory of the 'Canaanite Hittites'.

[112] Suggested by Hoffner (1973: 213).

a passage of time, is detectable in many instances. His contention is that through many years of contact with cities in Syria and Phoenicia (Carchemish, Aleppo, Ugarit) Hittite civilization left its marks there. From there Hittite influences may have filtered southwards to Israel just prior to beginning of the kingdom of David.[113]

---

[113] Thus Hoffner (1973: 214, 221). Further on the whole question of the Hittites in biblical tradition, see Kempinski (1979).

CHAPTER 14

The Trojan War: Myth or Reality?

The Enduring Fascination of Troy

The citadel with which the name Troy is associated lies in the north-west corner of Anatolia in the region called the Troad, so named by Graeco-Roman writers who believed that the whole area was controlled by Troy. The Troad forms a fairly clearly definable geographical unit. It is bounded on three sides by sea—the Hellespont (modern Dardanelles) to the north, and the Aegean Sea to the west and south. The whole area is mountainous and dominated in the south by the Mount Ida massif. It has two major rivers, the Simois and the Scamander. At the confluence of these rivers lies the site of Troy itself, on a mound called Hissarlık, the modern Turkish word for fortress.[1]

The mound overlooks the Hellespont/Dardanelles, which is to-day about 7 kilometres north of the site. Much of the flood-plain which lies in between was probably a large harbour during the Bronze Age, which would have provided an excellent anchorage in the Hellespont for the Trojan fleet of Homeric tradition.

For almost 3,000 years, the story of the Trojan War has provided one of the western world's most important sources of inspiration in the realms of art and literature. Amongst the ancient Greeks and Romans, episodes from Homer's account of the war offered many themes for artistic expression and philosophical reflection. The story of Troy's destruction provided the Augustan poet Vergil with the starting point for his great epic the *Aeneid*, a literary achievement which was tempered, perhaps enhanced, by its underlying political motives. In later European art and literature the tradition once again captured the imagination of a succession of writers, artists, philosophers, and political theorists.

But behind the artistic reflections of the tradition, there has been since the time of the Classical Greeks one persistent question. Did the Trojan War really happen? In the history of Classical

---

[1] On the topography of Troy and its environs, see Cook (1984).

scholarship, whether ancient or modern, there has seldom been a time when this question has not been asked. In recent years in particular, Homeric scholars have devoted much effort to speculating on whether or not there is any historical basis for the tradition of a Trojan War. Numerous books, articles, and public media programmes have been devoted to the topic, and in recent years the tradition has been scrutinized in great detail at a number of international conferences.[2]

Fascination with the possibility that Homer's account in the *Iliad* is based on fact is bound to continue, and scholars will continue to probe for the truth behind the legend. Moreover, Heinrich Schliemann's excavation of the mound at Hissarlık[3] provided, apparently, a specific physical setting for the conflict, and seemed to dispel for all time the belief that the *Iliad* was no more than a literary fantasy.

There are those scholars who firmly believe that the story in the *Iliad* is based on fact—that there was indeed a major conflict between Bronze Age Greeks and Trojans, that the Greeks were united under the command of Agamemnon, that there really was a massive Greek armada of 1,000 or more ships, and that the cause of the conflict was the abduction of Helen of Sparta by the Trojan prince Paris. Schliemann himself was in no doubt about this. Nor was Carl Blegen, the American archaeologist who continued the excavations at Hissarlık from 1932 to 1938. Blegen commented: 'It can no longer be doubted, when one surveys the state of our knowledge today, that there really was an actual historical Trojan War, in which a coalition of Achaians, or Mycenaeans, under a king whose overlordship was recognized, fought against the people of Troy and their allies.'[4] But other scholars are sceptical. One of them comments: 'Our faith in a historical Trojan war is founded above all on Homer, but Homer is not a historian. First of all he is a poet; what he relates is not history but myth.'[5]

---

[2] For example, those held in Sheffield, 1977, Liverpool, 1981, and Bryn Mawr, 1984. Proceedings of the latter two have been published by Foxhall and Davies (1984), and Mellink (1986).

[3] He conducted seven campaigns, from 1871 to his death in 1890. Following his death two further campaigns were conducted by his assistant Wilhelm Dörpfeld.

[4] Blegen (1963: 20).

[5] Hiller (1991: 145). Cf. Finley *et al.* (1964: 9): 'Until (new Hittite or North Syrian texts are produced), I believe the narrative we have of the Trojan War had best be removed *in toto* from the realm of history and returned to the realm of myth and poetry.'

We may well attribute many details of the tradition to a creative imagination, or to borrowings from other times and other places. But if we strip away all these details, are we still left with a core tradition, based on historical fact, of a Greek–Trojan conflict which ended in the destruction and abandonment of Troy?

Possible Anatolian Sources on Troy

Since the conflict is set in Late Bronze Age Anatolia, our Anatolian sources provide an obvious starting in our search for an answer to this question. Do these sources throw any light on the possibility that the tradition of the Trojan War was based on historical fact?

Most scholars agree that Homer's Troy did exist, and can be identified with the Late Bronze Age remains of Hissarlık. And it is generally accepted that the region around Hissarlık provided a plausible setting for a conflict between Mycenaean Greeks and local Anatolians towards the end of the Bronze Age. If this region was in fact the location of an important kingdom during the Hittite period, then we might expect to find references to it in the Hittite texts.

The Swiss scholar Emil Forrer claimed to have found such references. In the course of his discussions of Ahhiyawa in the 1920s and 1930s,[6] Forrer drew attention to the place-names Wilusiya and Taruisa, which are mentioned together in the *Annals* of the Hittite king Tudhaliya I/II. These names appear last in a list of countries in western Anatolia which had rebelled against Hittite rule early in the New Kingdom (see Ch. 6). According to Forrer, they were the Hittite way of writing Troia (Troy) and (W)ilios (Ilion).[7] Forrer noted references in other texts to the vassal kingdom Wilusa, particularly in the treaty drawn up early in the thirteenth century between the Hittite king Muwatalli and the Wilusan king Alaksandu. The latter recalls the name of the Trojan prince Alexander Paris in the *Iliad*.[8] Other identifications of Homeric names with Anatolian names have been suggested. Thus Priam(os), the

---

[6] See e.g. Forrer (1924*b*).

[7] In Homeric tradition, Troy and (W)ilios were two names for the same place. Wilios was an early form of the name Ilios before the initial w, representing the archaic Greek digamma, was dropped.

[8] On the equation, see Güterbock (1986*a*: 33 n. 1), who comments that the similarity between the names had been noted as early as 1911.

name of the Trojan king has been equated with *Pariya-muwa*[9] or even *Piyamaradu*,[10] and Eteocles (*Etewoclewes), son of Andreus, king of Orchomenos, with *Tawagalawa*.[11]

In spite of Forrer's arguments, many scholars have dismissed the Wilus(iy)a–(W)ilios/Taruisa–Troia equation as improbable, or at best unprovable.[12] One of the main problems with the equation is that until recently the Hittite texts gave no clear indication where the kingdom of Wilusa was located, beyond the fact that it was somewhere in western Anatolia.

However, the discovery of a text-join to the so-called Manapa-Tarhunda letter may have thrown additional light on this matter.[13] As we have noted (Ch. 9), the letter was written by Manapa-Tarhunda, vassal ruler of the western Anatolian kingdom called the Seha River Land. There now seems little doubt that this king-dom lay in western Anatolia to the north of the region of Milawata (Miletos). The Seha River itself was almost certainly the river known in Classical times as the Caicos.[14] And it is clear from the text-join that the kingdom of Wilusa lay *beyond* the Seha River Land, i.e. further to the north and in close proximity to the Land of Lazpa, the island of Lesbos off the north-west coast of Anatolia.[15] Almost certainly, then, Wilusa lay in the Troad, in the same region as Homeric Troy. This must considerably strengthen the possibility that the two were directly connected, if not identical.

Further, it is clear from the Hittite texts that Wilusa suffered a number of attacks during the thirteenth century, attacks which may well have involved or been supported by the king of Ahhiyawa, and which in the reign of Hattusili III or Tudhaliya IV resulted in the overthrow of the Wilusan king Walmu. If we accept that the Ahhiyawans of the Hittite texts were Mycenaean Greeks, it is possible that the conflicts, or one of the conflicts, in which Wilusa

---

[9] See Laroche (1972*b*: 126 n. 32).

[10] The suggestion is referred to by Morris (1989: 532).

[11] Thus Forrer (1924*a*); see Košak (1980*c*: 38), Güterbock (1984: 122 n. 26), Morris (1989: 532).

[12] But see Güterbock (1986: 35), who proposes Wilusa > *Wiluwa > *Wiluas > Wilios and Truisa > Truiya > Tröie. *Contra* the latter, see Gurney (1990: 46).

[13] The augmented text has recently been published and discussed by Houwink ten Cate (1983–4: 33–9).

[14] See Gurney (1992: 221).

[15] On the identification of Lazpa with Lesbos, see most recently Houwink ten Cate (1983–4: 44).

was involved in the thirteenth century provided at least part of the historical foundation for the tradition of a Trojan War.

From Hittite sources we learn that Mycenaean involvement in Anatolian affairs covered a period of some 200 years, roughly from the last quarter of the fifteenth to the last quarter of the thirteenth century, and reached its peak during the first half of the thirteenth century. Both documentary and archaeological evidence indicate that Milawata (Miletos) became the most important base for Mycenaean activity in western Anatolia.[16] As we have seen, it was from this base that the king of Ahhiyawa sought to extend his influence through adjacent regions in western Anatolia—regions which in some cases at least were subject to the overlordship of the Hittite king.

Troy's Role in Anatolian Affairs

Where does Troy fit into this picture? To begin with, we should be aware that Troy has assumed an importance in modern scholarship, as well as in popular belief, which may well be out of proportion to its actual importance in its contemporary context. This of course is partly due to its literary associations, but also to the fact that when Schliemann excavated the site of Hissarlık, little else was known of the Bronze Age civilizations of Anatolia.

The discoveries during the last century of a number of these civilizations, most notably the kingdom of the Hittites, have helped provide a more balanced perspective of Troy's role and status in the Bronze Age—though the romantic image of the kingdom of Priam lives on. In political terms, it was clearly not a major Anatolian state or kingdom, even amongst its western Anatolian neighbours. But it was by no means insignificant.

There can be no doubt that Hissarlık-Troy was the centre of a prosperous if not politically powerful northern Anatolian kingdom, and lay in a zone of dense population amid great expanses of rich, arable soil, according to the surveys conducted by John Bintliff in the region.[17] Through most of the Bronze Age, it had widespread commercial and cultural contacts. Significant quantities of

---

[16] See Bryce (1989c: 2), and the references cited therein.
[17] J. Bintliff, 'Environmental Factors in Trojan Cultural History', paper presented at the IVth International Colloquium on Aegean Prehistory, Sheffield University, April 1977.

Mycenaean pottery in various sub-levels of Level VI[18] indicate close contacts between Troy and the Mycenaean Greek world.[19] Contact between mainland Greece and Troy is attested even in the Middle Bronze Age.[20]

Yet if we can identify Troy with the kingdom of Wilusa, then it is clear from our Hittite records that it suffered a number of military attacks and occupations during the thirteenth century, attacks which apparently had at least the support of the Ahhiyawan king if not the direct involvement of Ahhiyawan forces. We have equated these Ahhiyawans with Mycenaean Greeks. Thus long-standing peaceful commercial intercourse between Greeks and Trojans seems to have been interrupted on a number of occasions, particularly in the thirteenth century, by disputes and perhaps open conflict between them. Indeed on one occasion, the Hittite king Hattusili III had apparently come close to war with his Ahhiyawan counterpart over Wilusa, possibly because of the latter's aggression towards it.[21]

A number of reasons have been suggested for a Mycenaean assault, or series of assaults, on Troy, most of them rather more prosaic than a desire to revenge an outraged husband and recapture a beautiful Mycenaean queen. Perhaps Mycenaean aggression was due to a squabble over use of the Hellespont by Greek merchant ships; Troy may have used its strategic location on the Hellespont to prevent Greek vessels sailing through the straits to the Black Sea, or to impose heavy tolls on ships to which it did grant safe passage. Its location on an alleged major route linking Anatolia with central Europe may also have made it an attractive target for Greek conquest. Perhaps the war had something to do with attempts to gain control of the excellent fishing grounds provided by the Hellespont: 'Troy with its former large bay would not only have formed an ideal harbour base for fishing, but the bay itself would almost certainly have been seasonally full to bursting

[18] See Mee (1978: 146–7), and (1984: 45). Note, however, Mee's comment (1978: 148) that this constitutes only a fraction of the pottery from the site dating to this period.

[19] Mellink (1986: 94) notes that Aegean interests in Troy increase at the time of Achaian expansion to Crete, Rhodes, and the Anatolian coast, as attested by archaeological evidence for trade and settlement in the Halikarnassos peninsula, Iasos, Miletos, Ephesos, Klazomenai, Smyrna, and the Larissa area. This expansion was strongest in LH IIIA, from c.1425 on.

[20] Mee (1984: 45).

[21] The reference to this occurs in the Tawagalawa letter, IV 7–10.

with fish shoals.'[22] Another suggestion is that the conflict arose over access to copper resources.[23]

All these suggestions are very speculative. There are those who still firmly maintain, perhaps not without justification, that the war was fought over the abduction of a Mycenaean queen, even if she were a willing abductee. Hittite kings were certainly prepared to go to war to reclaim subjects who had been removed, whether forcibly or voluntarily, from their kingdom. But all speculations about the possible reasons for a Greek–Trojan conflict bring us back to the basic question of whether the tradition of the Trojan War has an authentic historical basis. Can we relate what we learn from Hittite records to such a tradition? Further to this, can we provide a specific archaeological setting in which the tradition originated?

The Identification of 'Homeric' Troy

According to Blegen, Homer's Troy was the first phase of the seventh of the nine major settlements on the site—Troy VIIa.[24] This conclusion, though long accepted, is no longer in favour. At this stage of its existence, Troy has been described as little more than a 'shanty town', markedly inferior to its immediate predecessor.[25] And its destruction has now been dated to *c*.1200—at the very earliest[26]—too late to be associated with a major Mycenaean assault from the Greek mainland.

The more likely candidate for Homeric Troy is the final phase of the sixth level of the city—Troy VIh. This level, with its imposing towers and sloping walls, accords much better with the Homeric description of Priam's Troy than its successor level. Blegen argued

---

[22] Bintliff in his 1977 Sheffield Colloquium paper on Troy. See also Mee (1978: 148). But note the comments of Muhly (1992: 17), who cites Bloedow, 'Fishing in Troubled Waters', *Echos du Monde Classique*, NS 6 (1987), 179–85.

[23] A theory cited but opposed by Muhly (1992: 17).

[24] For a general account of Troy and the University of Cincinnati's excavations of the site, see Blegen (1963).

[25] See Mellink (1986: 97), Muhly (1992: 17). Easton (1985: 189) comments that the LH IIIC sherds among deposits of VIIa suggest that the destruction took place at a date later than that of the Mycenaean palaces, when Mycenaeans ought not to have been able to muster a coalition of the sort described by Homer. Cf. Mee (1978: 147; 1984: 48–50), Podzuweit (1982: 80). *Contra* Podzuweit's ceramic dating, see Hiller (1991: 153).

[26] Thus Podzuweit (1982: 80). Cf. Korfmann (1986*b*: 25–6).

that there were clear signs that VIh was destroyed by earthquake rather than by human agency, as indicated by cracks in the tower and wall of the citadel and evidence of floor subsidence. However while allowing for the possibility that this damage was caused by earthquake activity,[27] we cannot be sure whether this happened in the last phase of Troy VI or the first phase of Troy VII, or on a scale large enough to cause the destruction of the whole site.[28] By way of compromise, it has been suggested that Troy VIh could still have been brought to an end by enemy action—*perhaps* assisted by an earthquake which made the city vulnerable to conquest.[29]

The archaeological record provides no precise information on when Troy VIh was destroyed. All we learn from pottery found in this level is that it occurred some time within the first seventy years or so of the thirteenth century,[30] probably around the middle of the century.[31] This was the period of the most intense Ahhiyawan activity on the Anatolian mainland, when the Hittite texts record attacks made on the kingdom of Wilusa and the overthrow of the Wilusan king Walmu. New text discoveries may throw further light on this matter.[32]

Let us review at this point what we learn from our Anatolian sources which may have some bearing on the Trojan War tradition:

1. Mycenaean Greeks were closely involved in the political and military affairs of western Anatolia, particularly in the thirteenth century.
2. During this period the Hittite vassal state Wilusa was the subject of a number of attacks in which Mycenaeans may have been directly or indirectly involved. On one occasion, its

[27] The earthquake theory was revived by Rapp and Gifford (1982).
[28] Thus Easton (1985: 190–1).
[29] See Easton (1985: 189–90). See also Sperling (1991: 156), and the references cited by Morris (1989: 533). Morris further comments that new ceramic evidence and analysis associate VIIa with the LH IIIc era, and VIIb now appears sub-Mycenaean, eliminating phases of the citadel later than VI from the Homeric experience.
[30] i.e. during the LH IIIb period. Cf. Mee (1978: 146; 1984: 45), Easton (1985: 191), Mellink (1986: 94).
[31] See Korfmann (1990: 232) (who also suggests a date of *c*.1180 for the destruction of VIIa), and cf. Hiller (1991: 146).
[32] Watkins (1986: 58–62) has suggested that the remains of an Anatolian prototype of the *Iliad* are to be found in a Hittite ritual text, KBo IV 11 (*CTH* 772.1). But at present only a very small fragment of this text is known—far too little to justify serious consideration of Watkins' suggestion. Cf. the comment by Macqueen (1986: 166 n. 81).

territory was occupied by the enemy; on another occasion its king was dethroned.

3. Wilusa lay in north-western Anatolia in the region of the Classical Troad.
4. In philological terms, Wilusa can be equated with the Greek (W)ilios, or Ilion.
5. Within the period of the attacks on Wilusa, archaeological evidence indicates that the destruction of Troy VIh occurred. This is the level which best accords with Homer's description of the citadel of Troy.

Do these points add up to some kind of proof of a 'Trojan War' as depicted in the *Iliad*? Let us review the negative arguments:

1. Our Anatolian written sources provide no evidence for a single, major, extended attack by invading Greeks on an Anatolian kingdom which led to the eventual destruction of that kingdom. Rather the pattern is one of a number of limited attacks carried out over several decades or more, and perhaps an occasional temporary occupation of a beleaguered kingdom.
2. In some cases, Mycenaean Greeks may have been directly involved in the attacks. But in other cases, the attacks were carried out by Anatolian forces under the command of local leaders.
3. While Troy VIh was certainly destroyed during the period in question, we have no clear evidence that it was destroyed by enemy attack.
4. Contrary to Homeric tradition, archaeological evidence indicates that after the destruction of Troy VIh its successor Troy VIIa followed almost immediately after. The site was apparently occupied by the same population group.

If we take all this into account, the most we can say is that our Anatolian evidence provides evidence for a conflict, or series of conflicts, in which Mycenaean Greeks may have played some role, against a north-western Anatolian kingdom towards the end of the Late Bronze Age.

Did this, then, provide the raw material for Mycenaean ballads and lays about the exploits of Mycenaean kings and noblemen on the Anatolian mainland, and ultimately the kernel of the 'historical tradition' in the *Iliad*?

The Making of an Epic

The assumption that the Homeric epics were in a sense an end-product of at least several centuries of oral tradition rests to some extent on the evidence, though slight, of balladists or minstrels performing as entertainers at the banquets of Mycenaean kings and noblemen.[33] The case for a significant body of Mycenaean poetry has been argued by Webster, who states: 'We may suppose that there were three main kinds of poetry at every Mycenaean palace—cult songs, songs about the great kings of the past sung on their anniversaries, and songs sung at banquets which dealt with the international present but laid a strong emphasis on the exploits of the present local king.'[34]

Of course we have no actual Mycenaean ballads or tales or songs, and we can only deduce what their contents and themes might have been. To do this, we try to work backwards from the 'final product', so to speak, making assumptions about the starting point of the Homeric tradition, and hypothesizing about various 'in-between' stages before the epic reached the form in which we know it. In this respect, it might be useful to compare the development of the Mesopotamian Gilgamesh epic. The genesis of the epic dates back probably to the middle of the third millennium, when contemporary evidence indirectly attests to the existence of a king called Gilgamesh of the Sumerian city-state Uruk. The general view is that a body of legendary tales gradually arose about this king which were orally transmitted over a period of perhaps 500 years prior to the composition of the first version of the epic early in the second millennium.[35]

But can we determine a specific starting point for the *Homeric* tradition? Our Greek sources assign various dates to the Trojan War, mostly between the fourteenth and the early twelfth centuries.[36] Mycenaean involvement in western Anatolian affairs reached its peak in the same period. But the history of conflict between Mycenaean Greeks and native Anatolians in western Anatolia goes back at least to the early fourteenth century when

---

[33] See e.g. *Odyssey* 9. 1–11, together with evidence provided by Mycenaean vase-paintings.
[34] Webster (1958: 133).
[35] For a comprehensive treatment of the development of the epic, see Tigay (1982).
[36] These sources are collected and discussed by Forsdyke (1956: 62–86).

Attarsiya, a 'man of Ahhiya' was involved in military action with 100 chariots against the Hittites on the Anatolian mainland (see Ch. 6). It is just possible that *Attarsiya* was the Hittite way of writing the Greek name Atreus, a name borne in Greek tradition by one of the early rulers of Mycenae.[37] Could the Trojan War tradition have begun with a military engagement between Mycenaean Greeks and Anatolians in the fifteenth century?

Professor Emily Vermeule has argued that there are linguistic as well as other elements in the *Iliad* which could well be dated to this period. From a study of a number of passages in the *Iliad*, she concludes that the deaths of 'Homeric' heroes like Hector and Patroclos were already sung in the fifteenth or fourteenth centuries. Thus Homer's epic contained elements which go back a century, or perhaps much more, before the period when the Trojan War was alleged to have taken place.[38] Ballads and lays celebrating Greek heroic exploits against an Anatolian population may well have been sung at the courts of Mycenaean kings and noblemen in the thirteenth century. But they could have reflected episodes from a distant as well as a more recent past. The tradition on which the *Iliad* was based may have begun much earlier than many scholars currently believe. With each succeeding generation, new episodes, new elements were added to the ongoing saga of conflict between Greeks and Anatolians.[39]

The process continued beyond the end of the Bronze Age. This is apparent in a number of matters of detail in both the *Iliad* and the *Odyssey*. Attention has often been drawn to various inconsistencies in detail, which have led to the conclusion that 'Homeric society' was really an amalgam of three different periods—the Mycenaean Age, the Dark Age, and the early Iron Age. These inconsistencies support the notion of a dynamic oral tradition, in which details can readily be adapted to accord with contemporary fashions, practices, and beliefs.

We should think of Homeric tradition as consisting of a number of chronological layers covering a period of many centuries, with

---

[37] However Güterbock (1984: 119) comments that while the name sounds Greek it is hardly Atreus.

[38] Vermeule (1986: 85–6). See also Hiller (1991: 145), regarding the tradition of an earlier Trojan War, and Muhly (1992: 16).

[39] Cf. Macqueen's comments in Foxhall and Davies (1984: 84).

each layer adding to or blending in with preceding layers, with Bronze Age warriors inhabiting a Dark Age world, and vice versa. Finally the tradition of a Greek–Anatolian conflict was distilled in Greek literature into the story of a single major conflict. But it needed a specific setting—a citadel in north-western Anatolia whose population was subjected to a ten-year siege by Achaian Greeks. The citadel was finally occupied and destroyed by the Greeks, and its population was dispersed—according to Homeric tradition. Is such an event purely the result of a creative poetic imagination?

Perhaps not entirely. We have suggested a link between Homer's Ilion and the Anatolian state of Wilusa, and noted the attacks on Wilusa in which Mycenaean Greeks may have been directly or indirectly involved. Yet it is clear from the Hittite records that Wilusa survived these attacks. That is also borne out by the archaeological record if we link Wilusa with the site identified as Troy. Troy too rose again after its destruction at the end of Level VI.

But there did come a time when Troy was destroyed and apparently abandoned by its population—at the end of level VIIb, some time between 1100 and 1000. This was after the collapse of the major Bronze Age civilizations in the Near East. A few sherds of LH IIIC type from this level reflect the final degradation of the Mycenaean civilization.[40] We certainly cannot rule out the possibility that an episode or episodes from this period contributed significantly to the tale of conflict in the *Iliad*.[41]

All this may have provided the raw material for the making of the epic—a tradition of Greek–Anatolian conflict, a north-western Anatolian state which on several occasions in the thirteenth century was one of the victims of this conflict, the eventual destruction of the citadel of that state. It was the ruined abandoned site that greeted the Aiolian and the Ionian Greeks when they came to western Anatolia after the Bronze Age. Tradition associated this site with a long conflict between the Greek immigrants' Bronze Age ancestors and the local population and their allies. They now saw before them Troy's ultimate fate—its destruction and

[40] Jansen (1995: 1127).
[41] This would not be inconsistent with the views expressed by Finley *et al.* (1964: 1–9).

abandonment.[42] Perhaps it was in this context that the epic of the Trojan War first began to take shape.

In this respect, then, the story of the Trojan War is almost certainly a literary conflation—one which was several hundred years in the making. During this period, there was a gradual accumulation of traditions, many of which may have been inspired by a range of historical incidents. Some of these may have extended well back before the period when the war was alleged to have taken place. At some point, a selection was made from amongst these traditions, and those selected were woven into a continuous narrative. Yet the long-standing belief that this was the achievement of a single great creative genius of the late eighth century, a blind Ionian poet called Homer, may well be an over-simplification. As Vermeule points out, 'it seems fairly clear that no one used the name 'Homer' to refer to an individual person until, *c*.500 BC, Xenophanes and Herakleitos created him to find fault with him.'[43] It could be that there were a number of 'creative geniuses' who contributed significantly to the development of the epic. Quite possibly this part of the process began long before the late eighth century. There may have been one or more Dark Age poets to whom the bard's mantle should be assigned, or at least with whom it should be shared.

---

[42] It should, however, be noted that Troy was not entirely deserted. In a second phase of VIIb a coarse ceramic knobbed ware referred to as *Buckelkeramik* makes it appearance, perhaps reflecting the arrival of an immigrant population group from south-eastern Europe. And some rebuilding near the wall of the citadel around this time has been associated with Aiolian Greeks. Thus there appears to have been some reoccupation of the site, immediately or almost immediately after the destruction of VIIb. If so, it was on a much more modest scale than in the past, and was due to a different population group than its Bronze Age inhabitants. It was not until the campaigns of Alexander the Great in the 4th cent. that Troy VIII became a settlement of some significance. A useful summary of the final stages of Bronze Age Troy and what followed in its aftermath is provided by Jansen (1995: 1126–7).

[43] Vermeule (1986: 86).

A Final Comment

With the reign of Suppiluliuma II, we have reached the final pages in the saga of Hittite rule in the Bronze Age Near East. The kingdom over which Suppiluliuma and his predecessors held sway for some five centuries came abruptly to an end. Hattusa, the royal capital, was destroyed and its population dispersed. So much we conclude from the archaeologically attested catastrophe which befell Hattusa early in the twelfth century, so much from the absence of any evidence to indicate that the Hattusa-based kingdom of the Hittites continued beyond the reign of Suppiluliuma.

For almost 500 years the Hittites were the dominant power in Anatolia, and for much of this period controlled substantial amounts of territory extending south-eastwards to the Euphrates and down through northern Syria. Yet in their progress from petty kingdom to political and military supremacy over much of the Near Eastern world, they experienced dramatic fluctuations in their fortunes. Periods of internal political stability and great military triumphs abroad alternated with periods of internal political upheavals, rebellions in the subject territories, and invasion of the homeland by foreign powers. Indeed on more than one occasion, the kingdom of Hatti was brought close to extinction, by disruptive and destablilizing forces within it as well as by a range of external forces which threatened to engulf it.

When we consider the kingdom's vulnerability to such forces, it seems remarkable that it survived even the first few decades of its existence, let alone continued for a period of half a millennium. The power structure which the kings of Hatti built up in the wake of their conquests always remained precarious, given their difficulty in mounting major campaigns in more than one region of their kingdom simultaneously, their manpower shortages, their dependence on the loyalty of often unreliable vassal rulers, and the everpresent danger of powerful enemies implacably opposed to them. That their lease of power in the Near East lasted so long was an achievement due as much to their political and diplomatic astuteness in their dealings with vassal states and foreign kingdoms as to military prowess. In the field of international diplomacy they were clearly at the forefront of the peoples of the ancient world.

In other respects, they left some enduring legacies to later civilizations long after they themselves had disappeared from human memory. The neo-Hittite civilization of Iron Age Syria provides one of the immediate and most tangible examples of this. But there were other, less easily definable legacies. Hittite civilization drew much from the cultural traditions—social, religious, literary, artistic—of both earlier and contemporary Near Eastern civilizations. In this respect the Hittites were not themselves, apparently, a highly innovative or creative people. Yet by absorbing and preserving many elements of the civilizations of their neighbours, they helped ensure the preservation and transmission of these elements for later civilizations.

Customs, traditions, and institutions which first appeared in the earliest historical societies of Mesopotamia passed from one generation to another and from one civilization to another through the entire Near Eastern world over a period of several thousand years. The Hittites played an important part in this process. They absorbed within the fabric of their own civilization cultural and ethnic elements drawn from the wide range of civilizations with which they came into contact, either directly or through cultural intermediaries. Their religion was a composite of rituals and beliefs made up of native Hattian, Indo-European, Hurrian, and early Mesopotamian elements. Hittite 'literature' was also multi-cultural, consisting largely of folk tales, legends, and myths which were Hattian, Sumerian, Akkadian, Babylonian, and Hurrian in origin, and included a Hittite version of the epic of Gilgamesh. The Hittite collection of laws carried on a long line of legal tradition which extended back through the Code of Hammurabi to the reform texts and legal proclamations of the rulers of the Sumerian city-states in Early Bronze Age Mesopotamia. And aspects of Hittite laws and Hittite diplomatic contracts, which drew at least some of their inspiration from earlier Mesopotamian societies, left their mark on biblical laws and covenants.

More speculative, but perhaps no less important, is the role the Hittites may have played in the transmission of Near Eastern cultural traditions westwards to the Greek world. Graeco-Roman divination procedures had their prototypes in the procedures which are described in detail in Babylonian and Hittite texts. Significant elements of Greek mythology, first appearing in Hesiod's *Theogony*, can be traced back to Near Eastern mythological traditions, some of which are preserved in Hittite texts. Nor can we rule out the possibility that the Gilgamesh epic directly or indirectly influenced the Homeric epics, and that the Hittite version of the former was known in the early Greek world.

The possible reasons for the fall of the Hittite kingdom have provided grounds for much inconclusive theorizing and debate. Yet we should give as much if not more attention to the question of how the kingdom managed to survive so long. Against many odds, its timespan considerably exceeded that of a number of other Near Eastern kingdoms—Akkadian, neo-Sumerian, Babylonian, Assyrian, and the later Chaldaean and Persian empires—and matched that of New Kingdom Egypt.

In the final analysis we might compare the kingdom of Hatti with a living organism that grows and flourishes for a time before succumbing to its inevitable end. The kingdom had emerged and developed, it had survived a number of setbacks which might have brought its life to a premature end, it had reached its prime, and for a relatively long period flourished in its prime. In its later years, when decline appeared to be setting in, it had enjoyed a brief but vigorous new lease of life. Finally and inevitably its time ran out. There were others to take its place. But even after its demise, its progeny lived on, until this progeny too succumbed to other forces which were to shape the Near Eastern world in the decades and centuries to follow.

APPENDIX I
Chronology

Relative and Absolute Chronology

In attempting to construct a time-framework for the history of the Bronze Age kingdoms, scholars use the terms relative and absolute chronology. Broadly speaking, the former refers to the sequence in which events, including the reigns of kings, took place within a particular period, and any degree of coincidence or overlap between them. But such sequences, and the periods to which they belong, are left floating in time until they are anchored by absolute chronology. It is the latter which provides a quantitative, numerically measurable dimension to studies in chronology.

As an initial basis for absolute chronology, a fixed point in history needs to be chosen, from which time-spans for events which occurred before or after it can be calculated. Most civilizations, ancient and modern, have used a year of 365 days as the basic time-unit in such calculations. But a variety of starting points have been chosen. For example, peoples of several of the early Mesopotamian civilizations dated events by noting the year of a particular king's reign in which they occurred; thus the year of the king's accession became the fixed point for dating purposes. The Romans used the legendary date of the founding of Rome as the starting point for their dating system. The ancient Greeks calculated their dates in terms of Olympiads, periods of four years beginning with the date of the first Olympic Games. For the last 2,000 years, however, the Christian tradition has led to the year of Christ's birth being widely used as the chronological point of reference in calculating absolute dates for the course of human history.

Studies in the complementary areas of relative and absolute chronology provide the foundation for reconstructing the time-framework within which the Bronze Age kingdoms of the Near East rose, flourished, and fell. We shall consider below the methods used in arranging in their correct sequence the events which made up the histories of these kingdoms, and in assigning absolute dates to these events, calculated in terms of the number of years they occurred before the beginning of the Christian era.

Hittite Chronology

The chronology of the Hittite kingdom presents scholars with a number of problems. To begin with, Hittite records have left us no comprehensive king-lists, comparable to those of Egypt, Assyria, or Babylon. What are sometimes misleadingly called the Hittite king-lists are in fact royal offering lists—records of sacrificial offerings to be made to dead kings and members of their families during the course of religious festivals.[1] The information which we can obtain from these lists is very limited, and sometimes unreliable. They provide us only with the names of the recipients, they leave out (perhaps deliberately in one or two cases) persons we know occupied the throne, the names are not always in the correct chronological order, and there are inconsistencies between the seven different versions of the lists. Further, the lists end with the reign of the king Muwatalli II who died *c.*1272 BC, thus omitting the last five or six kings of the New Kingdom. In effect, the historical validity of the lists depends essentially on the extent to which the information they contain can be checked against other independent sources of information.

Hittite scholars thus have to construct their own list of Hittite kings, based on information derived from both tablets and seal impressions. This task is often facilitated by the inclusion of genealogical information in these sources, which sometimes traces a particular king's ancestry back several generations to his great-grandfather, or even earlier. By collating this information, we can in most cases arrange the known kings in their correct order, and determine their relationship with their most recent predecessors on the throne.

But problems sometimes arise with a number of kings who had the same name. Thus we know of at least two kings called Hattusili, at least three called Tudhaliya, and three called Arnuwanda. In most cases we have little difficulty in determining whether a particular king was the first, second, or third of that name, particularly if his father's name is given. But there are significant exceptions. For example, there were two kings called Arnuwanda, one of whom reigned early in the New Kingdom another towards its end, whose father was called Tudhaliya. Until comparatively recent times, historical events associated with the first father–son pair had been mistakenly assigned to the second. Further, there has been debate over how many homonymous kings there were. Two Hattusilis or three? Three Tudhaliyas or four? Were there two Hantilis, Zidantas, and Huzziyas who occupied the throne, or only one of each?

The lengths of the various reigns are also problematical. In contrast to information provided in Egyptian, Assyrian, and Babylonian records, we

---

[1] *CTH* 661. See Otten (1951*b*; 1968: 122–6), Kitchen (1962: 53–5). Lists A, C, E, and D were published in full in Haas and Wäfler (1977: 107–13).

have no explicit information on how long each Hittite king reigned. But in some cases we do have a range of information, both Hittite and foreign, on which we can draw in making our calculations. The inevitable margin of error is probably quite small in these cases. But again there are exceptions. For example, we can only guess at how long most of Suppiluliuma I's predecessors reigned. And several scholars have proposed that Suppiluliuma's reign, long assumed to have lasted some forty years, should be reduced to about half this period.[2] Obviously adjustments of this kind have important implications, not only for Hittite chronology *per se*, but also for synchronisms with the reigns of foreign rulers and with political and military developments elsewhere in the Bronze Age Near East.

Historical Synchronisms

In attempting to establish an absolute chronology for the reigns of the Hittite kings, and the events which took place during their reigns, we have to rely very largely on a small number of synchronisms with events recorded in texts from contemporary Near Eastern kingdoms. The following are some of the best known examples:

1. The sack of Babylon by the Hittite king Mursili I occurred in the reign of Samsuditana, the last member of the dynasty of Hammurabi.
2. The pharaoh Tutankhamun died in the year the Hittite king Suppiluliuma I conquered the Mitannian kingdom of Carchemish, which was some six years prior to Suppiluliuma's own death.
3. The Amarna letters provide a series of important synchronisms between events in Suppiluliuma's reign and the reigns of contemporary Near Eastern rulers—the kings of Mitanni, Babylon, and Assyria, and the rulers of Hittite, Egyptian and Mitannian vassal states in Syria.
4. The battle of Kadesh was fought between the Hittite king Muwatalli II and the pharaoh Ramesses II in the fifth year of the latter's reign.
5. The battle of Nihriya was fought between the Hittite king Tudhaliya IV and the Assyrian king Adad-Nirari probably early in the latter's reign and provides useful synchronistic data on the kingdoms of Hatti, Assyria, and Ugarit in the final decades of the Late Bronze Age.[3]

---

[2] Wilhelm and Boese (1987/9) followed, with suggested modifications, by Bryce (1989*b*). *Contra* the model proposed by Wilhelm and Boese, see Astour (1989: 7–8), Freu (1992: 88). For a response to Astour's criticisms of Wilhelm and Boese's chronology, see Wilhelm (1991: 473–4).

[3] See Singer (1987: 414).

Theoretically, correlation of events in Hittite history with the better established chronologies of the kingdoms of Babylon, Egypt, and Assyria should help provide some important fixed dates in Hittite history, given the use that can be made of astronomical phenomena in compiling absolute dates for the history of these kingdoms along with the information which they provide about the lengths of their kings' reigns. Yet the astronomical data are open to different interpretations, and have led to different conclusions about absolute dating. Thus a range of dates have been proposed for the sack of Babylon by the Hittite king Mursili I—as early as 1651, and as late as 1531. These differences have arisen for a number of reasons.

For Babylonian history, date calculations are based on a study of astronomical observations recorded on tablets now surviving in neo-Assyrian copies of the seventh century BC. The originals date back to the Old Babylonian period. These indicate the observations made of the planet Venus in the eighth year of the reign of the Babylonian king Ammisaduqa, the fifth and second-last member of the dynasty of Hammurabi.[4] In theory, correlation of the recorded positions of Venus with recorded lunar calendar dates should enable us to calculate an absolute date for the eighth year of Ammisaduqa's reign. And since we know his position in the Babylonian dynasty, and the length of the reign of each king who belonged to it, we should be able to establish a series of absolute dates for the entire dynasty.

Unfortunately the calculation is not quite so simple. The complete cycle of upper and lower conjunctions of Venus recurs every 275 years, and similar positions of the planet also repeat themselves in two shorter cycles, one of 56 years, the other of 64 years.[5] This has given rise to three possible chronologies, with variations in between—what is commonly referred to as a High, a Middle, and a Low chronology. With the help of Assyriological data contained in the Mari archives, we can at least establish upper and lower limits, in terms of absolute chronology, for the period of the Old Babylonian dynasty. Information from these archives indicates that the Assyrian king Samsi-Adad was contemporary with Hammurabi, whose reign can on other grounds be dated to the late nineteenth–early eighteenth centuries.[6] On the basis of this information, plus the astronomical data, three possible dates have been calculated for the end of the dynasty, and thus the Hittite conquest of Babylon—1651, 1595, 1531. Even then, allowance still has to be made for unknown variables, such as the locations where the astronomical observations were made, the possibility of corruption in the transmission of the records between the time of their

---

[4] The information is recorded on the 63rd tablet of the *Enuma Anu Enlil*, a collection of divine omens.

[5] See Astour (1989: 1–2).   [6] See Cryer (1995: 658).

composition and the time when they finally resurfaced in the neo-Babylonian texts, and sheer human error—or fabrication.[7]

Egyptologists have also attempted to establish an absolute chronology for Egyptian history by combining information from king-lists and other textual data with recorded observations of astronomical phenomena. A starting point for studies in Egyptian chronology was provided by the remains of a work called the *Aegyptiaca* (History of Egypt), compiled in the third century BC by the Egyptian priest Manetho. In this work, Manetho listed 31 Egyptian royal dynasties, from mythical times down to 323 BC (to the reign of Nectanebo II). We will leave aside here the question of the reliability of this list. In the main, dates in Egyptian history have been calculated by comparing data provided by the Sothic calendar (based on observations of the heliacal rising of the dog-star Sirius—called Sothis in Greek, Sopdet in Egyptian) with data from the Egyptian civil calendar. This was made possible by using the information that a Sothic cycle was of *c.*1,460 years' duration,[8] and that a new cycle began in 139 AD;[9] hence the previous cycle began *c.*1320 BC. It then became possible, at least in theory, to calculate a set of absolute dates for events in Egyptian history on the basis of recorded synchronisms between civil calendar dates and the Sothic cycle.[10]

Once again, however, this is complicated by the fact that we cannot be certain where in Egypt particular astronomical observations were made. Clearly, calculations based on the Sothic cycle are dependent on where the observations of the heliacal rise of Sothis occurred. Opinion is largely divided between Thebes and Elephantine. Sightings at the latter (which lay on Egypt's southern frontier) would produce a lower, i.e. later, date than the former. The overall result is that Egyptologists have produced a range of possible dates for various significant events in Egyptian history, including the royal accession dates. Thus we have three possible dates for Ramesses' accession—1304, 1290, 1279, and five possible totals, ranging from 225 to 175, for the number of years between the accessions of Tuthmosis III and Ramesses II.[11]

In view of these uncertainties, most Egyptologists now make little use of astronomical data, and are focusing their attention purely on internal evidence, i.e. the evidence provided by the texts themselves. In this context, the Manethonian tradition still continues to surface.[12] Yet the internal

---

[7] See Cryer (1995: 658).

[8] Based on the fact that every four years the Egyptian civil calendar gained on the Sothic calendar by one day, so that it took 365×4 years ($= 1,460$ years) for a full cycle to be completed. For more precise calculations, see Ingham (1969).

[9] According to the Roman grammarian Censorinus.

[10] See further on this Cryer (1995: 659).

[11] See further on this Krauss (1978: 173), Harrak (1987: 34).

[12] Note in particular Krauss (1978).

evidence presents a further set of variables. As we have noted, the Egyptians have left us detailed king-lists which generally provide data about the lengths of individual reigns. But not always. And the chronology is made more complicated by the co-regency question. How many co-regencies were there, and how long were these co-regencies? Does the stated length of a particular reign include a period of co-regency, or does it indicate the length of a reign after a period of joint rule?

These questions have a bearing on attempts to construct an absolute chronology for Hittite history. For no dates in this history can be established with any degree of confidence or precision independently of the synchronisms provided by the Hittites' Near Eastern neighbours. One may hope that further attention to correlations between Babylonian, Egyptian, and Assyrian data may help eliminate at least some of the uncertainties and variables in the task of establishing a firm absolute chronological framework for the history of the Near East during the Late Bronze Age.[13] Currently, three main chronologies have been developed, and scholars differ on which of the three they support—High, Middle, or Low. The periods between the established historical synchronisms, and the time-frame of events which occurred during these periods, have to be compressed or expanded accordingly.[14] Scholars often show remarkable ingenuity in doing so, in accordance with their own preferred scheme.[15]

There is, however, a current tendency for scholars progressively to lower absolute dates, and in a number of cases to compress the lengths of reigns or a sequence of historical events into a shorter time-frame. Thus there is general (though not universal) support for lowering the accession date of the pharaoh Ramesses II from an originally proposed 1304 BC to a presently favoured 1279 or 1274 BC.[16] This consequentially leads to a lowering of the dates of his immediate royal predecessors and successors, and because of historical synchronisms between Egypt and Hatti, to a number of revisions to the dates of the reigns of the thirteenth- and twelfth-century Hittite kings.

Further revisions may of course be necessary in the light of subsequent developments in the general field of Bronze Age chronology. There is also the question, still to be effectively addressed, of the degree of compatibility between dates established by the analysis of texts and astronomical phenomena on the one hand and dates established by archaeological analysis (including, for example, dendrochronology) on the other. We might note

---

[13] Cf. Harrak (1987: 36), Freu (1992: 41).
[14] This is well illustrated by the papers produced at the 1987 conference in Gothenburg, published by Åström (1987/9).
[15] As Güterbock and Gurney remarked, more than 20 years ago; see Gurney (1974: 105), citing also a comment made by Güterbock some years earlier.
[16] See Bolger (1991: 426).

in passing that while many Near Eastern historians are busily lowering dates, techniques used by Aegean archaeologists suggest that these dates should be pushed in the other direction!

It should be stressed, then, that the dates used throughout this book are provisional, will be disagreed with by a number of scholars, and may need revision or refinement in the light of subsequent developments in the field of Bronze Age chronology. For the present, the chronology used here arises largely from several points of reference—three assumed dates associated with three of the synchronisms referred to above: (*a*) 1595 for the fall of Babylon; (*b*) 1327 for the death of the pharaoh Tutankhamun; (*c*) 1279 for the accession of the pharaoh Ramesses II. In terms of the three proposed basic chronologies, my own chronological scheme might best be described as falling within the Middle to Low range.

Redating of Hittite Texts[17]

We have referred above to the difficulties of assigning to particular reigns a number of texts associated with a name borne by more than one Hittite king. This has applied particularly to a small group of important texts in which the names Tudhaliya and Arnuwanda appear. As we have noted, there were two occasions on which a king Tudhaliya was succeeded by a son called Arnuwanda. In the past, the texts in question were commonly attributed to the second pair, and were thus considered to provide information about historical events in the thirteenth century, in the last decades of the Hittite New Kingdom. However, one of the texts, the so-called *Annals* of Tudhaliya, contains a reference to the king of the Hurrians, almost certainly a king of Mitanni. Since the Mitannian kingdom was destroyed by Suppiluliuma I in the fourteenth century, and was subsequently absorbed into the Hittite and Assyrian kingdoms in turn, then the reference to the Hurrian king raised serious doubts about assigning this text, along with a number of others, to the thirteenth century.

A study of the language of the texts was needed to help resolve the matter. No living language remains static. Over a period of several centuries it will undergo a number of changes in its modes of expression, its grammar, its orthography, and in the characteristics of the script used to write it (i.e. the *ductus*; see Appendix 2). We would have little difficulty today in determining whether a piece of English prose was written in Elizabethan, Victorian, or modern times, on the basis of style, idiom, vocabulary, and even handwriting. Similarly the Hittite language underwent a number of changes during the five centuries of the Hittite kingdom. How does knowledge of these changes assist with dating the texts?

---

[17] Further summary discussions of this topic can be found in Hoffner (1980: 309–10), Košak (1980*b*), Easton (1984: 30–4).

Many texts can of course be firmly assigned to the reigns of particular kings purely on the basis of the events which they record. This provided a useful starting point in using linguistic data for dating purposes. An analysis of the language of these texts, combined with the knowledge of when they were composed, enabled scholars to identify certain features of the language which were characteristic of particular periods in its development. The linguistic criteria which they established for each of these periods could then be applied to texts which proved difficult or impossible to date on other grounds. As a result, the texts were divided into three chronological categories—Old Hittite, the language of the Old Kingdom texts (broadly speaking, seventeenth–sixteenth centuries), Middle Hittite, the language of the texts of the first half of the New Kingdom (fifteenth–fourteenth centuries), and Late Hittite, the language of the texts of the second half of the New Kingdom (fourteenth–twelfth centuries). Pioneering studies in this area were carried out by a number of scholars.[18] The conclusions which they reached were reinforced by research on Hittite palaeography. This showed changes in writing styles over a period of time which were not simply due to idiosyncratic features of individual scribes.[19]

The redating of a number of texts through linguistic analysis has led to a revision of the chronology of some of the major events recorded in Hittite history. Thus texts which had long been assigned to the last decades of the Late Bronze Age, notably those associated with the names Tudhaliya and Arnuwanda, have been reassigned to a period some 150 or more years earlier, to the reigns of the first two kings of these names.[20] Most notable amongst the texts in question are the so-called *Indictments* of Madduwatta and Mita of Pahhuwa (*CTH* 147 and 146 respectively), and the *Annals* of Tudhaliya (*CTH* 142).[21] Clearly, the redating of these texts has important implications for our understanding of the course of Hittite history during the period of the New Kingdom.

---

[18] Notably Carruba (1969), Otten (1969), Houwink ten Cate (1970).

[19] See Rüster (1972), and Neu and Rüster (1975).

[20] There is, however, a school of thought which maintains the traditional dating of the above texts, and explains the apparent early forms as conscious archaising by the scribes. See Heinhold-Krahmer *et al.* (1979); but note the review of this work by Gurney (1982). Knapp (1980: 45–6), also maintains the traditional dating of the Madduwatta text.

[21] These texts are discussed in Ch. 6.

APPENDIX 2

Sources for Hittite History: An Overview

With the disappearance of the Assyrian colonies in the latter half of the eighteenth century, written records ceased in Anatolia, not to reappear until the emergence of the Hittite kingdom in the first half of the seventeenth century. The earliest known Hittite texts were composed in the reign of Hattusili I, who refounded the city of Hattusa and presumably established the first palace archives. The script used in writing these texts was cuneiform, the same as that used in the letters of the Assyrian merchants. But the cuneiform tradition was not inherited from the Assyrians. Rather, it was adopted from the scribal schools of northern Syria, probably through Hittite contact with them during Hattusili's campaigns in the region.[1] Some 5,000 or more clay tablets impressed with the cuneiform script have been unearthed in the Hittite capital Hattusa this century, in perhaps as many as 30,000 fragments. These provide us with our chief source of information on the history of the Hittite world.

The Tablet Archives[2]

The tablets were rectangular in shape, and generally the whole of their surface front and back (obverse and reverse) was closely covered with the cuneiform script. Each side of the tablet was divided into as many as four vertical columns, and the text was also divided into sections by ruled horizontal lines or 'paragraph dividers'. Three types of materials were used for the tablets—clay, wood, and metal. Until recently, we had no surviving examples of the last two types, although the use of wood and metal for writing was made clear by references in the clay tablets to wooden tablets[3]

---

[1] Cf. Güterbock (1964*b*: 108), Hoffner (1973: 204), Cornelius (1979: 104–5), Steiner (1981: 159–60), Beckman (1983*b*: 100).

[2] On tablet archives in general in the Near East, see Veenhof (1986), Otten (1986: 184–5).

[3] For example in a text which sets out procedures related to the purchase of certain goods: 'And what (the purchaser) buys should be set down in (the form of) a wooden tablet, and let that be provisionally(?) sealed. As soon as the King, however, comes up to Hattusa, he (the recipient of the gift) must produce it (for inspection) in the Palace and they must seal it for him (with a royal seal impression)!' (KUB XIII 4 (*CTH* 264A) II 39–44, 48–51, trans. Houwink ten Cate (1994: 237)). We also have references to 'scribes of the wooden tablets'; e.g. KUB XIII 35

and to treaties inscribed on silver and iron.[4] Treaties were also inscribed on bronze, as we know from the discovery in 1986 of the famous and already much-discussed bronze tablet.[5] It is a find of major, indeed unique importance.

The great majority of tablets so far discovered were housed in a number of buildings at Hattusa—several on the acropolis now called Büyükkale (Buildings A, D, E, and K), one on the 'House on the Slope', and one in the the city's most important temple, the temple of the Storm God. In recent years, tablet archives have also come to light during the course of excavations near the modern towns of Maşat, which lies 116 kilometres north-east of Hattusa,[6] Ortaköy, 50 kilometres south-east of Çorum,[7] and Kusakli, 50 kilometres south-south-west of Sivas.[8] The sites where they were unearthed were clearly regional administrative centres of the kingdom, although their Hittite names have yet to be firmly established.[9]

In the archive rooms, the clay tablets were stored on wooden shelves which were built above stone benches covered with mud plaster.[10] Originally the tablets were labelled and arranged according to content. This was the task of the 'tablet librarian'. Unfortunately we know little about the original arrangement or locations of the tablets. During the upheavals to which the capital was subject on several occasions throughout its history, the archives must have suffered substantial damage and disruption. Also, much of the archive material may have been shifted a number of times from one site to another—for example when the Hittite capital was relocated at Tarhuntassa early in the thirteenth century, and shifted back to Hattusa a few years later. Further, the buildings on Büyükkale were totally levelled and rebuilt in the reign of the king Tudhaliya IV not long before the kingdom's final collapse. This must also have led to temporary and perhaps haphazard storage of archive material until such time as a full and

(+) (*CTH* 293) IV 28, in the letter KBo IX 82 (*CTH* 197) where the 'chief of the wooden tablet scribes' is one of the court advisers, and in the treaty on the recently discovered bronze tablet where the holder of the same office appears amongst the list of witnesses to the treaty (Bo 86/299 IV 37). Further on this, see Otten (1963: 3). See also Veenhof (1995a: 312).

[4] On the use of metal tablets in Hittite diplomacy, see Watanabe (1989). Copies of the metal originals were made on clay.

[5] Published by Otten (1988a).

[6] The archive, which consists of correspondence between the king and his local officials, has been published by Alp (1991).

[7] See Süel (1992). The material from the archive has not yet been published.

[8] See Wilhelm (1995b: 37).

[9] For Maşat, Tapikka and Sapinuwa have been proposed. For the former, see the references cited by del Monte and Tischler (1992: 160), Alp (1991: 42–3); for the latter, see Houwink ten Cate (1992b: 133–7), I believe that Süel has proposed Ortaköy for the site of Sapinuwa.

[10] For a description of the archive rooms, see Neve (1982: 104–7), Bittel (1983c: 23–5, 110–11).

systematic reorganisation of the material could be undertaken. Very likely the Hittite capital fell before this happened.

All these factors make extremely difficult the task of determining what system was originally used in arranging archive material, and what the rationale was for its distribution over a number of locations. Were the tablets stored in one building of a particular character or group which distinguished them from those stored in another? Were there basic differences between the tablets housed in the buildings on the acropolis and those stored in the temple?[11] Or was the storage of archive material at the end of the kingdom's history so hasty and haphazard that it is impossible for us to draw any conclusions about their original arrangement? A detailed systematic investigation of the contents of each tablet repository is necessary before we can answer these questions.[12]

The Scribes

Reading and writing in the ancient Near East was a highly specialized occupation, and scribes may well have been the only literate members in their society. Hittite scribes had the responsibility of drawing up treaties, taking down the letters of the Hittite king to foreign or vassal rulers, recording important exploits of the king, revising and updating religious, legal, and administrative texts, copying and recopying them whenever necessary, and then storing the tablets away for future generations. Training for this occupation was provided by scribal schools. It involved learning and mastering the cuneiform script by copying existing texts, progressing from simple to more complex documents.[13] Student scribes must also have learnt at least one, and probably several foreign languages. Given that Akkadian was the international language of diplomacy, many if not all scribes may have been required to be fluent in this language.

No doubt there was a clear hierarchy within the scribal class, ranging at the bottom from persons engaged in mechanical tasks such as copying texts to those at the top who were amongst the most important consultants to the king. The chief scribes presumably had a detailed knowledge of foreign affairs, particularly Hatti's previous and current relationships with both foreign kingdoms and its own vassal states. They must at least have known where to find this information, for much of the detail contained in treaties and in the king's correspondence was probably based on information and

---

[11] The latter seems to have been the chief repository for the treaties with foreign kings and vassal rulers; see Bittel (1983c: 23). Presumably the sacred inviolate character of these treaties was the reason for this.

[12] Work has already begun on this task; see Košak (1995).

[13] On the Mesopotamian scribal school tradition, see Sjöberg (1974), and on the likely continuation of this tradition at Hattusa, see Beckman (1983b: 97).

advice which they provided. Records containing this information could only be consulted by those able to read them. It is likely that the kings themselves were illiterate. After consulting earlier treaties in the archives and extracting relevant clauses from them, the scribe drafted a treaty and read the draft to the king. In the light of changes, modifications, and special provisions required by the king, or agreed to by him after preliminary negotiations with his treaty-partner, the final version of the treaty was prepared.

The chief scribes held a position of considerable responsibility and trust—and influence. It was a highly privileged position, and usually an inherited one, passing from father to son. Some scribes rose to high eminence in the kingdom, as illustrated by the appointment of the chief scribe Mittannamuwa as the administrator of Hattusa when the royal capital was transferred by the king Muwatalli II to Tarhuntassa. In the Hittite-administered city of Emar on the Euphrates, the chief scribe's status was equivalent to that of 'son of the king'.[14]

We know the names of a number of scribes from their practice of signing documents which they had written, and often stating their official position and genealogy.[15] For example:

One tablet (single tablet) of the Presentation of the Plea to the Storm God, written down from the mouth of His Majesty. (Text) complete. (Written by) the hand of Lurma, Junior Incantation Priest, Appre[ntice of], Son of Aki-Tessub. (KBo XI 1, Colophon, rev. 24–7, trans. Houwink ten Cate and Josephson (1967: 119))

Sometimes, a scribe in one royal court appended at the end of an official letter a note to his counterpart in the recipient court:

May Ea the king of wisdom, and Istanu of the Gateway graciously protect the scribe who reads this tablet, and around you may they graciously hold their hands.

You, scribe, write well to me; put down, moreover, your name. The tablets that are brought here always write in Hittite! (*EA* 32, 14–20, trans. Haas in Moran (1992: 103))[16]

A double-dividing line separates this last note from the rest of the letter which is addressed by the king of Arzawa to the pharaoh of Egypt. It is most unlikely that it was read either to or by the king on whose behalf it was written.

[14] See Arnaud (1987: 11). Further on the status of the chief scribe, see Danmanville (1971: 10).

[15] Cf. Otten (1986b: 185).

[16] On the practice of scribes appending notes to each other, in the form of a postscript, see Otten (1956).

Scribal Handwriting

As we have noted, one of the important tasks of the scribes was to make copies of all treaties, and all other important documents, for future reference. Furthermore they were constantly involved in the copying and re-writing of old texts. Clay tablets were generally not baked, and thus had a limited life span. Hence it was necessary to copy and recopy them from one generation to another to ensure their survival.[17] This means that the earliest Hittite texts are available to us only in copies made by scribes of a later period. But at least this has ensured their survival. A further benefit of this scribal practice is that in many cases a particular text survives in a number of copies, known as exemplars. These copies are often fragmentary. But the fragments can sometimes be pieced together to give a more or less complete version of the original text.

Further, the texts which bear the signatures of particular scribes enable us to recognise distinctive features of the handwriting of these scribes, and perhaps more importantly distinctive features of handwriting in a particular period.[18] This helps establish what is known as a *ductus* for the period, i.e. 'the manner of impressing cuneiform signs on tablets',[19] which in turn helps us to assign a number of texts which we cannot date on other grounds to the periods when they were composed, or in many cases when they were copied from earlier compositions.

But the exercise is not a straightforward one. It is complicated by the fact that some of the later scribes had an apparent tendency to 'archaize'— that is, to use the vocabulary and *ductus* of an earlier period in their compositions. A further complication is caused by variations in handwriting between scribes of the same period. 'Different scribes clearly had different hands, even if they wrote on the same wet clay only a few seconds apart.'[20] This has to be taken into account by scholars in their attempts to establish the chronology of a number of texts not datable on other grounds.

The Languages of the Texts

When the texts from the archives at Hattusa began to come to light early this century, many of them were found to be written in Akkadian, which

---

[17] The reason why the great majority of clay tablets in the ancient Near East were not baked, particularly those that were to be stored for future reference, is somewhat puzzling. See the comments of Veenhof (1986: 1).

[18] Note in this respect the important studies of Rüster (1972), and Neu and Rüster (1975). These scholars took a number of datable texts ranging from the early to the later periods of Hittite history, and listed the sign shapes characteristic of these texts, and thus of the periods in which they were written.

[19] Hoffner (1977: 78).   [20] Ibid. 78–9.

had already been deciphered and thus could be read with ease. In fact most of the early Hittite documents were probably originally written in Akkadian, and were translated into Hittite when later copies were made. Throughout the Late Bronze Age Akkadian was used as a diplomatic *lingua franca*,[21] thus letters exchanged between a Hittite king and his Egyptian, Assyrian, or Babylonian counterparts were written in Akkadian, as also were the treaties drawn up with these kings. The same applied to correspondence and treaties between the Hittite kings and their vassal rulers in Syria.

But numerous other tablets came to light which initially could not be read since they were written in an unintelligible language. This was the language of Nesa, the name of the city which became the royal seat of Pithana and his son Anitta in the Assyrian colony period. As we have noted, from the large number of texts henceforth written in this language, it is clear that 'Nesite' became the official language of the Hittite kingdom.

The task was to decipher the Nesite—what we call the Hittite—language. To some extent this task was facilitated by the Hittites' use of the cuneiform script. Thus when the Czech scholar Bedrich Hrozný began working on the language in the 1910s, he was assisted by the fact that Nesite used many of the same ideograms, with the same meaning, as Sumerian and Akkadian. This enabled a number of scattered words and phrases in the texts to be translated, and in some cases helped establish the character of these texts. But significant progress on the decipherment depended in the first instance on establishing the language group to which Nesite belonged.

As his investigations proceeded, Hrozný kept coming back to a conclusion that had already been suggested by an earlier scholar, and discarded—that Nesite was an Indo-European language, and thus related to Greek, Latin, and other languages of the Indo-European family. Once this had been conclusively demonstrated, the decipherment of Nesite proceeded relatively quickly. This marked the genuine beginning of Hittite studies, for it provided the key that unlocked the vast range of information preserved in the archives of the Hittite capital.

But more was to follow. So far, two distinct languages, Akkadian and Nesite, had been identified in the archives. Yet a number of the tablets found at Hattusa were written in neither of these languages. In 1919 a Swiss philologist Emil Forrer identified six other languages in the archives, generally designated in the tablets by their adverbial forms—Hurrian (*ḫurlili*), Hattian (*ḫattili*), Luwian (*luwili*), Palaic (*palaumnili*), Sumerian, and a language apparently spoken by the kings of Mitanni.[22] One question which these 'minority languages' raise is the extent to which Hittite scribes

---

[21] See Labat (1962).
[22] Forrer (1919). On the 'Mitannian language', see Gurney (1990: 103–4).

were required to be multilingual. Or were specialist scribes employed for particular languages? As noted above, we might at least expect that training in Akkadian was a regular feature of the scribal schools, given its international importance and the regularity with which it appears in the archives.

The Hittite Hieroglyphic Script

One further task had to be undertaken—the reading and decipherment of the strange unintelligible hieroglyphic script that appeared on monuments throughout Anatolia and Syria, and had done much to stimulate the interest and the researches which had led eventually to the rediscovery of the Hittites. The earliest known example of the script appears on a seal impression of the sixteenth century, from the seal of Isputahsu, king of Kizzuwadna. But the majority of hieroglyphic texts date from the thirteenth to the eighth centuries BC.

The task of decipherment proved rather more difficult than the decipherment of the Nesite cuneiform language. It was, however, greatly facilitated by the discovery in 1946 of a bilingual text, in Phoenician and Luwian hieroglyphs, at Karatepe in eastern Cilicia.[23] More recent work on the language of the inscriptions has established its virtual identity with that of the Luwian cuneiform texts.[24]

The character of the script, which was perhaps initially inspired by the monumental script of Egypt, made it a more appropriate medium than cuneiform for recording important achievements on public monuments. In the last century of the Hittite New Kingdom, increasing use seems to have been made of the script for this purpose. This is illustrated by several important discoveries in recent years, including the Yalburt inscription (see Ch. 12), and the so-called Südburg inscription in Hattusa (see Ch. 13). Both date to the final decades of the Hittite kingdom.

After the fall of Hattusa, the practice of writing cuneiform on clay tablets ceased. However the surviving branches of the Hittite royal family in Syria and southern Anatolia continued to use the hieroglyphic script, primarily for monumental inscriptions on stone as in the past. But the script also appears in a small number of letters and economic texts, and on small votive objects.

[23] See Barnett (1953), Hawkins and Morpurgo-Davies (1978).
[24] Amongst recent studies of the hieroglyphic inscriptions those of J. D. Hawkins are of particular importance; see the relevant items listed under his name in the Bibliography, including Hawkins and Morpurgo-Davies (1986). A *Corpus of Hieroglyphic Luwian Inscriptions* is currently in preparation.

Hittite Seals

Seals were used as a form of personal signature, both on clay *bullae* as well as on a range of documents, including land-grants, other royal gifts, records of goods purchased, and treaties. Some of the *bullae* were affixed to important documents, others served to seal access to buildings or rooms within them and sometimes to chests or boxes. The inscriptions which they bear often provide useful supplementary information about their owners in addition to what we know of them from other sources. In one case a seal impression on a document discovered in Temple 8 at Hattusa in 1984 has enabled us to identify a hitherto unknown king (see Ch. 5). More generally seal impressions sometimes contain valuable information about their owners' genealogy. An excellent example is provided by a seal in the shape of a Maltese cross, the so-called cruciform seal. A number of impressions of this seal were discovered in 1986, during the course of a new excavation of Temple 3 at Hattusa.[25] On these impressions the genealogy of the king Mursili II appears, extending back through many generations to the early years of the Hittite Old Kingdom. The names of at least eight of Mursili's predecessors are recorded, along with their queens.[26]

The earliest Hittite seals known to us, dating to the late sixteenth and early fifteenth centuries, were engraved in the hieroglyphic script. Later, from *c.*1400 onwards, royal seals featured both hieroglyphic and cuneiform inscriptions. The hieroglyphic inscription recorded the name and titles of the king in an inner circle; the cuneiform inscription appeared in (usually two) rings around this circle. Such seals are known as 'digraphic'. Sometimes the name of the reigning queen appeared with that of the king on the seals. Sometimes the queen's name appeared alone. Other seals bear the names of palace functionaries, including princes. Royal seals often featured a winged sun-disc, used as a symbol of royalty, extending over the hieroglyphic inscription in the centre of the seal. Other pictorial motifs, including human and divine figures, are also found on a number of royal seals.

---

[25] See Neve (1987: 400–1; 1989–90: 10). The seal has the inventory number 573/z, and has been published by Boehmer and Güterbock (1987: 69 no. 214, with pl. 25).
[26] See Neve (1987: 400–3; 1988: 374), and the detailed treatment by Dinçol *et al.* (1993). Neve (1987: 401) provided preliminary readings of the names on the sealings, and assigned the seal to Suppiluliuma II. Revised readings have been provided by Dinçol *et al.* (1993: 89), who have reassigned the seal to Mursili II. They have identified the names as follows: side *a*: Suppiluliuma I surrounded by Labarna I, Hattusili I, Mursili I, and one still uncertain name; side *b*: Mursili II surrounded by Tudhaliya I/II, [Arnuwanda I], Tudhaliya III, and a still problematic space. They state that these identifications are supported by the corresponding identifications of all the Great Queens except the one with the uncertain Great King.

Until recently, only a few hundred Hittite seals were known to us. This number has now increased dramatically. Excavations conducted in 1990 on the site of Nişantepe, a rocky outcrop within the Lower City of Hattusa,[27] brought to light a 'seal archive' consisting of almost 3,300 items—3,268 clay *bullae* and 28 land-grant documents. All bear seal impressions which record the names and titles of the seals' owners.[28] The earliest date to the reign of the king Suppiluliuma I, the latest to his namesake Suppiluliuma II, the last known king who occupied the throne in Hattusa.

The Nişantepe archive still awaits detailed analysis and publication. But even apart from some surprises already revealed by a cursory examination of the archive's contents, its importance is evident from the sheer volume of new seal impressions which have come to light.

The Tablets as Sources for Hittite History

With the decipherment of the Hittite language, the many complexities of the field of Hittite studies soon became evident. From the tablets it was clear that Late Bronze Age Anatolia was occupied by a large, heterogeneous conglomerate of kingdoms, clusters of communities, and tribal groups that differed markedly in their size, ethnic composition, and political organization. The tablets range widely in their contents. They include annalistic records relating the achievements of the kings who composed them, decrees, political correspondence, treaties between kings and their foreign counterparts or vassal rulers, administrative texts, edicts, a collection of laws, ritual and festival texts, and a number of mythological and literary texts.

Obviously the most important texts for historical purposes are those which might be described as historical narrative texts. These include the annals composed or commissioned by various kings to record their military achievements, several decrees or proclamations, a fragmentary biography of the king Suppiluliuma I composed by his son Mursili, and a so-called autobiography of the king Hattusili III, designed to justify Hattusili's seizure of the throne and his arrangements for the succession. Valuable historical information is also provided by the preambles to a number of treaties. These often contain a résumé of past relations, sometimes peaceful, sometimes hostile, between the kingdom of Hatti and the country of the king's treaty-partner. From the preambles too, we learn much about political developments within the Hittites' vassal states.[29]

[27] The name comes from a stone located there bearing a very weathered hieroglyphic inscription.
[28] See the reports of the excavations by Neve (1991: 322–38; 1992a: 307–16).
[29] The information contained in the archives at Hattusa is supplemented by a number of relevant texts (letters, diplomatic and administrative records) from the archives discovered at Alalah, Ugarit, and Emar in Syria.

Correspondence between the Hittite king and his foreign counterparts, his vassal rulers, and his administrative officials is a further source of important historical information.[30] The large collection of letters which have survived in the archives of the Hittites and their contemporaries gives us considerable insight into the nature of the administration of the Hittite kingdom and the control of its subject territories, and more generally into the world of Late Bronze Age international diplomacy.

Of particular importance in this last respect are the numerous letters exchanged between Hittite kings and the pharaohs of Egypt. Many of these come from the fourteenth-century cache of tablets discovered in Egypt in 1887 at the site of El Amarna.[31] Of at least equal interest and importance are the numerous letters exchanged between the royal houses of Hatti and Egypt in the thirteenth century, during the reigns of the Hittite king Hattusili III and the pharaoh Ramesses II.[32]

The Hittite world has left us no historians or comprehensive histories, as we understand these terms, no Bronze Age Herodotos, Thucydides, or Livy to chronicle, interpret, and critically assess for us the raw factual data which provide the basis of Hittite history. We have to do this for ourselves. And in taking on this task, we have always to bear in mind the limitations of the material with which we are working. The annalistic compositions contain little more than bald records of military enterprises, highlighting for posterity the successes of the kings who undertook them. While they sometimes contain admissions of failures, they are none the less highly selective in the information which they convey and that which they exclude. In diplomatic texts—treaties and royal correspondence—the authors almost invariably had one or more political axes to grind. In communications with their subject rulers, their allies, their enemies or potential enemies, they obviously sought to present their actions and policies and grievances in a light most favourable to themselves. Undoubtedly this sometimes led to the omission of relevant facts, or the distortion of facts, if it suited their purposes. Of course in this respect they were no different from kings, politicians, and diplomats in any age. And in many cases they were probably a good deal more honest.

But while the material from the Hittite archives has many limitations, it also has a number of advantages when compared with written source

---

[30] Much of this correspondence is catalogued in *CTH* 151–210. Many of the letters have most recently been ed. by Hagenbuchner (1989).

[31] Ancient Akhetaten, the city built by Akhenaten. For the most recent edition of the Amarna letters written predominantly in the reign of the pharaoh Akhenaten, see Moran (1992). In addition to the Egyptian–Hittite correspondence, the cache of more than 350 tablets also contains letters written to and received from Egypt's vassals and the kings of Assyria and Babylon.

[32] The full corpus of this correspondence has now been published by Edel (1994), cited as *ÄHK*.

material in later ages. Our histories of Greece and Rome are based largely on the works of ancient writers who for all their claims to impartiality none the less have presented us with subjective, biased and often conflicting treatments of the periods about which they wrote. In making use of their works for the purposes of modern scholarship, we are already at least one step removed from the primary sources on which they were based.

For writing a history of the Hittite world, we have much more direct access to primary data—the *original* sources—and much less need of a Bronze Age Thucydides to relay to us, in a selective way, information derived from such sources. We can read them for ourselves. Indeed in some cases our primary sources take us back one step further, since we have drafts of a number of documents, like letters and treaties, which were corrected and edited before final versions were made: what was corrected can often be as instructive as the correction itself.

In reconstructing a history of the Hittite world, we also make use of texts which may at first sight appear less relevant to our task. Of particular interest and importance in this respect are a number of prayers and votive texts. For example, we learn from a series of prayers composed by the king Mursili II of a plague which devastated the homeland for many years. Other religious texts inform us of various misfortunes suffered by the royal family—illness and death, political intrigues, family feuds. Many of these texts are extremely personal in nature, confidential communications between a member of the royal family and a relevant deity. Thus we learn of the possible Hittite violation of a treaty with Egypt, not publicly admitted, of a conspiracy leading to the assassination of Suppiluliuma I's brother, of a speech affliction suffered by Mursili II, of the illness and death of Mursili II's wife and the alleged complicity of his stepmother, of the arraignment and banishment of two Hittite queens, of the foot and eye illnesses suffered by Hattusili III, of tensions and intrigues in the royal family around the time of Hattusili III's death. These matters were aired in the context of prayers which reflect the belief that misfortunes suffered by the Land of Hatti, or by particular members of the royal family, were attributable to divine wrath.

In order to appease the offended deity, the reason for his or her wrath had first to be determined through oracular consultation. One by one the possible reasons were stated, an animal sacrificed, and its entrails consulted to determine the god's response. A negative response meant that the process had to be repeated with another possible reason stated. And so on, until an affirmative response was obtained and appropriate expiation made. Alternatively, a number of votive texts sought the god's cooperation in curing an illness which had afflicted a member of the royal family, with the promise of gifts to the god in the event that the illness was cured.

Religious texts provide us with valuable insights into the lives of many of the chief participants in the rise and fall of the Hittite kingdom, and into the fortunes and misfortunes of the dynasty to which they belonged. In so doing they help flesh out the history of this kingdom in ways which generally lie well outside the scope of the more overtly historical documents on which our knowledge of it largely depends.

Bibliography

AKURGAL, E. (1962), *The Art of the Hittites*, London.

——(1989), 'Are the Ritual Standards of Alacahöyük Royal Symbols of the Hattian or the Hittite Kings?', *Fs Özgüç*, 1–2.

——(1992), 'L'Art Hatti', *Fs Alp*, 1–4.

ALBRIGHT, W. F. (1944), 'An Unrecognised Amarna Letter from Ugarit', *BASOR* 95: 30–3.

——(1975), 'Syria, the Philistines, and Phoenicia', *CAH* II.2: 507–36.

ALDRED, C. (1975), 'Egypt: the Amarna Period and the End of the Eighteenth Dynasty', *CAH* II.2: 49–97.

ALP, S. (1950), 'Die soziale Klasse der Namra-Leute', *JKF* I: 113–35.

——(1974), 'Eine neue hieroglyphenhethitische Inschrift der Gruppe Kizildağ-Karadağ aus der Nähe von Aksaray und die früher publizierten Inschriften derselben Gruppe', *Fs Güterbock* I: 17–27.

——(1980), 'Die hethitische Tontafelentdeckungen auf dem Maşat-Hüyük', *Belleten* 44: 25–59.

——(1991), *Hethitische Briefe aus Maşat-Höyük*, Ankara.

ALTMAN, A. (1977), 'The Fate of Abdi-Ashirta', *UF* 9: 1–11.

ARCHI, A. (1966), 'Trono regale e trono divinizzato nell'Anatolia ittita', *SMEA* 1: 76–120.

——(1971), 'The Propaganda of Hattusilis III', *SMEA* 14: 185–215.

——(1979), 'L'Humanité des Hittites', *Fs Laroche*, 37–48.

ARNAUD, D. (1987), 'Les Hittites sur le Moyen-Empire: protecteurs et indigènes', *Hethitica* 8: 9–27.

ASTOUR, M. C. (1965), 'New Evidence on the Last Days of Ugarit', *AJA* 69: 253–8.

——(1969), 'The Partition of the Confederacy of Mukis-Nuhasse-Nii by Suppiluliuma. A Study in Political Geography of the Amarna Age', *Or* 38: 381–414.

——(1972), 'Hattusilis, Halab, and Hanigalbat', *JNES* 31: 102–9.

——(1978), 'Les Hourrites en Syrie du Nord', *RHA* 36: 1–22.

——(1979), 'The Kingdom of Siyannu-Usnatu', *UF* 11: 13–28.

——(1980), 'King Ammurapi and the Hittite Princess', *UF* 12: 103–8.

——(1989), *Hittite History and Absolute Chronology of the Bronze Age*, Partille.

—— (1994), Rev. of Wilhelm (1989), *JNES*, 53: 225–30.

ÅSTRÖM, P. (ed.) (1987/9), *High, Middle or Low? Acts of an International Colloquium on Absolute Chronology held at the University of Gothenburg, 20–2 August 1987*, Gothenburg.

BALKAN, K. (1955), *Observations on the Chronological Problems of the Karum Kanish*, Ankara.

—— (1957), *Letter of King Anum-Hirbi of Mama to King Warshama of Kanish*, Ankara.

—— (1973), *Eine Schenkungsurkunde aus der althethitischen Zeit, gefunden in Inandık*, Ankara.

—— (1974), 'Cancellation of Debts in Cappadocian Tablets from Kültepe', *Fs Güterbock* I: 29–41.

BARNETT, R. D. (1953), 'Karatepe, the Key to the Hittite Hieroglyphs', *AS* 3: 53–95.

—— (1975a), 'The Sea Peoples', *CAH* II.2: 359–78.

—— (1975b), 'Phrygia and the Peoples of Anatolia in the Iron Age', *CAH* II.2: 417–42.

BARTL, K. (1995), 'Some Remarks on Early Iron Age in Eastern Anatolia,' *Anatolica* 21: 205–12.

BEAL, R. (1983), 'Studies in Hittite History', *JCS* 35: 115–26.

—— (1986), 'The History of Kizzuwatna and the Date of the Sunassura Treaty', *Or* 55: 424–45.

—— (1992a), 'The Location of Cilician Ura', *AS* 42: 65–73.

—— (1992b), *The Organisation of the Hittite Military*, Heidelberg.

—— (1993), 'Kurunta of Tarhuntassa and the Imperial Hittite Mausoleum', *AS* 43: 29–39.

BECKMAN, G. (1982), 'The Hittite Assembly', *JAOS* 102.3: 435–42.

—— (1983a), *Hittite Birth Rituals* (*StBoT* 29), Wiesbaden.

—— (1983b), 'Mesopotamians and Mesopotamian Learning at Hattusa', *JCS* 35: 97–114.

—— (1986), 'Inheritance and Royal Succession among the Hittites', *Fs Güterbock II*, 13–31.

—— (1989/90), Rev. of Otten (1988b), *WO* 20/21: 289–94.

—— (1995a), 'Hittite Provincial Administration in Anatolia and Syria: the view from Maşat and Emar', *Atti del il Congresso Internazionale di Hittitologia* (*Studia Mediterranea* 9), Pavia, 19–37.

—— (1995b), 'Royal Ideology and State Administration in Hittite Anatolia', in J. M. Sasson, 529–43.

—— (1996), *Hittite Diplomatic Texts*, Atlanta.

BERAN, T. (1967), *Die hethitische Glyptik von Boghazköy* (= *WVDOG* 76), Berlin.

BEYER, D. (1982), *Meskéné-Emar, Dix ans de travaux 1972–82*, Paris.

BILGIÇ, E. (1945–51), 'Die Ortsnamen der "kappadokischen" Urkunden im Rahmen der alten Sprachen Anatoliens', *AfO* 15: 1–37.

——(1992), '"Ebla" in Cappadocian Inscriptions', *Fs Alp*, 61–6.

BIN-NUN, S. R. (1972), 'The Anatolian Background of the Tawananna's Position in the Hittite Kingdom', *RHA* 30: 54–80.

——(1974), 'Who was Tahurwaili, the Great Hittite King?' *JCS* 26: 112–20.

——(1975), *The Tawananna in the Hittite Kingdom*, Heidelberg.

BITTEL, K. (1970), *Hattusha, the Capital of the Hittites*, Oxford and New York.

——(1972–5), 'Hattusa', *RlA* 4: 162–72.

——(1976a), *Die Hethiter*, Munich.

——(1976b), 'Das Ende des Hethiterreiches aufgrund archäologischer Zeugnisse', in H. Müller-Karpe, 36–56.

——(1983a), 'Quelques remarques archéologiques sur la topographie de Hattusa', *CRAI*, 485–509.

——(1983b), 'Die archäologische Situation in Kleinasien um 1200 v. Chr. und während der nachfolgenden vier Jahrhunderts', in Deger-Jalkotzy, S., 25–65.

——(1983c), *Hattuscha, Haupstadt der Hethiter*, Cologne.

BITTEL, K., HOUWINK TEN CATE, PH. H. J., and REINER, E. (eds.) (1974), *Anatolian Studies presented to Hans Gustav Güterbock on the occasion of his 65th Birthday*, Istanbul (cited as *Fs Güterbock I*).

BLEGEN, C. (1963), *Troy and the Trojans*, London.

BOEHMER, R. M., and GÜTERBOCK, H. G. (1987), *Glyptik aus dem Stadgebiet von Boğazköy*, Berlin.

BÖRKER-KLÄHN, J. (1995), 'Malnigal', *IM* 45: 169–73.

BOLGER, D. (1991), Rev. of Åström, 1987/9, *CR* 41: 426–9.

BREASTED, J. H. (1906), *Ancient Records of Egypt* (7 vols.), Chicago.

BRENTJES, B. (1986), 'Archäologisches zu den Wanderungen der Indoiraner', *AOF* 13: 224–38.

BRIEND, J., LEBRUN, R., and PUECH, É. (1992), *Traités et serments dans le Proche-Orient Ancien*, Paris.

BRINKMAN, J. A. (1976), *Materials and Studies for Kassite History*, vol. i, Chicago.

——(1976–80), 'Kadasman-Turgu', 'Kadasman-Enlil II', *RlA* 5: 285, 286.

——(1980–83), 'Kudur-Enlil', *RlA* 6: 266–7.

——(1983), 'Istanbul A. 1988, Middle Babylonian Chronology, and the Statistics of the Nippur Archives', *ZA* 73: 67–74.

BROOKE, G. J. (1979), 'The Textual, Formal and Historical Significance of Ugaritic Letter RS 34.124 (= *KTU* 2.72)', *UF* 11: 69–87.

BRYCE, T. R. (1974a), 'Some Geographical and Political Aspects of Mursilis' Arzawan Campaign', *AS* 24: 103–16.

—— (1974*b*), 'The Lukka Problem—and a Possible Solution', *JNES* 33: 395–404.

—— (1979*a*), 'The Role of the Lukka People in Late Bronze Age Anatolia', *Antichthon* 13: 1–11.

—— (1979*b*), Rev. of Heinhold-Krahmer (1977), *BiOr* 36: 60–4.

—— (1981), 'Hattusili I and the Problems of the Royal Succession', *AS* 31: 9–17.

—— (1983), *The Major Historical Texts of Early Hittite History*, Brisbane.

—— (1985*a*), 'A Suggested Sequence of Historical Developments in Anatolia during the Assyrian Colony Period', *AOF* 12: 259–68.

—— (1985*b*), 'A Reinterpretation of the Milawata Letter in the Light of the New Join Piece', *AS* 35: 13–23.

—— (1986*a*), Rev. of Hoffmann (1984), *BiOr* 43: 747–54.

—— (1986*b*), 'Madduwatta and Hittite Policy in Western Anatolia', *Historia* 35: 1–12.

—— (1986*c*), *The Lycians in Literary and Epigraphic Sources*, Copenhagen.

—— (1986–7), 'The Boundaries of Hatti and Hittite Border Policy', *Tel Aviv* 13–14, 85–102.

—— (1988*a*), 'Tette and the Rebellions in Nuhassi', *AS* 38: 21–8.

—— (1988*b*), Rev. of Mellink (1986), *BiOr* 45: 668–80.

—— (1989*a*), 'Ahhiyawans and Mycenaeans—An Anatolian Viewpoint', *OJA* 8: 297–310.

—— (1989*b*), 'Some Observations on the Chronology of Suppiluliuma's Reign', *AS* 39: 19–30.

—— (1989*c*), 'The Nature of Mycenaean Involvement in Western Anatolia', *Historia* 38: 1–21.

—— (1990), 'The Death of Niphururiya and its Aftermath', *JEA* 76: 97–105.

—— (1992*a*), 'Lukka Revisited', *JNES* 51: 121–30.

—— (1992*b*), 'The Role of Telipinu, the Priest, in the Hittite Kingdom', *Hethitica* 11: 5–18.

BURNEY, C. (1989), 'Hurrians and Proto-Indo-Europeans: the Ethnic Context of the Early Trans-Caucasian Culture', *Fs Özgüç*, 45–51.

CANCIK, H. (1976), *Grundzüge der hethitischen und alttestamentlichen Geschichtsschreibung*, Wiesbaden.

CARPENTER, R. (1968), *Discontinuity in Greek Civilization*, New York.

CARRUBA, O. (1969), 'Die Chronologie der hethitischen Texte und die hethitische Geschichte der Grossreichszeit', *ZDMG* Suppl. 1.1: 226–49.

—— (1974), 'Tahurwaili von Hatti und die hethitische Geschichte um 1500 v. Chr. G.', *Fs Güterbock I*, 73–93.

—— (1977*a*), 'Beiträge zur mittelhethitischen Geschichte: I—Die Tuthalijas und die Arnuwandas', *SMEA* 18: 137–74.

CARRUBA, O. (1977*b*), 'Beiträge zur mittelhethitischen Geschichte II—Die sogenannten "Protocoles de succession dynastique" ', *SMEA* 18: 175–95.

——(1979), *Studia Mediterranea*, Pavia (cited as *Fs Meriggi*).

——(1990), 'Muwattalli I', *X. Türk Tarıh Kongresi*, TTKB, Ankara, 539–54.

——(1992), 'Die Tawannannas des Alten Reiches', *Fs Alp*, 73–89.

——(1993*a*), 'Zur Datierung der ältesten Schenkungsurkunden und der anonymen Tabarna-Siegel', *Fs Neve*, 71–85.

——(1993*b*), 'Der Stamm *pišeni-/pišn-* "vir" im Hethitischen', *IF* 98: 92–7.

CHADWICK, J. (1976), *The Mycenaean World*, Cambridge.

CHILDE, V. G. (1954), *What happened in History*, Harmondsworth.

CIFOLA, B. (1988), 'Ramesses III and the Sea Peoples: A Structural Analysis of the Medinet Habu Inscriptions', *Or* 57: 275–306.

CLINE, E (1991*a*), 'Hittite Objects in the Bronze Age Aegean', *AS* 41: 133–43.

——(1991*b*), 'A Possible Hittite Embargo against the Mycenaeans', *Historia* 40/1: 1–9.

COOK, J. M. (1984), 'The Topography of the Plain of Troy', in L. Foxhall, and J. K. Davies, 163–72.

CORNELIUS, F. (1958*a*), 'Geographie des Hethitherreiches', *Or* 27: 225–51, 373–98.

——(1958*b*), 'Zur hethitischen Geographie: die Nachbarn des Hethiterreiches', *RHA* 16: 1–17.

——(1959), 'Die Annalen Hattusilis I', *Or* 28: 292–6.

——(1979), *Geschichte der Hethiter*, Darmstadt.

CORNIL, P. (1990), 'Liste des noms géographiques des textes hittites. KBo XXII–XXX, XXXIII, KUB XLV–LVII', *Hethitica* 10: 7–108.

CORNIL, P. and LEBRUN, R. (1972), 'La Restauration de Nérik', *Hethitica* 1: 15–30.

CROSSLAND, R. A., and BIRCHALL, A. (1974), *Bronze Age Migrations in the Aegean*, London.

CRYER, F. H. (1995), 'Chronology: Issues and Problems', in J. M. Sasson, 651–64.

DANMANVILLE, J. (1971), 'État, Économie, Société Hittites', *RHA* 29: 5–15.

DARGA M. (1974), 'Puduhepa: an Anatolian Queen of the 13th Century B.C.', *Fs Mansel*, 939–61.

DAVESNE, A., LEMAIRE, A., and LOZACHMEUR, H. (1987), 'Le Site archéologique de Meydancikkale (Turqie): du royaume de Pirindu à la garnison ptolémaïque', *CRAI* 359–83.

DEGER-JALKOTZY, S. (1983), *Griechenland, die Ägäis und die Levante während der 'Dark Ages' vom 12. bis zum 9. Jh. v. Chr.*, Vienna.

DEL MONTE, G. F. (1974), 'Mashuiluwa, König von Mira', *Or* 43: 355–68.

——(1981), 'Note sui Trattati fra Hattusa e Kizuwatna', *OA* 20: 203–21.

——(1986), *Il Trattato fra Mursili II di Hattusa e Niqmepa di Ugarit*, Rome.

DEL MONTE, G. F., and TISCHLER, T. (1978), *Répertoire Géographique des Textes Cunéiformes Bd. 6 Die Orts- und Gewässernamen der hethitischen Texte*, (suppl. 6/2, 1992), Wiesbaden.

DIAKONOV, I. M. (1985), 'On the Original Home of the Speakers of Indo-European', *JIES* 13: 92–174.

DIETRICH, M., and LORETZ, O. (1978), 'Das "Seefahrende Volk" von Sikila (RS 34.129)', *UF* 10: 53–6.

——(1985), 'Die "Autobiographie" des Königs Idrimi von Alalah (Idrimi-Stele), *TUAT* 1/5: 501–4.

DINÇOL, A., DINÇOL, B., HAWKINS, J. D., and WILHELM, G. (1993), 'The "Cruciform Seal" from Boğazköy-Hattusa', *Fs Neve*, 87–106.

DONBAZ, V. (1989), 'Some Remarkable Contracts of 1-B Period Kültepe Tablets', *Fs Özgüç*, 75–98.

DREWS, R. (1993), *The End of the Bronze Age*, Princeton.

DROWER, M. S. (1975), 'Ugarit', *CAH* II.2: 130–60.

EASTON, D. F. (1981), 'Hittite Land Donations and Tabarna Seals', *JCS* 33: 3–43.

——(1984), 'Hittite History and the Trojan War', in Foxhall, L., and Davies, J. K., 23–44.

——(1985), 'Has the Trojan War Been Found?' (rev. of Wood, M., *In Search of the Trojan War*, London, 1985), *Antiquity* 59: 188–96.

EDEL, E. (1948), 'Neue keilschriftliche Umschreibungen Aegyptischer Namen aus den Boğazköytexten', *JNES* 7: 11–24.

——(1950), 'KBo I 15 + 19, ein Brief Rameses' II mit einer Schilderung der Kadesschlacht', *ZA* 49: 195–212.

——(1953), 'Weitere Briefe aus der Heiratskorrespondenz Ramses' II.: KUB III 37 + KBo I 17 und KUB III 57', *Geschichte und Altes Testament (Beiträge zur historischen theologie 16, Festschrift Albrecht Alt)*, 29–63.

——(1958), 'Die Abfassungszeit des Briefes KBo I 10 (Hattusili—Kadasman-Ellil) und seine Bedeutung für die Chronologie Ramses' II', *JCS* 12: 130–3.

——(1960), 'Der geplante Besuch Hattusilis III. in Ägypten', *MDOG* 92: 15–20.

——(1976), *Ägyptische Ärtze und ägyptische Medizin am hethitischen Königshof*, Göttingen.

——(1994), *Die Ägyptisch-hethitische Korrespondenz aus Boghazköy, (Bd I Umschriften und Übersetzungen; Bd II Kommentar)*, Opladen (cited as *ÄHK*).

EISELE, W. (1970), *Der Telipinu-Erlass*, Munich.

EMRE, K., HROUDA, B., MELLINK, M. J., and ÖZGÜÇ, N. (eds.) (1989), *Anatolia and the Near East* (Tahsin Özgüce Armağan), Ankara (cited as *Fs Özgüç*).

ERTEKIN, A., and EDIZ, I. (1993), 'The Unique Sword from Boghazköy/ Hattusa', in M. J. Mellink *et al.* (eds.) *Aspects of Art and Iconography: Anatolia and its Neighbours*, Ankara, 719–25 (*Fs Nimet Özgüç*).

FAULKNER, R. O. (1975), 'Egypt: From the Inception of the Nineteenth Dynasty to the Death of Ramesses III', *CAH* II.2: 217–51.

FECHT, G. (1984), 'Ramses II und die Schlacht bei Qadesh', *Göttinger Miszellen* 80: 23–53.

FEDERN, W. (1960), 'Dahamunzu (KBo v 6 iii 8)', *JCS* 14: 33.

FINKELBERG, M. (1988), 'From Ahhiyawa to Achaioi', *Glotta* 66: 127–34.

FINLEY, M. I., CASKEY, J. L., KIRK, G. S., and PAGE, D. L. (1964), 'The Trojan War', *JHS* 84: 1–20.

FORLANINI, M. (1979), 'Appunti di Geografia Etea', *Fs Meriggi*, 165–85.

——(1988), 'La regione del Tauro nei testi hittiti', *Vicino Oriente* 7: 129–69.

——(1995), 'The Kings of Kanis', *Atti del II congresso internazionale di Hittitologia* (*Studia Mediterranea* 9), Pavia, 1993: 123–32.

FORLANINI, M., and MARAZZI, M. (1986), *Atlante storico del Vicino Oriente antico, Fascicolo 4.3, Anatolia: l'Impero Hittita*, Rome.

FORRER, E. (1919), 'Die Acht Sprachen der Boghaz-köi Inschriften', Berlin.

——(1922–6), *Die Boghazköi-Texte im Umschrift, WVDOG*, 41, 42.

——(1924*a*), 'Vorhomerische Griechen in den Keilschrifttexten von Boghazköi', *MDOG* 63: 1–22.

——(1924*b*), 'Die Griechen in den Boghazköi-Texten', *OLZ* 27: 113–18.

——(1926*a*), *Forschungen I.1*, Berlin.

——(1926*b*), *Forschungen II.1*, Berlin.

——(1937), 'Kilikien zur Zeit des Hatti-Reiches', *Klio* 30: 135–86.

FORSDYKE, E. J. (1956), *Greece Before Homer*, London.

FOXHALL, L., and DAVIES, J. K. (1984), *The Trojan War, its History and Context*, Bristol.

FREU, J. (1987), 'Problèmes de chronologie et de géographie hittites: Madduwatta et les débuts de l'empire', *Hethitica* 8: 123–75.

——(1990), *Hittites et Achéens Donées nouvelles concernant le pays d'Ahhiyawa*, Document XI, Centre de Recherches Comparatives sur les Langues de la Mediterranée Ancienne, Nice.

——(1992), 'Les Guerres syriennes de Suppiluliuma et la fin de l'ère amarnienne', *Hethitica* 11: 39–101.

——(1995), 'De' l'ancien royaume au nouvel empire: les temps obscures de la monarchie hittite', *Atti del il Congresso Internazionale di Hittitologia* (*Studia Mediterranea* 9), Pavia, 133–48.

FREYDANK, H. (1959/60), 'Eine hethitische Fassung des Vertrages zwischen dem hethiterkönig Suppiluliuma und Aziru von Amurru', *MIO* 7: 355–81.

FRIEDRICH, J. (1926–30), *Staatsverträge des Hatti-Reiches in hethitischer Sprache*, 2 Parts, Leipzig.

GARDINER, A. (1960), *The Kadesh Inscriptions of Ramesses II*, Oxford.

——(1965), *Geschichte des alten Aegypten*, Stuttgart.

GARELLI, P. (1963), *Les Assyriens en Cappadoce*, Paris.

GARSTANG, J., and GURNEY, O. R. (1959), *The Geography of the Hittite Empire*, London.

GIORGADZE, G. G. (1991), 'The Hittite Kingdom' in I. M. Diakonov, *Early Antiquity*, Chicago, 266–85.

GOETZE, A. (1925), *Hattusili* (*MVAG* 1924, 3, 29. Jahrgang), Leipzig.

——(1927), *Madduwattas* (*MVAG* 32.1), Leipzig, repr. Darmstadt 1968.

——(1928–9), 'Die historische Einleitung des Aleppo-Vertrages (KBo 1 6)', *MAOG* 4: 59–66.

——(1933), *Die Annalen des Mursilis*, (*MVAG* 38), Leipzig, repr. Darmstadt, 1967 (cited as *AM*).

——(1936), 'Philological Remarks on the Bilingual Bulla from Tarsus', *AJA* 40: 210–14.

——(1940), *Kizzuwatna and the Problem of Hittite Geography*, New Haven.

——(1947*a*), Rev. of Bozkurt *et al.*, Istanbul Arkeoloji Müzerlerinde Bulunan Boğazköy Tableterinden Seçme Metinler, Maarif Matbaasi, Istanbul, 1944, *JCS* 1: 87–92.

——(1947*b*), 'A New Letter from Ramesses to Hattusilis', *JCS* 1: 241–52.

——(1951), 'The Problem of Chronology and Early Hittite History', *BASOR* 122: 18–25.

——(1957*a*), 'On the Chronology of the Second Millennium B.C.', *JCS* 11: 53–73.

——(1957*b*), 'The Roads of Northern Cappadocia in Hittite Times', *RHA* 15: 91–102.

——(1957*c*), *Kulturgeschichte Kleinasiens*, Munich.

——(1959), Rev. of von Schuler (1957), *JCS* 13: 65–70.

——(1964), 'State and Society of the Hittites', in G. Walser, *Neuere Hethiterforschung* (*Historia, Einzelschriften Heft* 7), 23–33.

——(1975*a*), 'The Struggle for the Domination of Syria (1400–1300 BC)', *CAH* II.2: 1–20.

——(1975*b*), 'Anatolia from Shuppiluliumash to the Egyptian War of Muwatallash', *CAH* II.2: 117–29.

——(1975*c*), 'The Hittites and Syria', *CAH* II.2: 252–73.

GOETZE, A., and PEDERSEN, H. (1934), *Mursilis Sprachlähmung*, Copenhagen.

GOLDMAN, H. (1935), 'Excavations at Gözlü Kule, Tarsus, 1935', *AJA* 39: 526–49.

GONNET, H. (1979), 'La titulature royale hittite au IIe millénaire avant J.-C.', *Hethitica* 3: 3–108.

—— (1987), 'Tabarna, Favori des Dieux?', *Hethitica* 8: 177–85.

GORDON, E. I. (1967), 'The Meaning of the Ideogram ᵈKASKAL.KUR = Underground Water-Course and its Significance for Bronze Age Historical Geography', *JCS* 21: 70–88.

GRAYSON, A. K. (1972–6), *Assyrian Royal Inscriptions*, i–ii, Wiesbaden.

—— (1975), *Assyrian and Babylonian Chronicles*, New York.

GRÉLOIS, J.-P. (1988), 'Les Annales Decennales de Mursili II (*CTH* 61.1)', *Hethitica* 9: 17–145.

GÜNBATTI, C. (1992), 'Some Observations about the Commercial Activities of Women in the Light of the Kültepe Tablets', *Fs Alp*, 229–34.

GURNEY, O. R. (1940), *The Hittite Prayers of Mursili II, LAAA* 27.

—— (1948), 'Mita of Pahhuwa', *LAAA* 28: 32–47.

—— (1958), 'Hittite Kingship', in S. H. Hooke (ed.), *Myth, Ritual and Kingship*, Oxford, 105–21.

—— (1973*a*), 'Anatolia *c*.1750–1600 B.C.', *CAH* II.1: 228–55.

—— (1973*b*), 'Anatolia c.1600–1380 B.C.', *CAH* II.1: 659–85.

—— (1974), 'The Hittite Line of Kings and Chronology', *Fs Güterbock I*, 105–11.

—— (1979*a*), 'The Hittite Empire', in M. T. Larsen, 151–65.

—— (1979*b*), 'The Anointing of Tudhaliya', *Fs Meriggi*, 213–23.

—— (1982), Rev. of Heinhold-Krahmer *et al.* (1979), *OLZ* 77: 560–3.

—— (1983), 'The Hittite title *Tuḫkanti-*', *AS* 33: 97–101.

—— (1990), *The Hittites*, London.

—— (1992), 'Hittite Geography: Thirty Years On', *Fs Alp*, 213–21.

—— (1993), 'The Treaty with Ulmi-Tesub', *AS* 43: 13–28.

GÜTERBOCK, H. G. (1934–8), 'Die historische Tradition und ihre literarische Gestaltung bei Babyloniern and Hethitern bis 1200', *ZA* 42: 1–91; 44: 45–149.

—— (1940), *Siegel aus Boğazköy I* (*AfO* Beiheft 5), Berlin (cited as *SBo* I).

—— (1942), *Siegel aus Boğazköy II* (*AfO* Beiheft 7), Berlin (cited as *SBo* II).

—— (1954*a*), 'Authority and Law in the Hittite Kingdom', *JAOS* suppl. 17: 16–24.

—— (1954*b*), 'The Hurrian Element in the Hittite Empire', *JWH* 2/2: 383–94.

—— (1956*a*), 'The Deeds of Suppiluliuma as told by his Son, Mursili II', *JCS* 10: 41–68, 75–98, 101–30 (cited as *DS*).

—— (1956*b*), 'Notes on Luwian Studies', *Or* 25: 113–40.

—— (1956c), 'L'Inscription hiéroglyphique hittite sur la matrice du sceau de Mursili II provenant de Ras Shamra', in Schaeffer, *Ugaritica III*, 161–3.

—— (1958), 'Kanes and Nesa: Two Forms of One Anatolian Place Name?', *Eretz-Israel* 5: 46*–50*.

—— (1961), 'The North-Central Area of Hittite Anatolia', *JNES* 20: 85–97 (rev. of Garstang and Gurney, 1959).

—— (1964a), 'Sargon of Akkad Mentioned by Hattusili I of Hatti', *JCS* 18: 1–6.

—— (1964b), 'A View of Hittite Literature', *JAOS* 84: 107–15.

—— (1965), 'A Votive sword with Old Assyrian Inscription', *Studies in Honour of Benno Landsberger on his Seventy-Fifth Birthday*, 197–8, Chicago.

—— (1967a), 'The Hittite Conquest of Cyprus Reconsidered', *JNES* 26: 73–81.

—— (1967b), 'Lexicographical Notes III', *RHA* 25: 141–50.

—— (1969), 'Ein neues Bruchstück der Sargon-Erzählung "König der Schlacht"', *MDOG* 101: 14–26.

—— (1970a), 'Some Aspects of Hittite Festivals' (Proceedings of the 17th Rencontre Assyriologique Internationale, Brussels, 1969), Brussels, 175–80.

—— (1970b), 'The Predecessors of Suppiluliuma Again', *JNES* 29: 73–7.

—— (1973a), 'Hattusili II Once More', *JCS* 25: 100–4.

—— (1973b), 'Hittite Hieroglyphic Seal Impressions from Korucutepe', *JNES* 32: 135–47.

—— (1978), 'Die Hieroglyphenschrift von Fraktin', *Assyriologia* 4 (*Fs Lubor Matous*), Budapest, 127–36.

—— (1983a), 'The Hittites and the Aegean World: Part 1. The Ahhiyawa Problem Reconsidered', *AJA* 87: 133–8.

—— (1983b), 'Hittite Historiography: A Survey', in H. Tadmor, and M. Weinfeld, *History, Historiography, and Interpretation*, Jerusalem, 21–35.

—— (1984), 'Hittites and Akhaeans: A New Look', *Proceedings of the American Philosophical Society* 128: 114–22.

—— (1986), 'Troy in Hittite Texts? Wilusa, Ahhiyawa, and Hittite History', in M. J. Mellink, 33–44.

—— (1989), 'Survival of the Hittite Dynasty', in W. A. Ward, and M. S. Joukowsky, 53–5.

—— (1990), 'Wer war Tawagalawa?', *Or* 59: 157–65.

—— (1992), 'A New Look at One Ahhiyawa Text', *Fs Alp*, 235–43.

HAAS, V. (1970), *Die Kult von Nerik*, Rome.

—— (1972–75), 'Hakmis(sa)/Hakpis(sa)', *RlA* 4: 49–50.

—— (1977), Rev. of Bin-Nun (1975), *WZKM* 69: 150–6.

HAAS, V. (1984), *Die Serien itkahi und itkalzi des AZU-Priesters, Rituale für Tasmisarri und Tatuhepa sowie weitere Texte mit Bezug auf Tasmisarri, Corpus der hurritischen Sprachdenkmaler*, I. Abteilung: *Die Texte aus Boğazköy*, Band I, Rome.

——(1985), 'Betrachtungen zur Dynastie von Hattusa im Mittleren Reich (ca. 1450–1380)', *AOF* 12: 269–77.

HAAS, V., and WÄFLER, M. (1977), 'Bemerkungen zu ᴱḫestī/ā (2. Teil)', *UF* 9: 87–122.

HAGENBUCHNER, A. (1989), *Die Korrespondenz der Hethiter* (2 Parts), Heidelberg.

——(1992), 'War der ᴸᵁ*tuḫkanti* Neriqqaili ein Sohn Hattusili III?', *SMEA* 29: 111–26.

HARDY, R. S. (1941), 'The Old Hittite Kingdom, a Political History', *American Journal of Semitic Languages and Literatures*, 58: 177–216.

HARRAK, A. (1987), *Assyria and Hanigalbat*, Zurich and New York.

HAWKINS, J. D. (1974), 'Assyrians and Hittites', *Iraq* 36: 67–83.

——(1988), 'Kuzi-Tesub and the "Great Kings of Karkamis"', *AS* 38: 99–108.

——(1990), 'The New Inscription from the Südburg of Boğazköy-Hattusa', *AA* 1990: 305–14.

——(1992), 'The Inscriptions of the Kizildağ and the Karadağ in the light of the Yalburt Inscription', *Fs Alp*, 259–75.

——(1995*a*), 'Karkamish and Karatepe: Neo Hittite City-States in North Syria', in J. M. Sasson, 1295–307.

——(1995*b*), '"Great Kings" and "Country-Lords" at Malatya and Karkamish', *Fs Houwink ten Cate*, 73–85.

——(1995*c*), *The Hieroglyphic Inscription of the Sacred Pool Complex at Hattusa (SÜDBURG) (StBoT* Beiheft 3), Wiesbaden.

HAWKINS, J. D., and MORPURGO-DAVIES, A. (1978), 'On the Problems of Karatepe: The Hieroglyphic Text', *AS* 28: 103–19.

——(1986), 'Studies in Hieroglyphic Luwian', *Fs Güterbock II*, 69–81.

HECKER, K. (1981), 'Der Weg nach Kanis', *ZA* 70: 185–97.

HEINHOLD-KRAHMER, S. (1977), *Arzawa, Untersuchungen zu seiner Geschichte nach den hethitischen Quellen*, Heidelberg.

——(1983), 'Untersuchungen zu Piyamaradu (Teil I)', *Or* 52: 81–97.

——(1986), 'Untersuchungen zu Piyamaradu (Teil II)', *Or* 55: 47–62.

HEINHOLD-KRAHMER, S., HOFFMANN, I., KAMMENHUBER, A., and MAUER, G. (1979), *Probleme der Textdatierung in der Hethitologie*, Heidelberg.

HELCK, W. (1961), *Urkunden der 18. Dynastie: Übersetzung zu den Heften 17–22*, Berlin.

——(1963), 'Urhi-Tesup in Aegypten', *JCS* 17: 87–97.

——(1971), *Die Beziehungen Ägyptens zu Vorderasien im 3. und 2. Jahrtausend v. Chr.*, 2nd edn., Wiesbaden.

——(1983), 'Zum ältesten Geschichte des Hatti-Reiches', *Fs Bittel*, 271–81.

——(1984), 'Die Sukzija-Episode im Dekret des Telepinus', *WO* 15: 103–8.

——(1994), 'Ägyptologische Bemerkungen zu dem Artikel von J. Freu in *Hethitica* XI 39', *Hethitica* 12: 15–22.

HELTZER, M. (1977), 'Metal Trade of Ugarit and the Problem of Transportation of Commercial Goods', *Iraq* 39: 203–11.

HILLER, S. (1991), 'Two Trojan Wars? On the Destructions of Troy VIh and VIIa', in M. Korfmann, *et al.*, 145–54.

HOFFMANN, I. (1984*a*), *Der Erlass Telipinus*, Heidelberg.

——(1984*b*), 'Einige Überlegungen zum Verfasser des Madduwatta-Textes', *Or* 53: 34–51.

HOFFNER, H. A. (1973), 'The Hittites and Hurrians', in D. J. Wiseman, *Peoples of Old Testament Times*, Oxford, 197–228.

——(1975), 'Propaganda and Political Justification in Hittite Historiography', in H. Goedicke, and J. J. M. Roberts, *Essays in the History, Literature and Religion of the Ancient Near East*, Baltimore and London, 49–62.

——(1977), Rev. of several Hittite studies, including Neu (1974), Rüster (1972), and Neu and Rüster (1975), *BASOR* 226: 78–9.

——(1980), 'Histories and Historians of the Ancient Near East: The Hittites', *Or* 49: 283–332.

——(1982), 'The Milawata Letter Augmented and Reinterpreted' (Proceedings of the 28th Rencontre Assyriologique Internationale, Vienna, 1981), *AfO Beiheft* 19, Horn, 130–7.

——(1983), 'A Prayer of Mursili II about his Stepmother', *JAOS* 103: 187–92.

——(1989*a*), 'The Ulmi-Tesub Treaty (KBo 4.10 = *CTH* 106), with a New Join', *Fs Özgüç*, 199–203.

——(1989*b*), 'The Last Days of Khattusha', in W. A. Ward, and M. S. Joukowsky, 46–51.

——(1992), 'Advice to a King', *Fs Alp*, 295–304.

HOFFNER, H. A, and BECKMAN, G. M. (1986), *Kaniššuwar. A Tribute to Hans G. Güterbock on his Seventy-Fifth Birthday*, Chicago (cited as *Fs Güterbock II*).

HOOKER, J. T. (1976), *Mycenaean Greece*, London.

HOUT, T. VAN DEN (1984), 'Kurunta und die Datierung einiger hethitischen Texte', *RAss* 78: 89–92.

——(1989*a*): KBo *IV 10 + (CTH 106). Studien zum Spätjunghethitischen. Texte der Zeit Tuthaliyas IV* (Dissert.), Amsterdam.

——(1989*b*), 'A Chronology of the Tarhuntassa-Treaties', *JCS* 41: 100–14.

HOUT, T. VAN DEN (1991), 'Hethitische Thronbesteigungsorakel und die Inauguration Tudhalijas IV', *ZA* 81: 274–300.

—— (1994), 'Der Falke und das Kücken: der neue Pharao und der hethitische Prinz?, *ZA* 84: 60–88.

—— (1995*a*), *Der Ulmi-Tesub-Vertrag* (*StBoT* 38), Wiesbaden.

—— (1995*b*), 'Khattushili III, King of the Hittites', in J. M. Sasson, 1107–20.

—— (1995*c*), 'Tuthalija IV. und die Ikonographie hethitischer Grosskönige des 13. Jhs.', Rev. of Neve (1993*b*), *BiOr* 52: 545–73.

HOUT, T. VAN DEN, and DE ROOS, J. (eds.) (1995), *Studio Historiae Ardens (Ancient Near Eastern Studies Presented to Philo H. J. Houwink ten Cate on the Occasion of his 65th Birthday)*, Istanbul (cited as *Fs Houwink ten Cate*).

HOUWINK TEN CATE, PH. H. J. (1963), Rev. of Kitchen (1962), *BiOr* 20: 270–6.

—— (1965), *The Luwian Population Groups of Lycia and Cilicia Aspera during the Hellenistic Period*, Leiden.

—— (1966), 'A New Fragment of the "Deeds of Suppiluliuma as told by his Son Mursili II"', *JNES* 25: 27–31.

—— (1967), 'Mursilis' North-Western Campaigns—A Commentary', *Anatolica* 1: 44–61.

—— (1970), *Records of the Early Hittite Empire*, Istanbul.

—— (1973), Rev. of von Schuler (1965), *BiOr* 30: 77–9.

—— (1974*a*), 'The early and late phases of Urhi-Tesub's Career', *Fs Güterbock I*, 123–50.

—— (1974*b*), 'Anatolian evidence for Relations with the West in the Late Bronze Age', in R. A. Crossland and A. Birchall, 141–61.

—— (1979*a*), 'Mursilis' Northwestern Campaigns—Additional Fragments of his Comprehensive Annals Concerning the Nerik Foundation', *Fs Laroche*, 157–67.

—— (1979*b*), 'The Mashuiluwa Affair: A Join (KBo XIX 46), and a Duplicate (KBo IX 77), to Mursilis's Comprehensive Annals (12th year of his reign)', *Fs Meriggi*, 267–92.

—— (1983), 'The History of Warfare according to Hittite Sources: the Annals of Hattusilis I', *Anatolica* 10: 91–109.

—— (1983–4), 'Sidelights on the Ahhiyawa Question from Hittite Vassal and Royal Correspondence', *JEOL* 28: 33–79.

—— (1984), 'The History of Warfare according to Hittite Sources: the Annals of Hattusilis I (Part II)', *Anatolica* 11: 47–83.

—— (1992*a*), 'The Bronze Tablet of Tudhaliyas IV and its Geographical and Historical Relations', *ZA* 82: 233–70.

—— (1992*b*), 'The Hittite Storm God; His Role and his Rule according to Hittite Cuneiform Sources', in D. Meijer (ed.), *Natural Phenomena*

Their Meaning and Depiction in the Ancient Near East, Amsterdam, Oxford, New York, and Tokyo, 83–148.

——(1994), 'Urhi-Tesub Revisited', *BiOr* 51: 233–59.

——(1995), 'Ethnic Diversity and Population Movement in Anatolia', in J. M. Sasson, 259–70.

HOUWINK TEN CATE, PH. H. J., and JOSEPHSON, F. (1967), 'Muwatallis' Prayer to the Storm-God of Kummanni (KBo xi 1)', *RHA* 25: 101–40.

HUXLEY, G. L. (1960), *Achaeans and Hittites*, Oxford.

IMPARATI, F. (1974), 'Una concessione di terre da parte di Tudhaliya IV', *RHA* 32 (whole issue).

——(1992), 'À propos des témoins du traité avec Kurunta de Tarhuntassa', *Fs Alp*, 305–22.

——(1995), 'Apology of Hattusili III or Designation of his Successor?', *Fs Houwink ten Cate*, 143–57.

IMPARATI, F., and SAPORETTI, C. (1965), 'L'Autobiografia di Hattusili I', *Studi Classici e Orientali* 14: 44–85.

INGHAM, M. F. (1969), 'The Length of the Sothic Cycle', *JEA* 55: 36–40.

IZRE'EL, S., and SINGER, I. (1990), *The General's Letter from Ugarit*, Tel Aviv.

JANSEN, H. G. (1995), 'Troy: Legend and Reality', in J. M. Sasson, 1121–34.

JESUS, P. DE (1978), 'Metal Resources in Ancient Anatolia', *AS* 28: 97–102.

JEWELL, E. R. (1974), *The Archaeology and History of Western Anatolia during the Second Millennium B.C.*, Ann Arbor.

KAMMENHUBER, A. (1959), 'Das Palaische', *RHA* 17 (whole issue).

——(1968), *Die Arier in Vorderen Orient*, Heidelberg.

——(1976), *Orakelpraxis, Träume und Vorzeichenschau*, Heidelberg.

——(1977), 'Die Arier im Vorderen Orient und die historischen Wohnsitze der Hurriter', *Or* 46, 129–44.

KAPTAN, E. (1995), 'Tin and Ancient Mining in Turkey', *Anatolica* 21: 197–203.

KEMPINSKI, A. (1979), 'Hittites in the Bible—What Does Archaeology Say?', *Biblical Archaeological Review* 5, no. 4: 20–45.

KEMPINSKI, A., and KOŠAK, S. (1970), 'Der Ismeriga-Vertrag', *WO* 5: 191–217.

——(1982), 'CTH 13: The Extensive Annals of Hattusili I (?)', *Tel Aviv* 9: 87–116.

KESTEMONT, G. (1974), *Diplomatique et droit international en Asie Occidentale*, Louvain-la-Neuve.

KITCHEN, K. A. (1962), *Suppiluliuma and the Amarna Pharaohs*, Liverpool.

——(1982), *Pharaoh Triumphant: The Life and Times of Ramesses II*, Warminster.

——(1985), Rev. of Krauss (1978), *JEA* 71: 43–4.

KITCHEN, K. A. (1995), 'Pharaoh Ramesses II and his Times', in J. M. Sasson, 763–74.

KITCHEN, K. A., and GABALLA, G. A. (1969–70), 'Ramesside Varia II', *Zeitschrift für Ägyptische Sprache und Altertumskunde* 96: 14–28.

KLENGEL, E., and H. (1975), *Die Hethiter*, Vienna and Munich.

KLENGEL, H. (1963), 'Der Schiedsspruch des Mursili II. hinsichtlich Barga und seine Übereinkunft mit Duppi-Tesup von Amurru (KBo III 3)', *Or* 32: 32–55.

——(1964*a*), 'Ein neues Fragment zur historischen Einleitung des Talmisarruma-Vertrages', *ZA* 56: 213–17.

——(1964*b*), 'Aziru von Amurru und seine Rolle in der Geschichte der Amarna-zeit', *MIO* 10: 57–83.

——(1965*a*), 'Die Rolle der "Ältesten" (LÚ^MEŠ ŠU.GI) im Kleinasien der Hethiterzeit', *ZA* 57: 223–36.

——(1965*b*), *Geschichte Syriens im 2. Jahrtausend v.u.Z.*, Part 1: *Nordsyrien*, Berlin.

——(1968), 'Die Hethiter und Isuwa', *OA* 7: 63–76.

——(1969), *Geschichte Syriens im 2. Jahrtausend v.u.Z.*, Part 2: *Mittel- und Südsyrien*, Berlin.

——(1970), *Geschichte Syriens im 2. Jahrtausend v.u.Z.*, Part 3: *Historische und allgemeine Darstellung*, Berlin.

——(1974), ' "Hungerjahre" in Hatti', *AOF* 1: 165–74.

——(1979*a*), 'Die Hethiter und Babylonien', *AO* 47: 83–90.

——(1979*b*), 'Handel und Kaufleute im hethitischen Reich', *AOF* 6: 69–80.

——(1989), 'Nerikkaili. Zum Problem der Homonymie im hethitischen Anatolien', *AOF* 16: 185–8.

——(1991), 'Tudhalija IV von Hatti: Prolegomena zu einer Biographie', *AOF* 18: 224–38.

——(1992), 'Die Hethiter und Syrien: Aspekte einer politischen Auseinandersetzung', *Fs Alp*, 341–53.

——(1995), 'Historischer Kommentar zum Sausgamuwa-Vertrag', *Fs Houwink ten Cate*, 159–72.

KLINGER, J. (1995), 'Das Corpus der Maşat-Briefe und seine Beziehungen zu den Texten aus Hattusa', *ZA* 85: 74–108.

——(1996), *Untersuchungen zur Rekonstruktion des hattischen Kultschicht* (*StBoT* 37), Wiesbaden.

KLINGER, J., and NEU, E. (1990), 'War die erste Computer-Analyse des Hethitischen verfehlt?', *Hethitica* 10: 135–60.

KNAPP, A. B. (1980), 'KBo I 26: Alasiya and Hatti', *JCS* 32: 43–7.

——(1983), 'An Alashiyan Merchant at Ugarit', *Tel Aviv* 10: 38–45.

KORFMANN, M. (1986*a*), 'Troy: Topography and Navigation', in M. J. Mellink, 1–16.

——(1986*b*), 'Beşik Tepe: New Evidence for the Period of the Trojan Sixth and Seventh Settlements', in M. J. Mellink, 17–28.

——(1990), 'Altes und Neues aus Troia', *Das Altertum* 36: 230–40.

KORFMANN, M., LATACZ, J., and CHRISTOPHERSON, A. (1991), *Studia Troica I*, Mainz.

KOROŠEC , V. (1960), 'Les Hittites et leurs vassaux syriens à la lumière des nouveaux textes d'Ugarit (*PRU* IV)', *RHA* 18: 65–79.

KOŠAK , S. (1980*a*), 'The Rulers of the Early Hittite Empire', *Tel Aviv* 7: 163–8.

——(1980*b*), 'Dating of Hittite Texts: A Test,' *AS* 30: 31–9.

——(1980*c*), 'The Hittites and the Greeks', *Linguistica* 20: 35–47.

——(1981), 'Western Neighbours of the Hittites', *Eretz Israel* 15: 12–16.

——(1986), 'The Gospel of Iron', *Fs Güterbock II*, 125–35.

——(1995), 'The Palace Library "Building A" on Büyükkale', *Fs Houwink ten Cate*, 173–9.

KRAUSS, R. (1978), *Das Ende der Amarnazeit*, Hildesheim.

KÜHNE, C. (1973*a*), 'Ammistamru und die Tochter der "Grossen Dame"', *UF* 5: 175–84.

——(1973*b*), *Die Chronologie der internationalen Korrespondenz von El-Amarna*, *AOAT* 17.

KÜHNE, C., and OTTEN, H. (1971), *Der Sausgamuwa-Vertrag* (*StBoT* 16), Wiesbaden.

KÜMMEL, H. M. (1985), 'Zwei Berichte von der Unterwerfung Zyperns durch Suppiluliama II.', *TUAT* I/5: 492–5.

——(1987), 'Rituale in hethitischer Sprache', *TUAT* II/2: 282–92.

KUPPER, J.-R. (1973), 'Northern Mesopotamia and Syria', *CAH* II.1: 1–41.

LABAT, R. (1962), 'Le Rayonnement de la langue et de l'écriture akkadienne au deuxième millénaire avant notre ère', *Syria* 39: 1–27.

LACKENBACHER, S. (1982), 'Nouveaux documents d'Ugarit', *RAss* 76: 141–56.

LANDSBERGER, B. (1954), 'Assyrische Königsliste und "Dunkles Zeitalter"', *JCS* 8: 31–45, 47–73, 106–33.

——(1965), 'Tin and Lead: the Adventures of Two Vocables', *JNES* 24: 285–96.

LAROCHE, E. (1947–48), 'Un point d'histoire: Ulmi-Tessub', *RHA* 8: 40–8.

——(1953), 'Suppululiuma II', *RAss* 47: 70–8.

——(1956), 'Documents hiéroglyphiques hittites provenant du palais d'Ugarit', in Schaeffer, *Ugaritica III*, 97–160.

——(1958), 'Études sur les hiéroglyphes hittites', *Syria* 35: 252–83.

——(1966), *Les Noms des Hittites*, Paris.

——(1971), *Catalogue des textes hittites*, Paris (cited as *CTH*).

——(1972*a*), *Catalogue des textes hittites, premier supplément*, *RHA* 30: 94–133.

LAROCHE, E. (1972*b*), 'Linguistique asianique', *Minos* 11: 112–35.

——(1976), 'Lyciens et Termiles', *RA* fasc. 1: 15–9.

——(1977), 'Glossaire de la langue hourrite', *RHA* 35.

——(1979), *Florilegium Anatolicum* (Mélanges offerts à Emmanuel Laroche), Paris (cited as *Fs Laroche*).

——(1982), 'Documents hittites et hourrites', in E. Beyer, 53–60.

——(1987–90), 'Luwier, Luwisch, Lu(w)iya', *RlA* 7: 181–4.

LARSEN, M. T. (1967), *Old Assyrian Caravan Procedures*, Istanbul.

——(1972), 'A Revolt Against Hattusa', *JCS* 24: 100–1.

——(1974), 'The Old Assyrian Colonies in Anatolia' (rev. article of Orlin (1970)), *JAOS* 94: 468–75.

——(1976), *The Old Assyrian City-State and its Colonies*, Copenhagen.

——(1979), *Power and Propaganda (Mesopotamia 7)*, Copenhagen.

LEBRUN, R. (1979), 'Considerations sur la femme dans la société hittite', *Hethitica* 3: 109–25.

——(1980), *Hymnes et prières hittites*, Louvain-la-Neuve.

LEWY, H. (1963), 'Nesa', *JCS* 17: 103–4.

——(1971), 'Anatolia in the Old Assyrian Period', *CAH* 1.2: 707–28.

LEWY, J. (1962), 'Old Assyrian Evidence concerning Kussara and its Location', *HUCA* 33: 45–57.

LIVERANI, M. (1978), 'L'élément hourrite dans la Syrie du nord (*c.*1350–1200)', *RHA* 36: 149–56.

——(1988), 'The Fire of Hahhum', *OA* 27: 165–72.

——(1990), *Prestige and Interest: International Relations in the Near East ca. 1600–1100 B.C.*, Pavia.

LLOYD, S. (1967), *Early Highland Peoples of Anatolia*, London.

——(1989), *Ancient Turkey*, London.

LORETZ, O. (1984), *Habiru-Hebräer. Eine sozio-linguistische Studie über die Herkunft des Gentiliziums 'ibri vom Appellativum habiru*, Berlin.

LUCKENBILL, D. D. (1926–7), *Ancient Records of Assyria and Babylonia*, i–ii, Chicago.

MACHINIST, P. (1982), 'Assyrians and Hittites in the Late Bronze Age', *Mesopotamien und seine Nachbarn* (Proceedings of the 25th Rencontre Assyriologique Internationale, Berlin, 1978), Berlin, 265–7.

MCMAHON, G. (1989), 'Hittite History', *Biblical Archaeologist* 52: 62–77.

MACQUEEN, J. G. (1986), *The Hittites and their Contemporaries in Asia Minor*, London.

——(1995), 'The History of Anatolia and of the Hittite Empire', in J. M. Sasson, 1085–105.

MAKKAY, J. (1993), 'Pottery Links between Late Neolithic Cultures of the NW Pontic and Anatolia, and the Origins of the Hittites', *Anatolica* 19: 117–28.

MARAZZI, M. (1984), 'Überlegungen zur Bedeutung von *pankus* in der hethitisch-akkadischen Bilinguis Hattusili I', *WO* 15: 96–102.

MARGUERON, J. (1982*a*), 'La Recherche sur le terrain', in D. Beyer, 11–14.

—— (1982*b*), 'Architecture et urbanisme', in D. Beyer, 23–39.

—— (1995), 'Emar, Capital of Astata in the Fourteenth century BCE,' *Biblical Archaeologist*, 58, 126–38.

MARTINO, S. DE (1991), 'Alcune osservazioni su KBo III 27', *AOF* 18: 54–66.

MASSON, E. (1979), 'Les Inscriptions hiéroglyphiques d'Emirgazi', *Journal des Savants*, 3–49.

MEE, C. B. (1978), 'Aegean Trade and Settlement in Anatolia in the Second Millennium B.C.', *AS* 28: 121–55.

—— (1984), 'The Mycenaeans and Troy', in L. Foxhall, and J. K. Davies, 45–56.

MELCHERT, H. C. (1978), 'The Acts of Hattusili I', *JNES* 37: 1–22.

—— (1991), 'Death and the Hittite King', in *Perspectives on Indo-European Language, Culture, and Religion (Studies in honor of Edgar C. Polomé)*, i, *JIES* Monograph no. 7, Bochum, 182–7.

MELLAART, J. (1971*a*), 'Anatolia *c*.4000–2300 B.C.', *CAH* I.2: 363–416.

—— (1971*b*), 'Anatolia *c*.2300–1750 B.C.', *CAH* I.2: 681–706.

—— (1974), 'Western Anatolia, Beycesultan and the Hittites', *Fs Mansel*, 493–526.

—— (1981), 'Anatolia and the Indo-Europeans', *JIES* 9: 135–49.

—— (1984), 'Troy VIIA in Anatolian Perspective', in L. Foxhall, and J. K. Davies, 63–82.

—— (1986*a*), 'Hatti, Arzawa and Ahhiyawa; a Review of the Present Stalemate in Historical and Geographical Studies', *Fs Mylonas*, 74–84.

—— (1986*b*), 'Some Reflections on the History and Geography of Western Anatolia in the Late 14th and 13th Centuries B.C.', *Anadolu* 10: 1986, 215–30.

MELLINK, M. J. (1983), 'Archaeological Comments on Ahhiyawa-Achaians in Western Anatolia', *AJA* 87: 138–41.

—— (1986), (ed.), *Troy and the Trojan War*, Bryn Mawr.

—— (1995), 'Comments on Continuity and Discontinuity in South Anatolian Coastal Toponymy', *Fs Houwink ten Cate*, 187–94.

MERIGGI, P. (1962), 'Über einige hethitische Fragmente historischen Inhaltes', *WZKM* 58: 66–110.

MEYER, G. R. (1953), 'Zwei neue Kizzuwatna-Verträge', *MIO* 1: 108–24.

MILLARD, A. R. (1984), 'Events at the End of the Late Bronze Age in the Near East', in L. Foxhall, and J. K. Davies, 1–15.

MORA, C. (1987), 'Una probabile testimonianza di coreggenza tra due sovrani ittiti', *Rendiconti Istituto Lombardo* 121: 97–108.

—— (1992), 'KUB XXI 33 e l'Identità di Mursili III', *SMEA* 29: 127–48.

MORAN, W. (1969), 'The Death of 'Abdi-Asirta', *Eretz-Israel* 9: 94–9.

MORAN, W. (1987), *Les Lettres d'El Amarna*, Paris.

——(1992), *The Amarna Letters* (English language edition), Baltimore.

MORRIS, S. P. (1989), 'A Tale of Two Cities: The Miniature Frescoes from Thera and the Origins of Greek Poetry', *AJA* 93: 511–35.

MUHLY, J. D. (1973), 'Copper and Tin: The Distribution of Mineral Resources and the Nature of the Metals Trade in the Bronze Age,' *Transactions of the Connecticut Academy of Arts and Sciences* 43, New Haven, 155–535.

——(1984), 'The Role of the Sea Peoples in Cyprus during the LC III Period', in V. Karageorghis, and J. D. Muhly, *Cyprus at the Close of the Late Bronze Age*, Nicosia, 39–56.

——(1992), 'The Crisis Years in the Mediterranean World: Transition or Cultural Disintegration?', in A. W. Ward, and M. S. Joukowsky, 10–26.

MUHLY, J. D. *et al.* (1985), 'Iron in Anatolia and the Nature of the Hittite Iron Industry', *AS* 35: 67–84.

——(1991), 'The Bronze Metallurgy of Anatolia and the Question of Local Tin Sources', *Archaeometry* 90: 209–20.

——(1992), 'Comment on the Discussion of Ancient Tin Sources in Anatolia', *JMA* 5: 91–8.

MÜLLER-KARPE, H. (1976), *Geschichte des 13. und 12. Jahrhunderts v. Chr.*, Jahresbericht des Instituts für Vorgeschichte der Universität Frankfurt A. M., Munich.

MUNN-RANKIN, J. M. (1975), 'Assyrian Military Power 1300–1200 B.C.', *CAH* II.2: 274–306.

MURNANE, W. J. (1985), *The Road to Kadesh*, Chicago (revised 2nd edn., 1990).

NA'AMAN, N. (1974), 'Syria at the Transition from the Old Babylonian Period to the Middle Babylonian Period', *UF* 6: 265–74.

——(1980), 'The Historical Introduction of the Aleppo Treaty Reconsidered', *JCS* 32: 34–42.

NASHEF, K. (1991), *Répertoire Géographique des Textes Cunéiformes Bd. 4 Die Orts- und Gewässernamen der altassyrischen Zeit*, Wiesbaden.

NEU, E. (1974), *Der Anitta-Text* (*SBoT* 18), Wiesbaden.

——(1995), 'Hethiter und Hethitisch in Ugarit', in M. Dietrich, and O. Loretz (eds.) *Ugarit, Bd I, Ugarit und seine altorientalische Umwelt*, Münster, 115–29.

NEU, E., and RÜSTER, C. (1973*a*), *Festschrift Heinrich Otten*, Wiesbaden (cited as *Fs Otten I*).

——(1973*b*), 'Zur Datierung hethitischer Texte', *Fs Otten I*, 221–42.

——(1975), *Hethitische Keilschrift-Paläographie II* (*StBoT* 21), Wiesbaden (see also Rüster, 1972).

——(1988), *Documentum Asiae Minoris Antiquae*, Wiesbaden (cited as *Fs Otten II*).

NEVE, P. J. (1982), *Büyükkale: Die Bauwerke (Boğazköy-Hattusa 12)*, Berlin.

——(1984), 'Die Ausgrabungen in Boğazköy-Hattusa 1983', *AA* Heft 3: 329–81.

——(1987), 'Die Ausgrabungen in Boğazköy-Hattusa 1986', *AA* Heft 3: 381–412.

——(1988), 'Die Ausgrabungen in Boğazköy-Hattusa 1987', *AA* Heft 3: 357–90.

——(1989), 'Die Ausgrabungen in Boğazköy-Hattusa 1988', *AA* Heft 3: 271–337.

——(1989–90), 'Boğazköy-Hattusha: New Results of the Excavations in the Upper City', *Anatolica* 16: 7–19.

——(1990), 'Die Ausgrabungen in Boğazköy-Hattusa 1989', *AA* Heft 3: 267–303.

——(1991), 'Die Ausgrabungen in Boğazköy-Hattusa 1990', *AA* Heft 3: 299–348.

——(1992a), 'Die Ausgrabungen in Boğazköy-Hattusa 1991', *AA* Heft 3: 307–38.

——(1992b), 'Suppiluliuma I. oder II.?' *Fs Alp*, 401–8.

——(1993a), 'Die Ausgrabungen in Boğazköy-Hattusa 1992', *AA* Heft 4: 621–52.

——(1993b), *Hattusa Stadt der Götter und Tempel*, Mainz am Rhein.

NOUGAYROL, J. (1956), *Le Palais Royal d'Ugarit IV* (Mission de Ras Shamra Tome IX), Paris (cited as *PRU* IV).

——(1970), *Le Palais Royal d'Ugarit VI* (Mission de Ras Shamra Tome XII), Paris (cited as *PRU* VI).

NOUGAYROL, J. *et al.* (1968), *Ugaritica V* (Mission de Ras Shamra Tome XVI), Paris.

OPPENHEIM, A. L. (1956), *The Interpretation of Dreams in the Ancient Near East*, Philadelphia.

——(1967), *Letters from Mesopotamia*, Chicago and London.

ORLIN, L. L. (1970), *Assyrian Colonies in Cappadocia*, The Hague and Paris.

OTTEN, H. (1951a), 'Ein althethitischer Vertrag mit Kizzuvatna', *JCS* 5: 129–32.

——(1951b), 'Die hethitischen Königslisten und die altorientalische Chronologie', *MDOG* 83: 47–70.

——(1951c), 'Zu den Anfängen der hethitischen Geschichte,' *MDOG* 83: 33–45.

——(1953), 'Die inschriftliche Funde', *MDOG* 86 (Vorläufiger Bericht über die Ausgrabungen in Boghazköy im Jahre 1952)': 59–64.

——(1955), 'Inschriftliche Funde der Ausgrabung in Boğazköy 1953,' *MDOG* 87: 13–25.

OTTEN, H. (1956), 'Hethitische Schreiber in ihren Briefen', *MIO* 4: 179–89.

——(1957–58), 'Bemerkungen zu den hethitischen Instruktionen für die LÚ.MEŠSAG' (rev. of von Schuler (1957)), *AfO* 18: 387–90.

——(1958), 'Keilschrifttexte', *MDOG* 91: 73–84.

——(1959), 'Korrespondenz mit Tukulti-Ninurta I. aus Boghazköy', in E. Weidner, 64–8.

——(1959–60), 'Ein Brief aus Hattusa an Bâbu-aḫu-iddina', *AfO* 19: 39–46.

——(1962), 'Die Textfunde der Campagnen 1958 und 1959', *MDOG* 93: 75–7.

——(1963), 'Neue Quellen zum Ausklang des Hethitischen Reiches', *MDOG* 94: 1–23.

——(1964), 'Der Weg des hethitischen Staates zum Grossreich', *Saeculum* 15: 115–24.

——(1967), 'Ein hethitischer Vertrag aus dem 15./14. Jahrhundert v. Chr. (KBo XVI 47)', *IM* 17: 55–62.

——(1968), *Die hethitischen historischen Quellen und die altorientalische Chronologie*, Mainz and Wiesbaden.

——(1969), *Sprachliche Stellung und Datierung des Madduwatta-Textes (StBoT 11)*, Wiesbaden.

——(1971), 'Das Siegel des hethitischen Grosskönigs Tahurwaili', *MDOG* 103: 59–68.

——(1973), *Eine althethitische Erzählung um die Stadt Zalpa (StBoT 17)*, Wiesbaden.

——(1975), *Puduhepa, eine hethitische Königin in ihren Textzeugnissen*, Mainz.

——(1976), 'Zum Ende des Hethiterreiches aufgrund der Boghazköy-Texte', in H. Müller-Karpe, 22–35.

——(1981), *Die Apologie Hattusilis III (SBoT 24)*, Wiesbaden.

——(1983), 'Die letzte Phase des hethitischen Grossreiches nach den Texten', in S. Deger-Jalkotzy, 13–24.

——(1984), Rev. of Tischler (1981), *IF* 89: 298–301.

——(1986), 'Archive und Bibliotheken in Hattusa' in *Cuneiform Archives and Libraries* (Proceedings of the 30th Rencontre Assyriologique Internationale, Leiden, 1983), Leiden, 184–90.

——(1987), 'Das hethitisches Königshaus im 15. Jahrhundert v. Chr.: Zum Neufund einiger Landschenkungsurkunden in Boğazköy', *Anzeiger der phil.-hist. Klasse der Österreichischen Akademie der Wissenschaften* 123, Vienna, 21–34.

——(1988a), *Die Bronzetafel aus Boğazköy: ein Staatsvertrag Tuthalijas IV*, Wiesbaden.

——(1988b), *Madduwatta*, *RlA* 7: 194–5.

——(1989a), *Die 1986 in Boğazköy gefundene Bronzetafel. Zwei Vorträge*, Innsbruck.

—— (1989*b*), 'Die Hieroglyphen-luwische Inschrift', *AA* Heft 3: 333–7.

—— (1990), 'Bemerkungen zur Überlieferung einiger hethitischer Texte', *ZA* 80: 224–6.

—— (1991), 'Excurs zu den Landschenkungsurkunden', *AA* Heft 3: 345–8.

—— (1993*a*), *Zu einigen Neufunden hethitischer Königssiegel*, Stuttgart.

—— (1993*b*), 'Ein Siegel Tuthaliyas IV. und sein dynastischer Hintergrund', *IM* 43: 107–12.

—— (1994), 'Die hethitische Grosskönig Henti in ihren Siegeln', *ZA* 84/2: 253–61.

—— (1995), *Die hethitischen Königssiegel der frühen Grossreichzeit*, Stuttgart.

OTTEN, H., AKURGAL, E., ERTEM, H., and SÜEL, A. (1992), *Hittite and Other Anatolian and Near Eastern Studies in Honour of Sedat Alp*, Ankara (cited as *Fs Alp*).

OTTEN, H., and SOUCEK, V. (1965), *Das Gelübde der Königin Puduhepa an die Göttin Lelwani* (*StBoT* 1), Wiesbaden.

ÖZGÜÇ, T. (1956), 'The Dagger of Anitta', *Belleten* 20: 29–36.

—— (1963), 'An Assyrian Trading Outpost', *Scientific American* 208: 97–102.

—— (1964), 'The Art and Architecture of Ancient Kanish', *Anadolu* 1st ser. 8: 27–48.

—— (1986), *Kültepe-Kanis II: New Researches at the Trading Center of the Ancient Near East*, Ankara.

—— (1988), *Inandıktepe*, Ankara.

PARDEE, D. (1977), 'A New Ugaritic Letter', *BiOr* 34: 3–20.

PIRENNE, J. (1950), 'La Politique d'expansion hittite envisagée à travers les traités de vassalité et de protectorat', *AO* 18: 373–82.

PODZUWEIT, C. (1982), 'Die mykenische Welt und Troja', in Hänsel, B., *Südosteuropa zwischen 1600 und 1000 vor Chr.*, Berlin, 65–88.

PRITCHARD, J. B. (1969), *Ancient Near Eastern Texts relating to the Old Testament*, 3rd edn., Princeton.

PUHVEL, J. (1989), 'Hittite Regal Titles: Hattic or Indo-European?', *JIES* 17: 351–61.

RAPP, G., and GIFFORD, A. (1982), 'Earthquakes in the Troad', in *Troy, the Archaeological Geology*, Princeton, 43–58.

RENFREW, C. (1987), *Archaeology and Language: The Puzzle of Indo-European Origins*, London.

RIEMSCHNEIDER, K. K. (1958), 'Die hethitischen Landschenkungs-urkunden', *MIO* 6: 321–81.

—— (1962), 'Hethitische Fragmente historische Inhalts aus der Zeit Hattusilis III', *JCS* 16: 110–21.

—— (1971), 'Die Thronfolgeordnung im althethitischen Reich', in H. Klengel, *Beiträge zur Sozialen Struktur des alten Vorderasien*, Berlin, 79–102.

Röllig, W. (1972–5), 'Heirat', *RlA* 4: 282–7.

——(1974), 'Politische Heiraten im Alten Orient', *Saeculum* 25: 11–23.

——(1988), 'Lukka, Lukki', *RlA* 7: 161–3.

Roos, J. de (1985), Rev. of Tischler (1981), *BiOr* 42: 128–33.

——(1985–86), 'Who Was Kilushepa?', *JEOL* 29: 74–83.

——(1989), 'KBo 33–216. A votive text of Tuthaliyas IV', *JAC* 4: 39–48.

Rowton, M. B. (1959), 'The Background of the Treaty between Ramesses II and Hattusili III', *JCS* 13: 1–11.

——(1966), 'The Material from Western Asia and the Chronology of the Nineteenth Dynasty', *JNES* 25: 240–58.

——(1967), 'The Physical Environment and the Problem of the Nomads', (Proceedings of the 15th Rencontre Assyriologique Internationale, Liège, 1966), Paris.

Rüster, C. (1972), *Hethitische Keilschrift-Paläographie I* (*StBoT* 20), Wiesbaden (see also Neu and Rüster, 1975).

——(1993), 'Eine Urkunde Hantilis II', *Fs Neve*, 63–70.

Sandars, N. K. (1985), *The Sea Peoples*, London.

Sasson, J. M. (ed.) (1995), *Civilizations of the Ancient Near East* (4 vols.), New York.

Schaeffer, C. F.-A. (1956), *Ugaritica* III (Mission de Ras Shamra Tome VIII), Paris.

Schuler, E. von (1956), 'Die Würdenträgereide des Arnuwanda', *Or* 25: 209–40.

——(1957), *Hethitische Dienstanweisungen für höhere Hof- und Staatsbeamte* (*AfO* Beiheft 10), Graz.

——(1965) *Die Kaškaer* , Berlin.

——(1980–3), 'Landschenkungsurkunden', *RlA* 6: 468–70.

Singer, I. (1981), 'Hittites and Hattians in Anatolia at the Beginning of the Second Millennium B.C.', *JIES* 9: 119–34.

——(1983*a*), 'Western Anatolia in the Thirteenth Century B.C. according to the Hittite Sources', *AS* 33: 205–17.

——(1983*b*), 'Takuhlinu and Haya: Two Governors in the Ugarit Letter from Tel Aphek', *Tel Aviv* 10: 3–25.

——(1985*a*), 'The Battle of Nihriya and the End of the Hittite Empire', *ZA* 75: 100–23.

——(1985*b*), 'The Beginning of Philistine Settlement in Canaan and the Northern Boundary of Philistia', *Tel Aviv* 12: 109–22.

——(1987), 'Dating the End of the Hittite Empire', *Hethitica* 8: 413–21.

——(1988*a*), 'Megiddo Mentioned in a Letter from Boğazköy', *Fs Otten II*, 327–32.

——(1988*b*), 'Merneptah's Campaign to Canaan and the Egyptian Occupation of the Southern Coastal Plain of Palestine in the Ramesside Period', *BASOR* 269: 1–10.

——(1988c), 'The Origin of the Sea Peoples and their Settlement on the Coast of Canaan', in M. Heltzer, and E. Lipinski (eds.), *Society and Economy in the Eastern Mediterranean (c.1500–1000 B.C.)* (Proceedings of the International Symposium, University of Haifa, April–May 1985), Leuven, 239–50.

——(1991a), 'A Concise History of Amurru', Appendix III (pp. 135–95), to Izre'el, S., *Amurru Akkadian: A Linguistic Study* (vol. ii), Atlanta.

——(1991b), 'The "Land of Amurru" and the "Lands of Amurru" in the Sausgamuwa Treaty', *Iraq* 53: 69–74.

——(1991c), 'The title "Great Princess" in the Hittite Empire', *UF* 23: 327–38.

——(1995a), ' "Our God" and "Their God" in the Anitta Text', *Atti del il Congresso Internazionale di Hittitologia* (*Studia Mediterranea* 9), Pavia, 343–9.

——(1995b), 'A Hittite Seal from Megiddo', *Biblical Archaeologist*, 58: 91–3.

SJÖBERG, A. (1974), 'The Old Babylonian Eduba', in *Sumerological Studies in Honor of Thorkild Jacobsen* (Assyriological Studies No. 20), Chicago, 159–79.

SMITH, S. (1949), *The Statue of Idrimi*, London.

SOMMER, F. (1932), *Die Aḫḫijavā Urkunden*, Munich, repr. Hildesheim 1975.

SOMMER, F., and FALKENSTEIN, A. (1938), *Die hethitisch-akkadische Bilingue des Hattusili I. (Labarna II.)*, Munich.

SOYSAL, Ö. (1990), 'Noch einmal zur Sukziya-Episode im Erlass Telipinus', *Or* 59: 271–9.

SPALINGER, A. (1979), 'Egyptian-Hittite Relations at the Close of the Amarna Period and some notes on Hittite Military Strategy in North Syria', *Bulletin of the Egyptological Seminar* 1: 55–89.

——(1981), 'Considerations of the Hittite Treaty between Egypt and Hatti', *SAK* 9: 299–358.

SPERLING, J. (1991), 'The Last Phase of Troy VI and Mycenaean Expansion', in M. Korfman, *et al.*, 155–8.

STARKE, F. (1981a), 'Die Keilschrift-luwischen Wörter für Insel und Lampe', *Zeitschrift für Vergleichende Sprachforschung*, 95: 142–52.

——(1981b), 'Zur Deutung der Arzawa-Briefstelle VBoT 1, 25–7', *ZA* 71: 221–31.

——(1983), 'Labarna', *RlA* 5: 404–8.

STEFANINI, R. (1964), 'KUB xxi 33 (Bo 487): Mursili's Sins', *JAOS* 84: 22–30.

STEINER, G. (1964), 'Die Ahhijawa-Frage heute', *Saeculum* 15: 365–92.

——(1981), 'The Role of the Hittites in Ancient Anatolia', *JIES* 9: 150–73.

STEINER, G. (1984), 'Struktur und Bedeutung des sog. Anitta-Textes,' *OA* 23: 53–73.

——(1989*a*), ' "Schiffe von Ahhijawa" oder "Kriegsschiffe" von Amurru im Sauskamuwa-Vertrag?' *UF* 21: 393–411.

——(1989*b*), 'Kültepe-Kanis und der "Anitta-Text" ' in *Fs Özgüç*, 471–80.

——(1990), 'The immigration of the first Indo-Europeans into Anatolia Reconsidered', *JIES* 18: 185–214.

SÜEL, A. (1992), 'Ortaköy: Eine hethitische Stadt mit hethitischen und hurritischen Tontafelentdeckungen', *Fs Alp*, 487–91.

STURTEVANT, E. H., and BECHTEL, G. (1935), *A Hittite Chrestomathy*, Philadelphia.

SÜRENHAGEN, D. (1981), 'Zwei Gebete Hattusilis und der Puduhepa', *AOF* 8: 83–168.

——(1985), *Paritätische Staatsverträge aus hethitischer Sicht*, Pavia.

——(1986), 'Ein Königssiegel aus Kargamis', *MDOG* 118: 183–90.

——(1992), 'Untersuchungen zur Bronzetafel und weiteren Verträgen mit der Sekundogenitur in Tarhuntassa', *OLZ* 87: 341–71.

TIGAY, J. H. (1982), *The Evolution of the Gilgamesh Epic*, Philadelphia.

TISCHLER, J. (1981), *Das hethitische Gebet der Gassulijawija*, Innsbruck.

——(1988), 'Labarna', *Fs Otten II*, 347–58.

——(1991), *Hethitisches Etymologisches Glossar, Teil III Lieferung 8*, Innsbruck.

——(1993), *Hethitisches Etymologisches Glossar, Teil III Lieferung 9*, Innsbruck.

TOORN, K. VAN DER (1994), 'Gods and Ancestors in Emar and Nuzi', *ZA* 84: 38–59.

ÜNAL, A. (1974), *Hattusili III. Teil I Hattusili bis zu seiner Thronsbesteigung, Band I: Historischer Abriss, Band II: Quellen und Indices*, Heidelberg.

——(1978), *Ein Orakeltext über die Intrigen am hethitischen Hof* (KUB *XXII* 70 = Bo *2011*), Heidelberg.

——(1980–3), 'Kussara', *RlA* 6: 378–82.

——(1989), 'On the Writing of Hittite History', (rev. of J. Macqueen (1986), *JAOS* 109: 283–7.

ÜNAL, A., ERTEKIN, A., and EDIZ, I. (1991), 'The Hittite Sword from Boghazköy-Hattusa, found in 1991 and its Akkadian Inscription', *Museum* 4: 46–52.

VEENHOF, K. R. (1972), *Aspects of Old Assyrian Trade and its Terminology*, Leiden.

——(1982), 'The Old Assyrian Merchants and their Relations with the Native Population of Anatolia', *Mesopotamien und seine Nachbarn* (Proceedings of the 25th Rencontre Assyriologique Internationale, Berlin, 1978), Berlin, 147–60.

——(1986), 'Cuneiform Archives', in *Cuneiform Archives and Libraries* (Proceedings of the 30th Rencontre Assyriologique Internationale, Leiden, 1983), Leiden, 1–36.

——(1989), 'Status and Offices of an Anatolian Gentleman: Two Unpublished Letters of Ḫuḫarimataku from Karum Kanish', *Fs Özgüç*, 515–25.

——(1995*a*), 'Old Assyrian *ISURTUM*, Akkadian *ESERUM* and Hittite GIŠ.ḪUR', *Fs Houwink ten Cate*, 311–32.

——(1995*b*), 'Kanesh: An Assyrian Colony in Anatolia', in J. M. Sasson, 859–71.

VERMEULE, E. (1960), 'The Mycenaeans in Achaia', *AJA* 64: 1–21.

——(1986), 'Priam's Castle Blazing', in M. J. Mellink, 77–92.

WALSER, G. (ed.) (1964), *Neuere Hethiterforschung*, (*Historia*, Einzelschriften Heft 7), Wiesbaden.

WARD, A. W., and JOUKOWSKY, M. S. (1989), *The Crisis Years: The 12th Century B.C.*, Dubuque.

WATANABE, K. (1989), 'Mit Gottessiegeln versehene hethitische "Staatsverträge"', *Acta Sumerologica* 11: 261–76.

WATERHOUSE, S. D. (1965), *Syria in the Armana Age: A Border-land between Conflicting Empires* (Ph.D. Diss.), Ann Arbor.

WATKINS, C. (1986), 'The Language of the Trojans', in M. J. Mellink, 45–62.

——(1987), 'Questions linguistiques palaites et louvites cunéiformes', *Hethitica* 8: 423–6.

WEBSTER, T. B. L. (1958), *From Mycenae to Homer*, London.

WEIDNER, E. F. (1923), *Politische Dokumente aus Kleinasien*, Leipzig, repr. New York, 1970 (cited as *PD*).

——(1930–1), 'Wasasatta, König von Hanigalbat', *AfO* 6: 21–2.

——(1959), *Die Inschriften Tukulti-Ninurtas I. und seiner Nachfolger* (*AfO* Beiheft 12), Graz.

——(1969), 'Assyrien und Hanigalbat', *Ugaritica* VI, 519–31.

WEIHER, E. VON (1973), 'Mitanni', *Fs Otten I*, 321–6.

WENTE, E. F., and VAN SICLEN III, C. C. (1977), 'A Chronology of the New Kingdom', in *Studies in Honor of George R. Hughes*, Chicago, 217–61.

WESTBROOK, R., and WOODARD, R. (1990), 'The Edict of Tudhaliya IV', *JAOS* 110: 641–59.

WILHELM, G. (1988), 'Zur ersten Zeile des Sunassura-Vertrages', *Fs Otten II*, 359–70.

——(1989), *The Hurrians*, Warminster.

——(1991), 'Probleme der hethitischen Chronologie' (rev. of Astour, 1989), *OLZ* 86: 469–76.

——(1995*a*), 'The Kingdom of Mitanni in Second-Millennium Upper Mesopotamia', in J. M. Sasson, 1243–54.

WILHELM, G. (1995*b*), 'Die Tontafelfunde der 2. Ausgrabungskampagne 1994 in Kusaklı', *MDOG* 127: 37–42.

WILHELM, G., and BOESE, J. (1979), 'Assur-Dan I., Ninurta-Apil-Ekur und die mittelassyrische Chronologie', *WZKM* 71: 19–38.

——(1987/9), 'Absolute Chronologie und die hethitische Geschichte des 15. und 14. Jahrhunderts v. Chr.', in P. Åström, 74–116.

WINKELS, H. (1985), Rev. of Tischler (1981), *Kratylos* 30: 183–5.

WISEMAN, D. J. (1953), *The Alalakh Tablets*, London.

WOUTERS, W. (1989), 'Urhi-Tesub and the Ramses-Letters from Boghazköy', *JCS* 41: 226–34.

YAKAR, J. (1976), 'Hittite Involvement in Western Anatolia', *AS* 26: 117–28.

——(1981), 'The Indo-Europeans and their Impact on Anatolian Cultural Development', *JIES* 9: 94–112.

——(1993), 'Anatolian Civilization Following the Disintegration of the Hittite Empire: An Archaeological Appraisal', *Tel Aviv* 20: 3–28.

YAMADA, M. (1995), 'The Hittite Social Concept of "Free" in the light of the Emar Texts', *AOF* 22: 297–316.

YARON, R. (1963), 'A Royal Divorce at Ugarit', *Or* 32: 21–31.

YENER, K. A. (1986), 'Tin in the Taurus Mountains: The Bolkardağ Mining Survey (Abstract)', *AJA* 90: 183.

ZACCAGNINI, C. (1990), 'The Transition from Bronze to Iron in the Near East and in the Levant: Marginal Notes', *JAOS* 110: 496–7.

ZGUSTA, L. (1984), *Kleinasiatische Ortsnamen*, Heidelberg.

Index

Bold figures indicate main references.